Participation in Petroleum Development

PARTICIPATION IN PETROLEUM DEVELOPMENT

Towards Sustainable Community Development in the Niger Delta

EDWARD T. BRISTOL-ALAGBARIYA

Foreword by George (Rock) Pring
Introduction by Peter Cameron

Centre for Energy, Petroleum and Mineral Law and Policy
University of Dundee

First published in Great Britain in 2009 by
CEPMLP, University of Dundee
Dundee DD1 4HN
Reprinted with corrections (Second Impression) 2010

http://www.dundee.ac.uk/cepmlp

ISBN: 978 1 84586 085 1

British Library Cataloguing-in-Publication Data
A catalogue record for this book is available on request from the British Library

Typeset by IDSUK (DataConnections) Ltd
Printed and bound in Britain by
CPI Antony Rowe, Chippenham, Wiltshire

To the ethnic minorities of the Delta and other regions of Nigeria, and citizens of major natural resources-rich communities who are neglected in the decision-making processes of the development of these resources in developing countries.

Contents

PART C

Abbreviations

ASOPADEC	Abia State Oil Producing Areas Development Commission
APEI	Action Plan on the Environment Initiative
ANWLGA	Akoko North West Local Government Area
ADR	Alternative Dispute Resolution
AG	Attorney General
ABI	American Biographical Institute
AC	Appeal Court (*Also see* CA:– Court of Appeal)
ATCA	Alien Tort Claims Act
ADF	Akassa Development Foundation
ADP	Asset Development Plan
AFR	African Region
ARAC	African Regional Aqua Centre
ASC	African Studies Centre
AG	Action Group
AGG	Academic Advisory Group (*Also see* Associated Gas Gathering)
AIC	Amanyanabo-in-Council (*Also see* the BKCTR:– Bonny Kingdom Council of Traditional Rulers and the King-in-Council – KIC)
AJEAM	African Journal of Environmental Assessment and Management
ALGE	Association of Local Government Ecologists
Alta. L. Rev.	Alberta Law Review
AMCEN	African Ministerial Conference on the Environment
ANEEJ	African Network for Environment and Economic Justice
Anor	Another
APRM	African Peer Review Mechanism
ASQ	American Society for Quality
ATNS	Agreements, Treaties and Negotiated Settlements
AU	African Union (ie, former Organisation of African Unity, OAU)
BBC	British Broadcasting Corporation
BIOFOR	Biodiversity and Sustainable Forestry

BCC	Bonny Chiefs' Council (*Also see* the BKCTR:– Bonny Kingdom Council of Traditional Rulers)
BOCCIMA	Bonny Chamber of Commerce, Industry, Mines and Agriculture
BCF	Bonny Community Front
BCOGT	Bonny Crude Oil and Gas Terminal
BCOT	Bonny Crude Oil Terminal
BEB	Bonny Employment Bureau
BECC	Bonny Environment Consultants Committee
BEEF	Bonny Educational Endowment Fund
BERP	Bonny Emergency Response Plan
BGT	Bonny Gas Transport
BGL	Bonny Gentlemen's League
BGF	Bonny Graduates Forum
BIA	Bonny Improvement Association
BIFA	Bonny Indigenous Fishermen Association
BIPF	Bonny Indigenous People's Federation
BIBC	Bonny Integrated Business Complex
BIF	Bonny Island Foundation
BKDC	Bonny Kingdom Development Committee
BMP	Bonny Master Plan
BRT	Bonny River Terminal
BTIP	Bonny Terminal Integrated Project
BUC	Bonny Utilities Company
BVC	Bonny Vocational Centre
BWPM	Bonny Women Patriotic Movement
BYF	Bonny Youths Federation
BC	British Columbia
BCSD	Business Charter for Sustainable Development
BPD	Business Partners for Development
BPE	Bureau for Public Enterprises
BCLR	Butterworths Constitutional Law Reports
Brook. L. Rev.	Brooklyn Law Review
CAPP	Canadian Association for Petroleum Producers
CEAA	Canadian Environmental Assessment Agency
CIDA	Canadian International Development Agency
CLEAA	Capacity Development and Linkages for EIA in Africa (*also abbreviated in some records as* CLEIAA)
CEE	Central and Eastern Europe
CASS	Centre for Advanced Social Sciences
CEPR	Centre for Economic Policy Research
CEHRD	Centre for Environment, Human Rights and Development
CEEPEDS	Centre for Petroleum, Environment and Development Studies

CEPMLP	Centre for Energy, Petroleum & Mineral Law & Policy
CCI	Chamber of Commerce and Industry
CEO	Chief Executive Officer
CPI	Centre for Petroleum Information
Civ	Civil
CS	Civil Suit
CAJE	Coalition for Access to Justice for the Environment
CARE	Community Action for a Renewed Environment
CC	Community Consultation
CBOs	Community-Based Organisations
CD	Community Development
CDC	Community Development Committee
CDF	Community Development Foundation
CDI	Community Development Initiative
CDO	Community Development Officer
CDP	Community Development Plan
CI	Community Involvement
CR	Community Relations
CLO	Community Liaison Officer
Cmnd	Command
CAMA	Companies and Allied Matters Act (*also refers to* Companies and Allied Matters Decree)
CC	Constitutional Court
C/f	Compare
COR	Cross River, Ogoja and Rivers
SEDCOSND	Council for the Socio-economic Development of the Coastal States of the Niger Delta
CAS	Country Assistance Strategy
CPS	Country Partnership Strategy
CRC	Council of Rivers Chiefs
CAC	Corporate Affairs Commission
CSR	Corporate Social Responsibility
CVI	Corporate Voluntary Initiative
CA	Court of Appeal (*also refers to* Community Assistance)
DSE	Department of Sustainability and Environment
DESA	Department of Economic and Social Affairs
DEFRA	Department for Environment, Food and Rural Affairs
DfID	Department of International Development
DNL	Datson Nigeria Limited
DESOPADEC	Delta State Oil Producing Areas Development Commission
DPR	Department of Petroleum Resources
DFID	Department for International Development
DRC	Democratic Republic of Congo
DTIE	Division of Technology, Industry and Economics

D&DA	Drought and Desertification Amelioration
EGGS	Eastern Gas Gathering Systems
ECI	Earth Charter Initiative
EDSOPADEC	Edo State Oil and Gas Producing Areas Development Commission
E & P	Exploration and Production
E&P Forum	Oil Industry International Exploration and Production Forum
EA	Environmental Assessment
EBR	Environmental Baseline Report
EPA	Environmental Protection Agency
EPJ	Environmental Justice Project
EBRD	European Bank for Reconstruction and Development
EC	European Commission (*Also see* European Community [EC] and European Union [EU])
ECA	Economic Commission for Africa
EFCC	Economic and Financial Crimes Commission
ECA	Export Credit Agency
ECG	Electrocardiogram (machine)
ECHR	European Court of Human Rights
EEZ	Exclusive Economic Zone
EF&CZM	Erosion and Flood Coastal Zone Management
ECCIMA	Enugu Chamber of Commerce, Industry, Mines and Agriculture
EDF	Environmental Defense Fund
EGASPIN	Environmental Guidelines and Standards for the Petroleum Industry in Nigeria
EHS	Environment, Health and Safety
ESHA	Environmental, Social and Health (Impact) Assessment
EIA	Environmental Impact Assessment (*Also see* Environmental Assessment, EA)
EIAR	Environmental Impact Assessment Report
EI	Extractive Industries
EIO	Extractive Industrial Operation(s)
EIR	Extractive Industries Review
EIS	Environmental Impact Statement
ELI	Environmental Law Institute
ELM	Environmental Law and Management
EMP	Environmental Management Plan (*Also see* Environmental Management Programme)
EMS	Environmental Management System
EOCDF	Eastern Obolo Community Development Foundation
EPA	Environmental Protection Agency
EPC	Engineering, Procurement and Construction
EPCL	Eleme Petrochemicals Company Limited

EPIC	Engineering, Procurement and Installation Contract
ERA	Environmental Rights Action
ES	Environmental Statement (*Also see* Environmental Impact Statement, EIS)
ESC	Economic, Social and Cultural
ESCAP	Economic and Social Commission for Asia and the Pacific
ESCR-Net	The International Network for Economic, Social and Cultural Rights
ESDD	Environmental and Sustainable Development Division
ENCAP	Environmentally Sound Design and Management Capacity-Building for Partners and Programs in Africa
ESMAP	Energy Sector Management Assistance Programme
EU	European Union (*Also see* European Community, EC)
EITI	Extractive Industries Transparency Initiative
FCPA	Foreign Corrupt Practices Act
F	Forestry
FCNM	Framework Convention for the Protection of National Minorities (ie, the European Framework Convention for the Protection of National Minorities)
FCT	Federal Capital Territory
FEPA	Federal Environmental Protection Agency
FEPEN	Friends for the Preservation of the Niger Delta
FG	Federal Government
FGN	Federal Government of Nigeria
FHC	Federal High Court
FSC	Federal Supreme Court
FCIArb	Fellow of the Chartered Institute of Arbitrators
FID	Final Investment Decision
FMEnve	Federal Ministry of Environment
FMEHUD	Federal Ministry of Environment, Housing and Urban Development
FMPR	Federal Ministry of Petroleum Resources
UNFAO	Food and Agricultural Organisation of the United Nations
FOI	Freedom of Information
FNI	Fridtjof Nansen Institute
FNP	Finima Nature Park
FoE	Friends of the Earth
FoEI	Friends of the Earth International
FRC	Finima Re-location Committee
FIELD	Foundation for International Environmental Law and Development
FRIN	Forest Research Institute of Nigeria
FRN	Federal Republic of Nigeria
FWLR	Federation Weekly Law Report

GTS	Gas Transmission System
GDRC	Global Development Research Centre
GMOU	Global Memorandum of Understanding
GEF	Global Environment Facility
GPF	Global Peoples Forum
GG	Good Governance
GNA	Good Neighbour Agreement
GRA	Government Reserved Area
GSR	Government Social Responsibility
GLO	Glossary
Hon	Honourable
HC	Host Country (*Also see* High Court)
HCJ	High Court of Justice
HRW	Human Rights Watch
HEC	Hyundai Engineering Company Limited
HEPP	Hydroelectric Power Project
HG	Host Government
HHI	Hyundai Heavy Industries
HIA	Health Impact Assessment
Hon	Honourable
HL	House of Lords
HMSO	Her Majesty's Stationery Office
HSE	Health, Safety and the Environment
HYSON	Hydrocarbon Services Nigeria Limited
ISOPADEC	Imo State Oil Producing Areas Development Commission
IPA	Ijaw People's Association
IA	Impact Assessment (*Also see* Environmental Impact Assessment [EIA] and Environmental Assessment [EA])
Inc.	Incorporated
IQC	Indefinite Quantity Contract
ICPC	Independent Corrupt Practices and Other Related Offences Commission
INFED	Informal Education Homepage
IADWP	International Association of Educators for World Peace
IAIA	International Association for Impact Assessment
IAP2	International Association for Public Participation
IAP3	International Association of Public Participation Practitioners
IBA	International Bar Association (*Also see* Impact-benefit Agreement
IBC	International Biographical Centre
IBRD	International Bank for Reconstruction and Development (*ie*, the World Bank)
ICC	International Chamber of Commerce
ICCSR	International Centre for Corporate Social Responsibility

ICFNL	International Centre for Nigerian Law
ICPS	International Centre for Participation Studies
ICMM	International Council on Mining and Metals
ICG	International Crisis Group
IDA	International Development Association
IDCC	Industrial Development Coordination Committee
IDSL	Integrated Data Services Limited
IEE	Initial Environmental Examination
ICFAI	Institute of Chartered Financial Analysts of India
IEEP	Institute of European Environmental Policy
ISS	Institute for Security Studies
IFBWW	International Federation of Building and Wood Workers
IFAD	International Fund for Agricultural Development
IFC	International Finance Corporation
IGOs	Intergovernmental Organisations
ITDG	Publishing, Intermediate Technology Development Group
IIED	International Institute for Environment and Development
IICD	International Institute for Communication and Development
IISD	International Institute of Sustainable Development
IITA	International Institute of Tropical Agriculture
ILO	International Labour Organisation
IMF	International Monetary Fund
IMO	International Maritime Organisation
INCEED	International Conference on Energy, Environment and Disasters
Int'L	International Law
INECE	International Network for Environmental Compliance and Enforcement
IOC	International Oil Company
IPIECA	International Petroleum Industry Environmental Conservation Association
IRR	Impoverishment Risks and Reconstruction
ISO	International Organisation for Standardization
IUCN	International Union for the Conservation of Nature and Natural Resources (*ie*, the World Conservation Union)
JCA	Justice of the Court of Appeal
JIC	Joint Industry Companies
JOA	Joint Operating Agreement
JPL	Journal of Planning and Environmental Law
JENRL	Journal of Energy and Natural Resources Law
JSC	Justice of the Supreme Court
JV	Joint Venture
JVA	Joint Venture Agreement

KB	King's Bench
KIC	King-in-Council – KIC (*Also see* AIC:– Amanyanabo-in-Council, and the BKCTR:– Bonny Kingdom Council of Traditional Rulers)
km	Kilometres
kWh	Kilowatt-hour
Ltd.	Limited
LACA	Local Government Action Committee on AIDS
LCV	Local Content Vehicle
LEEMP	Local Empowerment and Environmental Management Project
LUA	Land Use Act
LFN	Laws of the Federation of Nigeria
LGA	Local Government Area
LSE	London School of Economics
LNG	Liquefied Natural Gas
LPG	Liquefied Petroleum Gas
LRCN	Law Reports of Courts of Nigeria
LRHL	Law Reports, English and Irish Appeals and Peerage Claims, House of Lords (England)
LTC	Leadership Training Centre
MD	Managing Director
MIT	Massachusetts Institute of Technology
MW	Megawatts
MTPA	Metric Tonnes Per Annum
MDGs	Millennium Development Goals
MEAs	Multilateral Environmental Agreements
MEG	Macdonald Engineering Group
MEND	Movement for the Emancipation of the Niger Delta
MEnve	Ministry of Environment
MILD	Master of International Law and Diplomacy
MMSD	Mining, Minerals and Sustainable Development
MNCs	Multinational Companies
MNOCs	Multinational Oil Companies (*also refers to* 'Multinational Oil and Gas Companies' and 'Multinational Oil Operators' or Multinational Oil Operating Companies)
MSP	Multi-Stakeholder Partnership
MOSOP	Movement for the Survival of the Ogoni People
MoU	Memorandum of Understanding (*plural*, Memoranda of Understanding – MoUs)
MPN	Mobil Producing Nigeria Unlimited
MVP	Millennium Villages Project
MPR	Ministry of Petroleum Resources (*Also see* Ministry of Energy)

MRF	Mineral Resources Forum
MRGI	Minority Rights Group International
NACA	National Action Committee on AIDS
NPRC	National Constitutional Political Reform Conference
NAFCON	National Fertilizer Company of Nigeria
N-AGENDA	NLNG Agro Development Action
NANS	National Association of Nigerian Students
NICC	Nigeria Independent Constitutional Conference
NAPIMS	National Petroleum Investment Management Services
NIS	Newly Independent States
NCNC	National Council of Nigeria and the Cameroons (*Also see* National Council of Nigerian Citizens
NCP	Nigerian Content Policy (*Also see* Local Content Policy/ National Content Policy, and National Council on Privatisation)
NCWS	National Council for Women Societies
NEPA	National Electric Power Authority (ie, now Power Holding Company of Nigeria Plc). (*Also see* National Environment Policy Act (USA).
ND HDR	Niger Delta Human Development Report
NDBDA	Niger Delta River Basin Development Authority
NDC	Niger Delta Congress
NDDB	Niger Delta Development Board
NDDC	Niger Delta Development Commission
NDES	Niger Delta Environmental Survey
NDFI	Niger Delta Fund Initiative
NDHDR	Niger Delta Human Development Report
ND-HERO	Niger Delta Human and Environmental Rescue Organisation
NDNF	Niger Delta National Forum
NDPEHRD	Niger Delta Project for the Environment, Human Rights and Development
NDPVE	Niger Delta Peoples Volunteer Force
NDRDMP	Niger Delta Regional Development Master Plan
NDVS	Niger Delta Volunteer Service
NDWC	Niger Delta Wetland Centre
NDWJ	Niger Delta Women for Justice
NEDECO	Netherlands Engineering Company
NEPAD	New Partnership for Africa's Development
NAOC	Nigerian Agip Oil Company
NCF	Nigerian Conservation Foundation
NEPD	Nigerian Enterprises and Promotion Decrees
NES	Nigerian Environmental Society
NEITI	Nigerian Extractive Industries Transparency Initiative
NETCO	National Engineering and Technical Company Limited

NGC	Nigerian Gas Company
NMMA	Nigerian Minerals and Mining Act
NPA	Nigerian Ports Authority
NGL	Natural Gas Liquids
NGOs	Non–Governmental Organisations
NIC	National Intelligence Council
NIEO	New International Economic Order
NIPC	Nigerian Investment Promotion Commission
NISD	Network of Institutions for Sustainable Development
NISSCO	Nigerian Services and Supply Company Limited
NLC	Nigeria Labour Congress
NLNG	Nigeria Liquefied Natural Gas Limited
NNOC	Nigerian National Oil Company
NNPC	Nigerian National Petroleum Corporation
NNRA	Nigerian Nuclear Regulatory Authority
NOC	National Oil Company
NOIP	National Office of the Industrial Property
NOTAP	National Office of Technology Acquisition and Promotion
NPC	Northern Peoples Congress
NPDC	Nigerian Petroleum Development Company
NPPG	National Planning Policy Guideline
NPS	National Parks Service
NRC	Natural Resources Cluster
NRF	Natural Resources Forum
NRRR	National Reconciliation, Reconstruction and Rehabilitation
NSC	Nigerian Supreme Court
NUCEWWO/ NUCECFWW	National Union of Civil Engineering, Construction, Furniture and Wood Workers
NWLR	Nigerian Weekly Law Report
OD	Operational Directive
OECD	Organisation for Economic Cooperation and Development
OEL	Oil Exploration Licence
OGC	Oil and Gas Commission
OGIC	Oil and Gas Sector Reform Implementation Committee
OGEL	Oil, Gas & Energy Law Intelligence
OGP	International Association of Oil & Gas Producers
OHCHR	Office of the United Nations High Commissioner for Human Rights
Ok	Olokola
OKFTZ	Olokola Free Trade Zone
OLGA	Bonny Local Government Area

OML	Oil Mining Lease
OMPADEC	Oil Minerals Producing Areas Development Commission
OND	Our Niger Delta
OPEC	Organisation of Petroleum Exporting Countries
OPL	Oil Prospecting Licence
OPTS	Oil Producers Trade Section
OSCOM	Oslo Commission
OSOPADEC	Ondo State Oil Producing Areas Development Commission
OPI	Oxford Policy Institute
PARA	Paragraph (*plural*, paras)
PNG	Papua New Guinea
Pt.	Part
PAC	Project Advisory Committee
PAR & E	Participator Action Research and Evaluation
PIRC	Pensions & Investment Research Consultants Limited
PSNR	Permenent Sovereignty Over Natural Resources
PDP	Peoples Democratic Party
PEF	Petroleum Equalisation Fund
PIB	Petroleum Industry Bill
PSTF	Petroleum (Special) Trust Fund
PTDF	Petroleum Technology Development Fund
PC&EH	Pollution Control and Environmental Health
3P +	Pollution Prevention Pays Principle
PH	Port Harcourt
PHC	Port Harcourt High Court
PhD	Doctor of Philosophy
PPA	Post-Project Analysis
PA	Preliminary Assessment
PAIA	Promotion of Access to Information Act
PMC	Project Monitoring Committee
PI	Public Involvement
PP	Public Participation
PPMC	Products and Pipelines Marketing Company
PPP	Policy, plan and programme/project (*also refers* to Public-Private-Partnership, and Polluter Pays Principle)
PR&S	Departments of Planning Research & Statistics
PRA	Participatory Rural Appraisal
Precom	Pre-conference
PRSP	Poverty Reduction Strategy Paper
PTF	Presidential Task Force
PTI	Petroleum Training Institute
PSC	Production Sharing Contract
QB	Queen's Bench (*ie*, Queen's Bench Division within the Royal Courts/Queen's Bench Law Reports)

Q & A	Question and Answer
R&D	Research and Development
RA	Residential Area
RAID	Rights and Accountability in Development
RAP	Resettlement Action Plan (also refers to Resettlement Management Plan, RMP)
RBD	Rights-Based Development
RBDA	River Basin Development Authority
RCPC	Rivers Chiefs and Peoples' Conference
RSTRC	Rivers State Truth and Reconciliation Committee
RSSDA	Rivers State Sustainable Development Agency
RIIA	Royal Institute of International Affairs
RMP	Resettlement Management Plan
ROW	Right of Way
RSC	Rivers State Congress
RSEC	Rivers State Employment Centre
RSG	Rivers Sate Government
Rt. Rev.	Right Reverend
RMMLF	Rocky Mountain Mineral Law Foundation
SCNL	Saipem Contracting Nigeria Limited
Sess	Session
SCIN	Shell Companies in Nigeria
SAN	Senior Advocate of Nigeria
SA/SALR	South African Law Reports
SA	South Africa
SACA	State Action Committee on AIDS
SADC	Southern African Development Community
SAIEA	Southern African Institute for Environmental Assessment
SARPN	Southern African Regional Poverty Network
SAP	Structural Adjustment Policy
Supp	Supplementary
SC	Supreme Court
SCC	Supreme Court of Canada
SCD	Sustainable Community Development
SCP	Sustainable Consumption and Production
SCNR	Supreme Court of Nigeria Report
SCR	Supreme Court Reports
SD	Sustainable Development
SDC	Sustainable Development Commission
SEA	Strategic Environmental Assessment
SEDCOSND	Council for the Socio-economic Development of the Coastal States of the Niger Delta
SEMS	Social and Environmental Management System
SERL	Section of Energy and Natural Resources Law

SFEM	Second Tier Foreign Exchange Market
SGBP	Shell General Business Principles
SIA	Social Impact Assessment.
SMEs	Small and Medium Enterprises
SPA	Sales and Purchase Agreement
SPDC	The Shell Petroleum Development Company of Nigeria Limited *ie*, Shell Nigeria
Sq	Square
SRC	Community Social Responsibility (*Also see* Social Responsibility of Communities – SRCs)
SRI	Socially Responsible Investment
SRJ	Conferences held at Stockholm, Rio de Janeiro and Johannesburg
SSPA	South-South People's Assembly
SDNY	Southern District of New York
SDN	Stakeholder Democracy Network
SSS	State Security Service
St.	State
TCND	Technical Committee on the Niger Delta
TSKJ	Technip, Snamprogetti, Kellog, and the Japanese Gas Corporation
TWN	Third World Network
Tcf	Trillion Cubic Feet
TNC	Transnational Corporation
TOC	Transnational Oil Company
TOT	Transfer of Technology
TI	Transparency International
UBC	University of British Columbia
UIPN	International Union for the Protection of Nature
UK	United Kingdom
UN	United Nations
UNCED	United Nations Conference on Environment and Development
UNCHE	United Nations Conference on Human Environment
UNCLOS	United Nations Convention on the Law of the Sea
UNCTAD	United Nations Conference on Trade and Development
UNECOSOC	United Nations Economic and Social Council
UNDESA	United Nations Department of Economic and Social Affairs
UNDP	United Nations Development Programme
UNECA	United Nations Economic Commission for Africa
UNECE	United Nations Economic Commission for Europe
UNEP	United Nations Environment Programme
UNESCAP	United Nations Economic and Social Commission for Asia and the Pacific

UNFCCC	United Nations Framework Convention on Climate Change
UNFAO	United Nations Food and Agricultural Organisation
UNGA	United Nations General Assembly
UNHCHR	United Nations High Commissioner on Human Rights
UNICEF	United Nations International Children's Emergency Fund
UNILAG	University of Lagos
UNPFII	United Nations Permanent Forum on Indigenous Issues
UNPO	United Nations and Peoples Organisation
UNRISD	United Nations Research Institute for Social Development
Upa J Int'l Econ L	University of Pennsylvania Journal of International Economic Law
UPS	Uninterruptible Power Supply
USA/US	United States of America
USAID	United States Agency for International Development
USD	United States Dollar
USEPA	United States Environmental Protection Agency
UHS	Urhobo Historical Society
UPP	User Pays Principle
VEAs	Voluntary Environmental Agreements
VOC	Volatile Organic Compound
Vol	Volume
WAGPP	West African Gas Pipeline Project
WBCSD	World Business Council for Sustainable Development
WBG	World Bank Group
WCED	World Commission on Environment and Development
WCSD	World Commission on Sustainable Development
WMA	Whitehorse Mining Accord
WMI	Whitehorse Mining Initiative
WEED	World Economy, Ecology and Development
WSSD	World Summit on Sustainable Development
WW	World War
WWF	Worldwide Fund for Nature
YAAC	Youths Against Aids Club
YDS	Youth Development Scheme
YEAA	Youths Earnestly Ask for Abacha
YES	Youth Empowerment Scheme

List of Decided Cases

Adefulu vs. Oyesile (1989) 12 SC, 43

Akilu vs. Chief Gani Fawehinmi (1989), 3 SC, Pt. 11, 1

Anglo-Algerian Steamship Co. Ltd. vs. Houlder Line Ltd. [1908] 1 KB, 657

Attorney-General of Ondo State vs. Attorney-General of the Federation & 33 Ors (2002) 9 NWLR (Pt. 772), 729

Attorney-General of the Federation vs. Attorney-General of Abia State & 35 Ors (No. 2) (2002) 6 NWLR (Pt. 764), 542–905

Chief (Aseme-Alabo) Edward T. B. A. Bristol-Alagbariya vs. Chief (Dr.) A. A. Ibiama-Finecountry and Chief D. I. Manilla-Pepple (For Themselves and on behalf of the Bonny Chiefs' Council), Suit No. PHC/399^{m}/2002 (Unreported)

Chief R. O. Nkwocha v. Governor of Anambra state (1984), 6 SC, 362, at p. 363

Chief Samuel O. Tobin & Ors vs. Chief Israel I. Brown & Ors (Unreported), Suit No. PHC/174/72

Elf Nigeria Limited vs. Sillo (1994) 6 NWLR (Pt.350), 258

Ekpendu vs. Erika (1959) 4 FSC, 79

Ex Parte Chairperson of the Constitutional Assembly: In Re Certification of the Republic of South Africa, 1996, (1996) 4 SA 744 (CC), (1996) 10 BCLR, 1253

Fayehun vs. Fadoju (2000) Vol. 77 LRCN, 714

Garuba Abioye vs. Sa'adu Yakubu (1991)5 NWLR (Pt. 190), 130 at pp. 231–232

McCarthy vs. Metropolitan Board of Works, LR8, CP 208, *209*

Metropolitan Board of Works vs. McCarthy, LR 7 HL, 243

Nkwocha vs. Governor of Anambra state (1984) 6 SC 362, at p. 392; (1984) 1 SCNR 634 at p. 647; (2001) FWLR (Pt. 48), 1386 at p. 1409

Oronto Douglas vs. The Shell Petroleum Development Company of Nigeria Limited & Ors. (1999), 2 NWL, 466–475, at pp.466–475

Re St. Pierre vs. Ontario (Minister of Transportation and Communication (1987)1 SCR, 906–917

Republic of South Africa and Ors vs. Grootboom & Ors (2001) 1, SARL, 46–87

The Shell Petroleum Development Company of Nigeria Limited vs. Abel Isaiah & 2 Ors (Representing Omuoda community of Aluu, Rivers state) [2001] FWLR (Pt. 56) 608

The Shell Petroleum Development Company of Nigeria vs. Chief N. Y. Allaputa (For himself, the Amanyanabo of Bonny in Council, Chiefs, Elders and the entire Bonny Kingdom) [2005] 9 NWLR, 475–525

The Shell Petroleum Development Company of Nigeria Limited (SPDC) vs. Farah (1995) 3 NWLR (Pt. 382), 148

Tijani Akinloye vs. Chief Oyejide Suit No. HCJ/9A/81 (of July 17, 1981, at the High Court of Justice, Ijero, Ondo state – now Ekiti state), (Unreported)

Savannah Bank of Nigeria Limited vs. Ammel O. Ajilo (1989) 1 NWLR (Part 97), 305 at p. 352–353

Ugo vs. Obiekwe (1989) 2 SC, Pt. 11, 41

Senator Adesanya vs. The Federal Republic of Nigeria (1979–1981) NSC, p. 146 at 147

Wiwa et al., vs. Royal Dutch Petroleum Company, et al., Case No. 96 Civ. 8386 (KMW) (HBP) (S.D.N.Y.)

Ken Wiwa et al., vs. Brian Anderson, Case No. 01 Civ. 1909 (KMV) (HBP) (S.D.N.Y.)

Wiwa vs. Shell Petroleum Development Company of Nigeria Limited (SPDC), 04 Civ. 2665, (S.D.N.Y.)

Acknowledgements

Since this book is the product of my post-doctoral programme, may I start by thanking the entire staff of the Centre for Energy, Petroleum and Mineral Law and Policy (CEPMLP), University of Dundee, where I accomplished this programme. My gratitude particularly goes to Professors Peter Cameron, Alice Belcher, Philip Andrews-Speed, including Chris Rogers, Dr. Elizabeth Bastida, Mrs. Christine Hulbert, M. A. G. Bunter & Dr. Melaku Desta. Other University of Dundee personalities whose encouragements are immensely appreciated include Dr. Ian Francis, Professor Christopher Whatley & Anna Day of the Dundee University Press Limited (DUP) and the University Library. May I also thank Professor George (Rock) Pring of the Sturm College of Law, University of Denver, Colorado, for his monumental encouragement.

This book would not have been published without the motivation of my beloved wife, Tumini, and the difficulties encountered in the process by my beloved children, Lauretta Aribim, David Bereibibo, and Michael Asembo-Ilowi, including the support and encouragements of the elders and entire people of the Bristol-Alagbarigha Royal House (Founder of Grand Bonny), Kuruama and Kuruama-Iwoama, over which I am traditional head. My gratitude also goes to Sir (Dr.) & Lady. T. A. T. Allison, Rt. Rev. & Dame Gabriel Pepple, Mrs. Tumini Dublin-Green and her beloved daughter Elsie, Peter Rano & Tony Dawson of CBI Nigeria Ltd., Sir Daibi Selema, Chief (Sir) & Lady O. B. Fubara, Chief Idamiebi Brown, and King E. A. W. D. Pepple. Others are Professors Chinua Achebe, Wole Soyinka, Itse Sagay, SAN, M. A. Ajomo, Ndi Okereke-Onyiuke, Pat Utomi, Wayne Visser, Ken Omeje, D. M. J. Fubara, J. F. Fekumo, Turner Isoun, and Adango Miadonye, including Funmi & Femi Falana, David Kirk, Mrs. Ednah Minah, Ere Bristol-Alagbariya, Ambassador Gordon H. Bristol-Alagbariya, H. C. Kurubo Bristol-Alagbariya, Mrs. Flora A. Lionel Finecountry and Mrs. Juliet Emelike. My appreciation goes to Lizzy & Eze Nwizu, Mrs. Barbara Illsley, Mrs. Margaret Hoskins, Muriel & Alabo T. O. Graham-Douglas, Taba & Lawrence A. B. Wilcox, Dokubo & Bassey Captain Briggs, Gogo & Boma Fiberesima, George Etomi, Lawrence Fubara Anga, Celestine Ogolo, ThankGod Echikwa, Pat Baxter, Ms Mairi Sutherland, Gesi Asamaowei, Jezberth Pepple, Camir Ogueri, Dr. M. T. Akobo, Dr. Leslie Green, Dr. K. S. A. Ebeku, Dr. A. A. Jackson, Dr. J. N. Hart, Dr. Jideofor Adibe, Dr. Engobo Emeseh, Dr. Furo Jumbo, Dr. Emmanuel Amadi, Dr. Kudo

Eresia-Eke, Dr. Aminu Kabir, Dr. Silva Opusunja, Dr. Onimi Wilcox, Dr. D. A. Omoweh, Dr. (Mrs) Doris Fisher and Sokari Andrew-Jaja. Remaining are the William-Jumbo family, Boma Jumbo, Dan Abbey, Dagogo Stowe, Lizzy Finecountry, Joyce Halliday, Chuks Nwokike, Chiji Nwaozuzu, Madaki Ameh, Julius Nayak, Adebayo Adaralegbe, Asembo Timon, Ugochukwu Beke, T. Iboroma Akpana, Owuna Fenibo, Sam Finel Hart, Ikpe Imeh, Ifeanyi Maduabuchi, Monima Abbey, Emma Oruebo, Vincent Ebirim and my colleagues at the CEPMLP and the Newcastle Chambers of Engineering Ltd, UK. My appreciation also goes to Otokini, Fafaa, Roselyn, & Ifirima Dan-Princewill, including my colleagues at the Bonny Kingdom Council of Traditional Rulers (BKCTR) and the Rivers State Economic Advisory Council (RSEAC).

May I also thank the Federal Government of Nigeria through the Petroleum Technology Development Fund (PTDF), Government of Rivers state led by the Governor, His Excellency, Rt. Hon. Chibuike Rotimi Amaechi, and his Deputy, Engr. Tele Ikuru; Government of Bayelsa state led by the Governor, His Excellency, Chief Timipre Sylva, and his Deputy, Rt. Hon. Peremobowei Ebebi, Admiral Mike O. Ahigbe (Rtd.), & Nigeria LNG Ltd. (NLNG), regarding their encouragements. Other Rivers state government officials worthy of mentioning include Chief Nyesom E. Wike, Hon. (Barr.) Magnus Ngei Abe, Hon. Dakuku Peterside, Hon. (Dr.) Sampson Parker, Hon. Fubara George Tolofari, Hon (Dr.) Tammy Danagogo, Hon. Barr. Kinsley Chindah, Hon. (Barr.) Alice Nemi, Hon. (Barr.) Ezemonye Ezekiel-Amadi, Hon. Patricia Simon-Hart, and Hon. George D. N. Feyii. May I accordingly thank the International Association for Public Participation (IAP2), International Association for Impact Assessment (IAIA), Canadian International Development Agency (CIDA), Africa Centre for Peace and Conflict Studies, Department of Peace Studies, Bradford University; Calabash Project, Southern African Region; Social Impact Assessment Center, New York; British Library, London; & Oxford Policy Institute (OPI), Oxford, England. Others are Human Rights Watch, Friends of the Earth (FoE), Greenpeace, Christian Aid, St. Paul's Episcopal Cathedral Church, Dundee; United Nations Environment Programme (UNEP), Department of Petroleum Resources (DPR), Southern Minorities Forum, Ijaw National Congress (INC), and a host of others whose names are inevitably not mentioned here.

The support of some individuals and organisations enhanced the publication of this impression of the book. They include Onyoma Research Publications led by Professor and Dame E. J. Alagoa, office of the President Umaru Musa Yar'Adua, Vice President Goodluck Jonathan, General Ibrahim Babangida (Rtd.), General Abdullahi Sarki Mukhtar (Rtd.) –National Security Adviser, Professor Yinka Omorogbe, Professor C. P. Wolf, Prince Uche Secondus, Mr. Odein Ajumogobia, SAN, Chief Dumo Lulu-Briggs, Dr. Jasper William-Jumbo, and Aseme-Alabo (Dr.) Asemeyibo Buowari Brown. Others are the Senate of the Federal Republic of Nigeria led by Senator (Dr.) David A. B. Mark, Federal House of Representatives led by the Rt. Hon. Demeji Bankole, and Niger Delta Development Commission (NDDC) led by its

Governing Board Chairman, Air Vice-Marshal Larry Koinyan, its MD/CEO, Chibuzor Ugwoha, & its Rivers State representative, Emmanuel T. Georgewill. May I also mention the RSEAC led by its Chair, Professor Nimi D. Briggs, Bonny Local Government Council led by its Chair, Edward Ebenezer Pepple, & its Vice Chair, Hon. Emmanuel John-Jumbo, JBN Nigeria Plc represented by Thomas Balzuweit & Christian Hausemann, Global Gas & Refining Ltd. (a subsidiary of Global Energy Group) led by its Founder & Chair, Kenneth Yellowe, Senator Joseph I. Kaagerger, Hon. Bassey Otu, Hon. Daemi Kunaiyi-Akpana, Hon. Sokonte Davies, & Hon. Chuma Nzeribe. Others are Dr. S. M. O. Amachree, Data Amachree, Donu Kogbara, Ann Kio-Briggs, Carol Allison, Fidel Pepple, Vivian Bristol-Awuzu, Elizabeth Odi Brown, Professor D. E. Ajakaiye, and Bof & Toru Ofili. The motivation of the CEPMLP, DUP and Birlinn Ltd. remained most encouraging during the publication of this second impression.

Above all, I owe the greatest thanks and appreciation to God Almighty.

Foreword

Company-community conflict has come to define natural resources development in the twentieth and twenty-first centuries. In particular, the vast oil and gas Delta region in southern Nigeria, one of the largest petroleum-exporting areas in the world, is an extreme example of this human, environmental, and economic tragedy. For over half a century, petroleum development has been occurring in this ethnic minority region – despite protests, demands for participation, and resistance by the affected local people. Mind-numbing charges proliferate of human rights violations, assassinations, kidnappings, arrests, forced relocations, property destruction, central government corruption, corporate force, failed efforts at compromise, and grave environmental and public health crises.

This book is a fresh voice with impeccable credentials and compelling solutions. Dr. Edward T. Bristol-Alagbariya is the paramount chief of the Bristol-Alagbarigha royal house of Grand Bonny kingdom – one of the most impacted oil-producing areas in the Niger Delta. Dr. Bristol-Alagbariya is a blood-descendant of King Perekule, and Priest-King Alagbariya (founder of Grand Bonny and one of the four founding fathers and premier-kings of Grand Bonny kingdom). Dr. Bristol-Alagbariya discusses Grand Bonny kingdom as occupying a significant place in the political economy of Nigeria, from the pre-colonial era. He describes the coast of Grand Bonny as one of Nigeria's most strategic seaports from the period of the Atlantic trade between Western Europe and West Africa. He discusses Grand Bonny as the first seat of the government of River state when the state was created in May 1967, during the Nigerian Civil War. He demonstrates Grand Bonny Island city as playing host to Nigeria's premier crude oil export terminal as well as Nigeria's premier LNG plant located at Finima, along the Island city. The perspective of this book is reinforced by case studies on Grand Bonny kingdom.

Dr. Bristol-Alagbariya is a member of the Historical Society of Nigeria, the Nigerian Bar Association and the International Bar Association, including the International Association for Public Participation, International Association for Impact Assessment, Society of Petroleum Engineers, and Friends of the Earth Scotland. He is also a member of the Social Impact Assessment Center, New York, and an associate of the Calabash project (of Southern African region) on citizens' participation in environmental assessment. He has served on significant government committees in Nigeria. This book is the outgrowth of his PhD Thesis (which I assessed as external examiner) at the world-famous Centre for Energy, Petroleum & Mineral Law & Policy (CEPMLP), University of Dundee. He is, therefore, not only an academic and legal expert of note on the issues discussed in this book, but also a genuine 'stakeholder' of the Niger Delta – the book's area of focus.

Dr. Bristol-Alagbariya brings to the protracted conflict in the Nigerian Delta region a commendably positive, solution-oriented perspective, seeing both the cause and the cure in 'the weakness of environmental democracy' in the region. As to cause, he presents impressive empirical and scholarly research on the historical, ethnological, and political realities of the oil-rich region and nation and finds that the crises are caused by inadequate public participation or community involvement on two levels – both in the regional development process and in national government decision-making processes.

Public participation is now widely viewed as one of the fundamental prerequisites for the achievement of successful sustainable development. It is recognised as a critical component in numerous international legal authorities and studies, including Principle 10 of the 1992 Rio Declaration, Rio's Agenda 21, the 1998 Aarhus Convention, and other sources, which the author analyses in depth. Public participation is not just limited to Western liberal democracies, as the author carefully shows by documenting the centrality of citizen participation in the Delta communities' historical and social framework. However, as he illustrates in various case studies, public participation has followed a failure model in the course of petroleum development in the Niger Delta, ranging from nonexistent to superficial 'consult-then-ignore'.

The solution, Dr. Bristol-Alagbariya concludes, is that change is needed in how both the companies and the central government engage in public participation with the affected communities. Mere 'consultation' without 'implementation' is not sufficient. He persuasively details the reforms needed both in corporate social responsibility and in government social responsibility to resolve the crises and to proceed with sustainable development of the resource in a way that protects the environmental, social, and public health values of the Niger Delta communities.

This is an extraordinary book which can and should be read by statesmen, government regulators, resource development interest groups, policymakers, and academics. Its groundbreaking approach constitutes a path for constructive engagement and sustainable development not only for the Niger Delta and other major natural resource-rich areas of Nigeria but also a potential blueprint for other resource-rich developing nations.

George (Rock) Pring
(Professor of Law, University of Denver Sturm College of Law, Denver, Colorado, USA, & Principal, Global Environmental Outcomes LLC, Consultant on Environment, Natural Resources, and Access to Justice), June 2009.

Introduction

It was my privilege and my pleasure to be the principal supervisor of the PhD thesis which has been revised and transformed into this book. While supervising this thesis at the Centre for Energy, Petroleum & Mineral Law & Policy (CEPMLP), University of Dundee, I realised that it had the potential to be published in the interests of the wider public (outside its immediate academic community). I am therefore delighted that it has, in the course of the author's post-doctoral studies, emerged as a highly-accessible contribution to the study of the sustainable development of the oil-producing communities of the Federal Republic of Nigeria, especially the communities of the oil-rich Delta ethnic minority region of the federation.

The adverse consequences of extractive industrial operations (*ie*, petroleum and other mining and mineral resources development operations) on the environment in resources-rich local communities and the welfare of the people of these communities in developing countries continue to attract interest across the globe. The author points out how the enormous but largely mismanaged wealth, derived from these operations in such countries, plays a key role in generating crises. He discusses how these crises, heightened by youth restiveness, in the Nigerian Delta region became so serious in the 1990s that they began to trigger the rise of crude oil prices in international markets as well as generate other negative consequences. These include insecurity of supply of Nigeria's petroleum resources to its consumer nations, and the insecurity of lives and property, especially the lives of expatriate personnel of multinational oil companies and citizens of the region, as well as the Federal Government's petroleum development Joint Venture assets in the region. Based on these and other identified imperatives, the author makes a scholarly contribution to the resolution of these protracted and devastating crises on the platform of the ongoing worldwide participation explosion (ie, citizens' or public participation in environmental decision-making, otherwise known as environmental democracy).

From the level of nation states of the world at the United Nations, to various international, national and local community levels, the participation of those adversely affected by extractive industrial operations is being advocated. Participation of stakeholders in the decision-making process of extractive industrial operations is advocated as a means of achieving environmentally-sound and socially-equitable sustainable development in the overall interest of mankind. On the strength of various standards, toolkits and other models and references provided, the author indicates that environmental democracy is an idea whose time has come in Nigeria in relation to petroleum development. It is on this premise that the author anchors his discussion on sustainable community development in the Delta region and Nigeria's other oil-producing areas, without disregarding the interests of other major stakeholders of the petroleum development business and overall public good in Nigeria.

I therefore recommend this book to academics on natural resources law and policy, and to planners, policy makers, statesmen and government officials in Nigeria and beyond. It deserves the attention of all Nigerians in the effort towards sustainable community development in the oil-producing areas, as well as transparency and accountability in governance associated with petroleum development in the country. For Nigerians and all parties having interest in this area, this book is a pioneering study of significant practical relevance to the stimulation of environmental democracy in major natural resources development projects in a developing nation.

Professor Peter Cameron, FCIArb.

(Professor of International Energy Law & Policy, CEPMLP and Director of Research at the Postgraduate School, University of Dundee), June 2009.

Preface

This book discusses environmental democracy (ie, public or citizens' participation [PP] in environmental decision-making) with regard to petroleum development in the Federal Republic of Nigeria (FRN). Community involvement (CI) is discussed as an aspect of PP so as to examine the role of corporate responsibility and impact assessment regarding petroleum development in the Niger Delta. It is on this note that sustainable community development (SCD) featured as a key issue, considering that sustainable development (SD) cannot be achieved in Nigeria and other nations without the existence of sustainable communities. The destiny and/or wellbeing of mankind is thus closely associated with or dependent on the nature of man's immediate environment, which includes man's place of habitation such as communities, cities, and provinces comprising global nations.

PP (also referred to as public involvement [PI]) presupposes that members of the public affected by a decision have the right to be involved in the making of such a decision. PI is thus defined as a problem-solving process which uses public input in decision-making, while environmental democracy is defined as an aspect of PI regarding development proposals capable of impacting adversely on the environment and SD. The degree of PI in environmental decision-making is required to be participatory (ie, interactive) in order to properly incorporate the views and concerns of the affected, concerned and/or interested public into the decision-making process.

The goal of PP expressed by the leading international civil society organisation on participation – the International Association for Public Participation (IAP2), referred to in Chapter 1, provides that participation includes the promise that the involvement of (ie, the views and concerns expressed by) the affected, concerned and/or interested public will influence the decision. Participation promotes sustainable decisions by recognising and communicating the needs and interests of all participants, including decision-makers. It generates and enhances the involvement of those potentially affected by, interested in or concerned about decisions. Participation seeks input from participants in designing how they participate. It provides participants with information which they need to participate in a meaningful way. PP communicates to participants how their inputs affect decisions. Consequently, based on Principle 10 of the Rio Declaration on Environment and Development, 1992, as elaborated in the Aarhus Convention of 1998, on access to information, PP in decision-making and access to justice in environmental matters, the author demonstrates that PP (*ie*, interactive PI) can enhance or generate environmentally-sound and socially-equitable SCD in the course of petroleum development in the Niger Delta.

Petroleum resources have, for the last four decades, been the economic mainstay of the FRN. The resources development operations commenced in the Niger Delta (ie, the Delta ethnic minority region of the Federation) in 1956. Shortly after the commencement of these operations, citizens of the Delta region, the main producers of the resources, started protesting about the adverse effects of the operations on the environment in the region and their welfare. These protests became serious from the 1990s, as the problems of the citizens of the region heightened by the adverse effects of petroleum development, are neither fully nor satisfactorily being addressed by the Federal Government (FG), other levels of government and the multinational oil companies (MNOCs) operating in the region. Citizens of the Delta region feel estranged, due to such factors as unitary rule, lack of transparency and accountability in governance, inequitable laws and practices, and weak policies, guidelines and regulations governing petroleum development in the Federation. To improve environmental democracy in their communities, citizens and citizen groups of the Delta ethnic minority region are demanding for such institutional development as full institutionalisation of environmental mediation, in order to enhance the effective resolution of environmental disputes and conflicts in the region. They believe that the existence of environmental mediation as in the United States of America (USA), Canada, and Australia, will enhance the wellbeing of the oil producing communities and their citizens.

The protests of citizens and citizen groups of the Niger Delta expressed in the form of incessant community crises, aggravated by youth restiveness, are articulated through the resource-control movement which has become a binding force in the region.

Protracted community crises in the Delta region, which have caused the fall of Nigeria's oil-production rate and certain previous increases in global oil prices, have several negative effects. They hinder the smooth development of petroleum resources, and security of supply to Nigeria's consumer-nations. These crises endanger lives and property (ie, the lives of local citizens, expatriate personnel of the MNOCs and the Federal Government's [FG's] petroleum development joint venture [JV] assets) in the region's communities. Insecurity of lives posed by frequent hostage-taking of expatriates of the MNOCs and local citizens, especially infants and the elderly in the region, has generated public outcry condemning hostage-taking as a crime against humanity. The resource-control movement thus seeks to address the protracted community crises by advocating improved CI in the decision-making process of petroleum development, so as to enhance the protection of the environment and thereby generate sound and equitable SD in the region.

The crises in the Delta region indicates what happens when participation, based on mutually beneficial partnership among directly-affected stakeholders, is either insufficient or non-existent. Consequently, this book argues that it is the absence or weakness of PI in environmental decision-making in poor, rural and neglected major natural resources-rich communities of developing countries, as identified by authorities on PP in environmental decision-making, that gives rise to community crises and failures of major natural resources development projects in these countries. Concerning the need for improved or active PI in environmental decision-making regarding petroleum resources development in the Nigerian Delta region, this book proffers a solution to community crises by stating that improved environmental democracy in the resources development projects will enable citizens of the region to benefit fairly from such development projects taking place in their communities. It argues that citizens are unlikely to disrupt the resources development operations from which they will benefit in a socially justifiable form and manner. Hence, improved environmental democracy is discussed as an enduring solution to community crises propelled by the resource-control movement in the Delta region. The book considers the roles of corporate responsibility and impact assessment (IA) towards sound and equitable SD, based on the need to integrate socio-political processes associated with the region into the biophysical aspects of Environmental Assessment (EA), so as to effectively address the adverse effects of petroleum development in the region. The scope of the book is wide, as it attempts to pin the weakness of environmental democracy regarding petroleum development in the Delta region to the lack of participation of the majority of Nigerian citizens in decision-making processes of nation-building. The book thus advocates the need for improved citizens' participation in governance, towards greater transparency and accountability at all levels of decision-making in the country.

Key findings and conclusions of the book include the need for improvement in environmental and social performances of the MNOCs. Although the MNOCs and governments are making efforts to enhance SD in the course of petroleum development, these are mainly in the realm of lip service, and centred more on the conceptual framework of SD than its actual realisation. Whereas the FG and other levels of government and government functionaries often emphasise the need for SD, they do so to promote their political image and the image of their administrations, while the MNOCs profess SD to promote their public relations profile in relation to their operational activities in the resources-producing communities. The concept or principle of SD is therefore diluted in the course of its implementation in Nigeria. As such, the MNOCs are yet unable or reluctant to adequately comply with the provisions of Article 27 of the Johannesburg Declaration on SD, 2002, and the government remains unable to evolve or develop a stable and transparent system for regulating petroleum development in the Federation in compliance with the provisions of Article 29 of the Johannesburg Declaration on SD. Another finding of the book is that PI or PP is a significant pillar of EA or Environmental Impact Assessment

(EIA), as well as a fundamental instrument for collective, sound and equitable decision-making towards SD. The EA process of petroleum resources development projects is therefore a medium by which SD can be achieved in the Delta region and other oil-producing areas of the FRN. However, because of the weakness of this process, it is directed more towards the provision of such impact-benefits as social amenities or public utilities which are lacking in the resources-producing communities. Since it is the traditional responsibility of government to provide social amenities or public utilities, the MNOCs operating in the Federation are unwilling to entirely assume the responsibility to provide these amenities or utilities for the oil-producing communities. Another finding of this book is that lack of government social responsibility (GSR) or the failure of governance arising from improper or lack of accountability and transparency is why public utilities are not being adequately provided in Nigeria. It is demonstrated that lack of implementation of the existing EIA process by government regulatory agencies, especially in terms of ensuring compliance of the MNOCs, and the implementation of robust, beautifully and expensively-published corporate social responsibility (CSR) measures by these companies are twin problems challenging sustainable petroleum resources development in the Delta region and other oil-producing areas of Nigeria. The conclusion is that, although there is need for improvement in CSR, there is a greater need for GSR embedded in good governance (GG). Hence the call for GSR, to empower Nigerian citizens to interactively engage in the decision-making processes of nation-building, in order to foster transparency, accountability and responsibility in governance. Interactive PI is thus central to Nigeria's true nationhood, prosperity and SD. SCD in the Delta region and other oil-producing areas therefore presupposes an improved degree of citizens' involvement in decision-making generated by GG. The need to resolve community crises associated with petroleum development in the Delta region thus poses a challenge to improve CSR backed by GSR, because CSR, no matter how well designed or how properly implemented, is not, and never can be, an alternative to good governance (GG). GG is required to generate, motivate and improve CSR and the social responsibilities of the communities (SRCs) in order to generate strategic partnerships among the three major stakeholders of the petroleum resources development business in Nigeria towards environmentally-sound and socially-equitable SCD. Strategic partnerships, based on mutual trust, cooperation and commitment among the major stakeholders (ie, the FG, MNOCs and the resources-producing communities), are capable of generating prosperity in the overall interests of Nigeria, the MNOCs and consumer-nations of the resources, including the citizens of these nations who rely on the uninterrupted development and security of supply of these resources. The book's front cover design thus depicts such partnerships as strategic alliances which are capable of giving birth to a green environment in the FRN as well as an era of green governance in the Federation.

The author identifies the FG, the MNOCs and the petroleum resources-producing communities as the three major stakeholders of the resources development business in Nigeria. As paramount chief of a principal founding chieftaincy house community of the Delta region's ancient kingdom of Bonny, hosting such giant multi-billion USD MNOCs as Shell Nigeria, Exxon-Mobil, and Nigeria LNG Limited, and as a specialist on PP and IA of major natural resources development projects, the author establishes himself as a stakeholder of the petroleum development business in Nigeria. To date, no author has addressed the protracted community crises associated with petroleum development in the Delta region based on the weakness of environmental democracy as demonstrated in this book. The author is therefore resolute in asserting that there is no alternative to interactive involvement of citizens in the decision-making processes of nation-building affecting their lives, wellbeing and future generations, as this is the best way to achieve consensus among citizens, accountability in governance, and peace derived through collaborative partnership and mutual trust towards SD in Nigeria. Consequently, Nigeria (the most populous black African nation), cannot afford to be regarded as a failed state in contemporary global history, nor would it want to be reckoned with as being unable to achieve the Millennium Development Goals (MDGs) by 2015.

Edward T. Bristol-Alagbariya
Centre for Energy, Petroleum & Mineral Law & Policy (CEPMLP), University of Dundee, June 2009.

PART A

Introduction

CHAPTER 1

The Issue and Perspectives of the Book

1.1 BACKGROUND TO THE BOOK: THE CONCEPTUAL AND HISTORICAL CONTEXT

The main issues or problems addressed in this book are the community crises hindering the smooth development of petroleum resources in the Nigerian Delta region, due to the adverse effects of the development operations on the environment, citizens and future generations of the region.[1] These crises in the Delta ethnic minority region are described in various ways such as 'the Niger Delta question', 'the Niger Delta problems', 'conflicts in the Niger Delta', 'community unrest in the Delta region', 'youth restiveness in the Niger Delta', 'anti-oil production conflicts', 'resistance or resource-control movement'[2] in the Niger Delta, and so forth. Notwithstanding how these crises are described, they indicate what happens when participation, based on partnership reinforced by mutual commitment and trust among directly affected stakeholders, is either insufficient or non-existent. Community participation referred to as community involvement (CI)[3] is thus discussed in a way to offer a solution to

---

1 *See* the pronouncements of the community groups of the Delta region regarding the adverse consequences of petroleum development and their positions on the way forward. These include the Ogoni Bill of Rights of 1990, the Kaiama Declaration of 1998, the Resolution of the First Urhobo Economic Summit, the Warri Accord, the Aklaka Declaration of the Egi People, the Oron Bill of Rights, the Demand of the First Niger Delta Indigenous Women's Conference for Women of Bayelsa state, the Declaration of the Ikwerre Rescue Charter, the Declaration of the Niger Delta Bill of Rights, and other related declarations and demands of other citizen groups of the region. *See* the 'Ethnic Declarations of the People of the Niger Delta', by the Niger Delta Women for Justice (NDWJ), found at http://www.ndwj.kabissa.org/Declarations/declarations.html visited on 16/05/05. *Also see* L. Westra, *Environmental Justice and the Rights of Unborn Future Generations: Law, Environmental Harm and the Right to Health*, London, Earthscan, 2006.

2 *See* S. Azaike, *Inequities in Nigerian Politics*, Yanagoa, Treasure Communications Resource, 2003, especially pp. 185–201.

3 *See* the 'International Conference on Engaging Communities: An Initiative of the United Nations and Queensland Government', 14–17 August, 2005, held at the Brisbane Convention & Exhibition Centre, Queensland, Australia, found at http://www.engagingcommunities2005.org/home.html visited on 03/09/08. *See* the Declaration of this Conference entitled the 'Brisbane Declaration on Community Engagement', found at http://www.getinvolved.qld.gov.au/share_your_knowledge/un_conference/brisbanedeclaration.html visited on 03/09/08. *See* the area of the International Association for Public Participation (IAP2) homepage entitled 'Resources', found at http://iap2.org/dispalycommon.cfm?an=1&subarticlenbr=242 visited on 03/09/08.

these crises which have caused the fall of Nigeria's oil production rate and certain previous increases in global oil prices.[4]

The Nigerian Delta region, the third largest wetland[5] after the Mississippi River Delta and the Pantanal wetland,[6] is naturally endowed as other delta regions of the world. The region, richly endowed with several natural resources, as well as cultural and traditional heritage, has vast development opportunities in sectors of Nigeria's political economy such as agriculture, livestock, solid minerals, petroleum, forestry, and tourism. The major challenges of the region include its difficult physical geographical features which impact negatively on the welfare of its inhabitants. Hence, communication is difficult, development is expensive and education is scanty in the region.[7] Other challenges and problems in the region range from the pitfalls of traditional development practices or processes, to poor governance and the need for the multinational oil companies (MNOCs) to improve on their social responsibility (*ie*, environmental and social performances) in the region.

The history of community crises in the Delta region dates back to the beginning of British colonial influence from 1884/85,[8] because citizens of the Delta

---

4 *See* the BBC news entitled 'Niger Delta Unrest Dampens Shell', found at http://newsvote.bbc.co.uk/mpapps/pagetools/print/news.bbc.co.uk/1hi/business/4971. . . visited on 26/03/09. *See* another BBC news entitled 'Oil Prices Rise on Nigerian Fears', found at http://newsvote.bbc.co.uk/mpapps/pagetools/print/news.bbc.co.uk/1/hi/business/6584. . . visited on 23/04/07.

5 *See* the area of the homepage of Pro-Natura International (Nigeria) captioned 'Conflict Resolution and Peace Building', found at http://www.pronatura-nigeria.org/conflict/resolvingconfict.html visited on 25/12/09. It is essential to state that Wetlands are links between land and water. *They are transition zones where the flow of water, the cycling of nutrients, and the energy of the sun meet to produce a unique ecosystem characterized by hydrology, soils, and vegetation – making these areas very important features of a watershed.* Wetlands are *areas where water covers the soil, or is present either at or near the surface of the soil all year or for varying periods of time during the year, including during the growing season See* the area of the United States Environmental Protection Agency (USEPA) homepage captioned 'Wetlands Overview', with the subtitle 'What is a Wetland?', found at http://www.epa.gov/owow/wetlands/pdf/overview.pdf visited on 01/06/09. *Also see* the area of the USEPA homepage captioned 'Wetlands, Oceans and Watersheds', with the subtitle 'What are Wetlands?', found at http://www.epa.gov/owow/wetlands/vital/what.html visited on 01/06/09.

6 *See* the article by Jide Ajayi of the Vanguard newspaper, entitled 'Niger Delta and the Funding NDDC Deserves', found at http://www.vangardngr.com/articles/2002/politics/p301072004.html visited on 17/04/06. *Also see* the NDDC's publication entitled 'The Niger Delta Development Commission: A Brief History' (which states that 'the Niger Delta is the world's third largest wetland, coming after Holland and Mississippi'), found at http://www.nddconline.org/The_Niger_Delta/index.shtml visited on 22/12/04. *See* '*Comparing Rivers: The Mississippi and the Niger Conference*', 2002, found at http://www.edwinlyon.com/comparingrivers.htm visited on 13/11/06.

7 *See* the *Nigeria Report of the Commission Appointed to Enquire into the Fears of Minorities and the Means of Allaying Them or The Willink Commission Report* (hereinafter called *The Willink Commission Report*), London, Her Majesty's Stationery Office (HMSO), 1958, (reprint by the Southern Minorities Movement, Port Harcourt, Nigeria, 1996), p. 51.

8 1884/85 witnessed the signing of negative sovereignty treaties between the British and the traditional rulers of the ancient Niger Delta trading states. The British also entered into such treaties with other pre-colonial Nigerian organic entities with which they had direct imperial relations, as a result of which British colonialism was introduced over the entire pre-colonial Nigeria with the birth of modern Nigeria as an organic entity comprising the entire pre-colonial Nigeria in 1914. *See* K. O. Dike, *Trade and Politics in the Niger Delta 1830–1885: An Introduction to the Economic and Political History of Nigeria*, Westport, Connecticut, Greenwood Press, 1981,

region and other Nigerians were denied the right to participate in the affairs of the colonial government which affected them.[9] Community crises and resistance movements continued in the Delta region after British colonialism due to the neglect and marginalisation of the interests of the region and its citizens in decision-making processes in Nigeria.[10] The fact that decision-making in Nigeria is traditionally handled in the interests of the three major tribes, is the root-cause of the crises in the Delta and other ethnic minority areas of the country.[11] Marginalising the interests of the minorities in the Delta region means that these minorities do not have the opportunity to interactively participate[12] in the

---

pp. 65–80 and 217–218. *Also see* E. J. Alagoa and A. A. Derefaka (eds), *The Land and People of Rivers State: Eastern Niger Delta*, Port Harcourt, Onyoma Research, 2002, pp. 324–326, and 333. *See* E. T. Bristol, 'The Validity and Enforceability of the Oil Rivers Treaties of Protectorate', being a dissertation submitted to the Faculty of Law, Rivers State University of Science and Technology, Port Harcourt, in partial fulfilment of the requirements for the award of the Degree of Bachelor of Laws (LL B), 1990. *Also see* A. Oyebode, 'Treaties and the Colonial Enterprise: The Case of Nigeria', African Journal of International and Comparative Law, Vol, 2, Part 2, 1990, pp. 17–36.

9 *See* the publication entitled 'History of Nigeria', found at http://www.historyworld.net/wrldhis/PlainTextHistories.asp?historyid=ad41 visited on 26/10/05. *Also see* M. Crowther, *The Story of Nigeria*, London, Faber and Faber, 1978. *See* 'Empowering People – A Guide to Participation' authored by A. Clayton *et al*, under the auspices of the United Nations Development Programme (UNDP), found at http://www.undp.org/csopp/paguide.htm visited on 13/07/04.

10 *See* The Willink Commission Report, *op cit. Also see* E. J. Alagoa and A. A. Derefaka (eds), *The Land and People of Rivers State: Eastern Niger Delta, op cit*, pp 321–357. The main decisions regarding petroleum resources development may be considered as the Joint Venture (JV) and other operating agreements and documentations regarding the grant of the resources development rights to multinational oil companies (MNOCs). The oil-producing communities do not participate in the grant of these rights, as these are sovereign rights of Nigeria exercised by the Federal Government (FG). Besides, community involvement (CI) in the decision-making process of such institutions as the NDDC, established to develop the oil-producing communities in the course of petroleum development, may be described as weak. The Niger-Delta Development Commission (Establishment, etc) Act, (hereinafter called 'the NDDC Act'), Laws of the Federation of Nigeria (LFN) 2004 (formerly Cap. 6 LFN 2000), is weak for not empowering citizens of the oil-producing communities to participate in the discharge of the functions of the NDDC. *See* K. S. A. Ebeku, 'Appraising Nigeria's Niger Delta Development Commission Act, 2000', Statute Law Review, Vol. 25, No. 1, 2004, p. 89.

11 *See* R. T. Suberu, *Ethnic Minority Conflicts and Governance in Nigeria*, Ibadan, Spectrum, 2003. *Also see* The Willink Commission Report, *op cit*.

12 *See* the UN Economic and Social Commission for Asia and the Pacific (UNESCAP), *Public Involvement Guideline for Natural Resource Development Projects*, New York, UN, 1997, pp. 4 –5. *Also see* D. N. Zillman *et al* (eds), *Human Rights in Natural Resources Development: Public Participation in Sustainable Development of Mining and Energy Resources*, New York, Oxford University Press, 2002, especially the preview and pp. 1–76. *See* E. Bastida *et al* (eds), International and Comparative Mineral Law and Policy: Trends and Prospects, The Hague, Kluwer Law International, 2005, pp. 65–281. *See* J. L. Creighton, *The Public Participation Handbook: Making Better Decisions through Citizen Involvement*, San Francisco, Jossy-Bass, 2005, especially p. 1. *Also see* T. C. Beierle and J. Cayford, *Democracy in Practice: Public Participation in Environmental Decisions*, Washington, DC, Resources for the Future, 2002. *See* Section 39 of the 1999 Constitution of the FRN, entitled 'Right to Freedom of Expression and the Press'. The proposed Freedom of Information (FoI – *vis-à-vis* citizens' right-to-know) Act may thus be a stepping stone to participatory democracy as well as transparency and accountability in the governance of Nigeria, if its provisions can guarantee Nigerian citizens unfettered access to information. *See* the Promotion of Access to Information Act (PAIA), No. 2, 2000, of the Republic of South Africa, which was enacted *to give effect to the constitutional right of access to any information held by the State and any information that is held by another person and that is required for the exercise or protection of any rights; and to provide for matters connected therewith.*

decision-making processes of the country, especially the processes regarding petroleum development adversely affecting the environment and their wellbeing. Interactive community involvement (CI) in petroleum development in the Delta region is being hindered by such factors as unitary rule, lack of transparency and accountability in governance, inequitable laws and practices, and weak policies, guidelines and regulations associated with the *rentier* politics of petroleum development in the Federal Republic of Nigeria (FRN). As a result, citizens of the region from whose communities petroleum resources are mainly being produced in the federation, complain that the laws and practices governing petroleum development in their communities are socially unjust, inequitable and unfair.[13] The petroleum resources (*ie*, oil) producing communities spearheaded by citizens and citizen groups of the Delta region, Nigeria's main oil producing region, are agitating for the enactment of a better (*ie*, equitable) petroleum law which is capable of addressing their age-long plight, fears and concerns in the FRN.[14] Citizens of the Nigerian Delta region contend that some aspects of Nigeria's policy on the environment and sustainable development (SD) are weak, especially when considered in the context of existing laws, regulations and

---

13 *See* the newspaper report entitled 'N-Delta, Victim of Inequitable Laws – Ibori', found at http://www.feedsfarm.com/article/04c99c9b8145f60ce10efea5b17c2f568b8044e3.html visited on 20/10/06. *Also see* the recommendations of L. S. Pyagbara, in the publication entitled 'The Ogoni of Nigeria: Oil and Exploitation' (being the micro-study of the Minority Rights Group International (MRGI) produced in partnership with the Movement for the Survival of the Ogoni People [MOSOP]), found at http://www.minorityrights.org/Dev/mrg_dev_title6_nigeria/mrg_dev_title6_nigeria_pf.htm visited on 09/11/06. *See K. S. A.* Ebeku, *Oil and the Niger Delta People in International Law – Resource Rights, Environmental and Equity Issues*, Koln, Rudiger Koppe Verlag, 2006.

14 It is, in this regard, significant to note that although the Nigerian Minerals and Mining Act (NMMA), 2007, and the Petroleum Industry Bill (PIB), 2009, deal with extractive industrial operations, the provisions of the former tend to protect the interest of the solid minerals producing communities more than those of the latter, designed to protect the interest of the oil producing communities. For instance, Section 102 of the NMMA 2007 states that ... *The Minister shall, before granting a mining lease on any private or any State land – (a) cause the owner or occupier of the land to be informed of the intention of the Minister to grant the lease;* ... The replica of this good Section and some other good provisions of the NMMA regarding CI and community wellbeing are not in the draft PIB. Such inequitable treatments or gaps identified between the NMMA and the PIB tend to undermine the ongoing global efforts aimed at achieving environmentally-sound and socially-equitable sustainable development (SD) in local communities endowed with major natural resources in developing countries. Besides, it must be mentioned, even as they are, that the provisions the NMMA and those of the BIP on environmental democracy are short of the globally agreed degree of environmental democracy expressed in Principle 10 of the Rio Declaration on Environment and Development, 1992, as elaborated in the Aarhus Convention on Participation, 1998. This Law and the Bill are therefore incapable of guaranteeing sustainable community development (SCD) in the interest of the solid minerals producing areas of Northern Nigeria and oil producing communities of Southern Nigeria. The best way for extractive industrial operations to help contribute to SD, is for such operations to conform to agreed standards under the UN system. Vesting community wellbeing and other SD responsibilities on the Minister as, for instance, expressed in Section 4 of the NMMA 2007, may not suffice in terms of realising SCD in the solid minerals producing areas of Northern Nigeria. The existence of appropriate policies, laws and regulations regarding major natural resources development alone cannot guarantee SCD in the major natural producing areas of Nigeria. Appropriate government regulation, embedded in GSR and enhanced by good governance

practices.[15] Citizens of the Delta region feel that sufficient efforts are not being made by the relevant government departments, including regulatory authorities, to ensure that the MNOCs comply with the emerging policy and regulatory processes on environmental protection and SD. They complain that there are gaps between Nigeria's policies regarding its responsibilities as a member state of the United Nations (UN) and the African Union (AU),[16] and the regulatory practices regarding petroleum development in the region. They see that petroleum development is primarily designed to aid Nigeria's economic development at the expense of the region.[17]

(GG), is required to achieve SD in the course of these major natural resources development operations. Broadly speaking therefore, governance, being the key aspect or sphere of SD, requires appropriate fine-tuning, in order to achieve transparency and accountability in decision-making, especially at strategic levels of decision-making, so as to enhance the achievement of SD in the course of major natural resources development vis-à-vis extractive industrial operations in Nigeria. Corporate responsibility can then be more properly enhanced and enforced on the platform of a transparent and stable regulatory system established under GG. The need thus arises to amend the NMMA, 2007, as well as a drastic review of the PIB, 2009 (presently before the National Assembly) so as to harmonise them in the mutual interest of the entire resources producing areas, in conformity with the prevailing standards agreed under the UN system. Nigeria, should, in other words, improve the wellbeing of its oil producing areas and their people as well as those of its other major natural resources producing areas, such as the solid minerals producing areas, in the effort to achieve SD in the collective interest of all her component areas/regions and citizens, especially her poor citizens. *See* the 'Speech by the Chairman, General Ibrahim Babangida, Former President and Commander-in-Chief of the Armed Forces, Federal Republic of Nigeria, on the Occasion of the Launching of *Participation in Petroleum Development: Towards Sustainable Community Development in the Niger Delta*, by Aseme-Alabo Edward T. Bristol-Alagbariya, at the Transcorp Hilton, Federal Capital Territory (FCT), Abuja, on Thursday, 26 November 2009.'

15 *See* Y. Belgore, 'Problems with Oil Pollution Injury Litigation in the Nigerian Legal System: Can Nigerian Litigants Gain Access to Courts in England and the USA?', being a thesis submitted to the Centre for Energy, Petroleum & Mineral Law & Policy (CEPMLP), University of Dundee, in fulfilment of the award of the Degree of PhD, July 2003, p. 30. *Also see* the draft report of the 'National Oil and Gas Policy', prepared by Nexant Limited under the auspices of the Bureau of Public Enterprises (BPE), found at http://www.bpeng.org/sectors/National%20Oil%20&%20Gas%20Policy%2007.pdf visited on 28/09/03, p. 2–2. *See* V. E. Eromosele, *Nigerian Petroleum Business: A Handbook*, Surulere-Lagos, Advent Communications, 1997, pp. 26–28. *See* the article by O. Makinde *et al*, on Oil Regulation in Nigeria, in C. Campbell (ed), 'Getting the Deal Through: Oil Regulation in 14 Jurisdictions Worldwide', London, Global Competition Review, Law Business Research, 2004, pp. 45–48, at p. 45. *Also see* the Leadership newspaper report entitled 'Petroleum', found at http://www.leadershipnigeria.com/product_info.php?products_id=1501&osCsid=a3ce... visited on 23/04/07, p. 4 subtitled 'Petroleum Policy'.

16 *See* Article 29 of the Johannesburg Declaration on SD, 2002, on the role of government to develop a transparent and stable regulatory framework to enforce corporate accountability. *Also see* the New Partnership for Africa's Development (NEPAD) 'Action Plan for the Environment Initiative', Midrand, NEPAD, 2003, found at http://www.unep.org/roa/Docs/pdf/nepad/Action_Plan_for_the_Environment_Initiative.pdf visited on 12/04/06, which provides for the Strategic Environmental Assessment (SEA) that Nigeria is yet to introduce to enhance SD in its municipality.

17 *See* P. Schwartz, *Sustainable Development and Mining in Sierra Leone*, Belvedere Kent, Pneuma Springs, 2006, pp. 7 and 21. *Also see* N. Echefu and E. Akpofure, 'Environmental Impact Assessment in Nigeria: Regulatory Background and Procedural Framework', found at http://www.iaia.org/Non_Members/EIA/CaseStudies/EIANigeria.pdf visited on 24/08/04. *See* the report of S. Oley and K. Rubin on the summary of panel discussion of Theme No. 1 captioned 'Driving Forces Behind Environmental Compliance and Enforcement Programs' (at the Fourth

Nigeria's policy on the environment actually provides for citizens' participation in environmental decision-making and this is further expressed in certain environmental laws,[18] regulations, and sectoral and procedural guidelines of the country. Nigeria's policy on the environment provides that its success must be built on SD principles. One of the SD principles outlined in the policy is the Principle of Participation,[19] which is described *inter alia* as the principle 'which requires that decisions should, as much as possible, be made by communities affected or on their behalf by the authorities closest to them'.[20] Other principles of SD outlined are the Precautionary Principle, Pollution Prevention Pays Principle (3P +), Polluter Pays Principle (PPP), User Pays Principle (UPP), Principle of Inter-Generational Equity, and the Principle of Intra-Generational Equity. These principles convey the links between development processes, environmental factors and human and natural resources.[21] In spite of these, public participation (PP, ie, public involvement, PI) is still being weakly practised in Nigeria in ways which are incapable of fulfilling the globally identified need and widely accepted principles of PP in environmental decision-making. Citizens of the Delta region are thus insisting that the widely prevailing environmental protection and SD measures associated with major natural resources development should apply to petroleum development operations in the region.[22]

The minorities of the Delta region complain about the frustration caused by limited access to judicial justice[23] as well as the lack of administrative justice to enable them to seek redress from the MNOCs operating in their communities. These and other hindrances such as the expensive nature of litigations, delay

---

International Conference on Environmental Compliance and Enforcement organised by the International Network for Environmental Compliance and Enforcement [INECE], April 22–26, 1996, Chiang Mai, Thailand), found at http://www.inece.org/4thvol1/sumth1.pdf visited on 11/12/06. *See* G. S. Akpan, 'The Failure of Environmental Governance and Implications for Foreign Investors and the Host State – A Study of the Niger Delta Region of Nigeria', Oil, Gas & Energy Law Intelligence (OGEL), Vol. 3, Issue 3, October 2005. *See* The World Bank Research publication entitled *Oil Windfalls: Blessing or Curse?* New York, Oxford University Press, 1998. *Also see* the UN General Assembly (UNGA) Resolution 3281 (XXIX) adopted at the 29th Session of the Assembly, 1974, on the Economic Rights and Duties of states. *See* Article 17 of the UN Universal Declaration of Human Rights, 1948, and Article 21 of the African Charter of Human and Peoples Rights, Cap. 10, LFN 1990. *See* N. Schrijver, *Sovereignty over Natural Resources: Balancing Rights and Duties*, Cambridge, Cambridge University Press, 1997, especially pp. 390–395.

18 *See* the functions and powers of the Federal Environmental Protection Agency (FEPA) expressed in Sections 5 and 6 of the FEPA Act, LFN 2004.

19 *See* the revised edition of Nigeria's *National Policy on the Environment*, Abuja, FEPA, 1999, p. 1.

20 Ibid

21 Ibid.

22 *See* the joint publication of the International Petroleum Industry Environmental Conservation Association (IPIECA) and the Oil and Gas Producers Association (OGP), entitled 'Oil and Gas Sector Report Card', found at http://www.ipieca.org/downloads/general/ipieca_ogp_report_card .pdf≡arch=%22Oil%20and%20Gas%20Sector%20Report%20Card%22 visited on 27/07/06.

23 The Federal High Court (FHC) has exclusive jurisdiction over matters pertaining to mines, minerals, oil fields and oil mining. *See The Shell Petroleum Development Company of Nigeria Limited vs. Abel Isaiah & 2 Ors (representing Omuoda Community of Aluu, Rivers state)* [2001] F. W. L. R. (Pt. 56) 608 S. C.

and other procedural and technical encumbrances of the courts system regarding the relatively few cases they are able to institute against the MNOCs, are frustrating citizens of the region.[24] They feel that the MNOCs are conniving with the Nigerian state, represented by the Federal Government (FG), to prevent them from having proper access to justice.[25] The Delta ethnic minorities are agitating against protracted litigation and the intervention of the MNOCs in their internal affairs, especially the affairs of their communities associated with the operations of these companies. By the connivance of the MNOCs and the FG, the fundamental and environmental rights of these minorities are being abused. The Delta minorities are often threatened, intimidated, manhandled, detained, arrested and judicially tried and executed maliciously without fair hearing, as a result of the connivance of the FG and the MNOCs operating in the region.[26] Citizens of the Delta region also complain about lack of political will and sustained commitment on the part of the FG to act in their interest, so as to properly ensure their well-being.[27] As minorities who do not have the numerical strength and political power to promote their interests, they feel they are being ignored by the FG, controlled by the elite of the major ethnic groups.[28] The Delta minorities are thus concerned that the affairs of the FRN are being directed by the elite of the three major hegemonic tribes involved in cut-throat competition, to the detriment of the minorities.[29]

Citizens of the oil-rich but violent crises-riven Delta region feel estranged due to unitary rule (ie, over-centralisation) in the FRN and the *rentier* politics[30] of petroleum development operations, including the mismanagement of the wealth

---

24 *See The Shell Petroleum Development Company of Nigeria Limited (SPDC) vs. Farah)* (1995) 3 NWLR, Pt. 382, p. 148.

25 *See* J. G. Frynas, *Oil in Nigeria: Conflict and Litigation between Oil Companies and Village Communities*, Piscataway, Transaction, 1993, pp. 8, 59 and 98. *Also see The Price of Oil: Corporate Responsibility and Human Rights Violations in Nigeria's Oil Producing Communities*, New York, Human Rights Watch (HRW), 1999, pp. 156–158.

26 *See The Price of Oil: Corporate Responsibility and Human Rights Violations in Nigeria's Oil Producing Communities, op cit*, pp. 123–158.

27 *See* the report entitled 'Oil for Nothing: Multinational Corporations, Environmental Destruction, Death and Impunity in the Niger Delta', found at http://www.waado.org/Environment/OILCOMPANIES/oilForNothing.html visited on 08/08/2004. *Also see* the Vanguard newspaper report entitled 'Stop Treating Niger-Delta People like Animals, 4 American Hostages Tell FG', found at http://www.vanguardngr.com/articles/2002/headline/f119052007.html visited on 19/05/07.

28 *See* O. Nnoli, *Ethnic Politics in Nigeria*, Enugu, Fourth Dimension, 1978, especially pp. 140–168. *Also see* A. A. Ikein, *The Impact of Oil on a Developing Country: The Case of Nigeria*, New York, Praeger, 1990, p. 38. *See* Ike Okonta, 'The Lingering Crisis in Nigeria's Niger Delta and Suggestions for Peaceful Resolution' (being a working paper prepared for the Centre for Democracy and Development), found at http://www.cdd.oreg.uk/rsources/workingpapaers/niger_delta_eng.htm visited on 01/11/06.

29 *See* K. Saro-Wiwa, *On A Darkling Plain: An Account of the Nigerian Civil War*, London, Saros International, 1989, especially p. 11.

30 *See* K. Omeje, *High Stakes and Stakeholders: Oil Conflict and Security in Nigeria*, Aldershot, Ashgate, 2006, pp. ix–x, especially p. ix. *Also see* K. Omeje (ed), *Extractive Economies and Conflicts in the Global South: Multi-Regional Perspectives on Rentier Politics*, Aldershot, Ashgate, 2008. *See* J. G. Frynas, *Oil in Nigeria: Conflict and Litigation between Oil Companies and Village Communities, op cit*, pp. 8, 59 and 98.

accruing from these operations in the federation.[31] They complain about the divide and rule tactics and the partial and palliative measures of the FG in the region.[32] Considering the amazing paradoxes[33] characterising their region, the Delta minorities are lamenting that they are poor in the midst of the plentiful wealth being derived by the federal and state governments from the development of the abundant petroleum resources of their communities.[34] The Delta region's minorities are agitating for an increase in the revenues accruing to their states under the principle of derivation, considering that the FG is continually changing the revenue allocation formula based on the principle of derivation against their interests, contrary to what prevailed in the regional era when the major ethnic groups produced the wealth of Nigeria. The Delta minorities complain about how they are being inadequately compensated for adverse

---

31 When General Yakubu Gowon was head of State in Nigeria, he was quoted as saying 'our problem is not money . . ., but how to spend it'. *See* A. R. Na'Allah (ed), *Ogoni's Agonies: Ken Saro-Wiwa and the Crisis in Nigeria*, Asmara, Africa World Press, 1998, p. 133.

32 The plight of citizens of the oil-rich Delta is the same as that of a mother whose breast milk is being used to feed other children of the family, while her children are largely deprived of being nourished by same. The children of the Nigerian family who are robustly feeding from the petroleum breast-milk of mother-Delta at the expense of Nigeria's poor masses are the country's corrupt political rulers and their cohorts. Interestingly, C. Achebe identifies the leadership question as the core problem of Nigeria. According to Achebe, 'the trouble with Nigeria is simply and squarely a failure of leadership'. *See* C. Achebe, *The Trouble with Nigeria*, Enugu, Fourth Dimension, 1983, p. 1. Thus, based on the enlarged/ancillary hypothesis of this book, there is a need for improved social responsibility of the MNOCs in the Delta and other oil-producing areas in the course of petroleum development in these areas. Accordingly, there is a greater need for GSR embedded GG, in the interest of the oil-producing areas and all other areas of Nigeria, and the entire citizens of the country and humanity at large. *See* J. Agyeman *et al* (eds), *Just Sustainabilities: Development in An Unequal World*, London, Earthscan, 2003, pp. 269–288.

33 *See* the *Niger Delta Human Development Report*, Garki-Abuja, UNDP Nigeria, 2006, p. 9.

34 Nigeria has thus enacted the Nigeria Extractive Industries Transparency Initiative (NEITI), Act, 2007, as its version of the global EITI, to ensure extractive resources aid SD in the country. This Act empowers the NEITI to promote accountability and transparency regarding revenues paid to and received by government from Nigeria's extractive industrial operations. However, the NEITI Act has no provision to guarantee the prudent management and administration of the revenues received by governments from these operations. *See* the NEITI homepage, found at http://www.neiti.org/index.html and the area of this homepage captioned 'About NEITI', found at http://www.neiti.org/about.htm both visited on 17/07/07. The NEITI Act is therefore not a sufficient check on governments' proper management of Nigeria's revenues from its extractive industries, regardless of the existence of anti-corruption bodies as the Economic and Financial Crimes Commission (EFCC) and the Independent Corrupt Practices and Other Related Offences Commission (ICPC) which may assist in the enforcement of the NEITI Act. *See* the Nigerian Tribune newspaper report entitled 'Ribadu Seeks Amendment to Transparency Initiative Act', found in the area of the NEITI entitled 'NEITI Related News', found at http://www.neiti.org.ng/news/bautribune310807.pdf visited on 10/09/08. The NEITI Act is particularly weak due to Nigeria's refusal to ratify the African Union Convention on Preventing and Combating Corruption and Other Related Offences, 2006. *See* the ThisDay newspaper report entitled 'Nigeria, 37 Others Reject Anti-Corruption Convention', found at http://www.thisdayonline.com/nview.php?id=55104&printer_friendly=1 visited on 09/08/06. *Also see* Christian Akani, 'Preserving the Niger Delta for the Future +' (being a paper presented at the 14th edition of the International Association of Educators for World Peace [IADWP], August 22–28, 2004), found at http://www.nu.ac.za/ccs/files/Preserving%20the%20Niger%20Delta.pdf visited on 23/03/06. *See* the article by E. Duruigbo, entitled *The World Bank, Multinational Corporations and the Resource Curse in Africa*, 26 U. Pa. J. Int'l Econ. L., 2005, pp. 1–67.

consequences of petroleum development affecting them and their aquatic and terrestrial means of livelihood.[35] They are demanding equity participation,[36] improved Local Contents such as impact-benefits which include infrastructural development,[37] in the course of petroleum development in their communities.

In order to improve environmental democracy in their communities, citizens and citizen groups of the Delta ethnic minority region are demanding for such

35 The farmlands, fisheries and other aquatic and terrestrial livelihoods of the Delta minorities are being destroyed. The Delta minorities are witnessing oil pollution, gas flaring, deforestation, biodiversity loss, flooding and erosion, communicable diseases and infections and other health problems, including other deplorable circumstances and situations inflicting poverty and misery on them in the course of petroleum development in their communities. *See* A. Ogbuigwe, *Offended: Legal Issues in the Niger Delta Struggle*, Port Harcourt, Anpez Centre for Environment and Development, 1999, especially pp. 11–26. *Also see* the article by G. G. Darah, entitled 'Derivation is Not Resource Control', found at http://www.nigerdeltacongress.com/darticles/derivation_is_not_resource_contr.htm visited on 03/05/05.

36 The oppressive measures of the FG controlled by the major tribes continue to deny citizens of the Delta region equity participation in petroleum development, in spite of the participation arrangement initiated in the course of the proposed Olokola (*ie*, Ok) LNG project consequent upon which the FG recognised the host Ondo and Ogun states, including Delta state, as strategic stakeholder investors to have a measure of shareholding in the project. *See* the report of the Guardian newspapers entitled 'Govt Targets N1.3t from LNG, signs Pact on Olokola Project', found at http://www.guardiannewsngr.com/news/article06 visited on 19/04/07. The need thus arises for Nigeria to be guided on its ethnic minority issues by the declaration of the rights of persons belonging to national or ethnic, religious and linguistic minorities, adopted by the UNGA, in its Resolution 47/135 of December 18, 1992. *Also see* Section 7 of the repealed Minerals and Mining Decree, Cap 34 LFN 1999, and the Nigerian Minerals and Mining Act (NMMA), 2007, which repealed this Decree.

37 The provision of infrastructures and other public utilities may be considered under economic and socio-cultural (ESC) rights. In Nigeria, these rights (which include the right to development under economic objectives and the right to the protection of the environment under the environmental objectives provided for in Sections 16 and 20 respectively) are all under Chapter 2 (*ie*, Sections 13 to 24) of the 1999 Constitution of the Federation entitled 'Fundamental Objectives and Directive Principles of State Policy'. As these rights (considered as second generation human rights), impose no corresponding duties on government to observe in favour of the citizens, they are non justiciable. *See Attorney-General of Ondo state vs. Attorney-General of the Federation & 33 Ors.* (2002) 9 N. W. L. R. (Pt. 772), 729. *Also see* J. O. Akande, *Introduction to the Constitution of the Federal Republic of Nigeria 1999*, Ebute-metta, Lagos, MIJ, 2000, p. 63. This situation in Nigeria is, for instance, different from that of the Republic of South Africa, where the Bill of Rights enshrined in Chapter 2 (*ie*, Sections 7 to 39) of the 1996 Constitution of the Republic, may be enforced by the law courts, subject to the limitations imposed under Section 36 of the Constitution. The socio-economic rights of citizens of South Africa are thus justiciable, depending on the merit of each case. Hence, in *Government of the Republic of South Africa and Ors vs. Grootboom & Ors* (2001) 1, The South African Law Reports, pp. 46–87, the Supreme Court of South Africa held *inter alia* that the issue of whether socio-economic rights are justiciable at all in South Africa was put beyond question by the text of the Constitution as construed in the judgement of *Ex Parte Chairperson of the Constitutional Assembly: In Re Certification of the Republic of South Africa*, (1996) 4 SA 744 (CC), (1996) 10 BCLR, 1253. There are thus suggestions that Chapter 2 of the Nigerian Constitution require amendment, so as to impose a duty on government to observe the provisions of the chapter based on the merit of each case. *See* S. Tar. Hon, *Constitutional Law and Jurisprudence in Nigeria*, Port Harcourt, Pearl, 2004, pp.60–66. *Also see* D. Bilchitz, *Poverty and Fundamental Rights: The Justification and Enforcement of Socio-economic Rights*, Oxford, Oxford University Press, 2007. *See* M. A. Baderin and R. Mccorquodale (eds), *Economic, Social and Cultural Rights in Action*, Oxford, Oxford University Press, 2007. ESC rights in the FRN may in effect be considered in the context of GSR. *See* M. Lessonoff (ed), *Social Contract Theory*, Oxford, Basil Blackwell, 1990. *Also see* the Black's *Law Dictionary*, St. Paul, West (A Thomson Business), 2004, p. 1424. *See* the *New Shorter Oxford Dictionary*, Oxford University Press, 2002, p. 273.

institutional development as full institutionalisation of environmental mediation as a form of Alternative Dispute Resolution (ADR), to enhance the resolution of increasing environmental disputes and conflicts in the region.[38] They believe that extensive institutionalised environmental mediation, similar to that which exists in such jurisdictions as the United States of America (USA), Canada, and Australia,[39] will boost the wellbeing of the oil producing communities and their citizens.[40] The Delta minorities want government social responsibility (GSR), embedded in good governance (GG) and enhanced by the practice of true federalism and stable democracy, to properly cater for their interests and the interests of other Nigerian poor masses.[41] Considering that petroleum is a finite resource[42] and prevailing environmental hazards of former mining operations in the Jos Plateau ethnic minority area are not being addressed by the FG, the Delta minorities are afraid that their complaints about the adverse effects of the petroleum resources development may be ignored or

---

38 *C/f*, for instance, the provisions of Section 33 of the Environmental Impact Assessment (EIA) Act, Vol. 6, LFN 2004, on mediation. *See* R. Sidaway, *Resolving Environmental Disputes from Conflicts to Consensus*, London, Earthscan, 2005, pp. xxi, 64, 66, 73, 194–195, 258 and 261.

39 *See* N. Sipe, 'Environmental Mediation in Australia: Comparisons and Contrasts with the US', Alternative Dispute Resolution (ARD) Bulletin, Vol. 2, No. 4, 1999, abstract and pp. 1-3. *Also see* L. K. Patton, 'Settling Environmental Disputes: The Experience with and Future of Environmental Mediation', Environmental Law, Vol. 14, 1983–84, pp. 547–554. *See* the area of the USEPA homepage on 'Settlement', under 'Compliance and Enforcement', captioned 'Mediation', found at http://www.epa.gov/ebtpages/compsettlementmediation.html visited on 23/12/09.

40 *See* the panel report entitled 'Putting Community First: A Promising Approach to Federal Collaboration for Environmental Improvement (An Evaluation of the Community Action for a Renewed Environment [CARE] Demonstration Programme), National Academy of Public Administration, 2009, found at http://www.napawash.org/pc_management_studies/CARE/5-13-09_Final_Evaluation_Report.pdf visited on 23/12/09. *See* U. C. Ilegbune, 'Mediating Community/Company Environmental Disputes in the Oil and Gas Industry: A Guide for Promoting Environmental Mediation in Emerging Economies – Focus on Nigeria', Being A dissertation submitted in partial fulfilment of the requirements of Master of Laws (LLM) in Petroleum Law and Policy, CEPMLP, University of Dundee, March 2004.

41 *See* I. Sagay, 'Needs of the SouthSouth in a Federal Setup: Why SouthSouth is Aggrieved', found at http://www.vanguardngr.com/articles/2002/politics/april05/22042005/p222042005.html visited on 24/04/05.

42 Citizens of the Delta region are worried that governments exercising jurisdiction over areas of the region do not make enough effort to vitalise their traditional means of livelihood. They feel that the FG, along with their state and local governments, needs to diversify the petroleum resource-based Nigerian economy by, for instance, reviving agriculture, embarking upon more industrial developments and developing renewable sources of energy towards a sustainable future for Nigeria and Nigerians. Regarding renewable sources of energy, *see* the presentation of the Director of Energy Planning and Analysis Energy Commission of Nigeria, O. C. Iloeje (at the Renewable Energy Conference captioned 'Energetic Solutions', held at Abuja/Calabar, November 21–26, 2004) entitled 'Overview of Renewable Energy in Nigeria, Opportunities for Rural Development and Development of Renewable Energy Master Plan', found at http://www.onesky.ca/RE&DevAbuja2004_Iloeje.pdf visited on 31/12/06. The UNDP recommends that sustainable livelihoods in the Delta region must be accompanied by industrial diversification and economic growth, and be grounded in several capital assets (namely the natural, human, physical, social, and financial capital) which are fundamental to the development of communities in the region. *See* the *Niger Delta Human Development Report, op cit*, 130.

disregarded after the era of the development of these resources in their communities.[43]

The plight of citizens of the Delta region and the state of affairs in the region are complex and complicated due to certain factors. These include the existence or dominance of social capital relations which undermines the equitable spread of ongoing intervention and other related social investment initiatives of the various levels of government and the MNOCs, such as community development (CD) and economic empowerment measures directed towards sustainable human and CD.[44] Among other negative effects, social capital relations undermine sound and equitable sustainable human and CD in the region. Social capital relations, thriving all over the FRN, serves as the basis upon which certain internal contradictions such as intra- and inter-communal disputes and other state of affairs in the communities, Local Government Areas (LGAs) and states of the region may be appreciated or understood. Social capital relations determine how some civil and traditional governments, public institutions and community-based organisations (CBOs) either function or are organised and administered in the region. By and large, social capital relations determine how the relationships among citizens and groups thrive, especially the relationship between some influential citizens and citizen groups, relative to the advantages or benefits they are deriving from governments as well as the impact-benefit initiatives or social investments of the MNOCs operating in the Delta region.

Community and other leaders of the Delta region appropriate compensation and development funds meant for their communities. Youth leaders, elders and other leaders and giants in the communities connive with the MNOCs and government officials to divert social investments meant for the communities.[45] Leaders, especially political leaders, intimidate, oppress, suppress and even kill or abet in the killing of their citizens who protest that they should be accountable to their people. Community, youths and other leaders who try to ensure that corporate social responsibility (CSR) and GSR investments are

---

43 *See* B. A. Fubara, 'Niger Delta Economic Development without Crude Oil', being a draft position paper for the Economic Association of the Niger Delta states, dated December 2008. *Also see* A. Etekpe, *et al, Harold Dappa-Biriye: His Contributions to Politics in Nigeria*, Port Harcourt, Onyoma Research, 2003, especially pp xii–xiii. On tin mining in the Jos Plateau ethnic minority area during the colonial era, *see* 'Tin Mining and Processing Related Environmental Impacts and Associated Hazards on the Jos Plateau, North-Central Nigeria', being a paper presented by A.E. Ogezi, at the International Conference on Energy, Environment and Disasters (INCEED 2005), Bridging the Gaps for Global SD, at Charlotte, North Carolina, USA, July, 24–30, 2005. *Also see* the publication of the Third World Network (TWN) by A. Raufu, entitled 'Tin Mining Wreaks Havoc on 'Beautiful' Nigerian City', found at http://www.twnside.org.sg/title/1878-cn.htm visited 17/05/05.

44 *See* A. Dale and J. Onyx (ed), *A Dynamic Balance: Social Capital and Sustainable Community Development*, Vancouver, University of British Columbia (UBC) Press, 2005. *Also see* R. A. Irvin and J. Stansbury, 'Citizen Participation in Decision-making: Is It Worth the Effort?' Public Administrative Review, Vol. 64, Issue 1, 2004, pp. 55–65.

45 These are some issues discussed at the plenary session of the Shell Nigeria 2004 stakeholders' workshop held at the Petroleum Training Institute (PTI), Effurun, (near Warri), Delta State, 24–26 February, 2004.

driven in the interest of the poor populace are abused, threatened and sometimes killed by those who feel differently. The instances in the Delta region and other oil-producing areas of how the interests of the poor masses are undermined by their privileged citizens due to social capital relations are legion. Social capital relations generate contradictions which worsen the crises in the region.

Another aspect of internal contradiction relates to the principles of social justice, equity and fair play upon which the Delta region's resource-control movement is anchored. While certain citizens and citizen groups of the region point out that these principles should govern their relations with the FG and other issues affecting them in the FRN, they are either unable or reluctant to enforce these principles among themselves. By not doing so, they are worsening the state of deprivation, marginalisation, neglect, underdevelopment, poverty and misery in or among the communities and ethnic groups of the region. Ironically also, the resource-control movement fostered through violence rather than due process impedes genuine public participation.[46] Under cover of the resource-control movement, individuals and groups in the Delta region are threatening and killing themselves, and destroying communities and other ancient landmarks in the region.

Among other challenges of the Delta region is the fact that some appointed and elected citizens of the region are unable to satisfactorily promote the region's interest in the course of nation-building. More challenging among the internal complexities and contradictions in the Delta region is corruption in governance. Whereas the Delta minorities are agitating for GG in Nigeria, some of their traditional rulers and political leaders are not able to deliver this in the interest of their people. Most political leaders of the Delta region, presiding over the affairs of their states and LGAs, are as corrupt as their counterparts from the major ethnic groups and other parts of the federation.[47] Thus, while accusing governments in the region for the mismanagement of the wealth accruing to them from petroleum development, it was reported that out of a total of N16.447 trillion shared among the federal states and local governments from June 1999 to May 2007 from the federation account, over N2.5 trillion was allocated to the states in the region. This implies that the six states of the region

46 *See* the publication of the Department of Peace Studies, Bradford University, entitled 'Department of Peace Studies International Centre for Participation Studies (ICPS) Aims and Ethics', p. 2.

47 Also, there are their traditional rulers diverting compensation, development projects, development funds, and trust funds, etc, accruing to their people in the course of petroleum development in the communities of the Delta region. Certain youth leaders as well as a measure of other leaders in the region are not left out in this game of diverting public benefits into private gains in the course of petroleum development in their communities. They do so, with the aid of corrupt MNOCs officials who connive with them, contrary to the acclaimed social responsibilities and commitments of these companies and thus worsening the state of poverty and crises in the region. See the publication by J. Osai, entitled 'Shell as Agama Lizard' found at http://www.waado.org/Environment/OilCompanies/Shell-Communities/ShellsFalsePR.html visited on 22/03/04. *Also see* the 'Other Shell Reports' by the Friends of the Earth (FoE), especially the 2004 report entitled 'Lessons Not Learned: The Other Shell Report', found at http://www.foe.co.uk/resource/reports/lessons_not_learned.pdf 30/07/06.

received over 12.25 % of the above-stated total amount.[48] Constitutional powers and control over public funds are not being properly exercised to ensure or enhance responsibility, transparency and accountability of governments in Nigeria.[49] Consequently, there is absence of GSR or the failure of governance in the states and LGAs of the Delta region.[50] Due to these and other related internal

---

48 *See* the Daily Trust newspaper report entitled 'Federation Account: Niger Delta Benefit most from Obasanjo', found at http://www.dailytrust.com/news2d.htm visited on 18/06/07. Due to the mismanagement of the revenues accruing to the oil-producing states by the governments of these states, some are agitating that oil-producing communities, including land-owning families in these communities, should directly benefit from these revenues as, for example, is the case in Papua New Guinea (PNG). Also, due to corruption in Nigeria, most of the over USD 1.6trillion so far derived from the five decades of petroleum development in the country has either been stolen or wasted by governments. Thus, about 80% of oil monies flow to 1% of the population, whereas about 75% of Nigerians live on roughly US$1 per day. *See* the BBC news entitled 'Nigerian Leaders 'Stole' $380bn', found at http://newsvote.bbc.co.uk/mpapps/pagetools/print/news.bbc.co.uk/1/hi/world/africa/6. . . visited on 22/10/2006. *Also see* the BBC news entitled 'The Day Oil Was Discovered in Nigeria', found at http://news.bbc.co.uk/1/hi/world/africa/7840310.stm visited on 01/04/09. *See* the Vanguard newspaper report entitled 'Oil Ruins Us', found at http://www.vanguardngr.com/content/view/24320/68/ visited on 20/12/08. Regarding corruption by governments in Rivers state of the Niger Delta, see the HRW report entitled 'NIGERIA CHOP FINE: The Human Rights Impact of Local Government Corruption and Mismanagement in Rivers state, Nigeria', Vol. 19, No. 2 (A), dated January 2007, found at http://www.hrw.org/reports/2007/nigeria0107/ visited on 03/02/07. Pages 1–2 of the summary of this report states that *Nigeria has produced several hundred billion dollars worth of oil since independence in 1960, but ordinary Nigerians have derived appallingly little benefit from all that wealth. This situation exists primarily because successive governments, both military and civilian, have stolen or misused much of Nigeria's tremendous oil wealth. . . . The human rights impact of those losses has been profound, as funds that government could have spent on basic health care and primary education for Nigeria's citizens have instead been squandered or embezzled. Nigeria's public schools and clinics have been left to crumble and wither away and Nigerians have suffered greatly from the decay of those vital public services. Accurate statistics do not exist, but one million Nigerian children are believed to die each year before the age of five, and most of those children lose their lives to diseases that are easily preventable or treatable at low cost. The country is also thought to have the world's second-highest number of maternal deaths each year, trailing only India. Public schools have reached the point of near collapse in many areas, with many children passing through the system without learning to read. . . . use of public resources has been characterised by extravagance, waste and opacity; . . . Human Rights Watch investigated these . . . in Rivers state, . . . the heart of Nigeria's oil industry and its state government is wealthier than that of any other Nigerian state. The contradiction between Rivers' wealth and the material deprivation experienced by many of its people could not be any starker.*

49 *See* Sections 80–89 with respect to powers and control over public funds at the FG level, and Sections 120–129 at the level of state governments, as well as Sections 162–168 on public revenue, of the 1999 Constitution of the FRN.

50 The above-stated HRW report entitled 'NIGERIA CHOP FINE: The Human Rights Impact of Local Government Corruption and Mismanagement in Rivers state, Nigeria', *op cit*, pp. 1 and 4 provides that . . . *corruption has undermined public accountability and fuelled political violence and other forms of human rights abuse. Those who speak out against the conduct of those in power have often been targets of violence or intimidation [outright murder by hired assassins], and officials who commit such abuses are often able to enjoy complete impunity. In mid-2006, one local government chairman in Rivers state shot three of his constituents following an argument about a broken electrical transformer. He continues to occupy his office. . . . Human Rights Watch calls upon the Nigerian government to attack the roots of the country's corruption epidemic with more resolve; . . .* There is need therefore for good and socially responsible governments in the Delta region. GSR examples such as the establishment of the Ondo State Oil Producing Areas Development Commission (OSOPADEC), Delta State Oil Producing Areas Development Commission (DESOPADEC), Edo State Oil and Gas Producing Areas Development Commission (EDSOPADEC)

complexities and contradictions, the crises in the region and the plight of its poor and neglected citizens and communities are more complex and complicated than members of the public who are not citizens of the region may appreciate.

CSR and Impact Assessment (IA) or Environmental Assessment (EA) are cardinal to this book and hence require some measure of attention. Regarding CSR currently, one major issue is the enlargement of the social responsibilities of multinational extractive industries such as petroleum and mining companies operating in poor, rural and neglected resource-rich areas of developing countries.[51] In Nigeria, MNOCs are considered as paying their long overdue debt of not being good neighbours to the poor and marginalised oil-producing communities of the Delta region in the course of their operations in these communities. Thus, in the words of the Niger Delta Development Commission (NDDC),

> . . . *For the oil companies, it is a very complex, no-win situation. They are not the best suited to provide these services effectively. Nor are they seen as neutral and genuine development support providers. They are perceived as paying a long overdue debt, an obligation they are not seen to be doing enough to sufficiently redeem them* . . .[52]

As distinct from what prevails in developing countries like Nigeria, business accountability in the advanced countries is, for instance, enhanced by taxation.[53] Although MNOCs in Nigeria and other developing countries provide social investments for their host communities, it is the traditional responsibility of government (ie, GSR) to provide these investments and other public utilities. The joint contribution of the MNOCs and the FG, as for instance expressed in the NDDC Act,[54] deserves not to be interpreted or extended to mean the MNOCs taking over government's traditional responsibility to provide public utilities. Hence, this book will argue that CSR is distinct from GSR, and thus not an alternative to GSR. That GSR, as a mark of GG, is capable of providing viable and efficient public utilities and public institutions which are lacking in most developing countries.[55] Accordingly, corporate accountability will be

---

and the Rivers State Sustainable Development Agency (RSSDA), are required to be effective to enhance SCD in the region. *Also see* the Imo State Oil Producing Areas Development Commission (ISOPADEC) and the Abia State Oil Producing Development Commission (ASOPADEC).

51 The pendulum of social responsibility is currently swinging between governments of major natural resources-rich countries and the multinational companies (MNCs) extracting these resources. *See* A. Kabir, 'Social Responsibility of Governments in Mineral Resource Development', *op cit*

52 *See* the NDDC's publication entitled 'The Niger Delta Development Commission: A Brief History', *op cit.*

53 Ibid.

54 *See* Section 14 (2) of the NDDC Act, LFN 2004.

55 *See* the article by O. Arowolo entitled 'Social Responsibility of Multinational Oil Companies and the Challenge of Local Communities – Any Prospects for Reconciliation?', *op cit. Also see* Section 14 (2) (a) and (b) of the 1999 Constitution of the FRN.

considered in the context of the ability of host governments to evolve a transparent and stable regulatory framework to enhance the operation of companies, including MNOCs.[56] The role of governments in Nigeria is particularly significant given the commitment expressed by developing countries to govern better – pursuant to which commitment rich countries pledged to support poor countries[57] in the global effort to achieve the Millennium Development Goals (MDGs).[58]

This book will also focus on Impact Assessment (IA), a significant pillar of SD and PP. IA will be considered as an aspect of government's environmental regulation as expressed in Chapter 5, as well as a process by which public and in effect community involvement becomes part of the mindset of the MNOCs in the course of their operations in the communities. The book will thus consider the role of government in enhancing CI in the course of petroleum development in the FRN.

It may appear easier to describe citizens' involvement or PP than to define it, considering the ongoing participation opportunities occurring world-wide. Participation is the right of citizens to be heard in decisions that affect them. It may be considered as any process, including problem solving mechanisms, which uses public input in decision-making.[59] It is a framework for strengthening governance, especially grass-root democracy.[60] It may be described as *the involvement of individuals and groups that are positively or negatively affected by, or that are interested in [or concerned about], a proposed [or ongoing] project, program, plan, or policy that is subject to a decision-making process*.[61] The UN Environment Programme (UNEP) defines PI as 'a range of techniques that can be used to inform, consult or interact with stakeholders

56 *See* Articles 27, and 29 and 30 of the Johannesburg Declaration on SD, 2002.

57 This book considers the MNOCs operating in Nigeria as part and parcel of the rich countries, while sharing the opinion that business is key to Africa's development through the help of the advanced world and Africans in diaspora. *See* W. Visser *et al* (eds), *Corporate Citizenship in Africa: Lessons from the Past; Paths to the Future*, Sheffield, Greenleaf, 2006, pp. 12–17.

58 *See* the *Nigeria Millennium Development Goals 2006 Report*, Abuja, The National Planning Commission, 2007. Regarding the UNMDGs, *see* the UNGA Resolution 55/2 of 8 September, 2000, and the roadmap for the implementation of the Millennium Declaration expressed in the report of the then UN Secretary General (as a follow-up to the outcome of the Millennium Summit), during the 56 Session of the GA, on September 6, 2001. *Also see* the homepage of the UNMDGs, found at http://www.un.org/millenniumgoals/index.shtml visited on 24/03/09.

59 *See People and Participation: How to Put Citizens at the Heart of Decision-making*, London, Involve, 2005, especially p. 2.

60 *See* Section 14 (2) (c) of the 1999 Constitution of the FRN which provides that 'the participation of the people in their government shall be ensured in accordance with the provisions of this Constitution'. Given that participation is the 'voice of the citizens', this and other related provisions of the law cannot, especially where implementation processes are lacking, sufficiently generate the degree or level of PI capable of guaranteeing transparency, accountability and responsibility in the governance of the federation. *See* the African (Banjul) Charter on Human and Peoples' Rights (Ratification and enforcement) Act, Cap A9, LFN 1990.

61 *See* P. Andre *et al*, '2006 Public Participation: International Best Practice Principles', Special Publication Series No. 4, Fargo, International Association for Impact Assessment (IAIA), August 2006, p. 1.

affected by a proposal'.[62] The UNEP defines the word or term 'proposal' as 'any project, policy, programme, plan or other activity'.[63] PI or PP responds to the rights of individuals and groups affected by development proposals. Participation involves the form or method employed to engage individuals or group of individuals, who may be citizens or other members of the public.[64]

PP is particularly considered in this book in the context of environmental decision-making, otherwise referred to as environmental democracy, expressed in Principle 10 of the Rio Declaration on Environment and Development, 1992, and elaborated in the Aarhus Convention on Public Participation, 1998. The law, principle and practice of environmental democracy require the involvement of the public or citizens affected by development proposals, capable of impacting on the environment, in the decision-making process of such proposals, in order to achieve environmentally-sound and socially-equitable SD.[65] Thus, while considering PP in the context of the levels of PI, the UN Economic and Social Commission for Asia and the Pacific (UNESCAP) states that PI 'can be defined as a process through which the views of all interested parties (ie, stakeholders) are integrated into project decision-making'.[66] The best examples of PI are where involvement becomes part of the developer's state of mind rather than simply following a set of guidelines or procedures associated with it. The UNESCAP highlights that PI includes a number of levels, namely information gathering, information dissemination, consultation and participation.[67] Considering the involvement of stakeholders in these four levels, the UNESCAP offers the following definitions and/or descriptions:

1. *Information gathering: involving a systematic analysis of existing social, cultural and economic conditions about directly-affected groups of stakeholders (such as farmers or indigenous minorities).*

---

62 *See* M. McCabe and B. Sadler (eds.), *Environmental Impact Assessment Training Resource Manual*, Geneva, The Economic and Trade Branch, Division of Technology, Industry and Economics (DTIE), United Nations Environment Programme (UNEP), 2002, p. 560.

63 Ibid.

64 *See* J. Petts and B. Leach, *Evaluating Methods for Public Participation: Literature Review* (a Research and Development (R & D) Technical Report, E135), Bristol, Environmental Agency, 2000, p. 57.

65 *See* D. N. Zillman *et al* (eds), *Human Rights in Natural Resources Development: Public Participation in Sustainable Development of Mining and Energy Resources, op cit*, p.4. *Also see* N. Roberts, 'Public Deliberation in an Age of Direct Citizen Participation', the American Review of Public Administration, Vol. 34, No. 4, December 2004, pp. 315–353. *Also see* the article by D. A. Rondinelli and M. A. Berry, 'Environmental Citizenship in Multinational Corporations: Social Responsibility and Sustainable Development', *European Management Journal*, Vol. 18, No. 1, 2000, pp. 70–84. *See* the article by D. Mebratu, 'Sustainability and Sustainable Development: Historical and Conceptual Review', found at http://www.gena.ucl.ac.be/siteunite/article%20Mebratu.pdf visited on 18/09/06. *Also see* the area of the IAIA homepage captioned 'About the IAIA', found at http://www.iaia.org/Non_Members/About%20IAIA/about_iaia.htm visited on 17/09/06.

66 *See* UNESCAP, *Public Involvement Guideline for Natural Resource Development Projects, op cit*, p. 4.

67 Ibid.

2. Information dissemination: referring to the provision of information about a project to all interested parties (stakeholders). Stakeholders cannot genuinely be consulted or participate if they are not fully informed about the objectives of a project.

3. Consultation: where decision-makers listen to the views of other stakeholders in order to improve project design prior to implementation, or to make necessary changes during implementation. Consultation should involve government, affected parties, donor agencies, mass awareness organisations and NGOs (Local and/or international).

4. Participation: is an extension of consultation where directly-affected groups become joint partners in the design and implementation of projects. They participate in 'making' the decisions.[68]

The UNESCAP highlights that the first level is necessary in order to reach the next level and other subsequent levels in a graduated sequence. Hence, participation cannot take place without consultation, and consultation cannot occur without information dissemination. Given that participation is the highest level of PI, the UNESCAP states that it should be the objective of most large-scale natural resources development projects.[69]

While adopting the foregoing definition and/or description of PI or PP in the context of the ongoing 'world-wide participation explosion' and major natural resources development of which petroleum development constitutes part and parcel, it may be highlighted that participation implies the engagement or interactive involvement of all the interested, affected and/or concerned stakeholders of development proposals in a way that enables them to legitimately and mutually influence the decision-making process of the proposals.[70]

PI or PP is increasingly being designed to include the involvement or engagement of citizens, civil society groups and other members of the public, such as indigenous people, local communities, minorities, women, youth, as well as Non-governmental Organisations (NGOs) that are affected by development

---

68 Ibid.

69 *See* UNESCAP, *Public Involvement Guideline for Natural Resource Development Projects, op cit*, pp. 4, and 9–10. *Also see* S. Bass and B. Dalal-Clayton, 'Participation in Strategies for Sustainable Development', Environmental Planning Issues, No. 7, May 1995. *See* B. Dalal-Clayton and S. Bass, *Sustainable Development Strategies: A Resource Book*, London, Earthscan, 2007, pp. 177–225.

70 *See* Article 2 (5) of the Aarhus Convention (otherwise known as the Convention of the UN Economic Commission for Europe [UNECE]) on access to information, PP in decision-making and access to justice in environmental matters, 1988. *Also see* the goal of PP expressed in the 'IAP2 Spectrum of Public Participation' (depicting the increasing level of public impact on participation), in the area of the IAP2 homepage captioned 'Practitioner Tool' with the subtitle 'Spectrum', found at http://www.iap2.org/associations/4748/files/IAP2%20Spectrum_vertical.pdf visited on 17/09/08. *See* R. Sidaway, *Resolving Environmental Disputes from Conflicts to Consensus, op cit*, pp. 115–190. *See* D. Wilcox, 'Guide to Effective Participation', found at http://www.partnerships.org.uk/guide/index.htm visited on 21/09/08. *See The World Bank Participation Sourcebook*, Washington DC, The World Bank, 1996.

proposals, but are however traditionally marginalised in the decision-making process of such proposals.[71] Citizens of the Delta ethnic minority region and those of other oil-producing areas (ie, Ondo, Abia and Imo states) are directly affected, concerned and/or interested members of the public in the context of citizens' or PI in the decision-making process of petroleum development in the FRN.[72] The oil-producing communities in the nine states of the FRN are thus identified as comprising one of the three major stakeholder groups of the petroleum development business in the federation. The other two major stakeholders identified by the author are the MNOCs operating in the federation, and their Joint Venture (JV) partner (ie, the Nigerian National Petroleum Corporation, NNPC, which represents the FG for and on behalf of the FRN).[73]

Having discussed the genesis of the community crises in the Delta region and the concept of PP anchored on environmental decision-making in the context of major natural resources development of which petroleum development is an aspect, it may be reiterated that these crises disrupting the smooth process of petroleum resources development have several negative effects. These crises constitute a great problem which must be addressed to enhance the smooth development of the resources in the region, in the interest of the three major stakeholders and greater or overall public good in Nigeria.

1.2(I) QUESTIONS POSED

From the foregoing, the main questions posed are:

1. What are the identifiable forms and/or measures of citizens' involvement in petroleum resources development in Nigeria, considering the community

---

71 *See* M. Lee and C. Abbot, 'The Usual Suspects? Public Participation Under Aarhus Convention', Modern Law Review, Vol. 66, Issue 1, January 2003, pp. 107–108.

72 *See* Article 2 (5) of the Aarhus Convention of 1998, on access to information, PP in decision-making and access to justice in environmental matters, regarding the definition of the phrase '*public concerned*', which includes Non-Governmental Organisations (NGOs). *Also see* M. McCabe and B. Sadler (eds), *Environmental Impact Assessment Training Resource Manual, op cit*, p. 159, regarding the phrase '*affected and interested public*'.

73 By extension, citizens of the oil-producing communities, along with their future generations and the environment in the communities, as well as the oil-producing states and local governments, are considered as integral part and parcel of the communities, while the MNOCs are considered as part and parcel of the rich countries. Similarly, the entire citizens of the FRN including those of the oil-producing communities are considered in relation to the federation, as a major stakeholder. Thus, in the overall interest of the federation, the FGN is represented in petroleum JV partnerships by the Nigerian National Petroleum Corporation (NNPC). *See* M. M. Gidado, *Petroleum Development Contracts with Multinational Oil Firms: The Nigerian Experience*, Maiduguri, Ed-Linform Services, 1999, pp. 105–107. *Also see* the Joint Operating Agreement (JOA) between the NNPC, the Shell Petroleum Development Company Nigeria Ltd (SPDC/Shell Nigeria), Agip Oil Company Ltd., and Elf (Nigeria) Ltd., dated July 11, 1991, and made pursuant to the deeds of assignment and memorandum of understanding (MoU) signed by the parties on August 1, 1989, expressing their desire for the joint operation, development and production operations and management of certain designated concessions.

involvements (CIs) taking place in the course of the resources development in the Delta region?

2. Do the identifiable forms and/or measures of CI fulfil the globally identified need and widely accepted principles of PP in environmental decision-making?
3. If they do not, what improvements may be made to help remedy the community crises hindering the smooth development of the resources in the Delta region?

1.2(II) ISSUES REGARDING QUESTIONS POSED

The globally identified need and widely accepted principles of PP in environmental decision-making are stated in Principle 10 of the Rio Declaration on Environment and Development, 1992,[74] and elaborated in the Aarhus Convention on participation, 1998.[75] This book will consider this Principle, elaborated in the Aarhus Convention, as the benchmark for environmental democracy evolved from the effort of the UN in a bid to achieve SD. SD, from

74 This Principle provides that *Environmental issues are best handled with participation of all concerned citizens, at the relevant level. At the national level, each individual shall have appropriate access to information concerning the environment that is held by public authorities, including information on hazardous materials and activities in their communities, and the opportunity to participate in decision-making processes. States shall facilitate and encourage public awareness and participation by making information widely available. Effective access to judicial and administrative proceedings, including redress and remedy, shall be provided.* The Rio Declaration on Environment and Development, 1992, was made during the United Nations Conference on Environment and Development (UNCED) (informally called the 'Earth Summit'), held at Rio de Janeiro, in Brazil, from June 3–14, 1992. The resulting documents of the UNCED are Agenda 21, the Rio Declaration of Environment and Development, the Statement of Forest Principles, the UN Framework Convention on Climate Change and the UN Convention on Biological Diversity. Agenda 21 is a comprehensive plan of action to be taken globally, nationally and locally by organisations of the UN system, governments, and major groups in every area of human impact on the environment. Chapters 1, 8, 36, 38 and 40 of Agenda 21 of the UNCED, 1992, are respectively captioned 'Preamble', 'Integrating Environment and Development in Decision-making', 'Information for Decision-making', 'Promoting Education, Public Awareness and Training', and 'International Institutional Arrangements'. *See* the publication of the UN entitled 'UN Conference on Environment and Development (1992)', found at http://www.un.org/geninfo/bp/enviro.html visited on 22/02/06. *Also see* the area of the UN Economic and Social Affairs homepage, captioned 'Agenda 21', found at http://www.un.org/esa/sustdev/documents/agenda21/index.htm visited on 31/12/06.

75 *See* the Aarhus Convention adopted on June 25, 1998, in the Danish City of Aarhus, at the Fourth Ministerial Conference in the 'Environment for Europe' process. The former UN Secretary General, Kofi Annan, describes the Convention in the following words: . . . *although regional in scope, the significance of the Aarhus Convention is global. It is by far the most impressive elaboration of Principle 10 of the Rio Declaration, which stresses the need for citizens' participation in environmental issues and for access to information on the environment held by public authorities. As such, it is the most ambitious venture in the area of environmental democracy so far undertaken under the auspices of the United Nations. See* the area of the UNECE website captioned 'Aarhus Convention', found at http://www.unece.org/env/pp/ visited on 23/03/06. *Also see*, S. Stec *et al*, *The Aarhus Convention: An Implementation Guide*, Geneva, The UNECE, 2000.

which the term 'sustainable community development' (SCD) is derived, is considered from the report of the World Commission on Environment and Development (WCED, otherwise known as the Brundtland report) entitled *Our Common Future.*[76] This report defines SD as the 'development which meets the needs of the present without compromising the ability of future generations to meet their own needs'.[77] The author's perspective of SCD in the course of petroleum development in the Niger Delta is thus considered in the context of the progressively continuing effort of the UN on the environment and development to achieve SD in the interest of mankind. Given that SCD is a key feature of this book, it may be stated, following the definition of communities expressed hereunder, that the destiny and/or wellbeing of mankind is closely associated with the nature of man's immediate environment. Thus, there cannot be a sustainable world without sustainable communities, towns and cities. Given that communities exist within nations, nations deserve to be governed in a socio-economically and environmentally sound manner. Nations require being governed in ways that utilise science in a sound and responsible manner to evolve a strong, healthy, safe, just, equitable and inspirational society capable of thriving within environmental limits by, for instance, relying more on renewable energy and natural resources in the course of changing unsustainable patterns of consumption and production.[78] SCD thus requires communities to be eco and people friendly. It requires communities to be cornerstones (ie, models) of civilisation so as to enable them to achieve the needs and/or overcome the concerns and challenges of mankind through new and practical ways of livelihood. SCD requires GG, interactive PI/consensus-building in decision-making, partnerships (including strategic developmental partnerships) based on shared responsibility, mutual cooperation and trust, greater public interest (as against the needs and interests of few), efficient public utilities, civic pride, learning from past mistakes and the encouragement of good practices, so as to

---

76 The WCED (otherwise known as the Brundtland Commission) was established by the UN in 1983 to address growing concern about the accelerating deterioration of the human environment and natural resources and the effect of that deterioration for economic and social development. While establishing the Commission, the UNGA recognised that environmental problems were global in nature, and that it is in the common interest of all nations to establish policies for SD. *See* The WCED, *Our Common Future*, Oxford, Oxford University Press, 1987, especially pp. x–23.

77 Ibid, p. 43.

78 *See* the area of the UN Economic and Social Affairs: Division for SD homepage, regarding the 'Johannesburg Plan Implementation' on 'Changing Unsustainable Patterns of Consumption and Production', found at http://www.un.org/esa/sustdev/documents/WSSD_POI_PD/English/POIChapter3.htm visited on 05/03/09. *Also see* the homepage of the Sustainable Consumption and Production (SCP) Branch of the UNEP DTIE, especially the area of this homepage captioned the 'Marrakech Process: Towards a Global Framework for Action on Sustainable Consumption and Production', found at http://www.unep.fr/scp/marrakech/ visited on 05/03/09.

effectively design and implement development policies, plans and programmes/projects to achieve mankind's wellbeing.[79]

While considering the foregoing and other related issues towards SCD in the Delta region,[80] it must be noted that the Brundtland Commission's idea presents a radical agenda for social change in attitudes. Such a change, based on a strategic national approach (ie, the development of a National Strategy for SD [NSSD]),[81] requires indicators to monitor and evaluate ongoing SD initiatives.[82]

---

79 Wellbeing may be considered as a *positive physical, social and mental state; it is not just the absence of pain, discomfort and incapacity. It requires that basic needs are met, that individuals have a sense of purpose, that they feel able to achieve important personal goals and particulate in society. It is enhanced by conditions that include supportive personal relationships, strong and inclusive communities, good health, financial and personal security, rewarding employment, and a healthy and attractive environment.* Consequently, numerous factors may influence an individual's wellbeing. *See Sustainable Development Indicators in Your Pocket 2009: An Update of the UK Government Strategy Indicators*, Department for Environment, Food and Rural Affairs (DEFRA), 2009, p. 119. Although SD has its economic, social, environmental and governance aspects (*ie*, spheres or components), including its cultural and ecological components as some identify; its governance sphere (*ie*, the role of GG), is very significant. Thus, as the WCED put it, '. . . in the final analysis, sustainable development must rest on political will'. *See* The WCED, *Our Common Future, op cit*, especially pp. x–23, in particular p. 9. *Also see* J. Blewit, Understanding Sustainable Development, London, Earthscan, 2008. *See* S. Bell and S. Morse, *Sustainability Indicators: Measuring the Immeasurable?*, London, Earthscan, 2008. *See* S. Dresner, *The Principles of Sustainability*, London, Earthscan, 2008. *Also see* B. Dalal-Clayton and S. Bass, *Sustainable Development Strategies: A Resource Book, op cit*. The Earth Charter Initiative (ECI) expresses the values and principles for a sustainable future. *See* the ECI homepage found at http://www.earthcharterinaction.org/content/ visited on 23/12/09.

80 *See* the UNDP Millennium Villages Project (MVP) in Nigeria, found (in the area of the UNDP Nigeria homepage) at http://www.ng.undp.org/projects/mvp.shtml visited on 05/03/09. *Also see* the Pampaida MVP in Kaduna state, and the Ikaram-Ibaram MVP covering seven villages (ie, Eresu, Iyani, Ikram, Ase, Gedegede, and Ajowa) of the Akoko North West Local Government Area (ANWLGA) of Ondo state, found (in the area of the UNDP Nigeria homepage) at http://www.ng.undp.org/projects/poverty/docs/MYR_2008.pdf and at http://www.ng.undp.org/projects/poverty/docs/Bantanse_Oct14.pdf both visited on 05/03/09. *See* H. Girardet, *Schumacher Briefings 2: Creating Sustainable Cities*, Foxhole, Green, 2008. *See* H. Girardet, *CitiesPeoplePlanet*, Chichester, Wiley-Academy, 2004. *See* H. Barton (ed), *Sustainable Communities: The Potential for Eco-Neighbourhoods*, London, Earthscan, 2005. *See* R. Register, *Ecocities: Rebuilding Cities in Balance with Nature*, Gabriola Island, New Society, 2006. *See*, D. L. Christian, *Creating a Life Together: Practical Tools to Grow Ecovillages and Intentional Communities*, Gabriola Island, New Society, 2008. *See* J. Dawson, *Schumacher Briefings 12: Ecovillages: New Frontiers for Sustainability*, Foxhole, Green, 2006. *See* J. M. Bang, *Ecovillages: A Practical Guide to Sustainable Communities*, Edinburgh, Floris, 2005. *See* D. Warburton (ed), *Community & Sustainable Development: Participation in the Future*, London, Earthscan, 1998. *Also see* J. M. Bang, *Growing Eco-communities: Practical Ways to Create Sustainability*, Edinburgh, Floris, 2007. *See* D. N. Zillman *et al* (eds), Human Rights in Natural Resources Development: Public Participation in Sustainable Development of Mining and Energy Resources, *op cit*, pp. 580–582.

81 *See*, B. Dalal-Clayton and S. Bass, 'National Strategies for Sustainable Development: The Challenge Ahead', March 2000, found at http://www.nssd.net/pdf/Issues2.pdf visited on 04/05/09. *Also see* B. Dalal-Clayton and S. Bass, *Sustainable Development Strategies: A Resource Book, op cit*, p. 6.

82 *See* S. Baker, *Sustainable Development: Routledge Introductions to Environment Series*, London, Routledge, 2006, especially pp. 211–218. *Also see* G. Atkinson *et al*, *Measuring Sustainable Development: Macroeconomics and the Environment*, Cheltenham, Edward Elgar, 1999. *See* S. Bell and S. Morse, *Sustainability Indicators: Measuring the Immeasurable?*, London, Earthscan, 2008.

Considering that the problems confronting developed and developing countries are different, as a result of which countries are fine-tuning their SD strategies accordingly,[83] the efforts towards SD in the Niger Delta require being driven by the NSSD designed to tackle the SD problems and challenges confronting Nigeria.[84]

The existing forms and/or measures of community involvement (CI) in petroleum resources development in Nigeria are basically those designed by government and those increasingly being designed by the MNOCs operating in the country. On one hand, these measures are designed to implement certain relevant but scattered policies, regulations and laws, including the practices of various levels of governments. On the other hand, they are increasingly being designed to realise certain policy objectives, business statements, guidelines and standards, codes of conduct and other related corporate responsibility documents of the MNOCs, some of which are those of industry groups, corporate groups, and sectoral measures that are yet to be properly translated into the framework of the individual MNOCs. With the exception of CI in the Environmental Impact Assessment (EIA) of petroleum development projects, these measures are not being implemented in a way that is clear to or properly understood by members of the public in the country, especially those of the oil-rich Delta region. These measures are not being coordinated into a comprehensive whole.[85] The expectations of each of the major stakeholder-groups about these measures are yet to be appreciated by others, such that they often breed misunderstanding, scepticism, tension and confusion, which have the effect of worsening the already unclear picture about them.[86] There are thus no generally accepted ways of practising some or most of the existing forms and/or measures of CI. These forms and/or measures have not been

---

83 *See* B. Dalal-Clayton and S. Bass, 'Recent Progress and New Thinking on Strategies for Sustainable Development', being a paper presented at the Annual Meeting of the IAIA, Netherlands Congress Center, The Hague, June 15–21, 2002, p. 12. *Also see* B. Dalal-Clayton, K. Swiderska and S. Bass (eds), *Stakeholder Dialogues on Sustainable Development Strategies: Lessons, Opportunities and Developing Country Case Studies*, London, International Institute of Environment and Development, (IIED), 2002.

84 *See Nigeria's National Agenda 21*, Abuja, FEPA, 1999. The UN Agenda 21 calls all nations to develop and implement their own strategies, plans, policies and processes for SD in the interest of humanity. *See therefore Sustainable Development Indicators in Your Pocket 2009: An Update of the UK Government Strategy Indicators, op cit.*

85 *See* the non-coordination of the public hearings (discussed in Chapter 6) with other impact identification and mitigation processes of petroleum development proposals in the Delta region.

86 Various Memoranda of Understanding (MoUs) are being entered into between the MNOCs and the oil-producing communities, in the course of the operations of the MNOCs in the communities. Most often, these MoUs breed misunderstanding and confusion which occasion community crises and thereby threaten peace and security in the communities. Such MoUs may, in certain respects, be exemplified by that entered into on November 5, 1998, between Bonny kingdom and the Bonny Joint Industry Companies (JIC) led by the NLNG. This MoU, discussed in Chapter 9, generated the crisis occasioned by the Bonny community against the NLNG, in September 1999.

able to satisfy the communities neither have they been able to fulfil the expectations of the MNOCs and government. For instance, citizens of the communities regard them as partial and palliative measures. Detailed explanation is thus required in terms of discussing some of them; more so, as they are associated with other sectors of the Nigerian economy. Also, regarding the protection and regulation of the environment, certain gaps exist in terms of the environmental democracy measures initiated by the FG towards fulfilling the SD responsibilities of Nigeria as a member-state of the UN and the African Union (AU).[87] The present state of affairs regarding these forms and/or measures of PI is adversely affecting the smooth growth and advancement of environmental democracy which they are designed to promote. Besides, there has not been any deliberate effort of government or any known in-depth scholarly study designed to consider these forms and/or measures comprehensively.

From the foregoing and other related factors associated with the issue discussed in this and other chapters, it may be appreciated that the subject of CI in petroleum development in Nigeria is not as clear and simple as many would have thought. The existing forms and/or measures of CI in petroleum development need to be properly identified and categorised to enhance public understanding and consensus-building. They need to be assessed to verify whether or not they are capable of fulfilling the globally identified need and widely accepted principles of environmental democracy, to generate conclusions and recommendations towards resolving the crises in the Delta region.[88] These crises need to be resolved in the mutual interest of the three major stakeholders of the petroleum development business, including the interest of the poor citizens (who are being marginalised in decision-making processes in the country), and the consumer nations (along with the members of the public of these nations relying on the uninterrupted development and security of supply[89] of these resources). Community crises in the Delta

---

87 *See* the NEPAD 'Action Plan for the Environment Initiative', *op cit. See* L. M. Goodrich and W. T. R. Fox (eds), *Legal Effects of United Nations Resolutions*, New York, Columbia University Press, 1969. *Also see* Section 12 of the 1999 Constitution of the FRN, regarding the implementation of treaties entered into by Nigeria. Hence, regarding the 'Nature of the Plan of the Implementation and the Johannesburg Declaration', the USA is cited on page 146 of the report of the WSSD as follows: *The United States highlights the importance of the Plan of Implementation and the Johannesburg Declaration and notes that, like other such declarations and related documents, these documents adopted at this conference contain important political goals and coordinated plans of action, but do not create legally binding obligations on states under international law. See* the report of the WSSD, found at http://daccess-ods.un.org/TMP/6421712.html visited 31/12/06.

88 Regarding peace, environmental protection and SD, including SCD, in the Delta region and other oil-producing areas of Nigeria, Principle 25 of the Rio Declaration on Environment and Development, 1992, provides that 'peace, development and environmental protection are interdependent and indivisible'.

89 *See* D. R. Bohi and M. A. Toman, *The Economics of Energy Security*, Boston, Kluwer, 1996, p. 129. *Also see* F. Parra, *Oil Politics: A Modern History of Petroleum*, London, I. B. Tauris, 2004, p. 1.

region deserve to be urgently addressed in the interest of public good and Nigeria's future.[90]

1.3 AIMS AND OBJECTIVES

The aims and objectives of this book include examining the issues and circumstances which generated the crises in the Delta region, in a way to promote SD of petroleum resources and SCD in the Delta region and other oil-producing areas of Nigeria, including the security of supply of these resources to consumer-nations, as Nigeria's contribution to energy resources sustainability in the interest of mankind. The book will, in the process, also contribute to transparency and accountability in decision-making in Nigeria.[91] It is thus an academic and a practical contribution to environmental democracy regarding petroleum development in Nigeria.

From the foregoing aims and objectives, two hypotheses may be developed, namely the main/core hypothesis and the enlarged/ancillary hypothesis. The main hypothesis proposes that CI in petroleum development in the Delta region is consultative rather than being truly participatory, while the ancillary hypothesis provides that the majority of Nigerian citizens, especially the poor masses and those constituting Nigeria's intelligentsia, are not truly involved in decision-making processes as they are being marginalised in the governance of the country.

1.4 IMPORTANCE, JUSTIFICATION AND CONTRIBUTION

The author's perspective rests on the increasing role of the stakeholder theory in business relations, especially regarding major natural resources development in developing countries characterised by the resource curse and the existence of poor and neglected resources-producing communities. While considering the development of major natural resources as the foundation for the growth and/or advancement of developing countries, the author draws a connection between this state of affairs and the lack of participation of the citizens of the Delta region in the decision-making process of petroleum development in their communities. The author allows the book to home in on the role of corporate responsibility in terms of the MNOCs providing a measure of public utilities in the region, and impact assessment (of which participation is an important ingredient) as a significant pillar of SD. To the author's knowledge, no known scholarly work, especially at the doctorate

90 *See* the Guardian newspapers' editorial entitled 'Nigeria's Future and the Niger Delta', found at http://www.ngrguardiannews.com/editorial_opinion/article02//indexn2_html?pdate=180109&ptitle=Nigeria's%20Future%20And%20The%20Niger%20Delta visited on 18/01/09.

91 This is the basis for proposing the enlarged/ancillary hypothesis of the book.

level,[92] has addressed these problems.[93] This book is also important because it reinforces the view that Africa is a centre of crises and contradictions, and major natural resources development by extractive industries occupy a key place at the centre of these crises.[94] As a contribution to the resolution of the community crises occasioned by the adverse effects of petroleum development in the Delta region, this book is an idea whose time has come.[95] On this note, it addresses the problem of insecurity of supply of Nigeria's petroleum to its global consumer-nations and their consumer public, including the problem of insecurity of lives and property as the FG's petroleum development JV assets in the region. The deplorable state of insecurity in the region[96] has given rise to such social ills as hostage-taking of expatriate personnel of the MNOCs and

---

92 Related to this book, in the context of ethnic minority oil-producing areas, is the work of M. S. Steyn, entitled 'Oil Politics in Ecuador and Nigeria: A Perspective from Environmental History on the Struggles Between Ethnic Minority Groups, Multinational Oil Companies and National Governments', a PhD thesis submitted to the University of Free State, Bloemfontein, South Africa, in November, 2003. Based on the Herman Dooyeweerd philosophical postulation that human beings play a key role in caring for the earth, this thesis analyses the environmental and social impacts and the marginalisation of the oil-rich Nigerian Delta ethnic minority region. Steyn uses the studies of the indigenous Cofan and Siona-Secoya Indians of Ecuador in South America and the Ogonis of Nigeria to analyse the struggle of ethnic minority oil-producing communities in developing countries against MNOCs and their national governments. Whereas the struggle of the Ogonis is against Shell Nigeria with its parent companies in the Netherlands and the United Kingdom, the struggle of the Cofan and Siona-Secoya ethnic minorities of Ecuador is against Texaco Inc. of the USA. Steyn argues that it is the responsibility of national governments to pay attention to environmental and human rights abuse in their nations, while it is the responsibility of MNOCs to implement environmental protection measures in the course of their operations.

93 Other PhD studies relating to the oil-producing communities of Nigeria include that of J. G. Frynas on the conflicts between oil companies and village communities in Nigeria, submitted to the University of St. Andrews, Scotland. This study has been published as J. G. Frynas, *Oil in Nigeria: Conflict and Litigation between Oil Companies and Village Communities, op cit.* Another related book is the revised thesis of K. S. A. Ebeku, *Oil and the Niger Delta People in International Law – Resource Rights, Environmental and Equity Issues, op cit. Also see* A. Kabir, 'Social Responsibility of Governments in Mineral Resource Development', being a thesis submitted to the CEPMLP, University of Dundee, in fulfilment of the award of the Degree of PhD, June 2005. *See* E. Emeseh, 'Regulatory and Institutional Framework for Enforcing Criminal Liability for Environmental Damage', being a thesis submitted to the CEPMLP, University of Dundee, in fulfilment of the award of the Degree of PhD, December 2005.

94 *See* W. Visser *et al* (eds), *Corporate Citizenship in Africa: Lessons from the Past; Paths to the Future, op cit*, p. 13. *Also see* the discussion of K. Ballentine at the DESA Expert Group Meeting on 'Conflict, Peace-building and Development', on November 15, 2004, entitled 'Natural Resources, Governance, Development and Conflict', found at http://www.un.org/esa/peace-building/Action/DesaTaskForce/papersegm20041115/NaturalResourcesKBallentine.pdf visited on 10/05/05.

95 Thus, as the nineteenth century French poet and romantic writer, Victor Marie Hugo, put it, nothing is more powerful than an idea whose time has come. *See The New Encyclopaedia Britannica*, London, Encyclopaedia Britannica, 2002, Vol. 6, pp.125–127.

96 *See* the 2008 report of the Centre for Environment, Human Rights and Development (CEHRD), entitled 'Scorecard for 2008: A CEHRD Report on the State of Human Rights Abuse and Violence in the Niger Delta Region of Nigeria', found in the area of the homepage of the CEHRD captioned 'CEHRD's 2008 Human Rights Report', found at http://www.cehrd.org/files/Human_Rights_Report_2008.pdf visited on 29/03/09.

citizens (including infants, the elderly and traditional rulers in the region).[97] The book is thus a contribution to peace, in relation to the uninterrupted development of petroleum resources in the Delta region, in harmony with the findings of the continuing effort of the UN on the environment and development. The book is also a contribution to CSR and GSR, especially GG, including the social responsibility of the communities (SRCs), and SD, as well as true federalism and stable democracy in Nigeria.[98] It is a contribution to Nigeria's prosperity, as a way out of her resource curse and protracted ethnic minority question demonstrated by the Niger Delta crises. The ethnic thrust of the book is equally significant and justified, considering the argument of some that the prospects of Nigeria lie in its ethnic composition. Otherwise put, that Nigeria's federating units should be its component ethnic nationalities.[99]

This book is significant because it identifies several largely uncoordinated forms and/or measures of CI in petroleum development in Nigeria, to aid the understanding of members of the public, especially the major stakeholders of the resources development business. The identification of these measures of CI will help to address or at least minimise ongoing misunderstandings. It will provide the FG and other affected levels of government with an on-the-spot outline of these measures, so as to enhance the resolution of the crises in the Delta region. It is an effort to improve the frosty relationship[100] among the

---

97 Hostage-taking is thus being condemned as a crime against humanity undermining the positive values of the resource-control movement. *See* the ThisDay newspaper report entitled 'Dokubo Meets VP, Condemns Hostage-Taking', found at http://www.thisdayonline.com/nview.php ?id=83532&printer_friendly= visited on 13/07/07. *Also see* the Tide newspaper report entitled 'Children Protest Kidnapping in N' Delta', found at http://www.thetidenews.com/article.aspx ?qrDate=05/12/2008&qrTitle=Childrenprote... visited on 17/05/08. *See* the report of the Guardian newspapers, entitled 'Gunmen Abduct Opobo Chief, Free 2 French Sailors', found at http://www.guardinanewsngr.com/news/article05//indexn2_html?pdate=070908&ptitl... visited on 07/09/08. *Also see* C. Ogan, *Okrika: A Kingdom of the Niger Delta*, Port Harcourt, Onyoma Research, 2008, pp. xxxiv–xxxv. *See* the ThisDay newspaper report entitled 'Hostage Takers Are Criminals, Says Obasanjo', found at http://www.thisdayonline.com/nview.php?id+39478 visited on 31/01/06. *Also see* the 'Rivers State Kidnap (Prohibition) Law No. 3 of 2009', being a law to prohibit the act of kidnapping in Rivers State and the committing of any act as an explicit or implicit condition for the release of a person kidnapped, and for matters related thereto'.

98 Regarding the relationship of GG to SD, the former UN Secretary General, Kofi Annan, points out that 'good governance and SD are indivisible'. *See* the inaugural address of Kofi Annan at the UN 'International Conference on Governance for Sustainable Growth and Equity', held in New York, July, 28–30, 1997, found at http://magnet.undp.org/icg97/ANNAN.HTM visited on 29/09/06.

99 *See* the ThisDay newspaper report entitled 'Enahoro: Our Mistakes in the Founding of Nigeria', found at http://www.thisdayonline.com/nview.php?id=123647&printer_ friendly=1 visited on 28/09/08. *Also see* O. Awolowo, Awo*: The Autobiography of Chief Obafemi Awolowo*, Cambridge, Cambridge University Press, 1960, pp. 176–177.

100 These frosty relationships impose social responsibility on the international community, especially countries of the globe relying on Nigeria's petroleum resources to serve their needs, to persuade governments and MNOCs in Nigeria to properly fulfil their obligations and responsibilities to the resources-producing areas. *See The Price of Oil: Corporate Responsibility and Human Rights Violations in Nigeria's Oil Producing Communities, op cit*, pp. 189–199.

three major stakeholders, to enhance the realisation of tri-sector development partnerships.[101]

The significance and contribution of this book also hinge on its findings regarding the need to develop participation models (such as toolkits and guidelines),[102] and SD oriented good neighbour agreements[103] in place of the memoranda of understanding (MoUs) being entered into between the oil-producing communities and the MNOCs representing the joint venture partners of the petroleum development business (*ie*, the MNOCs and the FG represented by the Nigerian National Petroleum Corporation, NNPC). This book therefore aims to establish the relationship between research and development (R & D) regarding environmental democracy in major natural resources development.

---

101 *See* M. Warner and R. Sullivan (eds), *Putting Partnerships to Work: Strategic Alliances for Development between Government, the Private-Sector and Civil Society, op cit. Also see* the homepage of Business Partners for Development (BPD), found at *http://www.bpdweb.com/* visited on 25/12/09, regarding tri-sector partnerships aimed at providing win-win and long term benefits to business, civil society and government.

102 *See* the area of the IAP2 homepage captioned 'Practitioner Tools', and 'Toolbox', found at http://www.iap2.org/associations/4748/files/06Dec_Toolbox.pdf visited on 17/09/08. *Also see* the publication of the Australian Environmental Protection Agency (EPA), entitled 'Best Practice Environmental Management in Mining: Community Consultation and Involvement', dated 11/23/05, found, in the area of the Australian EPA homepage, at http://www.ret.gov.au/Documents/community_consultation_and_involvement20051124112825.pdf visited on 18/05/08. *See Doing Better Business Through Effective Public Consultation and Disclosure: A Good Practice Manual*, Washington DC, International Finance Corporation (IFC) Environment Division, 2000, found at http://ifcln.ifc.org/ifcext/enviro.nsf/AttachmentsByTitle/ppubconsult/$FILE/PublicConsultation.pdf visited on 29/10/04. *See* the 'Terms of Engagement: A Toolkit for Community Engagement for the Murray-Darling Basin' prepared by H. J. Aslin and V. A. Brown, under the auspices of the MurrayDarling Basin Commission, Department of Agriculture, Fisheries and Forestry, Australia, found at http://www.mdbc.gov.au/naturalresources/pdf/h-doment/Latesttoolkit.pdf visited on 06/09/05. *Also see* the UN Berlin Environmental Guidelines for Mining Operations, found at http://www.mineralresourcesforum.org/workshops/Berlin/index.htm especially the 'Berlin 11 Guidelines for Mining and Sustainable Development', 2002, found at http://www.mineralresources forum.org/workshops/Berlin/docs/Guidelines.pdf visited on 03/03/2006, concerning community consultation. *See* the 'Public Involvement Guideline: A Guideline to Involve the Public in Oil and Gas Operational Planning' (produced by the Oil and Gas Commission (OGC) of the Federal Republic of Canada, dated July, 2002, found at http://www.ogc.gov.bc.ca/documents/guidelines/revised-Public%20Inv.%20GL.pdf visited on 24/04/06. *Also see* G. McMahon and J. Strongman, 'The Rise of the Community', found at http://www.natural-resources.org/minerals/development/docs/pdfs/community.pdf visited on 22/02/06.

103 *See* the Agreements, Treaties and Negotiated Settlements (ATNS) with the Indigenous Peoples of Australia (*ie*, the Australian aboriginal minorities), found in the homepage of the ATNS project, at http://www.atns.net.au/default.asp, visited on 23/03/07. *Also see* M. Langton *et al*, (eds), *Honour Among Nations?: Treaties and Agreements with Indigenous Peoples*, Carton, Melbourne University Press, 2004. *See* M. Langton *et al*, (eds), *Settling with Indigenous People: Modern Treaty and Agreement-making*, Annandale, The Federation Press, 2006. *See* the area of the website of the Canadian Minerals and Metal Sector, captioned the 'Whitehorse Mining Initiative' (WMI), found at http://www.nrcan.gc.ca/mms/poli/wmi_e.htm visited on 31/12/06. *See* M. L. McAllister and C. J. Alexander, *A Stake in the Future: Redefining the Canadian Mineral Industry*, Vancouver, University of British Columbia (UBC) Press, 1997. Considering, however, that the Niger Deltans are not indigenous people, *see* N. Usman, 'The Rights of Indigenous Peoples and Mineral Resource Development: Global Trends and the Nigerian Question', being a thesis submitted to the CEPMLP, University of Dundee, in fulfilment of the requirements for the award of the Degree of PhD, June 2003. *See* the website of the 'United Nations Permanent Forum on Indigenous Issues (UNPFII)', found at http://www.un.org/esa/socdev/unpfii/ visited on 14/01/09.

1.5 METHOD AND STRUCTURE OF THE BOOK

Following the structure of the individual chapters discussed below, the book is methodically approached in a historical and logical sequence, in six parts and ten chapters. It discusses environmental democracy regarding petroleum development in the Delta region on the basis of the progressively advancing effort of the UN on the environment and development towards realising SD in the interest of mankind. The book considers the finding of experts on PP, that participation (*ie*, the right to be heard) has a distant historical origin dating back to the beginning of human civilisation and is thus deeply ingrained in some cultures, while it is non-existent in other cultures.[104] It thus examines whether or not the social systems of citizens of the Delta region are participatory, and the finding made is positive. This finding suggests that the answer to these protracted crises in the region is interactive CI in the decision-making process of petroleum development. Similar to the resistance movements of the British colonial era, the ongoing resource-control movement in the region is generated by lack of participation in such affairs of Nigeria as petroleum[105] development which directly impacts on citizens of the region. To examine the crises in the region in a wider, more proper, rational and realistic context of the FRN,[106] the author developed two hypotheses. Among other findings made, the concluding chapter confirms these hypotheses, and recommends the need for the improvement of CSR in the Delta region and other oil-producing areas,[107] and a greater

---

104 *See* D. N. Zillman *et al* (eds), *Human Rights in Natural Resources Development: Public Participation in Sustainable Development of Mining and Energy Resources, op cit*, preview.

105 'Petroleum' is variously referred to in this book as 'petroleum resources', 'resource', 'oil', 'crude oil', 'oil and gas', as well as oil and gas 'resources'; depending on the context in which it is used. Section 15(1) of the Petroleum Act, 1969, Cap 350, LFN 1990, defines petroleum as 'mineral oil (or any related hydrocarbon) or natural gas as it exists in its natural state in strata, and does not include coal or bituminous or other stratified deposits from which oil can be extracted by destructive distillation'. Since 1978, Nigeria has been Africa's largest oil-producing country and the world's eighth largest oil exporting country. Nigeria's petroleum reserves are about 34 billion barrels, while as one of the global top ten natural gas endowments, its proven natural gas is about 159 trillion cubic feet (Tcf). Petroleum development thus accounts for 95% of Nigeria's export earnings and 80% of its revenue. *See* the draft report of the 'National Oil and Gas Policy', prepared by Nexant Limited under the auspices of the BPE, *op cit*, p. 2–1. *Also see* the area of the NNPC website on 'Oil & Gas in Nigeria' captioned 'Development of Nigeria's Oil Industry' with the subtitle 'Oil and Gas Reserves', found at http://www.nnpcgroup.com/development.htm visited on 31/12/06. *See* the BBC report entitled 'Oil Prices Rise on Nigerian Fears', with the subtitle 'Global Oil Prices have Risen on the Back of Violence and Political Turmoil in Nigeria, the World's Eighth Largest Crude Oil Exporter', found at http://newsvote.bbc.co.uk/mpapps/pagetools/print/news.bbc.co.uk/1/hi/business/6584. . . visited on 23/04/07. *Also see* the article entitled 'Angola Surpasses Nigeria as Top Africa Oil Producer', found in the area of the homepage of Reuters, under the Energy section of 'Business and Finance', at http://www.reuters.com/article/rbssEnergyNews/idUSL1590863520080515 visited on 27/09/08.

106 The author developed these hypotheses in the wider context of the FRN because decisions associated with the development of petroleum and other major natural resources are primarily taken at the federal/central level of government.

107 *See* R. Welford, *Hijacking Environmentalism: Corporate Responses to Sustainable Development*, London, Earthscan, 1997, especially pp. x, the back-cover, and 179–210.

need for GSR embedded in GG in Nigeria.[108] The book found that the crises in the Delta region are due to the absence of GG. This is more so, because decision-makers merely listen to the concerns of the communities of the region during community involvements (CIs) without properly acting on these concerns in the course of the implementation of petroleum development projects[109] in the region. Accordingly, due to the absence of GG, the book found that the majority of Nigerian citizens are marginalised as appropriate opportunities are not provided by government to enable them make inputs into decision-making processes in the country. These findings establish the core and ancillary hypotheses of this book in the affirmative by narrowing the overall problem of Nigeria to that of bad governance (ie, the failure of political leadership) identified by Chinua Achebe, as expressed in this chapter and Chapter 10. A form of citizens' participation, by which citizens of Nigeria, including those of the Delta region, are empowered to make input in an interactive manner in the decision-making processes, is therefore recommended as the solution to the problem of environmental democracy in the region and the overall governance of Nigeria.

Apart from empowering citizens in decision-making processes, there are other attributes of GG in the interest of a nation and its citizens. GG can generate a stable and transparent regulatory environment to enhance SD of petroleum resources in Nigeria and sound and equitable SCD. GG is the solution to the petroleum resource curse in Nigeria. GG is the solution to the poverty plaguing Nigerian citizens in the midst of the plentiful wealth being generated from the development of the abundant petroleum resources of the country from the Delta region and other oil-producing areas.[110] GG is capable of generating SRCs as well as the promotion and maintenance of CSR, to foster win-win or collaborative partnerships among the major stakeholders of the petroleum development business, towards the resolution of the crises in the Delta region.[111] GG can distinguish the true ethnic minority Delta region from the artificial or politically diluted Niger Delta created by virtue of the NDDC Act, so as to properly address the problems of the region and its people on the basis of the Nigerian ethnic minority question. GG can generate a stable and transparent regulatory system to enhance the effectiveness of the impact assessment of petroleum development proposals, to achieve sound and equitable SCD. SD of petroleum resources will enhance security of supply of these resources to Nigeria's consumer-nations and thereby

---

108 In the perspective of the book, GG implies governance which is transparent and accountable in decision-making, and enhanced by true federalism and stable and sustained democracy. The recommendations of the book are thus made in the broader context and interest of all the oil-producing areas and the entire FRN. *See* R. T. Suberu, *Ethnic Minority Conflicts and Governance in Nigeria, op cit*, especially p. 83.

109 *C/f* F. A. Wilson (ed), *Towards Sustainable Project Development*, Cheltenham, Edward Elgar, 1997.

110 *See* the report of the International Crisis Group (ICG) on Nigeria, entitled 'Nigeria: Want in the Midst of Plenty', Africa Report No. 113–19, July 2006, found at http://www.crisisgroup/library/documents/africa/westafrica/113nigeriawantinthemidstofplenty.pdf visited on 21/11/06.

111 *See* R. Sidaway, *Resolving Environmental Disputes from Conflicts to Consensus, op cit*, pp. 115–190. *Also see* A. Onuoha, *From Conflict To Collaboration: Building Peace in Nigeria's Oil-Producing Communities*, London, Adonis & Abbey, 2005.

enlist Nigeria's contribution to sustainability in the interest of humanity in these nations, in conformity with Principle 1 of the Rio Declaration on Environment and Development, 1992. GG, generated by interactive PI, can enhance the practice of true federalism and transparent, accountable and sustained democratic governance in Nigeria. Based on these and other attributes and advantages of GG, PP or PI is bound to become not only a requirement of policy and law, but also an accepted cost of doing business and a proper way of life in Nigeria.[112] The various conclusions and recommendations of the book are therefore reached on the basis of logical and legal deductive reasoning.

Still on methodology, the author adopted a multiple research method[113] involving the use of library and desk-top sources, and e-mail, letter writing and telephone conversation processes so as to bridge gaps and to clarify grey and/or unclear areas identified in published works and other documents.

A major difficulty encountered is not having access to certain research resources in the custody of governments, the MNOCs and other institutions associated with the Nigerian petroleum industry, as some of these resources constitute classified information (in the country) not released to researchers and other members of the public. To remedy this difficulty, the author complemented accessible key resources with other relevant and readily available resources such as those of the media and civil society such as NGOs, CBOs and civil rights activists.[114] Besides, certain footnotes of this book are precisely written, while others are expressed in great detail. Those expressed in detail mostly relate to issues which, in the perspective of the author, are of interest to community stakeholder groups and individuals.[115]

---

112 *See* E. Bastida *et al* (eds), *International and Comparative Mineral Law and Policy: Trends and Prospects, op cit*, p. 279. *Also see*, the area of the homepage of 'Involve', entitled 'About Us', found at http://www.involve.org.uk/index.cfm?fuseaction=main.viewSection&intsectionid=368 visited on 30/08/08.

113 *See* D. E. Gray, *Doing Research in the Real World*, London, Sage, 2004, p. 33. *Also see* R. Churchill, 'Some Notes on PhD Research Methodology', being a paper delivered during the Ph D Easter Training Research Seminar of the CEPMLP, University of Dundee, 09/04/07. *See* G. Rugg and M. Petre, *A Gentle Guide to Research Methods*, Berkshire, Open University Press, 2007. *See* N. Moore, *How to Do Research: A Practical Guide to Designing and Managing Research Projects*, London, Facet, 2006. *See* R. Kumar, *Research Methodology: A Step-by-Step Guide for Beginners*, London, Sage, 2005.

114 These and other sources indicated above helped to bridge the gaps created by non-access to information in government and MNOCs' sources.

115 These include footnotes on Bonny kingdom, the area of emphasis of the book in the Delta region. Military Decrees mentioned are also referred to as Acts, where they have been revised and/or adopted as Acts of Parliament. Other methods used include tactful accounts on Finima without undermining the interest of any of its two incumbent paramount chiefs unusually installed by the Buoye-Omuso Brown major house, and the abbreviation of regularly used words, phrases and terms which are tabled for easy reference. Regarding abbreviations having more than one meaning, not more than one of them is used in a chapter, as demonstrated in the case of NCP meaning National Council on Privatisation in Chapter 2 and Nigerian Content Policy in Chapters 6 and 7. Also, PPP refers to Polluter Pays Principle in Chapters 1 and 10, Public-Private-Partnership in Chapter 2, and Policy, Plan and Programme in Chapter 5. In Chapter 4, the fourteen major chieftaincy houses of Bonny kingdom are discussed following the methodology of G. I. Jones, *The Trading States of the Oil Rivers: A Study of Political Development in Eastern Nigeria*, New Brunswick, Transaction, 2000, cited in the chapter. These houses are discussed in two broad divisions (*ie*, as 'duawaris' and 'opuwaris') based on their origins and traditional nomenclatures.

Chapter 1, the introductory part of the book, is, as described above, a conceptual and historical account of the crises in the Delta region in the context of the FRN. The chapter identifies the Nigerian minority question as the basis of the marginalisation of the citizens of the Delta region and other Nigerian ethnic minorities, as decision-making in Nigeria is mainly dictated by the interests of the three major ethnic groups whose elites mastermind the affairs of the country. This chapter identifies the petroleum resources-producing communities, the Federal Government (FG) and the MNOCs as the three major stakeholders of the resources-producing business in Nigeria. It discusses the stakeholder perspective, its growing recognition in the context of major natural resources development in developing countries, in the interest of the poor and marginalised resources-producing communities of these countries. It establishes two hypotheses. These are the core/main hypotheses anchored on lack of CI in petroleum development in the Delta region, and then the enlarged/ancillary hypothesis anchored on the lack of involvement of majority of Nigerian citizens in the decision-making processes of the country. Thus, the key proposition of the book is that neither CI in petroleum development (as exemplified by the state of affairs in the Delta ethnic minority region) nor overall PI (as evidenced by the plight of a vast majority of Nigerian citizens) in the governance of the country, has, so far, been able to properly integrate the concerns and other inputs of the affected public into decision-making processes, so as to arrive at transparent and accountable decisions. Improvement in CI (*ie*, interactive CI) is thus demonstrated as a means of addressing the crises in the Delta region, while improvement in PI (*ie*, interactive PI) is demonstrated as a means of addressing the Nigerian national question centred on bad governance.

Part B, made up of Chapters 2 and 3 is entitled 'Assessment of the interface between specific initiatives and trends in international environment and development policy, and stakeholder decision-making'. Chapter 2 consolidates the background analysis of Chapter 1 and discusses stakeholder concerns and actions in the Delta region in the context of the ongoing effort of the UN on the environment and development. The chapter discusses the twin relationship of the environment and development in relation to the environmental and developmental problems, socio-economic concerns and political aspirations of citizens of the Delta region, as well as GSR and CSR. It investigates the plight of the people of the Delta ethnic minority region worsened by the adverse effects of petroleum development in the region. This demonstrates the failure of successive FG's intervention measures in the region due to lack of sustained political will and commitment of the government controlled by ethnic majority elite and their associates. Aggravated by the absence of true federalism and transparent democratic governance, these FG measures have not sufficiently addressed the plight and concerns of Delta minorities as, for instance, expressed in the Willink Commission report of 1958. This Commission found that the Niger Delta was 'poor, backward and marginalised' in the course of nation-building in Nigeria.[116] Chapter 3 discusses

116 *See* The Willink Commission Report, *op cit*, pp. ii and p. 94 paragraph 27.

the 'Approaches to promoting the participation of stakeholders in business: A critical review of three dominant international initiatives'. The chapter discusses the Aarhus Convention of 1998 on PP in environmental decision-making as an intergovernmental approach, and two mainly civil society-based as well as other two main industry-driven international initiatives. These are the initiatives of the International Association for Public Participation (IAP2) and the International Association for Impact Assessment (IAIA), and those of the Mining, Minerals and Sustainable Development (MMSD) project and the World Bank Group (WBG) Extractive Industries Review (EIR).

Part C, Chapter 4, discusses 'Citizens' participation in the Delta communities in a social and historical framework'. In order to prove that PP in decision-making is an integral feature of the social systems of citizens of the Delta region, this chapter discusses the traditional social systems of the communities of the region exemplified by the house system of governance of Bonny kingdom. The Bonny kingdom's representative decision-making process is an integral feature of the social systems of other ancient trading states of the Delta region (which were and are still mainly core politically-centralised societies). The chapter distinguishes the core centralised social system of the ancient Delta trading states from the two other traditional social systems identified in the Delta region. These are the egalitarian or republican village democratic systems of such ethnic groups as the Ikwerre ethnic nationality, and the relatively non-core (ie, partly centralised) social systems of such communities and communal groups as Kolokuma, Andoni, Abua and Eppie-Atissa. While noting that participation is an integral feature of the traditional social systems of the communities, kingdoms, tribes and ethnic groups of the Delta region, this chapter re-establishes lack of PI as a significant cause of the ongoing crises in the region. It thus recommends the need for Nigeria to grant a proper sense of belonging to the Delta and other ethnic minorities by properly integrating them into the mainstream of governance through interactive PI, especially regarding aspects of governance which directly affect them as Nigerian citizens.

Part D of the book, comprising Chapters 5-7, discusses the evolution of formal EIA in Nigeria and CI in petroleum development in the Delta region. While discussing the commencement of formal EIA in 1992, Chapter 6 associates EIA with Environmental Assessment (EA) and generic Impact Assessment (IA) and thus lays the foundation for considering the adverse effects of petroleum development projects in the oil-producing Delta region. Chapters 6 and 7 consequently proceed to identify other forms and/or measures of CI in petroleum development in the Delta region. As reinforced in Chapters 8 and 9, Chapter 5 demonstrates the importance of PI and IA in the effort towards SD of petroleum resources and SCD in the Delta region and other oil-producing areas of Nigeria, considering that PI is a significant pillar/promoter of IA and IA is a significant pillar of SD.

Part E, comprising Chapters 8 and 9, discusses CI in the IA of oil and gas development projects in the Bonny kingdom. One significant finding of this part is that through IA, the poor and marginalised petroleum resources-producing communities of the Delta region are able to derive IA benefits from the MNOCs. Thus, as in other areas of the Delta region, due to the lack of GSR in Bonny kingdom, the EIA mitigation measures of oil and gas development projects are directed by the MNOCs more towards providing social investments which are lacking in the kingdom. Emphasis on the provision of social investments thus tends to undermine the environmental stewardship of the MNOCs which is crucial in the effort towards SD in the Delta region.

Among other things, Part F (Chapter 10) concludes the book by recommending the need for interactive CI in petroleum resources development in the oil-producing areas, fostered by GSR, and improved CSR and SRCs, in the course of the resources development in these areas. The chapter recommends the need for improvement in PI in decision-making processes in Nigeria, so as to achieve greater accountability, transparency and responsibility in governance, towards achieving SD *vis-à-vis* the Millennium Development Goals by 2015, in the interest of the citizens and humanity at large.

1.6 THE NIGER DELTA REGION

The word 'delta', a Greek alphabet letter, describes a low-lying triangular plain which is composed of stream-borne sediments deposited by a river at its mouth. Although most of the world's deltas are triangular (*ie*, deltoid in shape) as is the Niger Delta, some exceptions exist.[117] Since prehistoric times, delta regions have been significant to mankind, as their sands, silts, clays and other sediments and resources are useful to society. Major civilisations flourished in the deltaic plains of the Nile and Tigris-Euphrates rivers. In recent years, geologists have discovered much of the world's petroleum in ancient deltaic rocks.[118]

The main focus of this book, the true Delta region, is known as the Southern ethnic minority zone as well as the South-South geo-political zone of the FRN.[119] This zone is ethnographically, historically and geographically distinct

---

117 *See The New Encyclopaedia Britannica*, *op cit*, Vol. 3, p. 979.

118 Ibid. The Delta represents the continuity of rivers and river systems to supply and deposit stream-borne sediments. The Niger, from which the Niger Delta evolved, constitutes a basin, the Niger River Basin. This basin traversing nine countries (namely Benin, Burkina Faso, Cameroon, Chad, Cote d'Ivoire, Guinea, Mali, Niger and Nigeria) is a vital asset for the West and Central African regions. *See* K. G. Golfzen (ed), *The Niger River Basin: A Vision for Sustainable Development*, Washington, DC, The World Bank, 2005.

119 The other five geo-political zones of the FRN are the North Central, North Eastern, North Western, South Western and the South Eastern zones. The federation has about 150 million people, a land mass of about 923,768 km^2 (ie, 356,669 sq. miles), and over 250 ethnic groups including the three major ones, Hausa-Fulani, Yoruba and Igbo groups. The federation has three tiers of government, namely the federal, states, and local governments. There are 36 states, along with the FCT, Abuja, and 774 local governments in the federation.

from the artificial Niger Delta created by the NDDC Act.[120] It is bordered to the south by the Atlantic Ocean and to the east by Cameroon. It covers the mouth of the River Niger and the areas to the east and west comprising six major oil-producing states of Nigeria, namely Rivers, Delta, Bayelsa, Akwa-Ibom, Edo and Cross-River states, including the oil-producing areas of Ondo state peopled by the Ijaw ethnic group. Conversely, the artificial Niger Delta is made up of the entire nine oil-producing areas (*ie*, Abia and Imo states and the seven other oil-producing states stated above), comprising 185 LGAs of the FRN.[121]

The true Delta region is a vast sedimentary basin comprising such deltaic deposits as medium to coarse unconsolidated sands, silt, clay, shale and peat. This region is mostly a flat, low lying swampy basin criss-crossed by a dense network of meandering rivers, creeks and rivulets, comprising a diverse mosaic of five ecological zones. These zones are the mangrove forest and coastal vegetation zone, the fresh-water swamp forest zone, the low rain forest zone, the derived savannah zone and the montane zone, comprising heterogeneous groups belonging to about 40 different ethnic groups. Major among these groups are five linguistic groups (*ie*, the Ijoid, Edoid, Delta Cross, Yoruboid and Igboid groups) each of which is comprised of numerous sub-linguistic groups. Among these five groups, the Ijoid (having the longest settlement history), is the most complex linguistic group.[122] The communities of the region occupying distinct geographical locations are broadly known as coastal and mainland communities or communal groups.[123]

---

120 *See* Sections 2 (1) (b) and 4 of the NDDC Act, LFN 2004. This Act and the jurisdiction of the Ministry of Niger Delta (created by the FG in September 2008) cover the artificial Niger Delta region made up of the entire present-day oil-producing states of Nigeria. Petroleum resources development in Nigeria began in the communities of the true Delta region in 1956 (ie, over two decades before the development of these resources commenced in such other areas of Nigeria as Abia and Imo states). *See Southern Minorities Movement, Roots, Appraisal of the Nigerian Crisis and Solution*, Port Harcourt, Southern Minority Movement, February, 1995. *Also see Southern Minorities Movement, Roots, the Struggle and the Future*, Port Harcourt, Southern Minority Movement, December, 1995.

121 *See* the popular version of the 'Niger Delta Regional Development Master Plan (NDRDMP)' prepared by the NDDC, 2006, p. 7.

122 *See* the *Niger Delta Human Development Report, op cit*, pp. 21–22. *Also see* the homepage of the Ijaw Nation, found at http://www.unitedijaw.com/ visited on 13/03/09.

123 The communities, village-communities and communal groups (namely, the kingdoms, clans and ethnic groups) of the region occupy distinct geographical locations. The word or term community may refer to *people who live within a geographically defined area and who have social and psychological ties with each other and with the place where they live. See* the Black's *Law Dictionary, op cit*, p. 297. *Also see* the *New Shorter Oxford Dictionary, op cit*, pp. 463–464. *See* P. Mattessich, *et al, Community Building: What Makes It Work: A Review of Factors Influencing Successful Community Building*, Saint Paul, Minnesota, Amherst H. Wilder Foundation, 1997, p. 56. *See* the presentation of the USEPA entitled 'Projecting Land-Use-Change: A Summary of Models for Assessing the Effects of Community Growth and Change on Land-Use Patterns', found at http://faculty.washington.edu/pwaddell/Models/REPORTfinal2.pdf visited on 26/07/04. *Also see* 'Community Participation Factsheet', found at http://www.lwa.gov.au/downloads/publications_pdf/PF010165.pdf visited on 13/08/04.

1.7(I) STAKEHOLDER PERSPECTIVE

The author conceives and discusses the term stakeholders as comprising groups or individuals that can affect or are affected by business (ie, business operations) and are thus concerned about such operations.[124] Examples of stakeholders are managers, employees, customers, suppliers, distributors, and host communities of companies, as well as government regulators, NGOs such as trade unions, and civil society activists whose activities can affect or influence business operations.[125] The European Commission (EC) Green Paper entitled 'Promoting a European Framework for Corporate Social Responsibility [CSR]' defines the term stakeholder in the following words:

> *an individual, community or organisation that affects, or is affected by, the operations of a company. Stakeholders may be internal (for example, employees) or external (for example, customers, suppliers, shareholders, financiers, the local community).*[126]

The UNESCAP provides the answer to 'who are stakeholders?' as follows:

> *Stakeholders include all individuals or groups with an interest in a project. They are sometimes divided into four categories including: public sector agencies (ministries, provincial or local government, mass organizations); directly effected parties (who live or work where the project will be located); indirectly affected parties (who live nearby or use resources from the project area); and others (such as NGOs, external advisors, and the business sector).*[127]

The stakeholder theory promotes strategic development alliances such as tri-sector partnerships between governments, the private sector and civil society

---

124 *See* J. Andiof *et al* (eds), *Unfolding Stakeholder Thinking: Theory, Responsibility and Engagement*, Sheffield, Greenleaf, 2002, especially pp. 7–8. *Also see* J. Andiof *et al* (eds), *Unfolding Stakeholder Thinking 2: Relationships, Communication, Reporting and Performance*, Sheffield, Greenleaf, 2003. *See* S. Sharma and M. Starik (eds), *Stakeholders, the Environment and Society: New Perspectives in Research on Corporate Sustainability*, Cheltenham, Edward Elgar, 2004, pp.178–179.

125 Ibid. *See* M. A. G. Bunter, *Host Communities, Native Title and Petroleum Licensing*, Dundee, Centre for Energy, Petroleum and Mineral Law and Policy (CEPMLP), 2003, pp. v–vi. *Also see* A. L. Friedman and S. Miles, *Stakeholders: Theory and Practice*, Oxford, Oxford University Press, 2006, pp. 13-14.

126 *See* The EC Green Paper entitled 'Promoting a European Framework for Corporate Social Responsibility', Belguim, Directorate-General for Employment and Social Affairs of the EC, July 2001, p. 28. *Also see* M. McCabe and B. Sadler (eds), *Environmental Impact Assessment Training Resource Manual, op cit*, pp. 164–165.

127 *See* UNESCAP, *Public Involvement Guideline for Natural Resource Development Projects*, New York, UN,1997, p. 10.

in extractive industrial operations, so as to enhance the interests of stakeholders affected by these operations in developing countries.[128]

1.7(II) GROWING RECOGNITION OF THE STAKEHOLDER THINKING REGARDING MAJOR NATURAL RESOURCES DEVELOPMENT IN DEVELOPING COUNTRIES

As indicated above, the stakeholders that are of interest to this book are the oil-producing communities and the joint venture (JV) partners of the petroleum development business in Nigeria (*ie*, the FG and the MNOCs).[129] The operations of companies such as MNOCs, in poor, rural and neglected communities of developing countries usually adversely affect the environment, ecosystem, lifestyles, livelihoods and SD in the communities. These operations are to some extent beneficial to the communities, just as much as they adversely affect them, as exemplified by the operations of MNOCs in the Niger Delta. Consequently, MNCs extracting major natural resources in developing countries either exercise a sense of social responsibility or are expected to be socially responsible to the resources-producing communities.[130]

Traditional company law and practice provide that companies owe a primary responsibility to their shareholders (*ie*, investors) whose objective of owning companies is wealth creation (*ie*, to make profit).[131] The interests of

---

128 Ibid. *Also see* J. Andiof *et al* (eds), *Unfolding Stakeholder Thinking: Theory, Responsibility and Engagement, op cit. See* J. Andiof *et al* (eds), *Unfolding Stakeholder Thinking 2: Relationships, Communication, Reporting and Performance, op cit. See* M. Warner and R. Sullivan (eds.), *Putting Partnerships to Work: Strategic Alliances for Development between Government, the Private Sector and Civil Society*, Sheffield, Greenleaf, 2004. *See* K. Omeje, *High Stakes and Stakeholders: Oil Conflict and Security in Nigeria, op cit. Also see* J. K. Gamman, *Overcoming Obstacles in Environmental Policymaking: Creating Partnership through Mediation*, Albany, State University of New York Press, 1994. *See* U. Petschow *et al, Governance and Sustainability: New Challenges for States, Companies and Civil Society*, Sheffield, Greenleaf, 2005. *See* Article 26 of the Johannesburg Declaration on SD, 2002.

129 As a citizen and traditional ruler of Bonny kingdom, a prominent oil-producing kingdom of the Delta region, the author considers himself as a stakeholder of the petroleum development business in Nigeria. The oil-producing communities' major stakeholder group, to which the author belongs, especially as a specialist on PP and impact assessment of major natural resources development projects, explains his perspective and compassionate disposition towards his stakeholder group. His perspective may thus be different from the perspective of other scholars centred, for instance, on Nigeria's ethnic majority background or the interest of the MNOCs. *See* M. S. Steyn, 'Oil Politics in Ecuador and Nigeria: A Perspective from Environmental History on the Struggles between Ethnic Minority Groups, Multinational Oil Companies and National Governments', *op cit. Also see* R. T. Suberu, *Ethnic Minority Conflicts and Governance in Nigeria, op cit*, especially p. 83.

130 Catering for the interest of stakeholders also ensures business sustainability. *See* L. Burke and J. M. Logsdon, 'How Corporate Social Responsibility Pays Off', Long Range Planning, Vol. 29, No. 4, 1996, pp. 495–502, especially pp. 495 and 501. *Also see* H. R. Bowen, *Social Responsibilities of Businessmen*, New York, Harper and Brothers, 1953.

131 *See* K. Midgley, *Companies and their Shareholders – The Uneasy Relationship*, London, The Institute of Chartered Secretaries and Administrators, 1975. *Also see* the report of the New York Times, entitled 'The Social Responsibility of Business is to Increase Profits', by M. Friedman, found at http://lst-kieser.bwl.uni-mannheim.de/Downloads/SS05/Text_Friedman.pdf visited on 24/07/06.

the directors and other employees (*ie*, the internal stakeholders) who do not form part of the ownership of companies, are, along with the external stakeholders of companies, considered secondary.[132] From the latter part of the twentieth century, the traditional orientation of company law and practice began to change and gave rise to the emergence of the stakeholder theory which dilutes the shareholder theory in business relations, as companies increasingly began to cater for the interests of other stakeholders.[133]

In spite of the dilution of the shareholders' theory, in African and other developing countries, which are richly endowed by major natural resources, the adverse effects of the development of these resources are not being properly addressed. Hence, the stakeholder approach is considered as a way forward.[134] This approach, enhanced by SD partnerships fostered by mutual trust and cooperation between resources-producing communities and JV and other development partners, is what this book is attempting to advocate regarding petroleum development in Nigeria.[135]

1.8 LIMITATION OF SCOPE

This book focuses on the Nigerian Delta region, with particular emphasis on Bonny kingdom. Consequently, the scope of the book covers developments up to December 2006, which marked the end of its basic data gathering,[136] including the necessary fall-outs of its first impression launch (which took place in November 2009).

The limited scope of the book extends to such issues associated with its specialised area as the use of various distinct but similar words, phrases or terminologies to analyse, define, describe and examine the ongoing

---

132 *See* E. Sternberg, *Stakeholding: Betraying the Corporation's Objectives*, London, The Social Affairs Unit, 1998, pp.5–6, 27–28. *Also see* J. F. Johnston, *No Man Can Serve Two Masters: Shareholders Versus Stakeholders In the Governance of Companies*, London, The Social Affairs Unit, 1998.

133 Ibid.

134 *See* W. Visser *et al* (eds), *Corporate Citizenship in Africa: Lessons from the Past; Paths to the Future*, Sheffield, Greenleaf, 2006, p. 8.

135 *See* D. A. Omoweh, *Shell, the State and Underdevelopment of Nigeria's Niger Delta: A Study in Environmental Degradation*, Trenton, Africa World Press, 2005, p. 271. *Also see* the 'Report of the Niger Delta Youths Stakeholders Workshop', Port Harcourt, April 15–17, 2004, found at http://www.aapw/nnpcreport.pdf visited on 10/08/06. *See* the presentation made by A. Ogbuigwe, entitled 'Perspectives from the Niger Delta on Partnership for Sustainable Development', during the plenary session of the Shell Nigeria Stakeholder Workshop, held at the PTI, Effurun, Delta state, February 24–26, 2004. *Also see Niger Delta Human Development Report, op cit*, pp. 172–175. *See* M. B. Umar, 'Legal Issues in the Management of Nigeria's Production Sharing Contracts from a Study of the Nigerian National Petroleum Corporation's (National Petroleum Management Services') Perspective', OGEL, Vol. 3, Issue 1, March 2004, p. 71–100, especially p. 87. *See* the *Proposed National Oil & Gas Policy*, Abuja, BPE, Vol. 2, 2004, p. 66, item 8.0.

136 This impression of the book incorporates necessary fall-outs of its first impression launch, which took place in November 2009.

world-wide participation explosion.[137] Hence, the book cites the above UNESCAP-outlined four levels of PI, namely information gathering, information dissemination, consultation and participation, to emphasise the need to improve CI in the Niger Delta and other oil-producing areas of Nigeria and PI in Nigeria, to reinforce the idea that the governed should be engaged in their own environmental governance. Regarding the use of various participation models such as guidelines and toolkits designed to improve PI, it is reiterated in Chapter 10 that they are required to suit particular local circumstances or situations,[138] especially as there is no consensus qualifying any of them as the best.[139]

Another basic issue associated with the scope of this book is the resource-control movement of the Delta region.[140] This movement, which does not have an official or formal definition, is a recent coinage of the people of the region, especially the governors of the states of the region. Thus, the movement was defined at the Third Summit of the 17 Southern Governors of Nigeria, at Benin, in Edo state, as:

---

137 PP/PI is thus an all-encompassing label used to describe the various forms/mechanisms that individuals or groups may use to communicate their views on public issues in the context of the worldwide emerging participation opportunities. These include 'citizens' participation', 'citizens' involvement', 'stakeholders engagement', 'indigenous peoples' rights', 'local community rights', 'SD agreements', 'public hearings', 'advisory councils', 'NGO intervention', 'right to information', 'right to participation', 'right to justice', 'right to environmental justice or environmental democracy', 'voting', 'decisional transfers', 'benefits sharing', and the establishment of participation groups and organisations. PP involves voting, demonstrating, petitioning, protesting, criticising, lobbying, writing and speaking to the media, political leaders and governments, publishing newsletters, pamphlets, brochures and other documentations, debating, campaigning, appearing and partaking in public hearings. Other forms of participation include citizens requesting access to government-held information, serving on citizens' advisory panels, instituting law suits on grounds of public interest, and all other variants of the concept that the governed should be engaged in their governance. *See* D. N. Zillman *et al* (eds), *Human Rights in Natural Resources Development: Public Participation in Sustainable Development of Mining and Energy Resources, op cit*, p. 1–120, especially pp. 12 and 17. *Also see* E. Bastida *et al* (eds), *International and Comparative Mineral Law and Policy: Trends and Prospects, op cit*, pp. 265–267 and 278–279, especially p. 265. *See* the publication of the International Centre for Participation Studies, Department of Peace Studies, Bradford University, entitled 'Participatory Theories, Values and Practices', dated 18/04/2005, p. 2.

138 *See* the PP resources, including those on engagement methods and toolkits, provided in the homepage of 'getinvolved', found at http://www.getinvolved.qld.gov.au/index.html visited on 03/09/08. This homepage offers opportunity for everyday Queenslanders (in Australia) to interact with their government and be involved in the affairs of their communities. *Also see* the toolkits and other PP resources provided by 'Involve', in the UK, through its homepage found at http://www.involve.org.uk/home visited on 30/08/08. *See* the publication of the Yorkshire Rural Community Council, UK, entitled 'Good Practice in Community Involvement' http://www.ynypu.org.uk/social%20inclusion/YRCCSummary.pdf visited on 15/03/06. *See* the 'Community Consultation and Involvement Strategy' of the Erewash Borough Council, Derbyshire, UK, found at http://www.erewash.gov.uk/NR/rdonlyres/D58D652D-2F72-48AF-A576-D3315C3277AA/0/Community_Involvement_Strategy.pdf visited on 15/03/06.

139 *See* J. L. Creighton, *The Public Participation Handbook: Making Better Decisions through Citizen*_Involvement, op cit, p. 2.

140 *See* E. Bastida *et al* (eds), *International and Comparative Mineral Law and Policy: Trends and Prospects, op cit*, 283–309, and 311–329.

the practice of true federalism and natural law in which the federating units express their rights to primarily control the natural resources within their borders and make agreed contribution towards the maintenance of common services of sovereign state to which they belong.[141]

Itse Sagay explains that the movement is directed to achieve true political and fiscal federalism, as recognised and implemented under the Nigerian Independence and the Republican Constitutions.[142] Similarly, Oronto Douglas explains what resource-control implies in the following words:

(a) 'Resource control' to the communities and peoples of the Niger Delta is not just 'oil and gas'. In fact, land, forests and the water came out pre-eminently as prime resources by the estimation of the people. (b) 'Control' is almost always equated and used interchangeably with ownership. To this extent, I draw the conclusion that communities talk and mean 'ownership and control' in their advocacy for resource control. (c) There is a burning desire, an almost fierce yearning to regain the use and management of these resources without external control and direction. This is in line with the historical position of the peoples of the region. . . . (d) The freedom to willingly dispose of these resources, to negotiate its alienation or extraction without reference to a violent and or an undemocratic controller beyond the seas and oceans or behind the forests and the savannahs. (e) A belief that these resources be returned to the communities and managed at the community levels with little or no outside direction. (f) Resource control in the simplest sense means survival.[143]

141 *See* I. A. Ojefia, 'The Nigerian State and the Niger Delta Question', being a paper delivered during the 22nd Annual Conference of the Association for Third World Studies, Americus, Georgia, USA, found at http://199.236.119.147/oyefia.htm visited on 31/12/06. *Also see* 'NIGERIA: Federalism, the Constitution and Resource-Control', being the text of a speech delivered by I. Sagay, SAN, at the sensitisation programme organised by the Ibori Vanguard, at the Lagoon Restaurant, Lagos, found at http://www.wadoo.org/NigerDelta/Essays/ResourceControl/Sagay.html visited on 07/08/2004.

142 *See* A. A. Ikein and C. Briggs-Anigboh, *Oil and Fiscal Federalism in Nigeria: The Political Economy of Resource Allocation in a Developing Country*, Vermont, Ashgate, 1998. *Also see* 'NIGERIA: Federalism, the Constitution and resource Control', being the text of a speech delivered by I. Sagay, SAN, at the sensitisation programme organised by the Ibori Vanguard, at the Lagoon Restaurant, Lagos, *op cit. Also see* I. Sagay, 'Nigeria: Federalism, the Constitution and Resource Control: My Response', found at http://www.waado.org/NigerDelta/Essays/ResourceControl/Sagay2.html visited on 07/08/04. *See* the Vanguard newspaper report entitled 'One Voice: Give Us True Federalism, Scrap Obnoxious Laws, Say N-Delta Leaders', found at http://www.vanguardngr.com/index.php?option=com_content&task=view&id=13971. . . visited on 16/08/08. *See* the publication by D. Dafinone, entitled 'Resource Control: The Economic & Political Dimensions', found at http://www.waado.org/NigerDelta/Essays/ResourceControl/Dafinone.html visited on 15/05/05. *Also see* E. E. Smith *et al, International Petroleum Transactions*, Rocky Mountain Mineral Law Foundation, Denver, 2000, p. 263. *See* O. Awolowo, Awo: *The Autobiography of Chief Obafemi Awolowo, op cit*, p. 174.

143 *See* O. Douglas, 'On the Question of Resource Control and Ownership: A Reply to Yadudu', being a memorandum submitted to the Committee on Environment & Natural Resources and the Committee on Revenue Allocation & Fiscal Federalism, National Political Conference, *op cit.*

The resource-control movement is thus an umbrella participation movement of the Delta minorities,[144] rooted in the past struggles of these minorities as demonstrated by the struggles of their monarchs, other citizens and citizen groups, in the events that led to the creation of modern Nigeria during British imperialism.[145] It postulates that legal justice is not always consistent with social justice, as was the case with the socially unjustifiable laws of the imperial powers which empowered slave trade. It demands the exercise of political power and authority on the bedrocks of social justice, equity and fair-play, in the overall interest of all citizens and groups, in order to enhance mutual cooperation and understanding and enduring sustainable peace in the federation.[146] It represents the march of the oil-rich Delta region towards interactive CI and sound and equitable SCD in the course of petroleum development in the region, and the march of Nigeria towards true federalism and grass-root citizen-oriented democracy. It is thus more beneficial to other parts of Nigeria whose natural resources are yet to be harnessed for the development of such areas and the entire federation.[147]

Among other issues and challenges confronting it, some consider the resource-control movement as impinging on Nigeria's sovereignty over the ownership and control of its petroleum resources. As this book is not contending Nigeria's sovereignty[148] over these resources, the movement is delimited by the scope of

144 It is promoted by citizens and citizen groups in the region, including the region's youth emancipation groups, as the Movement for the Emancipation of the Niger Delta (MEND), the South-South Liberation. Movement and the Niger Delta Volunteer Force (NDVF). It, at the Nigerian Supreme Court, generated Suit No. S. C. 28/2001, between *Attorney-General of the Federation vs. Attorney-General of Abia State & 35 Ors* (No. 2) (2002) 6 NWLR. (Pt. 764). 542–905, discussed in Chapter 2. *See* I. Bannon and P. Collier (eds), *Natural Resources and Violent Conflicts: Options and Actions, Washington DC*, The World Bank, 2003. *Also see* the report of the HRW entitled 'Rivers and Blood: Guns, Oil and Power in Nigeria's Rivers State: A Human Rights Watch Briefing Paper', dated February 2005, found (in the publications area of the HRW homepage) at http://www.hrw.org/legacy/backgrounder/africa/nigeria0205/nigeria0205.pdf visited on 13/03/09. *See* J. J. Abubakar, *Guns and Wars: Proliferation of Small and Light Weapons in Internal Conflicts in Nigeria*, London, Adonis & Abbey, 2008.

145 *See Niger Delta Human Development Report, op cit*, pp. 16–17. *Also see* U. Ukiwo, 'From 'Pirates' to 'Militants': A Historical Perspective on Anti-state and Anti-Oil Company Mobilisation among the Ijaw of Warri, Western Delta', African Affairs, Vol. 106, No. 425, 2007, pp. 587–610.

146 The movement may thus be seen as querying the democracy and social justice principles expressed in Section 14 (1) of the 1999 Constitution of the FRN, in order to promote citizens' participation in governance, to ensure the security, welfare and sense of belonging and loyalty of the citizens. *See* S. Ajayi (ed), *Attah On Resource Control*, Lagos, Bangee Ventures, 2004, pp. v-vi. *Also see* J. I. Elaigwu, *The Politics of Federalism in Nigeria*, London, Adonis & Abbey, 2007, pp. 312–315.

147 *See* S. Ajayi (ed), *Attah On Resource Control, op cit*, pp. 1–15. *Also see* Dappa-Biriye, 'Resource Control, Beneficial to Nigerian state', found at http://www.nigerdeltacongress.com/rarticles/resource_control.htm visited on 25/01/06.

148 *See* Section 44 (3) of the 1999 Constitution of the FRN. *Also see* Section 1(1) of the Petroleum Act, 1969. *See* Section 1(1) of the Minerals and Mining Decree, Cap 34 LFN 1999. This book thus focuses on the resource-control movement as one generated by lack of interactive CI in petroleum resources development in the Delta region, and highlights the need for SD of these resources towards sound and equitable SCD in the Delta region, in the interest of social justice, equity and fair play in the FRN. *See* Y. Omorogbe, *Oil and Gas Law in Nigeria*, Lagos, Malthouse Press, 2001, pp. 143–157, especially p. 151. *Also see* N. Schrijver, *Sovereignty over Natural Resources: Balancing Rights and Duties*, Cambridge, Cambridge University Press, 1997. *See* O. O. Oshita, *Conflict Management in Nigeria: Issues and Challenges*, London, Adonis & Abbey, 2007, p. 95.

this book as explained in Chapter 10. Accordingly, given that the world is in an era of peak oil and climate change,[149] and SD is an illusion or incompatible with petroleum and other extractive industrial development operations in developing countries suffering from the resource curse,[150] there is urgent need for future studies on other ways and aspects of evolving sustainable communities, towns and cities based on the prevailing situations in Nigeria.

1.9 CONCLUDING REMARKS

This chapter introduces the issues or problems addressed, and the perspectives of the book. The chapter indicates that the book is centred on the true Nigerian Delta region rather than the artificial Niger Delta created by the NDDC Act. It is on this note that the author attempts to rationalise the marginalisation of the Delta ethnic minorities in the decision-making process of petroleum development and the overall governance of the FRN, and thereby identifies the need for the federation to properly address its lingering ethnic minority question. By and large, in this and other chapters, the true Delta region is considered along with other oil-producing areas (*ie*, the oil-producing states of Ondo, Abia and Imo states) as major stakeholders of the petroleum development business in Nigeria. The chapter notes that as Africa's largest and the world's eighth exporter, Nigeria's petroleum reserves are about 34 billion barrels; while, as one of the global top ten natural gas endowments, its proven natural gas is about 159 trillion cubic feet (Tcf). As its economic backbone therefore, petroleum development accounts for 95 per cent of Nigeria's export earnings and 80 per cent of its revenue.

The chapter has briefly examined the resource-control movement in the Delta region and the diverse issues associated with the same in the region and the entire FRN. In this way, the core/main hypothesis and the enlarged/ancillary hypothesis of the book were developed, in order to suggest or recommend ways to address the questions, aims and objectives outlined. Improved

---

149 *See* the DEFRA publications entitled *Guidance on How to Measure and Report your Greenhouse Gas Emissions*, London, DEFRA, 2009, and *Environmental Key Performance Indicators: Reporting for UK Business*, London, DEFRA, 2006. *Also see* T. Jackson, A *Sustainable New Deal*, London, Sustainable Development Commission (SDC), 2009.

150 The resource curse hypothesis states *that the wealth of mineral resources might be a disadvantage to mineral resource-dependent economies because it distorts the structure of national economies, decreases international competitiveness of other economic sectors, and discourages the adoption of policies designed to secure long-term development. Numerous examples of economic mismanagement with mineral revenues and comparatively poor performance of mineral-rich developing countries since the 1960s seem to support this [hypo]thesis. See* N. Mirovitskaya and W. Asher (eds), *Guide to Sustainable Development and Environmental Policy*, Durham, Duke University Press, 2001, pp. 9 and 17. *Also see* P. J. Stevens, 'Resource Curse' and How to Avoid It', *The Journal of Energy and Development*, Vol. 31, No. 1, 2006. *Also see* W. Ascher, *Why Governments Waste Natural Resources: Policy Failures in Developing Countries*, Baltimore, John Hopkins University Press, 1999. *See* R. Hannesson, *Investing for Sustainability: The Management of Mineral Wealth*, Norwell, Kluwer, 2001. *See* T. Jackson, *Prosperity without Growth?: The Transition to a Sustainable Economy*, London, SDC, 2009.

CI is prompted by agitation of the citizens and citizen groups of the Delta region that they, and by extension those of other oil-producing areas, are entitled to be more properly involved in the decision-making process of petroleum development operations and to benefit more as those directly suffering from the adverse effects of these operations in their communities. Improved CI is allied to the need for SD of petroleum resources and environmentally-sound and socially-equitable SCD in the oil-producing areas. Improved CI in petroleum development is thus required to fulfil the globally identified need and widely accepted principles of environmental democracy, expressed in Principle 10 of the Rio Declaration on Environment and Development, 1992, and elaborated in the Aarhus Convention of 1998 on participation. The ancillary hypothesis of the book is developed with regard to the need for improved PI in the overall governance of the FRN, so as to achieve accountability and transparency in the decision-making processes of the federation. Hence, the key proposition of the book is that neither CI in petroleum development (as exemplified by the state of affairs in the Delta ethnic minority region) nor overall PI (as evidenced by the plight of a vast majority of Nigerian citizens) in the governance of the country, has properly integrated the concerns and aspirations of the affected public in decision-making processes, to arrive at transparent and accountable decisions. Thus, while improved CI in petroleum development is considered as a means of addressing the crises in the Delta region, improved PI in the governance of Nigeria is considered as a means of addressing the Nigerian national question, in the overall interest of the country and its entire citizens, especially the plight of the impoverished citizens suffering in the midst of the enormous revenues being derived from petroleum development in the country. The recommendations of this book for the improvement of CI in the oil-producing areas and improvement of citizens' involvement in the entire FRN, are thus directed towards empowering Nigerian citizens, so as to enable the federation to overcome its resource curse. Considering that petroleum is a finite resource, this chapter establishes the concern of citizens of the Delta region and other oil-producing areas that the federal and other levels of government presiding over their affairs need to diversify their traditional sources of livelihood. Accordingly, the chapter establishes the need for the diversification of the Nigerian economy and the development of alternative energy resources towards a sustainable future in the country.

The chapter presents the plight of citizens of the Delta region, the main producers of Nigeria's petroleum resources, as that of the proverbial mother whose abundant breast-milk is being used to feed other children of the family, while her children are largely deprived of being nourished by the same. It states that the children of the Nigerian family who are robustly feeding from the petroleum breast-milk of mother-Delta at the expense of the poor masses are the corrupt political leaders of the country and their cohorts. Hence, as identified by Chinua Achebe in his book entitled *The Trouble with Nigeria*, it examines the leadership question as the key problem of Nigeria. This question requires to be addressed via improved PI in the overall governance of Nigeria, in the interest of social justice, equity and fair play between and among the ethnic minorities and the three major ethnic groups as well as between and among Nigerian citizens in government (*ie*, the governors) and the governed. The leadership (*ie*, governance) question requires to be addressed through the improvement of environmental governance and SD of petroleum resources, so as to overcome insecurity of supply to the resources consumer-nations, in the interest of humanity in these nations. Nigeria would thus be contributing towards SD in compliance with Principle 1 of the Rio Declaration on Environment and Development, 1992, which provides that 'Human beings are at the centre of concerns for sustainable development. They are entitled to a healthy and productive life in harmony with nature'.

Based on the enlarged/ancillary hypothesis, this chapter proposes the need for improvement in CSR in the Delta and other oil-producing areas; and a greater need for GSR embedded in GG, in the collective interests of the oil-producing and other areas of Nigeria *vis-à-vis* the collective interests of Nigerian citizens and all mankind. Based on the increasing impact of the stakeholder theory in major natural resources development in poor, rural and neglected areas of developing countries, the chapter identifies the oil-producing communities, the FG and the MNOCs as the three major stakeholders of the petroleum development business in Nigeria. By extension, citizens of the oil-producing communities, along with their future generations and the environment in the communities, including the oil-producing states and local governments, are identified as integral parts and parcels of the communities, while the MNOCs are considered as components of the world's rich countries. Accordingly, the chapter considers the entire citizens of the FRN (which includes those of the oil-producing areas), as major stakeholders by virtue of the stakeholder status of the FG which is represented in the resources development business by the NNPC. On this note, the chapter identifies a need for the consummation of SD-oriented development partnerships or other forms of good neighbour agreements to enhance mutual trust and commitment between the major stakeholders of the petroleum development business. Based on the stakeholder status of the Delta region, the author, as paramount chief of a principal founding chieftaincy house community of the region's ancient kingdom of Bonny and a specialist on PP and IA of major natural resources development projects, establishes himself as a stakeholder of the petroleum development business in Nigeria. The author's perspective and compassionate disposition regarding the interests of the crises-riven Delta region may thus be appreciated in this exploratory and cross-disciplinary discourse.

PART B

Assessment of the Interface between Specific Initiatives and Trends in International Environment and Development Policy and Stakeholder Decision-making

CHAPTER 2

Stakeholder Approaches in the Delta Region and Efforts of the United Nations on the Environment and Development

2.1 INTRODUCTION

The environment and development are twin issues continually influencing the needs, concerns and aspirations of citizens of the Niger Delta region. This chapter will discuss the challenges arising from the environment and development in relation to agitation by citizens of the Delta region for social justice, equity and fair play in the course of nation-building in Nigeria. The context of this discourse is the continuing effort of the United Nations (UN) on the environment and development as addressed by its three landmark Conferences and their ongoing processes to achieve sustainable development (SD). These Conferences, referred to as the SRJ process (from the initials of the cities in which they were held), are the Conferences on the Human Environment (UNCHE), held at Stockholm, Sweden, in 1972; on Environment and Development (UNCED), held at Rio de Janeiro, Brazil, in 1992; and the World Summit on SD (WSSD), held at Johannesburg, South Africa, in 2002. Consequently, the chapter will demonstrate how the oil-rich Delta region is being marginalised in decision-making processes in Nigeria, based on the failure of successive intervention measures by the Federal Government (FG) in the region to establish the responsibilities of government and the MNOCs in the form of Government Social Responsibility (GSR) and Corporate Social Responsibility (CSR) in the region.

2.2 (I) TWIN RELATIONSHIP OF THE ENVIRONMENT AND DEVELOPMENT IN THE HISTORY OF THE DELTA REGION

The SRJ process and the ongoing aftermath of this process in the UN system demonstrate the twin relationship of the environment and development in the global effort to achieve SD.[1]

1 *See* A. C. Kallhauge *et al*, *Global Challenges: Furthering the Multilateral Process for Sustainable Development*, Sheffield, Greenleaf, 2005. *Also see*, M. A. Ajomo and O. Adewale (eds.), *Environmental Law and Sustainable Development in Nigeria*, Lagos, Nigerian Institute of Advanced Legal Studies and the British Council, 1994, pp. 1–10, especially p. 2.

Development may be considered as a many-sided process.[2] Thus, in the light of the definitions and descriptions of the term 'environment' expressed in Chapter 5, it may, in the words of the World Commission on Environment and Development (WCED), namely the Brundtland Commission report, be stated that *the 'environment' is 'where we live', and the term 'development' is 'what we do in attempting to improve our lot within that abode. The two are inseparable.*[3]

From the period of the convention of the UNCHE up to the WSSD and thereafter, the UN has been making consistent effort to encourage and persuade global nations, sectors of society and peoples of the world to fully integrate the environment into every aspect of the socio-economic livelihood of mankind so as to achieve SD. Hence, the Declaration of the UNHE (otherwise referred to as the Stockholm Declaration), 1972, proclaimed that 'Man is both the creature and moulder of his environment' and that 'of all things of the world, people are the most precious . . .'[4] This Declaration provides that *the protection and improvement of the human environment is a major issue which affects the wellbeing of people and economic development throughout the world; it is the urgent desire of the peoples of the whole world and the duty of all Governments.*[5]

The physical environment may thus positively or negatively affect mankind. Considering that the environment is natural and there is need for man to live in harmony with his natural environment to enhance his progress and development, the provisions of Principle 1 of the Rio Declaration on Environment

2 *See* W. Rodney, *How Europe Underdeveloped Africa*, Washington DC, Howard University Press, 1982, p. 3. *Also see* A. Gilpin, *Dictionary of Environmental Law*, Cheltenham, Edward Elgar, 2000, p. 81. *See* A. Gilpin, *Environmental Impact Assessment: Cutting Edge for the Twenty-First Century*, Cambridge, Cambridge University Press, 1995, p. 170.

3 *See Our Common Future: The World Commission on Environment and Development* (hereinafter called '*Our Common Future*'), Oxford, Oxford University Press, 1987, p. xi.

4 *See* Proclamations 1 and 5 of the Stockholm Declaration, 1972.

5 *See* Proclamation 2 of the Stockholm Declaration, 1972. This Declaration further provides that: *Man has constantly to sum up experience and go on discovering, inventing, creating and advancing. . . . A point has been reached in history when we must shape our actions throughout the world with a more prudent care for their environmental consequences. . . . To defend and improve the human environment for present and future generations has become an imperative goal for mankind – a goal to be pursued together with, and in harmony with, the established and fundamental goals of peace and of worldwide economic and social development. To achieve this environmental goal will demand the acceptance of responsibility by citizens and communities and by enterprises and institutions at every level, all sharing equitably in common efforts. Individuals in all walks of life as well as organizations in many fields, by their values and the sum of their actions, will shape the world environment of the future. Local and national governments will bear the greatest burden for large-scale environmental policy and action within their jurisdictions. International cooperation is also needed in order to raise resources to support the developing countries in carrying out their responsibilities in this field. . . . The Conference calls upon Governments and peoples to exert common efforts for the preservation and improvement of the human environment, for the benefit of all the people and for their posterity. See* Proclamations 3, 6 and 7 of this Declaration.

and Development, (*ie*, the Rio Declaration), 1992, expressed in Chapter 1, is instructive.[6] Hence, for instance, chapter 8 of the UN Agenda 21 entitled 'Integrating Environment and Development in Decision-making' emphasises the need for integrating the environment and development in decision-making at the policy, planning and management levels of society. The efforts of the UN thus explain the need for environmental factors to influence the planning and decision-making processes of socio-economic developments so as to achieve SD.[7]

Consequently, regardless of the positive aspects of the environment in the Nigerian Delta region, the fragile and unfriendly attributes of the physical environment in the region have from the era of the British colonial administration been identified as posing developmental difficulties and challenges for the region's citizens.[8]

2.2 (II) DELTA REGION IN THE REGIONAL ERA (DURING THE ADVENT OF NIGERIA'S POLITICAL INDEPENDENCE)

The minorities of the Delta region continued to canvass issues regarding their marginalisation during the advent of Nigeria's political independence, especially at the Nigeria Independence Constitutional Conferences [NICCs]), and thereafter, up to date in post-colonial Nigeria. The NICCs started between 1953 and 1954 and continued up to 1958, consequent upon which political independence was granted to Nigeria in 1960.[9] The main objective of the Delta minorities during these Conferences was to achieve self governance from British colonialism to enable them to participate actively in the decision-making processes of their affairs, as well as the affairs of the Federal Republic of Nigeria (FRN) into which they had been politically amalgamated, along with other pre-colonial Nigerian ethnic groups. They saw the NICCs as providing a platform by which they could overcome the oppressive and repressive measures of British colonialism as well as their marginalisation by the three major tribes (ie, ethnic groups) in the federation. The agitation of the Niger Delta minorities thus started in the British colonial era, when regionalism was introduced in

6 *Also see* W. P. Birnie, and A. Boyle, *Basic Documents on International Law and the Environment*, New York, Oxford University Press, 1995, p. 11.

7 *See* N. A. Robinson (ed), *Agenda 21: Earth's Action Plan*, New York, Oceana, 1993, pp.115–136. *Also see* D. Ghai, *Development and Environment:* Sustaining People and Nature, Oxford and Cambridge, Blackwell, 1994. *Also see* M. Oxford, *Developing Naturally: A Handbook for Incorporating the Natural Environment in Planning and Development*, Somerset, The Association of Local Government Ecologists (ALGE), 2000.

8 *See The Willink Commission Report*, London, Her Majesty's Stationery Office (HMSO), 1958, (reprint by the Southern Minorities Movement, Port Harcourt, Nigeria, 1996), pp. 50–51. *Also see* A. Etekpe *et al*, *Harold Dappa-Biriye: His Contributions to Politics in Nigeria*, Port Harcourt, Onyoma Research, 2003, pp. 111–134 and 200.

9 *See* E. J. Alagoa and A. A. Derefaka, *The Land and People of Rivers State: Eastern Niger Delta*, Port Harcourt, Onyoma Research, 2002, pp. 343–346.

1939.[10] At the time, the Delta minorities came under the Eastern and Western regions of the federation which were dominated by the Igbo and Yoruba ethnic majority groups respectively.[11]

The three regions (ie, the Eastern, Western and Northern federating units) of Nigeria were dominated by three major political parties, namely the National Council for Nigeria and the Cameroon[12] (NCNC, 1944–1966), the Action Group (AG, 1950–1966), and the Northern Peoples Congress (NPC, 1951–1966). Each of these parties was controlled or dominated by the major ethnic group in each of the regions, namely the Igbo of the south-east in the case of the NCNC, the Yoruba of the south-west with respect to the AG, and the Hausa/Fulani of the north with regard to the NPC. Although each of the three political parties had national or countrywide objectives in varying degrees, the interests of the major ethnic groups remained paramount in their affairs.[13] The key problems of regionalism were the unhealthy competition among the three major tribes and the marginalisation of the ethnic minorities by these major tribes. The ethnic minorities in the three regions were thus more or less at the mercy of the major tribes.[14] To counter the domination of the major tribes, some ethnic minority political parties were formed. In the Rivers territorial area of the Niger Delta under the Eastern region, the Niger Delta Congress (NDC) headed by Chief H. J. R. Dappa-Biriye was formed similar to the Northern ethnic minority Middle-Belt Congress formed and led by Joseph Tarka.[15]

Besides protesting, during the NICCs, about how the Federal Republic of Nigeria was being governed at their expense, the Delta minorities complained

---

10 The regional era in Nigeria thrived between 1939 (during the British colonial era) and 1970 (when states were first created in post-colonial Nigeria). *See* E. J. Alagoa and A. A. Derefaka (eds), *The Land and People of Rivers State: Eastern Niger Delta, op cit*, pp. 331–342, especially pp. 333, and 339–342. *Also see* U. Udoma, *History and the Constitution of Nigeria*, Lagos, Malthouse Press, 1994, p. 143. *See* I. James, 'Road to Nigeria's Independence', sourced from the library area of the homepage of 'Citizens for Nigeria', found at http://www.citizensfornigeria.com/index.php?option=com_content&task=view&id=28&Itemid=43 visited on 31/12/06. *Also see* the publication compiled by N. Omoigui, entitled 'Gowon's Broadcast to the Nation – May 27, 1967', found at http://www..dawodu.com/gowon.htm visited on 08/11/06. This broadcast of General Yakubu Gowon, made during the Nigerian civil war, brought regionalism to an end by dividing the four regions which existed at the time into twelve states.

11 The NICCs commenced at the time of the three regions. This was before the creation of the Mid–Western region in June, 1963, for the minorities of the Western region (who were in the Benin and Delta provinces of the time). *See* the publication entitled 'Mid–Western Region, Nigeria', found at http://en.wikipedia.org/wiki/Bendel_State visited on 16/08/05.

12 This political party was later renamed the National Convention of Nigerian Citizens.

13 *See* E. J. Alagoa and A. A. Derefaka (eds.), *The Land and People of Rivers State: Eastern Niger Delta, op cit*, pp. 331–342. *Also see* U. Udoma, *History and the Constitution of Nigeria, op cit*, pp. 142–194.

14 *See* K. Saro-Wiwa, *On the Darkling Plain: An Account of the Nigerian Civil War*, Port Harcourt, Saros International, 1989, p. 10–13.

15 *See* E. J. Alagoa and A. A. Derefaka (eds), *The Land and People of Rivers State: Eastern Niger Delta, op cit*, pp. 342 and 345. *Also see* A. Etekpe, *et al, Harold Dappa-Biriye: His Contributions to Politics in Nigeria, op cit*, pp. 54–57 and 195–243. *See* P. Brass (ed), *Ethnic Groups and the State*, London, Croom Helm, 1985.

about the fragile and unfriendly nature of their physical environment. Among other things, they explained that their physical environment made transportation, communication and physical development difficult for their areas.[16] They also explained that the ethnic majority regional governments administering the region from their respective regional capitals in the interior mainland areas, namely Enugu, in the case of the Eastern region, and Ibadan, in the case of the Western region, neither appreciated nor understood the plight of the people of the region. They explained that their needs, concerns and challenges (as those who live mainly in the creeks, swamps and mangrove forest areas of the Delta) are different from those of the major ethnic groups in the Eastern and Western regions who live in mainland areas outside the Delta.[17] Consequently, the Delta minorities in the Cross-River, Ogoja and Rivers (COR) provinces made certain political demands as part of their COR state political movements.[18] They demanded the creation of states in their favour so as to allay their fears and to encourage them to accept political independence in union with the three major tribes. The entire Nigerian ethnic minorities consider the creation of states as a means of improving their welfare.

The compelling nature of the issues raised by the ethnic minorities of the three regions during the 1957 NICC forced the Conference to adjourn until 1958, following the appointment of a Special Commission of Enquiry by the departing British colonial government set up to enquire into the fears of the ethnic minorities and the means of allaying them in independent Nigeria. The Commission, headed by Queen's Counsel, Sir Henry Willink, was popularly known as the Willink Commission. For five weeks, between November and December, 1957, the Commission sat in more than six centres covering the Eastern, Western and Northern regions, to receive memoranda and collate other forms of complaints from the minorities. The Commission's report was submitted to the Colonial Office between April and July, 1958, and then onward to Parliament by the Secretary of State for the Colonies, following which the NICC resumed in September 1958.[19]

---

16 *See The Willink Commission Report, op cit*, pp. 50–51.

17 Ibid.

18 The movements are the COR State movement led by Sir Udo Udoma and the movement for the creation of a separate Rivers state represented by Chief H. J. R. Dappa-Biriye, for and on behalf of the Rivers Chiefs and Peoples Conference (RCPC). Citizens of the Rivers territory favoured the movement for a separate Rivers state in preference to the larger COR state movement inaugurated (at Uyo, on December 19, 1953) for the entire Eastern regional ethnic minority areas. *See* Annex 11 of the Report of the Resumed NICC held in London, in September and October, 1958, London, HMSO, Cmnd 569, entitled 'Statement of the Secretary of State for the Colonies on the Treaties between the Crown and the Oil Rivers Chiefs', pp. 42–43. *Also see* E. J. Alagoa and A. A. Derefaka (eds), *The Land and People of Rivers State: Eastern Niger Delta, op cit*, pp. 339–350. *See* the commentary of M. T. Akobo, T. T. Issoun and S. Asemota, SAN (of the Southern Minorities Movement) in the Willink Commission Report. *See The Willink Commission Report, op cit*, p. ii.

19 *See The Willink Commission Report, op cit*, p. i–ii.

In its report, the Willink Commission described the Delta region as 'poor, backward, and neglected'.[20] The report, while describing the pitiable state of the environment in the Delta region and the attendant difficulties confronting citizens of the region, provides that:

> *We were impressed by arguments indicating that the needs of those who lived in the creeks and swamps of the Niger Delta are very different from those of the interior. We agree that it is easy for a Government or Legislature operating from the far inland to concern itself, or even fully understand, the problems of a territory where communications are so difficult, building so expensive and education so scanty.*[21]

Members of the Willink Commission concluded that:

> *. . . we had no doubt that a feeling of neglect and a lack of understanding was wide-spread in both Regions (Western and Eastern Deltas). We consider that a case has been made out for special treatment of this area. This is a matter that requires special effort because it is poor, backward and neglected.*[22]

Consequently, the Commission had to make recommendations for the creation of a physical developmental Board for the Delta region known as the Niger Delta Development Board (NDDB). The Board was directed to initiate schemes to supplement the normal development of the Delta region designated as a 'Special Area'.[23] The Commission did not, however, accede to the request of the minorities for the creation of new states before the attainment of Nigeria's political independence.[24] Instead of recommending the creation of states for the ethnic minorities, the Commission suggested a balance of political power and authority among the component pre-colonial ethnic groups, in an attempt to make it impossible for the major tribes or any one of them to control power and authority at the expense of other ethnic groups in the federation. On this note, the Commission recommended the creation of minority Area Councils for the entire ethnic minority areas in the three regions, to cater for their political development under each regional government.[25] The

20 Ibid, pp. ii and 94.
21 Ibid, pp. 50–51.
22 *See* Chief D. S. P. Alamieyeseigha, 'The Environmental Challenge of Developing the Niger Delta', found at http://www.gasandoil.com/goc/news/nta40214.htm visited on 09/06/05.
23 *See The Willink Commission Report, op cit*, p. ii.
24 Ibid, pp. ii, 50–51, and 88. *Also see* E. J. Alagoa and A. A. Derefaka (eds), *The Land and People of Rivers State: Eastern Niger Delta, op cit*, p. 344. *See* A. Etekpe, *et al, Harold Dappa-Biriye: His Contributions to Politics in Nigeria, op cit*, p. 73. *Also see* Ike Okonta, 'The Lingering Crisis in Nigeria's Niger Delta and Suggestions for Peaceful Resolution' (being a working paper prepared for the Centre for Democracy and Development), found at http://www.cdd.oreg.uk/rsources/workingpapaers/niger_delta_eng.htm visited on 01/11/06.
25 *See The Willink Commission Report, op cit*, pp. ii and 88.

Commission relied on a catalogue of other assumptions and Constitutional provisions including the provision of such remedial measures as fundamental rights and the enforcement of such rights in the federation.[26]

The recommendations of the Willink Commission and other consequential measures taken in the interests of the minorities were accepted in consensus by Nigerians at the 1958 resumed NICC, and political independence was granted to Nigeria in 1960. While fulfilling the conditions for political independence, further steps were taken in post-colonial Nigeria to implement the recommendations of the Willink Commission in the interests of the ethnic minorities. In the Delta region, these steps included the establishment of the NDDB in 1961.[27] By looking forward to the implementation of its recommendations, the Willink Commission had assumed that ten years of concerted development projects – physical, manpower and industrial, would bring the people of the region into the mainstream of federalism and democracy in post-colonial Nigeria.[28]

However, in spite of the establishment of the NDDB and sundry other measures taken in the interests of the ethnic minorities, the conditions needed to allay the fears of the minorities were far from being fulfilled in post-colonial Nigeria. Concerning the NDDB, it started with headquarters in Lagos, whereas its areas of operation were at some distance in the Western Ijaw Division of the Delta Province, and the Yenagoa and Degema Provinces and the Ogoni Division of the Port Harcourt Province. As it became very obvious that Lagos (in the Western region) was far too remote from the Niger Delta, the headquarters of the NDDB was moved to Port Harcourt. Despite this move, the Board was not motivated by the Federal, Eastern and Western regional governments to find solutions to the problems of the Delta region.[29] For instance, its funding, supposed to be derived from the FG and the Eastern and Western regional governments, was not realised. Besides, there was no representative from the Delta region at managerial level on the Board.[30] Eventually, in 1966, military intervention in politics, was not contemplated by the Willink Commission,[31] further frustrated the existence of the Board and it became a victim of the Nigerian civil war years, from 1967 to 1970. Thereafter, at the end of the civil war, the Board was left moribund by the Federal Military

---

26 Ibid, p.ii.

27 By virtue of Section 14 of the Nigerian (Constitution) Order in Council, 1960, which provided for its establishment and empowerment of the NDDB, the Board was established by an Act of the Federal Parliament, No. 19 of 1961, and subsequently the existence of the Board was provided in the 1963 Republican Constitution

28 *See The Willink Commission Report, op cit*, p. ii.

29 *See* A. Etekpe *et al, Harold Dappa-Biriye: His Contributions to Politics in Nigeria*', *op cit*, pp. 232–233.

30 *See* Chief D. S. P. Alamieyeseigha, 'The Environmental Challenge of Developing the Niger Delta', *op cit.*

31 *See Southern Minorities Movement, Roots, the Struggle and the Future*, Port Harcourt, Southern Minority Movement, December 1995, p. 13.

Government (FMG), whose programme of National Reconciliation, Reconstruction and Rehabilitation (NRRR) neglected the rationale for its establishment as well as other interests of the people of the Delta region.[32]

In terms of party politics in the Delta region, after the emergence of the COR and Separate Rivers State movements in the regional era of British colonialism, little was achieved by citizens of the region who joined the AG and the NCNC, as the trend of marginalisation and neglect of the region and other minority ethnic groups continued in post-colonial Nigeria. Among few achievements recorded was the political resistance fostered in the Rivers territory by the NDC established by Chief H. J. R. Dappa-Biriye, the delegate of the RCPC who represented the Rivers territory at the 1957/58 NICCs. The NDC established its integrity as an ethnic minority political party by agitating against the marginalisation of the Delta minorities in the Eastern region. It eventually aligned with the NPC, to foster its interest in the Rivers territory. Among other things, the NDC stressed that man is a product of the influence and challenges of his physical, social and political environment. Thus, apparently referring to the tribal majority orientation of the dominant political parties in the federation, the motto of the NDC was 'Live and let live'.[33]

Following the efforts of the NDC on resistance through party politics, the next resistance movement in the Rivers territory in the 1960s was that of Isaac Adaka Boro, namely the 12-day Niger Delta Revolution, which took place shortly after the January 1966 military coup in the federation. During this revolution, Boro recruited some 150 youths, trained them and called them the Niger Delta Volunteer Service (NDVS), under his command. The NDVS launched a guerrilla campaign from its base on the River Nun in the Yenagoa Province which culminated in the declaration of the 'Niger Delta Republic'.[34] In his proclamation of the Republic, Boro stated that '. . . today is a great day, not only in your lives, but in the history of the Niger Delta. We are going to demonstrate to the world what and how we feel about oppression'.[35] The NDVS overran most of the Ijaw territories, receiving tumultuous welcome everywhere in the Delta region until federal troops overcame Boro and his compatriots. They were tried for treason and convicted between June and December 1966. Providence later favoured them during the Nigerian civil war, as their death sentences were commuted to life imprisonment and they were

32 *See* the 'Niger Delta Regional Development Master Plan', found (in the area of the Niger Delta Development Commission (NDDC) homepage captioned 'Master Plan') at http://nddc.gov.ng/the%20web/master%20plan.html visited on 27/02/09. *Also see* Ike Okonta, 'The Lingering Crisis in Nigeria's Niger Delta and Suggestions for Peaceful Resolution' (being a working paper prepared for the Centre for Democracy and Development), *op cit.*

33 *See* A. Etekpe *et al, Harold Dappa-Biriye: His Contributions to Politics in Nigeria*', *op cit*, pp. 195–241, especially p. 196.

34 *See* E. J Alagoa and A. A. Derefaka (eds), *The Land and People of Rivers State: Eastern Niger Delta, op cit*, p.347.

35 *See Southern Minorities Movement, Roots, the Struggle and the Future, op cit*, p. 15.

eventually granted full amnesty. Boro went on to join the Nigerian Army as a major, and died in active military service (during the civil war) in 1969.[36]

So, despite the agitation and resistance movements of citizens and citizen groups of the Delta and other ethnic minority regions of Nigeria, the marginalisation of the minorities continued after political independence. Military intervention in governance from 1966 worsened the plight of the minorities as successive military rule entrenched unitary rule which continues to undermine true federalism and genuine democracy in post-colonial Nigeria. The next section will discuss how the adverse effects of over five decades of petroleum development in the hitherto peaceful Delta region have generated the ongoing resistance movement (*ie*, the resource-control movement) in the region.

2.2 (III) PETROLEUM DEVELOPMENT IN THE DELTA REGION AFTER THE REGIONAL ERA: FROM THE INTRODUCTION OF MILITARY RULE IN 1966 TO PRESENT-DAY

Petroleum was discovered in commercial quantities in the Delta region in 1956, during the period of the NICCs from 1953/54 (in Lagos) up to 1957/58 (at Lancaster House in London), after which independence was granted to Nigeria on October 1, 1960. From this time, the adverse consequences and challenges of petroleum development gradually began to be felt in the communities of the region.[37] This situation gradually worsened as the unitary administrative system of petroleum development during the British colonial era continued in post-colonial Nigeria, especially under successive military regimes.[38] The traditions of unitary governance generated by military decrees, edicts, and so forth, undermined the community involvement (CI) and community partnership in

---

36 *See* E. J Alagoa and A. A. Derefaka (eds), *The Land and People of Rivers State: Eastern Niger Delta, op cit*, p. 347.

37 *See* A. A. Ikein, *The Impact of Oil on a Developing Country: The Case of Nigeria*, New York, Praeger, 1990. *See* the report of I. Gary and T. L. Karl, regarding poverty in Africa entitled 'Bottom of the Barrel: Africa's Oil Boom and the Poor', Catholic Relief Services, June 2003, found at http://www.catholicrelief.org/get_involved/advocacy/policy_and_strategic_issues/oil_report_full.pdf visited on 22/07/04. *Also see* E. C. Onwuka on 'Oil Extraction, Environmental Degradation and Poverty in the Niger Delta Region of Nigeria', *International Journal of Environmental Studies*, Vol. 62, No. 6, December 2005, pp. 655–662. *See* O. Douglas and I. Okonta, *Where Vultures Feast: Shell, Human Rights, and Oil in the Niger Delta*, New York, Sierra Club, 2001.

38 The first military rule in Nigeria began by the military coup of January 15, 1966, and its counter-coup of July 29, 1966. Other military interventions in politics are those generated by the military coups of July 29, 1975, December 31, 1983, and that of August 27, 1985. Military involvement in governance militarised the FRN and politicised the military. *See* the publication entitled 'Nigeria: Military Intervention and Military Rule', at the Library of Congress Country Studies; CIA World Fact Book, http://www.photius.com/countries/nigeria/government/nigeria_government_military_interventio~10020.html visited on 07/08/08. *Also see* J. I. Elaigwu, *The Politics of Federalism in Nigeria*, London, Adonis Abbey, 2007, pp. 102–127. *See The Willink Commission Report, op cit*, p. ii. *Also see* the report of the International Crisis Group (ICG) on Nigeria, entitled 'Nigeria's Faltering Federal Experiment', Africa Report No. 119, October 25, 2006, found at http://www.crisisgroup.org/library/documents/africa/westafrica/119nigeriasfalteringfederalexperiment.pdf visited on 21/11/06.

petroleum development in the Delta region. The continuation of the adverse consequences of petroleum development in the region generated renewed agitation, pronouncements and demands on the FG and the MNOCS, as well as resistance movements which gave birth to the resource-control movement in the hitherto peaceful communities of the region.[39]

Considering the numerous issues associated with this chapter, further discussions will be limited in three ways. Firstly, to issues associated with the plight of the people of the region in the context of the FG's intervention measures earmarked to develop the region after the era of the NDDB. That means, from the period of the establishment of the River Basin Development Authority (RBDA) system in 1976, to the recent establishment of the Council for the Socio-economic Development of the Coastal States of the Niger Delta (SEDCOSND) in April, 2006. Secondly, the chapter will discuss the colonial origins of the Nigerian oil industry which links the industry with the Nigerian state, to the detriment of true federalism and the sub-national interests of such marginalised component groups as the oil-producing minorities of the Delta region. Thirdly, due to the prevailing consequences of petroleum resources development, this chapter will briefly consider the progressively-advancing effort of the UN on the environment and development towards achieving SD, in relation to the resources development operations in the Delta and other oil-producing areas of Nigeria.

2.2 (iii) (a) **Post-NDDB Era: from the RBDA System to the Establishment of the SEDCOSND**

The year 1976, which marked twenty years of petroleum development in the Delta region, is significant because this was when the FMG, headed by General Olusegun Obasanjo, transformed the NDDB by establishing the River Basin Development Authority (RBDA) system. In the process, the FMG created ten more RBDAs in other areas or parts of the federation, and changed the name of the NDDB to the Niger Delta River Basin Development Authority (NDBDA). Under the RBDA system, the NDBDA was undermined, as it was starved of funds, while most of the other ten RBDAs were generously funded by the Government.[40] The Southern Minorities Movement describes how the RBDAs were established in the following words:

---

39 *See* S. Azaike, *Inequities in Nigerian Politics*, Yenagoa, Treasure Communications Resource, 2003. *Also see* the report by Akpobibibo Onduku, entitled 'The Lingering Crisis in the Delta Region: Field Work Report', found at http://www.peacestudiesjournal.org.uk/docs/OilConflict.PDF visited on 20/04/05. *See* I. Bannon and P. Collier (eds.), *Natural Resources and Violent Conflicts*, Washington DC, The World Bank, 2003. *See* the report of the Environmental Rights Action (ERA)/Friends of the Earth (FoE), Nigeria on the Odi massacre, entitled 'A Blanket of Silence: Images of the Odi Genocide', 2003.

40 The establishment of the RBDAs was a negation of the developmental ideas for the Niger Delta as contained in the Willink Commission's report, as the system of these authorities undermined the interests of the Delta region from which these ideas evolved. *See* the NDDC's publication entitled 'Historical Background', found at http://www.nddconline.org/history.shtml visited on 30/04/03.

> *The Irikefe Commission of inquiry, for the creation of states, recommended the creation of the Niger Delta Basin Development Authority. This recommendation was considered by the Federal Executive Council and was approved. The quick thinking of responsible officials (who were mainly from the large ethnic nationalities) of the Ministry of Water Resources at the time resulted in another memo to the Executive Council for the establishment of 10 River Basin Development Authorities. Government approved all of them.*
>
> *As a result, the Decree for the 10 River Basins Development Authorities was passed on 15 June, 1976, and became Decree No. 25 of 1976, while the one for the Niger Delta recommended by Irikefe was passed on 3rd August 1976 and became Decree No. 37 of 1976.*
>
> *With the establishment of 11 River Basins Development Authorities, the intention for establishing the Niger Delta Basin Authority for a 'poor, backward and neglected area' was thwarted. The Niger Delta remained backward and neglected in that the Niger Delta Development Authority received a lower grading in the category of the 11 Basins Development Authorities and thereby remained one of the least funded up to now. The result is that the big tribes are getting richer while the small tribes are getting poorer.*
>
> *The amount of money spent by the Federal Government on these River Basin Development Authorities also depended on who was the head of the Executive, and nobody from the Niger Delta Area has ever been Head of State or President of the Country. The two Decrees – 25 and 37 of 1976 were harmonised into Decree No. 87 of 1979.*
>
> *The River Basins Development Authorities are Regional groupings as a result of identical Resources for Regional Development Policy. River Basins Development Authorities are now a permanent feature in our Laws, having been re-enacted under Chapter 396 of the Laws of the Federation of Nigeria. The struggle of minorities has been both political and economic. The minorities were marginalised politically, and deprived economically. The majority have dominated the minorities both politically and economically even when the minorities now produce the wealth of the nation.*[41]

By 1994, the River Basin Development Authorities (RBDAs), which were statutory companies of the FG, numbered 12.[42] They were eventually partially

41 *See Southern Minorities Movement, Roots, the Struggle and the Future, op cit,* pp. 20–21.

42 The 12 RBDAs are namely Sokoto Rima RBDA (covering Sokoto, Kebbi and Zamfara states), Hadjia Jama're RBDA (covering Kano, Jigawa and Bauchi states), Chad RBDA (covering Borno and Yobe states), Upper Benue RBDA (covering Adamawa and Taraba states), Lower Benue RBDA (covering Benue, Nassarawa and Plateau states), Upper Niger RBDA (covering Niger state and the Federal Capital Territory, FCT, Abuja), Lower Niger RBDA (covering Kwara and Kogi states), Ogun-Osun RBDA (covering Lagos, Ogun, Osun and Oyo states), Benin-Owena RBDA (covering Edo, Delta, Ondo and Ekiti states), Anambra-Imo RBDA (covering Anambra, Imo,

privatised and commercialised, under the ongoing privatisation and commercialisation programme of the FG initiated in 1999 to make government wholly-owned enterprises function better.[43]

Due to the agitation and demands of the Delta region's minorities regarding the adverse consequences of petroleum development in their communities, the FG decided to establish another regional developmental intervention body for the entire oil-producing areas in 1992, at which time Abia and Imo states had become oil-producing states in the federation. This intervention body known as the Oil Minerals Producing Areas Development Commission (OMPADEC) came into being due to the events which followed the setting up of the Dr. Pius Okigbo Commission under President Shehu Shagari and the Justice Alpha Belgore Commission under General Ibrahim Babangida's regime.[44] OMPADEC was established by General Babangida following the announcement during his tour to

---

Abia, Enugu and Ebonyi states), Cross-River RBDA (covering Cross-River and Akwa-Ibom states) and Niger-Delta RBDA (covering Rivers and Bayelsa states). *See* the publication of the BPE entitled 'River Basin Development Authority', found at http://www.bpeng.org/CGI-BIN/companies/Natural%20Resources/Agro%20Allied%20and%RBDAs/River%20Basin%20Development%20Authority.pdf visited on 20/12/06. *Also see* the BPE homepage entitled 'About the BPE: Introduction', and the 'Privatisation Policy', respectively found at http://www.bpeng.org/10/021062172300a.asp?DocID=33&MenuID=2 and at http://www.bpeng.org/10/021062172300a.asp?DocID=5&MenuID=2 visited on 20/12/2005.

43 The FG privatisation and commercialisation programme was introduced due to the failure of public sector enterprises and the effort to make the private sector the leading engine of the growth of Nigeria's economy. This programme was empowered by the Public Enterprises (Privatisation and Commercialisation) Act, Decree, No. 28 of 1999, LFN, 1999, to make government wholly-owned enterprises function better under some form of public-private partnerships (PPPs). In order to properly coordinate and implement the privatisation and commercialisation programme, the Decree empowers the creation of certain institutions/bodies among which is the National Council on Privatisation (NCP). The NCP is the apex body charged with responsibility for formulating and approving policies on the programme and the Bureau for Public Enterprises (BPE) which is the Secretariat for the NCP is charged with responsibility for implementing the policies and decisions of the NCP. The companies to be commercialised under this programme include Niger Delta River Basin Development Authority (NDBDA). *See* the publication of the BPE entitled 'River Basin Development Authority', *op cit*.

44 Whereas, Alhaji Shagari was the President and Commander-in-Chief of the Armed Force, FRN, between October 1, 1979 and December 31, 1983, General Babangida was the Military Head of state and Commander-in-Chief of the Armed Force, FRN, between August 27, 1985 and August 26, 1993. The Presidential Commission on Revenue set up under President Shehu Shagari, on November 23, 1979, was chaired by a renowned economist, Dr. Pius Okigbo. Hence, the Commission became known as the Okigbo Commission. Its report on June 30, 1980, recommended an upward review of revenue-allocation based on the principle of derivation, in the interest of the oil-producing areas. The Commission also recommended the allocation of 1 per cent of the Federation Account to cater for ecological problems in the country. Based on the 1980 white paper on the Okigbo Commission, a Presidential Task Force (PTF – popularly known as 'the 1.5 per cent Committee') was set up and allocated 1.5 per cent from the Federation Account to tackle the developmental problems of the oil-producing areas. The Committee or Task Force which existed between the Shagari era and that of Babangida was ineffective, as the plight and concerns of the citizens of the Delta region became intensified. The establishment of OMPADEC was directly based on the recommendation of the Justice Alpha Belgore Commission for the establishment of a development agency, to ameliorate the problems of the Delta region due to the adverse effects and challenges of petroleum development in the region. *See Southern Minorities Movement, Roots, the Struggle and the* Future, op cit, pp. 21–28.

Rivers state earlier that year[45] that his administration had resolved to establish such an intervention body.[46] OMPADEC was set up by Decree No. 23 of 1992, to physically and economically develop and rehabilitate the Delta region, and to make a better impact in the region than its predecessor, the NDDB.

However, after three years of existence, OMPADEC ended up not achieving its goals. It ultimately came to grief leaving behind several unfinished development projects and non-payment of contractors who were awarded development projects to execute in the oil-producing areas. Like the NDBRDA, among other reasons that led to its demise is the fact that OMPADEC was starved of funds by the FG which could not sustain its political will and commitment to ensure the continued existence of OMPADEC.[47]

Before and during the establishment of the OMPADEC, the FG had drastically and systematically reduced the revenue-allocation formula based on the principle of derivation to the detriment of the Delta region's main oil-producing minorities. Revenue derivable under the nation's principle of derivation was reduced from 50 per cent (at the time of political independence) to 0 per cent and 3 per cent for the petroleum producing states of the Delta region.[48] As was the case, when revenue allocation based on the principle of derivation was 1.5 per cent during the existence of the PTF of the President Shehu Shagari era and other related institutions set up by the FG to develop the Delta region, allocations to the OMPADEC based on 3 per cent accruals to the states of the region and other oil-producing states were rarely remitted to the Commission. The interest of the Delta region was undermined, considering how revenue allocations from the Federation Account were being dispensed with for the development of the region. Moreover, whereas between 1992 and 1995, the OMPADEC received N11 billion from the FG, the Petroleum (Special) Trust Fund, PSTF, (which many believe was again politically set up by the FG as were the ten other River Basin Development Authorities in 1976) received N346 billion from the government between 1994 and 1997. Most citizens of the Delta region were thus not in doubt that the dissolution of the OMPADEC was not enhanced by the setting up of the PSTF.[49]

---

45 Ibid.

46 Ibid.

47 *See* A. K. Horsfall, *The OMPADEC Dream*, West Sussex, Imprint, 1999, pp. 5–6.

48 Thus, the trend of derivation as basis for revenue-allocation provides as follows: 1953 (Chicks Commission) – 100%; 1960 (Independence Constitution/Alhaji Tafawa Balewa) – 50%; 1970–72 (Gowon) – 45%; 1975 (Murtala/Obasanjo) – 20%; 1982 (Shagari) – 2%; 1984 (Buhari) – 1.5%; 1986–91 (Babangida) – 0%; 1992 (Babangida/Abacha) – 3%, and 1999 – present (Abubakar/Obasanjo/Yaradua) – 13%. *See* Section 162 of the 1999 Constitution of the FRN. *Also see* A. Ogbuigwe, *Offended: Legal Issues in the Niger Delta*, Port Harcourt, Anpez Centre for Environment and Development, 1999, pp. 19–20. *See* C. U. Uche and O. C. Uche, 'Oil and the Policies of Revenue Allocation', being a working paper of the African Studies Centre (ASC), ASC Working Paper 54/2004, found at http://www.ascleiden.nl/GetPage.aspx?url=/publications/chibuikeuche visited on 31/12/06. *See* A. H. Ekpo, 'Intergovernmental Fiscal Relations: The Nigerian Experience', being a paper delivered at the 10th Year Anniversary of the Financial and Fiscal Commission of South Africa, Cape Town International Convention Centre, Cape Town, South Africa, August 10–12, 2004, p. 32.

49 *See* A. K. Horsfall, *The OMPADEC Dream, op cit*, p.5.

After the demise of the OMPADEC in the events that occurred after 1995, the peculiar problems of the Delta region became serious, and gave rise to more aggressive discontent, agitation, protests and conflicts among the people of the region against the FG and the MNOCs. The FG in its characteristic manner had to intervene in 2000, by establishing the Niger Delta Development Commission (NDDC).[50] However, the NDDC, as conceived and established by the FG under the leadership of President Olusegun Obasanjo, is different from the developmental institution that citizens of the Delta region required or demanded.[51] Without duly considering the expressions, explanations and demands of citizens of the region, the President Obasanjo-led FG, including the Federal Legislative arm of government, proceeded to establish the NDDC for the entire nine oil-producing states of the federation.[52] President Obasanjo's administration is thus said to have created a politically-redefined or artificial Niger Delta by the establishment of the NDDC.[53] The setting up of the FG's SEDCOSND, in April, 2006,[54] by President Obasanjo's administration made it imperative that the true Delta region was politically undermined by the establishment of the NDDC. This situation is similar to how the interests of the Delta region were undermined when the River Basin Authority system was established in 1976 by the same administration of Obasanjo, when he was Military Head of State of the federation.[55]

---

50 While submitting the NDDC Bill to the National Assembly in May 1999, President Olusegun Obasanjo remarked that the Commission was considered as an agency to implement a programme for SD of the Delta region based on the Presidential Marshall Plan for the development, reconstruction and rehabilitation of the region.

51 Based on the 'Special Area' status of the Delta region expressed in the Willink Commission report, citizens of the region stressed that their plight and challenges were distinct from those of other oil-producing areas. Hence, they demanded a distinct FG intervention agency, separate from the one the government was establishing for the oil-producing areas. *See* 'The Position of the Ogoni People on the Proposed Niger Delta Development Bill' delivered at the Suanu Finimale Hall, Bori, dated July 24, 1999, found in the area of the Sierra Club website on human rights, at http://www.sierraclub.org/human-rights/nigeria/mosop/position.asp visited on 16/05/05. *Also see* the publication entitled 'We Have No Faith in Obasanjo's NDDC', found at http://www.nigerdeltacongress.com/warticles/we%20have%20no%20faith.htm visited on 15/05/05. *See* the report of the 'Washington Times' on Nigeria by E. Yawe, entitled 'Finding Permanent Solution: New Bill on the Niger Delta Seeks to Address Years of Neglect through Consensus', found at http://www.internationalspecialreports.com/africa99/nigeria/18.html visited on 09/06/05. *See* the publication of the NDDC entitled 'Niger Delta Devt. Plan to Gulp N500BN', found at *http://www.nddconline.org/Press_Release/messages/36.shtml* visited on 01/02/06.

52 *See* Section 2(1) (b) of the NDDC Act, LFN 2004.

53 *See* A. Etekpe *et al, Harold Dappa-Biriye: His Contributions to Politics in Nigeria*, Port Harcourt, Onyoma Research, 2003, p. xii. *Also see* the publication of the Niger Delta Fund Initiative (NDFI), 'Political Definition of N-Delta', found at http://www.earthrights.net/nigeria/news/definition.html visited on 25/05/04.

54 *See* the ThisDay newspaper report entitled 'Obasanjo: We Have Failed Niger Delta', found at http://www.thisdayonline.com/nview.php?id=44800&printer_friendly+1 visited on 06/04/06.

55 After his tenure in office as the military head of state between February 14, 1976, and October 1, 1979, Olusegun Obasanjo was democratically elected twice as the civilian head of state, from 29 May 1999, to May 2003, and thereafter up to May 29, 2006, when he ended his second term as a civilian President.

While considering the establishment of the NDDC as yet another partial and palliative political promise to them by the FG, citizens of the Delta region doubted that it would successfully address their age-long environmental concerns and developmental needs. The majority of the region's citizens believe that the NDDC lacks the required sustained political will and commitment of the FG and its Joint Venture (JV) partners, the MNOCs, to develop the region properly.[56] Although it may appear early to assess the performance of the NDDC, it is important to state, as indicated in Chapter 1, that the NDDC Act does not have any provision regarding the participation of citizens of the oil-producing areas in the affairs or decision-making process of the Commission. Neither did the Act impose a duty on the Commission to engage citizens of the oil-producing communities, nor did it empower or accord citizens the right to contribute to the decision-making process of the Commission in the exercise of its statutory functions and/or responsibilities.[57] CI in the decision-making process of the Commission is significant, considering that the FG and the oil-producing companies are funding the Commission to develop the oil-producing communities.[58] The lack of provision for CI, along with the erroneous title of the Commission, makes it essential for the NDDC Act, to be amended.

The amendment of the NDDC Act will enable the FG to rename the Commission properly, as a Commission for the Oil-Producing Areas. Also, the proposed amendment needs to provide that the multinational gas-producing companies in the country are to contribute to fund the NDDC rather than the MNOCs alone.[59] Besides, it is imperative for the FG to enact another law to cater more properly for the development of the Delta region so as to satisfactorily fulfil the Nigerian independence protocol based on the recommendations of the Willink Commission regarding the region. Citizens and communities of the Delta region deserve better treatment from the FG and the MNOCs than the way in which they have half-heartedly been treated so far. President Obasanjo himself mentioned this while setting up the SEDCOSND[60] as a new and unique

---

56 *See* the publication by T. I. Etim, 'NDDC: The Making of a Difference', found at http://www.onelga.com/nddc_diff.htm visited on 31/07/04.

57 *See* K. S. A. Ebeku, 'Appraising Nigeria's Niger Delta Development Commission Act, 2000', Statute Law Review, Vol. 25, No. 1, 2004, pp. 85–89, especially p. 89. *Also see* the Vanguard newspaper report entitled 'Group Tasks FG on Security in N-Delta', found at http://www.vanguardngr.com/articles/2002/niger_delta/nd117052007.html visited 20/05/07.

58 *See* Section 14 of the NDDC Act, entitled 'Fund of the Commission', especially sub-sections 14 (2) (a) and (b) regarding the contributions of the FG and the oil-producing companies to the fund of the Commission.

59 *See* the decision of the Supreme Court in *Attorney-General of the Federation vs. Attorney-General of Abia State & 35 Ors.* (No. 2) (2002) 6 NWLR (Pt. 764), 542–905. This decision is to the effect that the 13 per cent revenue accruing as a derivation fund to the oi- producing states should include revenues being derived from the development of gas in the country. This decision resulted in the enactment of the Onshore/Offshore Oil Dichotomy Abolition Act, which was signed into law in mid February 2004. Section 162 of the Constitution is entitled 'Public Revenue'. *Also see* K. S. A. Ebeku, 'Nigerian Supreme Court and the Ownership of Offshore Oil', Natural Resources Forum (NRF), Vol. 27, Issue 4, December 2003, pp. 291–299.

60 *See* the ThisDay newspaper report entitled 'Obasanjo: We Have Failed Niger Delta', *op cit.*

way forward. Obasanjo lamented that the Nigerian nation has continued to fail the Delta region. Consequently, the efforts of successive governments aimed at addressing the marginalisation and underdevelopment of the region have made no appreciable impact on the lives of the people of the region.[61]

So far, the FG's establishment of one intervention institution after another in the interest of the Delta region (ie, from the setting-up of the NDDB up to the NDDC and the establishment of the SEDCOSND), has not adequately fulfilled the Willink developmental vision for the region. The plight of the citizens of the region has deteriorated during the five decades of petroleum development in the communities of the region, regardless of any difference the Ministry of Niger Delta[62] created in 2008 by President Musa Yar'Adua may make; it may end up existing as a mere bureaucratic transformation, due to the usual lack of sustained political will on the part of the FG. There is thus a need for petroleum development to take place in the Delta region, in compliance with the stipulations of the continuing effort of the UN on the environment and development intended to achieve SD in the interest of humanity. To achieve SD in the interest of the Delta region and other regions and areas of Nigeria, lessons may be learnt from such international initiatives as those of the World Conservation Union (IUCN), the Ramsar Convention on Wetlands of 1971,[63] and the Conference on 'Comparing Rivers: The Mississippi and the Niger Conference',

---

61 Ibid. President Obasanjo was quoted as follows: *From pre-independence till today, what we must admit is that efforts made have not fully addressed the issues or have not fully satisfied the challenges, . . . The situation in the Niger Delta has been calling for attention since independence and different governments at different times have made attempts that have indicated that deaf ears have not been turned on issues of the Niger Delta. . . . stakeholders should perceive the problems as a national challenge that had transcended tribal or sectional lines, since they had ramifications that went beyond the borders of the country. . . . The Niger Delta needs special attention by all of us [all stakeholders]* . . . The function of the SEDCOSND is 'to assess and collate the short, medium and long-term definitive development programmes of the communities, local, state and federal governments, the . . . NDDC, oil companies and donor organisations towards addressing the challenges in the Niger Delta areas'. This Council was followed by the Ledum Mitee-led Technical Committee on the Niger Delta (TCND) created by President Yar'Adua. *See* K. S. A. Ebeku, 'Oil, Niger Delta and the New Development Initiative: Some Reflections from Socio-Legal Perspective', Oil, Gas & Energy Law Intelligence (OGEL), Vol. 4, Issue 3, September 2006, pp. 34, 49–51. *Also see* the report of the TCND, dated November, 2008. *See* the Guardian newspapers' report on the NDTC entitled 'What We Want Govt To Do Urgently, By Mitee', found at http://www.ngrguardiannews.com/news/article01//indexn2_html?pdate=071208&ptitl. . . visited on 08/12/08.

62 President Yar'Adua, succeeded President Obasanjo on May 29, 2006, and created the Ministry of the Niger Delta on September 10, 2008, as a FG's intervention measure in the Delta region. This Ministry, which the NDDC is placed under, is to coordinate the FG's environmental, infrastructural and youth development initiatives in the Niger Delta. It is the second Ministry to concentrate on a particular area in Nigeria. The first was that of the FCT, Abuja, created to address Abuja's developmental needs. *See* the ThisDay newspaper report entitled 'Yar'Adua Creates Ministry of N'Delta', found at http://www.thisdayonline.com/nview.php?id=122228&printer_friendly=1 visited on 11/09/08. *Also see* the report of the Guardian newspapers entitled 'Govt Creates Niger Delta Ministry, 27 Others', found at http://www.guardiannewsngr.com/news/article01//indexn2_html?pdate=110908&ptitl. . . visited on 11/09/08.

63 *See* the Convention on Wetlands, signed at Ramsar, Iran, in 1971, found at http://www.ramsar.org/ the initiatives of the World Conservation Union (IUCN), found at http://www.iucn.org/ the NEPAD Action Plan on the Environmental Initiative, found at http://wwwunep.org/roa/Docs/pdf/nepad/ActionPlanfortheEnviromentInitiative.pdf all visited on 13/11/06.

in 2002.[64] Lessons on how to protect the environment and to develop wetlands and other Deltaic regions of the world involving the institutional and sectoral strategies need to be applied in the Delta region.[65] These lessons deserve to be considered along with the environment initiatives of the New Partnership for Africa's Development (NEPAD), the International Association for Public Participation (IAP2), the International Association for Impact Assessment (IAIA), the Calabash Project of the Southern African region,[66] and the ongoing effort of the UN on environmental democracy, to achieve SD and sound and equitable sustainable community development (SCD) in the region.

2.2(iii) (b) Colonial Legacy of Petroleum Development in Post-colonial Nigeria

The Nigerian petroleum industry originated during the British colonial era when the ownership of mineral resources was vested in the British Crown, and the policies, laws and administrative practices governing the industry were based on the unitary or politically-centralised system of the colonial government in Nigeria. The first law on petroleum was the Petroleum Ordinance of 1889, which was followed by the Mineral Regulation (Oil) Ordinance, No 17 of 1914 (amended in 1925, 1950 and 1959). These laws aided the policies and administrative practices of the era. The centralised system of the industry grew on the attainment of Nigeria's political independence.[67] Thus, carried over from the provisions of the Minerals Act, 1946, after the attainment of Nigeria's political independence, mines, minerals, including oilfields, oil mining, geological surveys and gas were enshrined under the Exclusive Legislative List, under the 1960 and 1963 Constitutions of the FRN. Thereafter, even under democratic governance, all matters pertaining to major natural resources development have continued to be under the Exclusive Legislative List, and thus been legislated upon by the National Assembly.[68] Also, the Mineral Regulation (Oil) Ordinance of 1959 remained the principal legalisation in Nigeria until it was repealed by the Petroleum Act, 1969. The Oil Pipelines

---

64 *See* the Conference on 'Comparing Rivers: The Mississippi and the Niger Delta Conference', 2002, found at http://www.edwinlyon.com/comparingrivers.htm visited on 13/11/06.

65 In terms of lessons from other wetland regions of the world, certain lessons from the Mekong Delta in Vietnam, and the USA areas of the Mississippi river and the Florida Everglades may be considered relevant to the Nigerian Delta region. In terms of lessons of institutions established to manage Deltaic regions, certain lessons of the USA Tennessee Valley Authority may be considered relevant to the NDDC, as an institution established after the failures of the NDDB and OMPADEC to achieve the objectives for which they were established in Nigeria. *See* the email communication to the author by Professor C. P. Wolf, the Director of Social Impact Assessment Centre, New York, entitled 'Comparing Regions: Project Description', dated March 6, 2007.

66 *See* the discussions on the NEPAD, IAP2, IAIA and the Calabash Project in Chapters 3 and 5.

67 *See* D. N. Zillman *et al* (eds), *Human Rights in Natural Resources Development: Public Participation in the Sustainable Development of Mining and Energy Resources*, *op cit*, p. 553. *Also see*, M. M. Olisa, *Nigerian Petroleum Law and Practice*, Festac Town, Lagos, Jonia Ventures, 1997, pp. 9–13. *See* K. S. A. Ebeku, *Oil and the Niger Delta People in International Law – Resource Rights, Environmental and Equity Issues*, Cologne, Rudiger Koppe Verlag, 2006, pp. 74–75.

68 To this end, Part 1, Item 39 of the Second Schedule of the 1999 Constitution of the FRN, specifies mines and minerals, including oilfields, oil mining, geological surveys and natural gas, under the Exclusive Legislative list. This Second Schedule of the Constitution is entitled '*Legislative Powers*', whilst part 1 of it is entitled '*Exclusive Legislative List*'.

Act, 1956, also remained until it was amended and updated by the Oil Pipelines Act, 1965. This Act was eventually consolidated under Cap. 338, LFN, 1990, while the Petroleum Profits Tax Act, 1959, which prevailed after several amendments, was consolidated under Cap. 354, LFN, 1990.[69]

The period immediately after the Nigerian civil war (1967–70) is significant as regards the Nigerian petroleum industry. As a prelude to this period, the relevant events associated with the war may be discussed briefly. The war started in 1967 due to the secession of the Government of the South-Eastern region which culminated in the declaration of the Biafran Republic. From a political economy perspective, the main targets of the declaration of the Biafran Republic as an independent state from the FRN were the abundant petroleum resources of the federation discovered in the Niger Delta, part of which was under the South-Eastern region.[70] The declaration of the Republic of Biafra over the South-Eastern region by the Military Governor of the region, Lt. Colonel Emeka Ogumegu Ojukwu, meant the assumption of sovereignty, by the Igbo major ethnic group spearheading the Biafran Republic, over the petroleum resources of the Niger Delta.[71]

The minorities of the South-Eastern region expressed their unwillingness to be separated in this way from Nigeria, and this was the most significant reason relied upon by the federal forces to emancipate the Niger Delta from the Biafran Republic. Meanwhile, underlying the effort of the federal forces, led by the Hausa-Fulani Northern and the Yoruba South-Western major tribes, to emancipate the Niger Delta was their ambition to control the petroleum resources being discovered in the Delta communities.[72] This is why the continued cut-throat competition for political power among the three major ethnic groups in the federation is considered to be the main reason for the civil war.[73] Thus, the takeover by the federal forces of strategic petroleum development and installations in such

69 *See* D. N. Zillman *et al* (eds), *Human Rights in Natural Resources Development: Public Participation in the Sustainable Development of Mining and Energy Resources, op cit*, p. 553.

70 During the Nigerian regional years (before the creation of the Mid-Western region in 1963), part of the Delta ethnic minority region was under the Western and Eastern regional governments. The Mid-Western region, formed on 19 June 1963, from the Benin and Delta provinces of the Western region, became the fourth region of Nigeria. *See* the publication compiled by N. Omoigui, entitled 'Gowon's Broadcast to the Nation – May 27, 1967', *op cit*.

71 *See* E. J. Alagoa and A. A. Derefaka (eds), *The Land and People of* Rivers State: Eastern Niger Delta, op cit, p. 353. *Also see* the Ahiara Declaration of June 1, 1969, by Emeka Ogumegu Ojukwu, the Peoples' General of the Republic of Biafra (as he was then referred to). *See* the declaration entitled E. Ojukwu, 'The Ahiara Declaration (The Principles of the Biafran Revolution)' found at http://www.biafraland.com/AHIARA%20DECLARATION.rtf visited on 29/04/05. In the words of Ike Okonta, ... *This struggle for 'spoils' has created considerable tension and controversy, leading Nigeria's Northern Region to threaten to secede from the federation in 1953; the Western Region in 1954; and the Eastern Region to actually secede in 1967, which led to civil war. ...Politics turns on the struggle for spoils, while the state itself is the key arena for this struggle. See* I. Okonta, *When Citizens Revolt: Nigerian Elites, Big Oil and the Ogoni Struggle for Self-Determination*, Trenton, Africa World Press, 2008, pp. 4 and 7.

72 *See* E. J. Alagoa and A. A. Derefaka (eds), *The Land and People of Rivers State: Eastern Niger Delta, op cit*, pp. 351–357.

73 *See* K. Saro-Wiwa, *On the Darkling Plain: An Account of the Nigerian Civil War, op cit*, p. 11. *Also see* Ike Okonta, 'The Lingering Crisis in Nigeria's Niger Delta and Suggestions for Peaceful Resolution' (being a working paper prepared for the Centre for Democracy and Development), *op cit*. Several peace accords, especially the one held from January 5–7, 1967, at Aburi (*ie*, the Aburi

areas of the Delta as Bonny and Port Harcourt turned the tide of the war against the Biafran regime and as a result ended the war.[74]

The war, which lasted for 30 months (*ie*, from 6 July 1967, to 13 January 1970) ended as a family affair with the verdict of 'No-Victor-No-Vanquished'.[75] However, one of the first moves of the FMG which fought the war was the establishment of total control over the abundant petroleum resources of the Niger Delta, in order to prevent a repeat performance of the advantages taken against the FMG by the Biafran regime. The FMG, led by Lt. Col. (later General) Yakubu Gowon, reduced the power and influence of regional governments by bringing an end to regionalism through the creation of 12 states in place of the four regions which existed at the time. In the process, the powers of the states were reduced compared to those wielded previously by the regions which they replaced as geopolitical units.[76] The war thus offered the FMG not only a reason to establish greater sovereign control over petroleum development *vis-à-vis* the petroleum industry, but also a reason to do so under political centralisation (ie, unitary rule).[77] Furthermore, in order to strengthen its control over the petroleum resources of the federation in the Niger Delta, the FMG established the Nigerian National Oil Company, following which Nigeria became a member of the Organisation for Petroleum Exporting Countries (OPEC), in 1971.[78]

Most of the laws which came into place after the war to govern the petroleum industry were Military Decrees. These Decrees have subsequently been revised and updated (*ie*, transformed) into Acts of Parliament under democratic governments. So the Petroleum Decree (later known as the Petroleum Act) 1969,[79]

Accord) in Ghana collapsed. For instance, while Ojukwu relied on confederation reached at Aburi, considering the authority of the FMG in the regions, especially the South-Eastern region headed by Ojukwu, Gowon interpreted confederation differently. *See* the publication entitled 'Final Aburi Communiqué', found at http://www.dawodu.com/aburi1.htm visited on 22/03/08.

74 *See* E. J. Alagoa and A. A. Derefaka (eds), *The Land and People of Rivers State: Eastern Niger Delta, op cit*, p. 353.

75 It was on this basis that the NRRR programme of General Gowon's regime was designed to take effect immediately after the war in the interests of all Nigerians and Nigeria as a corporate entity. However, considering how this programme was improperly implemented in the context of ongoing calls for a Sovereign National Conference (SNC), it is essential for Nigeria to encourage an institutionalised conflict resolution system to avoid addressing prevailing conflicts improperly. *See* J. I. Elaigwu, *The Politics of Federalism in Nigeria, op cit*, p.148.

76 *See* the publication compiled by N. Omoigui, entitled 'Gowon's Broadcast to the Nation – May 27, 1967', *op cit*.

77 *See* S. A. Khan, *Nigeria: Political Economy of Oil*, Oxford, Oxford University Press, 1994, p. 22.

78 *Ibid. Also see* M. A. Ajomo, 'The Legal Framework of the Petroleum Industry', being a paper delivered at the Centre for Petroleum, Environment and Development Studies (CEEPEDS) Seminar on 'Essentials of Oil and Gas Law', Federal Palace Hotel, Victoria Island, July 21–22, 1999, p. 15.

79 A major element of this Decree/Act, now Cap 350 of the LFN, 1990, is its provision regarding the Nigerian state ownership and control of petroleum resource. The Act provides for the exploration, exploitation, prospecting and production of crude oil and natural gas. It vests the ownership of petroleum from the territorial waters and the continental shelf of Nigeria as well as all on-shore and off-shore revenues derived from petroleum resource, in the FG and for all other matters incidental thereto. The Act, which contains seven subsidiary regulations dealing with issues of oilfield operations, safety duties of managers, refining and other related issues or matters, was promulgated as Decree by the FMG headed by General Yakubu Gowon. The regulations under the Act are the Mineral Oil (Safety) Regulations, Petroleum (Drilling and Production) Regulations, Petroleum Refining Regulations, Crude Oil (Transportation and Shipment) Regulations, Petroleum Products (Prices of Automotive

Land Use Decree (also later known as the Land Use Act, LUA) 1978, and the Exclusive Economic Zone Decree, plus other Decrees (that are being transformed into Acts of Parliament)[80] which continue to govern petroleum operations, along with the various federal Constitutions (formulated during military regimes), played key roles to transform Nigeria into a unitary state. Other laws associated with petroleum operations in the FRN include the Oil Pipelines Act (Decree No. 31 of 1956), Cap 338, Oil in Navigable Waters Act (Decree No. 34 of 1968), Offshore Oil Revenue (Registration of Grants) Act, Cap. 336, and the Territorial Waters Act, Cap.428. Others are the Associated Gas Re-injection Decree Cap. 26, Lands Title Vesting etc. Decree, Cap. 52, National Inland Waterways Authority Decree, Cap 13, and the 1999 Constitution of the FRN, Cap. 24.[81]

Among the above-stated Decrees, the LUA 1978 remains one of the most controversial.[82] The LUA is considered as having a great impact on the existing land tenure systems, especially in Southern Nigeria,[83] since after Nigeria's attainment of modern nationhood.[84] The LUA has a great impact on major natural

---

Lubricating Oils) Order, and the Petroleum Products (Uniform Retail Prices) Order. *See* A. Ogbuigwe, 'Guide to Environmental Laws in Nigeria with Special Focus on Laws Applicable to the Petroleum Industry', Port Harcourt, Anpez Centre for Environment and Development, 2001. p. 24.

80 *See* LFN, Vol. 6, 2004, prepared under the authority of the revised edition (LFN) Act, 2004, by the law revision committee. Essentially, the FMG headed by General Yakubo Gowon (August 1, 1967 to July 29, 1975) promulgated the Petroleum Decree, Decree No. 51, 1969 (which is now Cap. 350, LFN, 1990), while the Military Government headed by Olusegun Obasanjo (which assumed power between February 14, 1976 and October 1, 1979) promulgated the Land Use Decree, Decree No. 6 of 1978, now Cap. 202, LFN, 1990. In the same year, 1978, the regime of General Obasanjo (which overthrew that of General Gowon) promulgated the Exclusive Economic Zone (EEZ) Decree, Decree No. 28 of 1978 (now the EEZ Act, Cap, 116 LFN, 1990, revised in 2004). The EEZ Act vests sovereign and exclusive rights in the Nigerian state over the exploitation of natural resources of the sea-bed, the subsoil and superjacent waters within the EEZ of the country.

81 *See* the Kaiama Declaration, being the Resolutions of the December 11, 1998, All Ijaw Youths Conference, held at Kaiama, Bayelsa state, Nigeria. *Also see*, the presentation entitled 'On the Question of Resource Control and Ownership: A Reply to Yadudu', being a memo submitted by Oronto Douglas, to the Committee on Environment & Natural Resources and the Committee on Revenue Allocation & Fiscal Federalism, National Political Reform Conference (NPRC), Abuja.

82 *See* D. N. Zillman *et al* (eds), *Human Rights in Natural Resources Development: Public Participation in the Sustainable Development of Mining and Energy Resources, op cit*, p. 564.

83 *See* Ogundare, J. (as he then was), in *Tijani Akinloye vs. Chief Oyejide* (Unreported), Suit No. HCJ/9A/81 of 17th July, 1981, at the High Court of Justice, Ijero, Ondo state (now Ekiti state). *Also see* Eso J. S. C., in *Nkwocha vs. Governor of Anambra state* (1984) 6 S. C. 362, at p. 392; (1984) 1 S. C. N. R. 634 at p. 647; (2001) F. W. L. R. (Pt. 48), 1386 at p. 1409. *See* Belgore J. S. C., in *Savannah Bank of Nigeria Limited vs. Ammel O. Ajilo* (1989) 1 N. W. L. R. (Pt. 97), 305 at p. 352–353. *Also see* Obaseki and Karibi-Whyte, JSC, in *Garuba Abioye vs. Sa'adu Yakubu* (1991)5 N. W. L. R. (Pt. 190), 130 at pp. 231–232. *See* J. F. Fekumo, *Principles of Nigerian Customary Law*, Port Harcourt, F & F., 2002, pp. 405–450. *See* M. Banaire, 'Towards Effective Control and Management of Land in Nigeria: A Re-Evaluation of the Land Use Act (1978)', Vol. 5 (2), *Oxford Commonwealth Journal*, 2005, pp. 257–286. *See* C. O'Faircheallaigh, 'Negotiating Cultural Heritage? Aboriginal-Mining Company Agreements in Australia', Development and Change, 39 (1), 2008, pp. 25–51. *Also see* L. Cotula and P. Mathieu (eds), *Legal Empowerment in Practice: Using Legal Tools to Secure Land Rights in Africa*, London, Food and Agricultural Organisation of the UN (UNFAO) and International Institute for Environment and Development (IIED), 2008.

84 *Per* Irikefe, JSC, in *Chief R. O. Nkwocha v. Governor of Anambra state* (1984), 6 S. C., 362, at p. 363. *Also see* J. F. Fekumo, *Principles of Nigerian Customary Law, op cit*, p. 405.

resources development.[85] Communities of the oil-rich Delta region regard the Act and other military enactments associated with petroleum development as having deprived them of their legitimate rights and interests in land in favour of the MNOCs being granted JV petroleum development rights by the FG. Customary rights and other interests of citizens of the Delta in and over land are being undermined in the course of petroleum development in the Delta communities.[86] M. G. Bunter describes this state of affairs in the following words:

> *Many of the grosser violations of native land rights and title result from the amalgamation of disparate peoples into convenient administrative units often under the exigencies of colonial rule. Upon independence from the colonial power such administrative units become independent nations and central government takes power over mineral resources. Acreage is defined by government for exploration, development and exploitation by international mining or oil companies. Areas are licensed, discoveries are made, development commences. The local people are not consulted. The trouble begins.*[87]

These words of Bunter describe the state of affairs in the Delta region which generated the resource-control movement of the region. The need thus arises for the FRN to address the resource-control movement on the basis of fair play, equity and social justice among the component ethnic nationalities and citizens of the federation.[88] The crises which generated the resource-control movement require to be resolved to achieve interactive CI and SCD in the Delta region and other oil-producing areas, and interactive citizens' participation in the entire FRN. These need to be achieved, in compliance with Nigeria's commitments and/or responsibilities arising from the progressive effort of the UN on the environment and development towards achieving SD in the interest of mankind.

2.3 THE ENVIRONMENT AND DEVELOPMENT IN A GLOBAL CONTEXT: EMERGING STANDARDS AND IMPLICATIONS IN THE NIGERIAN MUNICIPALITY

It is necessary to consider the developments being generated by the UN Conferences on the environment and development in Nigeria by recognising that the UN has from its inception in 1945 been concerned about the welfare

85 *See* D. N. Zillman *et al* (eds), *Human Rights in Natural Resources Development: Public Participation in the Sustainable Development of Mining and Energy Resources*, *op cit*, p. 564

86 *See* the report of the Ledum Mitee-led TCND, *op cit*, pp. 52–53.

87 *See* M. A. G. Bunter, *Host Communities, Native Title and Petroleum Licensing*, Dundee, Centre for Energy, Petroleum & Mineral Law & Policy (CEPMLP), 2003, p. 108.

88 *See* the ThisDay newspaper report entitled 'IBB Recommends Marshall Plan for N/Delta', found at http://www.thisdayonline.com/nview.php?id=119817&printer_friendly=1 visited on 16/08/08. *Also see* the report of the Guardian newspapers entitled 'U.S. Won't Back Military Option in N'Delta, says Carrington', found at http://www.guardiannewsngr.com/news/article03 //indexn2_htm?pdate=270808&ptitl. . . visited on 01/09/08.

of mankind. The UN has continued to focus on global peace and security, and the dignity of humankind through social progress and better standards of living as well as greater freedom through the employment of international mechanisms for the promotion of the socio-economic and political advancement of all peoples.[89] On this premise, the UN has, however, continually been faced with the challenges associated with the progressive course of human civilisation. These challenges include how to integrate environmental concerns into socio-economic development proposals based on the twin relationship of the environment and development, in order to achieve SD, as expressed by the general objects and purposes of the UN Charter.[90] The UN has thus been encouraging and persuading nations, sectors of society and peoples of the world to fully integrate the environment into every aspect of socio-economic livelihood.[91]

The UN appreciates that there are some sectors and organs of society whose roles are significant in the global effort to achieve SD. Hence, in July 2000, the then Secretary General of the UN, Kofi Annan, launched a voluntary initiative and non-regulatory instrument known as the Global Compact, to bring together with the UN agencies, companies, labour and civil society groups, to support universal environmental and social principles. The Global Compact was initiated so that private sector businesses can, in partnership with other social actors, help to achieve the vision of the UN to realise a more sustainable and inclusive global economy.[92] The Global Compact is thus a significant initiative of the UN in its progressively advancing and integrated effort towards SD.[93]

Furthermore, regarding this effort of the UN, the late 1960s onwards are significant. This was a period punctuated by emerging environmental problems and growing public awareness of the challenging issues of the deteriorating global environment in the course of socio-economic developments. The realities of this period sensitised various actors and segments of society, and caused the UN to convene its first formal Conference on the environment and development, namely the UNCHE held at Stockholm, Sweden, from June 5–16, 1972. This Conference ignited further actions and initiatives of the UN such as the convention of its tenth anniversary by the global community of nation states which took place at Nairobi, from May 10 to 18, 1982. It was

---

89 The inherent dignity of people and the values, legitimate aspirations, rights and responsibilities of all people expressed in the UN Universal Declaration of Human Rights (UNDHR), 1948, thus punctuates the universal interest and importance of citizens' or PP in decision-making.

90 *See* preamble, purposes and principles of the UN expressed in Chapter 1 (*ie*, Articles 1 and 2) of the *Charter of the United Nations*, 1945, found at http://www.un.org/aboutun/charter/ visited on 31/12/06.

91 *See* E. B. Barbier, *The Economics of Environment and Development: Selected Essays*, Cheltenham, Edward Elgar, 1998, p. 1. *Also see* M. A. Ajomo and O. Adewale (eds.), *Environmental Law and Sustainable Development in Nigeria, op cit*, pp. 1–2.

92 *See* the area of the UN Global Compact homepage, captioned 'What is the Global Compact', found at http://www.unglobalcompact.org/Portal/Default.asp? visited on 31/12/06.

93 Ibid.

followed by the convention of the UNCED held at Rio de Janeiro, Brazil, from June 3 to 14, 1992, and then the WSSD held at Johannesburg, South Africa, from August 26 to September 4, 2002, and the aftermath of these Conferences in the UN system. [94]

As the first formal Conference on the twin relationship of the environment and development, the Stockholm Conference represents an attempt by the UN to address the concerns of global nations about the deteriorating nature of the environment. In the process, what came to be known as the 'final documents' of the Conference emerged to constitute the general agreement among member-states and other interest groups of the UN (such as the intergovernmental and non-governmental organisations which were in attendance), to treat the environment and development as two sides of the same coin.[95] Following the Declaration of the Stockholm Conference (Stockholm Declaration), 1972, other follow-up steps and achievements made included the establishment of the UN Environment Programme (UNEP) at Nairobi, Kenya, in 1972.[96] Having been established as the voice of the environment within the UN system, the functions of UNEP constituted the focal objects for which the UN Commission on Environment and Development (WCED) was set up in 1983.[97]

---

94 As indications of widespread ecological problems became apparent in the 1960s, considering the general objectives, goals or purposes of the UN, proposals were made by global peoples and groups for the expansion of its activities by including environmental concerns so as to fulfil the overall intention of its Charter. *See* A. C. Kallhauge *et al, Global Challenges: Furthering the Multilateral Process for Sustainable*_Development, Sheffield, Greenleaf, 2005, pp. 16–19. *Also See* B. Linner and H. Selin, 'How It All Began: Global Efforts on Sustainable Development from Stockholm to Rio', (hereinafter called 'Global Efforts on Sustainable Development from Stockholm to Rio'), being the draft copy of a paper presented at the 6th Nordic Conference on Environmental Social Sciences, Abo, Finland, June 12–14, 2003, as part of the panel 'Johannesburg: A First Anniversary', found at http://www.cid.harvard.edu/cidbiotech/events/selinlinnerpaper100603.doc visited on 16/12/03. *See* B. Linner and H. Selin, [0]*The Thirty-Year Quest for Sustainability: A Historical Look at the 1972 Stockholm Conference and Beyond*, found at http://www.cid.harvard.edu/cidbiotech/events/selin_linner090603.htm visited on 05/12/03. *Also see* the area of the WSSD website captioned 'Summit Road Map', containing the key steps taken by the UN, as from the convention of the Stockholm Conference to the pre-conference arrangements of the WSSD, as well as parallel international social and environmental Summit processes and key Multilateral Environmental Agreements (MEAs), found at http://www.cebds.com/riomais10/summitroadmap.pdf visited on 10/12/03.

95 *See* M. A. Ajomo and O. Adewale (eds), *Environmental Law and Sustainable Development in Nigeria, op cit*, p. 2.

96 *See* M. T. Okorodudu-Fubara, *Law of Environmental*_Protection: Materials and Text, Ibadan, Caltop, 1998, pp. 38 and 914–920. *Also see* the publication of the UN Environment Programme (UNEP) on the Stockholm Conference, 'Constitution of the Conference', found at http://www.unep.org/Documents.multilingual/Default.asp?DocumentID=97&ArticleID=1496&l=en visited on 20/08/05. *Also see* the UN 'Nairobi Declaration' which expressed the role and mandate of UNEP, found at http://www.ourplanet.com/imgversn/86/nairobi.htm visited on 13/10/03. *See* these and more about the UNEP at http://www.wri.org/wr.org/wr2000/unep.html visited on 29/10/03.

97 *See* the website of the UNEP, found at http://www.unep.org/Documents.Multilingual/Default.asp?DocumentID=43 visited on 20/08/05.

Despite the bold steps of the UN in establishing the UNEP and the WCED, nothing more practically significant was achieved in terms of integrating global concerns for the development and protection of the environment in the context of economic planning and decision-making. Consequently, a UN Conference on the environment was held at Nairobi, Kenya, in 1982, to review the progress being made; thereafter by its resolution 42/228 of December 1982, the UN General Assembly (UNGA) called for another conference which was aimed at addressing the deteriorating state of the environment by establishing the basis for a sustainable way of life worldwide.[98] This resolution was moved to introduce certain measures to contain the challenges likely to deter global progress, as the world moves into the twenty-first century. This resolution was informed by the publication in 1987 of the report of the WCED entitled *Our Common Future* otherwise called the Brundtland Commission report or the Brundtland report.[99] This report widely appealed to individual global nations as well as prompted the UN into further action. In appealing to and sensitising the member-states of the UN, *Our Common Future,* which served as the basis of what became Agenda 21,[100] points out, as indicated in the introduction of this chapter, that the environment and development are inseparable.[101] SD requires a progressive transformation of economy and ecology as well as economy in relation to overall society, premised on good national governance and greater democratic international governance – 'what is needed now is a new era of economic growth – growth that is forceful and at the same time socially and environmentally sustainable'.[102] By being made so aware by *Our Common Future*, the UNGA had to call for the Convention of the UN Conference on Environment and Development (UNCED) on December 22, 1989. This Conference was held at Rio de Janeiro, Brazil, on June 3–14, 1992.[103]

98 *See* M. A. Ajomo and O. Adewale (eds), *Environmental Law and Sustainable Development in Nigeria, op cit*, p. 1.

99 *See* a publication on Dr. Brundtland, found at *http://www.tccge.org/include/pdf/Gro%20Harlem%20Brundtland%20June03.pdf* visited on 20/10/03. *Also see* the publication of the World Health Organisation (WHO) entitled 'Dr. Gro Harlem Brundtland, Director General', found at http://www.who.int/dg/brundtland/bruntland/en/print.html visited on 17/08/05. The WCED was set up to respond to the urgent call of the UNGA to examine the critical environment and development problems of the global community and formulate realistic proposals to solve them by formulating a global agenda for change towards SD. *See Our Common Future, op cit*, pp. xi and 8–9. *Also see* the publication of the UN Department of Sustainability and Environment (DSE) entitled 'Background: The Brundtland Report', found at http://www.brundtlandnet.com./brundtlandreport.htm visited on 25/05/04.

100 *See* the homepage of the 'UN Department of Economic and Social Affairs: Division for Sustainable Development', captioned 'Documents', with the subtitle 'Agenda 21', found at http://www.un.org/esa/sustdev/documents/agenda21/index.htm visited on 31/12/06.

101 *See Our Common Future, op cit*, p. xi. *Also see* the publication of the UN Department of Sustainability and Environment (DSE) entitled 'Background: The Brundtland Report', found at http://www.brundtlandnet.com./brundtlandreport.htm visited on 25/05/04.

102 *Further see Our Common Future, op cit*, pp. xi–xii, 8–9 and 43–46, especially p. xii.

103 *See* the area of the Earth Summit website, captioned 'UN Conference on Environment and Development (1992)', found at http://www.un.org/geninfo/bp/enviro.html visited on 23/10/06.

The UNCED, known as 'the Earth Summit', was intended to devise strategies, internationally and nationally, to fully integrate environmental protection into development in every aspect of economic life and behaviour.[104] The Rivers Chiefs and Peoples' Conference (RCPC) was among civil society groups that addressed the Summit. The address of the RCPC entitled the 'The Endangered Environment of the Niger Delta', could be described as a historical, geographic, political, environmental and socio-economic development account of the Niger Delta region. It is centred on the adverse effects of petroleum development in the region, as regards the desire, efforts and challenges of the people of the region to achieve environmentally sound and equitable SCD. It concluded by stating that the environment of the region is endangered, and that it is about the most endangered delta region in the world.[105]

At the Earth Summit, a comprehensive programme of action was put forward by governments, development agencies, UN organisations and independent sector groups in every area or locality where the economic activity of mankind impacts on the environment. The main resulting documents of the Earth Summit are Agenda 21, the Rio Declaration on Environment and Development, the Statement of Forest Principles, the UN Framework Convention on Climate Change and the UN Convention on Biological Diversity.[106] The Summit enlisted the agreement of the nations, key sectors of society and individuals in the world to a firmly-recognised idea of environmental protection in the course of socio-economic developments in the march towards SD through international partnerships and cooperation. Among other things, the Earth Summit recommended that all countries should establish programmes of integrated environmental and economic accounting, for use as a tool to enhance SD through policy making and planning and decision-making processes. Consequently, the World

---

104 *See* the report of Kofi Annan, the former UN Secretary General, entitled 'We the Peoples: The Role of the United Nations in the 21 Century', found at http://www.un.org/millennium/sg/report/full.htm visited on 31/12/06.

105 *See* D. M. J. Fubara (ed), 'The Endangered Environment of the Niger Delta: An NGO Memorandum of the Rivers Chiefs and Peoples' Conference', Port Harcourt, Nigeria, for the World Conference of Indigenous Peoples on Environment and Development and The United Nations Conference on Environment and Development, Rio de Janeiro, Brazil, 1992, (hereinafter called 'The Endangered Environment of the Niger Delta'), especially pp. 1 and 16. *Also see* the ThisDay newspaper report captioned 'N'Delta Commitment to Peace Doubtful – Clarke', found at http://www.thisdayonline.com/nview.php?id=113060&printer_friendly=1 visited on 03/06/08.

106 *See* the area of the Earth Summit website, captioned 'UN Conference on Environment and Development (1992)', *op cit*. While Agenda 21 is a comprehensive blue-print for global action in all areas of SD which included the formulation and elaboration of appropriate legal principles and rules, the Rio Declaration consists of several principles defining the rights and responsibilities of global nations regarding environmental protection and development; whilst the Forest Principles are a set of guidelines for the sustainable management of forests worldwide. *See* the publication of the UN Department of Public Information on the Earth Summit, entitled 'UN Conference on Environment and Development (1992)', found at http://www.un.org/geninfo/bp/enviro.html visited on 31/12/06. *Also see* E. T. Bristol, 'Global Consensus on Sustainable Development and Crude Oil Production in the Niger Delta', being a dissertation submitted to the Department of Jurisprudence and International Law, University of Lagos, Lagos-Nigeria, in partial fulfilment of the requirements for the award of the degree of Master of International Law and Diplomacy (MILD), 1995, p.xvii.

Commission on Sustainable Development (WCSD) was created in December 1992 to ensure effective follow-up on the agreements reached at the Earth Summit, and thereby monitor and report on implementation of these agreements at the local, national, regional and international levels of society.[107] Based on the recommendation of the UNGA Resolution 47/191 of 22 December 1992, the WCSD was empowered to promote the incorporation of the Principles of the Rio Declaration in the implementation of Agenda 21, to enhance public awareness on SD at all levels of society.[108]

The achievements recorded in fulfilment of the agreements reached at the Earth Summit lagged behind what was expected,[109] as the progress towards SD was disappointing. Hence, the rate of poverty was becoming higher and more deplorable, while the rate of environmental degradation was worsening. The UN, countries of the world and key sectors of society came to realise that SD is not an easy task to achieve, as more significant commitments are required to fully and sustainably integrate the economic, social, environmental, and governance spheres of development to meet the needs of mankind's present generation without sacrificing the ability of future generations to meet their needs. What the world, in effect, wanted was not a new philosophical or political debate but rather, a summit of actions and results.[110] Thus, ten years after the Rio de Janeiro first Earth Summit, the second Earth Summit (WSSD) was held at Johannesburg in South Africa, between August 26 and September 4, 2002. Indeed, while some refer to this Summit as the Johannesburg Summit, others call it the second Earth Summit or Conference.[111]

Debates at the WSSD were mainly held under tension because of the divide between governments and civil society groups, especially NGOs, the press and individuals. Besides, there was a great divide, mainly between the globally rich/developed countries and the poor/developing countries. Hence, the poor/global south countries accused the rich/global north countries of turning the Summit into a world trade affair.[112] Besides, civil society groups were

---

107 *See* the mission statement, goals and objectives of this UN Division for SD, found at http://www.un.org/esa/susdev/about_us/aboutus.htm visited on 30/10/03.

108 *See* N. A. Robinson (ed), *Agenda 21: Earth's Action Plan*, New York, Oceana, 1993, p. 115–136. *Also see* the publication of the University of Minnesota Human Rights Library, entitled 'Dissemination of the Principles of the Rio Declaration on Environment and Development, G. A. res. 48/190, 48 U. N. GAOR Supp. (No. 49) at 167, U. N. Doc. A/48/49 (1993)', found at http://www.1.umn.edu/humanrts/resolutions/48/190GA1993.html visited on 10/10/03.

109 *See* the article by R. Machemedze, entitled 'Global Peoples Forum Admits Failure in Implementing Agenda 21', found at http://www.solidaritetshuset.org/rorg/aktuelt/2002/dok/seatini17.htm visited on 21/2/03.

110 *See* the area of the website of the WSSD, captioned 'The Johannesburg Summit Test: What Will Change?', found at http://www.un.org/jsummit/index.html visited on 15/11/06.

111 *See* the website of the Summit entitled 'Johannesburg Summit 2002', found at http://www.johannesburgsummit.org/ visited on 13/08/05.

112 Whereas rich countries of the world are classified as the global North, poor countries are regarded as the global South. *See* S. Jones and G. Carswell (eds), *The Earthscan Reader in Environment, Development and Rural Livelihoods*, London and Sterling, Earthscan, 2004, p.193. *Also see* the article by P. Makombe, entitled 'WSSD Plan for Action Has No Action', found at http://www.solidaritetshuset.org/rorg/aktuelt/2002/seatine17.htm visited on 21/02/03.

critical about the Rio de Janeiro Earth Summit, in that it achieved or delivered much less than it promised.[113] These groups stated that governments of the world have, through their empty promises, lack of seriousness and tricky political posturing, refused to deliver the goals of SD as agreed upon at Rio de Janeiro.[114] The WSSD thus offered the participants and others present at the Summit an opportunity to network, and the global nations under the UN system to consider the achievement of SD more seriously. The Summit modestly explored the challenges towards achieving SD in line with the need to deliver the Millennium Development Goals (MDGs) in the interest of mankind.[115] The Summit culminated in the making of the Johannesburg Declaration on SD, 2002, on the basis of which follow-up measures are taking place in the UN system. It may therefore be concluded that the outcomes of the SRJ process, are still ongoing in the UN system.[116]

2.4 SD RESPONSIBILITIES OF GOVERNMENT AND THE MNOCS IN THE OIL-RICH DELTA REGION

The FRN, represented by the relevant government agencies and governments, and the MNOCs operating in the federation, owe the petroleum resources-producing communities certain responsibilities to ensure SD of these resources and SD in these communities, in compliance with the stipulations of the SRJ process and their progressively ongoing processes. Whereas the responsibilities of the governments arise from FRN's membership of the UN, the responsibilities of the MNOCs in a way arise from the UN Global Compact, of which Shell, Nigeria's leading multinational giant, is already a member.[117]

The Declarations of the UNCHE in 1972, its follow-up Conference at Nairobi in 1982, the UNCED in 1992, and the WSSD in South Africa, in

---

See the publication entitled 'World Summit on Sustainable Development . . . LIVE!', found at http://www.un.org/events/wssd/ visited on 18/08/05.

113 Ibid.

114 Ibid. *Also see* the article by R. Machemedze entitled 'Global Peoples Forum Admits Failure in Implementing Agenda 21', *op cit*.

115 *See* the publication entitled 'The Johannesburg Summit 2002: Basic Information' found at http://www.johannesburgsummit.org/html/basic_info/basicinfo.html visited on 18/08/05. *Also see* the homepage of the UN Millennium Development Goals (MDGs), found at http://www.un.org/millenniumgoals/, visited on 31/12/06. *See* the website of the WSSD captioned 'Key Outcomes of the Summit', found at http://www.un.org/jsummit/html/documents/summit_docs/2009_keyoutcomes_commitments.doc visited on 31/12/06. *See* the 'report of the World Summit on Sustainable Development', Johannesburg, South Africa, August 26, – September 4, 2002, New York, United Nations, found at http://daccessods.un.org/TMP/6421712.html last visited on 31/12/06.

116 *See* A. C. Kallhauge *et al*, *Global Challenges: Furthering the Multilateral Process for Sustainable Development*, *op cit*, pp. 17–20.

117 *See* the area of the UN Global Compact homepage captioned 'Participants and Stakeholders', found at http://www.unglobalcompact.org/ParticipantsAndStakeholders/search_participant.htm. . . visited on 31/12/06.

2002, have certain provisions which may serve as reference points or the basis for GSR and CSR. Briefly put, certain provisions of the Declaration of the WSSD (otherwise referred to as the Johannesburg Declaration on SD), 2002, captioned 'From Our Origins to the Future' are instructive. Thus, Article 26 of this Declaration emphasises the need for GSR and CSR by expressing the need for stable partnerships of major groups towards SD.[118] Also, while expressing the need for GSR and CSR, Article 29 of the Johannesburg Declaration on SD, 2002, provides that:

> *We agree that there is a need for private sector corporations to enforce corporate accountability which should take place within a transparent and stable regulatory environment.*

In effect, whereas it is the responsibility of governments in Nigeria[119] to provide a transparent and stable regulatory environment, it is the responsibility of the MNOCs in Nigeria to be environmentally and socially accountable and responsible for their operational activities. To do so, they are required to comply with government's policy, legislative and regulatory measures designed to address their operations in the oil-producing areas. Hence, Article 27 of the Johannesburg Declaration on SD, 2002, provides that:

> *We agree that in pursuit of its legitimate activities, the private sector, including both large and small companies, has a duty to contribute to the evolution of equitable and sustainable societies.*

On the other hand, regarding GSR, Article 30 of the Johannesburg Declaration on SD, 2002, provides as follows:

> *We undertake to strengthen and improve governance at all levels for effective implementation of Agenda 21, the Millennium Development Goals and the Plan of Implementation of the Summit.*

Besides, while emphasising the need for the entire global society to cooperate in order to achieve the MDGs by the year 2015, Article 36 of the Johannesburg Declaration provides as follows:

> *We commit ourselves to the Plan of Implementation of the World Summit on Sustainable Development and to expediting the achievement of the time-bound, socio-economic and environmental targets contained therein.*

---

118 *Also see* U. Petschow *et al* (eds.), *Governance and Sustainability: New Challenges for States, Companies and Civil Society*, Sheffield, Greenleaf, 2005.

119 *See* N. Schrijver, *Sovereignty over Natural Resources: Balancing Rights and Duties*, Cambridge, Cambridge University Press, 1997, especially pp. 390–395. *Also see* the provisions of Article 17 of the UN Universal Declaration of Human Rights, 1948, and Article 21 of the African Charter of Human and Peoples Rights, Cap. 10, LFN, 1990.

Thus, all nations, both poor and rich, have pledged to deliver the MDGs by the year 2015, in the interest of mankind. Briefly put, by virtue of the UNGA Resolution 55/2 of September 8, 2000, on the UN Millennium Declaration, and the roadmap towards the implementation of this Declaration, poor countries have pledged to govern better while rich countries pledged to support poor countries to achieve the MDGs. The pledge of governments of poor countries to govern their citizens and countries better[120] involves the provision of social investment or public utilities through good governance (GG), considering that SD is intricately associated with GG.[121]

In its effort to fulfil or implement its roles and responsibilities arising from its membership of the UN, the FRN produced its Local Agenda 21 entitled 'Nigeria's National Agenda 21'.[122] This was produced in order to improve the environmental governance effort of Nigeria, especially in relation to major natural resources development in the country. Thus, to fulfil its roles and responsibilities as a member-state of the UN, Nigeria's Agenda 21 is directed to achieve the following:

> *(i) to integrate the environment into development planning at all levels of government and the private sector, (ii) intensify the transition to sustainable development; (iii) address sectoral priorities, plans, policies and strategies for the major sectors of the economy; and (iv) simultaneously foster regional and global partnerships.*[123]

Accordingly, the mission statement on the 'rational use of oil and gas resources' expressed in Nigeria's Agenda 21, provides thus:

> *Produce the nation's oil and gas in an environmentally sustainable and socially nondisruptive way, ensuring long-term optimum returns from its exploitation and to invest the proceeds in the development of*

---

120 Rich countries undertook to support poor countries through aid, debt relief, and fair-trade, among other things. *See* the publication in the UN Development Programme (UNDP) website on the MDGs, captioned 'the Millennium Development Goals – MDGs', found at http://www.undp.org/mdg/ visited on 05/05/06. *Also see* the report of the UN Secretary General dated September 6, 2001, entitled the 'Road-Map towards the Implementation of the UN Millennium Declaration', found at http://ods-dds-ny.org/doc/UNDOC/GEN/NO1/526/07/PDF/NO152607.pdf?OpenElement and another report of the Secretary General dated September 2, 2003, entitled 'Implementation of the United Nations Millennium Declaration', found at http://ods-dds-ny.org/doc/UNDOC/GEN/NO3/481/57/PDF/NO348157.pdf?OpenElement both visited on 12/10/03.

121 *See* the inaugural address of Kofi Annan, the former UN Secretary General, at the UN 'International Conference on Governance for Sustainable Growth and Equity', held in New York, July, 28–30, 1997, found at http://magnet.undp.org/icg97/ANNAN.HTM visited on 29/09/06. *Also see* the Seoul Declaration on Participation and Transparent Government, made at the 6th Global Forum on Reinventing Governance, held at Seoul, Republic of Korea, on May 27, 2005.

122 *See* 'Nigeria's National Agenda 21', Garki-Abuja, The Presidency, Federal Environmental Protection Agency (FEPA), 1999.

123 Ibid, p. i.

> *sustainable projects and activities which improve the quality of life and the environment.*[124]

To achieve the foregoing objectives as reinforced by the mission statement, Nigeria's effort towards implementing the UN Agenda 21 in its municipality mainly revolves around four basic aspects of its Local Agenda 21 programme, namely the social, economic, natural resources and institutional aspects of the Agenda.[125] On institutional aspects, for instance, Chapter 5 is designed to discuss the effort of the FGN regarding the protection and development of the environment, biodiversity conservation and SD of Nigeria's natural resources, beginning with the promulgation of the FEPA Decree (Decree No. 58 of 1988) to the promulgation of the EIA Decree (Decree No. 86 of 1992), including the regulatory institutions created by the FG in this regard, pursuant to the efforts of the UN on the environment and development to achieve SD.

Also, in pursuance of the role of the UN's Agenda 21, Nigeria's Local or National Agenda 21 relies on the environmental aspect of Nigeria's VISION 2010 developmental programme.[126] This programme was carried out by a Committee set up in 1996 by the country's head of state, General Sani Abacha,[127] 'to look at all aspects of Nigerian society, helping to define for the country its correct bearing and sense of political, socio-cultural and economic direction'.[128] The VISION 2010 Committee was required to develop a blueprint that would transform Nigeria and place it firmly on the route to becoming a developed nation by the year 2010.[129]

---

124 Ibid, p. 17.

125 *See* the publication entitled 'Nigeria Country Profile Implementation of Agenda 21: Review of Progress Made since the United Nations Conference on Environment and Development, 1992', found at http://www.un.org/esa/earthsummit/nigeriac.htm visited on 20/11/02.

126 Ibid. On this note, *see* Nigeria's approach to SD in the context of the VISION 2010 programme, in the sub-section of the sub-heading (under the 'Economic Aspects of Sustainable Development in Nigeria') entitled 'International Cooperation: Decision-making', found at http://www.un.org/esa/agenda21/natlinfo/countr/nigeria/eco.htm visited on 20/11/02. This provides that *Nigeria's approach to sustainable development received a boost from the establishment of the VISION 2010 Committee, a body charged with the articulation of a long-term sectoral economic development programme designed to usher the nation into the millennium. The National Agenda 21 document has, therefore, been prepared to address the environmental implications of this development programme. See* the sub-section of the sub-heading (under the 'Economic Aspects of Sustainable Development in Nigeria') entitled 'International Cooperation: Decision-making', found at http://www.un.org/esa/agenda21/natlinfo/countr/nigeria/eco.htm visited on 20/11/02.

127 General Sani Abacha was the Military Head of state of the Federal Republic of Nigeria between November 17, 1993 and June 8, 1998.

128 *See* the 'VISION 2010 Report' found at http://www.vision2010.org/index.htm visited on 04/04/04, especially the introduction of this report.

129 Ibid, especially the mission statement of this Committee which is *to* help Nigeria become *'a united, industrious, caring and God-fearing democratic society, committed to making basic needs of life affordable for everyone, and creating Africa's leading economy'. Also see*, the Nigeria's Vision 2020 initiative launched by President Umaru Musa Yar'Adua, who assumed office as the President of the federation on May 29, 2007). This Vision is an economic and business plan to make Nigeria become a fully developed nation, in particular one of the 20 most developed global economies by the

To develop Nigeria, the VISION 2010 Committee states that its findings provide a clear route to the development of a stronger and more prosperous Nigerian nation, into the New Millennium.[130] VISION 2010 is identified to chart Nigeria's future social and economic development, and in the process usher in an era of cooperation between the public and private sectors of the country.[131] The progress report of Nigeria's Agenda 21 under the VISION 2010 programme provides that the country recognises the fact that broad public participation (PP) in decision-making is a fundamental prerequisite for achieving SD.[132] Among other things, the VISION 2010 Committee made recommendation for increased community stakeholder involvement and greater indigenous participation in the country's petroleum sector.[133]

Apart from the fact that the report of the VISION 2010 Committee expressed the need for broad PP in decision-making in order to achieve SD, environmental democracy based on stakeholder partnership regarding petroleum development in the Delta region and other oil-producing areas is increasingly being emphasised in Nigeria.[134] It is thus expected that governments and the MNOCs would be proactive in their efforts to achieve SD, by fully and effectively performing their respective roles and responsibilities arising from the UN system, considering the worldwide concerns about the crises in the oil-rich Delta region.[135] For instance, the concern of the USA about the crises in the region generated a partnership arrangement in December, 2005 between

---

year 2020. As the VISION 2010 programme, the success of the Vision 2020 initiative is dependent on government's will (*ie*, the will to enthronement of GG) in the country. *See* the newspaper report captioned 'Nigeria: Vision 2020 Depends On Political Will – ECCIMA', found at http://www.topix.com/world/nigeria/2008/01/nigeria-vision2020-depends-on-politica. . . visited on 02/06/08.

130 *See* the executive summary of the 'VISION 2010 Report' *op cit.*

131 Ibid.

132 *See* 'Nigeria's National Agenda 21', *op cit*, pp. 63–68.

133 *See* item 152 of Vol. 2, Book 4 of the VISION 2010 Report, captioned 'Sports, Ecology and Environment'. *Also see* the executive summary of the 'VISION 2010 Report' *op cit.*

134 These include the Niger Delta Youths Stakeholders Workshop, 2004, the Niger Delta Regional Development Master Plan, 2004/2005, the *Niger Delta Human Development Report*, Garki-Abuja, UNDP Nigeria, 2006, and the report of the Shell Nigeria 2004 Stakeholders Workshop discussed in Chapter 7. *See* the review of the book entitled *Assessing Participatory Development: Rhetoric Versus Reality*, by Martha ter Kuile (of the Canadian International Development Agency [CIDA], Hull, Quebec, Canada), in Society and Natural Resources, Vol. 5, 1992, p. 91, which provides that *You cannot achieve sustainable economic development without participation by people. You cannot achieve genuine participation without profound commitment and a change of heart. Even with such commitment, the costs are high. Also see* R. S. Sidaway, *Resolving Environmental Disputes: from Conflict to Consensus*, London, Earthscan, 2005, p. 115. *See* W. P Lineberry (ed), *Assessing Participatory Development: Rhetoric Versus Reality*, London, Westview Press/IFAD, 1989.

135 *See* the BBC news entitled 'Nigerian Oil Fuels Delta Conflict', found at http://newsvote.bbc.co.uk/mpapps/pagetools/print/news.bbc.co.uk/1/hi/world/africa/4617658.stm visited on 31/12/06. *Also see* D. Humphreys, 'Sustainable Development: Can the Mining Industry Afford It?' Resources Policy, Vol. 27, Issue 1, March 2001, pp. 1–7. *See* J. N. Ehanmo, 'Is Sustainable Development Compatible with Economic Growth in an Oil Dominated Developing Economy? (A Case Study of Nigeria)', being a dissertation submitted to the CEPMLP, University of Dundee, in Partial Fulfilment for the Award of MSc. Energy Studies with a Specialisation in Oil and Gas Economics, January 2006, pp. 58–59.

the USA and Nigeria, regarding how to enhance security, peace and prosperity in the region.[136] There is also the 2008 controversial bilateral partnership which was to be entered into between the British government and the FRN regarding the crises in the region.[137] Due to the crises in the Delta region and other unsustainable developments and conflicts plaguing Nigeria, the US National Intelligence Council (NIC) had in December, 2004 published a report entitled 'Mapping the Global Future: Report of the US National Intelligence Council's 2020 Project Based on Consultations with Nongovernmental Experts around the World'. This report presents the state of affairs in Africa and the pattern of conflicts as well as upside and downside surprises. On this note, the report predicts the collapse of Nigeria, considering that Nigerian leaders are locked in a bad marriage that they all dislike.[138] Furthermore, the US NIC report of November 2008, provides that although the Sub-Saharan African region will continue to be a major supplier of oil, gas and metals to global markets, it will remain the most vulnerable region on Earth. This may necessitate foreign military intervention to end the Niger Delta crises so as to stabilise petroleum exports in Nigeria. Precisely, as this report put it:

> *In 2025, Sub-Saharan African region will remain the most vulnerable region on Earth in terms of economic challenges, population stresses, civil conflict, and political instability. The weakness of states and troubled relations between states and societies probably will slow major improvements in the region's prospects over the next 20 years unless there is sustained international engagement and, at times, intervention. . . .*[139]

The challenges of conflicts arising from discords in Nigeria thus make it imperative for the crises in the Nigerian Delta region and other perennial

---

136 Based on this partnership, the governments of both countries established a joint committee charged with the task of coordinating a comprehensive action against insecurity in the petroleum rich Delta region. *See* the ThisDay newspaper article entitled '*Nigeria, US Sign Security Deal on the N/Delta*', found at http://allafrica.com/stories/printable/200512090398.html visited on 20/12/2005. *Also see* the report of the Guardian newspapers entitled 'Nigeria, U.S. Sign Pact on the Niger Delta, Gulf of Guinea', found at http://66.102.9.104/search?q=cache:KumVhRNT58J:www.guardiannewsngr.com/n. . . visited on 20/12/05. *See* A. Rowell *et al, The Next Gulf: London, Washington and Oil Conflict in Nigeria*, London, Constable & Robinson, 2005.

137 A news report on this states that . . . *Nigeria's decline in [petroleum] production worries the West, and the British government recently agreed to provide training and logistical support to the Nigerian military to combat rebel attacks and to protect its own interests – primarily British Petroleum's (BP) activities in the country. See* this news report by B. Smith, entitled 'Angola Becomes Africa's Largest Oil Producer', dated 4 September, 2008, found in the World Socialist Website, at http://www.wsws.org/articles/2008/sep2008/ango-s04.shtml visited on 27/09/08.

138 *See* this report found at http://www.dni.gov/nic/NIC_globaltrend2020.html visited on 31/12/06, particularly pp. 187–193, especially pp. 192–193.

139 *See* pp. iii and 56 of the US NIC November 2008 report entitled 'Global Trends 2025: A National Intelligence Council's 2025 Report', found at http://www.dni.gov/nic/NIC_2025_project.html visited on 30/11/08. *Also see* the Punch newspaper report entitled Why Foreign Military Intervention May be Necessary in Nigeria – US Analysts', found at http://www.punchontheweb.com/Article-print2aspx?theartic=Art2008113056873 visited on 30/11/08.

issues of the lingering Nigerian National Question to be addressed.[140] The Delta region's crises (occasioned by the adverse effects of petroleum development in the region), reinforce the view of Karen Ballentine, in her discussion paper on 'Natural Resources, Development and Conflict', that 'for developing countries, natural resources are (often) the "only game in town." '[141] Many are thus of the view that the Nigerian National Question needs to be properly addressed in a sovereign national dialogue[142] comprised mainly of the representatives of the component pre-colonial nationalities and activist civil society groups in the country. If such a dialogue is convened and decisions and understandings are amicably reached on the platforms of social justice, equity and fair play, a more prospective way forward may be arrived at in the overall interest of Nigeria. This way forward is capable of serving the collective interest of the poor citizens and the ethnic minorities (especially those of the Delta region) who have traditionally been deprived of proper participation in the decision-making processes of Nigeria's nation-building. It is capable of generating improved CSR,[143] integrative and restorative justice (RJ)[144] enhanced by GSR in the course of petroleum development in the Delta region.

---

140 *See* the report of the Guardian newspapers entitled 'Niger Delta Crisis is Real Danger, Says Eso', found at http://www.guardiannewsngr.com/news/article01//index2_html?pdate=030608&ptitl. . . visited on 03/06/08. *Also see* the ThisDay newspaper report entitled 'Growth of Africa's Oil Exporting Countries to Decline – IMF', found at http://www.thisdayonline.com/nview.php?id=126126&printer_friendly=1 visited on 24/10/08.

141 *See* the discussion paper of Karen Ballentine on 'Natural Resources, Governance and Conflict', delivered at the UN Department of Economic and Social Affairs (UNDESA) Expert Group Meeting on Conflict Prevention, Peace-Building and development', on November 15, 2004, found at http://www.un.org/est/peacebuilding/Action/DesaTaskForce/papersegm20041115/NaturalResourcesKBallentine.pdf visited on 10/05/05. *Also see* the report of the Human Rights Watch (HRW) entitled 'Engine of War: Resources, Greed, and the Predatory State', by A. Ganesan and A. Vines, dated January 2004, found at http://www.hrw.org/wr2k4/14.htm#_Toc58744963 visited on 21/08/08.

142 *See* the communiqué of the 'Conference of Nationalities' organised by the Campaign for Democracy in Nigeria, Lagos, Nigeria, from December 17 to 19, 1998, at the Century Hotel, Okota, Lagos, found at http://www.nigeriascholars.africanqueen.com/docum/confnation.htm visited on 22/11/02. *Also see* the homepage of the initiative for SNC in Nigeria, captioned 'Sovereign National Conference', found at http://www.ngex.com/snc/default.htm and at http://www.ngex.com/snc/ visited on 17/04/05.

143 *See* F. Bird, 'Wealth and Poverty in the Niger Delta: Reflections on the History of Shell's Operations in Nigeria', found at http://peace.concordia/pdf/GRSShellNigeriax.pdf visited on 06/05/05. *Also see* F. Bird, 'Ethical Reflections on the Challenges Facing International Businesses in Developing Areas' found at http://peace.concordia.ca.pdf/GRShellNigeria.pdf visited on 06/05/05. *See* the report of the Fridtjof Nansen Institute (FNI) prepared by Kristian Tangen entitled 'Shell: Struggling to Build a Better World?', found at http://www.fni.no/pdf/FNI-R0103.pdf visited on 25/11/04. *See* the reports of the Pensions & Investment Research Consultants Limited (PIRC), United Kingdom, on Shell, and in particular the report entitled the PIRC report 'Environmental and Corporate Responsibility at Shell: The Shareholder Role in Promoting Change', found at http://www.pirc.co.uk/shell.pfd visited on 01/09/04.

144 Restorative practices are underpinned by a set of values. These include empowerment, honesty, engagement, voluntarism, healing, restoration, accountability, inclusiveness, collaboration and problem-solving. These values are applied to resolve conflicts and to repair harm. RJ encourages those who have caused harm to acknowledge the impact of the harm and to remedy same in the interest of those who have suffered in the process, in a just and fair manner. *See* the homepage of Restorative Justice Consortium, found at http://www.restorativejustice.org.uk/? visited on 26/11/2008.

2.5 CONCLUSION

Similar to several other peoples of the world, citizens of the Nigerian Delta region are being influenced by the peculiar circumstances of the environment and the challenges of socio-economic developments in their communities. Due to the enormity of the adverse effects of petroleum development in the region, there is a need for the FG to exhibit political will and commitment to address the age-long concerns of citizens of the region, considering the status of Nigeria as a federation and its responsibilities arising from the efforts of the UN on the environment and development towards achieving SD in the interest of humanity. The MNOCs have a duty to contribute to the evolution of equitable and sustainable communities and societies in Nigeria, in compliance with Article 27 of the Johannesburg Declaration on SD, 2002. Also, the Government has responsibility to enforce corporate accountability by creating a transparent and stable regulatory environment for companies to operate, in compliance with Article 29 of the Johannesburg Declaration on SD, 2002. The need therefore arises for governments and the MNOCs operating in Nigeria to cooperate fully towards the realisation of environmentally-sound and socially-equitable SCD in the Delta region and other oil-producing areas of the country. Governments have a responsibility to lead the course of SD, so as to improve CSR and the social responsibility of the oil-producing communities (SRCs) in the course of petroleum resources development in the communities, especially by way of promoting interactive environmental democracy and tri-sector partnership among the identified major stakeholders, towards SD of the resources and SCD. Accordingly, there is a need for governments, especially the FG, to promote interactive PP nationwide, so as to enthrone transparency and accountability in all decision-making processes of nation-building, in the interests of all the ethnic groups and citizens, especially the poor and less-privileged citizens of the federation.

CHAPTER 3

Approaches to Promoting Stakeholder Participation in Business: A Review of Three Dominant International Initiatives

3.1 INTRODUCTION: THREE DOMINANT APPROACHES TO STAKEHOLDER PARTICIPATION

This chapter identifies three dominant approaches to promoting the participation of stakeholders in business. These are first – the Aarhus Convention of 1998, and second – the initiatives of the International Association for Public Participation (IAP2) and the International Association for Impact Assessment (IAIA), while the Mining, Minerals and Sustainable Development (MMSD) project and the World Bank Group (WBG) Extractive Industries Review (EIR) are identified as constituting the third category of approach. The chapter considers the Aarhus Convention of 1998 (on access to information, public participation [PP] in decision-making and access to justice in environmental matters) as an inter-governmental approach, the initiatives of the IAP2 and the IAIA as civil society-based approaches, and the initiatives of the MMSD project and the WBG EIR as industry-driven approaches.

First, the relevance of the Aarhus Convention demonstrates how it is the most impressive elaboration of Principle 10 of the Rio Declaration on Environment and Development, 1992. Hence, as indicated in Chapter 1, this Convention is considered as constituting the benchmark of environmental democracy initiated by the UN in order to achieve sustainable development (SD). Regardless therefore, of the fact that the Aarhus Convention is regional in scope (given that it is a Convention of the UN Economic Commission for Europe, UNECE), it has a global impact and significance. It is thus applicable to environmental democracy regarding petroleum development in Nigeria. Second, the relevance of the initiatives of the IAP2 and the IAIA demonstrates how these initiatives are promoting the participation of stakeholders in decision-making around the globe, as exemplified by the Calabash project on citizens' participation in Environmental Assessment (EA) in the Southern African region (*ie*, the Southern African Development Community [SADC]). The chapter considers the Calabash project as being worthy of emulation by other African regional groups and individual African countries such as Nigeria. The chapter also considers the significance of the Calabash project in the context of the New Partnership for Africa's Development (NEPAD) Action Plan on the Environment Initiative discussed in Chapter 5, given that NEPAD represents the framework of the African Union (AU) towards realising the SD initiatives of the UN in Africa. Third, the significance of the MMSD project and the WBG EIR (industry-driven initiatives) is based on how stakeholder engagement in extractive industrial operations (EIOs), such as oil, gas and mining projects may contribute to SD. Besides, the WBG EIR is considered on the basis of the role of the Bank Group as a dominant financier of international development projects in developing countries and thus a vital source of financial and technical assistance to these countries. These approaches are therefore discussed with a view to recommending how they might improve environmental democracy in relation to petroleum development in Nigeria.

3.2 (I) THE INTER-GOVERNMENTAL APPROACH: THE AARHUS CONVENTION

The Convention of the UNECE on Access to Information, PP in decision-making and access to justice in environmental matters was adopted on June 25, 1998, by 35 member countries of the UNECE and the European Community, in the Danish city of Aarhus at the Fourth Ministerial Conference in the Environment for Europe process.[1] This Convention is therefore, by orientation, an inter-governmental initiative.[2] The Convention, which came into force on October 30, 2001, was prepared under pressure from environmental Non-Governmental Organisations (NGOs) in Europe and negotiated in a remarkably open manner.[3] The birth of the Aarhus Convention started in 1996, in a participatory process among member states, including NGOs in these states. This process was fostered by certain preceding international efforts and instruments.[4]

---

1 *See* the area of the UNECE website captioned the 'Aarhus Convention on Access to Information, Public Participation in Decision-making and Access to Justice in Environmental Matters', with the subtitle 'Introducing the Aarhus Convention', found at http://www.unece.org/env/pp/ and the full text of the Convention found at http://www.unce.org/env/treatytext.html both visited on 30/11/06.

2 Ibid.

3 *See* the area of the UNECE website captioned the 'Aarhus Convention on Access to Information, Public Participation in Decision-making and Access to Justice in Environmental Matters', with the subtitle 'Introducing the Aarhus Convention', *op cit. Also see* the area of the 'Europa' (*ie*, the European Commission/Community) website, captioned 'The Aarhus Convention', found at http://ec.europa.eu/environment/aarhus/ visited on 30/11/06. *See* the publication entitled 'EC Lagging Behind on Aarhus Convention', found at http://www.eeb.org/press/2004/ec_lagging_behind_on_aarhus_conv.htm visited on 14/08/05.

4 These include the UN Stockholm Declaration on the Human Environment, 1972; the World Charter for Nature, 1982; the Report of the World Commission on Environment and Development, 1987; European Charter on Environment and Health, 1989; the UN General Assembly (UNGA) Resolution 45/94 of December 14, 1990, the UNECE Convention on Environmental Impact Assessment (EIA) in a Trans-Boundary Context, 1991; the UNECE Convention on the Protection and Use of the Transboundary Watercourses and International Lakes, 1992; the UN Rio Declaration on Environment and Development (especially Principle 10 of this Declaration), 1992; the UNECE (Sofia Guidelines) Guidelines on Access to Environmental Information and PP in Environmental Decision-making, 1995. *See* S. Stec *et al, The Aarhus Convention: An Implementation Guide, op cit,* pp. 2–4.

3.2 (II) OVERVIEW OF THE CONVENTION

Kofi Annan, the Secretary General of the UN between 1997 and 2006, had the following to say about the Aarhus Convention:

> *Although regional in scope, the significance of the Aarhus Convention is global. It is by far the most impressive elaboration of Principle 10 of the Rio Declaration, which stresses the need for citizens' participation in environmental issues and for access to information on the environment held by public authorities. As such, it is the most ambitious venture in the area of environmental democracy so far undertaken under the auspices of the United Nations.*[5]

The Convention dwells on Principle 10 of the Rio Declaration on Environment and Development, 1992, on the need for environmental democracy, and thereby focuses on the interactions between the public and public authorities in a democratic context. The Convention is a new kind of environmental agreement (*ie*, an environmental treaty) which links environmental rights and human rights, to improve PP in the negotiation and implementation of international agreements concerning environmental protection in relation to socio-economic development proposals.[6] By elaborating on the need for stakeholder participation with regard to accountability, transparency and responsiveness of governments (to citizens and the general public) towards environmentally sound SD, the Convention punctuates the heart of the relationship between people and governments.[7]

The universal context or feature[8] of the Aarhus Convention is exhibited by its rights-based and non-discriminatory[9] orientation and procedural requirement towards enhancing environmental democracy regarding the participation of citizens and the general public (including future generations).[10] Based on its universality feature, whereas most multilateral environmental agreements cover responsibilities that parties have to each other, the Aarhus Convention ascribes responsibilities of parties to the Convention to the public. By so granting the

---

5 *See* S. Stec *et al*, *The Aarhus Convention: An Implementation Guide*, *op cit*, p. v.

6 Ibid. *Also see* The MMSD project report entitled *Breaking New Ground: Mining, Minerals, and Sustainable Development: The Report of the MMSD Project*, London, Earthscan, 2002, pp. 296–297.

7 Ibid.

8 *See* the UNECE website captioned the 'The Content of the Convention', found at http://www.unece.org/env/pp/contentofaarhus.htm visited on 30/11/06. To this end, member nations of the UN that are not member nations of the UNECE or the European Community, may accede to be parties to the Convention subject to the provisions of Article 19, especially 19(3) and 19(4) of the Convention and by meeting other criteria expressed in other Articles of the Convention such as its Article 9 (3) concerning access to environmental justice.

9 *See* the Article 3 (9) of the Convention and the definition of the 'The public' and 'The public concerned' under Article 2 of the Convention. *Also see* the area of the UNECE website on the Aarhus Convention captioned 'The Content of the Convention', *op cit.*

10 *See* Article 1 of the Convention.

rights of access to information and PP in decision-making, the Convention imposes obligations on parties to it as well as on public authorities[11] concerning these rights by providing enforcement provisions on, or mechanisms for, access to justice in environmental matters. By implication, the rights-based approach of the Convention acknowledges that it is the responsibility of the present generation of mankind to achieve SD in the interest of future generations.[12]

Although the Aarhus Convention occupies a central place in discussions on environmental democracy around the world, it is regarded as 'a floor, and not a ceiling' [13], considering that it establishes minimum standards to be achieved.[14] Parties to the Convention may thus adopt further measures towards providing access to information which are relevant to the environment, PP in environmental decision-making and access to justice in environmental matters.[15]

3.2 (III) PILLARS OF THE AARHUS CONVENTION: ACCESS TO INFORMATION, PP IN DECISION-MAKING AND ACCESS TO JUSTICE IN ENVIRONMENTAL MATTERS

The Aarhus Convention has three broad themes (*ie*, it stands on three broad 'pillars'), namely access to information, public participation (PP) in decision-making and access to justice in environmental matters.[16] These pillars, which depend on each other for full implementation of the objectives of the Convention, are provided for under Articles 4 to 9 of the Convention.[17]

---

11 *See* the area of the UNECE website captioned the 'Aarhus Convention on Access to Information, Public Participation in Decision-making and Access to Justice in Environmental Matters', with the subtitle 'Introducing the Aarhus Convention', *op cit*. *Also see* Article 2 (2) of the Convention.

12 *See* the area of the UNECE website captioned the 'Aarhus Convention on Access to Information, Public Participation in Decision-making and Access to Justice in Environmental Matters', with the subtitle 'Introducing the Aarhus Convention', *op cit*.

13 *See* S. Stec *et al*, *The Aarhus Convention: An Implementation Guide*, *op cit*, p.5. *Also see*, the area of the UNECE website on the Aarhus Convention captioned 'The Contents of the Convention', *op cit*.

14 Ibid. *Also see* D. N. Zillman *et al* (eds), *Human Rights in Natural Resources Development: Public Participation in Sustainable Development of Mining and Energy Resources*, New York, Oxford University Press, 2002, p. 6.

15 *See* S. Stec *et al*, *The Aarhus Convention: An Implementation Guide*, *op cit*, p. 5. *Also see*, the area of the UNECE website on the Aarhus Convention captioned 'The Contents of the Convention', *op cit*.

16 *See* the area of the UNECE website on the Aarhus Convention captioned 'The Contents of the Convention', *op cit*. *Also see* S. Stec *et al*, *The Aarhus Convention: An Implementation Guide*, *op cit*, pp. 5–6. *See* the report by E. Petkova *et al*, entitled 'Closing the Gap: Information, Participation, and Justice in Decision-Making for the Environment', found at http://www.accessinitiative.org/publications.html visited on 01/12/06.

17 Ibid. Article 4 of the Convention is entitled 'Access to Environmental Information', Article 5 is entitled 'Collection and Dissemination of Environmental Information', and Article 6 is entitled 'Public Participation in Decisions on Specific Activities'. Furthermore, Article 7 is entitled 'Public Participation Concerning Plans, Programmes and Policies Relating to the Environment', Article 8 is entitled 'Public Participation During the Preparation of Executive Regulations and/or Generally Applicable Legally Binding Normative Instruments', while Article 9 is entitled 'Access to Justice'.

3.2 (iii) (a) First Pillar of the Convention: Access to Information

In several ways, limited access to environmental information stands as the main obstacle to improved environmental protection.[18] As expressed in Article 2 (3) of the Aarhus Convention, environmental information means 'any information in written, visual, rural, electronic or any other material form on', relating to or affecting the environment, as more widely expressed under sub-articles 2 (3) (a) to 2 (3) (c). For instance, information may be interpreted to include anything kept in any records, including registers, reports, returns and computer records.[19] Information in this regard refers to documents and any complete set of data which has not yet been compiled into a finished product, namely a concluded or completed document.[20] Access to information is usually defined broadly and with a presumption in favour of disclosure, to ensure that citizens are aware of the actual and threatened environmental impacts of development proposals, to enable them to address such impacts appropriately.[21]

The quality of information and its use, production, flow, accessibility and credibility affect the interaction of all actors involved in decision-making. Thus, access to environmental information, which stands out as the first pillar of the Aarhus Convention, generates or enhances trust and cooperation among stakeholders.[22] It enhances the realisation of the second and third pillars of the Convention, even though it can also stand independently. Considering that any natural or legal person is entitled to environmental information held by public authorities, there is no requirement to determine who has 'standing' (among members of the public) to have access to information as stipulated under Articles 4 and 5 of the Aarhus Convention.[23]

The access to information pillar may be divided into two parts.[24] The first part concerns the right of the public to request information from public

---

18 *See* D. J. Hughes *et al*, *Environmental Law*, London, Butterworths, 2002, pp. 151–152 and 165. *Also see* A. Gilpin, *Dictionary of Environmental Law*, Cheltenham, Edward Elgar, 2000, p. 91. *See* the publication of the European Commission entitled 'The Aarhus Convention and the Citizen', found at http://europa.eu.int/comm/environment/aarhus/ visited on 28/08/05. Limitations to information disclosure are exceptions based on public security, national defence, and international relations. *Also see* The MMSD project report entitled *Breaking New Ground: Mining, Minerals, and Sustainable Development: The Report of the MMSD Project*, *op cit*, p.297.

19 *See R vs. British Coal Corporation, ExParte Ibstock Brick Building Products Limited* (1955) 7 ELM, 202, the posture of the courts on the distinction between 'primary' information. *See* D. J. Hughes *et al*, *Environmental Law*, *op cit*, p. 155.

20 *Further see* D. J. Hughes *et al*, *Environmental Law*, *op cit*, p. 157.

21 *See* C. E. Bruch and R. Czebiniak, 'Globalising Environmental Governance: Making the Leap from Regional Initiatives on Transparency, Participation, and Accountability in Environmental Matters', found at http://www.inece.org/forumspublicaccess.pdf.pdf visited on 12/09/05.

22 *See* F. L. Careaga *et al*, 'Access to Information: A Key to Building Trust in the Minerals Sector. The Government Role', found at http://www.iied.org/mmsd.pdfs/018loayza.pdf visited on 15/09/05.

23 *See* D. J. Hughes *et al*, *Environmental Law*, *op cit*, p. 157. Requests for information in the context of Article 4 of the Aarhus Convention may be oral or written.

24 *See* S. Stec *et al*, *The Aarhus Convention: An Implementation Guide*, *op cit*, p. 6.

authorities and the obligation of the authorities to respond favourably to this request by providing the required information. This type of access to information covered under Article 4 of the Convention is regarded as 'passive'. The second part of the information pillar concerns the right of the public to receive information, based on the obligation of public authorities to collect and disseminate information of public interest in their possession (in an active manner) without the need for or waiting for any request from members of the public. This type of information covered under Article 5 of the Convention is regarded as 'active' .[25]

3.2 (iii) (b) Second Pillar of the Convention: PP in Decision-making

The second pillar of the Aarhus Convention is the PP pillar which grants the public and public interest-oriented environmental organisations the right to participate from an early stage in environmental decision-making.[26] This pillar relies on the two other pillars to be effective. This implies that it relies on the access to information pillar to ensure the participation of the public in an informed manner, while it relies on the access to justice pillar to ensure that participation takes place in an administratively and legally enforceable manner.[27]

The PP pillar is divided into three closely-related parts covered under Articles 6 to 8 of the Aarhus Convention.[28] These three parts set out procedural requirements for environmental decision-making in the participatory process, especially regarding who should be informed or notified in advance of such decisions.[29] The first part, covered by Article 6 of the Convention, concerns participation by members of the public who may be affected by or who are otherwise interested in the decision-making process of specific activities (such as socio-economic development proposals). In this case, the affected or concerned members of the public are required to be informed, either by public notice or individually, and in an adequate, timely and effective manner, early enough for them to prepare and participate effectively in environmental decision-making. Article 6 also sets out detailed procedures for PP towards securing permits regarding national or trans-boundary planning and decision-making procedures and/or processes for proposed activities listed in Annex 1 of the Convention which include such activities of the energy sector as oil and gas development projects. Whereas Article 6 involves the EIA process of the planning and development of proposed activities, the provisions of Article 7 are centred on PP concerning plans, programmes and policies relating to the environment. This Article thus sets the basis for the practice of Strategic

---

25 Ibid.

26 *See* the publication of the European Commission entitled 'The Aarhus Convention and the Citizen', *op cit.*

27 *See* S. Stec *et al, The Aarhus Convention: An Implementation Guide, op cit,* p. 6.

28 Ibid.

29 *See* D. J. Hughes *et al, Environmental Law, op cit,* p. 159.

Environmental Assessment (SEA), while Article 8 covers public or citizens' participation in the preparation of laws, rules and other legally binding normative instruments such as regulations.[30]

The participation of the public and public interest-oriented environmental organisations in the above-stated three parts, is to ensure adequate, timely and effective public input into the decision-making process.[31] To do so, information is required to be provided to the public and public interest-oriented environmental organisations on final environmental decisions and the reasons why such decisions are taken by public authorities.[32]

3.2 (iii) (c) Third Pillar of the Convention: Access to Justice in Environmental Matters

The Aarhus Convention is a treaty (which means it is in the domain of international law), albeit with aspects of municipal law which are applicable to member-states, and to a lesser extent non-member states of the Convention.[33]

This pillar, covered by Article 9 of the Convention, is about the right to administrative and judicial recourse to justice intended to enforce the first two pillars of the Convention, as well as decisions which are considered as contravening environmental law in general.[34] Hence, the Convention requires its state parties to establish publicly-accessible administrative and judicial review procedures that provide adequate and effective remedies (including injunctive remedies) which are appropriate and fair, as well as appropriate review mechanisms to remove or reduce the barriers capable of hindering access to justice.[35]

The main barriers inhibiting access to justice in the Aarhus Convention states include lack of judicial understanding of, and/or sympathy with, environmental issues; limited scope of judicial review process; and the absence of guaranteed place of standing (*ie*, '*locus standi*')[36] in the judicial review process. Others are the inability to obtain injunctive remedies in judicial review processes, and the unpredictable and prohibitive costs and expenses of

---

30 *See* S. Stec *et al*, *The Aarhus Convention: An Implementation Guide*, *op cit*, p. 6.

31 Ibid.

32 Ibid.

33 *See* the proposal for a Directive of the European Parliament and Council Directive on Public Access to Justice in Environmental Matters, found at http://www.defra.gov.uk/corporate/consult/aarhus/dir-accessjustice.pdf visited on 14/10/04. *Also see* the statement of the EC entitled 'Statement Summarising the Activities Carried out in Relation to the UN/ECE Convention on Access to Information, Public Participation in Decision-making and Access to Justice in Environmental Matters', found at http://www.unece.org/env/pp/national/ecommission.2.pdf visited on 14/10/05.

34 *See* S. Stec *et al*, *The Aarhus Convention: An Implementation Guide*, *op cit*, p. 6. *Also see* the publication of the European Commission entitled *The Aarhus Convention and the Citizen*, *op cit*. Article 9 of the Convention entitled 'Access to Justice'.

35 *See* Article 9(4) and (5) of the Convention.

36 *See The Black's Law Dictionary*, St. Paul, West (A Thomson Business), 2004, p. 960. *Also see* Article 9 (1) (a) of the Aarhus Convention.

environmental protection cases,[37] especially on public interest-oriented groups and individuals.[38]

3.2 (IV) CONCLUDING REMARKS ON THE CONVENTION

This brief discussion reveals that the Aarhus Convention has the potential of strengthening already established development-planning law procedures and judicial review processes in the Conventions member states.[39] Generally, in all nation-states of the UN, the Convention has the potential to improve environmental democracy.[40]

3.3 APPROACHES OF THE IAP2 AND THE IAIA ON PP IN DECISION-MAKING

The discussion under this sub-heading demonstrates the roles of the IAP2 and the IAIA in terms of promoting PP or citizens' involvement in decision-making.[41]

3.3 (I) THE IAP2 PROMOTING PP IN DECISION-MAKING

The International Association for Public Participation (IAP2), a global leader in PP whose international office is located in Denver, Colorado, USA, was established in 1990 as a non-profit corporation, in response to the rising global interest in PP. It is an association of people who participate in, as well as, implement public decision-making processes. Through its members, the IAP2 develops practical tools of and good practices on PP, to help businesses, communities, governments, and other institutional or organisational entities around the world to improve their decisions by involving those affected by such decisions.[42]

---

37 *See* the Lord Justice Brooke, 'David Hall Memorial Lecture: Environmental Justice: The Cost Barrier', Journal of Environmental Law, Vol. 18, No. 3, 2006, pp. 341–356.

38 *See* P. Davies report entitled 'European Community, Public Participation and the Aarhus Convention'. *See* this report in the MMSD project report No. 207, entitled 'Report of the Conference on the Role of Public Participation', Woodstock, dated May 25–27, 2001, found at http://www.iied.org/mmsd/mmsdpdfs/IBApublicparticipation.pdf visited on 15/09/05, pp. 19–20. *Also see* the article by C. Agnew, entitled 'Environmental Justice and Public Participation', found at http://www.ukela.org/Downloads/Crispin%20Agnew%20Speech.doc visited on 02/12/06. *See* the report by N. Sadeleer *et al*, entitled 'Access to Justice in Environmental Matters', found at http://www.oeko.de/elni/PDF-Files/Access%20to%20Justice%20-%20final%20report.pdf visited on 28/08/05.

39 *See* the article by M. Lee and C. Abbot, 'The Usual Suspects? Public Participation under the Aarhus Convention', Modern Law Review, Vol. 66 Issue 1, January, 2003, pp. 80–108, especially p. 106.

40 *See* S. Stec *et al*, *The Aarhus Convention: An Implementation Guide*, *op cit*, p. v. *Also see* Article 19 of the Convention.

41 *See* the description of civil society by the London School of Economics (LSE), in the area of the LSE homepage entitled 'What is Civil Society?', found at http://www.lse.ac.uk/collections/CCS/what_is_civil_society.htm visited on 30/12/06.

42 *See* the bulletin of the IAP2 entitled 'Good Decisions Don't Just Happen'. *Also see* the area of the IAP2 homepage captioned 'Welcome to the International Association for Public Participation!', found at http://www.iap2.org/index.cfm visited on 03/12/06.

The IAP2 is organised around the Executive Director, a high-calibre Board of Directors, a strong international headquarters, special committees, several professional sectors, country-wide chapters and the rest of its members from non-chapter countries,[43] conducts its activities to achieve the following objectives. These are to: (a) encourage and enhance the professional development of people working on PP; (b) educate decision makers about the value of PP; (c) help the public play an effective role in PP processes; and (d) continue to define, review and enhance best practices on PP.[44] The initial mission of the IAP2 includes convening annual conferences and the promotion of values and best practices associated with PP in government and industry decisions which affect the public.[45] Hence, the IAP2 promotes the fact that citizens' or public involvement (PI) in decision-making is not merely an attribute of democracy but an essential ingredient of good governance (GG) based on the transparency and accountability of governments to the governed. The existence of the IAP2 is thus directly or indirectly influencing the course of citizens' participation in the making of policies, plans and programmes which affect the citizens and society at large. Nations of the world, especially developing nations, are therefore being influenced by the IAP2 to imbibe the spirit of greater inclusiveness rather than excluding their citizens from decision-making processes, so as to promote GG and the global march towards SD.[46]

3.3 (II) THE IAIA PROMOTING PP IN THE IMPACT ASSESSMENT PROCESS OF DEVELOPMENT PROPOSALS

Similar to the role of the IAP2, the International Association for Impact Assessment (IAIA) promotes citizens' involvement or PP in environmental decision-making. The IAIA was organised in 1980 to bring together researchers, practitioners and users of various forms of impact assessment (IA) from all parts of the world. Its membership from over 100 global nations and well over 2,500 people belong to such professions, disciplines and works of life as corporate planners and managers, public interest advocates, government

---

43 The IAP2 has members in over 26 countries which include the United States of America (USA), Canada, Australia, United Kingdom, New Zealand, South Africa, Japan, Austria, China, Finland, France, Lebanon, Mexico, Poland, Slovenia and Thailand. *See* the area of the IAP2 homepage captioned 'About IAP2', found at http://www.iap2.org/displaycommon.cfm?an=3 visited on 03/12/06.

44 *See* the bulletin of the IAP2 entitled 'Good Decisions Don't Just Happen'. *Generally see* the area of the IAP2 homepage captioned "Resource database", found at http://iap2.civicore.com/index.cfm?fuseaction=resources.resources&checked=no visited on 30/05/09.

45 *See* the area of IAP2 homepage captioned 'About IAP2', *op cit. Also see* the Australasia chapter of the IAP2 homepage, captioned 'Australasia International Association for Public Participation', with the subtitle 'Welcome', found at http://www.iap2.org.au/ visited on 03/12/06. *See* the IAP2's publication entitled 'IAP2 Public Participation Spectrum: Increasing Level of Public Impact', found at http://www.iap2.org/displaycommon.cfm?an=5 visited on 02/08/04._

46 *See* T. C. Beierle and J. Cayford, *Democracy in Practice: Public Participation in Environmental Decisions*, Washington DC, Resources for the Future, 2002, pp. 1–33, especially, pp. 1 and 3.

planners and administrators, private consultants and policy analysts, college and university lecturers and their students.[47] The IAIA thus promotes IA with the aid of its membership from various disciplines and professions and by virtue of its activities which include annual and regional conferences, training programmes and publication of journals. Its remit is to provide outstanding opportunities for interchange to advance the state of the art and science of IA applications, ranging from local to global in developing international and local capability to anticipate, plan and manage the consequences of development proposals to enhance the quality of life for all.[48]

The activities of the IAIA are designed 'to (1) develop approaches and practices for comprehensive and integrated IA; (2) improve assessment procedures and methods for practical application; (3) promote training and public understanding of IA; (4) provide professional quality-assurance by peer review and other means; and (5) share information networks, timely publications, and professional meetings'. [49] The IAIA thus regards itself as the leading global authority on best practice in the use of IA for informed decision-making regarding policies, plans, programmes and projects, so as to advance innovation and/or improve local, regional, and global capacity in IA. In the process, the IAIA considers the assessment of the environmental, social, economic, cultural and health implications for development proposals as being significant in the decision-making process towards environmentally-sound and socially-equitable SD.[50]

3.3 (III) IMPACT OF THE IAP2 AND THE IAIA IN PROMOTING PP IN ENVIRONMENTAL DECISION-MAKING IN AFRICAN COUNTRIES

Considering the significance of the IAP2 and the IAIA globally, especially within their member countries which include those of Africa, is it obvious that

---

47 *See* the area of the IAIA homepage captioned 'About IAIA', found at http://www.iaia.org/modx/index.php?id=318 visited on 01/12/08.

48 The IAIA Conferences are organised annually. Thus, from 1990 to 2008, these Conferences were held as follows: Lausanne, Switzerland (1990), Champaign, Illinois, USA (1991), Washington DC (1992), Shangai, People's Republic of China – PRC, (1993), Quebec City, Canada (1994), Durban, South Africa (1995), Estoril, Portugal (1996), New Orleans, Louisiana, USA (1997), Christchurch, New Zealand (1998), Glasgow, Scotland (1999), Hong Kong, People's Republic of China – PRC (2000), Cartagena, Columbia (2001), The Hague, Netherlands (2002), Marrakech, Morocco (2003), Vancouver, Canada (2004), Boston, Massachusetts, USA (2005), Stavanger, Norway (2006), Seoul, Korea (2007), and Perth, Western Australia (2008). The IAIA's 2009 annual Conference is to take place in Accra, Ghana.

49 *See* the area of the IAIA homepage entitled 'About IAIA', *op cit. Also see* the area of the IAIA homepage entitled 'About US: Background and Purpose of IAIA', found at http://www.praxis.ca/iaiawnc/about.htm visited on 13/09/05.

50 Ibid. The members of the IAIA are spread among its affiliates. By June 2008, the IAIA has affiliates operating in Cameroon, China, Ghana, Korea, New Zealand, Ontorio and Quebec in Canada, Portugal, South Africa, Spain, and Western and Northern Canada. The IAIA's first Branch (a group comprised entirely of IAIA-International members), the Washington DC Area Branch, was organised in September, 2001, and its UK-Ireland pilot branch was launched in December 2005 and formalised in June 2008. Its evolving pilot branches include those of Nigeria, Senegal and Kenya.

their impact is being felt through their activities. The Calabash project, on PP in Environmental Assessment (EA) in the SADC region, thus suffices as a good example of these two associations.[51]

3.3 (IV) ROLE OF THE CALABASH PROJECT IN PROMOTING PP IN ENVIRONMENTAL DECISION-MAKING IN THE SOUTHERN AFRICAN REGION

The Calabash project was initiated by the Southern African Institute for Environmental Assessment (SAIEA) in 2003 to enhance PP in EA in the SADC region. This region is made up of 14 countries, namely Angola, Botswana, Democratic Republic of Congo (DRC), Lesotho, Malawi, Mauritius, Mozambique, Namibia, Seychelles, South Africa, Swaziland, Tanzania, Zambia and Zimbabwe.[52] The Calabash project is managed by the SAIEA with its headquarters in Windhoek, Namibia, and funded by the World Bank with support from the Canadian International Development Agency (CIDA).[53]

Studies are continually revealing that the results of development proposals are better when members of the public affected by such proposals are empowered to participate in the decision-making process of the proposals.[54] The objective of the Calabash project is to expand opportunities for civil society involvement in the decision-making processes of the EA development proposals in the SADC region. It identifies issues, options, approaches and tools for integrating environmental planning, assessment and management into small-scale community-driven developments. It focuses on how PP can be effectively used in community-generated projects as well as externally-sponsored projects. It is designed to develop capacity building and research programmes at community and government levels, to equip communities and government ministries involved in EA so as to close the gap hitherto existing between government regulators and community groups in the course of PP in EAs.[55]

Political, economic, social and cultural conditions vary from country to country within the SADC region, although there are common features of the countries in the region relating to EA and PP. Among these features are certain key problems and challenges which limit the benefits of PP from being fully

---

51 *See* the area of the Calabash website entitled 'About the Calabash Project', found at http://www.saiea.com/calabash/images/html/about.pdf visited on 17/09/05. *Also see* the homepage of the Southern Africa Institute for Environmental Assessment (SAIEA) on the Calabash project entitled 'The Calabash Project: Reports and Outputs', found at http://www.saiea.com/calabash/ visited on 09/12/2005. *Also see* Peter Tarr, *Environmental Impact Assessment in Southern Africa*, Windhoek, Southern African Institute for Environmental Assessment (SAIEA), 2003.

52 *See* the publication in the Calabash website entitled 'SADC – Southern African Development Community', found at http://www.saiea.com/calabash/images/html/sadc.html visited on 15/09/05.

53 *See* the area of the Calabash website entitled 'About the Calabash Project', *op cit*.

54 *See* the publication of the Network of Institutions for SD (NISD), Issue No. 1, dated May 2005, found at http://www.unep.ch/etb/areas/pdf/NISDnewsNo1.pdf visited on 17/09/05, p. 3. *See* the area of the SAIEA homepage entitled 'Calabash Products', found at http://www.saiea.com/calabash/final_report/html/products.html visited on 09/12/2005.

55 *See* the area of the Calabash website entitled 'About the Calabash Project', *op cit*.

realised. These include the issues of underdevelopment, limited capacity concerning the ability to guide and decide on EA processes, and the interference of high level politicians and traditional rulers who consider their opinions to be more important than those of the ordinary citizens in the course of PP, including PP in EA. Also, the poor citizens of the region are not aware of their rights to participate in EA processes, even as these processes are poorly organised. These and such other problems cutting across health, cultural, traditional, communication and literacy issues constitute barriers to interactive PP in EA,[56] in ways that undermine the independence and integrity of EA processes in the SADC region.[57]

So far, the Calabash project has recorded several achievements, four of which are the development of a contact group, a project advisory team, research and publication of a situation assessment, and the development of a communication strategy.[58] Other achievements of the Calabash project include the development of a Handbook entitled 'Calabash: A Guide to Opportunities for Public Participation in Environmental Assessment Processes in the Southern African Development Community'.[59] The project also developed generic PP terms of reference, published a report entitled *Calabash Case Studies Report: Public Participation in Environmental Assessment in the SADC Region*[60] and developed a guide or handbook on PP in EA entitled 'A One-Stop Participation: A Handbook for Public Participation in Environmental Assessment in Southern Africa'.[61] The project embarked on six research case studies on PP in EA in the region. It established an Electronic Library equipped with PP and Civil Society Engagement tools from around the world. In 2005, the project delivered a pilot course on EIA and PP in Windhoek for 27 participants from across the SADC region and other parts of Africa. To enhance PP in EA, the project established collaborative partnerships with a number of regional and international

56 *See* the publication of the Calabash project entitled 'SADC – Southern African Development Community', found at http://www.saiea.com/calabash/images/html/sadc.html visited on 15/09/05.

57 *See* the Calabash Participation Handbook, entitled 'One Stop Participation Guide: A Handbook for Public Participation in Environmental Assessment in Southern Africa', found at http://www.saiea.com/calabash/handbook/index.html, visited on 14/07/05, pp. 3–4.

58 *See* the area of the homepage of the SAIEA entitled 'Calabash Products', *op cit. Also see* the summary of the publication entitled 'Soul Beat Africa: Communication for Change – Experiences – Calabash – Southern Africa', found at http://www.comminit.com/africa/printversion.cgi?url=http://www.comminit.com/africa/experiences/pds62005/experiences-3213.html visited 17/09/05.

59 *See* this Handbook found in the Calabash project website, at http://www.saiea.com/calabash/pp_rights/pp_rights_guide.pdf visited 17/09/05.

60 *See* the 'Calabash Case Studies Report: Public Participation in Environmental Assessment in the SADC Region', found at http://www.saiea.com/calabash/casestudies/index.html visited on 17/09/05.

61 *See* the Calabash Participation Handbook, entitled 'One Stop Participation Guide: A Handbook for Public Participation in Environmental Assessment in Southern Africa', *op cit.* There are six main sections of this Handbook, including the section containing the figures used in the analysis and the annexures numbering from A to F. The main sections of the Handbook are entitled the introduction, practitioners, civil society, government, developers and managing conflict.

organisations[62] such as the IAP2, IAIA, the International Council on Mining and Metals (ICMM), and UN Environment Programme (UNEP). Considering these and other achievements of the Calabash project, NEPAD recognised it as a chapter (*ie*, a 'node') to assist its issues related to PP and EA issues.[63] Also, the IAP2 awarded the Calabash Governance Program the 2005 Core Values Award for 'Program of the Year'.[64]

The Calabash project has thus exhibited its potential in the use of EA as a catalyst for generating improved environmental democracy and environmental governance in the SADC region in a way that other African sub-regions and developing countries can emulate. The project has the potential to stimulate the NEPAD's 'Action Plan for the Environment Initiative'[65], so as to make the African Peer Review Mechanism (APRM), which is silent on environmental governance, be more forward-looking in the ongoing collective global effort to achieve SD.[66]

3.4 INTERNATIONAL INDUSTRY-DRIVEN INITIATIVES: THE MMSD PROJECT AND THE WBG EIR

The MMSD project and the WBG EIR are industry-driven approaches or initiatives designed to promote the participation of stakeholders affected by mining, minerals and other extractive industrial operations (EIOs), in order to make these operations contribute to SD.

3.4 (I) THE MMSD PROJECT

The Mining Mineral and Sustainable Development (MMSD) process found that the world around the mining and minerals sectors included a variety of stakeholders (*ie*, interest groups) such as host countries and their resources-producing communities. The global mining and minerals industrial sector, which is essential to contemporary societies and economies, found itself confronted by challenges that made the sector distrusted by many including its constituents and stakeholders, so that the sector lacked social licence to operate in many parts of the world.[67]

---

62 *See* the publication by the SAIEA, entitled 'Calabash Program – Increasing Capacity of Civil Society in the SADC Region to Participate in Environmental Decision-Making: Project Summary at Conclusion of 2 Year Contract Period, June 20, 2005'.

63 *See* the area of the Calabash website entitled 'About the Calabash Project', *op cit.*

64 Ibid.

65 *See* the NEPAD Action Plan on the Environment Initiative, found at http://www.unep.org/roa/Docs/pdf/nepad/ActionPlanfor the EnvironmentInitiative.pdf visited on 12/04/06.

66 The APRM, which is an ambitious and most innovative aspect of NEPAD, is an instrument voluntarily acceded to by member states of the African Union as an African self-monitoring mechanism. *See* the paper by J. Cilliers of the Institute for Security Studies (ISS), Southern Africa, entitled 'NEPAD's Peer Review Mechanism', found at http://www.iss.co.za/Pubs/Papers/64.html visited on 08/04/06.

67 *See* The MMSD project report entitled *Breaking New Ground: Mining, Minerals, and Sustainable Development: The Report of the MMSD Project, op cit*, p. xiv.

Based on the expectations of its stakeholders and society at large, and with the World Summit for Sustainable Development (WSSD) being planned for 2002, nine of the world's largest mining companies decided to initiate a project to examine the role of the minerals sector in contributing to SD, and how that contribution could be increased. Through the World Business Council for SD (WBCSD), they contracted with the International Institute for Environment and Development (IIED) to undertake a two-year independent process of research and consultation which came to be known as the MMSD project.[68] The MMSD process sought to create a picture of what the mining and minerals sector would look like if it could operate by addressing genuine concerns of the stakeholders affected by its operations and thereby contribute to SD.[69] The result of the MMSD project was published in its report captioned *Breaking New Ground: Mining, Minerals, and Sustainable Development: The Report of the MMSD Project*. This report illustrates the characteristically large and heterogeneous nature of the mining and minerals development sector, including the nature of the different stages of the sector involving its exploration, production, use, reuse, recycling, and final disposal stages.[70] It indicates that one of the greatest challenges currently facing the world is integrating economic activity with environmental integrity, social concerns, and effective governance systems. Thus, while emphasising the need for the sector to contribute to SD, it identified four spheres of SD, namely; economic, social, environmental and governance spheres.[71]

The report indicates that in the course of mining and mineral resources development operations, companies have learnt from political experiences of mineral resources-producing countries that there are significant benefits to good consultation processes at local levels. These processes have the potential to foster genuine relationships based on mutual respect, shared concerns, and shared objectives among host communities, host governments, companies and other stakeholders directly affected by mining and mineral resources development projects. Thus, regarding the participation of stakeholders, the MMSD report indicates that the sector needs to recognise the rights of stakeholders to participate in the decision-making process of its operations, in conformity with emerging international norms on environmental

---

68 The main components of the MMSD process included regional partnerships, national projects, global workshops, commissioned researches and presentations including communications made, as well as published bulletins. The regional partnerships based on research and consultation processes took place in Australia, North America, South America, and Southern Africa. These processes generated a picture of the contribution of the sector and specific actions required on the way forward towards SD. *See* The MMSD project report entitled *Breaking New Ground: Mining, Minerals, and Sustainable Development: The Report of the MMSD Project, op cit,* pp. vii–viii, xiv–xxxiv and 388–410.

69 Ibid, especially pp. xxxiv and 410.

70 Ibid, especially the table of contents of this report.

71 Ibid, p. xvi.

democracy.[72] Concerning the participation of the sector's resources-producing communities, especially indigenous communities, the report states as follows:

> *... decision-making needs to recognise the rights of communities to representation and engagement in processes that affect them, and bases the interaction between the mining project and the community on the values, goals, and aspirations of the community...*
>
> *The control over their own futures that such participation in decision-making engenders is particularly crucial to the sustainability and survival of indigenous communities.*[73]

The report of the MMSD project identifies nine key challenges associated with mining and mineral resources development. These challenges are (1) the viability of the minerals industry; (2) the control, use and management of land; (3) minerals and economic development; (4) local communities and mines; (5) mining, minerals and the environment; (6) an integrated approach to using minerals; (7) access to information; (8) artisanal and small-scale mining; and (9) sector governance: roles, responsibilities, and instruments for change.[74] The report concludes by recommending that it is crucial for community engagement, in the course of mining and mineral resources development projects, to start from the point of first contact between communities and companies, to enhance Integrated IA and sustainable community development (SCD).[75]

3.4 (II) THE WBG EIR

The World Bank Group Extractive Industries Review (WBG EIR) was initiated following the announcement of the Bank Group in 2000 that it would conduct

72 *See* The MMSD project report entitled *Breaking New Ground: Mining, Minerals, and Sustainable Development: The Report of the MMSD Project, op cit,* pp. xxxiv and 388–410, especially pp. xiv–xxxiv and 410. *Also see* the report of the Minerals and Energy Centre (MEPC), Randburg, South Africa, to the MMSD process, entitled 'A Case Study of Community Involvement in Developing the Minerals Policy in South Africa', MMSD report No. 172, October 2001, found at http://www.iied.org/mmsd/mmsdpdfs/172mepc.pdf visited on 15/09/05. *See* the publication of The MMSD project by L. Harding and C. Macdonald, entitled 'Developing Approaches for Stakeholder Engagement in the Minerals Sector', found at http://www.icmm.com/publications/153mmsdanstakeholder.pdf visited on 15/09/06.

73 *See* The MMSD project report entitled *Breaking New Ground: Mining, Minerals, and Sustainable Development: The Report of the MMSD Project, op cit,* p. 223.

74 Ibid, pp. xvii–xviii.

75 Ibid, pp. 226–27 and 399–400. *Also see* the area of the International Council on Mining and Metals (ICMM) homepage on SD good practice, captioned 'Good Practice: Sustainable Development in the Mining and Metals Sector', found at http://www.goodpracticemining.org/ visited on 14/04/09. *See* the area of ICMM homepage captioned 'Our Work', with the sub-title 'Industry Issues: Mining and Economic Development' (under 'Industry Issues'), found at http://www.icmm.com/page/4655/our-work/industry-issues/articles/mining-and-economic-development visited on 14/04/09.

a comprehensive review of its activities in the extractive industries sector.[76] In that year, while responding to the allegations of negative social and environmental impacts of extractive industries made by a variety of stakeholders, primarily environmental and human rights organisations, the Bank Group announced that it would conduct an assessment of its activities in the Extractive Industries (EI, *ie*, oil and gas, and mining production) sector with the aim of reviewing its future role in the sector.[77] The assessment involved an independent stakeholder consultation process directed to examine the role of the WBG in the industrial sector and to recommend changes to guide the Bank Group's future involvement in the sector towards poverty reduction and SD.[78] The then President of the WBG, James Wolfensohn, highlights that the role of the EIR is essential to developing countries, considering that the aim of the Bank Group (as a development institution) is to ensure that, along with governments, industry and the civil society, its activities are able to ensure that the sector makes the strongest possible contribution to sound economic growth and poverty reduction,[79] and thereby keep the needs of the poorest people in the forefront of the Group's deliberations and decisions.[80]

76 Although this sector involves quarrying and dredging operations, it is principally associated with oil and gas and mining operations. *See* the area of the International Finance Corporation (IFC) website on the EIR, captioned 'Extractive Industries', with the subtitle 'Extractive Industries Review', found at http://www.ifc.org/eir visited on 05/12/06. *Also see* the area of the homepage of the IFC, entitled 'Extractive Industries Review' with the sub-title 'Q & A', found at http://www.ifc.org/ifcext/eir.nsf/Content/Q&A visited on 30/12/06. *See* the area of The World Bank homepage captioned 'About Us', found at http://web.worldbank.org/WBSITE/EXTERNAL/EXTABOUTUS/0,,pagePK:50004410~piPK:36602~theSitePK:29708,00.html visited on 31/12/06.

77 James Wolfensohn committed to launch the EIR at the WBG's annual meetings in 2000. *See* the publication in the website of the Environmental Defense Fund (EDF), entitled 'Extractive Industries Review (EIR) Recommendations to The World Bank', found at http://www.environmentaldefense.org/article.cfm?contentid=3667 visited on 24/09/05. *Also see* the publication of the ICMM entitled '*World Bank Extractive Industries Review*', found (in the area of the ICMM homepage) at http://www.icmm.com/industry_world.php visited on 31/12/06.

78 The Review was to determine whether the WBG should continue to fund or lend money for the execution of extractive industrial projects and what conditions should guide or govern such funding or lending, considering the Bank Group's new posture of poverty reduction and SD. *See* the area of the WGB EIR website entitled 'Extractive Industries Review (EIR)', with the subtitle 'What is the EIR?', found at http://www.eireview.org/ visited on 24/09/04. *Also see* the final response of the management of the World Bank Group to the report of the EIR, referred to as the 'Final World Bank Group EIR Management Response (Full Report)', found (in the area of the WBG homepage captioned 'Oil, Gas, Mining and Chemicals', with the subtitle 'Extractive Industries Review', at http://siteresources.worldbank.org/INTOGMC/Resources/finaleirmanagementresponse.pdf visited on 04/04/05. This report is entitled 'Striking a Better Balance – The World Bank Group and Extractive Industries: The Final Report of the Extractive Industries Review, World Bank Group Management Response'.

79 *See* James Wolfensohn's letter, dated March 2, 2004, written in response to Dr. Salim's letter to him dated January 28, 2004, urging the WBG to accept the recommendations of the EIR. This response is found at http://www.ifc.org/ifcext/eir.nsf/AttachmentsByTitle/Salim/$FILE/EIR2.pdf visited on 07/10/05.

80 Ibid.

The WBG EIR was headed by Dr. Emil Salim[81] who was assisted by a small staff in a Secretariat initially situated in Washington, DC, USA, which office was later moved to Jakarta, in Indonesia, in February, 2002.[82] Over a period of two years, from July 2001 to December 2003, the EIR consulted with many stakeholder groups, including representatives of civil society, labour, industry, and government. The Secretariat held regional consultations in Latin America and the Caribbean, Africa, Asia-Pacific and Central and Eastern Europe. The EIR also conducted independent researches that analysed the social impacts of the sector's projects. The review, in which the WBG participated actively,[83] was completed in December 2003. Consequently, in January 2004, Dr. Salim presented the report of the Review entitled *Striking a Better Balance* to the WBG through its President, Mr. James Wolfensohn.

Following the period of public comments, the Management of the WBG responded to the recommendations of the EIR.[84] This response entitled 'Striking a Better Balance – The World Bank Group and Extractive Industries: The Final Report of the Extractive Industries Review, World Bank Group Management Response', dated September 17, 2004, is centred on the following subjects: strengthening governance and transparency; ensuring that extractive industrial projects benefit the poor; the participation and capacity building of members of the public and the communities, and the protection of the rights of people affected by EIOs. Others are the mitigation of environmental and social risks and the disclosure and transparency initiatives associated with EIOs; promotion of renewable energy and energy efficiency strategies aimed at combating climate change; improving organisational coordination and the ongoing learning process of the EIR. While indicating that the Bank Group will continue its investment in EIOs, the Management endorsed two fundamental messages expressed in the recommendations. These messages are that 'extractive industries can contribute to SD, when projects are implemented well and preserve the rights of affected people, and if the benefits they generate are well-used'; and that 'there is a continuing role for the Bank Group in supporting EI provided its involvement supports poverty

81 Dr. Salim was a former Minister of Environment in Indonesia, former Director of Indonesia's largest coal company, and the Chair of the WSSD held at Johannesburg in 2002.

82 *See* the publication in the Environmental Defence website entitled 'Extractive Industries Review (EIR) Recommendations to the World Bank', *op cit.*

83 Ibid.

84 *See* the report entitled 'Striking a Better Balance – The World Bank Group and Extractive Industries: The Final Report of the Extractive Industries Review, World Bank Group Management Response', *op cit. Also see* the civil society views on the Extractive Industries Review (EIR) entitled 'A Civil Society Analysis of the World Bank Group Response to the Extractive Industries Review, July, 2004', found at http://www.eireview.info/doc/Civil%20Society%20Analysis%20of%20Mgmt%20Response%20July%2019.doc visited on 07/10/05. *See* E. Bastida *et al*, *International Comparative Mineral Law and Policy: Trends and Prospects*, The Hague, Kluwer Law International, 2005, pp. 238–239.

reduction and SD'.[85] The WBG Management stressed that its future investments in extractive industry projects will be selective, as determined by the needs of poor people, stronger emphasis on GG and environmentally-sound and socially-equitable SD.[86]

The two recommendations of the EIR that attracted mixed feelings, about which governments and industry representatives expressed reservations, were the rule proposed for the WBG to require 'prior informed consent' of local residents as a precondition for investments, and the 'rights-based' approach to development. In spite of the mixed feelings generated by these and other recommendations of the EIR process, civil society groups showed their acceptance and support for them, and urged the WBG to fully implement them.[87] These groups assessed the response of the Management, and indicated that it consisted of statements of aspirations which did not confirm the Bank Group's commitment to implement a new and strong regime of environmental and social safeguard policies and procedures, capable of ensuring the effectiveness of its poverty reduction and SD strategies in EIOs, in poor and neglected rural communities of developing countries.[88]

3.4 (III) THE SCOPE OF THE MMSD PROJECT AND THAT OF THE WBG EIR

The scope of the MMSD project is broader than that of the WBG EIR. The MMSD project was broadly sector-based, involving the entire stakeholders of the global mining and minerals producing sector and thus stressed the need for cooperation among these stakeholders, while EIR was limited to the WBG's role in sponsoring future projects in the sector – where the Group is a key stakeholder. Despite this difference in scope, if the ideas and recommendations which emerged from the MMSD project and the EIR are taken on board and properly applied in Nigeria's extractive industrial sector, involving petroleum and other major natural resources development, they will improve environmental democracy towards environmentally-sound and socially- equitable SCD in the country.[89]

---

85 *See* the Executive Summary of the Response of the Management of the World Bank Group to the Recommendations of the Extractive Industries Review (EIR), found at http://siteresources.worldbank.org/INTOGMC/Resources/finaleirmanagementresponseexecsum.pdf visited on 04/04/05.

86 *See* the area of the IFC homepage on the EIR captioned 'World Bank Group Board Agrees Way Forward on Extractive Industries Review' found at http://www.ifc.org/ifcext/eir.nsf/content/pressrelease2 visited on 31/12/06. *Also see* the Executive Summary of the Response of the Management of the World Bank Group to the Recommendations of the Extractive Industries Review (EIR), *op cit.*

87 *See* the website entitled 'Civil Society Views on the World Bank's Extractive Industries Review', found at http://www.eireview.info/ visited on 07/10/05.

88 Ibid.

89 *See* the area of The World Bank homepage captioned 'Community Empowerment and Social Inclusion' with the subtitle 'Enhancing the Benefits to Communities from Extractive Industry Projects: Agenda and Summary', found at http://web.worldbank.org/WBSITE/EXTERNAL/WBI/WBIPROGRAMS/CESILPROGRAM/0,,contentMDK:20934624~pagePK:64156158~piPK:64152884~theSitePK:459661,00.html visited on 15/08/08. *Also see* K. McPhail and A. Davy, *Integrating*

3.5 CONCLUSION

The Aarhus inter-governmental Convention on citizens' or PP in environmental decision-making has reinforced the need for environmental democracy, expressed in Principle 10 of the Rio Declaration on Environment and Development, 1992, so that it will define the course of major socio-economic developments, especially major natural resources developments, within and among global nations. Based on the provisions of the Aarhus Convention and the ideas and recommendations of such international industry-driven initiatives as the MMSD project and the WBG EIR, environmental democracy involving stakeholders of EIOs is being practised more and more. Environmental democracy in EIOs will thus increasingly give rise to strategic development partnerships among such stakeholders as governments, private sector developers, and civil society groups such as communities, Community-Based Organisations (CBOs) and other NGOs. Consequently, the need for interactive citizens' or PI in environmental decision-making is becoming much more prominent not only as a matter of laws, policies and regulatory processes, but also as an accepted cost for doing business, a form of good practice and a general way of life towards environmentally-sound and socially-equitable SD.

Nigeria, as a member state of the UN, must, therefore, improve its existing methods of citizens' or PP in environmental decision-making so as to fulfil the provisions of Principle 10 of the Rio Declaration on Environment and Development, 1992, as elaborated in the Aarhus Convention. By so doing, Nigeria may improve on its degree of environmental democracy by complying with the provisions of Article 19 (3) and other relevant criteria of the Convention. Accordingly, it is needful for Nigeria to properly absorb and practise the ideas and recommendations made in the course of the MMSD project and the WBG EIR, along with other lessons being learned from the activities of the two identified international associations (ie, the IAP2 and the IAIA) on PP. Nigeria needs to improve environmental democracy in these and other related ways, towards sustainable petroleum development and environmentally-sound and socially-equitable SCD in its oil-producing and other major natural resources producing areas.

Social Concerns into Private Sector Decision-making: A Review of Corporate Practices in the Mining, Oil, and Gas Sectors, Washington DC., The World Bank, 1998. *See* the homepage of 'Good Practice – Sustainable Development in the Mining and Metals Sector', found at http://www.goodpracticemining.org/search.php?Query=examples visited on 15/08/08. *Also see* The MMSD project report entitled *Breaking New Ground: Mining, Minerals, and Sustainable Development: The Report of the MMSD Project, op cit*, pp. 226–228. *Also see* the *Community Development Toolkit*, London, Energy Sector Management Assistance Programme (ESMAP), 2005.

PART C

CHAPTER 4

Citizens' Participation in the Delta Communities: A Social and Historical Framework

4.1 INTRODUCTION

A key resource on the right to be heard (ie, citizens' or public participation [PP]) in natural resources development is a book edited by D. Zillman *et al*,[1] which states that participation . . . *is a fundamental principle of public law in most of the world's legal systems, even though in practice it ranges from being deeply-ingrained in some cultures while in other cultures it does not exist.*[2] With emphasis on Bonny kingdom (demonstrating a trend of traditional power game), this chapter will examine whether PP is rooted in the social system of the communities of the Delta region and how it is practised in the course of petroleum development to enhance sustainable community development (SCD) in the region.

4.2 AREA OF EMPHASIS: THE EASTERN DELTA KINGDOM OF GRAND BONNY

Grand Bonny kingdom, simply known as Bonny kingdom, is presently delineated by the Bonny Local Government Area (LGA). The kingdom is situated along the Eastern Delta Atlantic coast of Rivers state. Neighbouring areas to Bonny kingdom include the Andoni communities to the east, Kalabari kingdom (New Calabar) to the north west and Okrika kingdom to the north east, while on the southern part of Bonny kingdom is its Atlantic estuary called the 'Bight of Bonny'.[3]

Bonny kingdom is made up of fifty-six communities,[4] with a population of about 500,000 people.[5] The communities of the kingdom include the

---

1 *See* D. N. Zillman *et al* (eds), *Human Rights in Natural Resources Development: Public Participation in Sustainable Development of Mining and Energy Resources*, New York, Oxford University Press, 2002.

2 Ibid, the preview. *Also see* E. Bastida *et al* (eds), *International and Comparative Mineral Law and Policy: Trends and Prospects*, The Hague, Kluwer Law International, 2005, p. 267.

3 *See* E. J. Alagoa and A. Fombo, *A Chronicle of Grand Bonny*, Port Harcourt, Onyoma Research, 2001, pp. viii, 6, and 73–80. *Also see* the map in this book entitled 'Bonny and Her Neighbours'.

4 *See* the Shell Nigeria feasibility study of the 'BTIP Community Development Project', dated July 25, 2003, p. 1.

5 After the 1991 Nigerian census figures, the population of Bonny kingdom astronomically increased because of the influx of labour force such as petroleum development construction job seekers and business men and women, due to ongoing petroleum development projects in the kingdom.

kingdom's capital city, Grand Bonny, otherwise known as metropolitan Bonny.[6] As highlighted below, Bonny kingdom has thirty-five chieftaincy houses which include the George Pepple stock of the Perekule royal house from which the kings of the kingdom have recently been emerging.[7]

Bonny kingdom is one of the ancient Ijaw city/trading states of the Niger Delta. Others are the city states of Opobo (which emerged from Grand Bonny), Kalabari (New Calabar), Okrika and Nembe-Brass. These city states along with the Efik (ie, the Old Calabar) city state and the Itsekiri (Warri) trading kingdom made up the seven ancient Niger Delta trading states which existed like the ancient Greek city states.[8] Along with the ancient Benin/Edo kingdom, these ancient kingdoms or states existed as independent pre-colonial organic entities.[9] The ancient Ijaw nation/ethnic group, to which the Ijaw trading states belong, is the major ethnic group in the South-South geo-political zone as well as the fourth largest ethnic group in the Federal Republic of Nigeria (FRN).[10] As explained in Chapter 1, the South-South geo-political zone is the true Delta region of the federation.[11]

Bonny kingdom is a politically-centralised and socially-stratified[12] traditional polity practising patrilineal system of inheritance.[13] The kingdom's social system

---

6 Bonny or Grand Bonny (ie, '*Okoloama*', meaning 'curlew [*okolo*] town)', is the Island capital city of the kingdom and Local Government Area (LGA) of Bonny (OLGA). It is one of Nigeria's most strategic seaports from the period of the Atlantic trade between Western Europe and pre-colonial Niger Delta. Bonny was the first seat of the government of River state when the state was created by General Yakubu Gowon in May 1967, during the Nigerian Civil War. Virtually all Bonny kingdom's chieftaincy houses have compounds/seat of governance in Bonny. *See* E. J. Alagoa and A. Fombo, *A Chronicle of Grand Bonny, op cit*, pp. vii–viii and 3.

7 The title 'king' in Ibani (Bonny) language is 'Amanyanabo', meaning 'owner of the land'. This meaning of kingship derives from the fact that the natural owners of kingship and the kingdom are its founding fathers and premier kings. These are Kings Ndoli, Opuamakuba, Alagbariya and Asimini who ruled from the period of its foundation about the fourteenth century to the period of the arrival of the Western European explorers and merchants in the kingdom in the 15th century. *See* E.J Alagoa and A. Fombo, *A Chronicle of Grand Bonny, op cit*, pp. 3–5, 7, 16, 30–33, 45, 60–67. Regarding communal ownership of land based on foundation, *see* J. F. Fekumo, *Principles of Nigerian Customary Law*, Port Harcourt, F & F, 2002, pp. 1, 94–95.

8 According to K. O. Dike, *the Greek idea of city means a community of people rather than an area of territory; for although the Delta trading colonies were all outside her political boundaries, they were indissolubly bound by strong economic ties. See* K. O. Dike, *Trade and Politics in the Niger Delta 1830–1885: An Introduction to the Economic and Political History of Nigeria*, Westport, Connecticut, Greenwood Press, 1981, pp. 30–31, especially p. 31.

9 *See* M. Crowther, *The Story of Nigeria*, London, Faber and Faber, 1978, pp.188–206.

10 *See* E. J. Alagoa, 'The Ijaw in the New Millennium' (being a lecture given at the fourth convention of the Ijaw National Congress, at Yenagoa, Bayelsa state, on March 31, 2000 (hereinafter called *The Ijaw Nation in the New Millennium*), Onyoma Research, 2000, pp. 3–4. *Also see The Price of Oil: Corporate Responsibility and Human Rights Violations in Nigeria's Oil Producing Communities*, New York, Human Rights Watch, p. 8. *Also see* the report of the Human Rights Watch entitled 'NIGERIA: Human Rights Developments', World Report 1999, found at http://www.hrw.org/wr2k/Africa-07.htm visited on 31/10/05.

11 *See* the publication entitled *Southern Minorities Movement, Roots: the Struggle and the Future*, Port Harcourt, the Southern Minority Movement, 1995, especially pp. 5–6.

12 The hierarchy descends from the king to the chiefs and then down to the titled citizens and lineage heads, elders and other principal members, and finally down to the men, women and youths who are non-titled citizens. *See* E. J. Alagoa and A. Fombo, *A Chronicle of Grand Bonny, op cit*, p. 68.

13 By this system, children inherit from their fathers. Thus, children of an unmarried daughter inherit from their mother's father. This ancient inheritance system is, however, now being diluted.

(ie, how the people of the kingdom are organised in a characteristic pattern) is the 'house' system. This system, established by the kingdom's founding fathers and premier kings,[14] is a welfare system demanding loyalty, duty and responsibility from members in relation to their respective houses and the kingdom.[15]

4.2 (I) THE HOUSE OR CHIEFTAINCY HOUSE COMMUNITY IN GRAND BONNY KINGDOM

The term 'house' (*ie*, 'ward', 'family', or 'lineage') refers to a traditional administrative (*ie*, chieftaincy) unit. It is an extended family existing as the basic sociocultural, political, economic and any other conceivable institutional component unit of Bonny kingdom.[16]

From time immemorial, the house system has been existing as the basic social system of Bonny kingdom.[17] Thus, G. I. Jones identifies two main types of canoe houses in the trading states of Bonny and Kalabari. These are the consanguineous kinship units (of long ancestry – each of which has a common founding ancestor whose origin is traceable to the origin of these states) or the heterogeneous kinship units (comprised of consanguineous and non-consanguineous relatives whose affinity was established through a founding ancestor whose origin is not traceable to the origin of the states). The houses of Bonny kingdom are therefore either founding houses ('duawaris') or non-founding houses ('opuwaris'), including the minor houses ('kalawaris') which emerged from these two categories of houses.[18] Each house represents a chieftaincy unit whose people inhabit one or more communities, along with the fishing, farming and recreational or leisure settlements associated with the unit.

Article 4 (1) of the 'Constitution of the Bonny Youths Federation (BYF)', defines a Bonny youth to 'be a Bonny person by either or both parents being an indigene of Bonny and hold allegiance and loyalty to the Bonny kingdom'. This Article of the Constitution is captioned '*Basis for Affiliation and Membership of the Federation*'.

14 *See* G. I. Jones, *The Trading States of the Oil Rivers: A Study of Political Development in Eastern Nigeria*, New Brunswick, Transaction, 2000, p.198. *Also see* E. J. Alagoa and A. Fombo, *A Chronicle of Grand Bonny, op cit*, p. 45.

15 Houses assist their members in need or difficulty. Accordingly, duties and responsibilities accrue to individuals in relation to their respective houses and the kingdom. Regarding the duty of houses to launch war canoes in the interest of the kingdom during the Atlantic trade, *see* E. J. Alagoa and A. Fombo, *A Chronicle of Grand Bonny, op cit, p. 47.*

16 *See* G. I. Jones, *The Trading States of the Oil Rivers: A Study of Political Development in Eastern Nigeria, op cit*, pp. 18, 51, 55.

17 *See* E. J. Alagoa and A. Fombo, *A Chronicle of Grand Bonny, op cit*, pp. 45 and 67.

18 *See* G. I. Jones, *The Trading States of the Oil Rivers: A Study of Political Development in Eastern Nigeria, op cit*, pp. 53–62, especially p. 56. Beginning with the creation of the Allison (Nwaoju) major house by King Perekule, the 'opuwaris' were created in favour of the foster descendants of the founding folks due to the meritorious achievements of the founders of the 'opuwaris' to the development and/or advancement of the kingdom. Thus, the Ibiama (Finecountry) major house was created in favour of Igweyi, a foster son of King Bereibibo Alagbariya (who was initially the head of the Alagbariya house before he assumed kingship). Several major chieftaincy houses were also created out of the King Fubara Manilla Pepple house. These are the Captain Hart (Adango, Akunnayi) house, Jumbo (Sinaminasobo-ofori) house, Banigo (Ibaningo, Iringeresibo) house, Wilson Pepple (Oju-Igbe, Nkwerre) house and the Long-John (Amonibienye-ofori) house. *See* E. J. Alagoa and A. Fombo, *A Chronicle of Grand Bonny, op cit*, pp. 54–59, and 75.

G. I. Jones identifies the first four wards or component units of the Bonny kingdom thus:

> *according to Bonny tradition, the community consisted originally of four wards, derived respectively from Alagbaria, Opu Amakuba, Okpara Ndoli, and Asimini.*[19]

These four wards grew to become five after the foundation of Grand Bonny ('Okoloama') by Alagbariya. At the time, the founding group led by Priest-King Alagbariya met with the descendants of one of their kinsmen, Kongo, and realised that they all migrated from the same Central Delta Ijaw homeland. The descendants of Kongo were then integrated into Bonny kingdom as one of its founding units recognised as the Kongo ward.[20]

From its original four, and later five wards, Bonny kingdom grew after its post-settlement era to play a significant middleman role in the Atlantic trade which started in the fifteenth century.[21] During this trade, when the economy of Bonny and other ancient Delta states basically moved from fishing to middleman trading, their houses (which originated as lineages) also became trading companies or organisations and military units.[22] In the process, when Perekule assumed kingship in the eighteenth century, Bonny kingdom advanced further to have more chieftaincy houses, beginning with Perekule's creation of the Nwaoju (Allison) house[23] and the emergence of the houses of

19 *See* G. I. Jones, *The Trading States of the Oil Rivers: A Study of Political Development in Eastern Nigeria, op cit*, p. 198. Thus, G. Finapiri states that: *Historians used to think that it was Perekule who created the Ibani Chieftaincy Institution because he unilaterally appointed some slave chiefs. But this is not true; in fact, Perekule's action was revolutionary because chieftaincy had existed in Bonny among the Duowari houses (core Ijaw houses) in the formative years of the kingdom. So we can credit Perekule with initiating the policy of abolishing hereditary posts and creating a number of stools which were appointive rather than hereditary in order to counteract the powers of the hereditary chiefs. See* G. Finapiri, *Forgotten Heroes of Grand Bonny*, Lagos, CSS Press, 2001, pp. 19–20.

20 The descendants of Kongo migrated by sea route from Ebenitoru from the Central Niger Delta into the Eastern Delta province of Bonny kingdom – where they were integrated into the Alagbariya group. Whereas, the Alagbariya group originated from the Isedani lineage of Okoloba in Kolokuma, in the same Central Niger Delta, and migrated therefrom, by land route, to found Bonny kingdom. *See* the area of the Finima community website, captioned 'About Finima', found at http://www.bonnyisland.org/About%20Finima.html visited on 29/07/08. *Also see* E. J. Alagoa and A. Fombo, *A Chronicle of Grand Bonny, op cit*, pp. vii, and 4–5.

21 *See* E. J. Alagoa and A. A. Derefaka (eds), *The Land and People of Rivers State: Eastern Niger Delta*, Port Harcourt, Onyoma Research, 2002, p. 277.

22 Ibid, pp. 67–70. *Also see* the publication regarding G. I. Jones, 'The Trading States of the Oil Rivers: A Study of Political Development in Eastern Nigeria', found at http://www.amazon.com/gp/cdp/member-reviews/A3Q4A2SW1VVPZJ/102-2193900-5483327?_encoding=UTF8 visited on 14/04/05. *See* K. O. Dike, *Trade and Politics in the Niger Delta 1830–1885: An Introduction to the Economic and Political History of Nigeria, op cit*, p. 37. *See* R. Horton, 'From Fishing Village to City-State: A Social History of New Calabar', in M. Douglas and P. Kaberry (eds), *Man in Africa*, London, Tavistock, 1969, pp. 37–58.

23 The Nwaoju (Allison) house (sometimes associated with the Fubara Manilla Pepple group of houses) was thus the first created chieftaincy house ('opuwari') in the kingdom. The Fubara Manilla Pepple house and Opubo Anna Pepple house were the head houses of the 'opuwaris'. *See* E. J. Alagoa and A. Fombo, *A Chronicle of Grand Bonny, op cit*, pp. 45–59, and 75.

Perekule's two sons (Fubara [ie, Adum-Fubara] Manilla Pepple and Opubo [ie, Adum-Opu-bughu) Anna Pepple) as separate units of the Perekule lineage. More chieftaincy houses were created after the reign of King Perekule. Thus, King Fubara created the Captain Adango Hart (alias Akunnayi) house and the Wilson Oju-igbe Pepple (alias Nkwerre) house.[24] The houses of Bonny kingdom continued to expand during the Atlantic trade period until the departure of some of them during the civil crisis that gave rise to the foundation of the Opobo kingdom in 1869/70.[25] Following several continuities and changes from the late nineteenth century to date, Bonny kingdom now has thirty-five chieftaincy houses. These are the fourteen major houses, twenty minor houses, and the George Pepple unit of the Perekule royal house.[26] Among the fourteen major houses are five 'duawaris' (ie, the lineages of the founding fathers and premier kings, and those of their blood descendants), and nine 'opuwaris' (ie, the houses of the foster descendants of the founding stocks of the kingdom).[27]

Due to its all-embracing nature, the house system plays a dominant role in the lives of the people, communities, communal settlements and suburban

---

24 Ibid, pp. 56 and 59.

25 Ibid, pp. 47–48.

26 Ibid, p. 49. *Also see* the booklet entitled the '10th Coronation Anniversary of His Majesty, King E. A. W. D. Pepple III, Perekule XI, Amanyanabo of Grand Bonny kingdom', produced by the Bonny Chiefs' Council (BCC), p. 13. *Also see* E. J. Alagoa and A. Fombo, *A Chronicle of Grand Bonny, op cit*, pp. vii – 80, and p. 89.

27 The 'duawaris' are Bristol-Alagbarigha (alias Alagbariye, Alagbariya, Alagbaria), Halliday-Awusa, Dublin Green (alias Ebie, Oruapka), Tolofari (alias Oruasawor, Ndende Omuigbem), and Kongo (from which Buoye-Omuso Brown evolved). The 'opuwaris' are Fubara Manilla Pepple, Allison (alias Nwaoju), Captain Hart (alias Adango, Akunnayi), Jumbo (alias Sinaminasobo-ofori, Okponkata), Banigo (alias Ibaningo, Iringeresibo), Finecountry (alias Ibiama, Igweyi), Wilson Oju-igbe Pepple (alias Nkwerre), LongJohn (alias Amonibienye-ofori), and Wilcox (alias Wirikoma, Egede – which stands distinct between the 'duawaris' and the 'opuwaris'). The twenty minor houses are Willie-Pepple (which evolved from Prince Adasa Bereibibo Bristol-Alagbariya's lineage), Jim-Halliday, Attoni, Tobin, Jackmay, Jekey-Green, Christie-Wilcox, Dappa-Wilcox, Jack Manilla, Allaputa, Pollyn, Ada-Allison, Jamaica-Allison, Abbey-Hart, Abraham-Hart, Ezekiel-Hart, Dan-Jumbo, John-Jumbo, Stowe/Benstowe, and Dick-Obunku (Beresiri). Some of these minor houses sprang from the 'duawaris', while others emerged from the 'opuwaris'. Whereas, the 'duawaris' evolved naturally as the direct blood descendant houses of the founding fathers and premier kings, the 'opuwaris' were created (for the foster descendants of the founding folks of the kingdom). Also, as core Ijaw houses, the 'duawaris' are 'aboriginal/autochthonous canoe houses'; whereas, the 'opuwaris' are 'war canoe houses' created during inter-tribal wars era of the Atlantic trade in the Delta region. Furthermore, whereas the criterion for ascension to rulership in the 'duawaris' is primarily birth-right/hereditary, among the 'opuwaris' ascension is based on the popularity of aspiring candidates. Together, the 'duawaris' and 'opuwaris' are major houses. As fourteen major houses of present-day Bonny kingdom, they represent the ancient 'Okolo-ama-Ngiekiri-fajie' – the fourteen wards of Bonny. Besides, between the 'duawaris' (especially those of the founding fathers and premier kings) and the Perekule house, whereas the latter achieved the appellation royal in terms of producing kings in Bonny kingdom, the former are inalienably royal as the natural owners of kingship in the kingdom. The former are thus described in Ibani language as 'alayingifuro' (ie, originators/begetters of the royal/traditional institution) in the kingdom. *C/f* E. J. Alagoa and A. Fombo, *A Chronicle of Grand Bonny, op cit*, pp. 10, 17, 49, 54–66 and 75. *See* G. Finapiri, *Forgotten Heroes of Grand Bonny, op cit*, pp. 7–9, 19–20. *Also see* G. I. Jones, *The Trading States of the Oil Rivers: A Study of Political Development in Eastern Nigeria*, London, Transaction, 2000, pp. 25, 56–62, 161, 172, 174, 176, 196, 198, 202. *See The Constitution of Grand Bonny*. This Constitution, written in the 1970s without interactive public involvement, compromised the house system in relation to the origin of Bonny kingdom.

settlements of Bonny kingdom.[28] The system exists as a spiritual link from its founding ancestors to its present and continuing generations of people. Based on the system, each house or house community has a head – who may be a king or chief.[29]

4.2 (II) DECISION-MAKING BASED ON THE HOUSE SYSTEM OF GOVERNANCE IN BONNY KINGDOM

The house system has two basic levels of governance, namely governance at the level of the component chieftaincy houses or house communities and governance at the apex or central level of traditional rulership called the Bonny Kingdom Council of Traditional Rulers (BKCTR). This Council may be comprised of the king and chiefs (presented to the Council by their houses) who are assisted, since the reign of King Perekule, by the titled citizens and the 'Ibanise Kobiri'. Governance at the level of each chieftaincy house community is comprised of the king or a chief, who is the head, assisted by the elders (who are the heads of the component lineages), including other elders (who are principal members in their own rights and thus not representing any component lineage). Based on the hierarchical structure of the house system, decision-making flows from the people in a representative or limited democratic form or manner.[30] Thus, at the level of the component chieftaincy house community, the people make their input through their lineage heads into the deliberations of the house cabinet, where such input is considered as the collective will of the house. Towards kingdom-based decisions, the collective will or position of the house may, along with the positions of other houses, be taken to the BKCTR, where the collective will of the entire kingdom is determined. Where the BKCTR is comprised of chiefs alone (without a monarch or king), it is called the Bonny Chiefs' Council (BCC); whereas, where it is comprised of chiefs and the monarch (ie, an incumbent or a reigning monarch), it is called the Amanyanabo-in-Council (AIC – also known as the King-in-Council [KIC]). In other words, depending on how the BKCTR is constituted, it may either be called the BCC or the AIC/KIC.

---

28 The suburban settlements such as plantations and leisure/recreational areas are areas of economic and political influence outside the kingdom's traditional homeland. *See* E. J. Alagoa and A. Fombo, *A Chronicle of Grand Bonny, op cit*, p. 69. *Also see* G. I. Jones, *The Trading States of the Oil Rivers: A Study of Political Development in Eastern Nigeria, op cit*, p. 18.

29 Considering that Bonny kingdom was an independent organic entity during the pre-colonial era, the chieftaincy houses of the kingdom are still being referred to as 'country houses', while the chiefs of these houses are known as 'country chiefs' ('Ibani[se]-Alapu').

30 *See* N. Wariboko, 'Capability Distribution and Onset of the 1869 Bonny War', Nordic Journal of African Studies, 7 (2), 1998, p. 5. *Also see* G. I. Jones, *The Trading States of the Oil Rivers: A Study of Political Development in Eastern Nigeria, op cit*, pp. 57–61 and 128. *See* E. J. Alagoa and A. Fombo, *A Chronicle of Grand Bonny, op cit*, p. 17.

4.2 (III) DECISION-MAKING IN THE CHIEFTAINCY HOUSE COMMUNITY OF THE KINGDOM

Decision-making at the chieftaincy house level ends with the king or a chief who is the head of the house. Thus, while assisting their chief, the elders have the duty and responsibility to govern their respective lineages.[31] Accordingly, the chief, along with the elders and other principal members have the duty to govern the entire people of the house over which the chief is the head. It is the duty of the chief and elders to safeguard the properties and inheritance of the house, in accordance with custom and law. Members of the house (ie, be they individuals or groups) take advice and directives from their chief, along with their lineage heads and other principal members, regarding the general administration of the house.

The input, views or opinions of each lineage, which are taken or delivered to the house cabinet by a lineage head, may be different from the input, views or opinions that such a head may or would like to make as an individual not representing his lineage. In this way, the inputs gathered from the lineages are synthesised and harmonised to enable the cabinet (made up of the chief and the elders and other principal members) to arrive at final decisions representing the voice of their people. Thus, although the entire members of chieftaincy houses are not usually present at cabinet meetings where the decisions of their houses are made, their inputs are taken into consideration in decision-making processes.

Emergency decisions may, however, be taken by the chief alone, sometimes along with the lineage heads or at least some of them, without input from the entire members of the house. In such a situation, the chief would duly inform the elders and other principal members about his decision to enable them to ratify it[32] or make subsequent input where the need arises. The chief and lineage heads/elders would then inform the members of the component lineages about the decision, so as to enable them to make any subsequent inputs which might arise. Where subsequent inputs are required and where time permits, members of the component lineages are informed to express their opinions or views, and these are taken into consideration in the decision-making process. In this way, every member of each house is duly informed and involved in decision-making.

Although the foregoing represents the nature of the decision-making process in each chieftaincy house, the process may differ slightly in major chieftaincy houses made up of minor chieftaincy houses.[33] Decisions of the major or

31 In Ibani language, the lineages which are branches or component units of the house are called 'ikpangi' which is also now loosely called 'burusu'.

32 *See Ekpendu vs. Erika* (1959) 4 F. S. C., 79; and *Fayehun vs. Fadoju* (2000) 77 LRCN, p. 714.

33 The difference between major and minor chieftaincy houses depends on the nature of their past and continuing relationships. Thus, the relationship between the John Jumbo minor house and its Jumbo major house is more pronounced in various ways than the relationships between the Pollyn minor house and its Captain Hart major house, and those between the Tobin and Attoni minor houses and their Buoye-Omuso Brown major house.

parent house, presided over by its chief, are generally made up of inputs from its component lineages and those of its minor house or houses. Exceptions to this general rule include cases where minor houses may take independent decisions on issues exclusively affecting them.[34]

Considering that the communities of Bonny kingdom are communities belonging to its component chieftaincy houses, the general rule is that decision-making in each house community is the internal affair of the chieftaincy house to which the community belongs. As a rule, chieftaincy houses exercise exclusive jurisdiction over the affairs of their houses, house community and communities, as the case may be. This rule is however, for instance, subject to Bonny's customary principles of land ownership and ancillary interests in land, especially areas not allocated to houses (in the course of traditional land administration and management) in the kingdom. These principles are summarised as follows: 'tari piri sobo, piri omongibo', meaning 'he who first entered the bush-lands to found a community, has priority (*ie*, overriding) interest in terms of land ownership and ancillary land rights and interests in the community'.[35] Priority or overriding interest of a founding or other relatively ancient chieftaincy house in a community may express itself in such forms as land ownership and other related natural or inheritance rights and benefits being derived in the community.[36]

4.2 (IV) DECISION-MAKING FROM THE LEVEL OF THE COMPONENT CHIEFTAINCY HOUSES TO THE CENTRAL/APEX LEVEL OF TRADITIONAL GOVERNANCE

The introductory part of the above sub-heading has given an insight into the decision-making process at the house level of governance and at the central or

34 Some of such exclusive decisions may require the ratification, confirmation or support of their major houses. Hence, minor houses may appoint their chiefs independently, but the chiefs so appointed are installed with the knowledge and consent of their major houses so as to enable the major house chiefs to present their minors to the apex traditional ruling council of the kingdom. The relationship between minor houses and their majors may be elastic and remote in history, in the same way as between some principal major houses and subsequent major houses created from their stock.

35 This customary principle, subject to the Land Use Act, 1978, has three ambits, namely the above-stated summary and three others. One, 'kiri yanabo, piri yanabo', meaning, 'he who owns a communal land, owns its adjoining territorial bush-lands (ie, the bush-lands within the community's territory)'. Two, 'kiri yanabo bughu yanabo', meaning 'he who owns a communal land, owns its adjoining territorial mangrove swamp and forest areas (ie, the mangrove swamp and forest areas within the community's territory)'. And three, 'tari piri sobo, piri yanabo', meaning 'he who first entered the bush-lands to found a community, is the owner of the community's land and its adjoining bush-lands (ie, the bush-lands within the community's territory)'. In Bonny, the term 'community' represents the kingdom.

36 Regarding how community ownership of land is based on the foundation of the community, *see* J. F. Fekumo, *Principles of Nigerian Customary Law, op cit*, 91–96. Thus, claims of land ownership and the acquisition of same in the course of petroleum development to the deprivation and total exclusion of the kingdom's founding houses, constitute an aberration in fact, custom, and law. *See* the area of the Finima website captioned 'Memorandum of Understanding', entered into by the representatives of the three chieftaincy houses of Finima community, further to their pursuit of peace in the community, found at http://www.bonnyisland.org/MOU.html visited on 24/12/08.

apex traditional level of governance (ie, the BKCTR). Thus, the in the same way as emergency decisions taken at the level of the component chieftaincy houses, the BKCTR is duty-bound to inform the houses about emergency decisions taken without their requisite input, so as to enable the people to know about such decisions and to contribute to them where the need subsequently arises.

After the reign of the founding fathers and premier kings (ie, before the era of King Perekule) each king ruled in harmony with the nobles and the priests.[37] Heads among the nobles were 'amadapu', meaning 'subordinate heads' and 'regents'. The Amadapu were 'Aseme', meaning 'heads of royal descent' or 'hereditary lineage heads' (ie, present-day hereditary chieftaincy house heads – 'Aseme-Alapu').[38] At the time, governance thrived in accordance with natural law[39] and was thus characterised by virtue. Decisions were reached equitably among the kings, nobles (including other folks of the nobility kindred group) and the priests, especially the priests of 'Ikuba'. Such decisions were reached by considering people's welfare. Leadership was based on true service to the people, and this generated mutual respect, trust and cooperation (*ie*, consensus-building) in the kingdom.[40]

Thereafter, the apex traditional ruling council in its present form and character began in the eighteenth century during the reign of King Perekule. The original system,[41] as exemplified by kingship based on age and commitment to

---

37 These are priests of the kingdom's deity, 'Ikuba'. Alagbariya was the first high-priest of Ikuba. During the reign of Queen Kambasa, the sixth monarch of the kingdom, Prince Ndende from the Asimini lineage served as high-priest of 'Ikuba'. *See* E. J. Alagoa and A. Fombo, *A Chronicle of Grand Bonny, op cit*, pp. 6–8 and 24. Besides the high-priests of 'Ikuba', there were priests of other ancient deities such as those of 'Adumu' at Kuruama and 'Simingi' at Finima.

38 *See* E. J. Alagoa and A. Fombo, *A Chronicle of Grand Bonny, op cit*, pp. 6, 46–47 and 54. *Also see* G. I. Jones, *The Trading States of the Oil Rivers: A Study of Political Development in Eastern Nigeria, op cit*, pp. 57–62, 128, 161, 172, 174, 176 and 206. *See* G. Finapiri, *Forgotten Heroes of Grand Bonny, op cit*, pp. 19–20.

39 *See* J. Finnis (ed), *Natural Law: Volume I*, Aldershot, Dartmouth, 1991, p. xi. Natural law, which prevailed before the Atlantic trade era of positive law and re-emerged from the twentieth century, is determined by the connection of law to morality based on man's spiritual background. *See* J. E. Penner, *Mozley & Whiteley's Law Dictionary*, London, Butterworths, 2001, pp. 236–237.

40 Such decisions include the enthronement of Alagbariya, to succeed his elder brother, Opuamakuba, and the subsequent enthronement of Asimini who was crowned by his elder brother, Alagbariya. Other such decisions include Alagbariya offering his daughter, Princess Osunju, as sacrifice to achieve peace and good drinking water in Bonny. Asimini also offered his daughter, Princess Ogbolo, to the salt water deities, to achieve the widening of the Bonny estuary, so as to enable the Western European merchants to trade with the kingdom from the fifteenth century. There was also the resolution by King Halliday-Awusa and his kindred group (ie, the founding kindred group), to entrust kingship on Perekule during the seven-year war between Bonny and Andoni. King Awusa (who led Bonny kingdom until the seventh and final year of the war) agreed to confer kingship on Perekule. However, in the controversy that ensued between Awusa and Perekule regarding whether or not Perekule fully accomplished the conditions for the conferment, Awusa refused to deliver the traditional staff of office of kingship to Perekule when Perekule was to assume kingship. *C/f* E. J. Alagoa and A. Fombo, *A Chronicle of Grand Bonny, op cit*, pp. 6–7, 9–11, 14, 60–62, 75 and 89. *Also see* H. Crow, *Memoirs of the Late Captain Hugh Crow of Liverpool*, Frank Cass, 1970, pp. 211, and 215–217.

41 *See* E. J. Alagoa and A Fombo, *A Chronicle of Grand Bonny, op cit*, pp. 6–10, 15, 45, 54–55 and 74–75.

service (from the reign of the founding fathers up to the reign of King Awusa [Halliday]) now changed. This change was due to the display of political might and other traditions of positive international law which governed relations between the Western European powers and the Delta trading states including Bonny kingdom.[42]

After King Perekule's creation of the Nwaoju (Allison) major house[43] about 1740, more chieftaincy houses were created and other strategies designed by subsequent Perekule kings, to aid the continuation of their lineage over kingship. Consequently, divide and rule[44] crept into the traditional polity. This continues to undermine public good, even within the Perekule lineage, while lining the nests of those being favoured in the traditional power game. The compelling strength of Bonny's true social system based on fair play has

42 As expressed above, contrary to the dictates of natural law which prevailed during the era of the founding fathers and premier kings of the kingdom, positive law promoted the use of force and other ominous fratricidal means of conducting international relations by political authorities. *See* A. Oyebode, 'Treaties and the Colonial Enterprise: The Case of Nigeria', African Journal of International and Comparative Law, Vol, 2, Part 2, 1990, pp. 17–36.

43 Created chieftaincies started with King Perekule's creation of the Allison (Nwaoju) major house in acknowledgement of the role of Allison Nwaoju to the success of Bonny kingdom during the seven-year war between Bonny and Andoni. As E. J. Alagoa and A. Fombo put it: *Decisive change from strictly lineage set-up probably occurred in the reign of King Perekule. According to traditions of this House, the elevation of the founder, Allison Nwaoju to the chieftaincy was a revolutionary act on the part of King Perekule (King Pepple I). The king had got into trouble in a battle against the Andoni and was only saved by the timely and brave intervention of Allison Nwaoju and his retainers. The king thereupon empowered Allison Nwaoju to become head of his own house, to wear coral beads, ivory armlets, top hat, boots, an umbrella, and the special gown of a chief. The act was so revolutionary because Allison Nwaoju was a slave and it was a capital offence for a slave to wear any of these items of adornment, let alone to aspire to the rank of a house head. Allison Nwaoju had been a ward of the kings' daughter, Adumta but was sent away from the capital to Oloma because of stubbornness. There he accumulated wealth by trading and making canoes. By the time of the Andoni war, he already had a large following of slaves.* E. J. Alagoa and A. Fombo highlight that . . . *the war did not go all that well for King Perekule either. The king lost his two sons, Ibulu and Koronchi, and was himself barely saved from one engagement by the timely intervention of Allison Nwaoju (who thus won a chieftaincy title for himself and other deserving slaves)'. See* E. J. Alagoa and A. Fombo, *A Chronicle of Grand Bonny, op cit*, pp. 54 and 75.

44 During the Atlantic trade, divide and rule engulfed Bonny kingdom in the rivalry between the Fubara Manilla Pepple house and the Opubo Anna Pepple house (especially, as E. J. Alagoa and A. Fombo put it, during the era of ambitious leaders such as Ibaniburufigha and Oko Jumbo, and Maduka and Jack Jaja, as heads of these rival houses). This resulted in the foundation of the Opobo kingdom. *See* E. J. Alagoa and A. Fombo, *A Chronicle of Grand Bonny, op cit*, pp. 21–22, 25, 28–31, 47–48, 52–53, 68 and 111–112. Divide and rule continues to thrive in such a way that the 'opuwaris', along with their chiefs, are accorded discretions which undermine the natural rights and autochthonous customary status of the 'duawaris' and their hereditary heads. *See* G. Finapiri, *Forgotten Heroes of Grand Bonny, op cit*, pp. 19–20. *Also see* J. Finnis, *Natural Law and Natural Rights*, Oxford, Clarendon Press, 1980, especially pp. 18–19, 23–29, 198–199. Presently, as the kingdom is losing its dynamically-organised setting due to divide and rule, the welfare and security of its poor and neglected masses are at stake. *See* the BBC report regarding 'kidnapping, robbery, hijacking and rape' occasioned on water-transport passengers travelling from Bonny Island to Port Harcourt, entitled 'Nigerian Militants Rape Women', found at http://news.bbc.co.uk/1/hi/world/africa/7945820.stm visited on 16/03/09.

eventually generated awareness and agitation for greater public good in the governance of the kingdom.[45]

4.2 (v) (a) Setting-up of the Ibanise-Kobiri to Broaden Decision-making in the Kingdom

'Ibanise'[46] refers to the entire Ibani people (ie, Bonny and Opobo kingdoms). 'Ibanise Kobiri', meaning conference of delegates of the entire Ibani houses, evolved as a 'war council' and thereafter existed as the 'people's parliament', before assuming its present status (ie, the 'highest decision-making body of Bonny kingdom').

During the Atlantic trade in the Delta region, inter-tribal wars were rampant among the trading states of the region, as neighbouring kingdoms struggled to protect their middleman position. The states struggled for superior middleman position and to prevent their non-middlemen neighbours from either interfering with their position or having access to trade directly with the Western European merchants.[47] In Bonny kingdom, during these inter-tribal wars, certain foster descendants began to make significant achievements to complement those of the founding kindred group. In the perspective of this book, such achievements generated two results, namely, the evolution of the 'Ibanise Kobiri' and the creation of chieftaincy houses (*ie*, the 'opuwaris') exemplified above by King Perekule's creation of the Nwaoju (Allison) major house.

As serious emergency decisions were taken during the inter-tribal wars that took place during the Atlantic trade, it became necessary (after the reign of

---

45 *See* V. O. Bartkus and J. H. Davis (eds), *Social Capital: Reaching Out, Reaching In*, Cheltenham, Edward Elgar, 2009, especially pp. 239–259. *Also see* D. Castiglione *et al* (eds), *The Handbook of Social Capital*, Oxford, Oxford University Press, 2008, especially pp. 70–100. *See* J. A. Connor and S. Kadel-Taras, *Community Visions, Community Solutions: Grantmaking for Comprehensive Impact*, Saint Paul, Amherst H. Wilder Foundation, 2003, especially pp. 26–32. *See* P. Mattessich, *et al*, *Community Building: What Makes It Work: A Review of Factors Influencing Successful Community Building*, Saint Paul, Amherst H. Wilder Foundation, 1997, pp. 19–49, especially pp. 27–29. *See* J. F. Krile, *The Community Leadership Handbook: Framing Ideas, Building Relationships, and Mobilizing Resource*, Saint Paul, Fieldstone Alliance, 2006. *See* the Guardian newspaper editorial opinion by Pat Utomi entitled 'Everything Stands Or Falls on Leadership', found at http://wwwn.grguardiannews.com/editorial_opinon/article03//indexn2_html?pdate=2. . . visited on 23/03/09. According to Roscoe Pound: *In truth, in governance, as in all else that men do, balance is called for. . . . Ultimate perfection of mankind, if we may trust experience, can no more be achieved through government than through the other universal agencies of perfection in which men have believed in the past. See* R. Pound, *An Introduction to the Philosophy of Law: Based on the Storrs Lectures Delivered at Yale University*, New Haven, Yale University Press, 1965, p. 168.

46 'Ibanise' was derived from 'Beni' (now Ibani'), being the name of the ancestral father of Opuamakuba, Alagbariya and Asimini, the foremost founding ancestors and premier kings of Bonny kingdom. Alagbariya was thus named 'Kalabeni' meaning 'Junior Beni'. *See* the presentation at the 2004 Boro Day in the United States of America (USA), entitled 'Ijaw History (From Ijawnation Yahoogroups archive -posted by Benaebi Benatari of IPA [Ijaw People's Association], UK.)', found at http://www.ijaw-naa.org/ijaw/home.htm visited on 24/10/05.

47 *See* T. V. Erekosima *et al* (eds), *Hundred Years of Buguma History in Kalabari Culture: Buguma 1884–1894*, Lagos, Sibon, 1991, p.175. *Also see* E. J. Alagoa and A. Fombo, *A Chronicle of Grand Bonny, op cit*, pp. 73–80.

King Awusa [Halliday]) for individuals who had made prominent achievements to directly participate in decision-making at the apex level of governance. 'Ibanise Kobiri' was thus established as 'the kingdom's war council', and as it continued to be useful in Bonny kingdom's affairs (after Opobo had become a separate kingdom), it became a more permanent gathering or conference of the kingdom, comprising the king, chiefs, titled citizens and other representatives of the people. In the process, during the reign of King George Pepple (in the second half of the nineteenth century), 'Ibanise Kobiri' thrived as the 'people's parliament',[48] following which (from the late twentieth century) it became Bonny kingdom's 'national assembly'[49] considered as the 'highest decision-making body'.

Although decisions of the 'Ibanise Kobiri' are considered supreme, they are not truly free from interference by prominent chiefs and particularly kings. The doctrine of necessity which warranted the 'Ibanise-Kobiri's three transitional eras now requires that more rational and public-spirited decisions are taken at the central level of governance.

4.2 (v) (b): Further Broadening of Decision-making by the Appointment of Titled Citizens

To complement the role of the 'Ibanise Kobiri', the need to have a neutral party to resolve disputes[50] between and among members of the apex traditional ruling council generated the emergence of titled citizens. Titled citizenship is a status next to chieftaincy and kingship, accorded to reputable men and women in the kingdom. Besides maintaining cordial relations among members of the apex traditional ruling council, titled citizens take part in traditional administration at the central level of governance[51] and at the level of their chieftaincy houses.

4.2 (v) (c) Creation of an Employment Bureau in the Course of Petroleum Development Operations in the Kingdom

Unemployment is a perennial problem in post-colonial Nigeria. As the country is mainly unindustrialised, many youths remain unemployed even after university

48 At the time, the introduction of Christianity by King William Dappa Pepple in 1864, had diluted the significant roles and importance of priests of traditional deities in decision-making. *See* E. J. Alagoa and A. Fombo, *A Chronicle of Grand Bonny, op cit,* pp. 24–27, 34–36, especially p. 36.

49 Ibid, p. 39.

50 These are disputes between and among chiefs, and those between the chiefs and a reigning monarch.

51 Formal or institutionalised titled citizenship took place during the reign of King C. O. S. Pepple (1978–1993/1996). The most recent titled citizens were appointed during the tenth coronation anniversary of King E. A. W. D. Pepple, on December 23, 2006. *See* the booklet entitled the 'Tenth Coronation Anniversary of His Majesty, King E. A. W. D. Pepple III, Perekule XI, Amanyanabo of Grand Bonny Kingdom', produced by the BCC, pp. 47–49. A titled citizen may be an 'Ama-opusenibo' ('a senior male titled citizen') or an Ama-opuorubo' ('a senior female titled citizen'). Otherwise, a titled citizen may be an 'Ama-senibo' ('a junior male titled citizen') or an 'Ama-seniorubo' ('a junior female titled citizen'). There are thus two broad categories of titled citizens, namely 'Ama-opuseniapu' (senior titled citizens), and 'Ama-seniapu' (junior titled citizens).

careers.[52] As in most developing countries, unemployment in Nigeria is mainly due to the failure of governance.[53] Even though existing public sector employment opportunities are limited, governments in Nigeria lack the ability to boost private sector operations to enhance employment opportunities.[54]

While agriculture and other traditional means of employment are increasingly being abandoned in Nigeria, petroleum development in the oil-producing communities offers a measure of employment opportunities for the citizens, especially during the construction stage of development operations. Thus, among the concerns of citizens of the oil-producing communities when multinational oil and gas companies (MNOCs) arrive to operate in their communities, is the need for employment opportunities.[55] However, due to the industrialised and professionalised nature of the MNOCs' operations, they are only able to employ a few Nigerians. Unemployment gives rise to and also aggravates poverty among citizens.[56] The paradox of Nigeria is that poverty levels and their associated problems of unemployment contradict the country's immense wealth in human and natural resources, especially such major natural resources as petroleum and solid minerals. Thus, since the advent of Shell Nigeria (*ie*, the Shell Petroleum Development Company of Nigeria Limited – SPDC) in 1958, and in the 1990s the advent of other giant MNOCs such as Mobil Producing Nigeria Unlimited (MPN) and the Nigeria LNG Limited (NLNG), including their sub-contracting multinational and Nigerian firms in Bonny kingdom, citizens of the kingdom have been anxious to gain employment opportunities from these companies.

Shell started on a bad footing in Bonny kingdom, when it commenced production operations in 1961at its Bonny Crude Oil Terminal (BCOT), as it

---

52 Unemployment gives rise to several social problems, including crimes, especially in the absence of social security measures. *See* the *AllAfrica* (ie, African news and information for a global audience) online newspaper report entitled 'Social Security Summit: Stakeholders Link Crimes with Absence of Social Protection', found at http://allafrica.com/stories/printable/200511141308.html visited on 09/12/05. The crises in the Delta region are thus being aggravated by increasing unemployment in the region. *See* T. Adedoja, 'Niger Delta Crisis: Stakeholders Dialogue On Way Forward', found (in the area of the homepage of SPINWATCH, captioned 'all Africa.com') at http://www.spinwatch.org/content/view/435/9/ visited on 30/12/06. *Also see* F. Weston, 'Niger Delta, the Price of Oil and the Class Struggle', found at http://www.marxist.com/Africa/niger_delta.htm visited on 09/12/05. *Also see* A. Onduku, 'Environmental Conflicts: The Case of the Niger Delta', found in the area of the Urhobo Historical Society website at http://www.waado.org/NigerDelta/Essays/ResourceControl/Onduku.html visited on 09/12/05.

53 *See* an article by M. I. Obadan and A. F. Odusola, entitled 'Productivity and Unemployment in Nigeria', found at http://www.cenbank.org/OUT/PUBLICATIONS/OCCASIONALPAPERS/RD/2000/ABE-00-10.PDF visited on 09/12/05.

54 Ibid. *Also see* an article by M. I. Obadan, entitled 'Poverty Reduction in Nigeria: The Way Forward', found at http://www.cenbank.org/OUT/PUBLICATIONS/EFR/RD/2002/EFRVOL39-4-3.PDF visited on 09/12/05. *See* the Guardian newspapers report entitled '145 Outstanding Corps Members Get Jobs Today', found http://www.guardiannewngr.com/news/article04 visited on 19/12/05.

55 *See* S. Uwghevwe-Togbolo, 'Youths in the Niger Delta and Oil/Gas Companies', found (in the homepage of the Nigerian Village Square) at http://www.nigeriavillagesquare1.com/Articles/MYAI/2005/04/youths-in-niger-delta-region-and.html visited on 09/12/05.

56 *See* M. I. Obadan, 'Poverty Reduction in Nigeria: The Way Forward', *op cit.*

made no conscious effort to employ citizens of the kingdom. From 1958 to 1961, when the BCOT was being constructed, citizens of Bonny kingdom and those of other neighbouring areas were employed as construction workers. However, when crude oil export to consumer-nations started in 1961, the construction phase workers were laid off and production phase employees took over the BCOT operations. From then up to the 1990s, when other giant MNOCs began their operations, was a period of learning and unfulfilled hope for Bonny people. Due to pressures from the traditional rulers and other prominent Bonny people, the Rivers state government had to devise a means of redressing the unemployment situation in Bonny kingdom during the construction phase of the MPN Oso NGL (Bonny River Terminal – BRT) project and the NLNG plant complex at Finima, Bonny Island, which began in the 1990s. In order to share equitably any available employment opportunities in the process, the Rivers state government came up with a way to ensure that construction employment was offered by the companies in accordance with the relevant federal government (FG) guidelines. The government did this through the Rivers State Employment Centre (RSEC), by devising a formula for sharing construction employment opportunities among Nigerian citizens which in turn led to the establishment of the Bonny Employment Bureau (BEB).[57] The RSEC has responsibility for sourcing the required number of construction workers from Rivers state and other states of Nigeria while the BEB is responsible for sourcing the workers required from the kingdom and LGA of Bonny.[58]

The BEB, under the auspices of the apex traditional council of Bonny kingdom and the Bonny local government, is administered by Bonny citizens which for them counts as an aspect of traditional decision-making process.[59]

57 The BEB was formally inaugurated by the BCC in 1993, with Amaopusenibo Spurgean Green as its chairman.

58 For the smooth operation of the BEB, the employment sharing formula of 40 per cent to 60 per cent was evolved between the immediate chieftaincy house(s) or house communities/locality hosting the industrial operation and the rest of Bonny kingdom. As Finima community is the immediate host of these oil and gas industrial operations, the community has a 40 per cent allocation, while the rest of Bonny kingdom (outside Finima) is allocated 60 per cent of existing employment opportunities from these operations.

59 To protect the interests of the construction workers, the Rivers state government, under the auspices of the Rivers state chapter of the Nigerian Labour Congress (NLC), persuaded the MNOCs to enter into negotiation with the National Union of Civil Engineering, Construction, Furniture and Wood Workers (NUCEWWO). Project site construction agreements are thus being negotiated and put into effect between the representatives of the workers and the participating companies. The first of these agreements dated March 25, 1997, is entitled 'Agreement between the National Union of Civil Engineering, Construction, Furniture and Wood Workers (NUCEWWO) and the Participating Contractors Working on the NNPC/Mobil Producing Unlimited Oso 11 NGL (Bonny River Terminal – BRT) Project and on the Nigeria LNG Project for work on Bonny Island for Terms and Conditions for a Standard Wage on the Oso 11 NGL and NLNG Projects on Bonny Island, dated March 25, 1997'. This agreement is renewed from time to time. It was, for instance, renewed in 2000 (signed on February 8, 2000, and dated March 25, 2000), 2003 (signed December 5, 2002, and dated January 1, 2003), 2005 (signed on December 2, 2004, and dated January 1, 2005) and 2006/2007 (signed and dated January 1, 2007). Perhaps considering the ever-increasing inflation in Bonny due to the petroleum industry's

4.2 (v) (d) Establishment of the Bonny Youth Federation in Response to such Present-day Challenges as those of Petroleum Development

From time immemorial, young people in Bonny kingdom have been of immense assistance to their elders and society. Youngsters, whether males or females traditionally perform roles which their elders, as senior members of society, are considered too dignified or elderly to undertake. In the process, young people learn to assume positions of leadership through service. The role and importance of Bonny youngsters to society may be likened to those of age-grades in the mainland communities of the Delta region. Hence, based on age-settings, Bonny youngsters implement decisions of their elders/lineage heads, house communities and the apex traditional ruling council.[60]

Petroleum development operations, which began in 1957, in Bonny kingdom, gave rise to the need for more centralised and organised youth activities in the kingdom. The period from the late 1980s up to the early 1990s, enhanced by the creation of the Bonny LGA in 1991 by the Federal Military Government (FMG) led by General Ibrahim Babangida,[61] helped to boost organised youth activities in the kingdom. At the time, Nigerian youths were becoming active in governance, and this enhanced organised youth protests against MNOCs in the Delta region due to the adverse effects of the operations of these companies in the region. Thus, in 1992, the protests regarding the adverse effects of Shell Nigeria's operations at its BCOT, led to the death of a young man, Omusa Brown.[62]

The Bonny Youths Federation (BYF) consequently evolved following the nationwide nature of youth activism when General Sani Abacha was the military head of state from 1993 to 1998. Towards the end of the Abacha era, certain youths coordinated by Daniel Kanu established a political movement called 'Youths Earnestly Ask for Abacha' (YEAA). This movement planned and executed a well-supported 'two million man march', on March 3, 1998, at the Federal Capital Territory (FCT), Abuja, to prepare Nigeria for General

rapid expansion, the most prominent change in this series of renewed agreements is in the area of workers' wages. The agreements set terms for construction and contract works, including wages for the employees of the participating companies. They are earmarked to promote industrial relations between employers and employees, especially in the interest of the construction workers and the contractors engaged to render various works and services in the course of the projects.

60 *See* E. T. Bristol, 'Kuruama-Bonny: from Earliest Times to the Present', being an unpublished thesis submitted in partial fulfilment of the requirements for the award of the Bachelor of Arts Degree in History, University of Port Harcourt, July 1986, pp. 44–45.

61 *See* Section 7 of the 1999 Constitution of the Federal Republic of Nigeria (FRN), entitled 'Local Government System'. General Babangida governed the FRN from August 27, 1985 to August 26, 1993.

62 Omusa Brown died due to the over-reaction of government, especially the Nigeria Police Force, invited by Shell Nigeria to quell the agitation by youngsters. Gun shots by the police into the midst of the agitating youths, killed Omusa Brown. His death increased youth restiveness which later resulted in the death of a leader of the BYF, Kurubo Barasua, on September 27, 1998.

Abacha to continue as a civilian head of state.[63] YEAA was a revolutionary youth movement which intensified youth activism in the Delta region. Most youngsters of the region that attended the 'two million man march', saw, for the first time, how the revenues from petroleum resources development in their communities had been used to build a sophisticated federal capital for Nigeria, while their own environment, citizens and future generations face great uncertainty due to the adverse effects of the resources development operations in their communities. The stage was thus set for accelerated youth restiveness in the entire Delta region including Bonny kingdom.[64]

To formally establish the BYF in order to properly regulate youth activities in Bonny kingdom, the king and chiefs had to liaise with the Bonny local government council. Through the leadership of the council, the Constitution of the BYF was drawn up, to duly direct and guide youth activities in the kingdom and LGA of Bonny.[65] Entitled 'The Constitution of the Bonny Youths Federation (BYF)',[66] it was passed into law on September 12, 2001, under the administration of the Honourable Rodaford Opuwari Long-John, chair of Bonny LGA.

Leaders of the BYF are usually invited to take part in decision-making, especially during 'Ibanise-Kobiri' and special sessions of the apex traditional ruling council. This assists the traditional ruling council and the local government in the maintenance of peace, order and good governance (GG) in Bonny kingdom and LGA.

4.2 (v) (e) Establishment of Community-based Organisations (CBOs) to Enhance Physical Development and Environmental Protection in the Kingdom

In 1997, the challenges generated by the adverse consequences of petroleum development in Bonny kingdom made some public-spirited citizens and traditional rulers propose the creation of two CBOs to help the apex traditional ruling council to cater for physical development and environmental protection in the kingdom. This proposal led to the establishment, by the council, of the Bonny Kingdom Development Committee (BKDC) and the Bonny Environment Consultants Committee (BECC).

---

63 *See* the publication by Olisa Agbakoba, SAN, entitled 'Chima Ubani: End of An Era', found at http://allafrica.com/stories/200510040562.html visited on 19/10/05. *See* the counter youth movement to the Daniel Kanu coordinated YEAA formed by the National Association of Nigerian Students (NANS), presided over by Sunday Ogunlana, tagged 'Youths Earnestly Against Abacha [YEAA]', in a publication of the All-Africa Students Union, entitled 'Ambassador Sunday Oludare Ogunlana', found at http://www.aasu.org.gh/SOO.htm visited on 19/10/05. *Also see* the ThisDay newspaper report entitled 'PDP Rejects Omisore, Annuls Daniel Kanu's Bid Ticket', found at http://www.thisdayonline.com/archive/2002/12/22/20021222news01.html visited on 19/10/05.

64 *See* E. J. Alagoa, *The Ijaw in the New Millennium, op cit,* p. 8.

65 The joint effort of the traditional and civil governments of Bonny which resulted in the Constitution of the BYF lasted from July 1995 to September 2001.

66 The Constitution refers to 'youth as the strength of a nation' in the following Ibani words 'Asawo na ereawo ani ama kuro'. *See* the front cover of 'The Constitution of the Bonny Youths Federation (BYF)'.

The BKDC mainly liaises with the MNOCs operating in Bonny kingdom, and all relevant arms and institutions of government, to ensure that Bonny derives benefits from petroleum development in the kingdom. The BECC operates to ensure the protection of the environment in the kingdom. As petroleum development operations are central to the roles and responsibilities of the BKDC and BECC, these two CBOs deal more with the MNOCs than with the government.

Apart from the BKDC and BECC, there are other community-based trade, professional and other civil society organisations actively working in the interest of Bonny kingdom. Prominent among these CBOs are the Bonny Improvement Association (BIA), Bonny Community Front (BCF), Bonny Gentlemen's League (BGL), Bonny Women Patriotic Movement (BWPM), National Council for Women Societies (NCWS) – Bonny LGA chapter, Bonny Island Foundation (BIF), Bonny Chamber of Commerce, Industry, Mines and Agriculture (BOCCIMA), Bonny Graduates Forum (BGF), Bonny Indigenous People's Federation (BIPF), National Youth Council of Nigeria (NYCN) – Bonny LGA chapter, and a host of others. These include the Community Development Committees (CDCs), Project Advisory Committees (PACs) and Project Monitoring Committees (PMCs) initiated by the MNOCs operating in the kingdom. These CBOs contribute to decision-making by generating ideas or suggestions to address certain problems and challenges of the kingdom and LGA.

4.3 WHEN INCLUSION LEADS TO EXCLUSION IN DECISION-MAKING PROCESSES OF PETROLEUM DEVELOPMENT IN THE KINGDOM

The preceding account on decision-making under the house system of governance in Bonny kingdom, and how the system is attempting to adapt to promote environmental democracy regarding petroleum development in the kingdom, is illustrative of what is taking place in other kingdoms, tribes and communities of the Delta region.[67] The scope of decision making in Bonny kingdom is gradually being enlarged to involve more citizens and citizen groups than what prevailed in the past. In spite of this enlargement, there are certain problems associated with environmental democracy regarding petroleum development operations in the kingdom. These include the total or partial exclusion of the chiefs and citizens of certain chieftaincy houses and communities directly affected by these operations, in the course of environmental democracy at the level of apex traditional governance, where collective decisions on these operations are usually taken.

67 The soft law principle of PP is hardening national legislations, provisions of international development agreements and pre-conditions of funding agencies and other bodies whose supports are essential to development projects, especially major natural resources development projects. *See* D. N. Zillman *et al* (eds), *Human Rights in Natural Resources Development: Public Participation in Sustainable Development of Mining and Energy Resources, op cit*, p. 11. *Also see* E. Bastida *et al* (eds), *International and Comparative Mineral Law and Policy: Trends and Prospects, op cit*, pp. 265–281, especially p. 265.

The notion of how (or when) inclusion leads to exclusion means how (or when) citizens or members of the public who are directly affected by, interested in, or concerned about development proposals are excluded outright or marginalised from taking part in the decision-making process of such proposals, when in fact the process requires their inclusion. Certain factors may give rise to exclusion or partial inclusion in environmental democracy.[68] These include how public authorities define or constitute members of the public that the authorities are to engage or involve in environmental decision-making.[69] Exclusion may also arise because of the type of representation provided by developers, as well as that provided by affected citizen groups, when authorities engage in decision-making.[70]

Exclusion in Bonny kingdom suggests how the interests of some of the directly affected chieftaincy houses or communities are being marginalised in the decision-making process and are thus deprived of benefits from the projects.[71] Consequently, some chieftaincy houses and house communities have had to complain and to seek redress in the courts of law. These include such houses as the Buoye-Omuso Brown major house, the Bristol-Alagbarigha royal house,[72] the Jumbo major house,[73] and communities as Finima, Oloama, Peterside (Ayama), and Kuruama. This account will, however, concentrate on the Buoye-Omuso Brown major house, and its domain – Finima community.

---

68 Inclusion may be expressed in any policy, statutory and regulatory frameworks, or state-practice associated with environmental democracy.

69 *See* M. Barnes *et al*, 'Constituting 'the Public' in Public Participation', Public Administration, Vol. 81, Issue 2, June 2003, pp. 379–399. *Also see* A. G. McFarlane, '*When Inclusion Leads to Exclusion: The Uncharted Terrain of Community Participation in Economic Development*', 66 Brook. L. Rev. 861, 2000/2001, pp. 861–932.

70 Ibid. *Also see* U. Buhler, 'Participation "with Justice and Dignity": Beyond "the New Tyranny"', Peace, Conflict and Development, Issue 1, June 2002, pp. 1-16, found at http://www.peacestudiesjournal.org.uk/docs/Participation.PDF visited on 21/07/04.

71 *See* the area of the homepage of The World Bank captioned 'Community Empowerment and Social Inclusion', found at http://web.worldbank.org/WBSITE/EXTERNAL/WBI/WBIPROGRAMS/CESILPROGRAM/0,,menuPK:459702~pagePK:64156143~piPK:64154155~theSitePK:459661,00.html visited on 15/08/08.

72 *See* the publication of the Tide newspaper report entitled 'Court Restrains SPDC Payment of Royalties in Bonny', dated July 27, 2001, pp. 1-2. In this case, the Bristol-Alagbarigha royal house sought for an injunctive order from the Federal High Court sitting in Port Harcourt, in Suit No. FHC/PH/CS/116/2001. On July 20, 2001, the court granted an injunctive order restraining Shell Nigeria (SPDC) *to desist from holding further discussions and/or arrangements with any person and group of persons concerning lease agreement for right of way or payment of compensation or damages or royalty or royal rights or homage to any person or group of persons in connection with or in relation to the exploitation, extraction or production of minerals in Bonny town, Kuruama/Kuruama-Iwoama communities of Bonny kingdom*, to the exclusion of the house (as the founder of said Bonny town [ie, Grand Bonny], Kuruama and Kurua-Iwoama communities).

73 These three chieftaincy houses petitioned to Shell Nigeria and the Corporate Affairs Commission (CAC), FCT, Abuja, regarding their exclusion by the AIC in the registration of the Shell Nigeria Bonny Terminal Integrated Project (BTIP) Trust with the CAC. Whereas the Buoye-Omuso Brown and Jumbo Major houses petitioned that they are the immediate landlords of the Shell Bonny BGOT land, the Bristol-Alagbarigha royal house petitioned as the founder of Bonny Island community where the BGOT is situated.

Finima community occupies a distinct but adjoining area to Grand Bonny Island. However, in the course of modernisation, especially with regard to the location of major MNOCs in this adjoining area, the exact boundary between Finima and Grand Bonny is becoming obscure and a subtle source of controversy in Bonny kingdom. Including the Captain Hart major house relatives of the Buoye-Omuso Brown major house, other people of Finima community and sister houses of the Buoye-Omuso Brown major house are the Attoni and Tobin minor houses.[74] The three giant or major MNOCs operating in the kingdom, namely MPN (a subsidiary of ExxonMobil), the NLNG, and Shell Nigeria, are located in the adjoining area between Bonny Island and Finima but more in Finima's domain. Citizens and chiefs of Finima, especially the Buoye-Omuso Brown house (Governor of Finima), should, therefore, be contributing prominently, along with other citizens, chiefs and the king, in the decision-making process of the apex traditional ruling council regarding the operations of the MNOCs at Finima, Bonny Island.[75] This is, however, not the case, even when several major decisions regarding these operations are taken at the apex traditional ruling council. Moreover, since the stool of the Buoye-Omuso Brown major house at the council has intermittently been vacant, the interests of this house and Finima at large are being marginalised, despite any presence of the chiefs of the Tobin and Attoni minor houses in the council. Although it is not the responsibility of the council to install chiefs, the suspension[76] from the council of one chief of the Buoye-Omuso Brown major house after another, has worsened the ability of the house to maintain its presence in the council. By and large, members of the Buoye-Omuso Brown major house need to reunite their house so as to enable them to participate interactively in ongoing environmental democracy regarding petroleum development in Bonny affecting Finima directly, in the overall interests of Finima[77] and

---

74 *See* the area of the Finima community website, captioned 'About Finima', *op cit*. Regarding the relationship of the Tobin minor house and the Buoye-Omuso Brown major house, *see* Suit No. PHC/174/72, *Between Chief Samuel O. Tobin & Ors vs. Chief Israel I. Brown & Ors*, (Unreported). A section of the Captain Hart major house also inhabits Finima due to its affinity with the Buoye-Omuso Brown major house.

75 *See* Sections 33 to 46 of the 1999 Constitution of the FRN regarding fundamental rights, especially the rights of freedom of association and freedom from discrimination expressed in Sections 40 and 42.

76 The chiefs of the house (as exemplified by the cases of Chief Idamiebi Brown and Chief Yibo Buowari Brown) were suspended at different times from the council, due to internal politics in Bonny. Regarding Chief Buowari Brown, the contention at the AIC for suspending him was the non-fulfilment of some aspects of custom during his presentation to the council on April 6, 1996, when King E. A. W. D. Pepple, was proclaimed. Due to the proclamation, the BCC waived some customary requirements as water regatta display in lieu of which requirements the Buoye-Omuso Brown house was asked to pay the sum of 638,000 Naira to the BCC. About a year later, the non-fulfilment of these requirements was the reason for the AIC's suspension of Chief Buowari-Brown in the controversy generated at the council by Finima community's protest to MPN concerning the impact on Finima of the dredging of the Bonny River. *See* the interim injunction order of the Honourable Justice E. N. T. Ebete in Suit No. PHC/154/97, between Elder Bara Brown & Ors. vs. King E. A. D. Pepple III & Ors, dated February 6, 1997.

77 *See* the report of the Human Rights Watch, entitled 'Nigeria: Niger Delta: No Democratic Dividend', vol. 14, No. 7 (A) dated October 2002, found at http://www.hrw.org/reports/2002/nigeria3/ particularly at http://www.hrw.org/reports/2002/nigeria3/nigerdelta.pdf visited on 31/12/06, p. 11.

the entire Bonny kingdom. Besides, the MNOCs are required not to take sides in communal disputes in ways that undermine the interests of individuals and chieftaincy house communities directly affected by their operations in the kingdom.[78]

4.4 CONCLUDING REMARKS ON CITIZENS' INVOLVEMENT IN TRADITIONAL GOVERNANCE AND ENVIRONMENTAL DECISION-MAKING IN BONNY KINGDOM

So far, this chapter has discussed the house system of administration in Bonny kingdom. It has briefly demonstrated the character, quality and challenges of political leadership exemplified by kingship in relation to the prevailing traditional power game over the three identified periods or phases of the house system, in the context of classical natural law, positive law and re-emerging natural law. These three periods include the system's initial period (punctuated by classical natural law) which prevailed from the reign of the founding fathers and premier kings (about the fourteenth century) up to the reign of King Awusa (in the eighteenth century). The second and third periods of the system (punctuated by positive law) started with the reign of King Perekule, while its ongoing period is punctuated by re-emerging natural law.

As a form of representative democracy, the Bonny house system involves citizens in decision-making through the direct involvement of their traditional rulers, namely, the king, chiefs, elders and other principal members and titled citizens. These rulers engage their respective chieftaincy house communities in decision-making. Thus, the system's first period was when decision-making was equitably taken among the founding kindred groups. This period was characterised by leadership, particularly kingship, based on virtue, responsibility and selfless service to the people. Hence, Alagbariya offered his daughter, Princess Osunju, as sacrifice to the fresh-water deities to achieve peace and good drinking water; Asimini offered his daughter, Princess Ogbolo, as sacrifice to the salt-water deities for the Bonny Sea to widen so as to enable Bonny to take advantage of the Atlantic trade; and Awusa entrusted kingship to Perekule during the seven-year Bonny and Andoni war in the kingdom's overall interest. The second period which started with King Perekule's assumption of kingship, witnessed the creation of chieftaincy houses in recognition of the significant achievements of deserving foster descendants, exemplified by Perekule's creation of the Nwaoju (Allison) major chieftaincy house in favour of Nwaoju (Allison). This period was characterised by positive law and its promotion of political might and other ominous fratricidal means by political

---

78 *See* the International Association of Oil & Gas Producers (OGP) report no. 2.85/322 of October 2002, entitled 'Key Questions in Managing Social Issues in Oil & Gas Projects', found at http://www.ipeca.org/downloads/social/impact_assessment.pdf visited on 31/12/06. *Also see* K. McPhail and A. Davy, *Integrating Social Concerns into Private Sector Decision-making: A Review of Corporate Practices in the Mining, Oil, and Gas Sectors*, Washington DC, The World Bank, 1998.

authorities which laid the foundation for undermining the natural rights and customary status of the duawaris. Besides, it was during this period (ie, the Atlantic trade era of inter-tribal wars) that the 'Ibanise Kobiri' evolved as a child of necessity (*ie*, as a 'war council'), and subsequently became the 'people's parliament' during the reign of King George Pepple. The third and ongoing period of the Bonny house system, characterised by the continuation[79] of the reign of the Perekule lineage over kingship, is witnessing the need for more citizens and citizen groups to be directly involved in decision-making. This period has seen the establishment of such bodies as titled citizens, including the elevation of the status of the 'Ibanise Kobiri' to 'the highest decision-making body' in the kingdom. Punctuated by the prevailing adverse effects of petroleum development, this period has also witnessed the apex traditional council's creation of the BYF, BECC and the BKDC which are playing key roles in the kingdom, in the ongoing worldwide trend of PP in energy and major natural resources development. This trend, based on transparency and accountability in decision-making, is compelling Bonny traditional rulers, especially the king and chiefs, to be more accountable in a way that the voice of the rulers and other representatives of the people would be the true voice and will of the people. Indeed, against the background of divide and rule undermining public good, there is a yearning for good and dynamic leadership influenced by re-emerging natural law principles of fair-play, equity and social justice, towards collective public good, SD and environmentally-sound and socially-equitable SCD in the kingdom.[80]

79 Since Perekule assumed kingship, Bereibibo (ie, Adumtaye Bereibibo, – a maternal grandson of Perekule through Princess Adumta and head of the Alagbariya house – of whom the author is a blood-descendant), is the only one not exclusively of the Perekule lineage that has assumed kingship. *See* E. J. Alagoa and A. Fombo, *A Chronicle of Grand Bonny, op cit*, p. 60. *Also see* the Deed of Installation of Chief (Aseme-Alabo) Edward Tamunosiminikarama Bereibibo Adapa Bristol-Alagbariya, dated 12/10/96.

80 *See* P. Orebech *et al*, *The Role of Customary Law in Sustainable Development*, Cambridge, Cambridge University Press, 2005, especially the preview and pp. 449–450. Social concerns, especially the concerns of directly affected, marginalised and vulnerable groups, deserve to be integrated into the decision-making processes of petroleum development in Bonny kingdom, in compliance with the prevailing national and especially international standards on environmental democracy. Thus, to enhance the performances of such CBOs as the BECC and BKDC, they should be registered under Part C of the Companies and Allied Matters Act (CAMA), Cap 59, Laws of the Federation of Nigeria (LFN), 1990 (as amended), to change their committee status to duly incorporated CBOs, in compliance with the provisions of Part C of the Act, captioned 'Incorporated Trustees'. *See* Section 590 of the Act captioned 'Incorporation of Trustees of Certain Communities, Bodies, and Associations'. *See* the Akassa Development Foundation (ADF), Opobo-Nkoro Community Development Foundation and the Eastern Obolo Community Development Foundation (EOCDF). *Also see* the area of the Pro-Natura International (Nigeria) homepage on 'Institutions and Innovations for Sustainable Development', found at http://www.pronatura-nigeria.org/ visited on 29/12/08. Besides, the BECC can be incorporated into the framework of the Bonny local government, based on Section 25 of the Federal Environmental Protection Agency (FEPA) Act, Vol. 6, LFN, 2004, captioned 'Establishment of State and Local Government Environmental Protection Bodies'.

4.5 DECISION-MAKING BASED ON THE SOCIAL SYSTEMS OF OTHER NIGER DELTA AREAS

In the context of social system, two categories of neighbouring tribes and community groups to the ancient Delta trading states may be identified. These are those located in the creeks and mangrove forest areas of the Delta region (such as the communities of proto-Ijawland and Andoni) and others who are located between the coastline and mainland (*eg*, upland area) of the region (such as the Abua and Eppie-Atissa communities).[81] The tribes or communal groups inhabiting the mainland (*ie*, upland) area of the region are distinguished by their egalitarian (*ie*, republican) forms of village democratic social systems, exemplified by that of the Ikwerre ethnic nationality. Between the core politically-centralised social systems of the ancient trading states (exemplified by the system of Bonny kingdom) and the village democratic or republican social systems (exemplified by the system of the Ikwerre ethnic nationality) is the relatively non-core (*ie*, partly centralised) social system of such communal groups or communities as those of Andoni.

4.5 (I) THE ANDONI (OBOLO) COASTAL DELTA COMMUNITIES: FROM EARLY SEGMENTARY RULE TO A RELATIVELY POLITICALLY-CENTRALISED TRADITIONAL SOCIAL SYSTEM

The people of Andoni (*ie*, Obolo) communities mainly originated from ancestral Ijawland, while some of them originated from such other places as Itsekiri and Urombi in the Cameroons.[82] Several ancient communities such as Egwede, Asarama, Ukwa, Unyeada, Ekede, Agana and Ilotombi make up the Andoni or Obolo pre-colonial nation, located in Rivers state, in the Eastern Delta neighbourhood of Bonny kingdom.[83] As indicated above, the social system of the Andoni communities may be considered as an example of traditional social systems in the Delta region which are relatively non-core politically-centralised (as distinct from the social systems of the region's trading states).[84]

---

81 Eppie-Atissa is, for instance, made up of diverse village-communities and thus known as 'the home of all'. Tradition provides that fifteen of these village-communities originated from Engenni, six from Ogbia, five from Ijo, and one from Abua Odual. *See* E. J. Alagoa, (ed.), *The Land and People of Bayelsa State: Central Niger Delta*, Port Harcourt, Onyoma Research, 1999, pp. 81–82 and 218.

82 *See* S. Eneyo, *The Andoni Monarchy: An Introduction to the Kingship Institution of the Andoni People*, Port Harcourt, Riverside Communications, 1991, p. 10–31.

83 *See* S. Eneyo, *The Andoni Monarchy: An Introduction to the Kingship Institution of the Andoni People, op cit*, p. 10. *Also see* N. C. Ejituwu, *A History of Obolo in the Niger Delta*, Oron, Mason, 1991, pp. 56–57.

84 *See* G. I. Jones, *The Trading States of the Oil Rivers: A Study of Political Development in Eastern Nigeria, op cit*. The social system of Andoni communities appeared to be segmentary because they had no kings as conceived and practised in the ancient trading states. Hence, S. Eneyo maintains that 'Andoni moved from a segmentary stage to a unified kingship'. He indicates that 'changes in this segmentary nature of the tribe came with trans-Atlantic trade'. This implies that 'the Andoni monarchy evolved in response to pressures of the Atlantic trade'. *See* S. Eneyo, *The Andoni Monarchy: An Introduction to the Kingship Institution of the Andoni People, op cit*, pp. xiii, 36, 45, and 146–149. *Also see* N. C. Ejituwu, *A History of Obolo in the Niger Delta, op cit*, pp. 56–57.

Andoni established a patrilineal system of traditional governance that appeared to be segmentary among its component politically-independent or partially-independent communities. The traditional heads of the various Andoni communities usually assume headship through their lineages which are traced to the respective founders of their communities. In this way, each Andoni community, ruled by the founding families or lineages known as 'egwe', had a lineal system of traditional governance. 'Egwe' is the major unit of the house ('otoko') which is also made up of component family units known as 'uwu'. When more than one 'egwe' trace their ancestry to a common progenitor, they form a single cluster in the ward known as 'Ibirinya'.[85]

The village-community or town traditional council presided over by the ultimate community head, 'Okan Ama', is thus comprised of the head of each 'Ibirinya' called 'Okan Ibirinya'. Based on social structure, decision-making in the Andoni traditional setting derives input from the various family units, wards, and the village or town council of traditional rulers, presided over by their respective village or town community heads. On this basis, the various Andoni community or town traditional governments interrelated among themselves as component units of the Obolo nation or tribe.[86]

4.5 (II) SIMILARITY OF THE ANDONI SOCIAL SYSTEM WITH THE SYSTEMS OF SUCH OTHER NON-CORE POLITICALLY-CENTRALISED AREAS AS KOLOKUMA

The segmentary social system of the Andoni communities is similar to that of some fresh water Central Niger Delta Ijaw communities such as those of Kolokuma and Akassa.[87] The Buguma Internal Affairs Society has the following to say about the segmentary social system of these ancestral Ijawlands:

> *The farming communities of the Central Delta had no central political authority but autonomous settlements with a stateless organisation. The highest political authority was the Amagulu or village assembly. The oldest man in the settlement became the Amakosowei (town elder), and president of the assembly. The execution of decisions rested, however, with a younger leader, the Ogulosowei (spokesman). There was usually a priest or Orukarowei at the village level, while the ibe or clan level had a high priest, pere.*

85 Although there appear to be distinguishing features between the terms 'otoko' and 'egwe', they are used interchangeably with little or no practical distinction in the Andoni traditional polity. *See* S. Eneyo, *The Andoni Monarchy: An Introduction to the Kingship Institution of the Andoni People, op cit,* pp. viii–xiii, and 34–49.

86 *See* S. Eneyo, *The Andoni Monarchy: An Introduction to the Kingship Institution of the Andoni People, op cit,* pp. 34–35.

87 *See* E. J. Alagoa (ed.), *The Land and People of Bayelsa State: Central Niger Delta, op cit,* p.197.

> *In these settlements, rights accrued to individuals through their membership of lineage groups, wari, which formed residential wards of the village, polo or idumu. For example, farm plots were inherited on this basis.*[88]

Decisions of the segmentary communal areas of the Delta region thus derive more input from their citizens. These decisions are prone to being fairer, more equitable and more socially justifiable among the citizens and component communities of these areas than the decisions of the ancient Delta trading states which were and still are characteristically prone to generate despotism in traditional rulership.

4.5 (III) TRADITIONAL SOCIAL SYSTEM OF THE IKWERRE ETHNIC NATIONALITY

The Ikwerre ethnic nationality, along with such other communities, group of communities or minority tribes as Ekpeye, Etche, Ogba, Egbema and Ndoni inhabit the mainland (otherwise called 'upland') areas of the Delta region in present day Rivers state, whose languages are broadly Igboid in nature.[89]

The traditional social system of the Ikwerre ethnic nationality is akin to the traditional social system of other mainland Delta communal groups. There are thus some basic units of the social system of the Ikwerre nationality, as determined by its environmental challenges and the socio-economic needs and aspirations of its people. In the Diobu area of Ikwerreland, for instance, these units are four, namely the nuclear family or household ('oro'), extended family ('onu-ama'), larger extended family unit comprising two or more family units, ('mbu'), and then the village ('rumu').[90] These units constitute the Ikwerre village democracy which distinguished each Ikwerre village-community as being excessively democratic[91] (ie, republican, non-politically-centralised or stateless).

By virtue of the Ikwerre village democracy, the head of each village-community, namely the eldest male of the founding/ruling family in the village, is recognised as the owner of the land ('nye-nwe-ali'). He presides over the Village Assembly, 'Rumu-Oha', comprised of the eldest male members of the component families of

---

88 *See* T. V. Erekosima *et al* (eds), *Hundred Years of Buguma History in Kalabari Culture: Buguma 1884–1894*, op *cit*, p. 161.

89 Ikwerre is comprised of such major communities as Isiopko, Rumuji, Emohua, Ogbakiri, Aluu, Igwuruta, Akpor, and Obio. *See* E. J. Alagoa and A. A. Derefaka (eds), *The Land and People of Rivers State: Eastern Niger Delta, op cit*, pp. 175–177.

90 For instance, the first of these units, 'oro', is comprised of a husband and his wife or wives, including their children. This is a welfarist unit which regulates the conduct of its members through the leadership of the father as assisted by his wife or wives. Besides, 'mbu' is comprised of members who descended from a common ancestor by blood or an ancestor who is a mythical character. *See* E. T. Bristol-Alagbariya *'Nigerian Federalism and the Component Nationalities'*, unpublished book.

91 *See* K. O. Dike, *Trade and Politics in the Niger Delta 1830–1885: An Introduction to the Economic and Political History of Nigeria, op cit*, p. 37.

the village-community.[92] Despite the existence of the 'nye-nwe-ali', power and authority vis-à-vis decision-making are diffused at all governance levels of the village-community in such a way that the peculiarity of the system was often improperly appreciated or even misunderstood by foreigners.[93] Based on this system, each Ikwerre village administered law and order in ways which are distinct from their neighbouring Delta communities or ethnic nationalities with different social systems (ie, those with semi-politically-centralised systems such as Andoni and the core politically-centralised systems as those of the ancient Delta trading states and the ancient Benin Empire).

Generally, under the various pre-colonial Niger Delta social systems, people benefited from their lands and natural resources. Royalties accrued to the founders and sections of communities from which natural resources were derived.[94]

4.5 (IV) CONCLUSION ON THE TRADITIONAL SOCIAL SYSTEMS OF THE ANCIENT KINGDOMS, TRIBES AND COMMUNITIES OF THE DELTA REGION

Three basic forms of traditional social systems may be identified in the Delta region. These are the core politically-centralised systems of the ancient Delta trading states and the ancient Benin/Edo Empire; the relatively non-core (ie, partly-centralised) systems of such communities and communal groups as Kolokuma, Andoni, Abua and Eppie-Atissa; and finally the village democratic or republican systems of such ethnic groups as the Ikwerre ethnic nationality. Whereas decision-making processes under the republican and partly-centralised social systems are designed to derive more input from the citizens and consequently to generate more transparent, equitable and socially justifiable decisions, those of the core-centralised systems may prove otherwise (ie, where genuine PP is undermined). These three social systems, distinct as they are, reveal that the people of each system were traditionally involved in decision-making processes, in ways that are peculiar and suitable to each system. The Delta communities are thus cultural or ethnic groups, which traditionally involve their citizens in decision-making, as may be the case with other Nigerian communities and ethnic groups whose traditional systems are not discussed in this book.

4.6 ADVENT OF BRITISH COLONIALISM AND DECISION-MAKING IN THE COLONIAL ERA

The pre-colonial era of the communities, kingdoms and tribes of the Delta region and those of other component organic entities of modern Nigeria was succeeded by the British colonial era. British colonialism was established by

92 *See* E. T. Bristol-Alagbariya *Nigerian Federalism and the Component Nationalities*, unpublished book.

93 Ibid.

94 Ibid. *See* D. N. Zillman *et al* (eds), [0]*Human Rights in Natural Resources Development: Public Participation in Sustainable Development of Mining and Energy Resources*, *op cit*, pp. 550–552.

virtue of the negative sovereignty treaty-making and treaty-implementation processes between the British imperial authority and the pre-colonial Nigerian organic entities such as the Delta trading states with which the British established direct relations.[95]

British colonialism in Nigeria came into force after the Berlin West African Conference of 1885 on the partition of Africa among the Western European powers that attended the Conference. Colonialism was imposed on the component pre-colonial entities of Nigeria through a process which politically-amalgamated these entities into one British colony. In this way, based on the negative sovereignty treaties signed with the trading states of the Delta region, the British created in 1885 the protectorate of the Niger Districts over the region. This protectorate was renamed the Oil Rivers Protectorate in 1889, and Niger Coast Protectorate in 1893.[96] It was in 1906 amalgamated with other British colonial possessions in Southern Nigeria to give birth to the Colony and Protectorate of Southern Nigeria. In 1914, the Colony and Protectorate of Southern Nigeria was further amalgamated with that of the North to form the Colony and Protectorate of Nigeria, otherwise called modern Nigeria. From 1914 to 1960, British colonialism reigned over modern Nigeria until political independence was granted to the country on October 1, 1960.

4.7 DECISION-MAKING IN THE DELTA REGION UNDER BRITISH COLONIALISM THROUGH THE ERA OF THE THREE REGIONS TO THE PERIOD OF NIGERIA'S POLITICAL INDEPENDENCE

As indicated in Chapter 2, regionalism in Nigeria thrived from 1939 (during the British colonial era) to 1967 in post-colonial Nigeria (during the Nigerian civil war, when General Gowon's military regime created the first twelve states of the federation, on May 27, 1967).[97] Whereas in pre-colonial Nigeria, the ordinary citizens of the organic entities in the Delta region were involved in the decision-making process of these entities, this changed during the colonial era. The policies, laws, regulations and administrative practices of the British colonial government were directed to achieve the imperial objectives of the British in Nigeria.[98] By so doing, British colonialism excluded the rulers and

95 *See* K. O. Dike, *Trade and Politics in the Niger Delta 1830–1885: An Introduction to the Economic and Political History of Nigeria, op cit*, pp. 65–80 and 217–218. *Also see* A. Oyebode, 'Treaties and the Colonial Enterprise: The Case of Nigeria', *op cit*, pp. 17–36.

96 *See* E. J. Alagoa and A. A. Derefaka (eds), *The Land and People of Rivers State: Eastern Niger Delta, op cit*, pp. 324–326.

97 *See* E. J. Alagoa and A. A. Derefaka (eds), *The Land and People of Rivers State: Eastern Niger Delta, op cit*, p. 333. *Also see* the publication compiled by N. Omoigui, entitled 'Gowon's broadcast to the Nation – May 27, 1967', found at http://www.dawodu.com/gowon.htm visited on 08/11/06.

98 *See* D. N. Zillman *et al* (eds), [0]*Human Rights in Natural Resources Development: Public Participation in Sustainable Development of Mining and Energy Resources, op cit*, pp. 552–553.

people of the Delta region from the decisions taken about their communities. For instance, the colonial government used the house system of governance in the Delta trading states to serve its interests alone.[99] It proclaimed the Native House Rule Ordinance in 1901 and enforced it, among other things, to derive forced labour and to collate taxes in the trading states through the chiefs and other traditional house heads of these states. Where there were no such traditional heads to administer the affairs of a chieftaincy house community, the government created warrant chiefs to achieve the needs of its indirect rule. Similarly, in the Delta hinterland communities, where the social system was different and there were no traditional rulers as there were in the city states, the government created warrant chiefs to impose its indirect rule.[100]

As a result, various traditional rulers and their people in the Delta trading states and neighbouring areas lost their natural self governance under British colonialism, as decision-making in these states estranged these rulers and their people. In the process, the rulers and other citizens who were considered to have erred or not complied with the decisions of the government were punished. This was the fate that befell such kings as Dappa Pepple of Bonny in 1854, Jaja of Opobo in 1887, Nana Olomu of Itsekiri in 1894, Koko of Nembe (Brass) in 1895, and Overanwen of Benin in 1897. Reactions against oppressive decision-making under British colonialism led to such mass resistance movements as the 1895 Akassa Raid spearheaded by King Koko, and the women's riot at Igwenga (popularly called the Aba women's riot) of 1929.[101]

Due to these and other resistance movements in the Delta region and other parts of Nigeria at the time, the colonial government introduced certain steps. In the Delta trading states, when the colonial government realised that the Native House Rule Ordinance was bringing people into close contact and cooperation with their rulers, the government felt threatened and revoked the Ordinance in 1915.[102] Ultimately, the government introduced constitutional developments towards decolonisation in Nigeria. The decolonisation process gave rise to the making of the Clifford Constitution of 1922, Richard Constitution in 1944, Macpherson Constitution of 1951, and the Lyttleton Constitution (otherwise known as the Federal Constitution) of 1954.[103] The agitation of the nationalists which gave rise to the decolonisation process resulted in the formation of three dominant political parties in the interests of

---

99 *See* E. J. Alagoa and A. A. Derefaka (eds), *The Land and People of Rivers State: Eastern Niger Delta, op cit*, p. 327.

100 *See* A. E. Afigbo, *The Warrant Chiefs: Indirect Rule in Southern Nigeria 1891–1929*, London, Longman, 1972, especially pp. xi–xii, 112–113, 249–318.

101 *See* Alagoa E. J. (ed.), *The Land and People of Bayelsa State: Central Niger Delta, op cit*, pp. 203–204. *Also see* N. A. I. Waribere, *King Jaja The Great of Opobo*, Port Harcourt, Rivers State Newspaper Corporation, 1991, pp. 50–57.

102 *See* E. J. Alagoa and A. A. Derefaka (eds), *The Land and People of Rivers State: Eastern Niger Delta, op cit*, p. 328.

103 *See* I. James, 'Road to Nigeria's Independence', sourced from the library area of the homepage of 'Citizens for Nigeria', found at http://www.citizensfornigeria.com/index.php?option=com_content&task=view&id=28&Itemid=43 visited on 31/12/06.

the three major ethnic groups and hence their domination over the politics and governance of the country. From this period, it became clear to the ethnic minorities that British colonialism was about to be replaced with the hegemonic reign of the three major ethnic groups. So, beginning from the 1953/54 Nigerian Independent Constitutional Conferences, the ethnic minorities began to struggle to overcome their domination by the major ethnic groups. The domination of the major ethnic groups over the minorities, however, persisted until after the regional era in the FRN.[104]

4.8 CONTINUED MARGINALISATION OF THE INTERESTS OF CITIZENS OF THE DELTA REGION IN POST-COLONIAL NIGERIA IN THE COURSE OF PETROLEUM DEVELOPMENT IN THE REGION

During British colonialism, the FRN was transformed into a satellite area of metropolitan Europe. As such, by the time the federation attained political Independence in 1960, it had become dependent on the global north.[105] Marginalisation of the ethnic minorities by the major ethnic groups continued after the colonial era because such measures as constitutional, fundamental rights and the due process of law, put in place by the departing colonial government so as to stabilise governance, are not being enforced and improved upon in the light of present realities in the interests of the minorities and poor citizens of the country. Successive military interventions in governance, such as that from 1966, and Nigeria's corrupt political leaders[106] led by those of the major ethnic groups, continued to worsen the plight and predicaments of the poor citizens

---

104 *See* R. T. Suberu, *Federalism and Ethnic Conflict in Nigeria*, Washington DC, United States Institute of Peace Press, 2001.

105 *See* W. Rodney, *How Europe Underdeveloped Africa*, London, Howard University Press, 1972.

106 *See* The Mining Mineral and Sustainable Development (MMSD) project report, entitled *Meeting Report on Corruption Issues in the Mining and Minerals Sector*, report No. 205, Berlin, September 7, 2001, (co-hosted by Transparency International – TI), found at http://www.iied.org/mmsd/mmsdpdfs/corruptionissuesreport.pdf visited on 15/09/05. *Also see* The MMSD project report entitled 'Report of the Managing Mineral Wealth Workshop: How Can the Mineral Sector Support the Development of Mineral Economies and Contribute to Building Sustainable Communities, Especially in the Poorest Countries?', London, August 15–17, 2001, found at http://www.natural-resources.org/minerals/CD/docs/mmsd/workshops/mmwworkshopreport.pdf visited on 15/09/05. *See* The Extractive Industries Transparency Initiative (EITI) homepage, found at http://www.eitransparency.org/, visited on 31/12/06. *See* the publication of the Associated Press, entitled 'Oil-producing Nations Rank High in Corruption', found at http://www.msnbc.msn.com/id6288647/print/1/displaymode/1098/ visited on 11/01/05. *See* The Transparency International (TI) Corruption Perceptions Index 2002, found at http://www.transparency.org/pressreleasesarchive/2002/dnld/cpi2002.pressrelease.en.pdf visited on 18/12/04. *Also see* the ThisDay newspaper report entitled 'Nigeria, 37 Others Reject Anti-Corruption Convention', found at http://www.thisdayonline.com/nview.php?id=55104&printer_friendly=1 visited on 09/08/2006.

and the ethnic minorities.[107] The resulting dichotomies, crises and conflicts mainly exist between the minorities and the majorities on one hand, and on the other hand between governments and the governed. These dichotomies, crises and conflicts mainly characterise the divide between the corrupt and privileged few and the majority of the citizens who are being marginalised, neglected and deprived of proper participation in decision-making processes regarding nation-building in the federation.

4.9 CONCLUSION

This chapter demonstrates how PP or PI in decision-making is an integral component of the social systems of the ancient kingdoms, tribes and communities of the Delta region. Broadly, these systems range from areas where decision-making offers opportunities for limited citizens' involvement based on representative democracy, to other areas where decision-making widely involves the generality of the citizens. Whereas the former category of decision-making is exemplified by the core centralised social system of the ancient Delta trading states such as Bonny kingdom, the latter is illustrated by the village democratic or republican social system of the Ikwerre ethnic nationality. Between these two types of social systems are the relatively non-core (*ie*, partly-centralised) social systems of such communities and communal groups as Kolokuma, Andoni, Abua and Eppie-Atissa. It may thus be asserted that the kingdoms, tribes and peoples of the Niger Delta are among the ethnic groups and peoples of Nigeria that involve their citizens in decision-making. The practice or system of citizens' involvement, however, differs within and among the various Delta areas as well as within and among the different communities, clans, kingdoms and tribes of Nigeria.

This chapter has also shown that British colonialism denied citizens of the Delta region and their traditional rulers, as well as those of other component tribes and ethnic groups of Nigeria, the opportunity to duly or properly participate in the affairs of the colonial government regarding their homelands and the country. As a result, the traditional rulers of the Delta region and their various social systems as well as those of other pre-colonial Nigerian entities were used by the British colonial government as mere tools to promote colonial enterprise in the country.

Marginalisation of the interests of Nigerian citizens under British colonialism adversely affected the ethnic minorities more than citizens of the

107 *See* the *Nigeria Report of the Commission Appointed to Enquire into the Fears of Minorities and the Means of Allaying Them* or *The Willink Commission Report* (hereinafter referred to as *The Willink Commission Report*), London, Her Majesty's Stationery Office (HMSO), 1958 (reprint by the Southern Minorities Movement, Port Harcourt, Nigeria, 1996), p. ii. *Also see* E. E. Osaghae, 'Ethnic Minorities and Federalism in Nigeria', African Affairs, Vol. 90, 1991, pp. 237–258. *See* the report of the International Crisis Group (ICG) on Nigeria, entitled 'Nigeria's Faltering Federal Experiment', Africa Report No. 119, October 25, 2006, found at http://www.crisisgroup.org/library/documents/africa/westafrica/119nigeriasfalteringfederalexperiment.pdf visited on 21/11/06.

major ethnic groups, especially in the course of regional governance which took place from 1939 to 1967, and thereafter. Governance vis-à-vis decision-making processes in post-colonial Nigeria continues to thrive in favour of the major ethnic groups against the interests of the ethnic minorities; as well as in favour of the political elite in government (*ie*, the governors), against the interest of the governed, especially the poor citizens being marginalised and impoverished in the course of nation-building.

Nearly five decades after the attainment of Nigeria's political independence, the marginalisation of the interests of the ethnic minorities, especially the interests of those of the oil-rich Delta region, continues. Thus, despite the findings of the Willink Commission, the Delta region has remained poor, more backward and grossly neglected in post-colonial Nigeria. The region and its people are yet to be properly integrated into the mainstream federalism and democracy in post-colonial Nigeria. This is evidenced by decision-making regarding petroleum development in the region, which prevails contrary to the globally-recognised need and widely-accepted principles of environmental democracy.

Among other things, the aspect of this chapter on Bonny kingdom demonstrates that its apex traditional ruling council encouraged widening of the scope of environmental democracy associated with petroleum development in the kingdom. Consequently, the apex traditional rulers are required to abide by the decision-making tenets of the house system in conformity with what the founding fathers and premier kings who established the system truly intended and practised, and even improve on these, based on contemporary realities. The objective should be to ensure that the voice of the traditional rulers and other representatives of the people truly serve as the voice of the people, so as to help achieve environmentally-sound and socially-equitable SCD and overall public good in the course of petroleum development in the kingdom.

PART D

Evolution of Formal Environmental Impact Assessment and Community Involvement in Petroleum Development in the Delta Region

CHAPTER 5

Commencement of Formal Environmental Impact Assessment (EIA) in Nigeria and Public Involvement in the EIA Process

5.1 INTRODUCTION

Part D begins with this chapter, which will discuss the evolution of formal (*ie*, statutory) Environmental Impact Assessment (EIA) in Nigeria and how it allows public involvement (PI). Considering that community involvement (CI) is an aspect of PI, the main aim of this part is to identify the forms and measures of CI in the course of petroleum development in the Delta region, and to demonstrate how the statutory EIA process provides for CI in petroleum development in the communities of the region.

Project level statutory EIA in Nigeria started in 1992, during the ongoing effort of the United Nations (UN) on the environment and development, designed to address the deterioration of the global environment arising from unsustainable practices of mankind. This effort of the UN caused the Federal Government of Nigeria (FGN) to take concrete steps aimed at addressing Nigeria's environmental problems. These problems include the adverse effects of petroleum resources development in the oil-rich Delta region which generated community crises hindering the smooth development of resources in the region.

5.2 PROPER MANAGEMENT OF THE ENVIRONMENT AND ENVIRONMENTAL IMPACT ASSESSMENT

The need to properly manage the adverse effects of socio-economic developments on the environment so as to enhance or achieve sustainable development (SD), has given rise to various international and national initiatives and actions. These include the development of environmental and developmental policies, laws, guidelines and regulations, and the use of other environmental management tools, processes and practices. EIA is one of these tools or processes devised to regulate the adverse effects of development proposals on the environment and society at large.

Broadly, the term 'environment' refers to the surroundings or circumstances in which humanity struggles to survive and thrive.[1] The environment includes the

---

1 *See* A. Gilpin, *Dictionary of Environmental Law*, Cheltenham, Edward Elgar, 2000, p. 92. *Also see* M. McCabe and B. Sadler (eds), *Environmental Impact Assessment Training Resource Manual*, Geneva, The Economic and Trade Branch, Division of Technology, Industry and Economics (DTIE), UNEP, 2002, p. 557.

physical conditions or influences under or surrounding which any individual or thing exists, lives, or develops. These conditions or influences may be categorised into three: (1) the combination of physical conditions that affect and influence the growth and development of an individual or community; (2) the social and cultural conditions that affect the nature of an individual or community; and (3) the surroundings of an inanimate object of intrinsic social value.[2] The human environment includes the abiotic factors of land, water, atmosphere, climate, sound, odours, and tastes, the biotic factors of other humans, fauna, flora, ecology, bacteria, and viruses, and all the social factors which make up the quality of life.[3] These are the combination of elements whose complex interrelationships make up the settings, surroundings and conditions of life of the individual and of society, as they are or as they are felt.[4] The meaning of the environment is usually defined in environmental legislations of countries.[5] For instance, the Federal Environmental Protection Agency (FEPA) Act, Laws of the Federation of Nigeria (LFN) 2004, defines the 'environment' as including 'water, air, land, and all plants and human beings or animals living therein and the interrelationships which exist among these or any of them'.[6] Also, section 61 of the EIA Act, LFN 2004 (the revised enactment of the EIA Decree, Decree No. 86 of 1992) hereinafter referred to as 'the EIA Act', or 'the EIA Act, LFN 2004', defines the word 'environment' as

> *the components of the Earth, and includes – (a) land, water, and air, including all layers of the atmosphere, (b) all organic and inorganic matter and living organisms, and (c) the interacting natural systems that include components referred to in paragraphs (a) and (b).*

Thus, as the UN Economic Commission for Europe (UNECE) put it, the environment is about what we do to where we live.[7]

The foregoing definitions and descriptions of the environment reveal that the concept has emerged from the environment as a parcel of things which render a stream of beneficial services and some disservices to people, though largely without price, and which take their place alongside the stream of services rendered by real income, commodities, houses, infrastructure, transport and other people.[8] The idea of a beneficial environment thus relates

---

2 A. Gilpin, *Environmental Impact Assessment (EIA): Cutting Edge for the Twenty-First Century*, Cambridge, Cambridge University Press, 1995, p.1.
3 Ibid.
4 *See* Gilpin A., *Dictionary of Environmental Law, op cit*, p. 92.
5 Ibid, 92–93.
6 *See* section 41 the FEPA Act, Laws of the Federation of Nigeria (LFN) 2004. The FEPA Act was originally promulgated as a Decree (*ie*, the FEPA Decree, Decree No. 58 of 1988) which was later amended by Decree No. 59 of 1992. Thus, before the 2004 revision (affecting several other laws referred to in this book), the FEPA Act was Cap. 131, LFN 1990 (as amended) by Decree No. 59 of 1992.
7 *See* the publication of the UNECE entitled *Protecting Our Environment: How Environmental Impact Assessment Can Help*, New York, UNECE, 1998, p.1.
8 *See* A. Gilpin, *Dictionary of Environmental Law, op cit*, p. 92.

to the quality of life[9] that mankind is exposed to due to the state of the environment.

Relative to the term 'environment', EIA (also considered as Environmental Assessment [EA] or simply as IA),[10] may be defined or described in certain related ways. Section 61 of the EIA Act, LFN 2004, defines EIA in respect of a project as 'an assessment of the environmental effects of the project that is conducted in accordance with this Act and any regulations made thereunder'. The United Nations Environment Programme (UNEP) defines EIA as 'the systematic, reproducible and interdisciplinary identification, prediction and evaluation, mitigation and management of impacts from a proposed development and its reasonable alternatives.[11] The International Association for Impact Assessment (IAIA) thus simply defines IA as 'the identification of future consequences of a current or proposed action'.[12]

EIA is a planning tool as well as a regulatory, administrative and policy-appraisal process for decision-making regarding development proposals. It determines the likely effects of development proposals on the physical environment and the relationship of these effects with other associated aspects of and factors in society.[13] It is a valuable means of promoting the integration of environmental and natural resources development issues into planning and programme implementation.[14] It is a systematic precautionary process of

---

9 Ibid.

10 *See* M. McCabe and B. Sadler (eds), *Studies of EIA Practice in Developing Countries: A Supplement to the UNEP Training Resource Manual*, Geneva, DTIE, UNEP, 2002, pp. v and 558.

11 Ibid, p. 307. *Also see* the European Commission (EC) publication entitled 'Guidelines for the Assessment of Indirect and Cumulative Impacts as well as Impact Interaction', found at http://europa.eu.int/comm/environment/eia-studies-and-reports/guidel.pdf visited on 24/07/04. *See* the area of the EC website on the environment, entitled 'Environmental Assessment', found at http://europa.eu.int/comm/environment/eia/home.htm visited on 24/07/04. *See* J. Glasson *et al*, *Introduction to Environmental Impact Assessment*, Abingdon, Routledge, 2005, pp.3–4. *See* R. E. Munn (ed), *Environmental Impact Assessment: Principles and Procedures*, New York, Wiley, 1979. *See* the publication on EIA entitled 'What is Environmental Impact Assessment?: Definition, Background, Future', found at http://kurs.slu.se/kurser/LP0336/16214.0203/1Whatis EnvironmentalImpactAssessment.PDF visited on 08/05/04. *See* A. Gilpin, *Environmental Impact Assessment(EIA): Cutting Edge for the Twenty-First Century, op cit*, pp. 4–5. *See* Article 3 of the European Council EIA Directive 85/337/EEC of June 27, 1985. *Also see* A. Gilpin *Dictionary of Environmental Law, op cit*, pp. 5, 92–93, and 96–97.

12 The impact or effect is the difference between what would happen with the action (*ie*, the implementation of the development proposal) and what would not happen without it. The concept of the 'environment' in IA evolved from an initial focus on its biophysical components to a wider concept which includes the physical-chemical, biological, visual, cultural and socio-economic components of the environment. *See* the IAIA publication entitled 'International Association for Impact Assessment: Impact Assessment and Project Appraisal', found at http://www.iaia.org/Members/Publications/Guidelines_ Principles%20of%20IA.PDF visited on 09/05/04. *Also see* the publication of the IAIA entitled 'What Is Impact Assessment?', found in the area of the IAIA homepage captioned 'Special Publications', at http://www.iaia.org/publicdocuments/special-publications/What%20is%20IA_web.pdf visited on 25/12/09.

13 *See* P. W. Birnie and A. Boyle, *Basic Documents on International Law and the Environment*, Oxford, New York, Oxford University Press, 1995, p.27.

14 *See* A. L. Clark and C. J. Johnson, *Mineral Resource Assessment for National Planning and Policy Formulation*, Tokyo, Resource System Institute East-West Centre, 1988. *Also see* E. O. A. Aina and N. O. Adedipe (eds), *The Petroleum Industry and the Environmental Impact in Nigeria*, Abuja, Federal Environmental Protection Agency (FEPA), 1996, p.114.

environmental management, protection and regulation involving the examination, analysis and assessment of planned activities with a view to ensuring environmentally-sound and socially-equitable SD.[15] Thus, in order not to be considered as a mere servant of socio-economic development and growth, as well as an avenue for resource degradation and ecological devastation,[16] the EIA process needs to extend through the entire life-cycle of proposals' development, from the conception (*ie*, designing) and planning stages to the decommissioning stage of the proposals.

5.3 DISTINCTION BETWEEN EIA AND STRATEGIC ENVIRONMENTAL ASSESSMENT (SEA)

SEA is distinct from EIA, as it extends the aims and principles of EA beyond the project level by considering other possible alternatives.[17] Whereas, EIA is undertaken for individual projects, SEA integrates environmental considerations into policies, plans and programmes (PPPs),[18] to ensure that development proposals are ecologically, economically and socially sound. Thus, P. Caratti *et al* define SEA in the following words:

> *SEA is a systematic, on-going process for evaluating, at the earliest appropriate stage of publicly accountable decision making, the environmental quality, and consequences, of alternative visions and development intentions incorporated in policy, planning, or programme initiatives, ensuring full integration of relevant biophysical, economic, social and political considerations.*[19]

SEA evaluates the environmental consequences of proposed PPPs, to ensure that they are 'included and addressed at the earliest possible stage of decision-making'. It ensures that environmental and other aspects of sustainability are considered in PPP making.[20] In relation to EIA, UNEP describes SEA in the following words:

---

15 *See* Z. Gao, 'Environmental Regulation of Oil and Gas Industries, Vol. 2, Centre for Energy, Petroleum & Mineral Law & Policy (CEPMLP) Internet Journal, 1997, found (in the CEPMLP area of the University of Dundee homepage) at http://www.dundee.ac.uk/cepmlp/journal/html/vol2/article2-11.html visited on 31/12/06.

16 *See* A. Gilpin, *Dictionary of Environmental Law, op cit*, p. 97.

17 *See* M. McCabe and B. Sadler (eds), *Environmental Impact Assessment Training Resource Manual, op cit*, p. 561.

18 *See* the area of the EC website entitled 'Environmental Assessment', found at http://europa.eu.int/comm/environment/eia/home.htm visited on 18/02/05.

19 *See* P. Caratti *et al* (eds), *Analysing Strategic Environmental Assessment: towards Better Decision-Making*, Cheltenham, Edward Elgar, 2004, p. 7.

20 *See* B. Sadler, 'Environmental Impact Assessment in a Changing World: Evaluating Practice to Improve Performance, Final Report of the International Study of the Effectiveness of Environmental Assessment', Canadian Environmental Assessment Agency (CEAA), Ottawa, Canada, found at http://www.iaia.org/Members/Publications/Guidelines_Principles%20of%20IA.PDF visited on 09/05/04. *Also see* T. B. Fischer, *Theory and Practice of Strategic Environmental Assessment: Towards A More Systematic Approach*, London, Earthscan, 2007, p. 2.

> *In practice, EIA is applied primarily to prevent or minimise the adverse effects of major development proposals such as a power station, dams and reservoirs, individual complexes, etc. This process is also used as a planning tool to promote sustainable development by integrating environmental considerations into a wide range of proposed actions. Most notably, Strategic Environmental Assessment (SEA) of policies and plans focuses on the highest levels of decision making, when better account can be taken of the environment in considering development alternatives and options. More limited forms of EIA can be used to ensure smaller scale projects, such as dredging activities, road realignment and upgrading and housing subdivisions, conform to appropriate environmental standards or site and design criteria. . . .*
>
> *The term Strategic Environmental Assessment is variously defined and understood. It refers to a formal process of systematic analysis of the environmental effects of development policies, plans, programmes and other proposed strategic actions. This process extends the aims and principles of EIA beyond the project level and when major alternatives are still open.*
>
> *SEA represents a proactive approach to integrating environmental considerations into the higher levels of decision making, consistent with the principles outlined in Agenda 21. Often, broader, less detailed assessments are required at these levels compared to project EIA . . . Both processes have common elements, but increasing modification to procedure and methodology are necessary when moving from the project to the policy level.*[21]

SEA is therefore as a systematic, objective-led, evidence-based, proactive and participatory decision-making support process for the formulation of sustainable PPPs, leading to improved governance. It is a good governance (GG) instrument which characterises a more holistic approach to decision-making in EA towards SD.[22]

---

21 *See* M. McCabe and B. Sadler (eds), *Environmental Impact Assessment Training Resource Manual, op cit*, pp. 105, 493 and 561.

22 *See* T. B. Fischer, *Theory and Practice of Strategic Environmental Assessment: Towards A More Systematic Approach, op cit*, p. 6. *Also see* M. McCabe and B. Sadler (eds), *Environmental Impact Assessment Training Resource Manual, op cit*, pp. 5, 6 and 8. *See* K. Ahmed and E. Sanchez-Triana (eds), *Strategic Environmental Assessment for Policies: An Instrument for Good Governance*, Washington DC, The World Bank, 2008. *See* P. Caratti *et al* (eds), *Analysing Strategic Environmental Assessment: towards Better Decision-Making, op cit. See* B. Dalal-Clayton and B. Sadler, *Strategic Environmental Assessment: A Sourcebook and Reference Guide to International Experience*, London, Earthscan, 2005, pp. 366-370.

5.4 ENVIRONMENT INITIATIVE OF THE NEW PARTNERSHIP FOR AFRICA'S DEVELOPMENT (NEPAD)

NEPAD is an arm of the African Union (AU). NEPAD is a vision and strategic framework for Africa's renewal[23] and is promoted by the determination of Africans to extricate themselves and their continent from the malaise of under-development, unequal relations, and exclusion in an increasingly globalising world.[24] With regard to the environment, NEPAD developed an Action Plan on the Environment Initiative (APEI).[25] This is a coherent, holistic, integrated, strategic and long-term programme intended to promote SD in African countries. It takes full consideration of economic growth, income distribution, poverty eradication, social equity and better governance, as integral parts of Africa's sustainability agenda. In the context of EA of development proposals, the NEPAD APEI stipulates the use of strategic forms of EA (*ie*, SEA) at all levels of decision-making, to enhance or to achieve SD.[26]

Based on the overall objectives of NEPAD, the cluster of programme areas and project activities of the Action Plan, to be implemented over an initial period of ten years, cover the following areas of priority sectors and cross-cutting issues: combating land degradation, drought and desertification, wetlands,[27] invasive

---

23 *See* the area of the NEPAD homepage captioned 'NEPAD in Brief', found at http://www.nepad.org/2005/files/inbrief.php visited on 31/03/06. The primary objectives of NEPAD are: (1) to eradicate poverty; (2) to place African countries, both individually and collectively, on a path of sustainable growth and development; (3) to halt the marginalisation of Africa in the globalisation process and enhance its full and beneficial integration into the global economy; and (4) to accelerate the empowerment of women.

24 *See* the publication entitled 'The New Partnership for Africa's Development (NEPAD), dated October, 2001, found at http://www.org.resources/ConferenceReportandOtherDocuments/nepad/NEPAD.htm visited on 05/09/03.

25 *See* the NEPAD 'Action Plan for the Environment Initiative', Midrand, NEPAD, 2003, found at http://www.unep.org/roa/Docs/pdf/nepad/Action_Plan_for_the_Environment_Initiative.pdf visited on 12/04/06.

26 *See* an article authored by A. Weaver *et al*, entitled 'NEPAD and Environmental Assessment', African Journal of Environmental Assessment and Management (AJEAM), Vol. 7, 1–3 November, 2003, found at http://www.ajeam_ragee.org/vol17p1t13.htm visited on 12/09/04. For the application of SEA in Africa, *see* the ECA report entitled *Review of the Application of Environmental Impact Assessment in Selected African Countries*,Addis Ababa, ECA, 2005, p. xvii.

27 The Wetland component of the NEPAD Environmental Initiative is intended to enhance the contribution of wetlands in the socio-economic development of Africa as well as the conservation and SD of Africa's wetland areas. This initiative of NEPAD, as being encouraged and supported by UNEP and Contracting Parties of the Ramsar Convention, is important and relevant to the ongoing initiative of the Niger Delta Environmental Survey (NDES) and other initiatives earmarked to protect the environment and conservation of the ecology and ecosystem of the Niger Delta. *See* the Agenda and the Discussion papers of the 'Ramsar/UNEP Workshop on Africa's Wetland Management Strategy', held at Valencia, Spain, November 18–26, 2002, found at http://www.ramsar.org/cop8/cop8_nepad_agenda_e.htm visited on 12/04/06. *Also see* Section 1 of the report of the 'Thematic Workshop on Wetlands for the Finalisation of the Environment Initiative of the New Partnership for Africa's Development' (NEPAD), held at Nairobi, Kenya, February 10–11, 2003, found at http://www.environment-directory.org/nepad/documents/action/wetlands/Report.doc visited on 12/04/06. *See* 'Section 2 of the Action on Managing Africa's Wetlands as

species, marine and coastal resources, cross-border conservation of natural resources and climate change and cross-cutting issues. The Plan builds upon the related problems of pollution, forests and plant genetic resources, fresh water, capacity-building and technology-transfer.[28] It emphasises collective and individual responsibilities and actions of African countries to adopt and implement it to maintain the integrity of the environment and to ensure sustainable use of their natural resources so as to achieve the SD goals stipulated by the UN.[29] On its part, the UN acknowledges NEPAD as the framework of its support for Africa. Thus, from the period of its conceptualisation, especially through its specialist organ and voice on the environment – the UNEP, the UN has been supporting and encouraging the NEPAD APIE to reduce poverty and enhance SD in Africa.[30]

To implement the NEPAD APEI in individual African countries, the role of the African Peer Review Mechanism (APRM), intended to enhance GG in the member-states of the African Union (AU), is important. The APRM, an instrument voluntarily acceded to by member-states of the AU, is an African self-monitoring mechanism. It constitutes an attempt by participating African countries to bring to an end the problems of poverty and political instability in their countries. A major problem of the APRM is that it is voluntary for African countries to use it to improve their municipal systems. This implies that the implementation of the APRM rests on the political will and commitment of each participating country to thrive.[31] Despite this, the NEPAD APEI is capable of propelling African countries such as Nigeria to embrace SEA, to

---

Revised by the Thematic Working Group on Wetlands', found at http://www.environment-directory.org/nepad/documents/action/wetlands/ActionPlan.doc visited on 12/04/06. *See* the 'National Planning Tool for the Implementation of the Ramsar Convention on Wetlands', found at http://www.ramsar.org/cop9/cop9_nr_slovenia.pdf visited on 12/04/06, pp. 14–17, especially p. 16 on CI in EIA. *Also see* the Conservation of Nature and Natural Resources (IUCN – World Conservation Union) homepage, found at http://www.iucn.org/about/index.cfm visited on 06/01/09; especially the area of this homepage regarding Africa. *Also see* I. Hewawasam, *Managing the Marine and Coastal Environment of Sub-Saharan Africa: Strategic Directions for Sustainable Development*, Washington DC, The World Bank, 2002.

28 *See* the NEPAD *Action Plan for the Environment Initiative, op cit*, pp. 12–13.

29 Ibid, pp. 10–13.

30 *See* the 'United Nations Declaration on the New Partnership for Africa's Development, 16 September, 2002', found in the area of the homepage of the Department of Foreign Affairs, Republic of South Africa, found at http://www.dfa.gov.za/docs/2002/nepad0916.htm visited on 31/03/06. *Also see* the report of the UNEP entitled 'UNEP Support to NEPAD: Period of Report: 2004–2005,' with the subtitle 'Support for the Implementation of the Action Plan on the Environment Initiative of NEPAD', found at http://www.un.org/africa/osaa/2005%20UN%20System%20support%20for%20NEPAD/UNEP.pdf visited on 31/03/06.

31 *See* the publication on the APRM (under the '38th Ordinary Session of the Assembly of Heads of State and Government of the Organisation of African Unity (AU), 8 July, 2002' entitled 'The New Partnership for Africa's Development (NEPAD): The African Peer Review Mechanism (APRM)', found (in the . . . area of the official website of the 'South African Chairmanship of the African Union', 2002, captioned '*Documents and Speeches*') at http://www.au2002.gov.za/docs/summit_council/aprm.pdf visited on 08/04/06.

improve their EA processes, especially those regarding major natural resources development,[32] so as to enhance SD in their municipalities.

5.5 EA AS A KEY TO SD (EMPHASISING SD IN THE COURSE OF PETROLEUM DEVELOPMENT IN THE NIGER DELTA)

Based on the continuing effort of the UN on the environment and development, the definition of SD by the World Commission on Environment and Development (WCED) has already been stated in Chapter 1. EA is recognised as a key support tool for SD[33] through the balancing of local socio-economic, political and ecological priorities associated with the development proposals on the environment, humanity and society at large. SD seeks to establish a path along which development can progress by enhancing people's quality of life and ensuring the viability of natural systems on which development depends.[34] It has been established that SD depends on protecting natural resources which serve as a foundation for further development in society.[35] Given that petroleum is a major natural resource, petroleum resources development in Nigeria should be regarded as a foundation for further development in the interest of the Delta and other oil-producing areas, as well as the entire country and citizens of Nigeria.

Africans (more than some people from other parts of the world), are attached to their ancestry, traditional homelands and the natural environment, as these enable them to relate their past to the present as well as towards the future. Thus, nature is significant in many African social systems, because it is viewed as the mother of sustenance.[36] The march to achieve SD in African countries may require initiatives to accelerate economic development, growth and self reliance; improve health, income and living conditions of the poor majority; ensure equitable and sustainable use of the environment and natural resources for the benefit of the present and future generations; and the enthronement of GG enhanced by transparency and accountability in decision-making.[37] Broadly

32 *See* the Vanguard newspaper report entitled 'Nigerian Communities Ask Court to Stop West African Gas Pipeline Project', found at http://www.vanguardngr.com/articles/2002/ south-west/sw130032004.html visited on 19/04/04. *Also see* the 39 *See* the *Niger Delta Human Development Report*, Garki-Abuja, UNDP Nigeria, 2006, especially pp. iii–iv, 1–8, 6, and 147–176.

33 *See* Principle 17 of the Rio Declaration on Environment and Development, 1992. *Also see* M. A. Bekhechi and J. Mercier, *The Legal and Regulatory Framework for Environmental Impact Assessments: A Study of Selected Countries in Sub-Saharan Africa*, Washington DC, The World Bank, 2002, p. 9. *See* P. Tarr, *Environmental Impact Assessment in Southern Africa*, Southern African Institute for Environmental Assessment (SAIEA), 2003, pp. 5 and 9.

34 *See* P. Tarr, *Environmental Impact Assessment in Southern Africa, op cit*, p. 5.

35 *See* the publication entitled 'Defining Impact Assessment', found (in the IA page connected to the website of Hari Srinivas, Coordinator Global Development Research Centre, GDRC) at http://www.gdrc.org/uem/iaia/define.html visited on 07/08/06. *Also see* the '*Environmental Impact Assessment Sectoral Guidelines for Oil and Gas Industry Projects*', Abuja, FEPA, 1995, p. ii.

36 *See* P. Tarr, *Environmental Impact Assessment in Southern Africa, op cit*, pp. 5 and 9.

37 Ibid, p. 5. *Also see* the inaugural address of the former UN Secretary General, Kofi Annan, at the UN 'International Conference on Governance for Sustainable Growth and Equity', held in New York, July, 28–30, 1997, found at http://magnet.undp.org/icg97/ANNAN.HTM visited on 29/09/06.

put, the strategy for SD aims to promote harmony among human beings and between humanity and nature.[38]

Consequently, a UN Development Programme (UNDP) SD report on the Niger Delta region entitled the *Niger Delta Human Development Report*, recommends a seven-point agenda for sustainable human development in the region. This agenda emphasises peace as the foundation; governance based on genuine democracy, participation and accountability; an improved and diversified economy as a lever of progress; promoting social inclusion; the environment as a basis for sustainability; an integrated approach to dealing with HIV & AIDS; and partnerships for SD. The *Niger Delta Human Development Report* proposes full participation in development so as to ensure that everyone has a stake in the region's future. While emphasising a peopled-centred SD framework for the region based on the key roles of GG and partnership, the report proposes:

> *using the region's vast oil wealth to create an environment that allows people to flourish, live valued and dignified lives, overcome poverty, enjoy a peaceful atmosphere and sustain their environment. The agenda is a peopled-centred and sustainable framework requiring the involvement of all stakeholders, including local, state and federal governments, the NDDC, the oil companies and the entire private sector, civil society organisations, the people of the region and development partners.*[39]

One of the key problems affecting SD of petroleum resources in the Delta region is that governments and the multinational oil and gas companies (MNOCs) appear to be paying lip service to SD. By so doing, the Federal Government (FG), other governments and government agencies exercising jurisdiction over the region and the MNOCs operating in the region are committed to SD more as a concept rather than a necessity.[40] While government authorities are

---

38 *See* the WCED report entitled *Our Common Future*, Oxford, Oxford University Press, 1987, p. 65. *Also see* Principle 1 of the Rio Declaration on Environment and Development, 1992.

39 *See* the *Niger Delta Human Development Report*, Garki-Abuja, UNDP Nigeria, 2006, especially pp. iii–iv, 1–8, 6, and 147–176.

40 For instance, regardless of such achievements of the Niger Delta Development Commission (NDDC) as the production of the Niger Delta regional development master plan, the SD functions of the NDDC expressed in section 7 (1) (b) and (j) of the NDDC Act, LFN 2004, are far from being realised. Accordingly, the Rivers State SD Agency (RSSDA) Law, No. 3, of 2007, is narrow in scope and fluid in terms of the responsibilities placed on the Agency regarding, for instance, how to monitor and assess its performances. Besides, the Executive Board of the Agency do not require representatives of the oil and gas companies, as provided in section 5 (1) (g) of the law, considering that these companies are making no financial contribution to the Agency. Consequently, this law requires thorough review, to achieve a well designed and comprehensive SD agenda. Otherwise, it may be repealed, as what is required primarily is for governance in Rivers state and other states of the Niger Delta and the entire Nigerian nation to operate at a strategic level of decision-making, so as to harmoniously integrate policies, plans and projects/programmes. Governance at this level must be enhanced by interactive citizens' involvement, especially the involvement of experts and integration of research findings in decision-making processes, in the march towards SD. In the process, governments, especially governors, of the Delta region must be

seen expressing SD as a tool, identified more towards promoting their political image and the image of their administrations, the MNOCs are professing SD more towards promoting their community or public relations profile in the course of their petroleum development operations in the region and other oil-producing areas. The concept or principle of SD is thus being diluted in practice.[41]

SD has become a pillar of the UN system and thus efforts of global nations are earmarked to achieve the Millennium Development Goals (MDGs) in their municipalities.[42] SD has become significant in the context of petroleum and other major natural resources development in resources-rich developing countries. The ways in which the dilution of SD initiatives may therefore be addressed include life-cycle EA of petroleum and other major natural resources development projects and the formal introduction of SEA in Nigeria.

5.6 COMMENCEMENT OF FORMAL EIA IN NIGERIA

Formal or statutory EIA started in the USA with the enactment of the United States National Environmental Policy Act (NEPA) in 1969.[43] As indicated above, statutory EIA was introduced in Nigeria by the FG's promulgation of

---

financially disciplined and honest in the use of the wealth accruing to them from petroleum development in their communities, if the region is to develop. Massive capacity-building and the engagement of experts are required in the region. Capacity-building of the region's teeming poor and less privileged youngsters in the areas of basic vocational skills is required, in order to sustainably employ them in their own best and the overall interests of society. Capacity-building of target professionals, including the leadership and bureaucracy, is also required in the effort to develop the Delta region and to achieve the MDGs in the region. The eight UN MDGs are designed to: 1). eradicate poverty and extreme hunger; 2). achieve universal primary education; 3). promote gender equality and empower women; 4). reduce child mortality; 5). improve maternal health; 6). combat HIV-AIDS, malaria and other diseases; 7). ensure environmental sustainability; and 8). develop global partnership. *See* the homepage of the MDGs, found at http://www.un.org/millenniumgoals/index.shtml visited on 24/03/09. *Also see* the ThisDay newspaper report entitled 'Our Expectations from S'South Summit', found at http://www.thisdayonline.com/nview.php?id=141568&printer_friendly=1 visited on 23/04/09. *See* the homepage of South-South Nigeria, found at http://www.southsouthnigeria.org/ and the area of this homepage captioned 'News', for other reports and the 'Communiqué Issued at the End of the First South-South Nigeria Economic Summit, held at the Tinapa Business Resort, Calabar, April 22–25, 2009', found at http://messagewiseng.org/index.php?option=com_content&view=article&id=46&Itemid=18&showall=1 both visited on 30/05/09.

41 *See* N. De Sadeleer, *Environmental Principles: From Political Slogans to Legal Rules*, Oxford, Oxford University Press, 2002. *Also see* N. Carter, *The Politics of the Environment: Ideas, Activism, Policy*, Cambridge, Cambridge University Press, 2004, p. 191. *See* J. N. Ehanmo, 'Is Sustainable Development Compatible with Economic Growth in an Oil Dominated Developing Economy? (A Case Study of Nigeria)', being a dissertation submitted to the CEPMLP, University of Dundee, in Partial Fulfilment for the Award of MSc Energy Studies with a Specialisation in Oil and Gas Economics, January, 2006, especially pp. 58–59.

42 *See* M. Fitzmaurice and M. Szuniewicz (eds), *Exploitation of Natural Resources in the 21st Century*, The Hague, Kluwer Law International, 2003, p. vii.

43 This Act, which came into force in January 1970, provides for the EIA of all proposed major federal development actions in the USA having the potential of 'significant' effect or impact on the quality of the human environment. *See* A. Gilpin, *Environmental Impact Assessment (EIA): Cutting Edge for the Twenty-First Century, op cit*, pp. 2 and 5–7.

the FEPA Decree (Decree No. 58 of 1988). This Decree established the FEPA as the government's agency to protect and develop the environment in Nigeria. It was amended in 1992, when the EIA Decree (Decree No. 86 of 1992)[44] was promulgated as the core legislation governing formal EIA in Nigeria. The FEPA and EIA Decrees were revised and updated in 2004.[45] The promulgation of these Decrees, followed by the various sectoral and procedural guidelines and policy initiatives prepared by the FEPA (also referred to as 'the Agency'), and the guidelines and standards prepared by such other related arms and institutions of the FG as the Department of Petroleum Resources (DPR), may be considered as aspects of the efforts of the FG to protect and develop the environment, conserve biodiversity and ensure SD of natural resources in the federation. These efforts of the government were influenced by external and internal factors. Whereas, the main external influence is the effort of the UN on the environment and development, the main internal factors are the crises occasioned by the adverse effects of petroleum development in the Delta region.[46]

The progressive effort of the UN that influenced the FGN is traceable to the UN conferences on the environment and development referred to as the SRJ process in Chapter 2, and the follow-up measures of these conferences aimed at achieving SD in the interest of mankind. Besides, the crises in the Delta region which resulted in the promulgation of the FEPA and EIA Decrees, gave rise to a series of seminars, symposia and other related forums which were convened by government institutions and departments as well as by some civil society[47] groups and individuals whose activism attracted government's attention. Coupled with the effort of the UN at the time, these forums triggered the FGN to take the necessary steps to address the deteriorating state of the environment in the region. Among these forums was the first of a series of seminars convened by government institutions in 1979 which focused on the 'Oil Industry and the Niger Delta Environment'. The main objective of these forums was to educate and enhance public awareness of the environmental aspects of the operations of the petroleum industry in the Delta region.

44 *See* the FEPA (Amendment) Decree (Decree No. 59 of 1992 – Cap. 59 LFN 1992), and the EIA Decree, Cap. 86 LFN 1992.

45 *See* The EIA and FEPA Acts, Vol. 6, LFN 2004.

46 *See* A. C. Kallhauge *et al, Global Challenges: Furthering the Multilateral Process for Sustainable Development*, Sheffield, Greenleaf, 2005. *Also see* E. O. A. Aina and N. O. Adedipe (eds), *The Petroleum Industry and the Environmental Impact in Nigeria, op cit*, especially pp. vii, 221–231.

47 These civil society groups included the Environmental Rights Action (ERA), Nigeria, Friends of the Earth (FoE), Nigeria, and the Rivers Chiefs and peoples Conference (RCPC) whose representatives made a presentation at the WCED. *See* D. M. J. Fubara (ed.), 'The Endangered Environment of the Niger Delta: An NGO Memorandum of the Rivers Chiefs and Peoples Conference, Port Harcourt, Nigeria, for the World Conference of Indigenous Peoples on Environment and Development and The United Nations Conference on Environment and Development, Rio de Janeiro, Brazil, 1992'. *Also see* the communiqué of the two-day seminar organised by the Centre for Petroleum, Environment and Development, CEPEEDS, on 'Essentials of Oil and Gas Law', between July 20–21, 1999, at the Federal Palace Hotel, Victoria Island, Lagos.

The forums were also designed to stimulate the operators of the petroleum industry to take positive steps against the adverse effects of their operations on the environment, people and communities of the region. The forums succeeded in enlightening and sensitising the Nigerian public to better appreciate the adverse effects of petroleum development operations in the Delta region. The MNOCs operating there were equally sensitised and persuaded to take proactive steps to protect and rehabilitate the environment in the course of their operational activities in the communities of the region.[48]

The immediate factor which triggered the FG to promulgate the FEPA Decree was the secret dumping of toxic waste incident by an Italian vessel at the Koko port in Delta state, within the Delta region, in May 1988. The Federal Military Government (FMG – led by General Ibrahim Babangida) reacted against this incident by introducing the Harmful Waste (Special Criminal Provisions, etc.) Decree, Decree No. 42 of 1988. This Decree was followed by the FMG's promulgation of the FEPA Decree in the same year, and subsequently the EIA Decree in 1992.[49]

Section 2 of the revised EIA Decree (*ie*, the EIA Act, LFN 2004) is entitled 'Restriction on Public or Private Project without Prior Consideration of the Environmental Impact'. Sub-section 1 of this section of the Act, provides that 'the public or private sector of the economy shall not undertake or embark on or authorise projects or activities without prior consideration, at an early stage, of their environmental effects'. Furthermore, section 2 (3) of the EIA Act, LFN 2004, provides that 'the criterion and procedure under this Act shall be used to determine whether an activity is likely to significantly affect the environment and is therefore subject to an environmental impact assessment'. On the other hand, section 2 (4) of the EIA Act, provides that

> *All agencies, institutions (whether public or private) except if exempted pursuant to this Act, shall before embarking on the proposed project apply in writing to the Agency, so that subject activities can be quickly and surely identified and environmental assessment applied as the activities are being planned.*[50]

Following these and other relevant provisions of the EIA Act, LFN 2004, and what obtains in practice, the EIA process in Nigeria distinguishes between three types of projects: mandatory study activities, cases where EIA is

---

48 *See* E. O. A. Aina and N. O. Adedipe (eds), *The Petroleum Industry and the Environmental Impact in Nigeria, op cit*, p. vii.
49 *See* M. T. Okorodudu-Fubara, *Law of Environmental Protection: Materials and Text*, Ibadan, Caltop, 1998, p. vii, 315, 729, 744 and 804.
50 Section 2 of the EIA Act, LFN 2004, is entitled 'Restriction on Public or Private Project without Prior Consideration of the Environmental Impact'.

required, and projects excluded from the EA process.[51] Mandatory study activities or projects[52] are those which by orientation have adverse effects on the environment. The list under this first type of projects include those relating to agriculture, airports, land reclamation, logging and conversion of forestry to other uses, housing schemes covering more than 50 hectares, large industrial developments, infrastructural developments, mining, petroleum developments, power generation and transportation projects. The second category refers to cases where EA is required as specified under Section 13, and the excluded projects provided for in Section 14 of the EIA Act.[53] Cases for which EIA is not mandatory require screening reports to determine their status as to whether they indicate potential adverse effects on the environment. If they do,

51 *See* the draft report of the Nigerian '*National Oil & Gas Policy*', prepared by the Bureau of Public Enterprises (BPE) through NEXANT, found at http://www.nexant.com/docs/Nexantfactssheet01.pdf visited on 28/09/04, p.10–4. *Also see* M. A. Bekhechi and J. Mercier, *The Legal and Regulatory Framework for Environmental Impact Assessments: A Study of Selected Countries in Sub-Saharan Africa, op cit*, pp. 104–106. *See* the publication by the EIA Centre, Planning and Landscape, University of Manchester, entitled 'Recent Developments in EIA: Environmental Assessment in Nigeria', found at http://www.art.man.ac.uk/EIA/n112nig.htm visited on 18/11/02.

52 *See* section 12 of the Act is captioned 'Mandatory Study List Not to be carried out without the Report of the Agency', while section 22 is captioned 'Mandatory Study'. Section 61, the interpretation section, provides that 'mandatory study' means an environmental assessment that is conducted pursuant to Section 17 and that includes a consideration of the factors set out in Section 11 of this Decree. Sections 11 and 17 are captioned 'Notification of potentially affected States or Local Government Area, etc.', and 'Factors Not Included', respectively. *Also see* Section 12 of the schedule of the Act entitled 'Mandatory Study Activities'. Activity/item 12 of the schedule specifies 'petroleum'. Petroleum activities are thus detailed as follows: '(a) Oil and gas fields development. (b) Construction of off-shore pipelines in excess of 50 kilometres in length. (c) Construction of oil and gas separation, processing, handling, and storage facilities. (d) Construction of oil refineries. (e) Construction of product depots for the storage of petrol, gas or diesel (excluding service stations) which are located within three kilometres of any commercial, industrial or residential areas and which have a combined storage capacity of 60, 000 barrels or more. *Also*, the *Environmental Impact Assessment Procedural Guidelines* prepared by FEPA, specifies 21 categories of mandatory study activities. Number 15 in this category is entitled 'petroleum', and the items thereof are as follows: (a) oil and gas field development; b) construction of off-shore, on-shore, and overland pipelines; c) construction of oil and gas separation, processing, handling and storage facilities; d) construction of oil refineries; e) construction of product depots for the storage of petrol, gas or diesel which are located within three kilometres of any commercial, industrial or residential areas and which has a combined storage capacity of 60,000 barrels or more; and f) petroleum refining. *See* the *Environmental Impact Assessment Procedural Guidelines*, Abuja, FEPA, 1995, pp. 8–11.

53 This section captioned 'excluded projects' provides as follows: *(1) An environmental assessment of a project shall be required where – (a) in the opinion of the Agency the project is in the list of projects which the President or the Council is of the opinion that the environmental effects of the project are likely to be minimal; (b) the project is to be carried out during national emergency for which temporary measures have been taken by the Government; (c) the project is to be carried out in response to circumstances that, in the opinion of the Agency, the project is in the interest of public health or safety. (2) For greater certainty, where the Federal, State or Local government exercises power or performs a duty or function for the purpose of enabling projects to be carried out, an environmental assessment may not be required if – (a) the project has been identified at the time the power is exercised or the duty or function is performed; and (b) the Federal, State, Local government has no power to exercise any duty or perform functions in relation to the projects after they have been identified*'.

they have to undergo the EIA mediation and review process, depending on the level or nature of adverse impacts involved.[54]

Before the establishment of FEPA, there were sectoral environmental regulations with various significant responsibilities relating to environmental protection and improvement, along with the existence of commissions with advisory capacity in environmental matters and environmental non-governmental organisations (NGOs). At the time, project proponents were seen mainly as advocates in or judges of their own matters.[55] This situation changed with the promulgation of the EIA Decree in 1992, when the EIA process became recognised as the key tool for avoiding or mitigating unacceptable impacts of development proposals so as to properly regulate these proposals in a way to promote SD in the country.[56]

The amendment of the FEPA Decree in 1992 (after the UNCED), enlarged the powers and responsibilities of the FEPA.[57] Thus, Section 5 of the FEPA Act, LFN 2004, captioned 'Functions of the Agency', provides that:

> *The Agency shall subject to this Act, have responsibility for the protection and development of the environment and biodiversity conservation and sustainable development of Nigeria's natural resources in general and environmental technology, including initiation of policy in relation to environmental research and technology; . . .*[58]

The Agency was also empowered to accomplish the following duties:

> *(a) prepare a comprehensive national policy for the protection of the environment and conservation of natural resources, including procedure for environmental impact assessment for all development projects.*
>
> *(b) prepare, in accordance with the National Policy on the Environment, periodic master plans for the development of environmental science and technology and advise the Federal Government on the financial requirements for the implementation of such plans.*[59]

---

54 *See* sections 18, 19, and 20 of the Decree, respectively captioned 'Screening', 'Declaration of Class Screening Report', and 'Use of Previously Conducted Screening'. *Also see* section 33 of the Act regarding 'Mediation', and sections 34 to 36 regarding review processes.

55 *See* E. O. A. Aina and N. O. Aladipe, *The Petroleum Industry and the Environmental Impact in Nigeria, op cit*, p. 117. *Also see* M. McCabe and B. Sadler (eds), *Studies of EIA Practice in Developing Countries: A Supplement to the UNEP Training Resource Manual, op cit*, p. 65.

56 *See* A. Gilpin, *Environmental Impact Assessment (EIA): Cutting Edge for the Twenty-First Century, op cit*, pp. 2–3.

57 *See* the FEPA Decree (as amended) by Decree No. 59 of 1992. It was being referred to as the FEPA Act, Cap. 131, LFN 1990, before it was revised in 2004.

58 *See* the entire provision of Section 5 of the FEPA Act, LFN 2004.

59 *See* Section 5(a) and (b) of the FEPA Act, LFN 2004. *Also see* sub-sections 5 (c), (d), (e) and (f) of the Act.

The Agency was further empowered to advise government on the national environmental policies and priorities, as well as on environmental protection, conservation of natural resources and SD, including scientific and technological activities affecting the environment and natural resources. It was empowered to advise the President on the utilisation of the national ecological fund for the protection of the environment, and to cooperate with federal and states ministries, local governments, statutory bodies and research agencies, as well as other similar bodies in other countries and international bodies, on the protection of the environment and conservation of natural resources. The Agency was also empowered to carry out other activities which are necessary or expedient for the full discharge of its functions and responsibilities under the Decree.[60] The same FG which promulgated and amended the FEPA Decree, made the FEPA the regulatory agency of the EIA process when the government promulgated the EIA Act. By virtue of the amendment of the FEPA Decree, the Agency became an integral part of the Presidency.[61]

Section 24 of the FEPA Act, LFN 2004 captioned 'Co-operation with the Ministry of Petroleum Resources', (MPR) requires the FEPA to cooperate with the Ministry (now renamed Ministry of Energy) along with the Ministry's technical arm, the Department of Petroleum Resources (DPR).[62] The DPR performs wide and varied functions as the regulator (*ie*, watchdog) of the petroleum industry.[63]

Besides, in 1999, in the course of performing its roles and responsibilities, FEPA prepared *Nigeria's National Agenda 21, the* revised *National Policy on the Environment*, the EIA procedural guidelines and the sectoral guidelines

---

60 *See* sub-sections c, d, e and f of Section 5 of the FEPA Act, LFN 2004.

61 *See* supplement to Official Gazette Ex No. 68 Vol.79, 23rd December, 1992 – Part A, The Federal Environmental Protection Agency (Amendment) Decree No. 59 of 2nd August, 1992.

62 *Also see* the function of the NDDC to 'tackle environmental and ecological problems' arising from oil exploration in the Niger Delta, expressed in Section 7 (1) (h) of the NDDC Act, LFN 2004.

63 Whereas, the Nigerian National Petroleum Corporation (NNPC) was the commercial arm of the MPR, its technical arm was the DPR. The DPR assumed the role of the Petroleum Inspectorate and the powers which the Minister may delegate to the Chief Executive of the Inspectorate under Section 10 of the NNPC Act, LFN 1990. Such functions of the DPR as the issuing of environmental guidelines and standards governing the petroleum industry overlaps with those of the FEPA whose responsibilities are now carried out by the Federal Ministry of Environment, Housing and Urban Development (FMEHUD) created by the FG in December, 2006. *See* The Tide newspaper report entitled 'FG Reduces Ministries to 19', found at http://www.thetidenews.com/article.aspx?qrDate=12/14/2006&qrTitle=FGreducesm. . . visited on 15/12/06. *See* the NNPC Act, Cap. 320 LFN 1990. *Also see* the area of the official website of the Centre for Petroleum Information (CPI), under 'Regulators', captioned 'Department of Petroleum Resources', found at http://www.petroinfonigeria.com/dpr.html visited on 31/12/06. *See* the homepage of the DPR, found at http://www.dprnigeria.com/home.htm visited on 05/11/02. *See* the article by B. Adaralegbe, entitled 'DPR's Regulatory Powers Are Suspect', found at http://www.thisdayonline.com/nview.php?id=47617 visited on 31/12/06. It is important to note that compliance with the DPR and other guidelines do not in any way preclude development project proponents from complying with other applicable regulations and laws of the FRN. *See* the *Environmental Impact Assessment Procedural Guidelines, op cit*, p.1. *Also see* the *Environmental Impact Assessment Sectoral Guidelines for Oil and Gas Industry Projects*, Abuja, FEPA, 1995, p. 1.

for all the major sectors of the Nigerian economy, including the *National Guidelines on Environmental Management System in Nigeria* and the *National Guidelines on Environmental Audit in Nigeria*. Regarding petroleum development, FEPA formulated the EIA sectoral guidelines for oil and gas industry projects.[64]

FEPA continued to exist until June 1999, when its roles and responsibilities were taken over by the Federal Ministry of Environment (FMEnve) established at the time by the FG headed by President Olusegun Obasanjo, so as to ensure that environmental issues receive priority attention in the federation. Thus, the FMEnve absorbed the FEPA and other ministries and departments of the government which were carrying out functions and responsibilities relating to the environment. In turn, based on further reorganisation of the ministries, parastatals and agencies of the FG by the same President Obasanjo's administration in December 2006, a new ministry, namely the Federal Ministry of Environment, Housing and Urban Development (FMEHUD), was established. FMEHUD integrated the roles and responsibilities of the former Ministry of Environment and the housing component of the former Ministry of Housing and Urban Development.[65]

Considering various efforts of the FG towards the development and protection of the environment, especially in the course of formal EIA, it may ordinarily appear that the environmental problems and challenges of Nigeria have been fully addressed. This is not the case, as there are several EIA problems and challenges which are yet to be addressed. These include certain misunderstandings, confusion and other associated administrative bottle-necks, overlapping

---

64 *See* the revised Nigeria's *National Policy on the Environment*, Abuja, FEPA, 1999; *Nigeria's National Agenda 21*, Abuja, FEPA, 1999; the *Environmental Impact Assessment Procedural Guidelines, op cit*, the *Environmental Impact Assessment Sectoral Guidelines for Oil and Gas Industry Projects, op cit*, the *National Guidelines for Environmental Management System in Nigeria*, Abuja, FEPA, 1999; and the *National Guidelines for Environmental Audit in Nigeria*, Abuja, FEPA, 1999. These guidelines do not preclude project proponents from complying with other applicable regulations and laws. *See* the *Environmental Impact Assessment Procedural Guideline, op cit*, p.1.

65 The FMEnve's eight departments (subdivided into one administrative department and seven technical departments) are namely the Departments of Planning Research & Statistics (PR&S), Drought and Desertification Amelioration (D&DA), Environmental Assessment (EA), Environmental Conservation (EC), Erosion and Flood Coastal Zone Management (EF&CZM), Forestry (F), Pollution Control and Environmental Health (PC&EH), National Parks Service (NPS) and the Forest Research Institute of Nigeria (FRIN). Under the FMEnve, the Department of Environmental Assessment (EA) consisted of three divisions. These are the Environmental Standards and Monitoring Division (responsible for the development and management of reference laboratories, analytical services and environmental studies), Oil and Gas Pollution Control division (charged with the responsibility of developing and enforcing guidelines and standards for the oil and gas industry) and the EIA division (responsible for EIA processing and guideline development). *See* the report entitled 'Nigeria Environmental Analysis Final Report' (prepared under UDASI Contract No. LAG-1-00-99-00013-00, Biodiversity and Sustainable Forestry [BIOFOR] Indefinite Quantity Contract [IQC], dated April 2002), found at http://www.dec.org/pdf_docs/PNACP627.pdf visited on 25/03/04. *Also see* the publication entitled 'Achievements of the Ministry of Environment', found at http://www.nopa.net/ Environment/messages/2.shtml visited on 02/04/05.

areas and duplication of functions, adversely affecting the smooth administration of the EIA of development proposals. These misunderstandings and other related administrative bottlenecks exist between the DPR and the successive EIA administrative and regulatory bodies (ie, the FEPA, FMEnve and the FMEHUD) as well as between these regulatory bodies and the respective state Environmental Protection Agencies (EPAs) and local government council Environmental Protection units.[66] Besides, although the FEPA no longer exist, the FEPA Act still governs Nigeria's environmental protection and development issues.

Thus, Nigeria's EIA process is still developing, especially in terms of its implementation measures relating to monitoring and follow-up measures and PI, particularly due to poor access to information in favour of the public affected by development proposals.[67] The process is basically seen as servant to socio-economic developments and decisions already made. Learning experiences of the process witnessed the taking over of EIA administration or regulatory process by the FMEnve in June 1999, and thereafter by the Federal Ministry of Environment and Housing in December 2006.[68] The frequent shifts or changes from one EIA regulatory institution to another have weakened the implementation of the EIA process. Also, government ministries lack the requisite independence and professional expertise of independent regulatory agencies, especially when these ministries are headed by politicians who are non-experts on the environment. Besides, whereas based on Section 2 (4) of the EIA Act, the EIA process was initiated to assess all development projects, several government development projects, including those of the Niger Delta Development Commission (NDDC), and those being embarked upon by private individuals and groups are mainly not being subjected to the process. To overcome some problems of the EIA implementation process, the need arises for adequate follow-up and monitoring processes, and well designed EMPs and environmental management systems (EMS) covering the life-cycle of development projects.[69]

There are certain gaps between the provisions of the EIA Decree (as revised and transformed into an Act) and the policy on the environment associated with it, including the provisions of the EIA procedural and sectoral guidelines

66 *See* M. McCabe and B. Sadler (eds), *Studies of EIA Practice in Developing Countries: A Supplement to the UNEP Training Resource Manual, op cit*, p. 73. *Also see Nigerian Petroleum Law and Practice*, Festac Town – Lagos, Jonia Ventures, 1997, p. 56.

67 *See* the Nigerian *National Oil & Gas Policy*, prepared by the BPE through NEXANT, *op cit*, pp. 10–12 and 10–13.

68 Before 1999, when EIA was under the administration of FEPA, regular EIA publications were being produced by the Agency. This and some other related landmark achievements such as the preparation of policies, sectoral and procedural guidelines are not being followed, such that the situation is deteriorating.

69 *See* A. Morrison-Saunders and J. Arts (eds), *Assessing Impact: Handbook of EIA and SEA Follow-up*, London, Earthscan, 2006. *See* the ECA report entitled *Review of the Application of Environmental Impact Assessment in Selected African Countries, op cit*, especially pp. xvi, 46, 73–74, and 80. *Also see* Section 40(d) of the EIA Act, LFN 2004, on EIA follow-up programme.

on one hand, and what exists in practice (in the implementation of the process) on the other. For instance, whereas the FEPA sectoral and procedural guidelines indicate that certain development proposals require full-life or project-life assessment,[70] formally institutionalised, comprehensive and integrated EA processes do not exist in Nigeria. Nigeria's EIA thus requires effective implementation regarding follow-up and monitoring processes, and well designed EMPs and environmental management systems (EMS) covering the life-cycle of development projects.[71] Besides, Nigeria needs to upgrade its EA process by formally introducing SEA[72] in compliance with the NEPAD APIE. Nigeria's EIA process also requires such improvements as providing for capacity-building[73] and access to information for the public directly affected by development proposals. Regarding PI generally, PI models such as guidelines and toolkits need to be developed.[74] In addition, regarding future directions of the EIA process[75] in Nigeria, it is the responsibility of the government to develop a stable and transparent regulatory environment and to strengthen governance to effectively embark on the process.[76] Accordingly, it is the responsibility of development project proponents such as MNOCs to comply with government

---

70 *See* the *Environmental Impact Assessment Procedural Guideline, op cit*, p. 1. *Also see* p. 19 of the 'Sub-sectoral Guidelines for Petroleum Refining' in the *Environmental Impact Assessment Sectoral Guidelines for Oil and Gas Industry Projects, op cit. See* the *Environmental Impact Assessment Sectoral Guidelines for Oil and Gas Industry Projects, op cit*, p. 15. *Also see* the *National Guidelines for Environmental Management System in Nigeria*, FEPA, *op cit*, p. 1. *See* pp. 7–16 of the 'Sub-Sectoral Guidelines for Petrochemicals' in the *Environmental Impact Assessment Sectoral Guidelines for Oil and Gas Industry Projects, op cit. See* the *National Guidelines for Environmental Management System in Nigeria, op cit*, p. ii.

71 *See* A. Morrison-Saunders and J. Arts (eds), *Assessing Impact: Handbook of EIA and SEA Follow-up*, London, Earthscan, 2006. *See* the ECA report entitled *Review of the Application of Environmental Impact Assessment in Selected African Countries, op cit*, especially pp. xvi, 46, 73–74, and 80. *Also see* Section 40(d) of the EIA Act, LFN 2004, on EIA follow-up programme. *See* R. Therivel, *Strategic Environmental Assessment in Action*, London, Earthscan, 2004, pp. 254–256.

72 *See* Runhaar H. and Driessen P. P. J., 'What Makes Strategic Environmental Assessment? Successful Environmental Assessment? The Role of Context in the Contribution of SEA to Decision-making', Impact Assessment and Project Appraisal, Vol. 25, No. 1, March 2007, pp. 2–14. *See also*, J. F. Benson *et al*, 'Round Table: What is the Alternative? Impact Assessment Tools and Sustainable Planning', Impact Assessment and Project Appraisal, Journal of the International Association for Impact Assessment, Fargo, IAIA Headquarters, Vol. 21, No. 4, December 2003, pp. 261–6.

73 *See* the communiqué of the IAIA 2003 Conference on 'Impact Assessment and Capacity Building in Developing Countries' entitled the 'Marrakech Declaration', found at www.iaia.org/ . . ./CP%20Peter%20Leonard%20Follow-up%20on%20Marrakech% 20Declaration%20and% 20Action%20Plan.pdf visited on 31/12/05. *Also see* IAIA's publication entitled 'IAIA – From Marrakech to Vancouver and Beyond: Follow-up Marrakech Declaration – Draft Plan of Action (2004–2008)'.

74 *See* the Calabash Participation Handbook, entitled 'One Stop Participation Guide: A Handbook for Public Participation in Environmental Assessment in Southern Africa', found at http://www.saiea.com/calabash/handbook/index.html visited on 14/07/05.

75 *See* M. McCabe and B. Sadler (eds), *Environmental Impact Assessment Training Resource Manual, op cit*, pp. 110–111, and 551.

76 *See* Articles 29 and 30 of the Johannesburg Declaration on SD, 2002.

regulatory requirements, and prevailing CSR standards in compliance with the ongoing effort of the UN on the environment and development, especially regarding the UN Global Compact and Article 27 of the Johannesburg Declaration on SD, 2002. These responsibilities deserve to be fulfilled, to achieve environmentally–sound and socially–equitable sustainable community development (SCD) in the course of petroleum development in the Delta region and other oil-producing areas of Nigeria.[77]

5.7 GENERIC STEPS OR STAGES OF THE ENVIRONMENTAL ASSESSMENT (EA) PROCESS

Although detailed steps in EIA vary from country to country or jurisdiction to jurisdiction, there are a number of generic steps which are followed internationally. Briefly, these are screening (which follows after proposal identification), scoping, impact analysis, mitigation and impact management, reporting, review, decision-making, implementation and follow-up.[78] Nigeria's EIA procedural guidelines identify the stages of development proposals from project conception to commissioning stages, while the EIA sectoral guidelines for oil and gas industry projects further provides for remediation plans after decommissioning, closure or abandonment.[79] It is obvious that the EIA process in Nigeria follows the generic steps or stages of EA which obtain internationally, and that although life-cycle IA[80] and SD of natural resources[81] are required, SEA does not (as indicated above) exist in the country in compliance with the NEPAD APIE.

---

77 *See* the publication of the IAIA by E. Au entitled 'Impact Assessment, Sound Business Operation, and Corporate Responsibility for Sustainable Development', the IAIA Business & Industry Series No. 1, Fargo, IAIA Headquarters, May 2002, pp. 1 and 6.

78 *See* M. McCabe and B. Sadler (eds), *Environmental Impact Assessment Training Resource Manual, op cit. Also see* the UNEP publication entitled *Environmental Impact Assessment Training Resource Manual: Overhead Transparency Masters*, designed and typeset by A. Charlton and M. McCabe (hereinafter called '*Environmental Impact Assessment Training Resource Manual: Overhead Transparency Masters*'), Geneva, DTIE, UNEP. *See* P. Tarr, *Environmental Impact Assessment in Southern Africa, op cit*, pp. 6–7.

79 *See* the *Environmental Impact Assessment Procedural Guidelines, op cit*, pp. 1–6. *Also see* the 'Sub-Sectoral Guidelines for Petroleum Refining' in the *Environmental Impact Assessment Sectoral Guidelines for Oil and Gas Industry Projects, op cit*, p.19. *See* P. Tarr, *Environmental Impact Assessment in Southern Africa, op cit*, p. 7. *See* the *Environmental Impact Assessment Procedural Guideline, op cit*, pp. 1–6, and 12, especially p. 1.

80 *See* the 'Sub-Sectoral Guidelines for Petrochemicals' in the *Environmental Impact Assessment Sectoral Guidelines for Oil and Gas Industry Projects, op cit*, p.7, item 4.0. *Also see* Nigeria's *National Policy on the Environment, op cit. See* the *National Guidelines for Environmental Management System in Nigeria*, Abuja, *op cit. See* the *National Guidelines for Environmental Audit in Nigeria, op cit.*

81 *See* section 5 FEPA Act, LFN 2004 (*ie*, Section 4 of the FEPA (Amendment) Decree, Cap. 59 of 1992, LFN). *Also see Nigeria's National Agenda 21, op cit.*

5.8 PUBLIC INVOLVEMENT (PI), ACCESS TO INFORMATION AND ACCESS TO JUSTICE IN EIA PROCESS

Following the discussion in Chapter 3, it is necessary to consider how the three landmark pillars or principles of the Aarhus Convention of 1998 (*ie*, access to information, PP in decision-making and access to justice in environmental matters) prevails in Nigeria's EIA process, especially regarding petroleum development projects in the Delta region.

5.8(i)(a) PI in EIA Process

Besides the definition and levels of PI expressed in Chapter 1,[82] the UNEP indicates the following regarding PI in the EIA process. That PI typically involves:

> *determining the scope of the proposal, identifying interested and [directly] affected public, selecting appropriate techniques, considering the relationship to decision making, providing feedback to stakeholders, [and in terms of] undertaking the analysis of stakeholders inputs, keeping to budget and time lines.*[83]

In the EIA process of many countries, PI means engaging the affected, concerned and interested members of the public in the decision-making process of the planning and implementation of development proposals likely to have significant adverse effects on the environment, themselves and their society.[84]

The arrangements made by countries for PI vary significantly, reflecting traditions and styles of their governments.[85] Different levels of PI may, however, be relevant to different phases of an IA process,[86] although PI typically occurs during the scoping and review stages of the EIA process as well as at any other stage requiring the involvement of the public who may be affected by, concerned

---

82 *See* the United Nations Economic and Social Commission for Asia and the Pacific (UNESCAP), *Public Involvement Guideline for Natural Resource Development Projects*, New York, UN, 1997, p. 4.

83 *See* M. McCabe and B. Sadler (eds), *Environmental Impact Assessment Training Resource Manual, op cit. Also see Environmental Impact Assessment Training Resource Manual: Overhead Transparency Masters, op cit*, topic 3, slide 6.

84 *See* A. Gilpin, *Environmental Impact Assessment (EIA): Cutting Edge for the Twenty-First Century, op cit*, p. 63.

85 *See* M. McCabe and B. Sadler (eds), *Environmental Impact Assessment Training Resource Manual, op cit*, p. 137.

86 *See* P. Andre *et al*, '2006 Public Participation: International Best Practice Principles', Special Publication Series No. 4, Fargo, International Association for Impact Assessment (IAIA), August 2006, pp. 1–3. In this context, including the objectives of PP, P. Andre *et al* identifies the principles of PP best practice which include the basic principles of participation, operational principles of participation and the development of guidelines. Generally, good or best practice in PP includes the need to develop participation models such as toolkits and guidelines.

about or interested in development proposals.[87] The UNEP thus outlines PI in key stages of the EIA process.[88] During screening, PI is required in terms of determining the need for, and level of, the process. During scoping, involvement is required to identify the key issues and alternatives of given development proposals. During the stage of impact analysis, PI is required to identify the significant impacts and the mitigation measures. During the EIA review process, PI is required in order to comment on or respond to the EIA report. At the stage of proposal implementation, PI is required to check the EIA monitoring and follow-up measures by the proponent within the framework of the EMS/EMP designed by the proponent.[89] Regarding natural resource development projects, the UN Economic and Social Commission for Asia and the Pacific (UNESCAP) outlines members of the public who should be involved and the degree or form of and manner in which they should be involved in the following words:

> *All interested parties (stakeholders) should be involved (including those who may unknowingly be affected);*
>
> *Stakeholder Analysis is a powerful tool which enables PI practitioners to distinguish between stakeholder groups, each of which is likely to require different levels of PI;*
>
> *All interested parties should be given a fair opportunity to influence the design and implementation of a project;*
>
> *Directly affected parties (often poor or marginalised communities) are the most difficult to identify and involve in the PI process.*[90]

PI is thus designed to take account of the views, concerns and values of stakeholders, to ensure that the decision-making process is equitable and fair, towards realising more informed choice and better environmental outcomes. Involvement builds confidence and trust among stakeholders and thereby helps to prevent or reduce misunderstandings and conflicts plaguing several major natural resources development projects in poor-rural communities of developing countries.[91] PI is crucial for identifying issues and offering information, such as that based on local knowledge, as well as establishing priorities

87 *See* the chart entitled 'Generalised EIA Process Flow Chart', found between pp. 100 and 101 as well as pp. 159–187 of the *Environmental Impact Assessment Training Resource Manual. See* M. McCabe and B. Sadler (eds), *Environmental Impact Assessment Training Resource Manual, op cit. Also see Environmental Impact Assessment Training Resource Manual: Overhead Transparency Masters, op cit*, topic 3, slides 1–10.

88 *See* M. McCabe and B. Sadler (eds), *Environmental Impact Assessment Training Resource Manual, op cit. Also see, Environmental Impact Assessment Training Resource Manual: Overhead Transparency Masters, op cit*, topic 3, slides 5 to 6.

89 Ibid, topic 3, slide 5. *Also see* the UNESCAP, *Public Involvement Guideline for Natural Resource Development Projects, op cit*, p. 9.

90 *See* the UNESCAP, *Public Involvement Guideline for Natural Resource Development Projects, op cit*, p. 9.

91 *See* I. Bannon and P. Collier (eds), *Natural Resources and Violent Conflict: Options and Actions*, Washington DC, The World Bank, 2003.

regarding the EIA of development proposals. Many development proposals have failed because local or traditional factors were not taken into account or because such proposals never had public acceptance or support.[92] Thus, regardless of compliance with technical issues, when well provided for and implemented, PI is able to achieve its objectives of influencing the design and implementation of development proposals through generating better or well-informed, transparent and accountable decisions.[93]

5.8(i)(b) Provisions of Nigeria's EIA Process on PI

Given that PI is a significant pillar or principle of EIA as well as a fundamental instrument for collective, sound and equitable decision-making towards SD,[94] the EIA process in Nigeria provides for it in the EIA legislation and procedural guidelines of the process. Section 1(c) of the EIA Act, LFN 2004, indicates some of the objectives of the EIA process thus:

> ... *to encourage the development of procedures for information exchange, notification and consultation between organs and persons when proposed activities are likely to have significant environmental effects on boundary or trans-state or on the environment of bordering towns and villages.*[95]

Other provisions of the EIA Act on PI include Section 7 entitled 'Opportunity for Comments by Certain Groups', which provides that:

> *Before the Agency gives a decision on an activity to which an environmental assessment has been produced, the Agency shall give opportunity to government agencies, members of the public, experts in any relevant discipline and interested groups to make comment on environmental impact assessment of the activity.*

This section of the Act which grants rights to citizens of the Delta region and other oil-producing communities to comment on proposed petroleum development projects taking place in their domains, may be regarded as one of the main provisions of PI in the Act. Consequently, Section 8 of the Act which is captioned 'Decision Not to be given until the Appropriate Period has Elapsed' provides that:

---

92 *See* M. McCabe and B. Sadler (eds), *Environmental Impact Assessment Training Resource Manual, op cit*, pp. 145–146. *Also see* the UNESCAP, *Public Involvement Guideline for Natural Resource Development Projects, op cit*, p. 8.

93 *See* M. McCabe and B. Sadler (eds), *Environmental Impact Assessment Training Resource Manual, op cit*, pp. 145–146. *Also see* the UNESCAP, *Public Involvement Guideline for Natural Resource Development Projects, op cit*, p. 8.

94 *See* Chapter 36 of Agenda 21 entitled 'Promoting Education, Public Awareness and Training'. *Also see* the revised Nigeria's *National Policy on the Environment, op cit*, p. 1.

95 *See* Section 1 of the EIA Act, LFN 2004, entitled 'goals and objectives of environmental impact assessment'.

> *The Agency shall not give a decision as to whether a proposed activity should be authorised or undertaken until appropriate period has elapsed to consider comments pursuant to sections 7 and 17 of this Act.*

Also, Section 9 of the Act, is captioned 'Decision on the Effect of an Environmental Impact Assessment to be in Writing'. Sub-section (3) of this section provides thus:

> *If no interested person or group requests for the report, it shall be the duty of the Agency to publish its decision in a manner by which members of the public or persons interested in the activity shall be notified.*

Other relevant sections of the Nigerian EIA Act indicating PI in the EIA process include Sections 15, 16, 21, 24, 25, 26, 29, 32, 33, 36, 37, 38, 40, 43, 45, and 55 of the EIA Act.[96] The provisions of these sections reflect how and when members of the public, including citizens of the oil-producing communities, may be involved in the EIA of development proposals affecting them and about which they are interested or concerned. Thus, the EIA Procedural Guidelines outline such environmental protection requirements as up to date public consultation, public interest, short term and long term (adverse and beneficial) effects, reversible and irreversible effects, secondary/induced effects, cumulative effects, magnitude and distribution of effects, history of similar projects, and contractual controls, to be incorporated in the design and any further environmental implications of development projects. Other environmental protection requirements outlined include the use of best practicable means and best practical environment in measuring the ability to mitigate adverse environmental consequences of projects. These Guidelines require proponents of development proposals to submit to the regulatory body proceedings of public consultations and stakeholder comments in a public forum.[97]

5.8(i)(c) PI in the EIA Process Emphasising Involvement in Petroleum Development Projects

Considering that access to information discussed here is integral to PI, it may be mentioned that in the EIA process of oil and gas development projects in

---

96 The captions of the above-stated sections of the EIA Act are as follows: – Section 15 of the EIA Act is captioned 'Environmental Assessment Process'; Section 16 'Factors for Consideration of a Review Panel'; Section 21 'Decision of the Agency'; Section 24 'Public Notice'; Section 25 'Decision of Council'; Section 26 'Referral to Council.', and Section 29 of the Act is captioned 'Referral by Council'. Also, Section 32 of the Act is captioned 'Determination of Parties'; Section 33 'Mediation'; Section 36 'Assessment by Review Panel'; Section 37 'Hearing of Witnesses'; Section 38 'Public Notice'; Section 40 'Design and Implementation'; Section 43 'Joint Panel Review'; Section 45 'Conditions', and Section 55 of the Act is captioned 'Public Registry'.

97 *See* the *Environmental Impact Assessment Procedural Guidelines, op cit*, p. 14. *Also see* the 'Environmental Impact Assessment Sub-Sectoral Guidelines for Petroleum Refining', in the *Environmental Impact Assessment Sectoral Guidelines for Oil and Gas Industry Projects, op cit*, p. 7. *Also see* the *National Guidelines on Environmental Management System in Nigeria, op cit*, p. 1.

Nigeria, CI typically takes place during scoping,[98] review sessions, and project follow-up and monitoring processes.[99] On this note, the proponents of the oil and gas development projects initiate community consultations during the EIA process of their projects by addressing members of the affected and interested communities. They do so by first holding consultations with such key entry points as government ministries, agencies and units associated with the development and protection of the environment, community leaders and other directly-affected, concerned or interested stakeholder-groups such as relevant professionals, experts and NGOs[100] in the communities to be affected by their proposals. Initial consultation with the communities may include the convening of 'open public forums' by project proponents so as to inform the entire affected, concerned and interested public about their development proposals.[101] While project proponents convene some community open forums during the conception and planning stages of their proposals, they convene others during the construction phase of the proposals.[102]

PI may also take place where members of the public take the initiative to write and file their comments with the EIA regulatory body, following the display of public notices at strategic places within the affected state capitals and Local Government Areas (LGAs) on mandatory draft EIA study reports of development proposals prepared by project proponents in compliance with the provisions of Section 24(2) of the EIA Act, LFN 2004.[103] With the filing of such

98 Scoping identifies the issues that are likely to be of significant effect by eliminating issues of little concern in the EIA process, so as to safeguard effort, time and money in the process. *See* M. McCabe and B. Sadler (eds), *Environmental Impact Assessment Training Resource Manual, op cit*, pp. 225–251, especially p. 225. Hence, scoping is a mandatory step of the EIA process. *See* the 'Accompanying Guidelines for SPDC EIA Process, SCOPING', SPDC 2004-0002711 Volume 11, March 2004.

99 *See* O. Dada and A. Adoki, 'Scoping in the Shell Petroleum Company (SPDC): The Experience with the Major Trunk line Replacement Project', found at 'Impact Assessment for Industrial Development: Whose Business is It?', Abstract Volume, International Association for Impact Assessment (IAIA) 24th Annual Conference, Fargo, IAIA, p. 35.

100 *See* Section 7 of the EIA Act, LFN 2004, captioned 'Opportunity for Comments by Certain Groups' *Also see* Section 11 of the EIA Act, LFN 2004, captioned 'Notification to Potentially Affected States and Local Government Areas etc.' *See* Part III, Section 25 of the FEPA Act, LFN 2004, captioned 'Establishment of State and Local Government Environmental Protection Bodies'.

101 Project proponents often exclude some affected groups from their open forums while sometimes succumbing to the desire of other affected more powerful and influential groups. *See* the 'Public and Communities Consultation Programme' of the Shell Nigeria Shell Bonny Terminal Integrated Project (BTIP), reported under the 'Baseline Socio-Economics' of the BTIP EIA report, entitled 'The Shell Petroleum Development Company of Nigeria Limited Operator of NNPC/Shell/Agip/Elf Joint Venture, Bonny Terminal Integrated Project (BTIP) Environmental Impact Assessment', Final Report', dated October 2002 (hereinafter called the 'BTIP EIA report'), pp. 17-1–17-52.

102 *See* the letter from of the Manager, AGG projects, V. O. Dania, dated December 3, 1998, to the paramount ruler of the Kuruama communities, Chief (Barrister) E. T. B. A. Bristol-Alagbariya, where Shell Nigeria apologised for excluding Kuruama communities during the open forum of its AGG projects and thus promised to remedy the exclusion during its needs assessment programme for the communities conducted during the construction phase of the projects.

103 *See* M. McCabe and B. Sadler (eds), *Studies of EIA Practice in Developing Countries: A Supplement to the UNEP Training Resource Manual, op cit*, p. 69.

written comments within the time provided in the Act, or a report considered as a source of information within the contemplation of Section 18(2) of the Act (ie, the screening process of development proposals not indicated in the mandatory study list), mediation or panel review sessions or implementation follow-up programmes of the proposal's EIA process may be convened. EIA mediation and review sessions may be convened by the regulatory body in response to the comments, objections, reports or any other relevant information filed by members of the public such as EIA experts and practitioners, communities, community-based organisations and public-spirited environmental NGOs.[104] Besides, CI may take place when project proponents take steps to comply with the Oil Pipelines Act, Cap. 338, LFN 1990, which involves convening public hearings otherwise referred to as public objection hearing sessions discussed in Chapter 6.

It may be noted that Nigeria's biggest MNOC, Shell Nigeria, has outlined five steps of the EIA process of petroleum development projects which are especially fitting for stakeholder involvement. These are:

> *Stakeholder identification and planning for engagement . . . includes the various options for engaging with the different parties and identified stakeholders individually or in groups. This is to sensitise and inform them about the project – in some cases multiple meetings may be necessary. Scoping at multi-stakeholder meeting or workshops – provides good opportunity to get stakeholder input in the scoping of the EIA. (However, a one-to-one engagement is essential in providing gainful information and gaining confidence).*
>
> *Regular – a regular line of contact with stakeholders is established for the purposes of obtaining views of stakeholders and dissemination of factual information about the project to stakeholders.*
>
> *Constructive interaction – as the EIA proceeds (using SIA [Social Impact Assessment] and PRA [Participatory Rural Appraisal] techniques) and the project takes more detailed shape, engagement moves into a more constructive and interactive phase. This includes discussion of issues, concerns of likely effects of impacts and how they could be mitigated or enhanced, and*
>
> *Disclosure of draft EIA – a key opportunity for stakeholders to see that their issues have been addressed, and to comment further if necessary before EIA findings are translated into formal approvals and contractual documents.*[105]

---

104 *See* Sections 21(b) (ii) and 33 and 34 of the EIA Act, LFN 2004. EIA review process may be an in-house review, panel review or public review process. *See* M. McCabe and B. Sadler (eds), *Studies of EIA Practice in Developing Countries: A Supplement to the UNEP Training Resource Manual, op cit*, p. 69.

105 *See* the Shell Nigeria 'Accompanying Guidelines for SPDC EIA Process: STAKEHOLDER IDENTIFICATION AND INVOLVEMENT', SPDC 2004-0002710 Volume 1, March 2004, p. 6.

The sixth identified step associated with stakeholder involvement in the EIA process is the implementation of a review and audit process of development projects, which is designed to ensure the continuity of proponents' stakeholder involvement.[106]

Shell Nigeria indicates that its objective of stakeholder involvement may change as different stages of the EIA are reached, in order to achieve the maximum result expected in the involvement process, as it considers that 'consultation is required but engagement of stakeholders is preferable'.[107] Hence, Shell states that PI or stakeholder consultation does not end with the grant of EIA approval for the projects. Shell Nigeria emphasises that its PI or stakeholder consultation process continues and progresses, along with its other projects development efforts, in the following respects. These are during *compensation for land take and damages, assurance that impacts are being mitigated and any new issue is recognised, delivery of any sustainable community development (SCD) projects that have been agreed as part of the licence to operate; and hiring of local workers, contractors and suppliers.*[108]

The above steps and measures outlined by Shell Nigeria may give the impression that stakeholder involvement during the implementation of its petroleum development proposals takes place throughout the life-cycle of the proposals. This is not the case, as Shell Nigeria and other MNOCs do not completely or fully comply with these steps or forms of involvement in the course of their operations in the oil-producing areas.[109] Hence, CI in the

106 Ibid, p. 14.

107 Ibid, p. 6.

108 Ibid, pp. 6 and 14–15. CI in the course of the making of compensation to oil producing communities by Shell Nigeria and other MNOCs is not as easy as Shell may want the public to believe. *See* the discontinued *Suit No. FHC/PH/CS/CS/116/2001*, between *Chief E. T. B. A. Bristol-Alagbariya & Ors vs. The Shell Petroleum Development Company Nigeria Limited (SPDC)*, after an *Ex Parte* order of the Federal High Court sitting in Port Harcourt dated, July 16, 2001, against the SPDC not to make compensation payment until the determination of the matter before the court was ignored by the SPDC. *Also see* The Tide newspaper report entitled 'Court Restrains SPDC Payment of Royalties in Bonny', dated July 27, 2001, pp. 1–2. *See* The Tide newspaper report entitled 'SPDC Pays N30m Compensation in Defiance of Court Order?' dated September 13, 2002, p. 17. *See* the 'SPDC Land Acquisition and Compensation Policy' expressed in the 'BTIP EIA report', *op cit*, pp. A-49 – A-50. *See* however the report of the Conflict Expert Group, WAC Global Services, on 'Peace and Security in the Niger Delta', dated December, 2003. *Also see* the publication of Bloomberg on this report, entitled 'Shell 'Feeds' Nigeria Conflict, May End Onshore Work', found at http://www:bloomberg.com/apps/news?pid=71000001&refer=europe&sid=aC3m6AF visited on 06/01/05. Including other Friends of the Earth (FoE) reports entitled 'The Other Shell Reports', *see* the reports entitled 'Behind the Shine: The Other Shell Report', and 'Lessons Not Learned: The Other Shell Report 2004', found at http://www.foe.co.uk/resource/reports/behindshine.pdf and http://www.foe.co.uk/resource/reports/lessonsnotlearned.pdf respectively, visited on 30/07/06. *Also see* the Christian Aid report on Shell entitled 'Behind the Mask: The Real Face of Corporate Social Responsibility', found at http://.www.christianaid.org.uk/indepth/0401csr/csr_behindthemask.pdf visited on 31/12/06.

109 *See* the article of J. Osai, entitled 'Shell as Agama Lizard', found at http://www.waado.org/Environment/OilCompanies/Shell-Communities/ShellsFalsePR.html visited on 22/03/04. 'Agama' Lizard is a kind of self-praising creature.

EIA process of petroleum development proposals is mainly consultative rather than being truly participatory, given that the process is not entirely open, transparent and equitable, so as to constitute interactive engagement and partnership with the communities.[110] Project proponents and regulatory authorities mainly listen to the concerns and other views of the communities without properly addressing these in the planning and implementation processes of development proposals. Thus, as reinforced by the discussion in Chapters 8 and 9, PI or CI in the EIA process of petroleum development projects in Nigeria is primarily aimed at enabling the MNOCs to secure statutory permits from the regulatory authorities,[111] contrary to accepted and widely-recognised international standards and practices regarding major natural resources development.[112]

---

110 *See* P. Andre *et al*, '2006 Public Participation: International Best Practice Principles', *op cit*, pp. 3–4.

111 However, in response to the protracted crises in the Nigerian Delta region, efforts are made by the MNOCs to acquire social licence from citizens and citizens' groups of the communities of the region in the course of CI. *See* the SPDC 'Environmental Impact Assessment (EIA) Process: STAKEHOLDERS' *GUIDE'*, Document No.: SPDC 2003-069, 2003, p. 1. The increasing need for the MNOCs to obtain social licence from the communities, due to the crises disrupting their operations in the communities, requires them to embark on interactive CI processes by truly engaging and partnering with the citizens and citizens' groups of the communities in the course of operating in the communities. *Further see*, the SPDC 'Environmental Impact Assessment (EIA) Process: STAKEHOLDERS' *GUIDE'*, *op cit*, pp. 5–6. *See* the SPDC Environmental Impact Assessment (EIA) Process: STAKEHOLDERS' GUIDE, *op cit*, pp.1–2.

112 *See* M. McCabe and B. Sadler (eds), *Environmental Impact Assessment Training Resource Manual*, *op cit*, p. 177. *Also see* Chapter 7 of The World Bank Environmental Assessment Sourcebook, 1999, entitled 'Community Involvement and the Role of Nongovernmental Organisations in Environmental Assessment', found in the area of The World Bank homepage on EA at, http://web.worldbank.org/WBSITE/EXTERNAL/TOPICS/ENVIRONMENT/EXTENVASS/0,,contentMDK:20282864~pagePK:148956~piPK:216618~theSitePK:407988,00.html visited on 17/01/09. *See* 'Environmental Assessment Sourcebook Update: Public Involvement in Environmental Assessment: Requirements, Opportunities and Issues', dated October 1993, No. 5, found at http://siteresources.worldbank.org/INTSAFEPOL/1142947-1118039086869/20526290/Update5PublicInvolvementInEARequirementsOpportunitiesAndIssuesOctober1993.pdf visited on 11/04/06. *Also see* The World Bank publication entitled 'Environmental and Social Management Framework for Local Empowerment and Environmental Management Program (LEEMP)' bearing The World Bank Project Identification No. P069892, found at http://www-wds.worldbank.org/external/default/WDSContentServer/IW3P/IB/2002/04/26/000094946_0204170415492/Rendered/PDF/multi0page.pdf visited on 06/05/06. *See* the area of The World Bank homepage the 'Country Assistance Strategy (CAS): Background on Country Assistance Strategy' on Nigeria, found at http://web.worldbank.org/WBSITE/EXTERNAL/COUNTRIES/AFRICAEXT/NIGERIAEXTN/0,,menuPK:368909~pagePK:141132~piPK:141105~theSitePK:368896,00.html visited on 06/05/06. *See* the 'Public Involvement Guideline' of the Oil and Gas Commission (OGC) of the Federal Republic of Canada, dated July, 2002, found at http://www.ogc.gov.bc.ca/documents/guidelines/revised-Public%20Inv.%20GL.pdf visited on 24/04/06, especially pp.3 and 7. *Also see* the United States of America (USA) Emergency Response and Community Right-to-Know Act, 1986. *See* the emergency response system required to be put in place by the International Association of Oil and Gas Producers (OGP) 'Guidelines on Minimum Standards for HSE Governance in Joint Ventures', found at http://www.ogp.org.uk/pubs/331.pdf visited on 30/03/06.

5.8(II) ACCESS TO INFORMATION IN THE COURSE OF COMMUNITY INVOLVEMENT IN THE EIA PROCESS OF PETROLEUM DEVELOPMENT PROJECTS IN THE DELTA REGION

As in Chapter 3, access to information (the first pillar of the Aarhus Convention) should have, but for the structure of this chapter, been discussed before PI, as it enhances the realisation of public participation (PP) and access to justice in environmental matters (the second and third pillars of the Convention). Access to information is required in the public interest (to empower the public) to realise effective PI in the EIA process[113] and to enforce access to justice in environmental matters. Thus, while discussing PI in the EIA process of petroleum development proposals in Nigeria, some aspects of access to information, such as the display of public notices described under Section 24 of the EIA Act, were indicated. The provisions of Sections 55–57 of the EIA Act also deal with access to information in the EIA process of development proposals. Other provisions of the Act on access to information include Sections 24 and 38 and sub-sections 9(2), (3) and (4), 18(2), 21(3) and 36(a) of the Act.[114]

Notwithstanding the provision of any other enactment of the Federal Republic of Nigeria (FRN), Section 55(5) of the EIA Act protects the Agency or any person acting on its behalf or under its direction or that of the Nigerian state or any of its agencies, from any civil or criminal proceedings, for the consequences that flow from disclosure of information made in good faith of any record or part of a record required by the Act or failure to give any notice if reasonable care is taken to give the required notice.[115] Section 55 of the EIA

113 *See* J. A. Connor and S. Kadel-Taras, *Community Visions, Community Solutions: Grantmaking for Comprehensive Impact*, Saint Paul, Amherst H. Wilder Foundation, 2003, pp. 29–32.

114 *See* the SPDC *Environmental Impact Assessment (EIA) Process: STAKEHOLDERS' GUIDE, op cit. Also see* the 'Accompanying Guidelines for SPDC EIA Process, STAKEHOLDER IDENTIFICATION AND INVOLVEMENT', SPDC 2004-0002710 Volume 1, March 2004, p. 5. *See* The World Bank Environmental Assessment EA Sourcebook, 1991, and the Bank's Operational Policies on EA (ie, OP 4.01 of January 1999), and the Bank's procedures on EA (*ie*, BP 4.01 of January, 1999), respectively found at http://web.worldbank.org/WBSITE/EXTERNAL/TOPICS/ENVIRONMENT/EXTENVASS/0,,menuPK:407994~pagePK:149018~piPK:149093~theSitePK:407988,00.html, and http://wbln0018.worldbank.org/Institutional/Manuals/OpManual.nsf/toc2/9367A2A9D9DAEED38525672C007D0972?OpenDocument as well as http://wbln0018.worldbank.org/Institutional/Manuals/OpManual.nsf/toc2/C4241D657823FD818525672C007D096E?OpenDocument all visited on 11/04/06. The World Bank Operational Directive (OD) 4.01 on Environmental Assessment and its successor documents insist on access to information in the public interest, as a prerequisite for meaningful PI. *Also see* G. Gibson, 'Community Information Needs: Access to Information through the Mining Life Cycle', found at http://www.iied.org/mmsd/mmsdpdfs/a2icommunityinfo.pdf visited on 15/09/05.

115 To improve the situation of access to information in Nigeria, better instances of other jurisdictions may be considered. *See* Section 32(2) of the 1996 Constitution of the Republic of South Africa. *Also see* the 'Public Involvement Guideline' of the Oil and Gas Commission (OGC) of the Federal Republic of Canada, dated July, 2002, *op cit. See* the relevant aspects of the 'Guide to the OECD Guidelines for Multinational Enterprises' Complaint Procedure: Lessons from Past NGO Complaint', published by the OECD Watch, found at http://www.oecdwatch.org/docs/OW_publication_guide%20complaint%20procedure.pdf visited on 14/07/06.

Act generally provides for the role of the public registry. The existence of this is significant in terms of facilitating public access to written, visual, aural and electronic or any other material-related form of information associated with EAs.[116] In spite of the provisions of this section of the EIA Act, no well-equipped registry as contemplated by the Act has been established;[117] although, before its responsibilities were taken over by the FMEnve in June, 1999, FEPA made some effort in this regard. This effort is yet to be sustained and improved upon, to enhance easy access to information by the public during PI or CI in the EIA process of petroleum development proposals in Nigeria.

As indicated in Chapter 1, following the degree of PI required for involvement to become participatory as expressed by UNESCAP, PI is at its best when involvement becomes part of the developer's state of mind, rather than simply following a set of guidelines or procedures; participation is the degree of PI required of most large-scale natural resources development projects.[118] This is so, considering that in practice, PI in the EIA process largely corresponds to consultation,[119] as evidenced by the findings of the case studies in Chapters 8 and 9; thus confirming the hypothesis of this book that CI in petroleum development in the Niger Delta is more consultative than being truly participatory.

5.8(III) ACCESS TO JUSTICE IN THE COURSE OF COMMUNITY INVOLVEMENT IN THE EIA OF PETROLEUM DEVELOPMENT PROJECTS IN THE DELTA REGION

As expressed in Chapter 3, access to justice in environmental matters (ie, the third pillar of the Aarhus Convention), underpins the first two pillars of the Convention to enforce administrative and judicial justice in environmental matters. Access to judicial justice or judicial review in the domestic legal

116 Sections 57–59 of the EIA Act, LFN 2004, on '*Access to Information*'. Environmental democracy and accountability in governance may be enhanced by the proposed freedom of information (FoI) Act of the FRN. *See* the ThisDay newspaper report entitled 'FOI: To Be or Not to Be', found at http://www.thisdayonline.com/nview.php?id=125933&printer_friendly=1 visited on 24/10/08. A good FoI Act is thus capable of promoting unfettered access to information by Nigeria's public, and transparency and accountability in the governance of the country. *See* the Promotion of Access to Information Act (PAIA), No. 2, 2000, Republic of South Africa.

117 *See* p. 10–3 of the Nigerian 'National Oil & Gas Policy', prepared by the BPE through NEXANT, *op cit*.

118 *See* the UNESCAP, *Public Involvement Guideline for Natural Resource Development Projects, op cit*, p. 4.

119 *See* M. McCabe and B. Sadler (eds), *Environmental Impact Assessment Training Resource Manual, op cit*, pp. 161 and 163. *Also see Environmental Impact Assessment Training Resource Manual: Overhead Transparency Masters, op cit*, topic 3, slides 1–10. *See* the aspect on 'Community Involvement and Development' of the 'Berlin 11 Guidelines for Mining and Sustainable Development' (prepared by the UN pursuant to its ongoing effort on environment and development), found at http://www.mineralresourcesforum.org/workshops/Berlin/docs/Guidelines.pdf visited on 03/03/06, pp. 29–32.

system also involves the direct enforcement of environmental laws.[120] This discourse on access to justice will be limited to access to judicial review through the regular courts of law in Nigeria. Hence, it is considered that the mediation and panel review EIA administrative regulatory processes have been discussed above under public or CI in Nigeria's EIA process.[121]

Regarding access to justice of the oil-producing communities to judicial review through the regular courts of law, it is important to state that there are relatively few cases decided by the superior courts of law, especially those regarding the EIA process of petroleum development projects. Besides the issue of the exclusive jurisdiction of the Federal High Courts (FHCs) expressed in Chapter 1, another reason for the relatively few cases decided by the superior courts of law is the weak or unequal status of the communities in relation to the other identified major stakeholders of the petroleum development business in Nigeria. Consequently, due to the unequal relations between the MNOCs and the communities, cases instituted by the community-interest groups against the MNOCs are either resolved without the satisfaction of the communities, or abandoned – where they are not discontinued by these groups due to the encumbrances of the regular court processes. Out-of-court settlement of community-interest cases through the intervention of government, aimed at promoting industrial peace and harmony in oil-producing areas, is another reason accounting for few community-interest cases against the MNOCs. However, the communities consider various government intervention measures as being partial and palliative in terms of addressing their grievances and concerns against the MNOCs, due to the Joint Venture (JV) relationship of the FG and the MNOCs.[122] Other factors which account for why environmental protection cases instituted in the law courts to enforce the EIA process of petroleum development projects in Nigeria are rarely determined by the courts include the financial cost involved, delay and other encumbrances of the judicial review process, including the fact that legal aid is rarely available if not unavailable to the citizens. Also, as expressed in Chapter 3, public interest-oriented groups or individuals instituting public

---

120 *See* the area of the UNECE homepage on the Aarhus Convention captioned 'General Features, Access to Information, Public Participation, Access to Justice', with the subtitle 'Contents of the Convention: Access to Justice', found at http://www.unece.org/env/pp/contentAJ.htm visited on 31/12/06. *Also see* S. Stec *et al*, *The Aarhus Convention: An Implementation Guide*, Geneva, The UNECE, 2000, pp. v, 6, and 125–36. *See* the area of the homepage of the UNECE on the Aarhus Convention captioned 'General Features, Access to Information, Public Participation, Access to Justice', with the subtitle 'Contents of the Convention: Access to Justice', *op cit*.

121 *See* sections 24–38 of the EIA Act, LFN 2004.

122 *See* J. G. Frynas, *Oil in Nigeria: Conflict and Litigation between Oil Companies and Village Communities*, Piscataway, Transaction, 1993, pp. 8, 59 and 98. *Also see* the publication of the NDDC entitled 'The Niger Delta Development Commission: A Brief History', found at http://www.nddconline.org/The_Niger_Delta/index.shtml visited on 22/12/04. *See* the article of the Daily Independent newspaper entitled 'Niger Delta and Tokenism' (dated September 17, 2006, found at http://www.independentonline.com/print.php?a=11306 visited on 17/09/06.

interest cases, including those on environmental protection, require proof of their 'standing' or *locus standi*.[123]

The rule or principle of *locus standi* is at the core of judicial review associated with the enforcement of the environmental rights of citizens or other public interest rights in Nigeria.[124] A remarkable case on petroleum development in this regard is *Oronto Douglas vs. The Shell Petroleum Development Company of Nigeria Limited & Ors* (1999).[125] The Plaintiff/Appellant in this case is an environmental activist and a native of the Delta region. The Defendants/Respondents are JV partners in petroleum development. At the time, the respondents were engaged in the construction of the base project of the NLNG plant complex in Finima, Bonny Island, in the Bonny kingdom, Bonny Local Government Area of Rivers state. The Plaintiff sought for an injunctive order at the FHC, Lagos, to restrain the respondents from continuing with the construction of their base project until an EIA had been completed in compliance with the provisions of the EIA Decree. The first to fourth Respondents filed notices of preliminary objection contending that the appellant lacked *locus standi* to maintain the action against them. On that ground, the trial court upheld the Respondents' preliminary objection and struck out the Appellant's claim. The court held that it was erroneous for the trial court to conclude that the Appellant had no standing solely on the face of the writ of summons, without looking at the statement of claim. The Court of Appeal

123 *See* A. Murdie, *Environmental Law and Citizen Action*, London, Earthscan, 1993, pp. 87–88. *Also see* the article authored by J. E. Bonine, entitled 'Broadening "Standing to Sue" for Citizen Enforcement', found at http://www.inece.org/5thvol2/bonine.pdf visited on 07/04/04. In Nigeria, in *Senator Adesanya v. The Federal Republic of Nigeria* (1981), (1979–1981) NSC, pp. 146 and 147; or (1981) 5SC, p. 65, the Supreme Court held *inter alia* that the law is now well settled that the plaintiff will have standing in the matter only if he has a special right or alternatively if he has sufficient interest or special interest in the performance if the duty sought to be enforced or when his interest is adversely affected, or is about to be adversely affected. What constitutes all of the above will depend on the fact of each case, and whether an interest is worthy of protection is a matter of judicial discretion. *Also see Akilu vs. Chief Gani Fawehinmi* (1989), 3SC, Pt.11, p.1; *Adefulu vs. Oyesile* (1989) 12 SC p. 43; and *Ugo vs. Obiekwe* (1989) 2 SC, Pt. 11, p. 41.

124 Ibid. *See* Sections 6 and 36, and including Section 46, of the 1999 Constitution of the FRN, entitled 'Judicial Powers', 'Right to Fair Hearing', and 'Special Jurisdiction of the High Court and Legal Aid', respectively. Section 46 of the Constitution which deals with the principle or doctrine of access to justice otherwise referred to as *locus standi* is very restrictive, and mainly applicable to criminal matters. Section 46 (1) of the Constitution provides that *Any person who alleges that any of the provision of this Chapter has been, is being or likely to be contravened in any State in relation to him may apply to a High Court in that State for redress*. The key operative words or phrase of this sub-section or provision of the Constitution is 'in relation to him'. These words have been interpreted as restricting the rights of private citizens to file law suits only when they are personally affected by the act or omission complained of. The restrictive nature of this Constitutional provision does not guarantee wide environmental justice rights in favour of citizens or citizens' groups in Nigeria as distinct to wide powers under the Bill of Rights (*ie*, Sections 7 to 39) of the Constitution of the Republic of South Africa, 1996. *See* D. N. Zillman *et al* (eds), *Human Rights in Natural Resources Development: Public Participation in Sustainable Development of Mining and Energy Resources*, New York, Oxford University, 2002, pp. 554–557, and 578–579.

125 2 NWLR, pp. 466–475, especially pp. 466–467.

unanimously upturned the decision of the trial court. The Court of Appeal held that it was speculative for the trial court to decide that the Appellant did not sustain any injury, and that such a finding was not supported by any material before the court. However, the retrial ordered by the Court of Appeal was not achieved mainly due to the financial encumbrances on the Appellant, including the delay associated with the judicial review process in Nigeria.

As explained in Chapter 1, the foregoing and other concerns and challenges of petroleum development are sources of frustration, neglect and misery which have since the 1990s given rise to the incessant crises aggravated by the resource control struggle in the Niger Delta. EA, as a significant pillar of SD, thus has a key role to play to achieve its desired goals such as managing conflict in the participatory process of the assessment,[126] so as to realise collective, sound and equitable decisions towards SD in the Delta and other regions of Nigeria. Indeed, the EA process cannot succeed without political commitment, public support and adequate resources'.[127] The impact of development projects requires understanding and working out benefits and costs incurred by every stakeholder group'.[128] These costs and benefits are what IA should address; for IA to do so effectively, PI requires to be encouraged to flourish, as an instrument for transparent and accountable decision-making towards SCD in oil-rich developing countries such as Nigeria.[129]

5.9 CONCLUDING REMARKS

This chapter reveals that EA was developed as a planning tool, decision-making process, and a precautionary instrument for analysing the effects of development proposals on the environment and other aspects of society associated with the environment, and to mitigate the potential adverse effects of these proposals, so as to enhance SD. Formal or statutory EIA commenced in Nigeria due to the ongoing effort of the UN on the environment and development, and the crises in the Delta region. PI is developing as a significant pillar of the EIA process, in a way to enhance the so far frosty relationship among the three major stakeholders identified in Chapter 1, so as to enhance sustainable petroleum development and SCD in the oil-producing areas. The effectiveness of the EIA process thus greatly depends on the level or degree of

---

126 *See* the Calabash Participation Handbook, entitled 'One Stop Participation Guide: A Handbook for Public Participation in Environmental Assessment in Southern Africa', *op cit*, Chapter 6 entitled 'Managing Conflict [in the course of PP in EA]'.

127 *See* M. McCabe and B. Sadler (eds), *Environmental Impact Assessment Training Resource Manual, op cit*, p. 145.

128 *See* the publication of the IFC entitled *Sustainable Investment*, London, Newsdesk Communications, 2004, p. 20.

129 *See* K. McPhail and A. Davy, *Integrating Social Concerns into Private Sector Decision making: A Review of Corporate Practices in the Mining, Oil, and Gas Sectors*, Washington DC, The World Bank, 1998.

involvement of stakeholders, in a way that the views and concerns of the affected, interested and concerned public could be properly integrated into the decision-making process of development proposals, including petroleum and other major natural resources development proposals.

So far, based on the prevailing state of affairs in Nigeria, there is inadequate access to information, PP is lacking and access to justice is far from being achieved in the course of CI in petroleum development in the oil-producing areas. In the process, as indicated in Chapter 1 and reinforced in Chapters 8 and 9, petroleum development projects' proponents and regulatory authorities mainly listen to the concerns expressed by the oil-producing communities during the EIA process of development projects, without properly addressing these concerns in the course of the implementation of the projects. Thus, there is a gap between the provisions of the EIA Act on PI and what obtains in actual practice. This chapter also identifies certain gaps between the provisions of the EIA Act and the policies on SD which includes the SD elements expressed in *Nigeria's National Agenda 21*, and EIA procedural and sectoral guidelines, especially the sectoral guidelines for oil and gas industry projects. There is a need to improve upon the existing development project level EIA process, in order to bridge these gaps.

The improvement required indicates the need for effectiveness and to expand the scope of the EA process. Among other things, the effectiveness of the process requires human and financial resources as well as commitment on the part of practitioners, and the commitment and independence of the government regulatory authorities. These authorities and civil society groups need to develop good practice participation models such as guidelines and toolkits for PI in EAs, in order to boost CI in the course of major natural resources development proposals. There is also need for government's commitment in terms of harmonising the regulatory and other relevant institutional arrangements between the federal level and other levels of government (*ie,* the state and local governments) affected by development proposals. The effectiveness of the EA process requires the employment of sustainability indicators, including effective monitoring and follow-up measures built into the EMPs/EMSs of development proposals. Properly institutionalised and regulated life-cycle EIA of development projects is needed as well as upgrading of the existing project level EIA process by institutionalising SEA in compliance with the NEPAD APEI. By and large, government is required to improve on petroleum and other major natural resources development operations in Nigeria by developing a stable and transparent environmental regulatory framework in compliance with Article 29 of the Johannesburg Declaration on SD, 2002. The MNOCs operating in Nigeria are required to complement the effort of the government by enhancing the evolution of equitable and sustainable oil-producing communities in the country, in compliance with Article 27 of the Johannesburg Declaration on SD, 2002. The MNOCs, whose responsibility it is to subject their projects to the EIA process have the duty to complement the statutory permit issued by the regulatory authority for each of their projects with social licence from the oil-producing communities, so as to successfully implement these projects in the communities. Improved environmental protection and social performance measures, which include the MNOCs obtaining social licence from the oil-producing communities, have the potential to enhance environmentally-sound and socially-equitable SCD in the Delta region and other oil-producing areas, so as to help bring an end to, or at least minimise, the protracted community crises disrupting petroleum resources development in the FRN.

CHAPTER 6

Forms and Measures of Community Involvement in Petroleum Development in the Delta Region

6.1 INTRODUCTION

Chapter 5 demonstrates how the terms Environmental Impact Assessment (EIA), Environmental Assessment (EA), or Impact Assessment (IA) may be used interchangeably. It demonstrates IA as a significant pillar of sustainable development (SD), and PI as a significant pillar of the IA process as well as a fundamental instrument for collective, sound and equitable decision-making. PI thus becomes evident as a tool for building mutual trust, understanding and confidence among stakeholders, towards SD. This chapter will discuss other forms and measures of community involvement (CI) in petroleum development in the Niger Delta.

6.2 OTHER FORMS AND MEASURES OF COMMUNITY INVOLVEMENT IN PETROLEUM DEVELOPMENT IN THE DELTA REGION

Apart from EA, other forms of CI which takes place in the course of petroleum development in the Delta region include public objection hearings associated with town or country planning, and Nigeria's economic self-reliance policy. This policy, which has been in existence since the attainment of Nigeria's political independence, now particularly applies to her petroleum industry as a means of achieving equity participation in the context of the Nigerian (Local) Content Policy (NCP) in the industry.

6.2(I) PUBLIC OBJECTION HEARINGS REGARDING PETROLEUM PIPELINE PROJECTS AND THE GOVERNMENT TOWN/COUNTRY PLANNING SYSTEM IN RIVERS STATE (WITHIN THE DELTA REGION)

In the Nigerian Delta region, public objection hearings are organised for and on behalf of the Minister of Petroleum Resources by the Ministries of Land of the states in the region where petroleum development projects are taking place. These hearings and development-planning[1] verification sessions

1 *See* A. L. Clark and C. J. Johnson, *Mineral Resource Assessment for National planning and Policy Formulation*, Tokyo, Resource System Institute East-West Centre, 1988, regarding the need to extract mineral resources in conformity with national planning.

associated with land-use systems are statutorily provided for, in order to grant permits to survey the routes of pipelines in petroleum development projects, pipelines of the derivatives or components of crude petroleum and any other process of transportation connected with petroleum trade or operations in Nigeria.[2] These hearings are open to the affected public, and sometimes include other concerned and/or interested members of the public and citizens of the country. They constitute opportunities for those who are affected by, concerned with or interested in the subject matter of such hearings, to register and present their objections and substantiate them with relevant documentary or other forms of evidence.

Public hearings are required to be organised by impartial tribunals. These tribunals may be appointed by government for the purpose of specific hearings which may also be organised by government's administrative bodies acting within the ambit of their duties and responsibilities.[3] A. Gilpin, while discussing the procedures of public hearings and enquiries, points out that these hearings involve a spectrum of proceedings and principles that may be adopted, in public enquiry or hearing, into environmental issues and developmental applications. These occasions may include court-like procedures with evidence taken on oath, in which process cross-examination may be permitted without formal rules of admitting evidence. Submissions at public hearings are accepted verbally or in writing. Where submissions or the entire proceedings of public hearings are accepted in written form, admissions, answers to questions, and closing addresses may also be in writing.[4]

Regarding the public objection hearings organised by the Land Ministries of the states in the Niger Delta region and other oil-producing areas, Section 6 of the Oil Pipelines Act, 1990, is instructive. It stipulates that the holder of a permit to survey (*ie*, project proponent) wishing to 'enter any building or upon any enclosed court or garden attached to any building . . . [n]or any cultivated land' is required to give at least 14 days' notice to the owners, occupiers or persons in charge of any lands of its intention to do so (as expressed in subsection 6[1]), before entering into lands on the authority of Section 5. Prior assent of the owners or occupiers or other persons in charge of land is also

---

2 *See* sub-sections 4(1) and 11(2) of the Oil Pipelines Act, 1956, Cap. 338 Laws of the Federation of Nigeria (LFN), 1990. The Oil Pipelines Act (revised in 2004) came into being due to the necessity of transporting crude oil to long distances, for example, from the wellhead to the point of exportation/export terminals. *See* L. Atsegbua, 'The Development and Acquisition of Oil Licences and Leases in Nigeria', OPEC Review, Vol. 23, No. 1, March 1999, p. 58.

3 *See* the Black's *Law Dictionary*, St. Paul, West, 2004, pp. 737–738, and 1266.

4 Other procedural aspects of public hearings and enquiries concerning development proposals exist in other jurisdiction outside Nigeria. These include the Local Public Inquiry which takes place as a form of public environmental planning, under the housing, development and environmental legislation in Britain. *See* A. Gilpin, *Dictionary of Environmental Law*, Cheltenham, Edward Elgar, 2000, pp. 252–253.

required before a licensee or proponent takes possession or uses such lands as venerated land expressed in Section 15(1) (a) and (b) of the Act.[5]

Any person whose land or interest may be injuriously affected by the grant of a licence under the Oil Pipelines Act, is given an opportunity to lodge verbal[6] or written objection at a specified address, usually to administrative officers having responsibility in such area or to such other officers as the Minister may direct, as stipulated in Section 8(2) of the Act.[7] The notice of objection shall state the interest of the objector and the grounds for objection, as specified in Section 9(1) of the Act.[8]

---

5 Whereas, prior consent is required under Section 6(1), under Section 6(2) of the Act, prior assent of the owners, occupiers or persons in charge, is required, including compensation by proponents for unnecessary damage to any land entered upon and any buildings, crops or profitable trees thereon, as expressed in Section 6(3) of the Act. As stipulated in Section 6(4), in the event of dispute on the amount of compensation or to whom same may be paid, compensation shall be made in accordance with the provisions of Part IV of the Act. Section 15 of the Act captioned 'Restrictions upon Entry in Respect of Venerated Land', requires the prior assent of the owners or occupiers or persons in charge of certain public facilities as burial grounds or cemeteries, or lands containing any grave, grotto, area, tree, or any sacred thing or the object of veneration, in order for a licensee to enter upon, take possession of or use such lands in the course of their operational activities. *See* Section 4 of the Oil Pipelines Act, entitled 'Entitlement of Discoverer of Commercial Quantities of Oil to Permit to Survey', and Section 5 of the Act entitled 'Effect of Permit to Survey'. *Also see* Section 6 of the Act captioned 'Notice before Entry, Damage, Compensation, etc', Section 12 captioned 'Power to Impose Restrictions on Use of Adjoining Lands', and Part IV of the Act captioned 'compensation'. Under Section 6(3), the holder of a permit to survey under Section 6(3) is required to pay compensation to the owners, occupiers or any other persons in charge of lands as stipulated under Section 6, whereas the holder of an Oil Pipeline Licence is required under Section 11(5) of the Act, to pay compensation for persons injuriously affected by the rights conferred to the holder of the licence. The holder of an Oil Pipeline Licence has obligation to pay compensation to persons whose land or interest in land is injuriously affected. These include persons who have suffered damage due to neglect on the part of the holder or his agents, servants or workmen, and those who have suffered damage due to any breakage or leakage from the pipeline. Hence, owners of economic trees, crops, structures, appurtenance on land affected by onshore pipelines are entitled to compensation. Section 11 of the Oil Pipelines Act is captioned 'Rights and Obligations of the Holder of a Licence'. Compensation is also payable by the holder of an Oil Exploration Licence (OEL), Oil Prospecting Licence (OPL) and Oil Mining Lease (OML), by virtue of Paragraph 36, Schedule 1 of the Petroleum Act. This Paragraph provides for the payment of 'fair and adequate compensation for the disturbance of surface or other rights to any person who owns or is in lawful occupation of the licensed or leased lands'. The Paragraph is supported where the holder of the oil pipeline licence is a licensee under the OPL or OML, by Regulation 23 of the Petroleum (Drilling and Production) Regulations, 1969, which stipulates that fishing rights injured/unreasonably interfered with by the operation of the licensee or lessee shall be adequately compensated.

6 *See* Section 9(1) of the Oil Pipelines Act, regarding the duty of public officers regarding verbal objections.

7 Section 8 of the Oil Pipelines Act is captioned 'Application for Licence and Notice thereof'.

8 Section 9 of the Act, is captioned 'Notice of Objection'. Section 9(1) of the Act, regarding notice of objection, provides that *any person whose land or interest in land may be injuriously affected by the grant of a licence may within the period specified for objections lodge verbally or in writing at one of the specified addresses notice of objection stating the interest of the objector and the grounds of objection.*

Administrative officers or departments directed by the Minister to handle public objection hearings subject to Section 8(2) of the Oil Pipelines Act, are empowered to investigate the objections made to ascertain their compatibility, acceptability or otherwise in relation to the pipeline or other resource development rights specified in Section 8(2) (i) and (ii) of the Act.[9] The Permanent Secretary of the Lands and Survey Bureau of the Governor's Office in Rivers state, which organises the public hearing of objections filed by aggrieved oil-producing communities of the state in accordance with the provisions of the Oil Pipelines Act, states that the procedure for each hearing starts with the service of the notices required under Section 9 of the Act. Service of notices regarding each hearing must be by publication in the gazette and at least two daily national newspapers, and by radio,[10] with specific regard to Section 8(2) of the Act. The Bureau highlights that the recent policy of the state government is that radio announcements be made through media covering localities which pipelines cross. The Bureau suggests to project proponents that they serve notices directly at the headquarters of each Local Government Area (LGA) of the state and on all the community likely to be impacted by their pipeline projects.[11]

Public hearings are convened when the Department of Petroleum Resources (DPR) authorises or mandates the Bureau to do so. In practice, CI at public hearings usually begins with affected or interested communities, citizens' groups, and citizens lodging their complaints in the form of petitions or objections with the Lands and Survey Bureau. It would then examine the complaints in relation to interests in land and property which may include aquatic and terrestrial lives likely to be adversely affected in the course of oil and gas pipeline, or other related, petroleum development proposal. The examination of the Bureau is expected, among other issues raised, to involve

9 These development rights specified in Section 8(2) (c) (i) and (ii) of the Act are namely in relation to the (a) holders of exclusive prospecting licences, mining rights, OELs, and OPLs; and (b) lessees of mining leases, temporary mining leases or OMLs. *See* the letter of T. G. Ekine, Esq, for and on behalf of the Permanent Secretary, Lands and Survey Bureau of the Governor's Office, Rivers state, Nigeria, entitled 'Re: Our Bureau's Role in Organising Public/Objection Hearings in the Rivers state of Nigeria in Connection with the Minister's Grant of Petroleum Resources Development Rights', dated August 20, 2003, with reference no. RSL/41174/56, (hereinafter called the letter of T. G. Ekine, Esq, for and on behalf of the Permanent Secretary, Lands and Survey Bureau of the Governor's Office, Rivers state, Nigeria, entitled 'Re: Our Bureau's Role in Organising Public/Objection Hearings in the Rivers state of Nigeria in Connection with the Minister's Grant of Petroleum Resources Development Rights'.), item 3, p. 1.

10 Ibid.

11 Ibid. Section 8(3) of the Oil Pipelines Act provides that *Such notice shall contain a description of the proposed pipeline and its route and the proposed ancillary installations and shall set out a list of places and times at which copies of a plan sufficient to identify the land affected thereby may be inspected, and each copy of such notice shall require that objections (if any) shall be made at least seven days before the date to be appointed by the Minister for the hearing of objections and delivered at the places to be appointed by him for such lodgement.*

claims for compensation, excluding the 'quantum of compensation' as expressed in Section 9(2) of the Oil Pipelines Act.[12]

During hearings, claims for compensation are usually controversial between affected citizens and community groups and project proponents (*ie*, the MNOCs). The Bureau (acting under the influence of project proponents) is usually reluctant to address issues on non-payment of compensation by the proponents, when claims for compensation are made by affected citizens and community groups. Hence, by virtue of Section 9(2) of the Oil Pipelines Act[13] a need arises for clarification that the Bureau is to concern itself with non-payment of compensation but not 'quantum' of compensation.[14]

As expressed in Section 9(1) of the Oil Pipelines Act, one significant reason for registering objections is that of 'injurious affection' on the owner, occupier or any other person or persons having interest in land in the area affected by the grant of pipeline or other related petroleum development right by the government. The phrase or term 'injurious affection', is an all-encompassing one, having wide and complex interpretation.[15] Consequently, claims under this phrase may involve a wide variety of issues for damages affecting land and several other interests associated with land, which may include aquatic and

12 This section of the Act provides that 'matters relating to quantum of compensation shall not be material grounds to include a notice of objection under this section'.

13 This section of the Act provides that 'matters relating to 'quantum' of compensation shall not be material grounds for objection under this section'. On the other hand, Section 6(4) of the Act provides that 'in the event of dispute as to the amount of compensation to be paid as to whether or to whom any compensation shall be paid the provision of Part IV of this Act shall apply'.

14 The issue of compensation requires to be properly addressed to ensure compensation is adequate, prompt and effective. *See* Section 44 of the 1999 Constitution of the FRN entitled 'Compulsory Acquisition of Property'. *See Elf Nigeria Limited vs. Sillo* (1994) 6 N. W. L. R. (Pt.) 350, at 258. J. O. Akande states that this section of the Constitution *does not simply insist on the payment of compensation but the compensation paid must be adequate. This is in consonance with the common law presumption in the interpretation of statutes which leans against the taking away of proprietary vested rights without specific legal authority and the provision for compensation. See* J. O. Akande, *Introduction to the Constitution of the Federal Republic of Nigeria 1990*, Ebute-metta, Lagos, MIJ, 2000, pp. 106–114. *Also see* J. F. Fekumo, *Principles of Customary Land Law*, Port Harcourt, F & F, 2002, pp. xxiii and 450. In international law, compensation is required to be prompt, adequate and effective. *See* R. Higgins *Problems and Process: International Law and How We Use It*, Oxford, Clarendon Press, 1994, pp. 142 –145, especially p. 145. *See* G. Gilbert, 'Roselyn Higgins, 'Problems and Process: International Law and How We Use it', found at http://webjcli.ncl.ac.uk/articles4/gilbert4.html visited on 31/12/06.

15 Injury may mean a wrong or damage to a man's persons or goods. It can also be an infringement of some right considered as having monetary value which is not restricted to physical damage. The act of injurious affection on or relating to land is one which could otherwise not have been wrongful but for the Act or statute authorising it. *See* Bramwell B. in *McCarthy vs. Metropolitan Board of Works*, L. R. 8., C. P. 208, at 209. *Also see Anglo-Algerian Steamship Co. Ltd. vs. Houlder Line Ltd.* [1908] 1 K.B., 657, and *Metropolitan Board of Works* vs. *McCarthy*, L. R. 7 H. L. p. 243. *See Stroud's Judicial Dictionary of Words and Phrases*, Vol. 2, London, Sweet and Maxwell, 2000, pp.1295–1300. *See* A. Akinrele, *Nigeria Oil and Gas Law*, Dundee, Oil, Gas & Energy Law Intelligence (OGEL), 2005, p. 232.

terrestrial lives and property, as well as easement of affected citizens and community groups.[16]

After the lodging of objections by the affected, concerned or interested members of the public, the Bureau would request the project proponent to make its response on all the issues and concerns raised in each objection. Thereafter, most often, based on the assurance of the proponent that pending objections would be addressed in the interest of the objectors, the Bureau would send its report on the hearing to the DPR[17] to enable the DPR to make recommendations to the Minister by way of seeking the Minister's approval to grant the permit or licence being sought by the proponent. Hardly ever has the report of the Bureau been negative in a way which could delay the proponents or deter them from embarking on their proposals. This is why the Bureau intervenes to ensure that project proponents offer or agree to offer or guarantee that they would address the objections raised in the interest of the objectors. The Bureau may thus request members of the public who raised objections to write saying that their objections or concerns have been addressed or are being addressed by the proponents.[18]

---

16 In *Re St. Pierre vs. Ontario (Minister of Transportation and Communication* (1987)1 S. C.R., 906–917, the Appellants (Larry St. Pierre and Mary Grace St. Pierre) brought a legal action against the Respondent. In 1961, the Appellants bought land zoned as 'open space' in a quiet, rural neighbourhood near London and built their retirement home. Sometime before 1976, the Respondent acquired a strip of land adjoining the Eastern boundary of the land of the Appellants to construct a highway which was open to traffic in 1977. No part of the Appellant's land was acquired or taken. The Appellant brought a claim for *injurious affection* of their land caused by the acquisition of the adjoining land by the Respondent and the construction thereon of the public highway. The point in issue was whether the construction of the highway with its resultant damage to the Appellants' property was actionable at common law. The decision of the Lands Compensation Board, later renamed the Ontario Municipal Board, to allow the claim for compensation was upheld by the Divisional Court but overturned by the Court of Appeal. There are, however, examples of decided cases regarding how land has been *injuriously affected* on the basis of which claimants succeeded in their legal actions for the enforcement of their right to compensation. In *Re Masters and Great Western Railways* (1900) 2 Q. B., p. 677, the claim was based on the prevention of sinking a mine shaft at the spot compulsorily acquired or taken. Other cases include where claims may involve the inundation caused by raising the level of a stream and damage caused by insufficient drainage or protection of a railway. *See Stroud's Judicial Dictionary of Words and Phrases, op cit*, pp. 1295–1297.

17 See the letter of T. G. Ekine, Esq, for and on behalf of the Permanent Secretary, Lands and Survey Bureau of the Governor's Office, Rivers state, Nigeria, entitled 'Re: Our Bureau's Role in Organising Public/Objection Hearings in the Rivers state of Nigeria in Connection with the Minister's Grant of Petroleum Resources Development Rights', *op cit*, p. 2.

18 *See* the letter of the Bristol-Alagbarigha royal house (Founder of Grand Bonny) for and on behalf of its Kuruama and Kuruama-Iwoama communities, to the Legal Adviser Shell Nigeria, with reference no. BARH/KITC/SPDC/2002–016, dated October 14, 2002. This letter urged the Director of Lands and Survey Bureau to send a favourable report to the DPR, regarding the objection hearing session of the Bureau in respect of Shell Nigeria's application for OPL for its 14"Terminal trunk line project. However, after such letters of recommendation urging the DPR to issue the relevant permit or licence to project proponents (*ie*, the MNOCs), some proponents usually end up not fulfilling their promise to the affected public. Thus, in this instance, Shell Nigeria eventually refused to honour its promise to amicably resolve the matter with the Bristol-Alagbarigha royal house, as expressed in Shell's letter to the house, dated October 11, 2002. Shell's further verbal assurances to the house, which made the house withdraw its Suit No. FHC/PH/CS/116/2001 against Shell (to ensure amicable out-of-court settlement in 2006), did not persuade Shell to honour the said promise.

Apart from acting for and on behalf of the Minister, the various lands and survey Bureaux, ministries and other related arms of the government of each state in the Delta region and other oil-producing states have significant roles to play to ensure that MNOCs carry out their operations in compliance with development planning policies, laws and regulations of the Federal Republic of Nigeria (FRN). Thus, Paragraph 35 (b) of the First Schedule of the Petroleum Act, 1969, is instructive. This paragraph provides that the holder of an Oil Prospecting Licence (OPL) or Oil Mining Lease (OML)

> *... shall comply with any enactment to town or country planning or regulating the construction, alteration, repair or demolition of buildings, or providing for similar matters, which affects him in carrying out the operations authorised by the licence or lease.*[19]

Public objection hearings are, however, not being integrated into the EIA process of petroleum development projects in the FRN. Hence, the need to integrate the findings of these hearings into the EIA process, to ensure a comprehensive and integrated assessment of petroleum development projects, and to promote PI towards sustainable petroleum development and environmentally-sound and socially-equitable sustainable community development (SCD) in the Delta region and other oil-producing areas. Comprehensive and integrated EA centred on interactive PI is required in Nigeria, considering that PI stands at the apex of the EIA process.[20]

By and large, public objection hearings in the FRN constitute an attempt by the federal and affected state governments to ensure that proponents of petroleum development projects carry their petroleum pipeline and other related operations in compliance with the Oil Pipelines Act and other relevant laws, regulations, guidelines and policies of the federation governing these operations. For instance, proponents are required to comply with Nigeria's Oil and Gas Pipelines Regulations.[21] These hearings are also designed to enhance

19 This Schedule of the Petroleum Act is entitled 'Oil Exploration Licences, Oil Prospecting Licences, and Oil Mining Leases'.

20 *See* A. Gilpin, *Environmental Impact Assessment: Cutting Edge for the Twenty-First Century*, Cambridge, Press Syndicate of the University of Cambridge, 1995, p.171. Based on Section 44 of the EIA Act, LFN, Vol 6, 2004, entitled 'Substitute for Review Panel', public objection hearings may be substituted by EIA panel review process. Conversely, these hearings may complement Nigeria's EIA process to aid the proper integration of the public involvement (PI) into the process.

21 *See* the Oil and Gas Pipelines Regulations of the FRN, 1995, – the first set of regulations made under the Oil Pipelines Act. *See* M. M. Olisa, *Nigerian Petroleum Law and Practice*, Lagos, Martin Olisa, 1997, pp. 159–160.

industrial peace and harmony in the course of petroleum development in the oil-producing communities.[22]

The Petroleum Industry Bill (PIB), currently before the National Assembly, seeks to repeal the Oil Pipelines Act and several other laws governing the petroleum industry.[23] Considering Nigeria's responsibilities regarding ongoing international standards and practices on environmental democracy, her National Assembly is duty-bound to enshrine adequate provisions in the emerging petroleum law to improve environmental democracy and thereby enhance the reorganisation of her petroleum industry to enhance SD and SCD in the oil-producing areas.

6.3 BACKGROUND TO PARTICIPATION OF NIGERIA AND NIGERIANS IN THE CONTROL AND MANAGEMENT OF THE NIGERIAN PETROLEUM INDUSTRY

Petroleum development rights granted to MNOCs in Nigeria have witnessed a transition from the traditional concessions (which prevailed during British colonialism and shortly thereafter) to joint agreements which commenced by virtue of the promulgation of the Petroleum Decree, Decree No. 51 of 1969 (subsequently transformed into an Act, – *ie*, the Petroleum Act, 1969). This Act laid the foundation for equity participation in the Nigerian petroleum industry. The Act incorporates all the salient provisions of the previous laws under which the pre-1969 grants were made, and repealed the Minerals Oil Act, 1914.[24]

---

22 *See* the letter of T. G. Ekine, Esq, for and on behalf of the Permanent Secretary, Lands and Survey Bureau of the Governor's Office, Rivers State, Nigeria, entitled 'Re: Our Bureau's Role in Organising Public/Objection Hearings in the Rivers state of Nigeria in Connection with the Minister's Grant of Petroleum Resources Development Rights', *op cit*, p. 2. *Also see* Sections 49(d), 50, 52, and 164 to 179 of the PNG Oil and Gas Act, 1998 (as amended in 2002). *See* the Petroleum 'Policy Handbook' prepared by the Policy Branch of the Petroleum Division Department of Petroleum and Energy, PNG, dated April 2003. *See* M. A. G. Bunter, 'The Conquering of the 'Resource Curse' by Private Enterprise and Private Property', Vol. 2, Issue 3, OGEL, July 2004.

23 These include the Petroleum Act, 1969, Cap. 350 LFN 1990, Nigerian National Petroleum Corporation (NNPC) Act, 1977, Cap. 320 LFN 1990, NNPC (Amendment) Act, 2007, Oil Pipelines Act, Cap 338 LFN 1990, Petroleum Technology Development Fund (PTDF) Act, Cap. 355, LFN 1990, and a host of other petroleum laws (some of which were revised in 2004). *See* Section 478 of the Petroleum Industry (Draft) Bill (PIB), 2009, entitled 'Repeals'. *Also see* the commentary on this Bill entitled 'A Commentary on the Petroleum Industry Bill, the Oil and Gas Sector Reform Implementation Committee (OGIC)', 2009.

24 *See* G. Etikerentse, *Nigerian Petroleum Law*, London, Macmillan, 1985, p. 24. *Also see* G. Etikerentse, *Nigerian Petroleum Law* (2nd edn.), Dredew, 2005, p. 6. M. M. Olisa points out that equity participation had, however, been thought about as far back as 1962 in a concession agreement between the FG of Nigeria and Nigeria Agip Oil Company (NAOC) in which the Government was granted an option to acquire three per cent equity interest in the company. *See* L. A. Atsegbua, *Oil and Gas Law in Nigeria: Theory and Practice*, Benin City, New Era, 2004, pp. 87 and 89. *Also see* 'A Comparative Study of the Acquisition of Oil and Gas Rights in Africa', being an LLM Thesis by M. M. Olisa, submitted to the University of Alberta, Edmonton, Alberta, 1969, pp. 58 and 67.

The concessionary and other forms of legal relationships or arrangements governing the petroleum industry of the oil-rich developing countries determine the relationship between these countries and the MNOCs operating in them. Based on the Nigerian Petroleum Act, 1969, the arrangements which came into being between the Host Country ([HC], Nigeria), and the MNOCs are the joint ventures (JVs) or participation agreements, production sharing contracts, and risk contracts.[25] Equity participation may exist in any of these forms of arrangements when a HC or its national oil corporation has majority shareholding in the MNOCs as a means to achieve economic independence and thereby make the political independence of the HC more meaningful. Similar to the situation of other oil-rich developing countries, the transition (from the concessionary era as from 1969) took place due to Nigeria's need for equity participation to ensure the control and management of its petroleum industry.[26] Equity participation (*ie*, Nigerian indigenous participation) has traversed through the Nigerian Indigenisation era of the 1970s up to date. Currently, it is vigorously thriving in the framework of the Nigerian Content Policy (NCP).[27]

6.3 (I) INVOLVEMENT OF NIGERIA AND NIGERIANS *VIS-À-VIS* INDIGENOUS PARTICIPATION IN THE NIGERIAN PETROLEUM INDUSTRY DURING THE INDUSTRY'S TRADITIONAL CONCESSION ERA

The traditional concession, which continues to thrive in modern petroleum arrangements, may be explained in the following words of Y. Omorogbe:

> *The earlier type of petroleum arrangement between governments and companies was the traditional concession. This was an agreement whereby the oil company received the exclusive right to explore for petroleum and, if petroleum was discovered, to produce, market and transport the oil and gas. In return, the company paid some specified costs and taxes. These concessions had certain characteristics. First of all the contract area was often very large. In several instances, it extended over the whole of the national territory. Secondly, the duration was very long, typically between 40 years to 75 years.*
>
> *The company was often granted extensive rights over all the mineral deposits in the area. It was the exclusive owner and was free to dispose of them as it saw fit.*

---

25 *See* M. M. Gidado, *Petroleum Development Contracts with Multinational Oil Firms: The Nigerian Experience*, Maiduguri, Ed-Linform Services, 1999, p. xv.

26 Ibid, pp. 70–79, 140–142, and 218–226. *Also see* M. A. Ajomo, 'The Legal Framework of the Petroleum Industry', being a paper delivered at the Centre for Petroleum, Environment and Development Studies (CEEPEDS) Seminar on 'Essentials of Oil and Gas Law' (hereinafter called 'The Legal Framework of the Petroleum Industry'), Federal Palace Hotel, Victoria Island, July 21–22, 1999, pp. 13– 29.

27 *See* the area of the NNPC homepage, captioned 'Nigerian Content Development in the Oil and Gas Sector', found at http://www.nnpcgroup.com/faq.htm visited on 31/12/06.

> *Financial benefits accruing to the host states were usually minimal. In many cases, the companies paid a nominal rent of $150 and a bottle of rum for a whole concession. Royalties were based on volume, rather than value. For example, the Iraqi Agreement with the Khanaquin Oil Company in 1926 called for payment of four gold shillings per ton of crude oil produced and saved; the 1949 agreement between Saudi Arabia and Getty oil provided for royalty of US$0.50 per barrel. No income tax was levied until 1950 when it was frequently set at a rate of 50 per cent.*
>
> *These characteristic features were clearly inequitable and lopsided in favour of the oil companies, and therefore such arrangements were unable to survive decolonisation and the new international economic order. The traditional concession is therefore generally regarded as a discredited form of contract, and the very word 'concession' has a bad connotation in many countries.*
>
> *... In fact, concessions thrive all over the world today in a modernised form and often with a different name (licence, permit, lease or agreement).*[28]

Thus, the concessionary era during British colonialism witnessed the marginalisation of Nigeria and Nigerians. The grant of traditional concessionary rights by the colonial government to Shell-BP (ie, Shell Nigeria/the Shell Petroleum Development Company of Nigeria Limited, SPDC – a subsidiary of the Royal Dutch Shell group originally known as Shell D'Arcy) in November 1938 over the whole of Nigeria, covering 357,000 square miles, accounts for the company's dominance as the leading MNOC in the country. Consequently, Nigeria state and its citizens never had a proper or appreciable right to participate in their country's petroleum industry.[29]

---

28 Omorogbe distinguishes between the traditional and modern concessions in the following words: ... *The terms which characterise the oil concession are now changed. The duration is normally for an initial period of twenty years. The area is greatly reduced. ... The company is usually given rights only in respect of one mineral resource, crude oil, and sometimes, natural gas. Financial obligations are greatly increased. Companies are liable to rents, royalties, and a higher tax rate which captures between 55 and 90 per cent of the economic rent on the average for the state. Petroleum in situ remains at all times the property of the state, in almost all agreements of this nature. However, the contractor still has extensive rights over the petroleum, being granted the exclusive rights to explore, search and drill for, produce, store, transport and sell petroleum found within the concession area. ...* *See* Y. Omorogbe, *Oil and Gas Law in Nigeria*, Lagos, Malthouse Press, 2001, pp. 39–41.

29 *See* D. N. Zillman *et al* (eds), *Human Rights in Natural Resources Development: Public Participation in Sustainable Development of Mining and Energy Resources*, New York, Oxford University Press, 2002, pp. 552–553. C/f Omorogbe's analysis, in this regard, with that of L. Atsegbua, 'Development and Acquisition of Oil Licences and Leases in Nigeria', *op cit*, p. 57. *Also see* L. A. Atsegbua, *Oil and Gas Law in Nigeria: Theory and Practice*, Benin, New Era, 2004, pp. 41–42. *See* G. Etikerentse, *Nigerian Petroleum Law* (2nd edn.), *op cit, p. 53. Also see* M. A. Ajomo, 'The Legal Framework of the Petroleum Industry', *op cit*, pp. 1–2. *See* the 'New African Magazine' report entitled 'Niger Delta: Betrayal & Hope', London, IC Publications, Issue 469, January 2008, pp. 14–20. *Also see* W. Rodney, *How Europe Underdeveloped Africa*, London, Howard University Press, 1972, pp. 287–310, especially 287–288.

6.3 (II) INVOLVEMENT OF POST-COLONIAL NIGERIA AND ITS CITIZENS IN ITS PETROLEUM INDUSTRY: THE TRANSITION FROM TRADITIONAL CONCESSION TO EQUITY PARTICIPATION IN THE INDUSTRY

When Nigeria gained political independence in October 1960, the state of affairs in the country was similar to those of other newly politically independent states (NIS, *ie*, previously colonised) Afro-Asian countries. As Walter Rodney put it, 'social changes took place in the colonies, irrespective of the will of the colonialists. New social forces emerged – an industrial and agricultural proletariat, a national bourgeoisie and intelligentsia'.[30] In Nigeria, the new social forces led by the political elite persistently called for the nationalisation of the economy to enable Nigerians to take over dominant foreign-operating interests in the country. Hence, after the First Republic (1960 to 1966), the Federal Military Government (FMG) headed by General Yakubu Gowon from August 1, 1966 to July 29, 1975, took a bold step to respond to the persistent calls of Nigerians for the nationalisation of the economy. These calls, at the time when petroleum development had become the mainstay of Nigeria's economy, generated the promulgation of several Decrees between the late 1960s and 1970s, causing the period to be known as the 'indiginisation' era.[31] The MNOCs thus began to respond positively to the FMG's nationalisation process as they began to employ and train Nigerian citizens in the petroleum industry, and to enable the country to improve its technological base in the industry.[32] The FMG consolidated the process by promulgating the Petroleum Decree, 1969, which set the foundation for subsequent developments in the petroleum industry such as equity participation.[33] Post-colonial Nigeria consolidated upon the open-door policy granted from 1959 by the British colonial government, to overcome the imbalances of the traditional concessions on the platform of the New International Economic Order (NIEO) which gave rise to Nigeria's membership of the Organisation for Petroleum Exporting Countries (OPEC). While restructuring existing concession contracts, the 'most-favoured-nation' clause was introduced to arrange terms with the MNOCs just as favourable as those they were granting in other oil-producing countries in which they were operating.[34]

6.3 (ii) (a) Participation of Post-colonial Nigeria and Nigerians in the Nigerian Petroleum Industry

The participation of Nigerians in their petroleum industry is an aspect of Nigeria's economic self-sufficiency policy designed to indigenise the petroleum

30 *See* W. Rodney, *How Europe Undeveloped Africa, op cit*, pp. 287–288.
31 *See* L. A. Atsegbua, *Oil and Gas Law in Nigeria: Theory and Practice, op cit*, pp. 61–62.
32 *See* L. Atsegbua, 'The Development and Acquisition of Oil Licences and Leases in Nigeria', *op cit*, pp. 58–59. *Also see* G. Etikerentse, *Nigerian Petroleum Law* (2nd edn.), *op cit*, p.8.
33 *See* L. A. Atsegbua, *Oil and Gas Law in Nigeria: Theory and Practice, op cit*, pp. 60 and 87.
34 *See* L. Atsegbua, 'The Development and Acquisition of Oil Licences and Leases in Nigeria', *op cit*, p. 62.

industry, which, on the attainment of political Independence, became the mainstay of Nigeria's economy.[35] In the process there were six ways in which Nigeria's policy on manpower development and technology transfer in its petroleum industry was pursued (up to the ongoing NCP) towards self-reliance.[36] These ways, enhanced by the role of OPEC and the UNGA Resolution of 1962 on Permanent Sovereignty Over Natural Resources (PSNR), demonstrate the effort of post-colonial Nigeria towards equity participation in the industry.

First, Regulation 26 (1) of the Petroleum (Drilling and Production) Regulations, 1969, imposes obligations on the holders of OMLs and OPLs to employ and train Nigerians. The Regulations require the OML and OPL holders to prepare and submit to the Minister a detailed programme for the recruitment and training of Nigerians in all phases of petroleum development operations. MNOCs have an obligation to report on their training programmes and the progress of 'Nigerianisation' within a specified yearly duration.[37]

Second, in 1972, the Federal Government (FG) established the Petroleum Training Institute (PTI)[38] at Warri, in Delta state. The Government consolidated upon this in April 2007, by establishing the Federal University of Petroleum Engineering on the PTI campus.[39] Third, in 1973 the Government established the Petroleum Technology Development Fund (PTDF)[40] for the purpose of training and educating Nigerians in and about the petroleum industry. Fourth, between 1972 and 1997, the FG promulgated the Nigerian Enterprises and Promotion Decrees (NEPDs).[41] These Decrees, designed to

35 *See* M. M. Gidado, *Petroleum Development Contracts with Multinational Oil Firms: The Nigerian Experience, op cit*, pp. xiii, xiv, 34–40, and 70–72.

36 Ibid, pp. 70–72.

37 *See* Regulations 26 (1) and (2) and 27, 28 and 29 of these Regulations. *Also see* Paragraph 37 of the First Schedule of the Petroleum Act, 1969.

38 *See* the PTI Act, Cap. 356, LFN 1990.

39 *See* the report of the Guardian newspapers entitled 'Govt Sets Up Petroleum Varsity', found at http://www.guardiannewsngr.com/news/article33/140906 visited on 28/04/07.

40 *See* the PTDF Act, Cap. 355, LFN 1990. The PTDF, NNPC, Petroleum Equalisation Fund (PEF), Nigerian Nuclear Regulatory Authority (NNRA), PTI, and the Nigerian Liquefied Natural Gas Limited (NLNG) are parastatals under the Ministry of Petroleum Resources (MPR). *See* the area of the NNPC homepage captioned 'About NNPC', found at http://www.nnpcgroup.com/aboutus.htm visited on 31/12/06.

41 These Decrees were also called the Indigenisation Decrees. Following the First National Development Plan, the Second National Development Plan (which spanned from 1970–1974), conceived 'indigenisation' as a logical conclusion of the 'Nigerianisation' Policy. The NEPDs (which were repealed in 1995) were expressions of economic nationalism under political independence so as to provide for more participation of Nigerians in the economic life of the country, where Nigerians are yet unable to rely on themselves and thereby giving room for foreign participation or partnership in those areas of the economy where such participation or partnership is desirable. *See* M. M. Gidado, *Petroleum Development Contracts with Multinational Oil Firms: The Nigerian Experience, op cit*, p. 34. *Also see* the Nigerian Enterprises and Promotion (Repeal) Decree, Decree No. 7 of 1995. *See* the Nigerian Investment Promotion Commission (NIPC) Decree, Decree No. 16 of 1995 (ie, the NIPC Act, 1995). The latter legislation established the NIPC as the successor to the Industrial Development Coordination Committee (IDCC). The ongoing efforts of the NIPC are earmarked to encourage new investments and the expansion of existing ones in Nigeria, so as to enhance the investment climate in the country in the interest of Nigerian and foreign investors.

raise the proportion of indigenous ownership of industrial investments in Nigeria in defined degrees, required equity participation in the country's business enterprises.[42]

Fifth, the National Office of the Industrial Property (NOIP) Act, 1979, established the Office of Industrial Property to monitor the transfer of foreign technology to Nigeria. The administration of the Act was entrusted to the NOIP, recently renamed the National Office of Technology Acquisition and Promotion ('NOTAP'). NOTAP concerns itself with examining the quality of imported technology to determine its price and to check such abuses as the overpricing of real, fake or obsolete technology. The main concern of NOTAP is to register contracts and agreements regarding the transfer and acquisition of foreign technology.[43]

Sixth, the FG bargains for indigenous manpower training and technology transfer in the course of operations of the MNOCs in Nigeria, especially during specific oil and gas development projects by these companies.[44] Consequently, in 1989 the FG, through the Nigerian National Petroleum Corporation (NNPC), signed a technology transfer and manpower training agreement with BECHTEL, one of the world's premier engineering, construction and project management companies, with headquarters in San Francisco, USA.[45] This agreement led to the establishment of a company called NETCO. In the process, BECHTEL was to transfer petroleum industrial technology to NETCO through a specified training programme aimed at ensuring that the employees of NETCO and the NNPC benefited from the programme.[46]

---

42 *See* M. M. Gidado, *Petroleum Development Contracts with Multinational Oil Firms: The Nigerian Experience, op cit*, pp. 71–72.

43 *See* the area of the website on transfer of technology in Nigeria, captioned 'Transfer of Technology: National Office of Industrial Property Act', found at http://www.nipc-nigeria.org/property.htm visited on 31/12/06. *Also see* the homepage of NOTAP (of the Federal Ministry of Science and Technology), found at http://www.notap.gov.ng/index.php visited on 31/12/06.

44 *See* A. Acidah, 'Bringing Know-how Home', 'NLNG The Magazine', Vol. 2, No. 3, 2002, pp. 13–17.

45 *See* the homepage of BECHTEL, found at http://www.bechtel.com/default.htm visited 31/12/06.

46 *See* M. M. Gidado, *Petroleum Development Contracts with Multinational Oil Firms: The Nigerian Experience, op cit*, p. 72. *Also see* Y. Omorogbe, *Oil and Gas Law in Nigeria, op cit*, pp. 158–164. *See* Chapter 34 of the UN Agenda 21 entitled 'Transfer of Environmentally Sound Technology, Cooperation and Capacity-building', and Article 144 of the United Nations (UN) Convention on the Law of the Sea (UNCLOS 111) 1982 entitled 'Transfer of Technology'. *Also see* the full text of UNCLOS 111, found at http://www.un.org/Depts/los/convention_agreements/texts/unclos/unclos_e.pdf visited on 31/12/06. *See* E. E. Smith *et al, International Petroleum Transactions*, Rocky Mountain Mineral Law Foundation, Denver, 2000, pp. 494–542. *See* the UN Framework Convention on Climate Change (UNFCCC) guidebook for technology transfer, entitled 'Preparing and Presenting Proposals: A Guidebook on Preparing Technology Transfer Projects for Financing', found at http://unfccc.int/resource/docs/publications/pract_guide_06_en.pdf visited on 31/12/06. *Also see* the UN Conference on Trade and Development (UNCTAD), entitled 'Transfer of Technology: UNCTAD Series on Issues in International Investment Agreements', New York, UN, 2001, especially pp. iv–v, and 1–10.

In the course of Nigeria's economic self-reliant policy pursued under the NIEO, the UNGA Resolution on PSNR,[47] enhanced by OPEC, featured prominently in the country.

6.3 (ii) (b) Role of OPEC and the UNGA Resolution on Permanent Sovereignty over Natural Resources towards Equity Participation in Nigeria

'Participation' in the petroleum industry is a concept or term which describes a partnership arrangement in the ownership and control of petroleum contract or concession granted to MNOCs. State participation is a partnership arrangement where a developing state receives an equity or ownership interest in the rights[48] and obligations of a contract or concession directly or indirectly through its National Oil Company (NOC). Participation stems from the desire of developing countries producing petroleum resources to acquire a greater share of the profits from petroleum operations controlled and managed by MNOCs in their territories by exercising greater control over these companies. State owned or national oil companies were thus established to function as instruments for achieving effective state/government participation in the oil industries of major oil-producing countries.[49]

The establishment of OPEC in 1960 tilted the erstwhile contractual equilibrium in favour of its member-countries towards achieving equity participation in the petroleum operations in their municipalities.[50] Equity participation was

47 PSNR is a logical outcome of the principle of self-determination which led to the dissolution of the Western European colonial possessions in Africa and Asia. To newly independent developing countries sovereignty meant *inter alia* the freedom of a nation to exploit and dispose of its natural resources, unrestrained by any political, economic or legal limitations imposed or maintained by an external authority. Having achieved political independence, the newly independent-states (NIS)/-developing countries were eager to gain economic emancipation through the control and management of their natural resources being developed by multinational companies (MNCs). *See* the UN General Assembly (UNGA) Resolution 1803 (XVII) of 14 December, 1962 on PSNR. *Also see* J. Warden-Fernandez, 'The Permanent Sovereignty Over Natural Resources: How it Has Been Accommodated within the Evolving Economy', the Centre for Energy, Petroleum & Mineral Law & Policy (CEPMLP) Annual Review (CAR), 2000, Article 4, found in the area of the CEPMLP homepage, captioned 'CAR', at http://www.dundee.ac.uk/cepmlp/car/html/car4_art4.htm visited on 31/12/06. *See* L. A. Atsegbua, *Oil and Gas Law in Nigeria: Theory and Practice, op cit*, pp. 206–215. *See* N. Schrijver, *Sovereignty Over Natural Resources: Balancing Rights and Duties*, New York, Cambridge University Press, 1997.

48 Petroleum or oil rights granted by oil-producing countries may take one of three forms (*ie*, an exploration licence, a significant discovery licence, or a production licence). Section 2(1) of the Petroleum Act, 1969, provides that the Minister may grant an OEL, OPL, and OML. *See* L. A. Atsegbua, *Oil and Gas Law in Nigeria: Theory and Practice, op cit*, p. 65.

49 *See* M. A. Ajomo, 'The Legal Framework of the Petroleum Industry', *op cit*, p. 13. *Also see* L. A. Atsegbua, *Oil and Gas Law in Nigeria: Theory and Practice, op cit*, pp. 86–87. *See* M. M. Gidado, *Petroleum Development Contracts with Multinational Oil Firms: The Nigerian Experience, op cit*, pp. 140–154.

50 *See* the OPEC publication entitled 'OPEC General Information' dated 2005, found at http://www.opec.org/library/General%20Information/pdf/geninfo.pdf visited on 30/05/06. *Also see* the area of the OPEC homepage, captioned 'OPEC's Mission' found at http://www.opec.org/home/ visited on 31/12/06.

first proposed by OPEC in its 'Declaratory Statement of Petroleum Policy in Member-Countries' of January, 1968. Made to alter traditional concessions in favour of OPEC member-countries, the Declaratory Statement urged National Oil Companies (NOCs) of host governments (*ie*, the member-countries) to participate in producing operations guaranteed by the old concessions as well as those in the downstream refining, marketing and sales operations of the petroleum industry under new joint agreements with MNOCs. It was subsequently incorporated and adopted into the OPEC Resolution No. XVI.90 of June 25, 1968.[51]

From June 1968 onwards, OPEC took several steps to consolidate this Declaratory Statement. Along with its new policy guidelines regarding the changing pattern of the relationship between producer and consumer nations, the statement was adopted by the first Conference of the Sovereigns and Heads of State of OPEC member-countries in March 1975, in Algeria. The Statement indicated that OPEC should seek, in consultation and cooperation with the other countries of the world, the establishment of a NIEO based on justice, mutual understanding and a genuine concern for the well-being of all peoples.[52] Meanwhile, before its adoption in 1975, the Statement had (after its issuance in 1968 by OPEC) triggered Nigeria to take certain measures towards equity participation in its petroleum industry. These included the promulgation of Nigeria's Petroleum Decree in the following year (*ie*, 1969), the introduction of the Nigerian 'indiginisation' process or 'Nigerianisation' policy, and the establishment of the Nigerian National Oil Company (NNOC) early in 1971. As a result of these measures, Nigeria joined OPEC in July 1971 and became its eleventh member-country.[53] Equity participation promoted by the Nigerian Petroleum Act 1969 was thus inspired by the OPEC initiatives embedded in the principle of PSNR. This principle was initiated to spur developing countries to emancipate themselves economically through the control and management of their natural resources being developed by multinational companies (MNCs).[54]

---

51 *See* M. A. Ajomo, 'The Legal Framework of the Petroleum Industry', *op cit*, p.13. *See* the 'Press Background Information' of the 141 Extraordinary Meeting of the OPEC Conference scheduled to take place on June 1, 2006, Caracas, Venezuela, found at http://www.opec.org/home/Press%20Room/PressBack.pdf visited on 30/05/06.

52 *See* the 'Press Background Information' of the 141 Extraordinary Meeting of the OPEC Conference scheduled to take place on June 1, 2006, Caracas, Venezuela, *op cit. Also see* the OPEC publication entitled 'OPEC General Information', *op cit. See* Y. Omorogbe, *The Oil and Gas Industry: Exploration and Production Contracts*, Ikeja-Lagos, Malthouse Press, 1997, pp. 4–5. *See* A. Anghie, *Imperialism, Sovereignty and the Making of International Law*, Cambridge, Cambridge University Press, 2005, p. 211.

53 *See* M. A. Ajomo, 'The Legal Framework of the Petroleum Industry', *op cit*, p. 14. *Also see* Y. Omorogbe, *Oil and Gas Law in Nigeria, op cit*, pp. 93–94.

54 *See* M. A. Ajomo, 'The Legal Framework of the Petroleum Industry', *op cit*, p. 3. *Also see* H. S. Zakariya, 'Sovereignty, State Participation and the Need to Restructure the Existing Petroleum Concession Regime', *op cit*, p. 224.

6.3(ii) (c) Further Steps taken to Enhance Equity Participation in the Petroleum Industry

Nigeria's effort towards equity participation based on the Nigerianisation concept was strengthened in the Nigerian petroleum industry as the federal government (FG) began to enter into more beneficial arrangements by revising or redefining existing contracts with the MNOCs operating in the country.[55] M. A. Ajomo describes this new beneficial arrangement between the FG, through its newly established NNOC, and the MNOCs in the following words:

> *It was the Declaratory Statement of OPEC of 1968 that led the [Federal] Government on February 24, 1972, to issue Notice No. 311 in which it declared its decision not to grant any further petroleum licences or concessions of the old types whether to an individual or to a corporate body. It decided to vest all petroleum exploration rights over all unallocated acreages in the country in the newly established Nigerian National Oil Corporation (NNOC). NNOC was empowered to enter into new beneficial arrangements with interested companies for carrying out petroleum operations in Nigeria. And so new relationships were developed that would permit the full integration of the subsidiaries of the multinational companies into the economic strategies of the country.*
>
> *. . . following the establishment of the NNOC, Government decided to make a clean break from the traditional concession based on the Model OEL, OPL and OML. Any exploration was now to be based on a joint venture working relationship with the oil company concerned. In so doing, it was thought such arrangement would dismantle the enclave status enjoyed by the foreign oil companies operating in the country and ensure the proper exercise of sovereignty over the powerful multinationals.*[56]

The NNOC, the NNPC was established under Decree No. 33 of 1977, as a public organisation to manage the interest of the government in the Nigerian petroleum industry. Its establishment thus brought about a clean break from the traditional concession regime based on the model Oil Exploration Licence (OEL), OPL and OML, and gave rise to new modes of acquisition based on a joint working relationship between the NNPC and the MNOCs. These new

55 *See* M. M. Gidado, *Petroleum Development Contracts with Multinational Oil Firms: The Nigerian Experience*, *op cit*, pp. 34–40.

56 *See* M. A. Ajomo, 'The Legal Framework of the Petroleum Industry', *op cit*, pp. 17–18.

modes of acquisition are the JVs or participation contracts, production sharing contracts (PSCs) and risk service contracts.[57]

To know how these new modes of acquisition have favoured Nigeria, it is important to outline the objectives of state or equity participation, which started in the Latin American countries and India.[58] As evident above, these objectives which are political, economic and technological in orientation include the following:

> *to increase the HC's share of earnings of the industry; to give the HC a voice in the policy decisions of the company, and to exercise* de facto *control over the oil industry; and to develop technical and managerial skills in the oil industry.*[59]

In spite of revenue increase[60] accruing to Nigeria from the operations of the MNOCs, the manpower expertise and technology transfer being sought to aid Nigeria's control and management of her petroleum industry are far from being realised.[61] This is because the MNOCs are not eager to transfer managerial and technical skills, which constitute their strength in the petroleum development business, to Nigeria and other host countries (HCs).[62] Nigeria and other HCs are forced to remain as rentier states (*ie*, passive collectors of rents and royalties), while the MNOCs are focused on their objective of maximising profit through the domination of the petroleum development business in these

57 *See* M. M. Gidado, *Petroleum Development Contracts with Multinational Firms: The Nigerian Experience, op cit*, p. xv. Gidado highlights that *although Nigeria has improved its bargaining position through its membership of OPEC, . . . these contracts [often being subsequently amended by Memoranda of Understanding (MoUs), etc,] do not allow Nigeria enough opportunity to reduce its dependence on the Multinational Corporations.* Besides, PSCs and service contracts are not JVs in the strict sense, even though they are popularly referred to as contractual JVs. In true JV arrangements, co-ownership in the undivided percentage interest in OML or concession, and in the assets and funds employed in the JV arrangements, are vital elements, together with all the common law incidents and implications of co-tenancy, except to the extent modified by the JV arrangements. The usual elements of JV are (a) a community of interest in the object of undertaking; (b) an equal right to direct and govern the conduct of each other in the arrangement; (c) sharing of production; (d) shares in the loses, if any; and (e) a close and even fiduciary relationship between the parties. *See* M. M. Olisa, *Nigerian Petroleum Law and Practice, op cit*, p. 61. *Also see* L. A. Atsegbua, Oil and Gas Law in Nigeria: Theory and Practice, *op cit*, pp. 86, 206–227, especially pp. 219–220. *See* M. A. Ajomo, 'The Legal Framework of the Petroleum Industry', *op cit*, pp. 16–23. *See* Y. Omorogbe, *Oil and Gas Law in Nigeria, op cit*, pp. 47–54. *Also see* A. Akinrele, *Nigeria Oil and Gas Law, op cit*, pp. 8–16.

58 *See* L. A. Atsegbua, *Nigerian Petroleum Law – The Acquisition of Oil Rights in Nigeria*, Benin, Renstine, 1993, pp. 38–43.

59 *See* L. A. Atsegbua, *Oil and Gas Law in Nigeria: Theory and Practice, op cit*, p. 86. *Also see* M. A. Ajomo, 'The Legal Framework of the Petroleum Industry', *op cit*, pp. 16–17.

60 Revenue increase is being hindered by MoUs with the MNOCs. These MoUs undermine the efficacy of the PPTA. *See* M. A. Ajomo, 'The Legal Framework of the Petroleum Industry', *op cit*, p. 29.

61 *See* G. Etikerentse, *Nigerian Petroleum Law, op cit*, p. 10.

62 *See* M. A. Ajomo, 'The Legal Framework of the Petroleum Industry', p. 26.

countries.[63] Post-colonial Nigeria's decades-long effort towards equity participation has thus not given rise to the desired equal relationship between her and the MNOCs operating in her municipality. Nigeria's effort to achieve economic self-reliance is increasingly being undermined by the current trend of globalisation based on the free market (*ie*, free enterprise) system which gave rise to the privatisation and commercialisation[64] of public investments in the country. In the process, equity participation[65] in the Nigerian petroleum industry is being vigorously pursued in the context of the Nigerian Content Policy (NCP).

6.3(ii) (d) Equity Participation in the Nigerian Petroleum Industry in the Context of the NCP

The NCP, otherwise known as the 'Local Content Policy' or 'National Content Policy', is a redesigned form of the Nigerianisation process (*ie,* Nigeria's economic self-reliance policy) aimed at improving equity participation in the Nigerian petroleum industry. It is intended to promote added value in the Nigerian economy, by ensuring the use of local raw materials, goods and services, including local human resources, based on the required quality and standards in the industry.[66] It involves the promotion of a steady and measurable growth of Nigerian indigenous capacities (*ie*, Nigerian citizens and companies).[67] The FG has, therefore, made a rule requiring any foreign firm bidding for oil operation in Nigeria to protect the country's interest by involving a Nigerian investor to serve as its Local Content Vehicle (LCV).[68] The development in technology, skilled and

63 *See* K. Omeje (ed), *Extractive Economies and Conflicts in the Global South: Multi-Regional Perspectives on Rentier Politics*, Aldershot, Ashgate, 2008.

64 *See* Y. Omorogbe, *Oil and Gas Law in Nigeria, op cit, pp.* 178–190. *Also see* Nigeria's privatisation and commercialisation exercise through the homepage of the Bureau for Public Enterprises (BPE), found at http://www.bpeng.org/en/default.htm visited on 31/12/05. *See* A. Anghie, *Imperialism, Sovereignty, and the Making of International Law, op cit.*

65 Considering the state of affairs when it evolved in the indigenisation era of the late 1960s to the 1970s, Nigeria's economic self-reliance policy has from the mid-1980s been diluted or relaxed. This policy has been diluted from the 1980s (during the era of the military regime of General Ibrahim Babangida, when the IMF-World Bank economic liberalisation/reformation programme based on the Structural Adjustment Policy, SAP, was introduced). The dilution taking place is especially prevalent in the ongoing economic liberalisation programme centred on privatisation and commercialisation of government investments. This programme, vigorously pursued by the President Olusegun Obasanjo administration (May 29, 1999 to May 29, 2007), is earmarked to transform Nigeria's political economy, by increasing foreign participation in the economy. In the process, however, corrupt political rulers and their interest groups are those buying the government investments being privatised, while the majority of Nigerians are increasingly facing difficulties because of the ongoing global economic down-turn.

66 *See* the *AllAfrica* online newspaper report entitled 'Call for Bigger Stake in Oil Industry for Local Companies', found at http://allafrica.com/stories/200108010323.html visited on 05/09/04. *Also see* the report entitled *Enhancing of Local Content in the Upstream Oil and Gas Industry in Nigeria: a Comprehensive and Viable Policy Approach*, Lagos, Kragha & Associates, 2003, p.1.

67 *See* the area of the NNPC homepage, captioned 'Nigerian Content Development in the Oil and Gas Sector', *op cit.*

68 *See* the report of the Guardian newspapers entitled 'New Local Content Rule Out for Oil Investors', found at http://www.ngrguardiannews.com/news/article03 visited on 25/09/06. *Also see* the report entitled *Enhancing of Local Content in the Upstream Oil and Gas Industry in Nigeria: a Comprehensive and Viable Policy Approach, op cit,* p.v.

technical manpower, and increase in investment opportunities and wealth creation to be realised, are earmarked to boost Nigeria's industrial base.[69] The NCP is thus designed to transform Nigeria's oil wealth into revitalising its oil and gas and other sectors so as to diversify the country's economy towards sustainable growth and overall prosperity.[70]

So far, in the course of over fifty years of petroleum development activities in Nigeria, local involvement in the petroleum industry stands at about fifteen per cent.[71] Based on the recommendations of the Nigerian National Content Committee set up by the FG to review the situation of the NCP towards improvement, Nigeria has expressed its determination to achieve seventy per cent Local Content by 2010 in the country's upstream oil and gas operations.[72]

The overall success of NCP, however, depends largely on its implementation towards greater opportunities for competitive domestic value addition in the

---

69 Thus, regarding the development of indigenous companies, recent efforts of the FG include the allocation of marginal oil fields to Nigerian oil companies. Marginal fields are fields considered not productively robust for major MNOCs. These fields are governed by the Petroleum (Amendment) Decree, Decree No. 23 of 1996, which provides for the insertion of a new paragraph 16A, after paragraph 16, in Schedule 1 to the Petroleum Act. This Decree allows the holder of an OML, based on the consent of the Head of State, to farm out any marginal field which has been left unattended for at least ten years. The Head of State gives his consent to farm out when he is satisfied that it is in the public interest so to do, given also that the parties to the farming out are acceptable to the government. The allocation of marginal fields compliments previous allocation of oil blocks to Nigerian indigenous oil companies on sole risk basis. *See* Y. Omorogbe, *Oil and Gas Law in Nigeria, op cit*, pp. 170–177. *Also see* the leadership newspaper article entitled 'Petroleum', with the sub-title 'Petroleum Policy', found at http://www.leadershipnigeria.com/product_info.php?products_id=1501&osCsid=a3ce. . . visited on 23/04/07, p. 4.

70 *See* the report entitled *Enhancing of Local Content in the Upstream Oil and Gas Industry in Nigeria: a Comprehensive and Viable Policy Approach, op cit*, pp. v–vi. *Also see* the 'Report of the National Committee on Local Content Development in the upstream sector of the Nigerian Petroleum Industry', dated January 2002, pp. 1–5, and 34–38.

71 Some have in their assessment of the NCP blamed the low level of participation of Nigerian firms on the provisions of the JV Agreements (JVAs) between Nigeria and the MNOCs and certain other related factors. They consider the cosmetic provisions of existing JVAs as not being helpful to the growth of indigenous manpower and companies. *See* the Syndicate Session Report on 'Local Content' prepared by Professor G. E. D. Omuta, delivered at the Shell Nigeria Integrated Environment and Community Development Stakeholders' Workshop captioned 'Partnerships for Sustainable Development', held at the Petroleum Training Institute (PTI), Warri, Delta state, February 24–26, 2004. *Also see* 'Local Content in Nigerian Oil Industry: Dilemmas of a Good Corporate Citizen', by Per Heum (of the Institute for Research in Economics and Business Administration), found at http://program.forskningsradet.no/petropol/Heum-Nigeria.doc visited on 05/09/04. *See* the publication entitled 'Summary of the National Workshop on Improvement of Local Content and Indigenous Participation in the Upstream Sector of the Petroleum Industry', found at http://strategis.ic.gc.ca/epic/internet/inimr-ri.nsf/en/gr-78147e.html visited on 05/09/04. *See* the article entitled 'Putting the Oil Industry in Local Hands a Slippery Business', found at http://www.ipsnenews.net/africa/print.asp?idnews=23133 visited on 05/09/04. *Also see* the *AllAfrica* online newspaper report entitled 'Call for Bigger Stake in Oil Industry for Local Companies', found at http://allafrica.com/stories/200108010323.html visited on 05/09/04.

72 *See* the 'Executive Summary' of the 'Report of the National Committee on Local Content Development in the Upstream Sector of the Nigerian Petroleum Industry', *op cit*, pp. 1–4. *Also see* the area of the NNPC's Nigerian Content homepage captioned 'Directives and Regulations', found at http://www.nigcontent.com/index.php?option=com_content&task=view&id=29&Itemid=56 visited on 13/01/09.

petroleum industry, in order to balance local opportunities with existing foreign investment opportunities.[73] It is thus necessary for the FG to reward MNOCs which are excelling in terms of implementing the policy.[74] The FG may do so by granting such MNOCs incentives. It is also necessary for the Government to pay more attention to the development of technology, local capacity-building through local or indigenous participation in the petroleum and other local industrial sectors of the economy.[75] To enhance the implementation of the policy, the Local Content Division of the NNPC, the National Petroleum Investment Management Services (NAPIMS – the upstream arm of the NNPC overseeing government's investments in the MNOCs), and the Federal Ministry of Energy, particularly the DPR, have significant roles to play. Other required roles include the need to facilitate the transition of the Nigerian Content Development Bill, 2006, into law.[76] Based on the impact-benefit idea or rational of the EA process, it is essential for the proposed law to empower the public directly-affected by petroleum resources development operations to enable them to benefit more in the course of the development operations in their communities. Lessons from developing countries, as Chile and Indonesia, Malaysia and Botswana, on how to address the resource curse,[77] are also significant for Nigeria to imbibe.

At this juncture, it is essential to discuss how the MNOCs are implementing the NCP in the course of their operations, using the examples of Nigeria LNG Limited (NLNG) and Shell Nigeria.

6.3 (ii) (d) (i) Nigeria LNG Limited Re-engineering the NCP Based on Impact-benefit

To implement the NCP in the course of its construction and operational phases, the NLNG evolved its Local Content Plan,[78] designed from Shell

73 *See* the report entitled *Enhancing of Local Content in the Upstream Oil and Gas Industry in Nigeria: a Comprehensive and Viable Policy Approach, op cit*, pp. vi, 63, 64–69.

74 Ibid, pp. 68–69.

75 Ibid. pp. 22–23, and 46–69. *Also see* the research report by P. Ballantyne, entitled 'Collecting and Propagating Local Development Content' (being the report of a project carried out by the International Institute for Communication and Development (IICD) in association with the Tanzania Commission for Science and Technology and funded by the UK Department for International Development [DfID]), report No. 7, dated May 2002, found at http://www.ftpiicd.org/files/research/reports/report7.doc visited on 13/09/04.

76 *See* the Nigerian Content Development Bill, 2006, sponsored at the National Assembly by Senator L. Maeba (of the Rivers South East Senatorial District), entitled 'A Bill for an Act to make Provisions for Nigerian Content Development in the Upstream Sector of the Nigerian Petroleum Industry and for Matters Connected therewith'. *Also see* the ThisDay newspaper report entitled 'Executive Bill on Local Content Underway', found at http://www.thisdayonline.com/news/20040908news07.html visited on 08/09/04.

77 *See* P. J. Stevens, 'The Resource Curse and How to Avoid It', the Journal of Energy and Development, Vol. 31, No. 1, 2006.

78 *See* A. Acidah, 'Bringing Know-how Home', *op cit*, pp. 13–17. *See* the NLNG Local Content Plans entitled 'Nigeria LNG, Expansion Project, Local Content Plan, Revision A1', and the 'Nigeria LNG Plus Project, Project Plan 19, Nigerian Content Plan', JP 1000 LNG, Plan PL 19.

Nigeria's NCP, evolved in 1998, to enhance the capabilities, competencies and competitiveness of its Nigerian contractors in such a way as to boost Nigeria's industrial development in conformity with Shell's commitment to sustainable development (SD).[79]

The NLNG Local Content Plan ensures that Nigerian labour and material resources are fully used during the NLNG project, based on approved technical quality, schedule (including health, safety and environment [HSE] requirements) and cost requirements of the project. This Plan, developed in association with TSKJ Nigeria Limited ([TSKJN – the major engineering, procurement and construction [EPC] contractor of the Nigeria LNG project), is aimed at maximising the participation of indigenous local, regional and other Nigerian contractors in the course of the works contracted to TSKJN by the NLNG, during the construction and upgrade processes of the NLNG project.[80] All EPC contractors of the various NLNG trains or projects are made to comply with the NLNG Local Content Plan which has such community relations components as development projects for host communities.[81] The Plan is designed for the benefit of Finima/Bonny Island, Rivers and Bayelsa states as well as other neighbouring states and the whole of Nigeria whose contractors are classified into regional, indigenous and other Nigerian contractors.[82] It is on this premise that the NLNG defines the classes and categories of contractors being engaged in the course of its operations.[83]

Opportunities for participation of Nigerian engineers is given priority in the Plan to enable them to achieve construction and management skills which may be used in the course of other or future development projects in the country.[84] It identifies goods and services to be supplied from Nigeria, based on the specified conditions, terms and standards.[85] It requires all the NLNG's vendors and suppliers to register with the DPR, in compliance with the requirements of the Nigerian petroleum industry.[86] The NLNG encourages local or indigenous companies and suppliers to use Nigerian companies and manufacturers to

79 Shell thus ensures that its tenders for big Engineering, Procurement and Installation Contracts (EPICs) to foreign oil firms provide opportunities for Nigerian firms to be affiliated to the foreign firms. *See* the area of the Shell Nigeria homepage captioned 'Local Content', found at http://www.shell.com/home/Framework?siteId=nigeria&FC2=/nigeria/html/iwgen/leftnavs/zzz_lhn6_2_1.html&FC3=/nigeria/html/iwgen/society_environment/sust_dev/local_content.html visited on 01/08/06.

80 *See* the 'Nigeria LNG Plus Project, Project Plan 19, Nigerian Content Plan', *op cit*, especially pp. 3–10 and 33–34. *Also see* the NLNG Local Content Plan, PL 19–3 (*ie*, the 'NLNG's List of Potential Community Projects'), pp. 1–2. *See* the 'NLNG 2007: Facts and Figures on NLNG', p. 52.

81 *See* the 'NLNG 2007: Facts and Figures on NLNG', p. 52.

82 *See* the 'Nigeria LNG Plus Project, Project Plan 19, Nigerian Content Plan', *op cit*, pp. 8–13.

83 Ibid, p. 10. *Also see* A. Acidah, 'Bringing Know-how Home', *op cit*, pp. 14–17.

84 *See* A. Acidah, '*Bringing Know-how Home*', *op cit*, p. 17. *Also see* the 'Nigeria LNG Plus Project, Project Plan 19, Nigerian Content Plan', *op cit*, especially p. 49.

85 *See* the 'Nigeria LNG Plus Project, Project Plan 19, Nigerian Content Plan', *op cit*, p. 5.

86 Ibid, pp. 10–11. *See* A. Acidah, 'Bringing Know-how Home', *op cit*, pp. 14–17.

provide technical support, materials-sourcing and materials-servicing services. In the absence of capable Nigerian sub-contracting firms, the NLNG may engage foreign contractors or suppliers to provide spare parts and stockholdings, as well as trained field personnel.[87] Based on the importance of technology transfer, the Plan provides for training programmes for local and national unskilled workers at the construction site during the construction and expansion phases of the NLNG project.[88]

6.4 SHELL NIGERIA'S PROJECT ADVISORY COMMITTEE (PAC)

In or about 2002,[89] Shell Nigeria introduced the PAC system by which it involves the representatives of the Niger Delta oil-producing communities in ancillary decision-making processes of the construction phase of its development projects taking place in and environmentally impacting on the communities.[90] The PAC system is a community relations (CR), crisis prevention and partnership mechanism.[91] This system, introduced in Rivers state, comprises the representatives of Shell, its development projects' affected or impacted communities, and the host state government, including such government's security agencies as the State Security Service (SSS), the Nigerian Navy and the Nigeria Police).[92]

The benefits which communities derive from the PAC system include securing employment opportunities, sub-contracts, CD projects and youth training programmes and amenities. These benefits are often expressed in the Memoranda of Understanding (MoUs) usually signed between the contracting firms of Shell Nigeria and the participating communities. The responsibility of the communities to be peaceful, orderly and law abiding in the course of the

---

87 *See* the 'Nigeria LNG Plus Project, Project Plan 19, Nigerian Content Plan', *op cit,* pp. 10–11.
88 Ibid. *See* A. Acidah, '*Bringing Know-how Home*', *op cit,* pp. 14–17.
89 *See* the document entitled 'Procedural Guide for PAC Meetings', PAC.DOC2002 CCIP (SPDC), and having the names of A. E. Kinsipe, F. Fufeyin and Jegede, as Community Assistance (CA) Coordinators of the Eastern Division of the Shell Nigeria (SPDC) and Sullivan & Sullivan Consulting, as Consultants of the Rivers state government and facilitator of the government and the SPDC.
90 Ibid. The system was designed by Sullivan & Sullivan Consulting led by Nze Akachukwu Nwankpo, as conflict resolution machinery in the course of Shell's petroleum development projects in the Delta region. Some development projects in which Shell used the system include its Cawthorne Channel 2 further oil development drilling project and the SPDC/NISSCO/DAEWOO Cawthorne Channel integrated Associated Gas Gathering (AGG) project.
91 *See* I. T. Amachree, *Effective Community Relations: Focus on Project Advisory Committee (PAC) of the Cawthorne Channel Drilling Campaign and other Issues Affecting the Oil and Gas Industry PLUS A Practical Guide to Claims for Oil Spillages, Acquisitions, Blockades, Agency, etc,* (hereafter referred to as *Effective Community Relations: Focus on Project Advisory Committee (PAC) of the Cawthorne Channel Drilling Campaign and other Issues Affecting the Oil and Gas Industry,* Umuebule, I. T. Amachree, 2004, p. vii–viii, 23–25 and 50–52. *Also see* the document entitled 'Procedural Guide for PAC Meetings', PAC.DOC2002 CCIP (SPDC), *op cit.*
92 *See* I. T. Amachree, *Effective Community Relations: Focus on Project Advisory Committee (PAC) of the Cawthorne Channel Drilling Campaign and other Issues Affecting the Oil and Gas Industry, op cit,* pp. 24–25.

projects, forms part of the MoUs.[93] Conversely, the oil companies undertake in the MoUs not to intimidate, molest or frustrate the community workers.[94] The benefits Shell and its sub-contracting firms derive from the PAC system thus include smooth and uninterrupted operations, and the safety of their personnel at project sites. The system has an in-built mechanism for peace keeping, orderliness and conflict resolution facilitated by the involvement of the representatives of the communities. Parties to the system are able to build upon the smooth relationship already created in the course of future development operations, towards greater industrial peace and harmony in the Delta region.[95] The system enhances the role of the relevant government's peace keeping, security and law enforcement agencies in performance of their duties at project sites.[96] It also reduces the cost of projects by creating mutual understanding between Shell Nigeria and its sub-contractors, and the communities. The overall success of the PAC system in terms of the degree of CI however depends largely on the project management teams of Shell Nigeria and its subcontracting firms executing projects for which the system is designed.[97]

---

93 Hence, clause 4(2) of the MoU between Bonny cluster communities (*ie*, Kalaibiama, Kuruama, Kuruama-Iwoama, etc) and their Settlements, AND Saipem Contracting Nigeria Limited (SCNL) on the participation of the identified host communities of the Bonny cluster of the Gas Transmission System (GTS) project, implemented by SCNL for and on behalf of the NAOC, dated October 8, 2004, provides as follows: *The Community on its part shall ensure that community workers are properly advised to subject themselves totally to the provisions of the conditions of service of the company, and its rules and regulations. See* the clause 4(2) of this MoU, dated October 8, 2004. Also, clause 4(4) of this MoU, provides that *All workers both community and non-community, shall obey the company's regulations and be strictly bound by the company's conditions of service and where necessary disciplinary measures shall be meted out to all workers without discrimination.* Accordingly, clause 11(4) of the MoU between cluster 111 communities: (*ie*, Kalaibiama, Bikiri, Kuruama, Ijawkiri, Kuruama-Iwoama, etc, their settlements) all of Bonny kingdom, AND Nigerian Services and Supply Company Limited (NISSCO) on the Shell Nigeria Cawthorne Channel integrated projects, dated April 30, 2003, provides as follows: *All community workers shall obey company regulations and conduct themselves in a manner that shall promote mutual respect and non-violence in their relationship with other workers on site. Also see* the 'Memorandum of Understanding between Kuruama Community AND the Shell Petroleum Development Company of Nigeria Limited: SPDC MoU with Kuruama Community' which took effect from November 15, 2004, and to terminate on May 15, 2006, regarding the SPDC EGGS 1 project.

94 *See* clause 11(9) of the above-cited MoU between cluster 111 communities: (*ie*, Kalaibiama, Bikiri, Kuruama, Ijawkiri, Kuruama-Iwoama, etc, their settlements) all of Bonny kingdom, AND Nigerian Services and Supply Company Limited (NISSCO) on the Shell Nigeria Cawthorne Channel integrated projects, dated April 30, 2003. This clause provides that 'The Company or any of its officials shall not intimidate or frustrate any community worker in the course of its operations in clause No. 3'.

95 *See* I. T. Amachree, *Effective Community Relations: Focus on Project Advisory Committee (PAC) of the Cawthorne Channel Drilling Campaign and other Issues Affecting the Oil and Gas Industry, op cit*, pp. 24–25, 73–74, 105–107.

96 The roles of the respective parastatals and officers of government and the security agencies as well as that of the third party facilitator are important for the success and advancement of the system.

97 So far, from eye witness account, the system is used more or less as a palliative process of CI, towards enhancing peace and industrial harmony regarding the construction phase of oil and gas development projects taking place in the communities of the Delta region. The PAC does not extend beyond the construction phase of oil and gas development projects, and so the citizens employed in the process fall back into the unemployment fold after the construction phase of projects. Even for Shell Nigeria, it is still an experimental system. For the system to strive in the overall interest of

Consequently, it may be concluded that Shell Nigeria's NCP and the NLNG Local Content Plan, along with the Shell Nigeria PAC system, are voluntary (*ie*, corporate social responsibility [CSR]) measures designed by these MNOCs to enhance industrial peace and harmony in the Delta region. These CSR measures are designed to ensure that the oil-producing communities which are being adversely affected by operations of the MNOCs derive some measures of assistance and benefits in the course of these operations in the Niger Delta.

6.5 OTHER CORPORATE VOLUNTARY MEASURES OF COMMUNITY INVOLVEMENT IN THE DELTA REGION

Apart from the CSR measures discussed above, there are other voluntary measures initiated by the MNOCs to ensure the involvement of citizens of their host communities in the course of their operations in the Delta region and other oil-producing areas of Nigeria. Some of these measures to be discussed in the next chapter include the Shell Nigeria's stakeholders' workshops, engagement of community-based non-governmental organisations (NGOs) in community relations, and Shell's leadership role in the Niger Delta Environmental Survey (NDES). The voluntary measures of the NLNG, which is a member of the Shell companies (*ie*, the Royal Dutch Shell Group of Companies) in Nigeria,[98] include its stakeholders' workshops and other occasional briefings organised for citizens and CBOs of its host communities. Other CI measures designed by Shell Nigeria and the NLNG in the course of their operations in the communities are the signing of MoUs with their host communities, and the involvement of professional CBOs in the EIA process of their development projects. Some MNOCs also employ the services of their land-owning and environmentally impacted communities to provide surveillance services, as a means of protecting their oil and gas installations in the communities. These CSR CI measures (exemplified by those of Shell Nigeria and the NLNG) arises from their statements of general

stakeholders, it should be encouraged by government. I. T. Amachree thus suggests that the enactment of a law at the state level would further enhance the PAC system. According to him: *The Rivers state House of Assembly has already made laws requiring companies doing business in the state to reserve certain categories of work places for indigenes. . . . The Assembly cannot make laws on oil exploration but it can do so in relation to matters concerning breach of security around project sites in host oil communities. The Project Advisory Committees presently enhancing smooth operations of these companies should be given legal cover . . .' See* I. T. Amachree, *Effective Community Relations: Focus on Project Advisory Committee (PAC) of the Cawthorne Channel Drilling Campaign and other Issues Affecting the Oil and Gas Industry, op cit*, pp.74–75.

98 Shell Nigeria holds 25.6 per cent of the shares in the NLNG. *See* the area of the NLNG homepage, captioned 'The Company', found at http://www.nlng.com/NR/exeres/F48DE9A7-F3F3-4A8E-929A-0C34F1CFF92B%2Cframeless.htm visited on 31/12/07. *Also see* the area of the website of the Royal Dutch/Shell Group of Companies, found at http://www.shell.com/home/Framework?siteId=home visited on 31/12/06.

business principles',[99] and other social responsibility statements, policies, codes of conduct and voluntary standards and initiatives of the MNOCs designed by their parent companies and sectoral groups.[100]

6.6 CONCLUSION

This chapter demonstrates that apart from EIA, there are other forms and measures of CI associated with petroleum development in the Niger Delta. It will thus be more evident in Chapter 7 that CI based on EIA and public objection hearings are backed by statutes, while the NCP (being upgraded into a law) is backed by policy. As will be further demonstrated in Chapter 7, other identified forms and measures of CI are those voluntarily designed by the MNOCs in compliance with the initiatives of their parent companies and those of their sectoral groups. Chapters 8 and 9 will, among other things, demonstrate how these measures of CI being increasingly introduced by the MNOCs are designed to promote certain government policies, laws and intervention measures in the oil-producing communities. Thus, the NCP and National Content Plans of the MNOCs promote the impact-benefit idea or rationale of the EIA or IA process. This idea or rationale also promotes the poverty alleviation and economic empowerment programmes of FG in thc oil-producing communities.

So far, the prevailing situation regarding public objection hearings exemplifies it as a government CI initiative which is not properly understood by the oil-producing communities. Although the MNOCs are versed in these hearings, some of them occasionally undermine the interests of the communities affected by their operations by, for instance, refusing or being reluctant to pay compensation to the communities even at the instance of these hearings. Thus, to avoid or delay the payment of compensation to certain communities affected by their operations, MNOCs sometimes seek refuge under Section 9(2) of the Oil Pipelines Act (which provides for the 'quantum of compensation' and not non-payment of the compensation). Public objection hearings are also not being associated with nor integrated into other aspects of planning as well as other decision-making processes of petroleum development projects such as the EIA or IA process of development projects. Besides, the objectives of the NCP deserve to be more properly implemented to achieve the goals of the principles of PSNR and NIEO, including OPEC initiatives arising from these goals. Noteworthy however is the fact that the NIEO demanded by developing countries is now being challenged by the reintegration of these countries into the world's capitalist market based on free enterprise system.

---

99 *See* the 'Statement of General Business Principles' of the Royal Dutch/Shell Group of Companies, found at http://www.shell.com/static/media-en/downloads/sgbp.pdf visited on 31/12/06. *Also see* the SPDC 'Statement of General Business Principles' fashioned after those of its parent group, the Dutch/Shell Group of Companies.
100 Ibid.

CHAPTER 7

Social Responsibilities of the Multinational Oil Companies and the Government, and Community Involvement in Petroleum Development in the Delta Region

7.1 INTRODUCTION

Chapters 5, 6 and this chapter are related, because their objective is to identify the forms and measures of community involvement (CI) taking place in the course of petroleum development in the Delta region. Thus, as indicated in the concluding part of Chapter 6, this chapter will attempt to identify other industry-driven (*ie*, corporate social responsibility [CSR]) measures of CI designed in the course of the petroleum development projects of Shell Nigeria and the Nigeria LNG (NLNG) in the region. The chapter will, however, start with a background on CSR, including how it evolved to complement government social responsibility (GSR) so as to enhance business sustainability and sustainable development (SD) in the course of major natural resources development in developing countries.

7.2 CSR AND HOW IT EVOLVED TO COMPLEMENT GSR IN THE COURSE OF MAJOR NATURAL RESOURCES DEVELOPMENT IN DEVELOPING COUNTRIES

CSR is a broad, complex and increasingly dynamically-expanding subject from concept to cover.[1] It may be discussed from the perspective of its different names, factors associated with its evolution, its aspects or dimensions, and views on its contribution to society in relation to the social responsibilities of

1 *See Global Environmental Health in the 21st Century: From Governmental Regulation to Corporate Social Responsibility: Workshop Summary*, Washington DC, The National Academies Press, 2007, pp. 11 and 78. *Also see* D. Vogel, *The Market for Virtue: The Potential Limits of Corporate Social Responsibility*, Washington, DC, Brookings Institution Press, 2005, pp. x–xi. *See* A. Crane *et al* (eds), *The Oxford Handbook of Corporate Social Responsibility*, Oxford, Oxford University Press, 2008, pp. 3–5, and 568–574.

multinational companies (MNCs) designed to complement GSR in the course of major natural resources development in developing countries.[2]

The idea of CSR dates back to the 1930s.[3] It was coined in 1953 by Howard R. Bowen in his book entitled *Social Responsibilities of Businessmen.*[4] Its discourse may involve the use of a variety of terms, concepts, principles or names[5] which include 'business ethics', 'corporate responsibility', 'corporate accountability', 'corporate voluntary or self-regulatory measures' (ie, 'corporate self regulation'), 'environmental stewardship', 'corporate philanthropy', 'corporate social/public investments or interventions', 'socially conscious investment', 'corporate social performance' and 'corporate citizenship'.[6] Others are 'business for social responsibility', 'company obligations', 'public relations', 'community relations' (CR),[7] 'economic, legal, ethical and discretionary responsibilities of companies', 'corporate paternalism', and 'corporate sustainability initiatives'. These terms reflect a wide range of issues, including business in relation to public scrutiny (ie, the court of public opinion on business), business-society relationship,[8] and in the particular context of this chapter – the effects of business on the environment, human rights and poverty in developing countries.

CSR evaluates how companies manage their core business to add value to stakeholders such as consumers and other members of society affected by their value-chain, in order to promote business sustainability and to contribute to SD. CSR is the enlargement of the social responsibilities of companies to the public affected by their operations. These may imply the increasing social intervention measures of the MNCs designed over and above what the law and regulations provide in developing countries. CSR involves how business sustainability is intertwined with economic growth, social cohesion and environmental

---

2 *See* D. McBarnet *et al* (eds), *The New Corporate Accountability: Corporate Social Responsibility and the Law*, Cambridge, Cambridge University Press, 2007.

3 *See Global Environmental Health in the 21st Century: From Governmental Regulation to Corporate Social Responsibility: Workshop Summary, op cit*, pp. 10–11, and 78.

4 *See* the area of the website of Corporate Watch captioned 'The Evolution of CSR', found at http://www.corporatewatch.org/?lid+2682 visited on 12/07/06. *Also see* H. R. Bowen *Social Responsibilities of Businessmen*, New York, Harper and Brothers, 1953.

5 *See* the report of the Catholic Relief Services (by I. Gary and T. L. Karl), entitled 'Bottom of the Barrel: Africa's Oil Boom and the Poor', dated June 2003, found at http://www.catholicrelief.org/get_involved/adevocacy/policy_and_strategic_issues/oil_report_full.pdf visited on 22/07/04. *Also see* area of the homepage of the International Standards for Business, Government and Society (ISO) on ISO 26000 on Social Responsibility, found at http://isotc.iso.org/livelink/livelink/fetch/2000/2122/830949/3934883/3935096/07_gen_info/about.html visited on 30/08/08.

6 *See* W. Visser *et al* (eds), *Corporate Citizenship in Africa: Lessons from the Past; Paths to the Future*, Sheffield, Greenleaf, 2006. *Also see* the EC Green Paper entitled 'Promoting a European Framework for Corporate Social Responsibility', Belguim, Directorate-General for Employment and Social Affairs of the EC, July 2001, pp. 4–5.

7 *See* A. E. Nwokedi, *Community Relations in Oil Producing Companies in Nigeria*, Abuja, Daylight Media Services, 1999, especially pp. 2–3 and 5. *Also see* the report (by Caroll School of Management, Boston College Centre for Corporate Community Relations) entitled *Community Relations: Unleashing the Power of Corporate Citizenship: Consortium Benchmarking Study Best–Practice Report*, Houston, American Productivity and Quality Centre, 1998.

8 *See* M. Blowfield and A. Murray, *Corporate Responsibility: A Critical Introduction*, Oxford, Oxford University Press, 2008, pp. 40–43 and 381–382.

protection.[9] It involves environmental, social, ethical, governance, health, and other issues, in a way that its scope varies from country to country, region to region, and interest group to interest group, and so forth.[10] It examines 'the changing relationship between business, society, and government, environmental issues, corporate governance, the social and ethical dimensions of management, globalisation, stakeholder debates, shareholder and consumer activism, changing political systems and values, and the ways in which corporations can respond to new social imperatives'.[11] Companies are thus investing in their future by generating profits through socially and environmentally sound operations and thereby contributing towards the wellbeing of mankind and society.

The European Community (EC) outlines the factors and developments that generated CSR in the following words:

> *New Concerns and expectations from citizens, consumers, public authorities and investors in the context of globalisation and large scale industrial change;*
>
> *Social criteria are increasingly influencing the investment decision of individuals and institutions both as consumers and investors;*
>
> *Increased concerns about damage caused by economic activity to the environment; Transparency of business activities brought about by the media and modern information and communication technologies.*[12]

Increasing economic competition among MNCs, especially multinational extractive industries, is another reason accounting for the growth of CSR in developing countries richly endowed with major natural resources.[13] CSR

---

9 *See* B. E. Joyner and D. Payne, 'Evolution and Implementation: A Study of Values, Business Ethics and Corporate Social Responsibility', *Journal of Business Ethics*, Vol. 41, 2002, pp. 297–311, especially p. 297. *Also see Global Environmental Health in the 21st Century: From Governmental Regulation to Corporate Social Responsibility: Workshop Summary, op cit. See* L. Burke and J. M. Logsdon, 'How Corporate Social Responsibility pays Off', *Long Range Planning*, Vol. 29, No. 4, 1996, pp. 495–502, especially pp. 495 and 501.

10 *See Global Environmental Health in the 21st Century: From Governmental Regulation to Corporate Social Responsibility: Workshop Summary, op cit*, especially pp. 10–11, 78–79, and 84 and 87.

11 *See* A. Crane *et al* (eds), *The Oxford Handbook of Corporate Social Responsibility, op cit*, preview.

12 *See* the EC Green Paper entitled 'Promoting a European Framework for Corporate Social Responsibility', *op cit*, p. 5. *Also see* the area of the Mineral Resources Forum (MRF) homepage, captioned 'Corporate Social Responsibility: Driving Forces', found at http://www.natural-resources.org/minerals/csr/index.htm#Concept visited on 31/12/06. *See* P. Kotler and N. Lee, *Corporate Social Responsibility: Doing the Most Good for Your Company and Your Cause*', Hoboken, John Wiley & Sons, 2005.

13 *See* the area of the website of Corporate Watch captioned 'The Evolution of CSR', *op cit. Also see* V. Haufler, *A Public Role for the Private Sector: Industry Self-Regulation in a Global Economy*, Washington, D. C., Carnegie Endowment for International Peace, 2001, p. vii and the back cover preview. *See* the report of the Catholic Relief Services (by I. Gary and T. L. Karl), entitled 'Bottom of the Barrel: Africa's Oil Boom and the Poor', dated June 2003, *op cit. Also see Oil of Poverty in Niger Delta* (by the African Network for Environment and Economic Justice, ANEEJ), found at http://www.boellnigeria.org/documents/Oil%20of%20Poverty%20in%20Niger%20Delta.pdf visited on 08/08/04.

evolved to sustain the operations of MNCs extracting major natural resources in poor, marginalised and crises-riven rural communities in developing countries, so as to enhance SD of these resources and sustainable community development (SCD).[14]

CSR has internal and external aspects or dimensions. Internally, socially responsible practices involve employees in relation to the administration and management of company operations. Thus, while giving account of the internal dimension of CSR, the EC states that:

> *within the company, socially responsible practices primarily involve employees and relate to issues such as investing in human capital, health and safety, and managing change, while environmentally responsible practices relate mainly to the management of natural resources used in the production. They open a way of managing change and reconciling social development with improved competitiveness.*[15]

The external dimension of CSR extends beyond the doors of a company to involve the company's wide range of stakeholders other than its employees. In a world of multinational investments, global production and supply chains, the list of company stakeholders is wider and far more embracing than the immediate operational area of the company.[16] Thus, other stakeholders embraced in the course of CSR include the business partners and customers of companies, public authorities, and non-governmental organisations (NGOs) representing host communities and other affected local citizens' groups, including the environment in present and future generations of the host communities who may be affected by the operations of companies.[17] Due to stakeholder relations, MNCs operating in developing countries are increasingly embarking on social investments in the interest of their host communities. One problem with these

---

14 *See* W. Visser *et al* (eds), *Corporate Citizenship in Africa: Lessons from the Past; Paths to the Future, op cit*, especially, pp. 10–17. *Also see* B. Andersen, *Bringing Business Ethics to Life: Achieving Corporate Social Responsibility*, Milwaukee, American Society for Quality (ASQ) Quality Press, 2004. *See* the presentation of T. W. Stephens, 'Corporate Social Responsibility in the Oil Sector: Issues and Emerging Trends for Africa', dated November 30, 2004, found at http://www.africacncl.org/(vlzsp055zvxeqbms0ggg45)/downloads/Presentations/CSRStrephens.ppt~1 visited on 09/05/04. *See* A. Warhurst, 'Corporate Citizenship and Corporate Investment', found at http://www.greenleaf-publishing.com/content/pdfs/jcc01warh.pdf visited on 31/12/06. *See* L. S. Munilla and M. P. Miles, 'The Corporate Social Responsibility Continuum as a Component of Stakeholder Theory', Business and Society Review, Vol, 110, No. 4, December 2005, pp. 371–387.

15 *See* The EC Green Paper entitled 'Promoting a European Framework for Corporate Social Responsibility', *op cit*, p. 9.

16 Ibid. *See* R. Halfon, *Corporate Irresponsibility: Is Business Appeasing Anti-Business Activists?*, London, The Social Affairs Unit, 1998. *Also see* K. McPhail and A. Davy, *Integrating Social Concerns into Private Sector Decision-making: A Review of Corporate Practices in the Mining, Oil, and Gas Sectors*, Washington DC, The World Bank, 1998.

17 *See* The EC Green Paper entitled 'Promoting a European Framework for Corporate Social Responsibility', *op cit*, pp. 12–13.

investments of multinational extractive industries is that they are not sustainable, because of lack of good governance (GG), capacity or other forms of inability of their host resources-rich local communities to sustain them. Besides, in the course of relating to their host communities, some of these MNCs join forces with arbitrary community and government forces to undermine popular will or greater public interest. MNCs are thus being accused of embarking on social responsibility at the expense of required environmental protection measures and other internationally accepted and recognised norms, values and practices.[18]

The foregoing and other diverse views have been and still are being expressed in academic and non-academic writings regarding CSR in the context of MNCs. Thus, as civil society groups such as NGOs continue to identify the negative aspects and results of CSR, certain questions are being asked and concerns expressed.[19] These include whether CSR does not in fact constitute a breach of the fundamental capitalist model; if it does not give rise to false developmental promise; if it does not limit business initiatives; and so on. CSR is viewed as publicity or propaganda machinery for promoting the public image of companies. It is viewed as a means of avoiding or undermining regulatory processes as well as regulations, gaining legitimacy and access to markets and decision-makers, in their operational areas.[20] Besides, NGOs contend that CSR enables business to propose ineffective voluntary, market-based solutions to social and environmental crises under the guise of being responsible. It is thus arguable whether or not, between the objectives of maximising profit and maintaining social responsibility principles, there is no choice for MNCs, especially extractive industries, to promote environmentally sound and socially equitable SD. CSR is also being criticised as diverting attention, focus and interest in developing countries from the failures of the traditional roles of government. Indeed, it is considered that CSR may divert attention from broader political, economic and social solutions for

18 *See* the publication of Corporate Europe Observer, entitled 'Rio + 10 and the Corporate Greenwash of Globalisation', issue 9, June 2001, http://www.corporateeurope.org/observer9/index.html visited on 05/09/08. *Also see* the publication of the Corporate Europe Observer, entitled 'Industry's Rio + 10 Strategy: Banking on Feelgood PR', issue 10, December 2001, found at http://www.corporateeurope.org/observer10/basd.html visited on 05/09/08. *See* the Friends of the Earth (FoE) reports captioned 'The Other Shell Reports'. *Also see* the Christian Aid reports on Shell entitled 'Behind the Mask: The Real Face of Corporate Social Responsibility', found at http://.www.christianaid.org.uk/indepth/0401csr/csr_behindthemask.pdf visited on 31/12/06.

19 *See* the publication in Choike's homepage, entitled 'Oil Companies in Developing Countries', found at http://www.choike.org/nuevo_eng/informes/1283.html visited on 27/05/04.

20 *See* the report of Corporate Watch 2006 report on Corporate Social Responsibility entitled 'What's Wrong with Corporate Social Responsibility', found at http://www.corporatewatch.org/?lid=2670 visited on 14/07/06. *Also see* the 'Friends of the Earth (FoE) International: Proposed International Convention on Corporate Accountability', found in the area of the FoE homepage captioned 'Towards Binding Corporate Accountability', found at http://www.foei.org/publications/corporates/accountability.html visited on 27/07/06.

developmental problems.[21] Multinational oil companies (MNOCs) are thus being called upon to shun arbitrary operational approaches, such as supporting oppressive and unpopular regimes, human rights abuses and other forms of unsustainable development practices in their operational areas. Activists and civil society groups are calling for binding international rules on corporate activities and the review of municipal company laws designed to regulate corporate voluntary initiatives (CVIs, ie, corporate self-regulatory market and NGOs driven initiatives).[22] CSR is, however, considered as reinforcing rather than challenging the power of corporations, especially regarding MNCs operating in developing countries of the world.[23]

Regardless of the arguments for and against CSR, this discourse is primarily concerned about how CSR may complement GSR in the interest of poor and marginalised communities of developing countries, where MNCs are developing major natural resources. CSR is thus at the centre of ongoing debates on the relationship between the environment and development towards enhancing sustainable economic development in developing countries. This is particularly so on how the operations of multinational extractive industries may enhance SD and thereby generate CSR measures to improve the socio-economic and environmental conditions of the often poor and rural-host communities of these operations. Proponents of CSR are, therefore, of the view that the environmental and social responsibilities of MNCs in the course of these operations are in the interests of the stakeholders of these operations such as host communities and society at large, especially in African and other developing countries.[24] While considering the role of business in Africa's development over centuries, proponents of CSR contend that African countries can properly determine their future with the aid of advanced countries, along with the assistance of Africans in diaspora.[25] As regards petroleum development and CSR in Africa, it is said that 'the emerging social responsibility and environmental movements, as well as improvements in regulations

---

21 *See* J. G. Frynas, 'The False Developmental Promise of Corporate Social Responsibility: Evidence from Multinational Oil Companies', International Affairs, Vol. 81, No. 3, May 2005, pp. 581–598.

22 *See* the FoE report on Shell entitled 'Behind the Shine: The Other Shell Report 2003', found at http://www/foe.co.uk/resource/reports/behindshine.pdf visited on 23/12/04, p. 33.

23 *See* D. C. Korten, *When Corporations Rule the World*, California, Berret-Koehler, 2001. *Also see* D. Vogel, *The Market for Virtue: The Potential Limits of Corporate Social Responsibility, op cit*, pp. xi and 45. *See* J. A. Zerk, *Multinationals and Corporate Social Responsibility: Limitations and Opportunities in International Law*, Cambridge, Cambridge University Press, 2006.

24 *See* L. Burke and J. M. Logsdon, 'How Corporate Social Responsibility Pays Off', *op cit. Also see* the publication by N. A. Dentchev, entitled 'Integrating Corporate Social Responsibility in Business Models', found at http://www.feb.ugent.be/fac/research/WP/Papers/wp_05_284.pdf visited on 24/07/06. *See* J. E. Akude, 'The Failure of and Collapse of the African state: on the Example of Nigeria', found in the area of the homepage of FRIDE entitled 'Publications', http://www.fride.org/download/COM_Nigeria_ENG_sept07.pdf visited on 12/12/08.

25 *See* W. Visser *et al* (eds), *Corporate Citizenship in Africa: Lessons from the Past; Paths to the Future, op cit*, pp. 10 and 17.

in Africa, . . . show [sic] how oil development could be a positive force in the continent's emerging market'.[26]

The social responsibility of governments (GSR), especially in the context of the social contract of governance,[27] is weak in several developing countries endowed with major natural resources. The failure of government or public institutions to properly cater for the welfare of citizens in resources-rich developing countries is compounded by the influence of the MNCs developing major natural resources in these countries. The role of CSR in terms of complementing GSR thus becomes significant in these countries.[28]

7.2(I) CORPORATE VOLUNTARY OR SELF-REGULATORY INITIATIVES

Voluntary or self-regulatory initiatives by companies are components of CSR.[29] The use of voluntary initiatives (VIs) to improve the environmental and social performances of companies, to complement or improve government's traditional regulatory measures, may be traced to the period before the UN Conference on Environment and Development (UNCED) held at Rio de Janeiro, Brazil, in 1992. Based on the commitment of the entire global community at this Conference, otherwise called the Earth Summit, industry and governments began increasingly to use voluntary measures, in the course of socio-economic development proposals, to improve environmental performance and to help achieve SD.[30] Corporate voluntary iniatives (CVIs) exceed the social responsibility requirements of national sectoral legislations, regulations and practices, particularly in developing countries. These initiatives include codes of conduct, or other CSR or social investment initiatives such as policies, statements of business principles and practices, ranging from the

26 Ibid, p. 15.

27 *See* M. Lessonoff (ed), *Social Contract Theory*, Oxford, Basil Blackwell, 1990.

28 *See* O. Arowolo, 'Social Responsibility of Multinational Oil Companies and the Challenge of Local Communities – Any Prospects for Reconciliation?', Oil, Gas & Energy Law Intelligence (OGEL), Vol. 2, Issue 04, October 2004. *Also see* S. Sharma and M. Starik (eds), *Stakeholders, the Environment and Society: New Perspectives in Research on Corporate Sustainability*, Cheltenham, Edward Elgar, 2004, pp. 2–3. *See* E. T. Bristol-Alagbarya, 'Oil, Gas and NGOs – What Does the Future Hold?' being a presentation made at a dinner hosted by Bjorn Edmond, Vice President Communications, for the Royal Dutch Shell Group, at the St. Duke's Hotel, St. James Place, London, on July 13, 2006, pp. 1–2.

29 *See* the website of the UN Global Compact, found at http://www.unglobalcompact.org/ visited on 31/12/06. *C/f* S. Tully (ed.), *Research Handbook on Corporate Legal Responsibility*, Cheltenham, Edward Elgar, 2005, pp. 372–394, especially 378–380 and 391–392.

30 *See* the publication in the area of the website of the UNEP Division of Technology, Industry and Economics (DTIE – also referred to as the UNEP Industry Outreach), on voluntary initiatives (VIs), captioned 'Background on Voluntary Initiatives', found at http://www.uneptie.org/outreach/vi/background.htm visited on 01/10/04. *Also see* the publication in the area of the website of the UNEP DTIE, captioned 'About Voluntary Initiatives', found at http://www.uneptie.org/outreach/vi/about_vi.htm visited on 31/12/06.

commitments by individual companies to those adopted from their parent companies, sectoral groups and associations.[31]

Other aspects of CVIs are understandings and agreements on environmental performance targets which may be between groups of companies comprising an industry sector, as well as between government(s), an operating company and affected stakeholder groups such as resources-rich communities and labour. CVIs, often designed to reconcile the economic development objectives of major resources-rich developing nations suffering from the resource curse, include the environmental and social performance measures designed by MNCs operating in poor and marginalised resources-producing communities. Due to increasing competition among MNCs[32] in resources-rich developing countries, MNOCs design CVIs so as to derive social licence from their host communities. MNOCs are using CVIs to address such key global community's problems as environmental degradation, human rights abuse, poverty, climate change and HIV/AIDS. These are problems which central governments of developing countries are unable or unwilling to address in the interest of their resources-producing communities. In developing and developed countries, CVIs are increasingly being designed to achieve a balance (ie, win-win situations) among key stakeholders of major natural resources development such as governments, corporations, communities, and key civil society stakeholder groups such as industry and labour unions.[33] Thus, due to the significance of CVIs in the context of the progressively continuing effort of the UN on the environment and development towards SD, VIs have, since July 2000, been launched under the UN Global Compact, to promote ten universal principles in the areas of human rights, labour, the environment and anti-corruption.[34] Consequently,

31 *See* The Shell General Business Principles (SGBP) 1976 (last revised in 2005), found in the area of the Shell Global homepage captioned 'Our Values' with the sub-title ', found at http://www-static.shell.com/static/aboutshell/downloads/who_we_are/sgbps/sgbp_english.pdf visited on 31/01/09. *Also see* the 'Statement of SPDC Business Principles', signed by its former Managing Director, R. van de Berg, dated November 1997. *Also see* D. Leipziger, *The Corporate Responsibility Code Book*, Sheffield, Greenleaf, 2003.

32 *See* V. Haufler, *A Public Role for the Private Sector: Industry Self-Regulation in a Global Economy*, Washington DC, Carnegie Endowment for International Peace, 2001.

33 *See* sections 49(d), 170(3) and 164–179 of the PNG Oil and Gas Act, 1998 (as amended in 2002). *Also see* the Petroleum 'Policy Handbook' prepared by the Policy Branch of the Petroleum Division Department of Petroleum and Energy, PNG, dated April 2003. *See* I. Serageldin *et al*, 'Making Development Sustainable: From Concept to Action', occasional paper series, No 2, Washington DC, The World Bank, 1994. *See* the 2006 Annual Review of the International Council on Mining & Metals (ICMM), entitled 'Setting the Standard to Meet the Challenge of Sustainable Development', found at http://www.icmm.com/publications/15671CMMAR06.pdf visited on 31/12/06. *See* D. A. Rondinelli and M. A. Berry, 'Environmental Citizenship in Multinational Corporations: Social Responsibility and Sustainable Development', *European Management Journal*, Vol.18, No. 1, 2000, pp. 70–84. *See* N. Rogovsky, 'Corporate Community Involvement Programmes: Partnerships for Jobs and Development', Geneva, International Institute for Labour Studies, 2000. *Also see* M. C. G. Guerra, 'Community Relations in Mineral Development Projects', found at http://www.dundee.ac.uk/ceplmp/journal/html/vol11/article11-6.pdf visited on 31/12/06.

34 *See* the area of the UN Global Compact website captioned 'About the Global Compact: What is the Global Compact?' found at http://www.unglobalcompact.org/AboutTheGC/index.html visited on 31/12/06.

at the World Summit on Sustainable Development (WSSD) which took place at Johannesburg in 2002, CSR and the role of big business were deliberated upon by participants.[35] UNEP, which proposed a number of mutually supportive initiatives at the WSSD, played a significant role in facilitating the preparation of a series of sector reports, whereby industry organisations took stock of progress towards SD, and outlined future challenges and actions to be taken.[36] Although governments did not eventually commit themselves to any implementation process at the Summit, they reached an agreement that opened the door to binding corporate accountability measures.[37]

There are a number of advantages for companies and industry sectors that use voluntary approaches. These include greater flexibility regarding ways and means of reaching targets, and the opportunity to present a better public image. For governments, the benefits of voluntary approaches include their usefulness in terms of promoting dialogue with the private sector and in raising the awareness of industries' managements on environmental issues. CVIs may also serve as tools to push industry's environmental performance further and resource productivity beyond previously-agreed targets. These initiatives promote innovation. They limit the cost of enforcing environmental standards and compliance measures on governments. NGOs that are at the forefront of CSR recognise that the appropriate use of CVIs is desirable as these initiatives have proactive and progressive elements in terms of environmental protection, SD and the promotion of industrial peace and harmony between MNCs and their host communities in developing countries. Considering the significant role which business can play to enhance SD, NGOs insist on the sustenance and improvement of CVIs based on measurable targets and benchmarking (based on the review of performances on the strength of available good or best practices). NGOs also advocate that companies should evolve risk management plans, to prepare them ahead of any eventual conflicts and disasters in order to minimise the effects of such events. NGOs advocate that the implementation process of CVIs needs to be reported regularly, to properly assess and enhance the progress and improvements being made by companies. NGOs insist on the use of third party verification mechanisms of corporate responsibility initiatives.[38]

---

35 *See* the publication of the FoE International (FoEI) entitled 'Big Rules? Corporate Accountability and the Johannesburg Summit', found at http://www.foei.org/en/publications/corporates/rules.html visited on 31/12/06. *Also see* the FoEI position paper for the World Summit on Sustainable Development (WSSD) entitled 'Towards Binding Corporate Accountability', dated January 2002, found at http://www.foe.co.uk/resource/briefings/corporate_accountability.pdf visited on 30/01/09.

36 *See* the area of the website of the UNEP DTIE captioned 'UNEP Contribution for WSSD', found at http://www.uneptie.org/outreach/wssd/index.htm, visited on 31/12/06.

37 *See* Article 27 of the Johannesburg Declaration on SD, 2002. *Also see* the area of the WSSD website captioned 'Key Outcomes of the Summit', found at http://www.un.org/jsummit/html/documents/summitdocs/2009keyoutcomescommitments.doc visited on 31/12/06.

38 *See* the publication in the area of the website of the UNEP DTIE, captioned 'About Voluntary Initiatives', *op cit*. *Also see* B. Andersen, *Bringing Business Ethics to Life*, *op cit*, pp. 34–37.

From the foregoing, other CVIs designed by Shell Nigeria and the NLNG may be identified and briefly discussed.

7.3 OTHER SHELL NIGERIA'S VOLUNTARY OR SELF-REGULATORY COMMUNITY INVOLVEMENT INITIATIVES

Other aspects of Shell Nigeria's CI measures include its stakeholders' workshops, and its and other MNOCs' engagement of local NGOs and other community-based companies to execute certain aspects of their community development (CD) and community relations (CR) initiatives in the oil-producing communities. Shell Nigeria and other MNOCs also involve CD Committees (CDCs) to enhance the implementation of their CD initiatives in the communities. Besides, Shell is the leader of the Niger Delta Environmental Survey (NDES) which it set up in 1995 and is almost entirely funded by the MNOCs under the umbrella of the Oil Producers Trade Section (OPTS) of the Lagos Chamber of Commerce and Industry, to facilitate socio-economic development planning and SD in the Niger Delta.

7.3(I) SHELL NIGERIA'S STAKEHOLDERS' WORKSHOPS

Shell Nigeria's stakeholders' workshops which started in 1998 constitute a form of the company's voluntary or self-regulatory CI process. These workshops, temporarily suspended due to insecurity because of the Niger Delta crises, may be described as Shell's major annual stakeholders' consultation process,[39] with strategic and topical themes.[40]

The objectives of these workshops are to:

(a) continue engagement and partnership with communities, government, academia, local and international NGOs and donor organisations in the company's SD programme;

---

39 From 1998 to 2004, about eight stakeholders' workshops were convened by Shell Nigeria. *See* the Shell Nigeria '2002 Stakeholders' Workshop Report', the Shell Petroleum Development Company Limited (SPDC), Operator of the NNPC/Shell/Elf/Agip Joint Venture, A Dawn Function Production: 042-454267, p.6.

40 In 1998, the workshop was tagged 'Stakeholders' Environmental Workshop'. In 1999, it was tagged the 'Community Development Listeners' Forum'. In the year 2000, it was tagged the 'Integrated Environment and Community Development Stakeholders' Workshop'. In 2001, it was captioned the 'Integrated Environment and Community Development Stakeholders' Workshop', with the theme 'Working for the Sustainable Development of the Niger Delta'. In 2002, it was captioned the 'SPDC Environment and Community Development Stakeholders' Workshop', with the theme 'Building Partnerships for Sustainable Development'; and the last workshop held in 2004 was captioned the 'SPDC Integrated Environment and Community Development Stakeholders' Workshop', with the theme 'Partnerships for Sustainable Development'. The first Shell Nigeria stakeholders' environmental workshop held in April 1998 was followed by the October 1998 'Community Development Listeners' Forum' and a further Stakeholders' Environmental Workshop held in November that year. The year 2000 Workshop was the first to combine or integrate the topics of environment and CD, to reflect Shell Nigeria's new SD approach to business and the wishes of its stakeholders.

(b) improve the company's stakeholder engagement process for continuity and sustainability;
(c) review with stakeholders, progress made on the company's plans and commitments;
(d) consult with stakeholders on the company's environment and CD programmes;
(e) suggest ways for partnership towards SD in the Delta region;
(f) discuss other issues of major concern with the company's stakeholders.[41]

As these workshops have taken place over a number of years, some aspects of them as well as key issues associated with them have become part of Shell Nigeria's operational framework. In order to exercise a measure of control over the workshops, preparations for them, involving the selection of themes and key topics, are usually done by Shell Nigeria.[42] However, in order to enlist the involvement of other stakeholders, room is often given for participants to make inputs into Shell's agenda. To encourage the involvement of stakeholders, Shell despatches workshop booklets to invited delegates to inform them about each workshop and to enable them to discuss it with their constituency members while preparing for it. These booklets allow participants to make meaningful contributions in the interest of their constituencies or people, so as to enhance the success of the workshop.[43] At the start of each workshop, each participant is asked to complete a questionnaire. They are asked to indicate two or three topical issues or problems concerning the theme and subject matter of the workshop, and to give their opinions on how to address these issues or problems. While completing their questionnaires, participants are required to indicate any environmental problems and CD concerns associated with Shell Nigeria's operations and how they feel such problems and concerns may be addressed. The answers received are combined and categorised into specific subjects and themes. Some of these are considered as 'big ticket' items and thus tabled for deliberation during syndicate sessions of the workshop.[44] By collating and reviewing the delegates' points, Shell Nigeria ensures that significant issues are given appropriate attention at the workshop.[45]

Given that participants' presentations are often made as directed by Shell Nigeria, during plenary and syndicate sessions, participants are often given ample opportunity to address the sessions. These are followed by interactive discussion.[46] Syndicate sessions of each workshop usually start with an

41 *See* the Shell Nigeria '2002 Stakeholders' Workshop Report', *op cit*, p. 6.
42 Ibid, pp. 8–9.
43 Ibid.
44 Ibid.
45 Ibid.
46 Ibid.

introduction to the subject under discussion, often made by a member of Shell Nigeria or its facilitator, for the benefit of those participants who may not be experts or very knowledgeable about the subject. Delegates are encouraged to join syndicate groups of their choice, based on their concerns or areas of interest. Shell Nigeria assigns facilitators to the various syndicate groups, while the chair of each group is traditionally elected from its members. The facilitators and chairs carry out the responsibility of preparing each group's report, based on the guidelines provided by Shell Nigeria, to enable each syndicate group to present a good report. Among other responsibilities, the chairs deliver their respective reports to all participants at the plenary session. Summaries of these reports are then included in the communiqué of the workshop prepared by co-opted syndicate group chairs. Draft communiqués are prepared and discussed by the participants to make sure that the final communiqué to be published truly captures the deliberations and decisions of each workshop.[47]

Although these workshops enable stakeholders of the Delta region to discuss interactively, the decisions reached do not impose any obligation on Shell Nigeria. These decisions are left for Shell to implement voluntarily. In spite of this, stakeholders regard the workshops as a way of resolving the ongoing crises occasioned by the adverse affects of operations by Shell and other MNOCs in the Delta region.

7.3(ii)(a) The NDES Initiated by Shell Nigeria and other Major MNOCs

The Niger Delta Environmental Survey (NDES) is registered under the Companies and Allied Matters Act, 1990, as a company limited by guarantee. This Survey was begun on February 3, 1995, by Shell Nigeria, which announced its formation on behalf of its Joint Venture (JV) with the Nigeria National Petroleum Corporation (NNPC), Elf and Agip, in the wake of international criticisms of the adverse effects of its petroleum development in the Delta region. The formation of the Survey was particularly triggered by crises regarding the adverse effects of Shell's operational activities in the region.[48]

Following the initial environmental survey and network gathering system started in the Delta region during the British colonial era by the Netherlands

---

47 *See* the '2004 SPDC Integrated Environment and Community Development Stakeholders' Workshop', found (in the area of the Shell Nigeria homepage) at http://www.shell.com/static/nigeria/downloads/pdfs/Commuique1.pdf visited on 01/09/04.

48 *See The Price of Oil: Corporate Responsibility and Human Rights Violations in Nigeria's Oil Producing Communities*, New York, Human Rights Watch (HRW), 1999, p. 87. The crises in the Delta region culminated in the arbitrary arrest, unfair trial, sentencing and judicial murder by hanging of Ken Saro-Wiwa and his eight Ogoni kinsmen, on November 10, 1995, and thereafter the decision of Shell Nigeria to commence the multi-billion Naira NLNG project at Finima, Bonny Island. *See* the Greenpeace publication, entitled 'The Life & Death of Ken Saro-Wiwa: A History of the Struggle for Justice in the Niger Delta', found at http://www.remembersarowiwa.com/pdfs/LifedeathKSW.pdf visited on 31/12/06. *Also see* A. Rowell and S. Kretzmann, 'All for Shell: The Ogoni Struggle – A Project Underground Report', found at http://www.moles.org/ProjectUnderground/motherlode/shell/timeline.html visited on 31/12/06.

Engineering Company (NEDECO),[49] NDES was set up to build upon available data in the region and produce an integrated sustainable resource development management plan and report involving the participation of all major stakeholders of the region.[50] The Survey was to provide a framework upon which to understand and tackle the Delta region's environmental and socio-economic problems, from the background of physical environmental features to the problems associated with ongoing human actions and industrial activities in the region.[51]

The Survey's independent committee, made up of representatives of Shell, Nigerian and International conservationists, academics and the Nigerian affiliate of the World Wildlife Fund (WWF), was set up to manage the sum of $US 5m (about N520 million) budgeted by the major MNOCs to carry out the Survey.[52] The Survey's steering committee was made up of representatives from the Ministry of Petroleum and Energy Resources, Rivers, Bayelsa and Delta state governments, the World Bank, the Nigerian Conservation Foundation London, and the MNOCs operating in Nigeria under the umbrella of the OPTS of the Lagos Chamber of Commerce and Industry (CCI).[53] Stakeholder state governments such as Rivers and Bayelsa states promised to assist in funding of the Survey.[54]

7.3(ii)(b) Concerns about the NDES and Proposals for SD in the Delta Region

Although the MNOCs which almost entirely funded the NDES expressed optimism, the majority of the citizens and civil society groups in the Delta region were sceptical that the Survey would objectively address the problems and challenges outlined in a way to achieve SD in the region. All the more so, as the MNOCs led by Shell Nigeria were acting as judges on the complaints against them. The Survey was thus dismissed as a public relations ploy by the MNOCs.

A renowned academic, democrat and political economist of Africa, Professor Claude Ake, was among several prominent citizens of the region who were

49 *See* the *Niger Delta Human Development Report*, Garki-Abuja, UNDP Nigeria, 2006, pp. 91–92.

50 *See The Price of Oil: Corporate Responsibility and Human Rights Violations in Nigeria's Oil Producing Communities, op cit*, pp. 87–90. *Also see* the PIRC's report entitled 'Environmental and Corporate Responsibility at Shell: The Shareholder Role in Promoting Change', found at http://www.pirc.co.uk/shell.pdf visited on 01/09/04. *See* the PIRC's publication entitled 'Controversies Affecting Shell in Nigeria', found at http://www.pirc.co.uk/shellmar.htm visited on 20/09/04.

51 *See* the NDES publication entitled 'Niger Delta Environmental Survey: The Mission Statement', being the second briefing note of the activities and achievements of the NDES, Steering Committee, NDES, 1977, pp. 1 and 5–6. *Also see The Price of Oil: Corporate Responsibility and Human Rights Violations in Nigeria's Oil Producing Communities, op cit*, p. 88.

52 *See* the PIRC's publication entitled 'Controversies Affecting Shell in Nigeria', *op cit.*

53 *See* the NDES publication entitled 'Niger Delta Environmental Survey: The Mission Statement', *op cit*, p. 1.

54 *See The Price of Oil: Corporate Responsibility and Human Rights Violations in Nigeria's Oil Producing Communities, op cit*, p. 87.

critical about the Survey from outset. Claude Ake, who was appointed a member of the Survey's Steering Committee, observed the MNOCs' conflict of interest. In his article entitled 'Shelling Nigeria Ablaze', Ake stated that neither the NDES nor Shell's well-financed world-wide campaigns could hide the disaster Shell's petroleum development operations were perpetrating in the Delta region. His words were:

> *Shell Petroleum Development Company of Nigeria shows no sign of remorse for causing the strife in Ogoniland which has thrown Nigeria into one of the deepest crises of its history. It insists defiantly that it will not change its ways and denies any part whatsoever in the environmental degradation of the Niger Delta, which it blames on indigenes conniving at oil spills to collect compensation.*
>
> *Shell's vehement rejection of all blame has clearly undermined the Niger Delta Environment Survey, NDES, which it has been trying to sell as an independent and objective judge, for it has put [the] NDES under pressure to exonerate Shell. In any case, NDES has already ceased to be a serious proposition. The designated representative of the communities has resigned over Shell's role in the death of Ken Saro-Wiwa and his colleagues and doubts about the effectiveness of NDES. The World Conservation Foundation, represented on NDES to give it international legitimacy, is being asked by Nigerian and European environmentalists to resign amidst concerns of receiving funding from Shell. The NGO representatives in NDES in [sic 'is from'] the Nigerian World Conservation Foundation which was started by a former Nigerian Petroleum Minister who is now a director of Chevron. That leaves apart from the chairman just representatives of government and the oil industry.*
>
> *Neither the NDES nor Shell's well-financed campaigns across the world can hide the disaster it is perpetrating in the Niger Delta . . .*
>
> *Neither Shell nor other oil companies in Nigeria invest much in the treatment of effluents.*[55]

55 *See* this article published in the Tell Magazine of January 29, 1996, found at http://www.nigerdeltacongress.com/sarticles/shelling_nigeria_ablaze.htm visited on 21/07/07, p. 4. In its speech made during the first year anniversary of the execution of Ken Saro-Wiwa and his eight other Ogoni human and environmental rights' activists, Greenpeace International described the oil industry as an environmental destruction engine and questioned if continued petroleum development in Nigeria can be justified. Greenpeace International stated that certain conditions ought to be met to complement the NDES. These include: (1) a full and independent international inquiry into Shell's and other oil companies' operations in Nigeria, to determine whether they are complying with the environmental laws of Nigeria and the standards of the industry prevalent in Europe and North America; (2) Shell's public commitment to operate under the highest standards imposed on the industry world-wide; and (3) Shell's public condemnation of the judicial murder of the Ken Saro-Wiwa and his eight Ogoni kinsmen. *See* this speech of Greenpeace International entitled '10th November 1996: 1st Anniversary of the Death of Ken Saro-Wiwa', found at http://archive.greenpeace.org/comms/ken/anniv01.html visited on 21/07/06.

Ake lamented the extent of environmental degradation and human rights abuse of Shell Nigeria in the Delta region, including the privatisation of the instruments of political power and authority of the Nigerian state by the officers of Shell in the region. According to him:

> *While degrading the environment and abusing human rights, Shell and the other petroleum multinationals in Nigeria firmly discourage resistance against their misdeeds. Environmental Activism in Nigeria has thus become as hazardous as the environment [in] the Niger Delta. Ken Saro-Wiwa was not the only environmental activist charged with murder. Professor Jaja Ohinwa, a former Vice-Chancellor and spokesperson for the Obagi community in Rivers state, was also charged with murder and detained. He was lucky to escape [with] the dismissal from his university appointment.*
>
> *In the wake of the Ogoni crisis, another ugly aspect of the methods of Shell and the oil companies has come to light, namely bribing officials to terrorise environmental and human rights activists in the oil producing communities . . .*
>
> *On several occasions, I have raised the question of the privatisation of the state by Shell with Shell officials. The privatisation of the state is evident in the swarm of policemen and women in Shell residential headquarters and offices supposedly securing Shell; the presence of armed troops in the operational bases of the company, and in the prerogative of Shell and other oil companies to call on the police and the military for their security. In 1989, Shell called the Mobile Police Force into Umuchem where it was having problems with the community and blood was shed. . . .*
>
> *It is indicative of Shell's privatisation of the state and its prerogatives that it buys substantial quantities of firearms through open tender for its own use. ThisDay [Newspaper] of Friday, December 22, 1995, reports a case before a Lagos High Court in which an arms dealer, Humanitiex Nigeria Limited, sued Shell Nigerian for N100 million (?) for breach of contract in seeking to open again for its bidding an arms supply contract which Shell awarded in 1993. In a 17-paragraph affidavit sworn by the chief executive of the company, Gabriel Akinluyi, the company says that Shell was making the purchase to update firearms of its security forces across the country. We see here the bizarre and frightening novelty of accumulation of terror. I call for an independent inquiry into the acquisition and use of firearms by Shell.*
>
> *These tendencies have been replayed in Ogoniland on an extended scale with more tragic consequences. By all indications, there is worse to come. Shell remains unrepentant and belligerent. At the same time, consciousness and resentment [are growing] in the oil producing communities . . .*[56]

56 *See* the article of Professor Claude Ake entitled 'Shelling Nigeria Ablaze', published at p. 4 of the Tell Magazine of January 29, 1996, *op cit*.

Having described the Survey as merely representing an inventory of pollutants in the Delta region, Ake had to resign his appointment as a member of its Steering Committee.[57] In his resignation letter from the Steering Committee of the NDES, Ake stated that he had reconsidered his membership of the Committee because of the demise of the Ogoni activists including Ken Saro-Wiwa (whom Ake said hadencouraged him to accept his appointment onto the Committee). Ake pointed out that there was no reason to assume that the petroleum industry is concerned about the plight of the oil-producing communities, which are increasingly being alienated in the course of the operations of the industry. He said that he accepted the appointment to serve on the Committee towards reconciling the profit motive of the petroleum industry with its social responsibility, but that he was sceptical as the Survey appeared to be a cover-up. In his words:

> *In the light of the demise of Ken Saro-Wiwa and his colleagues, I have had to rethink NDES. For me, agreeing to serve in the Steering Committee of the NDES was a leap of faith. For if past experience is any guide, there is no reason to assume that the petroleum industry in Nigeria is the best concerned about the plight of oil producing communities including their susceptibility to environmental hazards and it was not reasonable to fear that NDES might be a cover-up.*
>
> *In the end, I decided to serve and allow for the possibility that the petroleum industry in Nigeria might have finally recognised the need to reconcile the profit motive with social responsibility. I have always felt that until this reconciliation is achieved, the oil producing communities will be increasingly alienated and hostile and all stakeholders will suffer in the rising tide of violent conflict. This is why I have been trying to initiate dialogue between them. The distinguished representative of the oil companies in the NDES Steering Committees can testify to these efforts.*[58]

Also, considering the need for a comprehensive and independent survey on the Delta region and how the structure of the NDES was a hindrance to its

---

57 Claude Ake's resignation from the membership of the Steering Committee of the NDES took effect from November 16, 1995. *See* the 'Letter of Resignation' of Professor Claude Ake directed to the chair of the Steering Committee of the NDES, Gamaliel Onosode, dated November 15, 1995 (contained in the press statement of Greenpeace, entitled 'Reasons for Resignation From Shell's Niger Delta Environmental Survey', dated November 23, 1995), hereinafter referred to as 'Letter of Resignation' of Professor Claude Ake directed to the chair of the Steering Committee of the NDES, Gamaliel Onosode, dated November 15, 1995', found (in the area of the Urhobo Historical Society homepage on Shell and Niger Delta Communities) at http://www.waado.org/Environment/OilCompanies/Shell-Communities/ClaudeAkeResignation.html visited on 07/09/08. *Also see* the article by L. Efana, entitled 'In Memoriam: Claude Ake (1939–1996', Nordic Journal of African Studies 5 (2), 1996, pp. 98–100.

58 *See* 'Letter of Resignation' of Professor Claude Ake directed to the chair of the Steering Committee of the NDES, Gamaliel Onosode, dated November 15, 1995', *op cit*.

success, the Human Rights Watch (HRW) doubted that the NDES would succeed. In its words:

> *A comprehensive and independent assessment of the impact of the oil industry on the ecology and communities of the Niger Delta that involves communities themselves is badly needed; the NDES was the first attempt to carry out such an assessment, but its structure was always problematic for this task and it has apparently failed.*[59]

Claude Ake contended that the NDES was morally unacceptable and diversionary, considering that what was needed was not a mere inventory of pollutants in the Delta region but conscientious solutions capable of healing the badly-damaged social and moral fabric of the operations of the industry in the region. Ake predicted that the crises in the region would escalate if the NDES became unsuccessful, especially as it does not have the enthusiastic support of the oil industry. In his words:

> *Unfortunately, the effort did not succeed and conflict escalates with unfortunate consequences. It is clear now that the NDES is too late and does not represent a change of heart. To begin with, it does not enjoy the enthusiastic support of the industry at large. Clearly there is nothing in the recent performance, of the oil companies, notably Shell, NAOC, Elf and Mobil, to suggest that the NDES is associated with increasing sensitivity to the plight of the oil producing communities. It is telling that as the tragedy unfolded in Ogoniland, Shell, whose perceived insensitivity engineered the conflict, in the first place did not intervene forcefully for reconciliation. And when the disaster occurred, Shell expressed regrets but pointedly stated, according to the British process, that it was not considering any change in its current practices.*
>
> *Considering the tragic enormity of recent happenings, and the crises of conscience arising from them, NDES now seems to my mind diversionary and morally unacceptable. By all indications, what we need now is not an inventory of pollutants, but to look at our selves in the face, reach down to our innermost resources and try to heal the badly damaged social and moral fabric.*[60]

Claude Ake predicted that the seed of more catastrophes has been sown by Shell Nigeria in the Delta region, and that unless the adverse consequences of petroleum development in the region is redressed, citizens of the region would continue to take action, as it is time to call Shell to order and to account. As he put it:

---

59 *See The Price of Oil: Corporate Responsibility and Human Rights Violations in Nigeria's Oil Producing Communities, op cit*, p. 90.

60 *See* 'Letter of Resignation' of Professor Claude Ake directed to the chair of the Steering Committee of the NDES, Gamaliel Onosode, dated November 15, 1995', *op cit*.

> *Unless something gives [way], there will be more strife and they will be far more catastrophic. What is at issue is nothing less than the viability of Nigeria, as oil is the real power and the stuff of politics in Nigeria as well as what holds the country in a fragile dialectical unity of self seeking. It is time to call Shell to order and to account*[61].

While commenting on the formation of the NDES up to the resignation and death of Claude Ake, the 'Third World Traveler' states that:

> *It is difficult to ascertain the full extent of environmental damage . . . throughout the Niger Delta because there has never been an independent environmental assessment conducted . . .*
>
> *In December 1994, Mr. J. P. Dessel, the Head of Environmental Studies for Shell Nigeria, resigned because 'I increasingly felt my professional and personal integrity was at stake'. In March 1996, he appeared on British television stating that 'it is clear to me that Shell was devastating the area'.*
>
> *For years, Shell denied that its operations in Nigeria caused any damage. Recently, they have responded to these revelations by promising to do better.*
>
> *. . . Surely, Shell does not need a decade to enact better practices.*
>
> *Shell has tried to portray their own study – the Niger Delta Environmental Survey (NDES) as an ongoing legitimate effort to assess the state of the environment. The NDES was launched with much fanfare in February 1995, but lost any legitimacy it might have had when Professor Claude Ake resigned following Saro-Wiwa's execution. Ake was the sole community representative on the study, a highly respected academic who was most recently a visiting Professor at Yale. Following this resignation, he denounced the NDES as a public relations ploy by the oil companies. In November 1996, Ake was killed when the 727 he was travelling in crashed for unknown reasons.*[62]

To prove Ake's concerns and predictions right about the imminent crisis in the Delta region, it was immediately after his sudden but tragic death on

---

61 *See* the article of Professor Claude Ake entitled 'Shelling Nigeria Ablaze', *op cit. Also see* the NGO reports on the NDES such as the one by Project Underground entitled 'U.N Report Calls for the Investigation of Shell in Nigeria', found at http://www.moles.org/ProjectUnderground/drillbits/980507/98050701.html visited on 21/07/06. *See* the report of the Sierra Club, on human rights and the environment, entitled 'International Campaigns: Nigeria: UN Report on Nigerian Human Rights Calls for Investigation of Shell', found at http://www.sierraclub.org/human-rights/nigeria/releases/boycott.asp visited on 31/12/06. *See* another Sierra Club report on human rights and the environment, entitled 'International Campaigns: Nigeria: Ogoni Tell Shell 'We Want a Clean Up, Not a Cover Up',' found at http://www.sierraclub.org/human-rights/nigeria/mosop/cover.asp visited on 31/12/06.

62 *See* the publication of the 'Third World Traveler', entitled 'The Flames of Shell: Oil, Niger Delta & the Ogoni: From the Project Underground Factsheet', found at http://www.thirdworld-traveler.com/Boycotts/Flames_Shell.html visited on 21/07/06.

November 7, 1996[63] that the resource control movement started in the region.

The resignation of Claude Ake from the Steering Committee of the NDES in November, 1995, and his death in November 1996, was followed by the publication of the 'Phase One Report' of the Survey in September, 1997.[64] This report attracted criticisms from independent peer review sources in Nigeria and overseas. The HRW expressed reservation about the Survey:

> *Nigerian environmentalists express great scepticism as to the independence of the NDES from the oil industry – which funds it – in practice, and its ability to carry out its mandate effectively. What was initially a promising project which Community members themselves, consulted for virtually the first time about their own environment, reportedly felt could make a positive contribution to improvement of their circumstances and the management of the Delta, has degenerated into an opportunity for patronage for its members.*[65]

Besides, the HRW has this to say about the initial two-volume report on the 'definition, description of the Niger Delta and the assessment of data':

> *the report was seriously criticized by Nigerian environmentalists involved in the process, and by some personnel within SPDC, for failing to provide a clear idea of what had been achieved so far and what the next stages should be. Although a follow up report was prepared, disagreements between Euroconsult and the Steering Committee continued, and the contract with Euroconsult was not extended'.*[66]

The Pensions and Investment Research Consultants Limited (PIRC), a guardian of good corporate governance and shareholder responsibility in the United Kingdom, was among the several civil society groups that were critical about the 'Phase One Report' of NDES. The PIRC analysed the reaction that led to the rejection of the NDES Phase One report and the retention of a Nigerian group towards the production of its final report. According to the PIRC:

> *The environmental survey had been initiated in February 1995 in an effort to reconcile the conflict between the environment and development process. The 'Phase One report' of the survey was published a year later than originally proposed, in December 1997, as the original study produced by managing consultants had been considered unacceptable*

---

63 Professor Claude Ake, a Nigerian National Merit Award Winner and the founder and chief executive for the Centre for Advanced Social Sciences (CASS) born on February 18, 1939, died on November 7, 1996, in a Boeing 727 plane crash on a flight between Port Harcourt and Lagos, Nigeria.

64 *See* L. Efana, 'In Memoriam – Claude Ake (1939–1996)', *op cit*.

65 *See The Price of Oil: Corporate Responsibility and Human Rights Violations in Nigeria's Oil Producing Communities, op cit*, p. 90.

66 Ibid, p. 89.

following independent peer reviews in Nigeria and overseas. It was judged that more work was required and a Nigerian group was retained which produced the final report.[67]

As a result of the criticisms which the NDES Phase One report attracted from independent peer review sources in Nigeria and overseas, a Nigerian group was retained to produce the final report of the Survey,[68] which is yet to be published. The UN Development Programme (UNDP) Nigeria describes how modern data was gathered and analysis made by local and international experts in the course of the NDES, but lamented how the final report of the Survey is yet to be published to enhance the development of the Delta region. As UNDP Nigeria put it:

Using the most modern data-gathering and analysis technology, and large number of local and foreign experts, the NDES has amassed, collated, classified and mapped vital data and information on various aspects of the Niger Delta environment. Sadly, however, this report has never been published, thus depriving the public of a rich source of data that could make major contributions to the development of the region.[69]

While commending Shell Nigeria and other major MNOCs for initiating the NDES and the effort of Shell regarding the production of the UNDP *Niger Delta Human Development Report* (NDHDR),[70] it may be echoed that the final report of the Survey deserves to be published to foster ongoing efforts towards SD in the Delta region.

7.3(ii)(b)(i) Proposal for an Integrated Survey

Briefly, what is needed is an independent cumulative and integrated environmental and socio-economic survey of the impact of the oil industry in the Delta region.[71] Such a survey requires the incorporation of previous efforts

---

67 *See* the PIRC's report, entitled 'Environmental and Corporate Responsibility at Shell: The Shareholders Role in Promoting Social Change', *op cit*, item 10:13, p. 28.

68 Phase two of the Survey, based on the findings of its first phase, started in September, 1997. This involved inputs of the Rivers State University of Science and Technology and the University of Port Harcourt, along with the NGO groups consulted, and the UN International Children's Emergency Fund (UNICEF).

69 *See* the *Niger Delta Human Development Report, op cit*, p. 92.

70 *Also see* the publication of the UNDP Nigeria on the launching of the NDHDR entitled 'ND HDR Launched by President Obasanjo', which describes the production of this report as an effort of the partnership between the UNDP and Shell Nigeria, found at http://web.ng.undp.org/index.php?name=News&file=article&sid=47 visited on 31/12/06.

71 A comprehensive and integrated impact assessment of petroleum development projects in the Delta region, fostered by interactive citizens' involvement, is capable of ushering equity, prosperity and tranquillity into the region. *See* 'Niger Delta Development: Can Impact Assessment Help?', being an address by C. P. Wolf, on the Occasion of the Launching of *Participation in Petroleum Development: Towards Sustainable Community Development in the Niger Delta*, by Aseme-Alabo Edward T. Bristol-Alagbariya, at the Transcorp Hilton, Federal Capital Territory (FCT), Abuja, on Thursday, 26 November 2009.'

and relevant lessons and initiatives derived from other jurisdictions.[72] Besides, such a survey deserves to be premised on the fact that SD is about long term (which brings together ideas from the long history of human development into a common framework) and that SD has four dimensions or spheres (ie, the economic, social, environmental and governance dimensions of which the governance dimension, namely responsible governance, is the core and engineering force to steer, integrate and harmonise other dimensions).[73] These

---

72 These include lessons learnt from such relevant international initiatives as the Ramsar Convention on Wetlands and the World Conservation Union. *See* the website of the Ramsar Convention found at http://www.ramsar.org/ and the key documents of this Convention as those concerning national wetland policies and strategies found at http://www.ramsar.org/wurc/wurc_library.htm#nwps both visited on 31/12//06. *Also see* the website of the International Union for the Conservation of Nature and Natural Resources (IUCN) otherwise known as the 'World Conservation Union', found at http://www.iucn.org/ visited on 31/12/06. *Particularly see* the 'Ramsar/UNEP Workshop on Africa's Wetland Management Strategy'. *See* the agenda for discussion of this Workshop found at http://www.ramsar.org/cop8/cop8_nepad_agenda_e.htm and the issues for discussion found at http://www.ramsar.org/cop8/cop8_nepad_issues_e.htm both visited on 31/12/06. *Also see* I. Hewawasam, *Managing the Marine and Coastal Environment of Sub-Saharan Africa: Strategic Directions for Sustainable Development*, Washington DC, The World Bank, 2002. *See* the series of international travelling seminars facilitated by the Social Impact Assessment (SIA) Center, New York (the details of which are provided via e-mail of March 6, 2007, entitled 'Comparing Regions', by the Director of the Center, C. Wolf, to the author, following a series of telephone conversations with the author). These seminars are (1) 'Comparing Rivers: The Mississippi and the Niger Delta', supported by the New Orleans District, U.S. Army Corps of Engineers and the World Bank Institute, held in November 2002 in New Orleans, USA; (2) 'Comparing Wetlands: The Florida Everglades and the Niger Delta', supported by the South Florida Water Management District and the Florida Earth Foundation, held in April, 2006, South Florida, USA; and (3) 'Comparing Institutions: The Tennessee Valley Authority and the Niger Delta Development Commission', which was scheduled to take place in July 2007. Lessons from these international visiting seminars on rivers, wetlands, and institutions within wetlands and Deltaic regions should enhance the application of the good lessons, while avoiding the pitfalls or any negative lessons of these external experiences in the Niger Delta. Such good lessons deserve to be continually assessed and enhanced by monitoring, reporting and capacity-building processes.

73 *See* D. Kaufmann *et al*, 'Governance Matters IV: Governance Indicators for 1996–2004', found at http://www.worldbank.org/wbi/governance/pdf/GovMatters_IV_main.pdf visited on 02/08/06. *Also see* D. Kaufmann *et al*, 'Governance Matters IV: Updated Data and New Results for 1996–2004', being a presentation made at the Centre for Global Development, Washington DC, May 18, 2005, found at http://www.worldbank.org/wbi/governance/pdf/GMIV.pdf visited on 02/08/06. *See* the MMSD project report entitled *Breaking New Ground: Mining, Minerals, and Sustainable Development: The Report of* the MMSD Project, London, Earthscan, 2002, pp. 15–30, pp. 23 and 30. *Also see* the inaugural address of the former UN Secretary General, Kofi Annan at the UN 'International Conference on Governance for Sustainable Growth and Equity', held in New York, July, 28–30, 1997, found at http://magnet.undp.org/icg97/ANNAN.HTM visited on 29/09/06. *See Our Common Future*, Oxford, Oxford University Press, 1987, especially pp. 8–9 and 43–65. *See* U. Petschow *et al* (eds), *Governance and Sustainability: New Challenges for States, Companies and Civil Society*, Sheffield, Greenleaf, 2005. *Also see* the report of the UN Economic Commission for Africa (UNECA), entitled 'Striving for Good Governance in Africa: Synopsis of the 2005 African Governance Report prepared for the African Development Forum 1V', found at http://www.uneca.org/agr/agren.pdf visited on 06/05/05. *See* the publication of the International Institute of Environment and Development (IIED) by N. Borregaard and P. Kapelus, entitled 'Corporate Citizenship – Revisiting the Relationship between Good Governance and Sustainable Development', found at http://www.iied.org/docs/cred/wssd_corporate.pdf visited on 27/01/05. *Also see* T. C. Beierle and J. Cayford, *Democracy in Practice: Public Participation in Environmental Decisions*, Washington DC, Resources for the Future, 2002.

dimensions of SD require to be considered in relation to the peculiar problems, challenges and needs of the Delta region.

As indicated in Chapters 1 and 2, in order for good governance (GG) to enhance the achievement of SD in the Delta region and other regions of the FRN, Nigerian political rulers are required to exhibit goodwill and commitment of government (*ie*, government social responsibility [GSR])[74] in the interest of the citizenry and entire mankind. It is for GSR to build and cement the social contract of governance with the entire citizens and humanity in Nigeria, and to stimulate and energise CSR (*ie* the responsibility of the MNOCs) in the interest of the petroleum resources-producing Delta region and other oil-producing areas of the country.

7.4 THE NLNG START-UP AND SCD WORKSHOPS

Similar to the Shell Nigeria stakeholders' workshops, Nigeria Liquified Natural Gas Limited (NLNG) started a number of interactive consultation processes by enlightening its community representations about its operations, so as to promote cordial relations with the communities.[75] The two community workshops so far convened by NLNG are its production phase start-up workshop (which took place in February 1999, prior to the commencement of the company's shipment of its product – LNG) and its SCD workshop (which took place in August, 2004).

7.4(I) THE NLNG PRODUCTION PHASE START-UP WORKSHOP

The role of this workshop which is interactively similar but less advanced in comparison to the Shell Nigeria's stakeholders' workshops, was to brief the NLNG plant site and pipeline communities about the company's production phase. To achieve the purpose of the workshop, a question and answer bulletin entitled 'CQ *Common Questions: NLNG START-UP*',[76] was published by NLNG to enlighten the representatives of NLNG's host communities and the general public about its production phase involving the export of gas to overseas buyers and consumers.

In the course of the workshop, NLNG mentioned certain effects which its operational phase would have on the communities. These included how its shipment of liquefied natural gas (LNG) would impact on the fishing occupation of citizens of the company's plant site Finima and Grand Bonny Island communities, including those of other adjoining communities of Bonny kingdom situated

74 *See* D. M. J. Fubara (ed.), 'The Endangered Environment of the Niger Delta', *op cit*, pp. v, and 66–68.

75 These are the plant site communities of Bonny kingdom and the pipeline (Gas Transmission System GTS) communities of the company.

76 *See* the NLNG publication, titled *CQ Common Questions: NLNG START-UP*, A KameraWorks Production '99, February 1999.

in the neighbourhood of the Bonny Sea. NLNG mentioned the issue of the exclusion zone created on the Bonny Sea and River to enhance its LNG shipments and indicated how that would obstruct deep sea fishing within and around the zone. NLNG highlighted that the exclusion zone is created as a safety measure to protect the fishermen from having contact with the LNG shipment process, as the process is considered dangerous to unauthorised members of the public who may be in the zone during NLG shipments. In response, community representatives from Bonny kingdom at the workshop indicated that the exclusion zone so created covers their traditional high fish catch zone, and asked how NLNG would compensate their fishermen from the permanent loss of their means of livelihood throughout the life of NLNG operations in the kingdom. NLNG responded by stating that it would address the issue as one of CR, rather than as a matter of legal or contractual responsibility to the fishermen.[77]

In the course of this workshop, NLNG explained that its operations during the production phase would involve the periodic dredging of the Bonny Sea to enhance gas shipments. Considering continuous dredging of the sea to enhance crude oil and LNG exports, the representatives of Bonny kingdom appealed to NLNG and by extension to other MNOCs involved to address the adverse effects of dredging. Especially affected are Grand Bonny Island, Finima and Peterside/Fibiri, Kuruama/Kuruama-Iwoama and other adjoining coastal areas and coastal activities of the people of the kingdom.[78]

The workshop enabled the NLNG host communities to have basic knowledge about the NLNG production phase.

7.4(II) THE NLNG SCD WORKSHOP

Also similar to the Shell Nigeria stakeholders' workshops, the NLNG two-day SCD workshop which took place at the NLNG residential area at Finima, Bonny Island, from August 17 to 18, 2004, was another form of voluntary consultation which involved participants from NLNG's host communities. This workshop, facilitated by Shell Global Solutions, was also intended to enable NLNG to derive community input into its SD strategy.[79]

---

77 Due to its willingness to assist the fishermen through community relation gestures, NLNG commissioned the Bonny Environmental Consultant Committee (BECC) to assess the impact of the exclusion zone created in the high fish catch/LNG loading area. One result of this study is the acquisition of fishing implements for the fishermen through the Bonny Indigenous Fishermen Association (BIFA).

78 One suggestion made regarding the frequent dredging of the Bonny Sea is the need for NLNG, Shell Nigeria and Exxon-Mobil, using the Sea to export oil and gas products to their overseas buyers and consumers, to jointly construct a concrete embankment around Bonny community as a shore protection measure, considering that the sea is increasingly overflowing its bounds. This suggestion arising from the complaint about the frequent dredging of the Bonny Sea is discussed in Chapter 8 regarding the Shell Nigeria Bonny Terminal Integrated project (BTIP).

79 *See* the report of this Workshop titled 'Communiqué Presented at the End of the Two Day Workshop on Sustainable Community Development, August 17–18, 2004, at the NLNG RA, Bonny', sourced from the Community Relations Department of NLNG.

The issues addressed include how SD can be achieved in the course of petroleum development in the communities, especially in the course of its operations. SCD was addressed on the basis of the needs of the communities (as could be implemented, based on NLNG's budget for CD), in relation to the traditional roles of the government in relation to the communities. Other issues addressed included community participation, community empowerment (including manpower development), community advocacy strategies, and the need for partnership, mutual respect and trust among stakeholders of the NLNG operations. The representatives of the host communities stated that citizens of the communities are required to actively participate rather than being merely consulted in the course of NLNG's operations. The workshop thus focused on tri-sector partnership involving MNOCs, the government (at all levels), and communities, including NGOs and other developmental institutions and agencies towards SCD.[80] On this note, while considering a strong SD strategy for NLNG, such issues as capacity-building (including manpower development), strategic stakeholder partnerships, and the need for NLNG to focus on catalytic CD projects for the communities featured prominently.[81]

7.5 BEGINNING OF ONGOING CSR IN THE NIGER DELTA

Various aspects of this book have demonstrated how CSR is becoming increasingly important in the course of petroleum development in the Delta region. It is thus necessary to discuss how the ongoing social responsibility agenda of the MNOCs led by Shell Nigeria began in the Delta region in this era of sustained global effort towards SD in the interest of mankind.

Shell Nigeria makes a case for SD, stating that it is the right thing to do in a properly regulated and stable economic environment in the interest of the present and future generations of Nigerian citizens. In the process, Shell attempts to showcase its ongoing CD process in the Delta region as one based on the principles of SD and best global practice. It identifies such pressing concerns in Nigeria as increasing poverty in the midst of plentiful wealth derived from petroleum development, population growth, biodiversity loss, deteriorating air and water quality, climate change and the abuse of human rights. Shell demonstrates its commitment to SD by considering these concerns

80 Ibid.

81 Ibid. To assess its performance, NLNG took stock of the positive and negative outcomes of the workshop and identified 46 issues in terms of what went well and 23 issues in terms of what went wrong. NLNG outlined these outcomes, after the workshop, in a document accompanying the workshop's communiqué entitled 'Post Workshop Evaluation'.

as constituting threat to life and the well-being of Nigeria.[82] Similarly, NLNG, to which Shell Nigeria is technical adviser, has published and publicised its mission statement, statement of business practice and ethics and environmental and community responsibilities, including its other social responsibility commitments, to showcase its effort towards SD and SCD.[83] Generally, wherever or whenever the MNOCs operating in Nigeria consider it necessary and expedient, especially during the construction phase of their petroleum development projects, they enter into memoranda of understanding (MoUs) with the oil-producing communities. These MOUs thus determine their CD and other CR agenda in the communities. On this note, Shell Nigeria and NLNG have, since the 1990s, been entering into MOUs with their host communities, as a result of which Shell recently introduced the global memoranda of understanding (GMOUs)[84] in the course of its relations with its host communities.

Following the background given in Chapter 1, the ongoing social responsibility efforts of the MNOCs operating in Nigeria obviously started as a result of the crises (ie, the resource control movement) in the Delta region which became globalised by active civil society campaigns against the MNOCs and the Federal Government (FG).[85] Consequently, Shell Nigeria and other MNOCs started being proactive in terms of addressing the needs and concerns of their host communities by strengthening their social responsibility

82 *See* the area of the Shell Nigeria homepage captioned 'Community & Environment', found at http://www.shell.com/home/content/nigeria/society_environment/dir_community_environment.html visited on 31/12/06. *Also see* the section of this area of Shell Nigeria homepage captioned 'Community Involvement', with the sub-title 'Community Development', found at http://www.shell.com/home/content2/nigeria/society_environment/dir_community_development.html visited on 31/12/06. *See* the 'Community & Environment' area of Shell Nigeria's homepage, subtitled 'Business Development', under Community Involvement, found at http://www.shell.com/home/Framework?siteId=nigeria&FC2=/nigeria/html/iwgen/society_environment/business_dev/zzz_lhn.html&FC3=/nigeria/html/iwgen/society_environment/business_dev/dir_business_dev.html visited on 31/12/06. *Also see* the area of the Shell Nigeria homepage captioned 'Community & Environment', with the subtitle 'Sustainable Development', found at http://www.shell.com/home/content/nigeria/society_environment/sust_dev/dir_sust_dev.html visited on 31/12/06.

83 *See* the area of the NLNG homepage captioned 'The Company' with the subtitle 'Statement of the NLNG's Business Principles and Ethics', found at http://www.nlng.com/NLNGnew/company-info/Statement+of+NLNG+Business+Principles+and+Ethics.htm visited on 31/12/06. *Also see* the area of the NLNG homepage captioned 'Nigeria LNG Limited', with the sub-titles 'Mission Statement', 'Our Commitment and Responsibilities', regarding the NLNG's 'Environmental Responsibilities' and 'Community Responsibilities', found at http://www.nlng.com/NLNGnew/default visited on 31/12/06.

84 Shell Nigeria defines GMOU as 'a comprehensive agreement between SPDC and any group of communities (cluster) within a geographical area. The agreement shall specify SPDC's activities, benefits to communities in terms of development and other basis for relationship between the two parties over a 5-year period'. *See* GMoUProject@shell.com visited on 31/12/06.

85 Outside Nigeria these campaigns include those of Greenpeace, HRW, Sierra Club, Environmental Rights Action (ERA), FoE, Christian Aid, Corporate Watch, African Writers Abroad, International PEN, English PEN, Minorities in Europe, Index on Censorship, People and Planet, SpinWatch and Stakeholder Democracy Network (SDN). Others are the Canadian International Development Agency (CIDA), Bloomberg, the Pensions Investment Research Consultants (PIRC), Limited UK. *See* the homepage captioned 'Remember Saro-Wiwa', found at http://www.remembersarowiwa.com/ visited on 08/09/08.

programmes in the communities.[86] These proactive measures of the MNOCs particularly began after Shell Nigeria's wake-up call occasioned by the Brent Spar incident which took place in 1995, in the North Sea, Europe, and the Ogoni crisis of the same year. The Brent Spar incident and Ogoni crisis (which culminated in Nigeria's FG judicial execution of Ken Saro-Wiwa and his eight Ogoni kinsmen) constituted a wake-up call to Shell Nigeria to evolve its ongoing SD-oriented social responsibility measures in the course of its operations in its host communities.[87] Similarly, the crisis of September 20–22, 1999,

---

86 *See* the Shell Nigeria SCD Policy and SCD 'Big Rules', found in its '2003 People and the Environment Annual Report', found at http://www.shell.com/static/nigeria/donloads/pdfs/annualreport2003.pdf visited on 27/11/04, pp. 16, 25 and 31. *Also see* Shell Nigeria homepage captioned 'Issues: The Ogoni Issues', found at http://www.shell.com/home/Framework?siteId=nigeria&FC2=/nigeria/html/iwgen/about_shell/issues/ogoni/zzz_lhn.html&FC3=/nigeria/html/iwgen/about_shell/issues/ogoni/ogoni.html visited on 28/02/07. *Also see* the message from the Managing Director of Shell Nigeria, Engineer Basil Omiyi, in the Shell Nigeria '2004 People and the Environment Annual Report', found at http://www.shell.com/static/nigeria/downloads/about_shell/2004_rpt.pdf visited on 14/07/05. *See* the area of the Shell Nigeria homepage captioned 'Community (Our Involvement with the Communities): Community Development', found at http://www.shell.com/home/Framework?siteId=nigeria&FC2=/nigeria/html/iwgen/society_environment/zzz_lhn.html&FC3=/nigeria/html/iwgen/society_environment/dir_community_development.html visited on 25/06/06. *See* the speech entitled 'Citizens Deserve More from Governments', being an acceptance speech of E. T. Bristol-Alagbariya, on the awards of 'Man of the Year 2005' and the 'Great Mind of the 21st Century', bestowed on him by the American Biographical Institute (ABI), at the World Forum of the ABI and the International Biographical Centre (IBC), held at St. Catherine's College, University of Oxford, England on July 8, 2006. *See* C. Hood and D. Heald (eds), *Transparency: The Key to Better Governance*, Oxford, Oxford University Press, 2007.

87 *See* F. Bird, entitled 'Wealth and Poverty in the Niger Delta: Reflections on the History of Shell's Operations in Nigeria', and 'Ethical Reflections on the Challenges Facing International Businesses in Developing Areas', found at http://peace.concordia.ca/pdf/GRBookintro.pdf both visited on 06/05/05. *Also see* the report of the Fridtjof Nansen Institute (FNI) by K. Tangen, entitled 'Shell: Struggling to Build a Better World?', found at http://www.fni.no/pdf/FNI-R0103.pdf visited on 25/11/05. Among other measures taken after its wake-up call, Shell Nigeria enlisted to become a participant and stakeholder of the UN Global Compact, on June 12, 2006. *See* the area of the UN Global Compact website captioned 'Participants and Stakeholders', found at found at http://wwwunglobalcompact.org/ParticipantsAnsStakeholders/search_participant.htm... visited on 31/12/06. Regarding Shell's complicity in the judicial execution of Ken Saro-Wiwa and his eight Ogoni kinsmen under Nigeria's military rulers, a fourteen-year landmark lawsuit instituted against Shell in New York was eventually settled out-of-court in favour of the Ogoni plaintiffs in June, 2009. In the process, Shell agreed to pay the sum of $15.5m (*ie*, £9.7m or N2.3bn) as compensation to the Ogonis, in order to settle the human rights charges brought against it. The settlement includes the setting up of a trust for the benefit of the Ogoni communities. *See* the publication entitled 'Royal Dutch Shell Forced to Settle Human Rights Case Out of Court' found (in the news area of the 'Remember Saro-Wiwa' homepage) at http://remembersarowiwa.com/ visited on 09/06/09. *Also see* Wiwa *et al.*, vs. Royal Dutch Petroleum Company, *et al.*, Case No. 96 Civ. 8386 (KMW) (HBP) (S.D.N.Y.); Ken Wiwa *et al.*, vs. Brian Anderson, Case No. 01 Civ. 1909 (KMV) (HBP) (S.D.N.Y.); and Wiwa vs. Shell Petroleum Development Company of Nigeria Limited (SPDC), 04 Civ. 2665, (S.D.N.Y.), found (in a document entitled 'Settlement Agreement and Mutual Release', made by the parties to these cases) at http://www.earthrights.org/files/Legal%20Docs/Wiwa%20v%20Shell/Wiwa-v-Shell-agreements-and-orders.pdf visited on 22/06/09. Although Shell denied complicity in the course of its defence, this settlement may in the parlance of CSR be interpreted as Shell's acceptance of guilt. *C/f* the report of the Guardian newspapers entitled 'Why Shell Opted for Out-of-Court Settlement with Ogoni, by Brinded', found at http://www.ngrguardiannews.com/news/article04//indexn2_html?pdate=120609&ptitl... visited on 12/06/09. Besides *see* the editorial opinion of the Guardian newspapers' entitled 'Thinking of the Ogoni Four' found at http://www.ngrguardiannews.com/editorial_opinion/article04//indexn2_html?pdate=1... visited on 17/06/09.

embarked upon by NLNG's host Bonny kingdom against NLNG, suffices as a wake-up call on NLNG. This crisis discussed in Chapter 9 triggered the NLNG to promote SD by improving its environmental and social performances in the course of its operations in its host communities.[88]

7.6 CSR: FROM HOW AND WHY IT IS CONSIDERED TO BE GOOD AND ITS LIMITATIONS

Originally CSR was considered as an initiative for business to embark on doing good; it is presently considered as the effort of business in doing good to do well. CSR is thus the premise upon which business either engages in doing good or a measure of good, at least.[89] Development policy and good practice demonstrate that CSR is good for business, especially in the interest of stakeholders. CSR is good not only in terms of business sustainability, but also in the interest of governments hosting business organisations, as well as citizens and communities of host governments affected by the production and distribution chains of business organisations. CSR promotes the cooperation, partnership and participation among stakeholders, especially major stakeholders, of business.[90] CSR is in the interest of the major stakeholders of Nigeria's petroleum development business, as each of these stakeholders needs the cooperation, understanding and goodwill of the others in their overall mutual interest. Thus, regardless of the factors or forces against it, there is a business case for CSR (*ie*, firms 'do well' [financially] by 'doing good' [acting responsibly] towards realising a better society).[91]

However, in spite of the business case for it, CSR has its limitations which adversely affect or undermine the interest of such stakeholders of business as host communities.[92] To overcome some of these limitations, MNCs should not introduce (in the course of their operations) measures that could dilute or undermine existing government regulations designed to, for instance, enhance environmental protection initiatives,[93] which could abuse human rights, or weaken

88 In spite of these wake-up calls and such governance reforms as the establishment of the NDDC and the Ministry of the Niger Delta discussed in Chapters 1 and 2, the Niger Delta crises largely remains unresolved. *See* J. G. Frynas and S. Pegg (eds), *Transnational Corporations and Human Rights*, Basingstoke, Palgrave Macmillan, 2003, pp. 99–114, especially pp. 111–112.

89 *See* the homepage of the World Business Council for Sustainable Development (WBCSD), found at http://www.wbcsd.org/templates/TemplateWBCSD5/layout.asp?type=p&MenuId=MQ&doOpen=1&ClickMenu=LeftMenu visited on 31/12/06.

90 *See* Principle 27 of the Rio Declaration on Environment and Development, 1992, and Article 26 of the Johannesburg Declaration on SD, 2002.

91 *See* A. Crane *et al* (eds), *The Oxford Handbook of Corporate Social Responsibility, op cit*, pp. 4–5, 83–112 and 569–570.

92 *See* J. G. Frynas, 'The False Developmental Promise of Corporate Social responsibility: Evidence from Multinational Oil Companies', Vol. 81, Issue 3, *International Affairs*, 2005, pp. 581–598.

93 *See* the ThisDay newspaper report entitled 'Oil Companies Shun Dialogue on Environment', found at http://www.thisdayonline.com/nview.php?id=72881&printer_friendly=1 visited on 14/03/07.

positive societal values in their operational areas in resources-rich developing countries.[94] CSR should not be a shield behind which MNOCs could misrepresent facts and figures about social investments published in their SCD reports.[95] MNCs avoiding tax in developing countries should not be validly laying claim to CSR.[96] CSR should not mean highly-placed company officials colluding with community leaders to undermine the interests of host communities. CSR should not mean propaganda fuelled by the MNCs to promote and project their operational interests in developing countries.[97] CSR should not be negatively explored and exploited by the MNCs to engage other forms of initiatives and practices which are detrimental to their poor, rural and marginalised host communities. In effect, although in most major natural resources-rich developing countries such as Nigeria the MNOCs operate as alternative governments, these companies are required to restrain themselves from acting negatively, to

94 *See* the report of the Conflict Expert Group, WAC Global Services, on 'Peace and Security in the Niger Delta', dated December, 2003, especially pp. 5 and 93. *Also see* the publication of Bloomberg on this report, entitled 'Shell 'Feeds' Nigeria Conflict, May End Onshore Work', found at http://www:bloomberg.com/apps/news?pid=71000001&refer=europe&sid=aC3m6AF visited on 06/01/05. *See* V. Haufler, *A Public Role for the Private Sector: Industry Self-Regulation in a Global Economy, op cit*, p. vii. *See* D. McBarnet *et al* (eds), *The New Corporate Accountability: Corporate Social Responsibility and the Law, op cit*, especially pp. 119–147.

95 *See* the Shell Nigeria '2003 People and the Environment Annual Report', *op cit*, pp. 28–29, regarding the Independent Assurance report of KPMG. *Also see* the Royal/Dutch Shell Group annual report entitled 'The Shell Report 1998: Profits and Principles – Does There have to be a Choice?,' found at http://www.shell.com/static/media/downloads/publications/shellreport1997.zip visited on 31/12/06. *See* the KPMG UK homepage found at http://www.kpmg.co.uk/index.cfm visited on 28/02/09.

96 *See* the article by O. M. Bakre, 'Tax Avoidance, Capital Flight and Poverty in Nigeria: The Unpatriotic Collaboration of the Elite, the Multinational Corporations and the Accountants: Some Evidence', found at http://visar.csustan.ed/aaba/Bakre2006.pdf visited on 30/12/06. *Also see* Snyckers T., 'Evading Corporate Social Responsibility through Tax Avoidance', *op cit*, pp. 67–79. *See* the businessdayonline report, entitled 'Institutions Indulge in Tax Evasion Despite Huge Profits They Make in Nigeria', found at http://www.businessdayonline.com/?c=54&a=8317 visited on 26/09/06. *See* the report of the Guardian newspapers (authored by A. Daniel), entitled 'Senate Panel Indicts NNPC, Shell, Others in Bonga Projects: Wants Shell to Pay N602 billion to govt: Seeks Reorganisation of NNPC', found at http://www.guardiannewsngr.com/news/article02 visited on 01/05/06. *See* the ThisDay newspaper report (by M. Oduniye), entitled 'Oil Majors to Refund N39.9bn to FG', found at http://allafrica.com/stories/printable/200508030570.html visited on 10/08/05. *Besides see* A. Akinrele, 'The Nigerian National Petroleum Company at a Crossroads: An Analysis of the Challenges of Funding, Commercialisation and Autonomy', OGEL, Vol. 1, Issue 02 of March 2003.

97 *See* the publication by J. Osai, entitled 'Shell as Agama Lizard' found at http://www.waado.org/Environment/OilCompanies/Shell-Communities/ShellsFalsePR.html visited on 22/03/04. 'Agama' Lizard is a self-praising creature. Jason Osai, a Professor of social sciences from the Delta region, describes the public relations of Shell Nigeria in the Delta region and likens these relations to the self-praising efforts of the Agama lizard. *Also see* the 'Other Shell Reports' published by the FoE.

undermine SD.[98] MNCs should not claim to know their host communities more than the people of those communities; (*ie*, as the saying goes, to be more Catholic than the Pope), in the course of embarking upon social investments in the communities.[99] Citizens of the resources-producing and other host communities know themselves and their communities better than the MNOCs operating there. Nevertheless, social investments from MNCs are needed to enhance the development of communities. Citizens of those communities are also in need of capacity development to enhance CSR and other forms of CI measures of the MNCs operating in their communities. Besides, it is important that in Nigeria, apart from the FG's JV partnership effort to provide social investments along with the MNOCs operating in the oil-producing communities, there are no consistent and dedicated efforts on the part of governments to sustain these investments. In most cases, such investments are abandoned without being duly executed by the MNOCs, or if they are executed, they are not maintained and sustained by governments. The MNOCs and development agencies are not well suited to sustain these investments, while communities lack the capacity financially, technically and otherwise, to do so. As expressed in Chapter 1, the duty to provide, maintain and sustain social investments or public utilities, regardless of the presence of the MNOCs in the oil-producing communities, is thus simply and squarely in the domain of government, especially GG enhanced by GSR.[100]

No matter how well designed or intended, and no matter how well implemented, CSR has a perennial limitation to the extent that it is not an alternative to GSR.[101] CSR is not an alternative to good (ie, accountable, transparent and responsible) government. GSR, particularly GG, is required to structure CSR and to boost well-designed and properly-directed CSR measures in

---

98 *See* A. Rowell *et al*, *The Next Gulf: London, Washington and Oil Conflict in Nigeria*, London, Constable & Robinson, 2005. *See* W. R. Blackburn, *The Sustainability Handbook: The Complete Guide to Achieving Social, Economic and Environmental Responsibility*, London, Earthscan, 2008.

99 *See* B. Andersen, *Bringing Business Ethics to Life: Achieving Corporate Social Responsibility*, *op cit*, pp. 316–317, especially p. 316.

100 However, due to such market peculiarities as good neighbourliness and law in Nigeria, the MNOCs operating in the country have responsibility to fund CD in the Delta region. Thus, section 14 (2) (b) of the NDDC (Establishment, etc) Act, 2004, Laws of the Federation of Nigeria (LFN), provides that the finances of the Commission include 'three per cent of the total annual budget of any oil-producing company operating onshore and offshore in the Niger-Delta Area; including gas processing companies'.

101 *See* the article by O. Arowolo, entitled 'Social Responsibility of Multinational Oil Companies and the Challenge of Local Communities – Any Prospects for Reconciliation?,' *op cit*. Nevertheless, as David Grayson of the Doughty Centre for Corporate Responsibility, Cranfield School of Management, put it, traditionally 'soft' issues for business like human rights, the environment, or diversity, have now become 'hard' for business to ignore, manage or get them wrong. *See* M. Blowfield and A. Murray, *Corporate Responsibility: A Critical Introduction*, *op cit*, preview.

developing countries endowed with abundant major natural resources.[102] CSR has the potential to encourage significant improvements in these countries only in concert with and by boosting traditional political processes, especially good and sustainable democratic governance.[103] Given therefore that CSR has limitations,[104] there should or ought to be limitations to the role of business in society, especially considering the ongoing effort of the entire global community to achieve SD.[105]

7.7 CONCLUSION

The introduction of this chapter indicates that Chapters 5 to 7 are interconnected in attempting to identify the forms and measures of CI taking place

102 *See* W. Ascher, *Why Governments Waste Natural Resources: Policy Failures in Developing Countries*, Baltimore, Johns Hopkins University Press, 1999, especially pp. 1 and 269–279. *Also see* W. Ascher and R. Healy, *Natural Resource Policymaking in Developing Countries: Environment, Economic Growth, and Income Distribution*, *op cit*, especially pp. ix–xi, and 181–202. Based on the provisions of Articles 27, 29 and 30 of the Johannesburg Declaration on SD, 2002, it is for governments to set regulatory standards and for MNCs to comply with and adapt towards them. Thus, in the context of PP in the decision-making process of democratic governance, V. Haufler states that: *Ultimately, much of the responsibility for resolving social problems in an accountable and democratic manner rests with governments. Democratic governments need to set minimum standards, appropriate to the level of the development of the state and in accordance with widely held values. Citizens must be empowered to determine their own fate through democratic political processes. Values cannot be imposed from abroad, from foreign activities, governments, or corporations. International industry self-regulation has the potential to encourage significant improvements but only in concert with traditional political processes. See* V. Haufler, *A Public Role for the Private Sector: Industry Self-Regulation in a Global Economy*, *op cit*, p. 122. *Also see* K. Ginther *et al* (eds), *Sustainable Development and Good Governance*, Dordrecht, Martinus Nijhoff, 1995.

103 Indeed, as V. Haufler put it, *There are – and should be – limits to the role of business in designing policy. At a practical level, there are economies of scale in regulation by governments and international organisations. Industry self-regulation works most effectively when there is some legal recourse. The problems of labour in the developing world, for instance, cannot be resolved entirely by business because the real issue is the lack of recourse in weak or politically repressive regimes. Most important, industry initiatives are not part of a political process in which accountability, equity, and participation are valued. What is good for a large corporation is not necessarily good for a particular country or for society in general. Ultimately, much of the responsibility for resolving social problems in an accountable and democratic manner rests with governments. Democratic governments need to set minimum standards, appropriate to the level of development of the state and in accordance with widely held values. Citizens must be empowered to determine their own fate through democratic political processes. Values cannot be imposed from abroad, from foreign activists, governments, or corporations. International industry self-regulation has the potential to encourage significant improvements but only in concert with traditional political processes. See* V. Haufler, *A Public Role for the Private Sector: Industry Self-Regulation in a Global Economy*, *op cit*, pp. 121–122.

104 *See* P. Crowson, 'Adding Public Value: The Limits of Corporate Responsibility', April 2007, being the report of a series of five workshops held at the Centre for Economic Policy Research (CEPR), London, between April and June 2006, entitled 'Adding Public Value: The Limits of Corporate Responsibility'.

105 *See* Articles 26, 27, 29 and 30 of the Johannesburg Declaration on Sustainable Development, 2002. *Also see* the UN Global Compact which brought corporations and business together with UN agencies, labour and civil society to support universal environmental and social principles. *See* the website of this Compact, *op cit*.

during petroleum development in the Delta region, and by extension in other oil-producing areas of Nigeria. The conclusion to this chapter will thus amplify some of the conclusions expressed in Chapters 5 and 6.

The forms of CI already identified may be divided into two broad categories: the statutory measures designed by the FG, and CSR measures increasingly being designed by the MNOCs in the oil-producing communities. These forms of CI are designed to enable citizens of the communities to be involved in ancillary decision-making processes of petroleum resources development projects sited in their communities. Since the 1990s, the CI measures increasingly being introduced by the MNOCs in the Delta region are mainly designed to address the adverse effects of the resources development operations causing crises in the region. The EIA process identified in Chapter 5 and the public objection hearing system identified in Chapter 6 are statutory forms of CI taking place in the Delta region and other oil-producing areas of Nigeria. The CSR measures of CI identified are those voluntarily designed by the MNOCs in conformity with the initiatives of their corporate groups, parent companies or sectoral groups, as influenced by socio-political, market and other prevailing forces and factors including government's policy, regulatory and legislative measures and state practice in Nigeria. For instance, regarding compliance with government policy initiatives, it may be noted that the Nigerian Content Policy (NCP) was redesigned by MNOCs such as Shell Nigeria and NLNG in ways to promote the poverty alleviation programme of the FG and the impact-benefit and impact-mitigation measures of the EIA process, in the interest of the oil-producing communities.

Other CVIs designed by the MNOCs during the construction phase of their petroleum development projects in the Delta region include the establishment of Project Advisory Committees (PACs), as well as encouraging the formation and sustenance of such community-based bodies as CD Committees (CDCs) to enhance the implementation of their impact-benefit and other forms of CD initiatives in the region. Chapter 6 indicates that the PAC system, evolved as Shell's voluntary initiative, is designed to facilitate community relations (CR), partnership, peace-keeping and crisis prevention decision-making systems during the construction phase of its petroleum development projects in the region. Other corporate voluntary forms of CI are the stakeholders' workshops centred on such topical issues as environmental protection, SD and SCD. These workshops, discussed in this chapter along with the initiative of the MNOCs led by Shell Nigeria to set up the NDES, may be considered as hybrid measures of CI involving the FG. Chapters 8 and 9 will demonstrate the social investment initiatives of the JV partners in the EIA process of their petroleum development projects in the Delta region, as exemplified by the Shell Bonny Terminal project and the NLNG project in Finima, Bonny Island.

It is noteworthy that regardless of the shortcomings of the project level EIA process, it features as the most potent form of environmental democracy regarding petroleum development in Nigeria. Thus, Chapter 5 recommends the need for the EIA process to be developed at the strategic levels of petroleum development proposals (*ie*, at the levels of policies, programmes and projects). Strategic Environmental Assessment (SEA) has the potential to enhance SD of petroleum resources and other major natural resources, including environmentally-sound and socially-equitable SCD in the resources-producing areas and SD in the whole of Nigeria.

Other significant findings in this part of the book include the fact that the NCP promotes equity participation of Nigerians in the Nigerian petroleum industry without placing preference on the participation of Nigerians from the oil-producing areas, based on the principle of impact-benefit and impact-mitigation. This chapter demonstrates that CSR is good for business, especially in the long-term, based on goodwill derived by business from stakeholders such as host communities and society at large. The need thus arises for MNOCs and other MNCs to improve on their corporate social and environmental performances, so as to derive social licence from their host communities; while GSR embedded in GG is required to stimulate and strengthen CSR in the interest of major natural resources-producing communities in developing countries. It has thus been demonstrated that no matter how well designed, intended and implemented, CSR is not, and should not be looked upon, as an alternative to GSR or GG.

It is, therefore, the traditional responsibility of government to provide public utilities. However, due to the failure of governance (*ie*, lack of GG) in Nigeria and other developing countries suffering from the resource curse, governments in these countries are unable or unwilling to fulfil their traditional responsibility to provide and sustain public utilities as is the case in the advanced countries where MNOCs also operate. Hence, even though, due to such market forces as law and good neighbourliness, the MNOCs provide public utilities in the oil-producing areas of Nigeria, CSR measures cannot independently remedy the ongoing crises occasioned by the adverse consequences of petroleum development in the Delta region. In effect, the achievement of a win-win situation between companies, central governments and communities, is the best desirable outcome in order to resolve the ongoing crises in the Delta region; considering that the FG and citizens of the communities are both unyielding, and the MNOCs are expected by governments and the communities to exhibit more social responsibility measures to achieve SCD. GSR embedded in GG is capable of generating such a win-win situation in the region.

By and large, GG has the potential to elicit the input of Nigeria's intelligentsia identified in Chapter 6, including the assistance and support of its citizens in diaspora indicated in this chapter, to generate sound decisions towards SD in the country. Indeed, as expressed in Chapter 1, considering the commitment of developing countries to govern better, GSR embedded in GG, is capable of attracting various forms of development assistance and partnerships from the advanced countries, to foster CSR in the Delta and other regions of Nigeria, so as to achieve SD *vis-à-vis* the millennium development goals (MDGs) in the country.

PART E

Community Involvement in Impact Assessment of Oil and Gas Development Projects in Bonny Kingdom

CHAPTER 8

Community Involvement in Impact Assessment of the Shell Bonny Oil and Gas Terminal Project and its Associated Social Investments

8.1 INTRODUCTION

This chapter will start with an account of Shell Nigeria's ongoing social responsibility measures in the oil-rich Delta region with emphasis on the Environmental Impact Assessment (EIA) process of Shell's oil and gas development projects in the communities of the region.

8.2 SHELL NIGERIA'S SOCIAL RESPONSIBILITY MEASURES IN THE DELTA REGION EMPHASISING THE EIA PROCESS OF ITS DEVELOPMENT PROJECTS IN THE COMMUNITIES OF THE REGION

Chapter 7, which along with Chapters 5 and 6 constitutes Part D of this book, examines the corporate social responsibility (CSR) measures of multinational companies (MNCs) in developing countries, especially those engaged in extractive industrial (ie, oil and gas and mining) development operations in poor, rural and marginalised communities of developing countries. One key issue discussed in Chapter 7 is how the multinational oil companies (MNOCs) operating in Nigeria, led by Shell Nigeria (*ie*, the Shell Petroleum Development Company of Nigeria Limited – SPDC), began to embark upon CSR measures in the 1990s, in order to address the protracted crises occasioned by the adverse effects of petroleum development in the Delta region. In 2003, in the course of its environmental stewardship in support of formal and regulatory EIA process in Nigeria, Shell Nigeria published certain EIA manuals. These are the 'Environmental Impact Assessment (EIA) Process: Stakeholders' Guide,[1] and its accompanying guidelines on 'Stakeholder Identification and Involvement'[2], 'Scoping'[3], 'Data

1 *See* the 'SPDC Environmental Impact Assessment (EIA) Process: STAKEHOLDERS' GUIDE', Document No.: SPDC 2003–069, 2003.

2 *See* the 'Accompanying Guidelines for SPDC EIA Process: STAKEHOLDER IDENTIFICATION AND INVOLVEMENT', SPDC 2004–0002710 Volume 1, March 2004.

3 *See* the 'Accompanying Guidelines for SPDC EIA Process, SCOPING', SPDC 2004–0002711 Volume 11, March 2004.

Collection'[4], 'Report Review'[5], and the accompanying guidelines on 'Preparation and Implementation of Environmental Management Plan'.[6] These manuals reveal the effort of Shell Nigeria towards 'Rebuilding Environmental Impact Assessment (EIA) so as to deliver true partnerships'.[7] Considering the internationalised context of Shell operations, Shell International states that Shell's Environmental Assessment (EA) has since the mid-1990s been focusing on the social dimension of business, more than ever before. Thus, in the words of M. G. Murray of Shell International:

> *Social impact Assessment (SIA) remains a weak link in the impact assessment process being applied to new projects . . . .*
>
> *From a business perspective, Shell International has, since the mid 1990s, provided increasing attention to the social dimension. The company has seen that social issues such as human rights, gender, marginalised peoples, economic development, resettlement, land acquisition and health impacts have all become of foremost importance to a wide variety of stakeholders. Indeed, environmental issues are now often looked at from the human direction as neighbours and communities look from the anthropogenic point of view toward the use of biodiversity, effects of low level toxic exposure, food chain effects of contamination of the environment and loss of human enjoyment resulting from destruction of wildlife.*
>
> *Accompanying the need for improved social impact assessment is the need to enhance the ability to consult and engage with a wide variety of stakeholders. Social impact assessment and consultation is essentially an unbreakable partnership. It is recognised that stakeholders are those who are impacted by a project but also those who can impact the project. A wide variety of voices is increasingly heard, with stress being placed on not limiting those that can be heard and should be involved, but listening and responding to all. . . .*
>
> *This process is of great importance to the company. Early identification of issues and resolution during the planning stages has shown to deliver projects on time and with much wider stakeholder support. It also minimizes delay further on due to surprises and allows for the incorporation of the communities into the benefit stream as a partner.*

---

4 *See* the 'Accompanying Guidelines for SPDC EIA Process, DATA COLLECTION', SPDC 2004–0002712 Volume 111, March 2004

5 *See* 'Accompanying Guidelines for SPDC EIA Process, REPORT REVIEW', SPDC 2004–0002713 Volume 1V, March 2004.

6 *See* the 'Accompanying Guidelines for SPDC EIA Process, PREPARATION AND IMPLEMENTATION OF ENVIRONMENTAL MANAGEMENT PLAN', SPDC 2004–0002714 Volume V, March 2004.

7 *See* the Shell Nigeria (SPDC) publications entitled 'Rebuilding Environmental Impact Assessment (EIA) to Deliver True Partnerships' and 'Executing EIAs – A Partnership Process: The New Vision for the Environmental Impact Assessment', dated November, 2001.

> *. . . Consultation and engagement [have] become the identified tools to ensure issues are identified and managed.*[8]

Shell Nigeria's mission statement on 'Community & Environment' also indicates that:

> *Shell Nigeria places great importance on making a difference in the environment in which people live and work, fostering and maintaining relationships with communities, taking care to be a good neighbour and contributing to sustainable development initiatives.*[9]

Given that the aim of Shell companies is to be good neighbours, the Shell Group states that:

> *We aim to be good neighbours in the communities where we operate. This means more than running our operations cleanly and safely; it also means working with local people to address their concerns and help them benefit from our activities.*[10]

Principle 6 of the revised 'Shell General Business Principles: Royal Dutch Shell Plc' captioned 'Local Communities', thus emphasises the following:

> *Shell companies aim to be good neighbours by continuously improving the ways in which we contribute directly or indirectly to the general well-being of the communities within which we work.*
>
> *We manage the social impacts of our business activities carefully and work with others to enhance the benefits to local communities, and to mitigate any negative impacts from our activities.*

---

8 *See* the publication of the International Association for Impact Assessment (IAIA), entitled 'Social Impact Assessment: More Than Ever Before a Business Need: Shell International Believes that Focused Attention to the Social Dimension Shows Definitive Business Returns' authored by M. G. Jones, the IAIA Business & Industry Series No. 1, Fargo, IAIA, May 2002, p.4. Regarding the role of SIA in the resolution of the crises in the Delta region, *see* The World Bank workshop in this regard tagged 'Workshop: Social and Conflict Analysis of the Nigerian Niger Delta', found (in the area of The World Bank website on Nigeria) at http://web.worldbank.org/WBSITE/EXTERNAL/COUNTRIES/AFRICAEXT/NIGERIAEXTN/0,,contentMDK:21276545~menuPK:368902~pagePK:64027988~piPK:64027986~theSitePK:368896,00.html visited on 23/06/07.

9 *See* the area of the Shell Nigeria's homepage captioned 'Community & Environment', found at http://www.shell.com/home/Framework?siteId=nigeria&FC2=/nigeria/html/iwgen/leftnavs/zzz_lhn6_0_0.html&FC3=/nigeria/html/iwgen/society_environment/dir_community_environment.html visited on 31/12/06.

10 *See* the area of the global homepage of the Shell Group captioned 'Environment and Society', with the subtitle 'Our Neighbours', found at http://www.shell.com/home/content/envirosoc-en/society/our_neighbours/dir_our_neighbours_18042007.html visited on 22/03/08.

> *In addition, Shell companies take a constructive interest in societal matters, directly or indirectly related to our business.*[11]

Based on emergent global trends, the policy initiatives and operational actions of Shell Nigeria witnessed a transition in 1998 from Community Assistance (CA) to Community Development (CD) and thereafter to Sustainable Community Development (SCD) in April 2003.[12] In this regard, Shell Nigeria states that it has commenced the EA of its CD interventions in the course of embarking on social investments which address the basic developmental needs of the citizens and communities of the Delta region, so as to ameliorate the degree of poverty and deprivation in the region. CSR measures include capacity-building, provision of micro-credit schemes, indigenous business and youth development programmes, as well as healthcare, education, women empowerment schemes, and other forms of CD and socio-economic empowerment projects, programmes and activities involving the engagement of CD partners to assist in the process.[13] The overall objective of the EA process of

---

11 Thus, Shell's responsibilities to society are '*to conduct business as responsible corporate members of society, to comply with applicable laws and regulations, to support fundamental human rights in line with the legitimate role of business, and to give proper regard to health, safety, security and environment*'. *See* the revised and updated 'Shell General Business Principles: Royal Dutch Shell Plc', signed by the Chief Executive of the company, Jeroen van de Veer, dated August 2005, found at http://www.shell.com/static/nigeria/downloads/pdfs/sgpb_300805pdf visited on 22/03/08. *See* the area of Shell Nigeria's homepage captioned 'About Shell Nigeria', with the subtitle 'How we Work: Business Principles', found at http://www.shell.com/home/Framework?siteId=nigeria&FC2=/nigeria/html/iwgen/about_shell/how_we_work/zzz_lhn.html&FC3=/global/about_shell/how_we_work/business_principles_ga.html last visited on 11/09/08.

12 *See* the Shell Nigeria '2003 People and the Environment Annual Report', found at http://www.shell.com/static/nigeria/downloads/pdfs/annualreport_2003.pdf visited on 27/11/04, pp. 15–16 and 25.

13 *See* the area of Shell Nigeria homepage captioned 'Community Involvement: Community Development', found at http://www.shell.com/home/Framework?siteId=nigeria&FC2=/nigeria/html/iwgen/leftnavs/zzz_lhn6_0_0.html&FC3=/nigeria/html/iwgen/society_environment/dir_community_environment.html visited on 31/12/06. *Also see* the report of the Guardian newspapers on Shell Nigeria's 'LiveWire' programme entitled '34 Delta Youths Get N7.5m Shell Lifeline to Begin Own Business' found at http://www.guardiannewsngr.com/news/article26 visited on 07/05/07. *See* the Shell Nigeria SCD Policy and SCD 'Big Rules', found in the company's '2003 People and the Environment Annual Report', *op cit*, p. 31. In contrast with what obtains in the various annual reports of Shell Nigeria and those of its Group, the Royal/Dutch Shell Group, see critical assessments of the following civil society activists and NGOs as Christian Aid and Friends of the Earth (FoE). *See* the FoE reports on Shell entitled 'The Other Shell Reports', particularly, 'The Other Shell Reports' entitled 'Behind the Shine: The Other Shell Report 2003', and 'Lessons Not Learned: The Other Shell Report 2004', respectively found at http://www.foe.co.uk/resource/reports/behindshine.pdf and http://www.foe.co.uk/resource/reports/lessonsnotlearned.pdf both visited on 30/07/06. *See* the FoE report entitled 'Royal Dutch Shell: Use Your Profits to Clean Up Your Mess!', as contained in a press release dated December 8, 2006, found at http://www.shellfacts.com/article.php?id=430 visited on 16/04/07. *Also see* the Christian Aid report on Shell entitled 'Behind the Mask: The Real Face of Corporate Social Responsibility', found at http://.www.christianaid.org.uk/indepth/0401csr/csr_behindthemask.pdf visited on 31/12/06, especially pp. 22–33 entitled 'Sustained Misery: Shell in the Niger Delta'. *See* the press release on this Christian Aid report, entitled 'Report Reveals the True Face of Corporate Social Responsibility', dated 21/01/04, found at http://www.christian-aid.org.uk/news/media/pressrel/

each of its petroleum development projects taking place in the oil-producing communities is to secure statutory permit from the regulatory authorities and social licence from the communities. As Shell Nigeria's Managing Director, Ron van den Berg, put it, when the company's EIA manuals were published:

> *We initiated steps to improve our EIA process, with workshops that engaged various stakeholders, in 1999. The new process focuses on the engagement and involvement of key stakeholders. It strives to achieve openness and transparency. Its mission is to secure statutory permit from regulatory authorities and 'social license' from project communities. We aspire to attain world-class standard in impact assessment and management. Also, we hope to create an enduring partnership with the project communities in order to achieve sustainable community development. . . .*
>
> *As a first step however, we need to inform our communities about the new EIA process and seek their involvement. Therefore, this manual is specially produced and distributed in order to inform our stakeholders about our EIA process, encourage their participation and create an atmosphere of mutual trust and understanding.*
>
> *For long, we have realized that we must continue with external stakeholders to manage the impacts of our operations on the environment in which we operate. If we do not get this process right, then, SPDC and its host communities may not achieve and realise a sustainable future. . . .*
>
> *Our desire is that partnership with communities in which we operate, our EIAs will address not only the natural environment but also the social and health aspects as well. . . . We understand that in our current operating circumstances, the impact of our activities on the communities is in many ways more critical to the success of a project than the impact on the natural environment . . .*[14]

Consequently, the vision of Shell Nigeria is 'to be the [Nigerian petroleum industry] leader, employer of first choice and a company that delivers as promised'.[15] This chapter will discuss the nature of CI in the EIA process of

---

040121p.htm visited on 31/12/06, where Christian Aid calls for laws to make multinational companies meet basic social and environmental standards in poor countries'. Chapter 2 of this press release regarding Shell Nigeria's operations in the Niger Delta provides thus: *Shell Nigeria claims it has turned over a new leaf there and strives to be a 'good neighbour'. Yet it still fails to quickly clean up oil spills that ruin villages and runs 'community development' projects that are frequently ineffective and which sometimes even widen the divide in communities living around the oil fields. Also see* the reports of the UK Pensions and Investment Consultants Limited (PIRC) on Shell Nigeria, especially the PIRC report entitled 'Controversies Affecting Shell Nigeria', found at http://www.pirc.co.uk/shellmar.htm visited on 20/09/2004. *See* the publication by J. Osai, entitled 'Shell as Agama Lizard' found at http://www.waado.org/Environment/OilCompanies/Shell-Communities/ShellsFalsePR.html visited on 22/03/04. These critical assessments of civil society activists and groups emphasise the inadequacies and limitations of CSR discussed in Chapter 7.

14 *See* the 'SPDC Environmental Impact Assessment (EIA) Process: STAKEHOLDERS' GUIDE', *op cit*, pp. 1–2.

15 *See* the statement of Shell Nigeria's vision in its poster entitled 'Our Vision: Let's Live Our Vision'.

the Shell Nigeria's Bonny Terminal Integrated project (BTIP) in the context of the social investments being provided by Shell under its joint venture (JV) operational framework, and thereby assess how the objectives of Shell Nigeria in the course of the EIA process are being achieved in the Delta region. Based on the findings of previous chapters, especially Chapters 1 and 7, on the significant role of government towards improved CSR in petroleum development in Nigeria, this chapter and Chapter 9 will attempt to provide a basis for the recommendation of the concluding chapter on the greater need for and challenge of Government Social Responsibility (GSR)[16] in the Delta region and other oil-producing areas of the country.

8.3 SHELL NIGERIA'S BONNY CRUDE OIL AND GAS TERMINAL (BGOT)

The Shell Nigeria Bonny Crude Oil Terminal (BCOT) is the largest of its kind in Africa.[17] What was originally known as the BCOT (from the onset of Shell's operation in Bonny in 1957/58), has become the Shell Bonny oil and gas terminal, BGOT (following the upgrade of the terminal which commenced in 1996).[18]

8.3(I) HISTORY OF THE BONNY TERMINAL

Oil exploration started in Nigeria in 1937. Following the discovery of crude oil in commercial quantities in the Delta region in 1956, the first crude oil

---

16 Regarding GSR in the Delta region, it may be noted that the ThisDay newspaper report captioned 'Okonjo-Iweala Partners Gallup for Polling in Nigeria: 92 Per cent Nigerians Worry Over N/Delta', states as follows: *Former Finance/Foreign Minister and founder of NOI Polls, Dr. Ngozi Okonjo-Iweala, has reached a partnership with Gallup Poll (USA) to develop opinion in Nigeria with the first result released. . . .indicating that 92 percent of Nigerians are concerned about developments in the Niger Delta. . . .major findings of the first ever country-specific polls conducted in Nigeria by NOI POLLS in partnership with Gallup, has revealed that 92 percent, representing overwhelming majority of Nigerians, are sympathetic to the cause of the Niger Delta people. The polls also showed that 92 percent of Nigerians say government is not doing enough for the region.* The NOI Polls is a Nigerian-based non-political, non-profit making polling organisation that is committed to giving the Nigerian people opportunity to air their views in decision-making. Gallup incorporated is a US-based company with its headquarters (HQ) in Washington DC, which specialises in opinion polling, strength management etc. *See* this report found at http://www.thisdayonline.com/nview.php?id=77863&printer_friendly- visited on 11/05/07. *See* the homepage of the 'NOI-POLS: Giving People Voice. . . Supporting Decision-making', found at http://www.noi-polls.com/ and the area of this homepage with the subtitle 'Press Releases', found at http://www.noi-polls.com/press.html both visited on 11/05/07.

17 *See* the area of Shell Nigeria homepage entitled 'About Shell Nigeria', with the sub-title 'Our Performance' and thereafter 'Briefing Notes' on the BTIP, dated January 2009, found at http://www.shell.com/static/nigeria/downloads/pdfs/brief_notes/bonny.pdf visited on 01/04/09.

18 *See* the Shell Nigeria bulletin entitled 'Bonny Crude Oil Terminal' (hereinafter called the 'Bonny Crude Oil Terminal' bulletin), p. 1, slides 2 and 3. *Also see* the EIA of the Bonny Terminal integrated upgrading project, entitled 'The Shell Petroleum Development Company of Nigeria Limited, Operator of NNPC/Shell/Agip/Elf Joint Venture, Bonny Terminal Integrated Project (BTIP) Environmental Impact Assessment', Final Report', dated October 2002 (hereinafter called the 'Bonny Terminal Integrated Project (BTIP) EIA report'), p.1–10.

shipment took place in 1958 from Port Harcourt through Bonny[19] (*ie*, Grand Bonny/Bonny Island – the capital city of Bonny kingdom and Local Government Area [LGA]) of Rivers state. At the time, it was realised that Port Harcourt had a number of disadvantages as a crude oil terminal. One of these disadvantages was the depth of water in the channel, which limited the size of oil tankers that could be used for purposes of crude oil export. A feasibility study on eleven potential sites was then conducted in order to identify the site for the construction of a crude oil terminal. Of the eleven coastline sites considered, the Bonny coastline was chosen as the best possible location to site Nigeria's premier crude oil terminal.[20]

The BCOT (now the BGOT) is located in Bonny, in an area delineated as 4° 25' north of the equator, 45 km downstream from Port Harcourt.[21] This location, by the Bonny Atlantic coastline, is mainly situated in Bonny.[22] The BCOT land was acquired in 1958, and signatories to the acquisition include the Buoye Omuso Brown major house of Finima and the Jumbo major house of Bonny.[23]

---

19 *See* M. A. Ajomo, 'The Legal Framework of the Petroleum Industry', being a paper delivered at the Centre for Petroleum, Environment and Development Studies (CEEPEDS) Seminar on 'Essentials of Oil and Gas Law', Federal Palace Hotel, Victoria Island, July 21–22, 1999 (hereinafter referred to as 'The Legal Framework of the Petroleum Industry'), p. 2.

20 *See* the 'BTIP EIA report', *op cit*, p. 1–1. *Also see* the area of the homepage of the NNPC captioned 'History of the Nigerian Petroleum Industry', consisting of the subtitle entitled 'Major Events in the History of the Nigerian Oil and Gas', found at http://www.nnpcgroup.com/history.htm visited on 28/10/05. *See* the area of the official website of the Bonny Island Foundation (BIF) captioned 'industry', found at http://www.grandbonny.org/industry.html visited on 31/12/06.

21 *See* the 'BTIP EIA report', *op cit*, p. 1–1.

22 Priest-King Alagbariya is the discoverer, founder and first indigene of Bonny, through whom the Bristol-Alagbarigha royal house evolved; whereas Finima was founded by the descendants of Kongo through whom the Buoye-Omuso Brown major house of the kingdom evolved. *See Suit No. PHC/174/72, Between Chief Samuel O. Tobin & Ors vs. Chief Israel I. Brown & Ors*, (unreported). *See* E. J. Alagoa and A. Fombo, *A Chronicle of Grand Bonny, op cit*, pp. viii and 7. *Also see* E. J. Alagoa, A History of the Niger Delta, Onyoma Research, 2005, pp. 151–152. *Besides see* K. O. Dike, Trade and Politics in the Niger Delta 1830–1885: An Introduction to the Economic and Political History of Nigeria, Westport, Connecticut, Greenwood Press, 1981, pp. 24 and 196. *See* G. Finapiri, *Forgotten Heroes of Grand Bonny*, Faghafagha Communications, 2001, pp. v, 7 and 9. *See* B. A. Obuoforibo, *Topics in Bonny Church History*, Port Harcourt, CSS Press, 2001, p. 259. *See* Kalada Israel Abbey, *A Spotlight on Grand Bonny*, p. 1. *Also see* the official website of the BIF, captioned 'Early Kings', found at http://www.grandbonny.org.org/history.html visited on 31/12/06.

23 The acquisition agreement has the names of the signatories written in longhand (rather than the individual signatures of the signatories), along with an interpretation clause in English without an illiterate jurat as required by law. The interpretation provides that *The foregoing having been first read over and interpreted to them when they appeared perfectly to understand the same, including the terms of Clause 3(1) the revision of the rental in the presence of: . . . SENIOR DISTRICT OFFICER & JUSTICE OF THE PEACE [DEGEMA]. Signatories to the acquisition/lease agreement are indicated as Chief Henry Buowari Brown for the Buoye Omuso Brown major house of Finima, and Chief Victor Fikuru Oko-Jumbo for the Jumbo major house of Bonny. The names of King Eugine William Dappa Pepple and Chief Francis Dibarigoma Fonyama Banigo appeared as consentors to the agreement for the king, chiefs and peoples of Bonny kingdom. See Deed made on the 22nd day of July 1958 between Chief Henry Buowari Brown (for himself and on behalf of the Brown House of Finima, Bonny and Chief Fikuro Oko Jumbo for himself and on*

The Shell Bonny terminal provides dehydration, storage and export facilities for crude oil production in the SPDC Eastern Division. The BCOT was built to process wet crude oil produced by Shell Nigeria's Eastern Division as well as from third parties such as TotalFinaElf (Elf) and Chevron Nigeria Limited. The Terminal was also designed to store processed crude oil and then export it via its offshore loading platform. The BCOT was built in accordance with the applicable environmental protection and industrial development standards in the 1960s, at which time the terminal was considered adequate in relation to the existing world standard. When the construction of the BCOT was completed in 1961, at a cost of £15m, it had four storage tanks with a combined capacity of 330,000 barrels of crude oil. About 30 per cent of Nigerian oil production and 50 per cent of Shell Nigeria's production are being exported from the Bonny terminal which is operated by Shell Nigeria on behalf of a consortium of the Nigerian National Petroleum Company (NNPC), Shell Nigeria, Elf and Nigerian Agip Oil Company Limited (AGIP).[24]

With the commissioning of the Shell Nigeria Bonny premier oil terminal on April 7, 1961, the export of crude oil started at the terminal in 1962.[25] After the construction phase of the terminal, its initial storage tanks were gradually increased from August 1966, when the capacity of the terminal was expanded to 3.5 million barrels, with 14 storage tanks serving the facility.[26] These storage tanks were gradually increased until they became 23, with a total storage capacity of 7.9 million barrels of crude petroleum. The terminal's ongoing upgrade commenced in 1996 (ie, after over 32 years of operation).[27]

---

behalf of the Jumbo House of Bonny. . . . and the Shell Petroleum Development Company of Nigeria Limited (otherwise referred to as the Shell Bonny Terminal (BCOT) land acquisition agreement), pp. 4–5. Among other things, this agreement provides for 60 per cent of the lease of the BCOT land payments to the Buoye Omuso Brown major house and the Jumbo major house, while the remaining 40 per cent was to be paid to the entire Bonny community, as compensation. When it became aware of the BCOT agreement, the Bristol-Alagbarigha royal house (which did not have a chief presiding over its affairs during the period of this agreement), complained about its marginalisation as the founder of and an aboriginal minority in Bonny whose natural right and interest deserves to be protected on the course of Shell Nigeria's operations in Bonny. *See* the publication of the IAIA entitled 'Social Impact Assessment: More Than Ever Before a Business Need: Shell International Believes that Focused Attention to the Social Dimension Shows Definitive Business Returns' by M. G. Jones, *op cit*, p.4. *Also see* the United Nations (UN) Declaration of the Rights of Persons Belonging to National or Ethnic, Religious and Linguistic Minorities, adopted by the General Assembly Resolution 47/135 of December 18, 1992, which applies to the ethnic minority Delta region and aboriginal minority groups in the region. Also, regarding customary land ownership based on foundation and the exceptions to same, *see* J. F. Fekumo, *Principles of Nigerian Customary Law*, Port Harcourt, F & F., 2002, pp. 1, 94–95.

24 *See* the 'Bonny Crude Oil Terminal' bulletin, *op cit*, p. 1, slides 2 and 3. *Also see* the 'BTIP EIA report', *op cit*, pp. 1–1 and 1–10. *See* the area of the Shell Nigeria homepage captioned 'About Shell', with the sub-sub-title 'Shell in Nigeria – History' (under the sub-title 'Who We Are'), found at http://www.shell.com/home/PrintFramework?siteId=nigeria&FC3=/home/nigeria/html/iwgen/about_shell/who_we_are/history/history.html visited on 30/05/09.

25 *See* the 'Bonny Crude Oil Terminal' bulletin, *op cit*, p. 1, slide 2.

26 *See* the 'BTIP EIA report, *op cit*, p. 1–10. *Also see* the area of the website of the NNPC captioned 'History of the Nigerian Petroleum Industry', consisting of the subtitle entitled 'Major Events in the History of the Nigerian Oil and Gas', *op cit.*

27 *See* the 'Bonny Crude Oil Terminal' bulletin, *op cit*, slide 2.

Following its piecemeal rehabilitation processes which started after 1961, the main construction and upgrade of the BCOT, involving its expansion and redevelopment, commenced in 2002.[28]

8.4 SOCIAL INVESTMENTS OF SHELL NIGERIA IN BONNY DURING THE CONSTRUCTION OF THE BCOT

Considering that the BGOT was built before the introduction of the formal EIA process in Nigeria, community involvement (CI) at the time was very minimal. CI, which took the form of consultation at the time of the BCOT construction, included the acquisition of the terminal land from the Bonny and Finima communities of Bonny kingdom. Another aspect of CI which took place during the construction was the provision of construction-phase employment opportunities for the people of Bonny kingdom and other Nigerian citizens who undertook manual work during the process. The overall process of community consultation (CC) which took place did not properly comply, for instance, with certain provisions or requirements of existing Nigerian legislation at the time, such as the Oil Pipelines Act 1990.[29] In terms of international standards (ie, considering it as a multinational enterprise), although the BCOT was looked upon as one of the most modern when it was built,[30] the conditions of service for the construction labour force did not, for instance, meet certain prevailing requirements of the International Labour Organisation (ILO),[31] especially the requirement for 'freedom of association and collective bargaining'.[32] Also,

---

28 *See* the 'BTIP EIA report', *op cit*, pp. 1–10. *Also see* the 'Bonny Crude Oil Terminal' bulletin, *op cit*, pp. 1–6, slides 3–12.

29 *See* the objection hearings discussed in Chapter 6. These hearings only came into the limelight in the wake of the crises in the Delta region, in spite of the existence of the Oil Pipelines Act, 1990.

30 *See* the 'BTIP EIA report', *op cit*, pp. 1–10.

31 *See* R. Blanpain (ed), *Multinational Enterprises and the Social Challenges of the XX1st Century: The ILO Declaration on Fundamental Principles at Work Public and Private Corporate Codes of Conduct*, The Hague, The Netherlands, 2000. *Also see* the area of the homepage of the ILO captioned 'About the ILO' and the 'History of the ILO', found at http://www.ilo.org/public/english/about/index.htm visited on 17/08/06. As distinct from contemporary realities, Nigerian workers were, at the time of the construction of the BCOT, not given the opportunity to form unions to enable them to demand the rights of workers. There were no workers' unions such as the National Union of Civil, Engineering, Construction, Furniture, and Wood Workers (NUCECFWW), – formerly known as the International Federation of Building and Wood Workers (IFBWW). Activist labour unionism only came into being when the Nigerian Labour Congress became formally constituted in 1978. *See* the area of the Nigeria Labour Congress (NLC) homepage captioned '*History of Nigeria Labour Congress*,' found at http://www.nlcng.org/PROFILE/historyofcongress.htm visited on 17/08/06.

32 This requirement may further be considered under the UN Global Compact, as freedom of association of workers and the effective recognition of the right of workers to collective bargaining, comprising one of the ten principles of the Global Compact, found at http://www.unglobalcompact.org/AboutTheGC/TheTenPrinciples/index.html visited on 31/12/06. *Also see* Article 28 of the Johannesburg Declaration on SD, 2002. *See* P. Muchlinski *et al* (eds), *The Oxford Handbook of International Investment Law*, Oxford, Oxford University Press, 2008, pp. 646–654.

when the BCOT was built between 1957/58 and 1961, there were no social investments considered such as impact-benefit schemes embarked upon by Shell in the interests of the host Bonny and Finima communities. There is therefore a difference between how the MNOCs in Bonny kingdom and other areas of the Delta region operated prior to 1990, and thereafter, when these companies began to embark on social investments in favour of their host communities.[33]

8.5 UPGRADE OF THE SHELL BCOT TO BGOT IN THE COURSE OF THE BTIP

After operating the BCOT for over thirty years, the objective of the terminal's integrated upgrade, rehabilitation, redevelopment and expansion includes the need to repair its obsolete equipment and installations, so as to enhance its operation for the next twenty-five years, in compliance with the prevailing world-class environmental and developmental standards recognised and implemented by Shell.[34] The upgrade was designed to more than double the terminal's capacity, so as to process and export about 1.25 million barrels per day, along with the associated production of gas being delivered to its neighbouring Nigeria LNG Limited (NLNG) for export.[35] It was designed to install necessary equipment and facilities in line with future oil and gas production forecasts. Shell Nigeria describes the main goals of the upgrade in the following words:

> *To prepare Asset Development Plan (ADP) for the terminal. To re-instate the technical integrity of the terminal. To maximise the utilisation of existing assets in the terminal. To provide, in a phased manner, the facilities required for the processing of planned future production.*[36]

Shell Nigeria states that its integrated upgrade of the BCOT also involves improvement of the terminal's environmental management system, and a new

---

33 *See* F. Bird, 'Wealth and Poverty in the Niger Delta: Reflections on the History of Shell's Operations in Nigeria', found at http://migs.concordia.ca/documents/GR_Shell_Nigeriax.pdf and F. Bird, 'Ethical Reflections on the Challenges Facing International Businesses in Developing Areas', found at http://peace.concordia.ca/pdf/GRBookintro.pdf both visited on 06/05/05. *See* L. S. Pyagbara, 'The Ogoni of Nigeria: Oil and Exploitation', found at http://www.minorityrights.org/admin/Download/pdf/NigeriaMicro.pdf visited on 31/12/06.

34 *See* the area of the Shell Nigeria homepage captioned 'How We Work' with the sub-title 'Our Values, Principles and Relationship with Our Partners', found at http://www.shell.com/home/Framework?siteId=nigeria&FC2=/nigeria/html/iwgen/about_shell/how_we_work/zzz_lhn.html&FC3=/nigeria/html/iwgen/about_shell/how_we_work/dir_how_we_work.html visited on 31/12/06. *Also see* the area of this homepage captioned 'The Shell General Business Principles [SGBP]', revised in 2005, after the last update made in 1997, found at http://www.shell.com/static/envandsoc-en/downloads/making_it_happen/sgbp.pdf visited on 31/12//06. *See* the 'Bonny Crude Oil Terminal' bulletin, *op cit*, pp. 1–6, slides 3–12.

35 *See* the BGOT internal document entitled 'NLNG Back-up Gas Supply Plant Document No. GEN-1104-PR-001 PROCESS Design Philosophy', dated 13/03/02, authored by IMPaC Offshore Engineering, p. 5.

36 *See* the 'Bonny Crude Oil Terminal' bulletin, *op cit*, pp. 1–6, slides 3–12.

phase of community relations (CR) and interface processes with citizens of Bonny kingdom intended to comply with the prevailing policy, legal and regulatory framework of the EIA process in Nigeria and internationally.[37] In the process of the upgrade, the conceptual design of the terminal was made to cover the installation of the requisite facilities. The installation is designed to be in phases: the reinstatement of integrity phase, which had already been completed at the close of 2003; the maintenance of the integrity/expansion phase earmarked to be completed in 2007; and the follow-up maintenance and integrity/expansion phase intended to be completed in 2013.[38] Hyundai Heavy Industries (HHI) of South Korea is Shell's contractor, executing the BTIP at the contract sum of $600m.[39]

8.6 COMMUNITY CONSULTATIONS (CCS) IN THE EIA PROCESS OF THE BTIP AND THE MITIGATION MEASURES AND SOCIAL INVESTMENTS DESIGNED FOR BONNY

Shell Nigeria occasionally consults the leaders and certain segments of Bonny community in the course of its operations at the BGOT. As a result, in the course of the BTIP, Shell Nigeria has been holding consultation with the leaders and certain target individuals and groups in Bonny and Finima communities. In the process, Shell is embarking on certain social investment projects, programmes and services in the interest of its host Bonny and Finima communities. The account of these social investments will focus on the EIA mitigation or impact-benefit measures designed in the interest of the citizens and residents of Bonny community.[40]

---

37 *See* the 'BTIP EIA report', *op cit*, p. 1–1. *Also see* the 'Bonny Crude Oil Terminal' bulletin, *op cit*, p. 1, slide 2. *See* the area on Nigeria in the publication entitled 'Country Analysis Briefs', found at http://www.eia.doe.gov/emeu/cabs/nigeria.html visited on 25/03/04.

38 Ibid, p. 5, slide 11.

39 *See* 'The Atlantic Oil and Gas Works Online – International News', especially the aspect of this news sub-titled 'Shell Awards Hyundai $600 Million Contract for Bonny Terminal Project (03/07/02)', found at http://www.oilworks.com/New/i030302.html visited on 04/10/03. *Also see* the Hyundai Heavy Industries Company Limited (HHI) news on the BTIP titled 'HHI Won $600 Mil. Oil Terminal Plant Project', found at http://www.hhi.co.kr/English/print.asp?dn=newsEng&Code=156&title=News+Flash, and http://www.hhiir.com/admin/admin_e/archive/data/MarEng_2002.pdf visited on the 07/04/04 and 01/09/04 respectively. *See* the article entitled 'Shell Awards HHI Bonny Terminal Project', found at http://www.rigzone.com/news/article.asp?a_id=2783 visited on 07/04/04. *Besides*, see the area of the Hyundai Engineering Company Limited (HEC) website captioned 'Upstream Oil and Gas', which contains information about the BTIP, found at http://www.hec.co.kr/homepage/eng/business/process1.htm visited on 04/10/03. *Also see* an overview of the BTIP, entitled 'Nigeria: Construction Contract Award for Planned $600, 000, 000 Oil Export Terminal Upgrading and Expansion Project, HYUNDAI HEAVY INDUSTRIES CO. LTD. (HHI). [SOUTH KOREA]', found at http://findarticles.com/p/articles/mi_go2264/is_200204/ai_n6853064/print visited on 31/12/06.

40 Regarding social investments for Finima community in the course of the BTIP, the paramount ruler of the community, Chief (Dr.) Yibo Buowari-Brown states in his response to an e-mail enquiry of the author to him, dated March 28, 2007, that 'there are no CD projects being executed or planned to our knowledge that are tied to the current BTIP'.

8.6(I) COMMUNITY CONSULTATION (CC) IN THE EIA PROCESS OF THE BTIP

Generally, Shell Nigeria's continuing community interfaces and other aspects of its CR in Bonny and Finima communities take place in the course of its social investment initiatives as a corporate citizen of Bonny kingdom.[41] Shell Nigeria CC regarding the BTIP began during the scoping process of the EIA of the project. While giving an account of community interfaces within CR, Shell Nigeria states that in Bonny these take place with target individuals and groups, such as traditional and political leaders, women and youth leaders and community-based organisations (CBOs). Examples of these are the king and chiefs comprising the apex traditional ruling council of Bonny kingdom,[42] the Bonny Environment Consultants Committee (BECC), the Bonny Kingdom Development Committee (BKDC), the Bonny Employment Bureau (BEB), and the Bonny Youths Federation (BYF), including other Community-Based organisations (CBOs) as the Bonny Women Patriotic Movement (BWPM).[43]

Between 1997 and 1999, when consistent CC associated with the EIA of the BTIP took place, there were several initial EIA scoping consultation processes. Hence, the king, Edward A. W. D. Pepple, was, for instance, consulted as a stakeholder on October 14, 1998 and on April 20, 1999. The latter consultation

41 The social investment and continuing corporate citizenship efforts of Shell Nigeria in Bonny may hardly be distinguished from its wider efforts on CR, and the same applies to such efforts of other MNOCs operating elsewhere in the Delta region. *See* A. E. Nwokedi, 'Community Relations in Oil Producing Companies in Nigeria', Abuja, Daylight Media Services, 1999. *Also see* the 'Bonny Crude Oil Terminal' bulletin, *op cit*, p. 11, slide 23. See the report of K. Tangen (of the Fridtjof Nansen Institute – FNI), entitled 'Shell: Struggling to Build a Better World?', found at http://www.fni.no/pdf/FNI-R0103.pdf visited on 25/11/05. *Also see* the publication of the IAIA entitled 'Social Impact Assessment: More Than Ever Before a Business Need: Shell International Believes that Focused Attention to the Social Dimension Shows Definitive Business Returns' authored by M. G. Jones, *op cit*, p. 4.

42 That is, the BCC or Amanyanabo-in-council (AIC). The leaders of Bonny kingdom which Shell Nigeria consulted in the course of its BTIP include King Edward A. W. D. Pepple, the Bonny Chiefs' Council (BCC) led by its Chair, Chief Reginald Abbey-Hart, the paramount chief of Finima community, Chief (Dr.) Yibo Buowari Brown, Chief (Apostle) S. T. Wilcox of Peterside community, the chair of the Bonny local government, Hon. Abinye Alex Hart, the BYF, and the community leaders of Oloama and Peterside communities, including the BECC and the BKDC. The NGOs which enlisted in the BTIP EIA process include the ANPEZ Centre for the Environment, Nigerian Environmental Society (NES), Friends for the Preservation of the Niger Delta (FEPEN), Niger Delta Wetlands, and the Niger Delta Human and Environmental Rescue Organisation (ND-HERO). *See* the 'BTIP EIA report', *op cit*, pp. 17-6 – 17-13, Table 17.1, entitled 'Summary of Community Liaison Meetings held for BTIP EIA'.

43 *See* the 'BTIP EIA report', *op cit*, pp. 17-6 – 17-13, Table 17.1, entitled 'Summary of Community Liaison Meetings held for BTIP EIA'. The social investment and continuing corporate citizenship efforts of Shell Nigeria in Bonny may hardly be distinguished from its wider efforts on CR, and same applies to such efforts of other MNOCs operating elsewhere in the Delta region. *See* A. E. Nwokedi, 'Community Relations in Oil Producing Companies in Nigeria', Abuja, Daylight Media Services, 1999. *Also see* the 'Bonny Crude Oil Terminal' bulletin, *op cit*, p. 11, slide 23. See the report of K. Tangen (of the Fridtjof Nansen Institute -FNI), entitled 'Shell: Struggling to Build a Better World?', found at http://www.fni.no/pdf/FNI-R0103.pdf visited on 25/11/05. *Also see* the publication of the IAIA entitled 'Social Impact Assessment: More Than Ever Before a Business Need: Shell International Believes that Focused Attention to the Social Dimension Shows Definitive Business Returns' authored by M. G. Jones, *op cit*, p. 4.

of Shell Nigeria with the king was made by Ann Jamieson, the Shell Nigeria EIA Project Manager contracted from the Macdonald Engineering Group Limited, (MEG) of the Federal Republic of Canada.[44] The summary of the consultation with the king shows that the king was informed about the progress of the EIA process of the BTIP, and in particular the intended date for the EIA public forum of the BTIP for members of the Bonny community. In response to the Shell Nigeria CC team, the king requested the company to convene the public forum and FEPA environmental hearings associated with the BTIP in Bonny rather than in Port Harcourt, and that the BCC should be consulted in advance.[45] Thereafter, on April 29, 1999, the BCC, made up of several chiefs of Bonny kingdom including the author, was briefed about the BTIP by the officers of Shell Nigeria. These officers included the Project Manager of the BTIP (and now a Senior Manager in charge of the project), Ted Ene, the Project Manager of the conceptual design team of the project, Okeh Elechi, the coordinator of the EIA process of the project, Steve Atemie of Shell Nigeria, and Ann Jamieson of MEG, Canada. In the process, members of the BCC were briefed on the scope of the BTIP. Many issues were raised by the BCC regarding past environmental adverse effects of the BCOT. On this note, the chiefs expressed concern about past emissions of toxic gases from the BCOT. Ann Jamieson addressed the chiefs by explaining to them that the purpose of the EIA was to address and mitigate potential and future environmental issues, and that past issues were beyond the scope of the BTIP EIA process. In terms of toxic gases from BCOT, Ann Jamieson explained that although benzene and other volatile organic compounds (VOCs) had been measured in the local study area (*ie*, the Bonny community area) during the data gathering for the BTIP EIA, the source of the VOCs was yet to be determined. She then assured the chiefs that VOC emissions from the redesigned terminal would be collected, condensed and used as fuel, and would thus no longer be emitted into the atmosphere to cause environmental hazards in Bonny.[46] Towards the end of the consultation process with the BCC, the chiefs requested an impact-benefit project for Bonny community which they named as the community's shoreline protection project so as to prevent the erosion of the community's shorelines into the Bonny Sea or Atlantic estuary.

Other BTIP EIA CCs included that with the paramount chief of the Buoye-Omuso Brown major house, governor of Finima, Chief (Dr.) Yibo Buowari Brown which took place on October 13 and 14, 1997. During this consultation, the Shell Nigeria BTIP EIA CC team also briefed certain representatives of the Buoye-Omuso Brown major house and the entire Finima community on the intended modernisation and expansion of the BCOT. In the process, Chief

44 MEG, a Canadian conceptual engineering design concern, was engaged for the overall BTIP EIA management and to support interaction between the BTIP Canadian Conceptual Engineering Team and the Shell Nigeria BTIP Team. *See* the 'BTIP EIA report', *op cit*, pp. iii –iv and J–4.
45 *See* the 'BTIP EIA report', *op cit*, p. 17–11.
46 Ibid, p. 17-11.

Buowari Brown emphasised the need for interaction between Shell and the Bonny people in the course of the company's operations. Chief Buowari Brown lamented the reduction of such fish and sea foods as periwinkles, oysters and crops in Bonny due to the adverse effects of the operations of Shell Nigeria at the BCOT, and that these and other related aquatic and ecological issues are yet to be addressed since Shell commenced its BCOT operations.[47]

Leaders of the BYF were also consulted by the Shell Nigeria BTIP EIA CC team on November 29, 1997. In the process, the Secretary-General of the BYF, Clinton Dan Jumbo, requested Shell Nigeria to employ the youths of Bonny in the course of the BTIP. The team assured the youths that Shell Nigeria would cooperate with them and all of the citizens of the kingdom.[48] Thereafter, the Shell Nigeria BTIP EIA CC team had consultation with the leaders of Oloama and Peterside communities on May 9, 1998. At Peterside, the team briefed the paramount chief of the Wilcox major house, Chief (Apostle) S. T. Wilcox, and a leading community politician, Reginald Wilcox. In the process, Chief Wilcox, a former employee of Shell Nigeria, registered his displeasure over Shell's previous CCs in Bonny kingdom.[49] On May 12, 1998, the Shell Nigeria BTIP EIA CC team also met with the chair of the Bonny local government council, Hon. Abinye Alex Hart and briefed him on the intended upgrade and expansion of the BCOT.[50] The Hon. Alex Hart expressed the need for Shell to pay attention to the concerns and needs of the citizens of Bonny and to properly consult them in future, to enhance the development of the kingdom and Local Government Area (LGA), especially in the areas of environmental protection, improved healthcare, education and public utilities.[51]

After the various consultations held with the traditional rulers, government officials and other key leaders of Bonny community, the Shell Nigeria BTIP CC EIA team held certain public forums in Bonny, during which the BECC and the BKDC played significant roles as key CBOs.

8.6(II) THE BTIP EIA PUBLIC FORUMS HELD IN BONNY

The main BTIP EIA public forum in Bonny community was held at the Government School Compound, on April 30, 1999, following the consultations held with the traditional, government and other key leaders of the community, as indicated above. Present at this public forum were leaders of

47 Ibid, p. 17-7.

48 Ibid, pp. 17-6 – 17-13.

49 Ibid, 17–8.

50 The Shell consultation team was made up of five representatives which included the community liaison officer (CLO) of its EIA team, I. T. Tamunoigoni, the EIA Field Manger, Dr. O. Amund, the EIA socio-economic team leader, Dr. Oruwari, and the EIA historical resources team leader, Dr. Eldred Green.

51 *See* the 'BTIP EIA report', *op cit*, p. 17–10.

the traditional[52] and local government councils, and of youth organisations and CBOs of Bonny kingdom such as the BECC, BKDC and the Bonny Improvement Association (BIA), including environmental protection and industry regulators, and NGOs. The forum created an opportunity for interested stakeholders to deal directly with the Shell Nigeria BTIP EIA CC team made up of management staff, engineers and conceptual designers, and environmental personnel of the company. The forum enabled Shell Nigeria to present an overview of the BTIP to members of the public and to solicit their support, while listening to their concerns towards the execution of the project.[53] The concerns of the citizens and residents of Bonny at the forum is summarised by Shell Nigeria in the following words:

> *SPDC began operating in Bonny in the early 1960s before environmental concerns were major priorities, even in most developed nations. Governments, industry and scientists, and the general public worldwide are now generally better educated, more aware of their rights, and less tolerant of the impacts that industry introduces into the environment. Additionally, the global drive for sustainable development has made people more aware of their environment. It had become clear that in order to operate cleanly, efficiently and peacefully, oil companies in Nigeria have to ensure that their facilities have the latest technology and that they operate in a safe and environmentally friendly manner.*[54]

Some specific issues about which citizens of the kingdom complained included air quality associated with the discharge of VOCs at the BCOT, the need to hold public forums and FEPA environmental hearings in Bonny rather than in Port Harcourt, and the need for sincerity of purpose of the Shell Nigeria EIA team. Other specific issues complained of are the need to protect the fisheries and other aquatic lives being poisoned by crude oil pollution in the course of Shell's operations in the kingdom, lack of interactive CI, employment and the award of contracts to citizens of the kingdom, the need to build an embankment to protect the shores of Bonny community and other CD projects

---

52 During this forum, the Chief Edward Bristol-Alagbariya represented the apex traditional council of the kingdom and thus had to speak at the forum. Chief Alagbariya thanked Shell for organising the forum and made an appeal for adequate protection and conservation of the environment in the course of Shell's operations in Bonny kingdom by interactively involving citizens of the kingdom in its environmental decision-making processes. Chief Alagbariya appealed to Shell to engage Bonny citizens through employment, award of contracts, and the provision of such essential social investments as the embankment of the Bonny community shoreline, in the course of its BGOT operations. *See* the 'BTIP EIA report, *op cit*, pp. Appendix J, p. J–1 and pp. J–9 to J–10, for the speech entitled 'Chief T. A. Edward [Bristol-Alagbariya] of BCC and a representative of the Amanyanabo'.

53 *See* the 'BTIP EIA report', *op cit*, p. 17-48. Members of the media along with two colourful dance groups of Bonny that entertained members of the public were also in attendance.

54 Ibid.

associated with the BTIP. Shell Nigeria responded by promising to address the various needs and concerns raised.[55]

8.6(III) THE BTIP EIA REVIEW MEETING HELD IN PORT HARCOURT

Following the BTIP EIA consultative meetings and public or open forums held in Bonny, the EIA review meeting of the project took place on September 24, 2002, at the Presidential Hotel in Port Harcourt.

Few stakeholders from Bonny attended this meeting, as compared to those that attended the public forum held at the Government School compound, Bonny. The meeting was attended by such CBOs of Bonny as the BECC and the BKDC as well as some citizens and representatives of Bonny kingdom, including certain environmental NGOs operating in the Delta region. Other stakeholders in attendance were three chieftaincy houses of Bonny kingdom (*ie*, the Buoye-Omuso Brown major house, the Jumbo major house and the Bristol-Alagbarigha royal house) which established their respective claims as being directly affected by the BTIP. These chieftaincy houses complained about their marginalisation, and that their protests regarding the BTIP were yet to be addressed.[56] In response, the Shell Nigeria EIA team stated that Shell would sufficiently address these protests soon.

Shell Nigeria also expressed its commitment to the BTIP EIA follow-up measures and to a continuous process of consultation with the citizens of Bonny kingdom in the course of its operations at the BCOT and elsewhere in the kingdom, to enable it to obtain social licence from the citizens to operate. Hence, one of the BTIP EIA CC follow-up measures which Shell convened took place on August 12, 2004, at the women's hall in Bonny.[57] During this meeting, Shell expressed its commitment to continue with its ongoing CC, especially its consultations with the traditional rulers of the kingdom, and that it will not undertake any new initiative at the terminal without consulting with the rulers.[58] However, in spite of its several assurances, the follow-up measures are, for instance, yet to address several concerns of Bonny citizens, including

---

55 Ibid, pp. 17-49 – 17-50.

56 The Jumbo major house representatives informed Shell Nigeria that Shell is yet to respond to its series of protest letters regarding the BTIP as a signatory of the terminal's 1958 lease agreement, while those of the Bristol-Alagbarigha royal house informed Shell that its protest is that Shell is undermining its God-given/natural right, as the founder of Bonny, in the course of its operations in Bonny.

57 *See* the report of this forum entitled the 'Report of the BTIP Public Enlightenment Forum. In this forum, Shell called upon its contractor implementing the BTIP – (ie, Hyundai Heavy Industries –HHI) – to address citizens of the community. Abel Attoni, the CLO of HHI, did so. Abel Attoni discussed the HHI's welders training programme for Bonny youths and its contact with the BKDC regarding the other CD programmes such as the building of a science block for the community's secondary school. Regarding the engagement of the community's contractors, following the prompting of Abel Attoni, Engineer Darbas Adabanya of Shell Nigeria, who represented the Deputy Manager of the Bonny Terminal at the forum, promised that Shell will discuss with HHI on ways to ensure that Bonny contractors are engaged in the course of the project.

58 *See* the 'BTIP EIA report', *op cit*, p.17–2.

those of the three chieftaincy houses directly affected by its operations at the BCOT.[59]

8.7 ESTABLISHMENT OF THE BONNY JOINT INDUSTRY COMPANIES (JIC) BY THE THREE MAJOR MNOCS TO PROVIDE SOCIAL INVESTMENTS IN BONNY

As a result of the relatively continuous CC process that began in Bonny kingdom from the 1990s, as distinct from the rareness of CI which characterised petroleum development operations by the MNOCs in the Delta region before then, the Bonny JIC evolved in 1998[60] during the BTIP. Shell Nigeria and the two other major MNOCs operating in Bonny Island community (*ie*, Mobil Producing Nigeria Unlimited – MPN, a subsidiary of Exxon-Mobil), and the NLNG, formed the JIC to enhance their social investment initiatives for Bonny kingdom in the overall interests of the kingdom. In the JIC, NLNG assumed a 50 per cent share, while Shell Nigeria and MPN took 30 per cent and 20 per cent shares respectively. The JIC set up the Joint Industry Committee which is made up of the representatives of these three major MNOCs and those of Bonny kingdom.[61] The Committee meets to embark upon social investments in the kingdom, especially in the Bonny and Finima communities of the kingdom.[62]

The initial social investments are the NLNG spearheaded Memorandum of Understanding (MoU) projects, by virtue of the MoU signed between the JIC and Bonny community on November 5, 1998.[63] The MoU projects include the Bonny

59 *See* A. Morrison-Saunders *et al*, 'EIA Follow-UP: International Best Practice Principles', Special Publication Series No. 6, Fargo, IAIA, July 2007.

60 *See* the bulletin of the JIC entitled 'Community Projects Status', with its main theme captioned 'BUC Surpasses Projection – Hits 5000 Customer Base', dated June 2004, p. 7.

61 Ibid, pp. 6–8.

62 *See* the 'BTIP EIA report', *op cit*, pp. 17-51 – 17-52. *Also, see*, the bulletin of the JIC entitled 'Community Projects Status', with its main theme captioned 'JIC MoU Projects AN UPDATE', dated December 2003.

63 This MoU is annexed to the BTIP EIA report as Appendix K of the report. *See* Appendix K of the 'BTIP EIA report', *op cit. Also see* references to this MoU on pp. 17–51 of the report. The preamble of the MoU between Bonny community and the JIC provides *inter alia* that *The Bonny kingdom, here represented by the Council of Traditional Rulers and the Bonny Kingdom Development Committee (BKDC), and the Bonny Joint Industry Companies, comprising Nigeria LNG Limited (NLNG), The Shell Petroleum Development Company of Nigeria Limited (SPDC) and Mobil Producing Nigeria Unlimited (MPN), in order to improve the economic and social life of Bonny people and to ensure that there is real and sustainable progress on Bonny Island, hereby jointly announce the following agreements and actions.* The MoU is entitled 'Memorandum of Understanding by the Bonny Community and the Bonny Joint Industry Companies (JIC) on Community Stakeholding in the Industry Sponsored 1998/1999 Community Development Projects,' is signed by the chair, BCC, the chair BKDC, on behalf of Bonny kingdom, and the representatives of the Bonny JIC. It is witnessed by the Government of Rivers state represented by the Secretary to the Government, the chair Bonny Local Government Council, and the king of Bonny kingdom. While the JIC sponsored these MoU projects for Bonny community, it sponsored electricity, road and water projects for Finima community.

road (ie, the Bonny-by-pass road and the Bonny-Abalamabie road) projects. Others are the Bonny Master Plan,[64] the Bonny electricity (*ie*, including the Bonny power supply and distribution) scheme, the Bonny water and its Abalamabie extension scheme, and the management consultancy of these schemes. Based on the provision for setting up a management consultancy in the MoU,[65] the Bonny Utilities Company (BUC) was established as a 'not for profit' CBO by the JIC in partnership with Bonny community, the Bonny local government and the Rivers state government.[66] The implementation of some of the MoU projects was unduly delayed due to certain unanticipated problems, before being commissioned on December 15, 2008.[67] These problems included contractual problems within the JIC and the difficulty of CD project contractors getting access to their project sites. An unmentioned problem was that unspent community investment funds are retired at the end of each year by the MNOCs before new budgets for each following business year are made by their JV partners to enable existing and new social investments to proceed.[68]

---

64 *See* the 'Bonny Master Plan, sponsored by the Joint Industry Companies at the request of the Bonny Kingdom Development Committee', dated July 2002.

65 The JIC undertook in the MoU to establish a utilities Board comprising members of the Bonny community, the Bonny Local Government, and the JIC. It also undertook to do the following: (a), to be responsible for the setting up of management committees to oversee the operation and maintenance of the water and electricity distribution schemes to be provided; (b), to be responsible for contributing to the cost of the operation and maintenance of the management committees through the payment of reasonable rates to be fixed by the utilities Board; and (c), to ensure the sustainable implementation of a business plan by the utilities Board, towards long-term electricity supply in Bonny beyond 2003 by consulting with the government and the National Electric Power Authority (NEPA – now Power Holding Company of Nigeria Plc).

66 The BUC, about 85 of whose employees are from Bonny, grants free electricity to cover basic consumption determined for the citizens and residents of the community. Beyond this basic consumption, consumption is paid for, in order to ensure sustainability. *See* the 'NLNG 2007: Facts and Figures on NLNG', p. 46. Other kingdoms, clans, and tribes in the Niger Delta that have established not for profit CBOs, in the course of their CD or SCD initiatives. *See* the Akassa Development Foundation (ADF), found on http://www.pronatura-nigeria.org/adf.htm Opobo-Nkoro Community Development Foundation, found at http://www.pronatura-nigeria.org/ondf.html and the Eastern Obolo Community Development Foundation, found at http://www.pronatura-nigeria.org/eodf.html all visited on 01/08/06. Certainly, the idea of incorporating 'not for profit' CBOs (under Part C of the Companies and Allied Matters Act [CAMA], 1990), is an idea whose time has come in the Delta region in the overall interests of the oil-producing areas of Nigeria.

67 *See* the booklet entitled 'the Bonny Kingdom Development Committee in collaboration with The Joint Industry Companies Official Commissioning of JIC MoU Projects'.

68 Thus, funds for uncompleted CD projects revert to the JV partners at the end of each year. This accounting process undermines the SCD and sustainability reporting initiatives of the MNOCs. *See* M. Warner, 'Bridging the Economic Benefits Gap: A Management Framework for Improved Economic and Socio-Economic Performance Reporting by Energy Companies', found at http://www.odi.org.uk/iedg/Business_Development_Programme/Papers/ODL_Extractive_Economic BenefitsStudy_execsumm.pdf visited on 31/12/06. *Also see* M. Warner, *Assessing Business Development Impact: A Management Framework for Improved Economic and Socio-Economic Performance Reporting*, London, Overseas Development Institute (ODI), 2008. Following the discussion (in Chapter 7) on misrepresentation of facts and figures regarding reports of MNOCs on social investments in the oil-producing communities, *see* the Shell Nigeria '2006 People and the Environment Annual Report', found at http://www.shell.com/static/nigeria/downloads/pdfs/2006_shell_nigeria_report.pdf visited on 28/02/09, where KPMG UK states on p. 35 that it is *unable to complete work required to form a conclusion on the data relating to the total number of completed SCD projects marked . . . on page 24 of the Report.*

8.8 CD INITIATIVES ASSOCIATED WITH THE BTIP

There are two main social investment or CD initiatives associated with the BTIP, namely the BTIP CD initiative and the Bonny integrated project business complex.

8.8(I) THE BTIP CD INITIATIVE

Due to lack of social public utilities in the oil-producing communities, one aim of Shell Nigeria's petroleum resources development EIA process is to embark on social investments in the communities, to enhance development of the resources-producing communities.[69] Thus, in the course of the BTIP, the apex traditional ruling council (ie, the Amanyanabo-in-council, AIC), and Bonny community, represented by the secretary of the BCC, Chief (Dr.) A. A. Finecountry, 'requested that such initiatives be translated into monetary donations to the Bonny community, to enable the community to decide for itself what beneficial projects to embark on'.[70] Shell undertook to donate the sum of 505m Naira (N505, 000, 000.00) into a community trust fund[71] to be established by the BCC, to ensure prudent management of the sum. The BCC 'assured Shell that the sum to be donated was sufficient to execute all the projects identified by the community and they should therefore not have recourse to Shell on the adequacy or otherwise thereof'.[72]

The Shell BTIP Bonny CD trust fund agreement (ie, the BTIP CDI) generated controversy at the AIC and in the Bonny community. At the community level, the three chieftaincy houses directly affected by Shell Nigeria's operations at the Bonny terminal queried their exclusion in CC processes of the donation of the trust fund.[73] In the wake of this controversy, Shell Nigeria refused to pay

---

69 See the 'BTIP EIA report, *op cit*, pp. 17-51 – 17-52.

70 *See* clause 2 of the recital of the agreement captioned 'Bonny Terminal Integrated Project Community Development Initiative (hereafter called the 'BTIP CDI'). This Initiative (consummated before December, 1999 but not dated) was signed for and on behalf of Shell Nigeria by Joshua Udofia, Deputy Managing Director and Senior Advisor of Shell Nigeria, in the presence of T. E. Ene (PTE, Shell Port Harcourt), while Chief D. I. Manilla Pepple signed for and on behalf of Bonny community, in the presence of Chief Dr. A. A. Finecountry).

71 *See* the homepage of the '*Alaska Permanent Fund Corporation*', found at http://www.apfc.org/home/Content/home/index.cfm visited on 31/12/06. *Also see* the community trust fund initiative in the Delta region, canvassed by the Niger Delta Fund Initiative (NDFI), found at http://www.earthrights.net/nigeria/exec.html visited on 25/05/04. Community trusts are ways to build strong and sustainable communities. *See* the area of the homepage of 'Development Trusts Association Scotland –The National Body for Trusts in Scotland', with the subtitle 'About Development Trusts', found at http://sitepreview.freecom.net/freecom17393/html/whatis.cfm visited on 18/09/08. *Also see* D. Wilcox, 'The Guide to Development Trusts Partnerships', found at http://www.partnerships.org.uk/pguide/index.htm visited on 23/09/08.

72 *See* clause 4 of the 'BTIP CDI'.

73 As indicated above, these chieftaincy houses are the Buoye-Omuso Brown major house, Jumbo major house and Bristol-Alagbarigha royal house. Notably, due to the secrecy surrounding the trust fund issue at the AIC, its member, Chief (Aseme-Alabo) E. T. Bristol-Alagbariya demanded that the issue be made open for deliberations by the beneficiaries represented by the entire chieftaincy houses of Bonny. Among various other decisions secretly taken at the AIC was the decision

the trust fund sum to the AIC except into a community trust fund, as agreed with the AIC. The AIC, represented by the BCC, then instituted a legal suit against Shell Nigeria demanding payment of the fund. This suit commenced at the Rivers state High Court sitting in Port Harcourt, to the Court of Appeal (CA), Port Harcourt, and then up to the Supreme Court (SC), at the Federal Capital Territory (FCT), Abuja, where the BCC and Shell Nigeria entered into an out-of-court settlement dated May 9, 2007, for the fund and interest accrued, by virtue of the order of the CA dated July 13, 2001.[74] Instead of adopting the out-of-court settlement as judgement of the Supreme Court in the

---

upon which a public notice was made in the Guardian newspaper of May 22, 2000, entitled 'Public Notice: Bonny Terminal Integrated Project Trust', by which three chiefs in the council were proposed as trustees without the knowledge and consent of the beneficiaries. For instance, Part C, sections 590–612 of the CAMA, 2004, pertains to 'Incorporated Trustees', in Nigeria. Section 591(2) of this Act provides for the requirements such as documents to be attached to the application for incorporated trustees. Sub-section 2(b) of this section requires the attachment of 'duly signed copies of the minutes of the meeting appointing the trustees and authorising the application, showing the people present and the votes scored.', while section 591(5) provides that *If any person knowingly makes any false statement or gives any false information for the purpose of incorporating trustees under this Part of the Decree, he shall be guilty of an offence and liable on conviction to imprisonment for one year or to a fine of N100. Also see* the area of the website of the Alaska Permanent Fund Corporation captioned 'Frequently Asked Questions', regarding 'Why did Alakans Create the Fund?' and 'Why is the Fund Successful?', found at http://www.apfc.org/theapfc/faq.cfm?srchhighlight=#successful visited on 31/12/06. Chief Bristol-Alagbariya opposed how the trust fund was being discretely negotiated at the AIC. To establish proper standing in law, Chief Alagbariya joined his primary constituency – the Bristol-Alagbarigha royal house, to question why the natural right of the house, as the founder of Bonny, should be neglected in the decision-making process of the fund. The BCC reacted and arbitrarily suspended him. Chief Alagbariya in turn reacted by instituting an action at the court of law, challenging the BCC that his suspension was contrary to his fundamental rights guaranteed under the 1999 Constitution of the Federal Republic of Nigeria (FRN). In an order dated July 31, 2002, the court restrained the BCC from impeding the fundamental rights of the Chief Alagbariya. The action consequently ended with a consent judgement, where the BCC undertook to reabsorb him. *See Suit No. PHC/399m/2002, Between Chief (Aseme-Alabo) Edward T. B. A. Bristol-Alagbariya vs. Chief (Dr.) A. A. Ibiama-Finecountry and Chief D. I. Manilla-Pepple (For Themselves and on Behalf of the Bonny Chiefs' Council)*, (Unreported). Besides, in the heat of the controversy at the AIC, Chief Alagbariya suggested that the fund should be in the custody of the king, to guarantee its safety. *Inter alia*, Chief Alagbariya suggested that at least 30per cent of the fund should be used to educate Bonny youths in specialised fields of oil and gas related studies in the world's best educational institutions. *See* the letter of Chief Bristol-Alagbariya to his colleagues at the AIC, dated August 18, 2003, is entitled, *inter alia*, 'Re: The Shell Petroleum Development Company of Nigeria Limited (SPDC) Donation of 505 Million Naira Bonny Community Development Trust Fund in the Course of the SPDC Ongoing Bonny Crude Oil Terminal Integrated Project', especially p. 2.

74 This order in *Suit No. SC/249/2005 (Appeal No. CA/PH/144/2001, Suit No. PHC/250/2000) between the Shell Petroleum Development Company of Nigeria vs. Chief N. Y. Allaputa (For himself, the Amanyanabo of Bonny in Council, Chiefs, Elders and the Entire Bonny Kingdom)*, signed by the Presiding Judge, the Hon. Justice J. O. Ogebe, and M. O. Atoyebi (for the Deputy Chief Registrar of the court), provides *inter alia* as follows: *IT IS ORDERED AS FOLLOWS: 1. That by consent of both parties the judgement sum of N420, 750, 000 (Four Hundred & Twenty Million Seven Hundred & Fifty Thousand Naira) Only shall be paid to the D. C. R. of this court on or before 31/08/2001 and he shall pay same into an interest yielding account in Zenith International Bank, Trans-Amadi, Port Harcourt, pending the determination of the Applicant's Appeal. 2. That both parties are encouraged to find ways of resolving the matter in dispute out of court in the interest of peace and harmony in the society [Bonny community]. See* the judgment of the CA in this Suit, reported in [2005] 9 N. W. L. R., 475–525. Besides, while responding to the protest of the Bristol-Alagbarigha royal house, Buoye-Omuso Brown major house, and Jumbo major house, regarding their exclusion from the proposed Board of Trustees of

overall interest of Bonny community, the BCC and Shell Nigeria filed a joint motion of discontinuance dated June 11, 2007, for the withdrawal of the suit and that was granted by the Court.

Due to the AIC's discreet nature of handling the trust fund issue, the controversy regarding it continued. The Bonny LGA chapter of the National Youth Council of Nigeria (NYCN) thus tabled the issue along with other issues generating crisis in Bonny, at the Rivers State Government Truth and Reconciliation Commission (RSGTRC) on August 5, 2008. While deliberating on Bonny kingdom issues, the AIC informed the Commission that it had filed a legal suit challenging its jurisdiction to entertain the issues. Having been so deprived of the opportunity to reconcile the people of Bonny on the issues before it, the Commission ended its public sittings on November 25, 2008 and delivered its report on March 10, 2009.[75] The military drafted by the FG in the wake of tension in Bonny continues to remain in order to safeguard the government's enormous JV petroleum investments in the kingdom, albeit at the expense of innocent citizens.[76]

8.8(II) THE PROPOSED BONNY INTEGRATED BUSINESS COMPLEX (BIBC)

Another Shell Nigeria CD project designed in the interest of the Bonny community is the BIBC conceived by Shell's micro-credit and business development team during the construction phase of the BTIP. The BIBC is a shared

the BTIP Bonny CD trust, the Corporate Affairs Commission (CAC), situated at the Federal Capital Territory (FCT), Abuja, had in its letter to these houses and the BCC, directed as follows: . . . *You are however advised to meet and resolve these issues amicably in the interest of the development of Bonny kingdom*. This advice was given by the CAC in a letter directed to the parties with reference number, CAC/IT/R/8524/VOL./1/123, dated December 6, 2001, and signed by Ekinyi Ogah, for the Registrar General of the CAC. This letter is entitled 'Re: Objections to the Registration of Bonny Terminal Integrated Project Trust under Part 'C' of the Companies and Allied Matters Act, 1990'.

75 *See* the Daily Sun newspaper report entitled 'Shell N.5b Windfall Tears Rivers Community Apart', found at http://www.sunnewsonline.com/webpages/news/national/2008/june/21/national-21-06-. . . visited on 21/06/08. *Also see* the ThisDay newspaper report entitled 'Bonny Youths Blame Crisis on N505m Shell Largesse', found at http://www.thisdayonline.com/nview.php?id=118904&printer_friendly=1 visited on 10/08/08. *See* the Vanguard newspaper report entitled 'Bonny Monarch Subpoenaed by Truth Commission', found at http://www.vanguardngr.com/content/view/22390/43/ visited on 22/11/2008. *Also see* another Vanguard newspaper report entitled 'Royal Father Shuns Rivers Truth Commission's Summons', found at http://www.vanguardngr.com/content/view/22728/42/ visited on 26/11/08. *See* the Vanguard newspaper report entitled 'Militant Group Threatens Bonny Monarch', found at http://www.vanguardngr.com/content/view/22823/42/ visited on 27/11/08. *Also see* the report of the Ibani Express entitled 'Bad Money? The Untold Story of the N505m that Ripped Bonny', Vol. 2. No. 3, April 7 – May 8, 2009, pp. 1 and 20. The report of the RSTRC entitled 'Speech made by the Hon. Justice Kayode Eso, CON, LLD, LITT.D, on the Occasion of the Submission of the Truth and Reconciliation Commission on Tuesday, 10th March, 2009', indicates anachronistic and prehistoric rule in Bonny kingdom contrary to what the Constitution of the FRN guarantees. The Rivers State Government White Paper on this report *inter alia* queries '. . . The erroneous claim of the Amanyanabo [King], that he could do anything without having to respond personally or be held accountable personally, . . .' *See* the 'Rivers State Government White Paper on Eso Panel', pp. 469–471, especially p. 470.

76 *See* The Times of Nigeria report entitled 'Nigerian Soldiers Caught On Video Executing Civilians! It Is War Crime – MEND', found at http://www.thetimesofnigeria.com/Article.aspx?id=1873&print=1 visited on 19/06/09.

vision of Shell Nigeria and the king of Bonny kingdom and the BKDC regarding socio-economic and infrastructural development in Bonny community. It was initiated as a springboard for economic development in Bonny, considering that business is an engine of growth and development in society.[77] The BIBC is considered to be a nucleus for current and future development of an area using a basic framework that would encourage (and promote) local self-employment and income generation.[78]

The BIBC, to be built on three hectares of land, is designed to have such projects as business enterprises, a fish canning factory, fish pond, fish smoking, cold storage facilities, deep sea fishing (trawling), petroleum products marketing station, training and business support facilities, business incubator centre, craft centre, multipurpose and cultural centre, sports and recreation facilities among other projects which may be determined by the people of Bonny, in accordance with the provisions of the feasibility report of the complex.[79] Furthermore, based on the CCs held in various citizen groups and communities of Bonny by Datson Nigeria Limited (DNL) so as to give its professional opinion on the BIBC, citizens of Bonny suggested including such other facilities as a community bank complex and bottled water and soft drinks industries.[80] Also, in the course of the CCs convened by DNL, citizens of Bonny complained that they had not been informed that the complex is intended to be built for them. Considering the several unfulfilled promises of Shell Nigeria since it commenced operations in Bonny, the people expressed reservation that the BIBC would eventually be built. They thus urged Shell Nigeria to be sincere about its promise to build the BIBC, to enable them to have confidence in the company.[81] In response, Shell urged the people to take ownership of the complex and use and maintain it to improve their well-being.[82]

---

77 It is considered that business performs an economic function through wealth creation and a social development function by distributing wealth through employment and other activities. Hence, *the concept is expected to provide a platform through which development concerns as outlined in the CD plan and stated above can be tackled simultaneously in an integrated manner. The underlying consideration is that an Integrated Business Complex will enable the community to assemble economic empowerment; social services and utilities-based projects using a common framework, in a designed area, from which economic activities can start and permeate the entire community. See* the Shell Nigeria feasibility study of the 'BTIP Community Development Project' designed by the Shell Nigeria micro-credit and business development team, dated July 25, 2003 (hereinafter referred to as the Shell Nigeria feasibility study of the 'BTIP CD Project'), p. 1.

78 Ibid, p. 2.

79 To comply with the BIBC feasibility study designed by Shell Nigeria, DNL was engaged by Shell as a consultant to prepare a professional opinion, informed by CC, on the study. *See* the opinion of Datson Nigeria Limited (DNL) expressed in its feasibility study of the BIBC, dated May 28, 2004, pp. 3–4.

80 Ibid, p. 4.

81 Ibid, pp. 3–4.

82 Ibid, p. 3. Shell Nigeria's view on community ownership of such social investments as the BIBC is indeed significant. However, effective community ownership of such social investments require human resources development (*ie*, capacity-building) and venture capital which may be provided for the communities by the JV partners of the petroleum development business, the state and local

8.8(III) THE BONNY CD PLAN (CDP)

In 2001, in the course of the BTIP, Shell Nigeria assisted the Bonny community to produce a CDP comprising the needs of the community for five years. The Bonny CDP begins with the profile of Bonny community which identifies the tribe, language, location, population, geographical features, literacy levels, and the traditional occupations and lifestyle of the people of Bonny kingdom. The plan also indicates existing public utilities in Bonny community.[83]

The CDP began with a session on Participatory Rural Appraisal (PRA) from June 6–8, 2001. The prioritisation of the needs of the people of the community is based on how important such needs are, and the availability of finance to provide them. While prioritising CD projects based on their level of importance, thirty projects[84] were outlined by the BKDC and the representatives of the men, women and young people of the community.

The objectives of the Bonny CDP arising from the Bonny Master Plan (BMP) include the promotion of the living conditions of the people and the creation of employment opportunities, especially skilled manpower recruitment. Other objectives of the plan are to establish income generating projects to promote even distribution of income among individuals and groups, and the need for effective participation of the people in the ownership and management of the CD initiatives designed for them. The plan is also designed to enable the community to sustain its pace of development, and to avert or minimise the crises occasioned against the MNOCs through the provision of gainful socio-economic engagements for restive young people in the community.[85] The Plan is also designed to empower Project Management Committees (PMCs) to take responsibility for the implementation and management of specific projects. It

---

governments of the communities. These are essential, in order that natural resources development could sustainably enrich the resources-producing poor and marginalised communities. In these and other essential ways, the efforts of the JV partners to enhance SCD in the oil-producing communities may be feasible through equipping the communities to produce some of their basic needs in the form of economic self-reliance. *See* T. Binns and E. Nel, 'Beyond the Development Impasse: The Role of Local Economic Development and Community Self-Reliance in Rural South Africa', The Journal of Modern African Studies, 37, 3 (1999), pp. 389–408, especially pp. 404–407. *See* P. Newman *et al*, *Resilient Cities: Responding to Peak Oil and Climate Change*, Washington DC, Island Press, 2009. *Also see* R. Hopkins, *The Transition Handbook: From Oil Dependency to Local Resilience*, Foxhole, Green, 2008.

83 *See* the CDP for Bonny community, pp. 1–3.

84 Ibid, pp. 4–5. The first ten projects so prioritised include the ring and link roads connecting the Bonny Island community with its 56 village communities. Others are the need for agricultural development and advancement, shore protection, micro-credit scheme, education, small scale/cottage industries, health/medical care system, drainage, women development centre and transportation system. The developmental need and priorities ranging from numbers 11–20 are the need for a recreation centre, water and water treatment plant, employment, stadium, youth development scheme (YDS), construction of canal, land reclamation by sand-filling, landing jetty, market and low cost housing. Finally, the needs of the people ranging from numbers 21–30 of the priority list are electricity, youth multipurpose centre, bridges, communication, warehouse, town hall, cold room, charity home, fire service station and public toilet facilities. *See* the CDP for Bonny community, pp. 3–9.

85 Ibid, pp. 6–8.

is designed to generate core and integrated CD projects capable of providing complementary services as well as the utilisation of local resources and the use of appropriate technology. The plan is dynamic in the sense that prioritised projects not executed (as planned), could be modified and rescheduled for implementation in future.[86]

The plan provides the strategies for its implementation. These are: (1) the involvement of the people themselves in participatory planning and decision-making; (2) incorporation of income generating projects; (3) incorporation of employment creation projects; and (4) involvement of stakeholder partners, namely the community, federal, state and local government, including the MNOCs operating in the community (*ie*, Shell Nigeria, Exxon-Mobil and the NLNG), as well as other business concerns such as the banks in the community. The Niger Delta Development Commission (NDDC), which is responsible for the development of the Delta region and other oil-producing areas of the country, is also stated as a potential stakeholder. Other groups whose roles are important in the context of implementation include NGOs and CBOs. Based on these implementation strategies, certain factors which may influence the plan's success are identified. These are the maintenance of peace in the entire Bonny kingdom; transparency, honesty and accountability on the part of the stakeholders; the availability of development funds and qualified personnel; the people's attitude towards self-help CD initiatives and the active participation of all stakeholders. Other identified factors are the need for the people to take ownership and management of their CD projects; and the existence of political stability, from the LGA, to the state and federal levels of government, in the country.[87] To enhance its implementation, the plan was signed on June 8, 2001, by the chairs of BCC and BKDC, including the women and youth leaders of the community.[88]

8.8(IV) COMMUNITY CONCERNS REGARDING ENVIRONMENTAL PROTECTION AND CALLS FOR SHELL'S ENVIRONMENTAL STEWARDSHIP

Environmental stewardship has already been discussed as an aspect of CSR in Chapter 7 and in the course of the social responsibility measures of Shell Nigeria at the beginning of this chapter.[89] Thus, regarding CI in environmental

---

86 Ibid.
87 Ibid, p. 11.
88 Ibid.
89 *See* the article by Claude Ake entitled 'Shelling Nigeria Ablaze', published in the Tell Magazine, 29 January 1996, found at http://www.nigerdeltacongress.com/sarticles/shelling_nigeria_ablaze.htm visited on 21/07/07, p. 4. *See* P. Kotler and N. Lee, *Corporate Social Responsibility: Doing the Most Good for Your Company and Your Cause*, Hoboken, John Wiley & Sons, 2005, pp. 207–276, especially p. 207. *Also see* W. Visser *et al* (eds), *Corporate Citizenship in Africa: Lessons from the Past; Paths to the Future, op cit*, especially, pp. 93–117. *See* the area of the Shell Nigeria homepage captioned 'Community & Environment', found at http://www.shell.com/home/Framework?siteId=nigeria&FC2=/nigeria/html/iwgen/leftnavs/zzz_lhn6_0_0.html&FC3=/nigeria/html/iwgen/society_environment/dir_community_environment.html visited on 31/12/06.

protection, Shell Nigeria consults the BECC in the same manner as it consults with the BKDC regarding CD in Bonny kingdom.

The environmental protection concerns expressed by citizens of Bonny during Shell's consultations with them include air and underground water pollution generated by the presence of VOC (Volatile Organic Compound) emission sources, especially the high volume of sludge[90] being emitted at the terminal into the community. These VOC emissions have, in the course of Shell's operations, been polluting the Bonny sea and mainland water table, as well as impacting adversely on fisheries and other sea food and aquatic lives and the terrestrial environment in Bonny. The sources of VOC emission are mentioned in the BTIP EIA report, which provides that they are treated to mitigate their adverse effects. Thus, regarding 'Existing VOC Emission Sources', the BTIP EIA report indicates that:

> *At the existing Bonny Terminal, there are several potential sources of fugitive volatile organic compound (VOC) emissions. These sources are mainly associated with the following:*
>
> - ***Tank Farm.*** *As indicated in Table 6.3, the existing Bonny Terminal Tank Farm is comprised of a total of 23 storage tanks. Two of the tanks have cone roof types, while the remaining tanks have floating roofs. The tanks, associated valves and venting systems are all potential sources of VOCs. Source characterization for the tank farm indicates that 164,000m3/d of VOCs are currently emitted from the Bonny Terminal.*
> - ***Sludge Holding Pits.*** *At the existing Bonny Terminal, sludge is removed from the storage tanks when they are cleaned. The sludge is then held in four sludge storage pits with a combined gross capacity of 7,000m3. In 1994, the total accumulated sludge was estimated by SPDC to have a volume of 3,000m3. The composition of the sludge was as follows:*
>
>   *>Solids 34%.*
>   *>Oil 35%.*
>   *>Water 31%.*
>
> *In 1995, SPDC estimated the total accumulated sludge to have a volume of 6,000m3. No emission estimates are available for the sludge holding pits . . .*
>
> - ***Emulsion Treatment.*** *At the existing Bonny Terminal, there are two tanks (ie, Tanks No. 601A and 601B)) associated with Emulsion Treatment Facility. Both tanks have cone roofs. The tanks are 9.9m high, with diameters of 33.48m. The gross and net storage capacities are 53,600 and 33,300 Blbs. The emulsion is drained from the tanks,*

90 Shell Nigeria defines sludge in the following words: *sludge derived from oil production typically consists of water, oil (particularly the heavier hydrocarbon molecules) and sediment (drilling mud and any solid particles carried out of the layers of rock that produced the oil). This material accumulates on the bottom of storage tanks. See* the 'BTIP EIA report', *op cit, p.* GLO–5. *Also see* pp. 6–11 to 16–17, regarding existing VOC emission sources and how sludge is being treated.

> *and is heated and separated into water and oil in two emulsion treatment units. The emulsion storage tanks and emulsion treatment units are all potential sources of VOC emissions. The emissions from the emulsion treatment tanks have been included in the overall tank farm emissions.*
>
> - ***Water Treatment.*** *Water from the oil storage tanks and emulsion treatment facilities is treated in the Titled Plate Interceptors. The treated water is allowed to settle in a holding basin and the effluent from the holding basin is eventually discharged into the Bonny River. The water treatment facilities are potential sources of VOC emissions. Although no emission estimates are available for the water treatment facilities, these emissions are insignificant as compared to the overall tank farm emissions, and furthermore will be reduced in the future because of improved technology included in the design of the upgraded Bonny Terminal.*
>
> *Other potential sources of VOCs at the existing Bonny Terminal may exist. However, in comparison to the above, these sources are also deemed to be insignificant. . . .*[91]

The BTIP EIA report states that fugitive VOC emission would be significantly reduced in the operations of the redesigned terminal based on improved techniques. The report states, in the following words, that Shell Nigeria will address the issue of sludge and other effluents in the course of its improved maintenance and environmental monitoring programmes:

> *. . . SPDC will be directly responsible for all of the preceding monitoring which will be considered within the Terminal property. SPDC will*

91 *See* the 'BTIP EIA report', *op cit*, pp. 6–11 to 16–17, regarding existing VOC emission sources and how they are being treated and how the new design of the terminal based on the use of new technology will substantially reduce their emission. The above-stated Table 6.3 is, in the EIA report, entitled 'Summary of Bonny Terminal Storage Tanks'. It may be recalled that while commenting on the treatment of effluents (emission) from the Shell Bonny terminal, Claude Ake states that: . . . *Neither Shell nor other oil companies in Nigeria invest much in the treatment of effluents. According to a European Community study 'Mangroves of Africa and Madagascar', the waters of the Niger Delta contain at least 6 percent of petroleum and often up to 60 ppm. An environmental impact study of Shell (Resigner Industries, 1993) put an average hydrocarbon content of petroleum hydrocarbons in waste water in Oloma Creek [Bonny kingdom] at 62.7 mg/1. At the Bonny Terminal in Rivers state where Shell does its separation of water from crude oil, the mud at the waste water at Bonny Terminal averages 7.8 mg/1. As the World Bank Report quoted above has noted, the industry is using API (techniques?) and TPF facilities which are unsuitable for separation of better than 50mg/1. See* the article of Professor Claude Ake entitled 'Shelling Nigeria Ablaze', *op cit*. The Baseline Report of the NLNG project also indicates the noticeable changes in the water quality in Bonny over the years. These changes are said to have arisen due to the increasing levels of oil and grease or increased nitrates traceable to the Shell Nigeria Bonny terminal operations, and changes in land use caused by increased farming in Bonny. *See* the 'Nigeria LNG Project: LNG Plant Environmental Baseline Report', dated 1995, prepared by SGS Environment Ltd., p. 11.

> *propose that the Joint Industry Companies (JIC) initiate a programme to monitor for volatile organic compounds (VOCs) on an annual basis within the Local Study Area. Additionally, SPDC will propose that the JIC also initiate a programme for continuous 24-hour per day monitoring of ambient air quality and meteorological parameters at a minimum of three sites within the Local Study Area. These could be used to assess cumulative impacts from all industries in the area.*[92]

In the course of the BTIP public forums, citizens of Bonny kingdom also complained about the adverse effects of the frequent dredging of the Bonny River. As a result, they requested an embankment project to protect the Bonny community's shores, which are gradually and consistently eroding. Citizens and residents of Bonny Island community also complained about land and air pollution, including a continuous rise in the cost of living since the influx of foreign construction workers into the Island community, due to Shell's operations at the BCOT. While complaining about the tokenistic nature of CC, the citizens of Bonny demanded to be interactively involved in the decision-making process of Shell Nigeria's operations at the BCOT.[93] They demanded adequate environmental protection in the course of these operations by use of new technologies. The overall demand of the citizens is for Shell's operations in Bonny kingdom to be governed by the good practices of the global petroleum sector.[94] Thus, the BTIP EIA report regarding 'Community Relations with SPDC' states that:

> *Many of the surveyed residents indicated that in their opinion, relations between SPDC and the Bonny community are strained. Table 17.4*

---

92 *See* the 'BTIP EIA report', *op cit*, pp. ES–13–14. Essentially, EIA monitoring should take place throughout the construction phase of development projects, whereas specific mitigation issues identified in EIA processes could be treated as EIA-follow-ups. Aspects of project monitoring may thus be integrated into the Environmental Management Plans (EMPs) of projects. VOC emissions could be specifically treated under EIA follow-up of the construction phase of the BTIP. Where these emissions are not completely addressed in the follow-up process, they could be treated under such monitoring programmes as the EMP/Environmental Management System (EMS) of the BGOT. For more distinctions between EIA monitoring and follow-up processes, *see* the presentation of O. J. Dada, entitled 'Moving the EMP from the Shelf to the Field In Shell Petroleum Development Company, Nigeria'. *Also see* the presentation of A. Morrison-Saunders, entitled 'Exploring the Dimensions of EIA Follow-up'. *See* the abstracts of these two presentations in the final programme of the 24th Annual Conference of the IAIA, 24–30th April 2004, Vancouver, Canada, pp. 18 and 100. *Also see* the report of the UN Economic Commission for Africa (ECA) entitled *Review of the Application of Environmental Impact Assessment in Selected African Countries, op cit*, especially pp. xvi, 46, 73–74, and 80. *See* section 40 (d) of the EIA Act, Vol. 6, Laws of the Federation of Nigeria (LFN) 2004, on EIA follow-up programme.

93 *See* R. Sidaway, *Resolving Environmental Disputes from Conflicts to Consensus*, London, Earthscan, 2005, pp. 115–190. *Also see* R. Ademokai and W. R. Sheate, 'Community Participation and Environmental Decision-making in the Niger Delta', *Environmental Impact Assessment Review*, Vol. 24, Issue 5, July 2004, pp. 516–517. *See* C. Lucas and L. Hoskins, *The Wilder Nonprofit Field Guide to Conducting Community Forums: Engaging Citizens, Mobilising Communities*, St. Paul, Amherst H. Wilder Foundation, 2003, especially p. 63.

94 *See* the BTIP EIA report', *op cit*, pp. 17-42 to 17-50.

presents the statistics from the Socio-Economic Survey with respect to this issue.

... The surveyed residents were asked to give suggestions with respect to how SPDC might improve relations with the community. The general feeling in the community is that although the cost of living is high because of the development of oil and gas industry in the area, residents have not benefited from this development, and therefore they suffer as a result of increased prices and decreased services. As such, local residents feel that the oil companies operating in the area should assist the general populace to ensure that their lives do not continue to be negatively impacted by continuing industrial development in their community.

... Many local residents are interested in the upgrade of the Terminal and indicated that SPDC should make more effort to meet the general public in Bonny in order to develop a better mutual understanding of community and Terminal issues. This is indicated clearly by the following direct quotations extracted from the Socio-Economic Surveys:

- *I would like SPDC to explain their plans for the Bonny Terminal to me for my understanding.*
- *SPDC should come down to the community and interact with the common man and not only with the Chiefs and Elders.*
- *The modernisation idea is good. We do not know the effects yet, but our concern is clean air, water and soil.*
- *SPDC should give us the best technology just as the white people do for their people. I do not know the technical details, but we want clean air and water and we want our marine animals to do fine and feed us.*
- *SPDC should try as much as possible to eliminate environmental pollution on Bonny land and rivers.*
- *SPDC should use the most environmentally-friendly technology of this century. They should consult international experts.*
- *SPDC should use dialogue and must change their attitude to a new and better improved attitude.*
- *SPDC should renovate the Terminal to an international standard. No oil spillage and every other environmental harzard[s] should be taken into consideration*
- *Pollution of the air and water and land should be considered and equipment should be installed to handle any hazards.*[95]

It may be remarked that the foregoing statements and views of the residents and citizens of Bonny community demonstrate a need for improvement in the social and environmental performance standards of Shell Nigeria in the course

95 Ibid, pp. 17-42 to 17-44.

of its operations at the BCOT and the entire Bonny kingdom.[96] These statements and views demonstrate the essence of PI or PP as a means of integrating social concerns into the environmental decision-making process associated with Shell operations in the kingdom.[97] Besides, these statements and views are important because CSR in African countries is seen to be driven by MNCs, whose operational standards other companies operating in these countries are either adopting or implementing.[98]

While responding to the above and other issues raised by the citizens and residents of Bonny community in these CI processes, Shell Nigeria states that 'many of the preceding issues were discussed with the community during the Public Forum held on April 30, 1999'.[99] Shell thus assured the citizens and residents of the community that their complaints would be timeously addressed. As Shell put it in the BTIP EIA report, 'All complaints from local residents will be addressed in a timely manner'.[100]

---

96 *See* the 'International Finance Corporation's Performance Standards on Social & Environmental Sustainability', dated April 30, 2006, found at http://www.ifc.org/ifcext/enviro.nsf/AttachmentsByTitle/pol_PerformanceStandards2006_full/$FILE+Performance+Standards visited on 31/12/06. *Also see* The World Bank Operational Policy/Bank Procedure 4.01 on Environmental Assessment (EA), dated January 1999, (updated in March 2007), found at http://wbln0018.worldbank.org/Institutional/Manuals/OpManual.nsf/toc2/9367A2A9D9DAEED38525672C007D0972?OpenDocument and at http://web.worldbank.org/WBSITE/ EXTERNAL/PROJECTS/EXTPOLICIES/EXTSAFEPOL/0,,contentMDK:20543912~menuPK:1286357~pagePK:64168445~piPK:64168309~theSitePK:584435,00.html visited on 26/04/07.

97 *See* the International Association of Oil & Gas Producers (OGP) Report No. 2.85/322 of October 2002, entitled 'Key Questions in Managing Social Issues in Oil & Gas Projects', found at http://www.ipeca.org/downloads/social/impact_assessment.pdf visited on 31/12/06. *See* K. McPhail and A. Davy, *Integrating Social Concerns into Private Sector Decision making: Review of Corporate Practices in the Mining, Oil, and Gas Sectors*, Washington DC, The World Bank, 1998. Besides, the above-stated statements and views of the citizens and residents of Bonny may be interpreted as evidence of the fact that Bonny kingdom is a typical example of where the traditional rulers and local government authorities deserve to be more socially responsible to the plight of the people, towards greater and more equitable public good.

98 *See* W. Visser *et al* (eds), *Corporate Citizenship in Africa: Lessons from the Past; Paths to the Future, op cit*, pp. 93–104, especially p. 93. There is thus need for the private sector organisations in Africa to give priority attention to environmental stewardship in the course of their operations. Thus, the concerns for improved environmental stewardship of corporations, especially extractive industrial companies, in African countries are particularly significant, considering the ongoing worldwide concern about climate change (ie, global warming) due to greenhouse gas emissions into the atmosphere especially through industrial operations in African and other developing countries and transition economies. *See* N. H. Ravindranath and J. A. Sathaye, *Climate Change and Developing Countries (Advances in Global Change Research)*, Kluwer, 2002. *Also see* D. N. Zillman *et al* (eds), *Human Rights in Natural Resources Development: Public Participation in the Sustainable Development of Mining and Energy Resources*, New York, Oxford University Press, 2002, pp. 249–263. *See* A. Markandya and K. Halsnaes (eds), *Climate Change & Sustainable Development: Prospects for Developing Countries*, London, Earthscan, 2002.

99 *See* the BTIP EIA report', *op cit*, p. 17–44.

100 Ibid, p. ES–9. Regarding abandonment (and by extension decommissioning) in the context of the BTIP, Shell Nigeria states that it would comply with best practice in accordance with statutory and mandatory requirements as well as those of the Royal/Dutch Shell Group's standards. *See* the BTIP EIA report', *op cit*, p. A–50. Shell Nigeria responded to the needs, concerns and other expressions made by the citizens and residents of Bonny community, in the context of the socio-economic studies

8.9 FREQUENT DREDGING OF THE BONNY RIVER BY SHELL AND OTHER MNOCS OPERATING IN BONNY

One obviously neglected aspect of Shell Nigeria's operations at the BCOT is the frequent dredging of the Bonny River (otherwise referred to as the Bonny Sea or Atlantic channel). Since the beginning of Shell's operations in Bonny, the river has been frequently dredged, especially with the start of operations of MPN at its Oso NGL Bonny River Terminal (BRT) site and the NLNG as from the 1990s.[101] The frequent dredging by the major MNOCs in Bonny (*ie*, the Bonny JIC) does not only adversely affect Bonny Island, but also the satellite communities of Bonny kingdom situated along or by the Bonny River. These include Finima community situated in the Southern part of Bonny kingdom, and the kingdom's Western Zone Peterside (Ayama), Fibiri and Kuruama communities which are confronted by perennial erosion. Besides, for citizens of Kuruama and Kuruama-Iwoama, Kalaibiama, Fibiri and Peterside communities who usually travel through the Bonny Sea to Bonny Island, there have been frequent boat mishaps. As such, fishermen from these communities are no longer able to engage in their traditional fishing and fish farming occupations along the Bonny River. Yet, the EIAs of the JIC of Bonny kingdom, have, if at all, only insufficiently addressed the adverse effects of the dredging of the Bonny River.[102] Although there is need for the EMPs of the JIC to address these adverse effects, the role of the Nigerian Ports Authority (NPA),[103] as the regulator of maritime activities in Nigeria, is also significant. The NPA, being a federal parastatal, is far more powerful and should therefore be active in terms of regulating the MNOCs than the activism of the poor and neglected oil-producing communities.

---

of the BTIP EIA report. Shell responded by stating that these studies are earmarked . . . . *to ensure that all community concerns relating to the future operation of the Terminal are incorporated into the project either as part of the Conceptual Engineering Design, Environmental Management Plan or Community Development Plan. See* the BTIP EIA report', *op cit*, p. 17–1.

101 *See* the MPN 'Environmental Impact Assessment for Capital Dredging of Approach Channel, Offshore Bonny, Rivers state, Nigeria', Final Report', prepared by Unilag consult, dated October 1996, especially pp. 79–80. *Also see* the ThisDay newspaper report entitled 'House, Oil Companies Agree on Host Communities', found at http://www.thisdayonline.com/nview.php?id=119163&printer_friendly=1 visited on 09/08/08.

102 *See* the letter of the paramount chief of Finima, Chief Idamiebi Brown, to the chair and members of the Finima Relocation Committee (FRC), entitled 'Dredging of Creek and Dredge-Filling of Land', dated February 20, 1985.

103 The NPA is a wholly government owned organisation under the supervision of the Federal Ministry of Transport with the responsibility of providing specific ports and harbour services for the countries maritime industry. *See* the area of the homepage of the NPA captioned 'History', found at http://www.nigerian-ports.net/flash/home/history.html visited on 31/12/06. *Also see* the area of the homepage of the NPA captioned 'Corporate Profile', found at http://www.nigerian-ports.net/flash/authority/profile.html visited on 31/12/06. This homepage provides that the responsibilities of the NPA include the fact that *many of the ports and terminals are directly geared to the requirements of major multinational companies in essential industries such as oil, gas, and steel production. This helps to ensure stability and long-term commitment.*

8.10 CONCLUSION

This chapter demonstrates that Shell Nigeria's ongoing upgrade of the BCOT, referred to as the BTIP, is designed to modernise the terminal so as to enable it to operate for the next 25 years – as a world-class crude oil and gas terminal. This largest terminal of its kind in Africa has, during its ongoing integrated modernisation, acquired a new name, BGOT, given that it has commenced associated gas production being exported from the neighbouring NLNG complex.

Considering the state of affairs when the BCOT was built between 1957/58 and 1961 (*ie*, when formal EIA process was non-existent), it is obvious that the nature of Shell Nigeria's CC is gradually improving, as enhanced by the PI component of Nigeria's formal EIA process. Also, whereas Shell Nigeria did not embark on social investments for Bonny and Finima communities when the terminal was built, the BTIP has some social investments for the communities. This confirms the observation made in Chapters 1 and 7 that, due to the wake-up call on Shell in the Delta region in 1995, its social responsibility measures and those of other MNOCs are improving in the interests of the Delta region and other oil-producing areas. However, considering the various concerns expressed by the citizens and other residents of Bonny kingdom in the course of the BTIP CCs, the MNOCs operating in the kingdom need to further improve on their social and environmental performances in the kingdom. Specifically, Shell Nigeria needs to improve its operations by addressing such concerns as the tokenistic nature of CCs, unemployment and other socio-economic empowerment needs, and the adverse effects of the frequent dredging of the Bonny River, so as to comply fully with its social responsibility commitments. As demonstrated in Chapter 7, these commitments include those of its Group (*ie*, the Royal/Dutch Shell Group) and the internationalised petroleum industrial sector. Other Shell's social responsibility commitments mentioned include those of the UN Global Compact, of which Shell Nigeria has been a participant and stakeholder since June 2006. The need thus arises for Shell Nigeria to improve on its social and environmental performances, in compliance with public outcries, especially those of civil society groups, in order to ensure that its enormous profits are used to address the social and environmental harms being occasioned by its operations in the oil-producing communities.

The chapter demonstrates that Shell Nigeria is far from accomplishing its social responsibility in favour of the ordinary citizens and residents of the Bonny community, including the three chieftaincy houses (*ie*, the Buoye-Omosu Brown major house, Jumbo Major house and the Bristol-Alagbarigha royal house) whose protests reveal that they are directly affected by its BGOT operations. In spite of the concerns expressed by the citizens and residents of Bonny during the CC process of the BTIP EIA, they supported Shell Nigeria by granting it social licence to embark upon the project. Shell is thus required to address the concerns of the Bonny public in the course of its BGOT operations, by, among other things, ensuring that the entire chieftaincy houses, citizens and residents of Bonny community benefit from these operations fairly and equitably, in compliance with its declared world-class corporate responsibility commitments. Notably, the BTIP EIA report provides that Shell would *ensure that all community concerns relating to the future operation of the terminal are incorporated into the project either as part of the Conceptual Engineering Design, Environmental Management Plan or Community Development Plan.* Also, the social licence granted by the Bonny public to support the BTIP is significant as it demonstrates that the commitment of citizens of the Delta region is to encourage MNOCs operating in the region. If the MNOCs are thus able to adequately accomplish their environmental and social responsibilities in the region, this will generate an end to, or at least minimise, the ongoing crises in the region. Besides, the concerns expressed by the citizens and residents of Bonny consulted in the BTIP EIA CC process regarding the need for greater environmental democracy concerning the operations of Shell and other MNOCs in Bonny, reveal the need for the traditional rulers of Bonny kingdom to be more socially responsible to the plight of their people.

The BTIP EIA process discussed in this chapter reinforces the conclusion reached in Chapter 5, that PI is a significant pillar of EIA, while the EIA process is a significant pillar of SD. Whereas the BTIP EIA report may suffice as evidence of the improving social and environmental performances of Shell Nigeria in Bonny, it also reflects Shell Nigeria's self-praising attitude expressed by J. Osai in his article entitled 'Shell as Agama Lizard'. Essentially, the state of affairs in Bonny regarding the operations of Shell Nigeria and NLNG respectively discussed in this chapter and Chapter 9, represent the general state of affairs regarding the operations of MNOCs in other oil-producing areas within and outside the Delta region.

CHAPTER 9

Community Involvement in Impact Assessment of the Nigeria LNG Finima-Bonny Project and its Associated Social Investments

9.1 INTRODUCTION

Following the background on Corporate Social Responsibility (CSR) given in Chapter 7, this chapter will begin with an outline of the vision, mission statement and statement of business principles of Nigeria LNG Limited (NLNG) characterising it as a responsible corporate citizen. Based on NLNG's responsibilities and commitments to its host communities, the chapter will examine its social investments, including those designed as impact-benefits, in the interest of its primary host Finima and Grand Bonny Island communities, and by extension its pipeline (*ie*, Gas Transmission System – GTS) communities of Bonny kingdom.

9.2 NLNG: ITS ORIGIN, ONGOING CONSTRUCTION AND PRODUCTION PHASES AND ENVIRONMENTAL IMPACT ASSESSMENT (EIA) PROCESS

The potential for an LNG project in Nigeria was conceived in 1969 but it was not until the 1980s that Philips Petroleum developed proposals for the multi-billion USD NLNG project, Finima, Bonny Island. The project became a reality in March 1985, with the formation of a working committee involving the Federal Government (FG), Shell, Elf (now TotalFinalELF) and Agip, which signed the framework agreement to exploit Nigeria's enormous gas reserves. NLNG was eventually incorporated as a private multinational company (MNC) on May 17, 1989, to harness these reserves to produce liquefied natural gas (LNG) and natural gas liquids (NGL) for export.[1]

---

1 *See* the area of the NLNG homepage captioned 'The Company', with the sub-title 'Shareholders', and another area of this homepage captioned 'EIA for NLNG Plus', with the subtitle 'Introduction and Background', respectively found at http://www.nlng.com/NLNGnew/companyinfo/Shareholders.htm and at http://www.nlng.com/NLNGnew/environment/EIA+For+NLNGPlus/ Introduction+and+Background.htm visited on 21/09/08. *Also see* 'NLNG 2007: Facts and Figures on NLNG', p. 3.

NLNG was incorporated as a multinational limited liability company owned by its joint venture (JV) partners subscribing to the following shares: the Nigerian National Petroleum Corporation (NNPC), 49 per cent; Shell Gas B.V. (Shell), 25.6 per cent; TotalFinalELF Ltd. (Elf), 15 per cent; and Eni/Agip International (Agip), 10.4 per cent.[2]

The FG, through the NNPC, acquired Finima community land for the construction of the NLNG plant complex which, together with the residential area – situated about 40 km south of Port Harcourt, the capital of Rivers – stretched from mainland Finima to its adjoining Grand Bonny Island. The utilities provided in the residential area are designed to accommodate some 3,350 employees during its operational phase.[3] The plant complex, covering about 2.27 km^2 of mainly reclaimed Finimaland, and the residential area were cleared in the 1980s,[4] resulting in Finima community being displaced. The people of Finima were involuntarily resettled in their ancestral area which is about 10 km away from Grand Bonny Island, now known as new Finima community.[5] The entire NLNG complex is situated along the Bonny Sea, between the Shell Nigeria Bonny Oil and Gas Terminal (BGOT) and Mobil Nigeria Unlimited (MPN)/NNPC Oso NGL Condensate recovery plant (at the Bonny River Terminal – BRT).

---

2 *See* 'NLNG 2007: Facts and Figures on NLNG', pp. 3–4.

3 The NLNG residential area was designed to contain 375 houses, a medical centre, school, shopping centre and such other utilities as leisure facilities. *See* the 'Nigeria LNG Project Environmental Statement LNG Plant HO2754/ES-LNG/v4/3-95' of the NLNG Base Project prepared by SGS Environmental Ltd., dated March 1995 (hereinafter called the 'Nigeria LNG Project ES of the LNG Plant Complex, prepared by SGS Environmental Ltd.'), Executive Summary.

4 Ibid. *Also see* the area of the NLNG homepage captioned 'EIA for NLNG*Plus*' with the sub-title 'Introduction and Background', found at http://www.nlng.com/NLNGnew/environment/EIA+For+NLNGPlus/Introduction+and+Background.htm visited on 31/12/06.

5 *See* the area of the NLNG homepage captioned 'Operations & Strategies', with the sub-title 'The Plant', found at http://www.nlng.com/NR/exeres/CD1A6522-614B-4835-8D68-42E5A02BF6FE%2Cframeless.htm visited on 31/12/06. The main elements of the NLNG project are a dedicated GTS, three LNG storage tanks with the capacity of 84,000 m^3 each, a common fractionalisation plant to process LPG, two condensate storage tanks with a capacity of 36,000 m^3 each, two new 65,000 m^3 LPG refrigerated tanks (for propane and butane), and eight generators with a total capacity of 320 MW. Other facilities are two LNG export jetties and one LPG and condensate export jetty situated by the plant complex, along the Bonny River. The jetties enhance LNG export, and are also used by the NLNG shuttle boats and for materials off-loading. The rest of the main elements of the NLNG project include 19 LNG ships and a 2.08 km^2 staff residential area. The Bonny Gas Transport (BGT) was established in 1989 as a wholly-owned subsidiary of NLNG, to cater for its shipments. The NLNG pipeline/GTS traversed over 110 contiguous communities situated in Bonny kingdom and other areas of River state. The pipeline/GTS stretched from Ubeta in the Ahoada West local government area (LGA) to Rumuji in the Emouha LGA and then through the Western Zone of Bonny kingdom from the Kuruama/Peterside axis across the Bonny Sea to Finima, Bonny Island, in Bonny kingdom, Bonny LGA (OLGA). The NLNG GTS communities in Bonny kingdom include Kuruama community (along with its Kuruama-Iwoama contiguous community, Peterside (Ayama) community, Ayaminima community, Akiama community and Orupiri community. *See* 'NLNG 2007: Facts and Figures on NLNG', pp. 3, 13 and 44.

To commence operation, the Final Investment Decision (FID) for the NLNG Base project, comprising its initial two trains, was made by its shareholders in November, 1995. The Base project involved the construction of its original water-cooled plant and about 201 km of dedicated pipeline/GTS route, transporting natural gas from gas fields all over Rivers state to the plant complex at Finima, Bonny Island, where liquefaction takes place to enhance bulk export.[6] The process started in January 1996, and was completed in August 1999. Thereafter, the start-up process began the production phase on September 15, 1999. Train 2 of the Base project came on stream on February 27, 2000, while train 3 (*ie*, the NLNG Expansion project) came on stream in November, 2002. Thereafter, the NLNG*Plus* (*ie*, the NLNG trains 4 and 5 projects) came on stream in November 2005 and February 2006, respectively. Train 6 came into operation in December 2007, while development planning is currently under way for train 7+, to further expand the NLNG plant complex to a total production capacity of 30 MTPA LNG by the end of the decade.[7]

The EIA process of the NLNG construction phase covers the NLNG Base project, the Expansion project, the NLNG*Plus* project, including train 6, and the upcoming *NLNG 7+ Project* (*ie*, trains 7 and 8 projects).[8] Separate EIAs were carried out during the Base project for the NLNG plant complex and GTS. These are reported in two parts (ie, an Environmental Baseline Report, EBR, and an Environmental Statement [ES]). Following a preliminary environmental study made at the conception stage of the project, intensive environmental studies were carried out and EIA reports prepared between 1987 and 2002.[9]

A typical NLNG EIA report covers the baseline data/report and the Impact Assessment (IA) report comprising the environmental, social and health IA of the train/project involved.[10] NLNG states that its EIA process abides by Nigeria's municipal regulatory measures and internationally accepted guidelines, including those issued by its shareholders. Thus, regarding the NLNG*Plus* project, NLNG states that:

---

6 *See* the 'Nigeria LNG Project ES of the LNG Plant Complex, prepared by SGS Environmental Ltd.', *op cit*, Executive Summary.

7 *See* the area of the NLNG homepage captioned 'Operations & Strategies', with the sub-title 'The Plant', *op cit*. *See* 'NLNG 2007: Facts and Figures on NLNG', pp. 12–13, and 16. *See* the area of the NLNG homepage entitled 'The Company' with the sub-title 'Milestones', found at http://www.nlng.com/NLNGnew/companyinfo/Milestones.htm visited on 31/12/06.

8 *See* 'NLNG 2007: Facts and Figures on NLNG', p. 19.

9 *See* the 'Nigeria LNG Project ES of the LNG Plant Complex, prepared by SGS Environmental Ltd.', *op cit*, Executive Summary. *Also see* 'NLNG 2007: Facts and Figures on NLNG', p. 39.

10 *See* the Environmental Baseline Report of the NLNG Base project entitled the 'Nigeria NLNG Project JP 9000 LNG Bonny Island, Rivers state, Nigeria, LNG Plant Environmental Baseline Report', prepared by SGS Ltd., 1995. *Also see* the area of the NLNG homepage captioned 'EIA for NLNG*Plus*', found at http://www.nlng.com/NR/exeres/5BAB0B5A-8F6F-4A76-A36D-55F8C728D3BC%2Cframeless.htm visited on 31/12/06.

For the NLNGPlus project, an environmental impact assessment was carried out in parallel with the development of the project. This assessment was conducted in accordance with the Federal Government of Nigeria legislation [EIA Decree No. 86 of December 1992 and the Federal Environmental Protection Agency (FEPA) 1995 Sectoral Guidelines for Oil and Gas Industry projects], internationally accepted (including World Bank) guidelines for environmental assessment and guidelines issued by NLNG's shareholders.[11]

On the involvement of stakeholders, NLNG's Train 7+ Plus Project 'Stakeholder Identification and Management Plan', which identified 80 stakeholders of the project, provides thus:

Key to delivering effective impact assessment and social performance is stakeholder engagement, of which the first step is a structured identification of stakeholders and a plan for engagement. . . .

About 80 groups of stakeholders have been identified and subsequently mapped with regard to their stake in the Project. . . . Based on this mapping, stakeholders have been grouped into three types, i.e.

- *Critical Stakeholders*
- *High Awareness Stakeholders*
- *Interest Group Stakeholders . . .*

Consultation with local communities and other stakeholders is a key feature of NLNG's corporate policy. The aim of consultation is to gather information on issues, concerns and successes by dialogue with the local communities and other stakeholders. The company then looks towards working with the stakeholders to identify methods of addressing any negative impacts and to identify ways to maximise the positive benefits.

Public consultation has been an integrated part of all projects developed by NLNG since the early nineties. However, with evolving knowledge of and requirements for stakeholder consultation, the intensity and quality of this process as part of successive ESHA has improved significantly over the years. . . .

The stakeholder consultation was designed:

- *to be transparent in order to build trust and also allow for effective communication channels to be set up between key stakeholders*
- *to be informative so that participants are kept fully aware of NLNG's activities*

---

11 *See* the area of the NLNG homepage captioned 'EIA for NLNG*Plus*' with the sub-title 'Introduction and Background', *op cit*.

- *to be iterative to allow sufficient time for participants to fully understand and respond to the issues.*[12]

Given NLNG's claim that it abides by Nigeria's regulatory measures and internationally accepted guidelines on EA/EIA, it is important to consider the social responsibility objectives and commitments in the context of its social investment efforts in its primary host Bonny kingdom.

9.3 MISSION STATEMENT, STATEMENT OF BUSINESS PRINCIPLES AND ETHICS OF NLNG AND COMMITMENTS TO ITS HOST COMMUNITIES AS EXEMPLIFIED IN BONNY KINGDOM

NLNG's view of CSR may be identified from its vision, mission statement, statement of business principles, ethics, and its environmental and social performance responsibilities and commitments, which include its community relations (CR) and sustainable community development (SCD) strategies. In Bonny kingdom, these responsibilities and commitments are discharged by the NLNG's CR and community development (CD) efforts in Finima and Bonny Island, and to a lesser degree in its GTS communities of the kingdom. Regarding its vision, NLNG aspires to be a global company helping to build a better Nigeria:

> *Nigeria LNG will be a global NLNG company renowned for its operational excellence, cost leadership, high HSE standards, honesty and integrity. We will be helping to build a better Nigeria by processing, shipping and marketing efficiently and profitably the country's gas resources, thereby diversifying the economy and minimising the environmental impact of our activities and product.*
>
> *We will set high standards in community relations and technology transfer, and actively promote the sustainable development of Nigerian businesses. . . .*
>
> *Finally, we will execute and operate our business in Nigeria with an international outlook and mindset.*[13]

12 *See* the NLNG Train 7+ Project, 'Stakeholder Identification and Management Plan', The Hague, Shell Global Solutions International B. V., 2005, especially pp. 2, 4, and 5–6, found (in the area of the NLNG homepage captioned 'EIA for NLNGSevenPlus', with the sub-title 'EIA for NLNGSevenPlus –Volume 2') at http://www.nlng.com/NR/rdonlyres/BFD298A3-EC70-4781-ACF7-E9A2D8FB4E2D/0/18_NLNG7_Stakeholder_Management_Plan_03.pdf visited on 21/09/08.

13 *See* the area of the NLNG homepage captioned 'EIA for NLNG*Plus*' with the sub-title 'Introduction and Background', *op cit. Also see* the area of the NLNG homepage captioned 'The Company', found at http://www.nlng.com/NR/exeres/F48DE9A7-F3F3-4A8E-929A-0C34F1CFF92B%2Cframeless.htm visited on 31/12/06. *See* 'NLNG 2007: Facts and Figures on NLNG', p. 3, and 'Facts and Figures on NLNG 2008', p. 7.

Accordingly, NLNG expressed its mission statement (which is compatible with its business principles and ethics) as follows:

> *To market, produce and deliver Liquefied Natural Gas and Natural Gas Liquids to buyers safely, reliably and profitably, growing our company and its people to their full potential, and being a trusted partner with all our stakeholders in sustainable development of Nigeria's gas industry and of NLNG's host communities.*[14]

The introduction of the 'Statement of NLNG's Business Principles & Ethics', including its core and professional values indicates that:

> *Nigeria LNG Limited (NLNG) is a private joint venture company, registered in Nigeria and formed by its shareholders to be World-class LNG Company helping to build a better Nigeria.*
>
> *Its mission is to produce and deliver LNG and NGL's to customers safely, reliably and profitably, grow our Company and its people to their full potential and to be a trusted partner with all our stakeholders in the sustainable development of Nigeria's gas industry and NLNG's host communities.*[15]

In terms of its social responsibility commitments to its host communities, NLNG, which in eight years earned over 187 billion Naira for Nigeria,[16] states that it is implementing a CR policy based on stakeholding for sustainability in the following words:

> *Corporate social responsibility is a principle NLNG holds dear. It dictates how it does its business and how it relates to its internal and external publics. NLNG believes that good moral behaviour builds trust, respect, goodwill and enlists employee loyalty.*
>
> *The company has a strong sense of community and respect for dignity of persons, which fosters motivation, teamwork, fulfilment, and productivity. With a dedicated 201 km pipeline route passing through more than 110 contiguous communities, the company sees itself as a corporate*

14 *See* the area of the NLNG homepage captioned 'Mission Statement', found at http://www.nlng.com/NLNGnew/default visited on 31/12/06.

15 *See* the area of the NLNG homepage entitled 'The Company', with the sub-title 'Statement of NLNG's Business Principles & Ethics', found at http://www.nlng.com/NLNGnew/company-info/Statement+of+NLNG+Business+Principles+and+Ethics.htm visited on 31/12/06. In this area, the 'core ethical values' of NLNG are listed as honesty, integrity, trust, mutual respect, and a drive for excellence, while its 'professional values' are listed as *respect for the Health and Safety of people and for the Environment; belief that we should work in ways which support Sustainable Development; Discipline, Professionalism and Teamwork; Openness and Accountability; Commercial Orientation; and Pride in all that we do.*

16 *See* the report of the Guardian newspapers entitled 'Nigeria Earns N187billion from Gas in Eight Years', found at http://www.guardiannewsngr.com/news/article01 visited on 23/02/07.

citizen of its pipeline communities and its primary host communities of Bonny and Finima.

The NLNG has a well-articulated community relations policy that is premised on participation, stakeholding and partnership, underpinned by the drive for sustainability. The company supports projects that communities need and are able to demonstrate ability to sustain. This concept ensures a long-lasting partnership between the company and the community with results that are mutually beneficial.[17]

Under CR and development, NLNG states that:

NLNG's corporate social responsibility programme is built on partnership and sustainability. All NLNG's projects are community driven and people-oriented. As a result, the company is not patronizing in its relationship with the communities. In pursuing its policy, the company provides support to the communities in two broad areas: business/human development, and the provision of infrastructure.

. . . To maintain close contact with the communities, community relations officers are assigned to specific settlements as liaison officers, covering the spreads within Bonny, Finima and the pipeline communities.

. . . The officers meet regularly with representatives of the host communities to maintain good relationships for the company's effective operations.[18]

---

17 *See* 'NLNG 2007: Facts and Figures on NLNG', p. 44. *Also see* the report entitled *Community Relations: Unleashing the Power of Corporate Citizenship: Consortium Benchmarking Study Best-Practice Report*, by the Caroll School of Management, Boston College Centre for Corporate Community Relations, Houston, American Productivity and Quality Centre, 1998.

18 *See* 'NLNG 2007: Facts and Figures on NLNG', pp. 45–46. The NLNG describes its CD policy as 'community self-help'. That means . . . *the concept of development by the NLNG for the development of her host communities. It involves the communities taking the initiative to develop projects for themselves. Under the program, communities only appeal to the company to assist them in the development of an ongoing project of theirs. The company gives only materials support while the communities supply the requisite labour, and supplementary material[s]. See* the NLNG 'Common Questions on Self-Help', regarding the answer to 'What Does NLNG Mean By Self-Help?'. The NLNG states that '*the size of support [given by the NLNG] is often commensurate to the size of community investment or stakeholding. The ones with higher stakes are likely to receive bigger support from the company*'. The NLNG explains that *stakeholding here is the community investment and responsibility in the execution and running of a project of its choice. This reinforces a sense of community ownership of the project. This way, communities are not onlookers in their own development, but active participants in the process.* Considering, however, that the communities lack financial resources, self-help projects involving financial expenses, such as for labour and logistic support on the communities, tend to hinder the smooth realisation of these projects. So far, NLNG has executed over 50 CD projects in Bonny Island and Finima community, including about 200 self-help projects such as the provision of health, roads, electricity, water and other social amenities in its pipeline communities. *See* the area of the NLNG homepage captioned 'Community Relations', with the subtitle 'Community projects', found at http://www.nlng.com/NLNGnew/community/Community+Projects.htm visited on 31/12/06.

NLNG highlights that its CR strategy is centred on CD and community empowerment through several social investments in its host communities. In Bonny kingdom, NLNG 'recognises that industry activities on Bonny Island will increase pressure on most aspects of community life [in its host communities]'.[19] Besides the Bonny Joint Industry Companies (JIC) Memorandum of Understanding (MOU) projects discussed in Chapter 8, NLNG has been embarking on other social investments in Bonny, Finima and its GTS communities on which NLNG expends over seven million dollars annually.[20] As regards health, NLNG's social investments include its Ibanise HIV-AIDS partnership, Roll Back Malaria Campaign, immunisation programme, and the provision of medical equipment. In the area of education, social investments by NLNG include the award of scholarships, provision of the Bonny Educational Endowment Fund (BEEF), and the establishment of the Bonny Vocational Centre (BVC). On economic empowerment, its social investments include its micro-credit scheme, youth empowerment scheme (YES), the NLNG Agro Development Action (N-AGENDA), business development/ advisory support services, and its impact-benefit strategy based on the Nigerian Content Policy (NCP) discussed in Chapter 6. Through this strategy, NLNG has improved the NCP by devising its Local Content Plan to give priority to awarding engineering, procurement and construction (EPC) contracts to contractors from its host communities, before considering the award of such contracts to other contractors from Rivers state, other states of Nigeria and other parts of the world.[21] Regarding environmental stewardship, NLNG's initiative on conservation resulted in its establishment of the Finima Nature Park (FNP), while its environmental partnership with the Bonny kingdom is fostered through the kingdom's Community-based Environmental Organisation – the Bonny Environment Consultants Committee (BECC).[22] Also, NLNG (which prides itself as an environmentally-friendly company),[23] has an Environmental Policy document based on engineering and environmental standards which provides that it will:

> *Realise protection of the environment through both preventive and curative measures; pertain conservation measures to minimisation of emissions, effluents and wastes which are known to have negative impact on the environment; strive at continuous improvement efficiency in the use*

19 *See* the area of the NLNG homepage entitled 'Our Commitments and Responsibilities,' with the subtitle 'Environmental Responsibilities', found at http://www.nlng.com/NLNGnew/default visited on 31/12/06.

20 *See* the area of the NLNG homepage entitled 'Community Relations' with the subtitle 'Community Projects,' *op cit.*

21 Ibid, p. 52.

22 Ibid, pp. 41–42.

23 *See* the area of the NLNG homepage captioned 'Environmental Management', found at http://www.nlng.com/NR/exeres/6FA7708A-AF4D-493A-8E09-8D91FEF5623F%2Cframeless.htm visited on 31/12/06.

of natural resources and energy; implement the environmental policy by means of Environmental Management System [EMS].[24]

Having been incorporated to set up an Environmental Management System to fully implement environmental requirements, NLNG indicates its environmental stewardship on Health, Safety and Environment (HSE) as follows:

> *NLNG places a premium on Health, Safety and the Environment (HSE) in its activities. The company has a well-articulated HSE policy anchored on the need to take proper care of the health and safety of its employees and of other persons, and to give proper regard to the conservation of the environment.*
>
> *The company aims to be among the leaders in the LNG industry in these matters. In line with this, NLNG plans its work to:*
>
> - *prevent injuries and ill-health;*
> - *prevent damage to assets and the environment;*
> - *meet requirements for demonstrable diligence.*
>
> *At the conception of the NLNG project, preliminary environmental [study] was the priority of the company. Between 1987 and 2002, intensive environmental studies were carried out and Environmental Impact Assessment (EIA) reports prepared.*
>
> *The reports were reviewed and certified by the Nigerian environmental governing body, the Federal Environmental protection Agency, (FEPA). Due processes were followed and in early 1997, the final EIA report was approved, making NLNG the first major project in Nigeria to complete the full EIA process before commencement of business.*
>
> *An important element of the EIA process is to mitigate potential impacts. For the Base Project, some probable impacts were identified and mitigation measures were immediately taken. To ensure adherence to EIA specification, an Environmental Management Plan with a major objective of ensuring compliance with legislation, and the NLNG Company policy was set up.*[25]

NLNG states that its environmental footprint is evident in its protection measures, which include its system of discharging water to mitigate adverse effects on the environment, its sewage disposal and solid waste management

---

24 *See* the 'Nigeria LNG Project ES of the LNG Plant Complex, prepared by SGS Environmental Ltd.', *op cit*, pp. 5–6. *See* the NLNG Environmental Policy document (NLNG 1992).

25 *See* 'NLNG 2007: Facts and Figures on NLNG', p. 19. *Also see* the new version of the World Bank Group (WBG), 'Environmental, Health, and Safety Guidelines' (ie, 'EHS Guidelines'), found at http://www.ifc.org/ifcext/enviro.nsf/Content/EnvironmentalGuidelines and particularly in compliance with the new WBG 'Environmental, Health and Safety Guidelines for Liquefied Natural Gas (LNG) Facilities', found at http://www.ifc.org/ifcext/enviro.nsf/AttachmentsByTitle/gui_EHSGuidelines2007_LNG/$FILE/Final++LNG.pdf visited on 30/12/07.

system, and its method of dispersing emissions into the air.[26] NLNG states that its HSE, environmental regulation and SD initiatives are designed to comply with world class standards such as those of the World Bank Group (WBG) and the Royal Dutch/Shell Group – to which it belongs.[27] NLNG indicates that its SD strategy is to integrate economic, social, health and environmental considerations in all project decisions and actions in ways that reflect its contribution under six sustainability principles. These are to respect and safeguard people, engage and work with stakeholders, minimise impact on the environment, use resources efficiently, maximise profitability, and maximise benefits to the community.[28] The NLNG declares its commitment to carry out its operations based on the worldwide experience of its shareholders in developing oil and gas projects, especially LNG businesses.[29] NLNG highlights its

26 *See* 'NLNG 2007: Facts and Figures on NLNG', pp. 39–42.

27 *See* the area of the NLNG homepage captioned 'EIA for the NLNG*Plus*', with the subtitle 'The Proposed Project', found at http://www.nlng.com/NLNGnew/environment/EIA+For+NLNGPlus/The+Proposed+Project+-+contd.htm visited on 31/12/06. *Also see* the area of the Royal Dutch/Shell Group website captioned 'About Shell' with the subtitle 'A Global Group', found at http://www.shell.com/home/PrinterFrameork?sitedId=royal-en&FC3=/home/royal-en/h. . . visited on 11/12/2004. Apart from being a shareholder in the NLNG, Shell Nigeria is technical adviser to the NLNG. Hence, the NLNG constitute part and parcel of the Shell companies in Nigeria as well as a member of the Royal Dutch/Shell Group. *See* 'NLNG 2007: Facts and Figures on NLNG', p. 4. *Also see* the Shell Nigeria 'People and the Environment' Annual Report, 2005, found at http://www.shell.com/static/nigeria/downloads/pdfs/2005shellnigeriareport.pdf visited on 31/12/06, p. 45, entitled 'Shell Companies in Nigeria', with the sub-title 'Nigeria Liquefied Natural Gas Company Ltd. (NLNG)'. Regarding the application of recognised international/world-class standards by the NLNG in the course of its operations, NLNG homepage captioned 'EIA for NLNG*Plus*, with the subtitle 'The Proposed Project – cont'., found at http://www.nlng.com/NLNGnew/environment/EIA+For+NLNGPlus/The+Proposed+Project+-+contd.htm visited on 31/12/06. *Also see* the 'Nigeria LNG Project ES of the LNG Plant Complex, prepared by SGS Environmental Ltd'., *op cit*, pp. 104–105. Other international standards and practices applicable to the NLNG include those of the WBG and the International Finance Corporation (IFC), the Shell Group HSE Policy and Commitment (1997), the Shell Group Procedure for an HSE Management System (1997), Shell group Approach to Global Environment standards (1998), Shell group Commitment to Climate Change (1998), Shell Group Statement on Biological diversity, and the Shell Group Statement on Sustainable Development: Our Aspirations, our Commitments. NLNG states that it has adopted and integrated these standards into its environmental, social and health protection measures for the design, construction, and operation phases of the NLNG project. *See* the area of the NLNG homepage captioned 'EIA for NLNG*Plus*', with the subtitle The Proposed Project – cont,' *op cit*. For NLNG and other MNOCs operating in Nigeria, it is also pertinent to consider the impact of such foreign laws as the US Alien Tort Claims Act (ATCA), 1789 and the US Foreign Corrupt Practices Act (FCPA), 1977. Regarding these two laws, *see* the Global Policy Forum homepage, entitled 'Alien Tort Claims Act' found at http://www.globalpolicy.org/intljustice/atca/atcaindx.htm visited on 30/12/06, and the publication of the Tim Riley Law firm entitled 'LNG Corruption Danger to Our Communities', found at http://timrileylaw.com/LNG_CORRUPTION.htm visited on 13/03/09. *Also see* A. Palmer, entitled 'Community Redress and Multinational Enterprises', Foundation for International Environmental Law and Development (FIELD), dated 2003, found at http://www.field.org.uk/PDF/redres.pdf visited on 17/04/04.

28 *See* the area of the NLNG homepage captioned 'EIA for NLNG*Plus*', with the subtitle The Proposed Project – cont', *op cit*.

29 *See* the area of the NLNG homepage captioned 'EIA for the NLNG*Plus*', with the subtitle 'The Proposed Project', *op cit*.

EIA commitments in the course of the NLNG*Plus* project in the following words:

> *. . . [The] NLNG is committed to carry out a full Environmental, Social and Health (Impact) Impact Assessment (ESHA), in parallel with the development of the project, in consultation with neighbours, interested parties and the public at large. . . . The sustainability principle 'engage and work with stakeholders' requires NLNG, during the ESHA, to consult project-affected groups and local non-governmental organisations (NGOs) about the project's environmental and social aspects and will take their views into account.*[30]

Also regarding SD, the EIA of the NLNG*Plus* project provides that NLNG adopts the generally accepted definition of the World Commission on Environment and Development (WCED, – the Brundtland's Commission). Concerning its SD responsibilities, NLNG states that it considers SD as comprising three closely linked areas of attention (ie, economic development, environmental protection and social responsibility).[31] It thus commits itself to contribute to SD in the following words:

> *. . . the NLNG aims to contribute to Sustainable Development (SD). This means that a strategy has been developed in line with current best practices to integrate economic, social and environmental considerations in all project decisions and actions and to work with the host communities while ensuring a lasting partnership.*[32]

Based on the foregoing environmental and social responsibility initiatives and commitments, it is important to discuss the Bonny kingdom versus the NLNG crisis, which the author described in Chapter 7 as the wake-up call of NLNG in the kingdom and its other host communities.

---

30 Ibid.

31 *See* the area of the homepage of NLNG entitled 'EIA for the NLNG*Plus*', with the sub-title 'Environmental, Social and Health Mngt', found at http://www.nlng.com/NLNGnew/environment/EIA+For+NLNGPlus/Environmental%2c+Social+and+Health+Mngt.htm visited on 31/12/06. *Also see* the report of the World Commission on Environment and Development (WCED) otherwise known as the Brundtland report, entitled *Our Common Future*, Oxford, Oxford University Press, 1987, especially pp. 8–9 and 43–66. It is pertinent to indicate the need for NLNG to broaden the spheres of SD which it has identified to include governance sphere. *See* Mining, Minerals and Sustainable Development (MMSD) project report entitled *Breaking New Ground: Mining, Minerals, and Sustainable Development: The Report of the MMSD Project*, London, Earthscan, 2002, pp. 23–25, especially, p. 25.

32 *See* the area of the NLNG homepage entitled 'EIA for NLNGSEVENPLUS,' with the sub-title 'EIA For NLNGSevenPlus – Volume 1,' Executive Summary, item 0.1.1, captioned 'Nigeria LNG Ltd and its Aspirations,' found at http://www.nigerialng.com/NR/rdonlyres/8E80D111-139C-433A-A0B4-6118CD971596/0/CExecutive_Summary_FINAL.pdf visited on 21/09/08.

9.4 BONNY KINGDOM VERSUS THE NLNG CRISIS OCCASIONED BY THE NON-IMPLEMENTATION OF THE EIA AND OTHER BASE-PROJECT COMMITMENTS OF THE NLNG TO ITS PRIMARY HOST GRAND BONNY AND FINIMA COMMUNITIES

As a preamble to the discussion on this crisis, it may be noted that prior to the commencement of the NLNG Base project in January 1996,[33] Finima community was involuntarily resettled. The people were displaced from their community (now called 'old' Finima) to an adjoining area of their domain (now called 'new' Finima), so as to provide space for the NLNG plant complex. The resettlement of the Finima people took place without the fulfilment of several of the NNPC's responsibilities to the people, inherited by NLNG when it came into operation. These responsibilities include such basic necessities of life as housing (considering that the replacement and modernisation of houses which existed in old Finima were not adequate or completed). Besides, the construction process of the NLNG Base project was concluded without the fulfilment of several mitigation measures[34] expressed in the project's EIA report, including NLNG's other commitments[35] in favour of its primary host Finima and Bonny Island communities. As a result, over 20,000 citizens of Bonny kingdom launched a peaceful protest against NLNG, from September 20–22, 1999.[36]

The Bonny kingdom versus NLNG crisis started with the declaration of an 18-point resolution by the kingdom. This resolution was ratified at the Ibanise Conference[37] of September 19, 1999, and read to the public by the chair of the BKDC, Dr. T.A.T. Allison. The Ibanise Conference resolved that Bonny people should call off the protest when the demands expressed in their resolution were accomplished. The protest, which started on September 20, became violent when some combat-ready policemen injured some of the protesters in the course of shooting to quell the protest. The protesters reacted by destroying several valuable assets at the NLNG plant complex, resulting in closure of the complex and its residential area, including the residential area of the NLNG

33 *See* the area of the NLNG homepage entitled 'The Company' with the sub-title 'Milestones', *op cit*.

34 *See* the 'Nigeria LNG Project ES of the LNG Plant Complex, prepared by SGS Environmental Ltd.', *op cit*, pp. 104–130.

35 These include the Memorandum of Understanding (MoU) projects of the Bonny JIC discussed in Chapter 8 as being spearheaded by NLNG.

36 *See* the area of the NLNG homepage captioned 'News & Media', with the subtitle 'Press Releases – 1999', for the publications entitled 'Incident at the NLNG Plant Site (i) [Statement I]' dated 20/09/1999, and 'NLNG Plant Shut-Down Incident at Bonny (ii) [Statement II]', dated 23/09/1999, found at http://www.nlng.com/NLNGnew/news/Press+Releases/1999/Plant+Shutdown1.htm and at http://www.nlng.com/NLNGnew/news/Press+Releases/1999/Plant+Shutdown2.htm visited on 31/12/06.

37 Chapter 4 discussed this Conference as the highest decision making body of Bonny kingdom, especially during periods of emergency.

main sub-contractor (*ie*, TSKJ Nigeria Ltd). Among other effects, this protest prevented the first shipment of LNG scheduled to take place on October 1, 1999, in commemoration of Nigeria's Independence celebrations of that year.[38] It took the intervention of the Governor of Rivers state, Dr. Peter Odili, to call off the protest and later, a visit by the President, Chief Olusegun Obasanjo, to Bonny community, on September 26, 1999, to ensure the resumption of peace and normality in the community. The Rivers State Government then had to set up a negotiation panel comprising delegates of Bonny kingdom, NLNG and representatives of the Government. The panel, chaired by the Deputy Governor, Gabriel T. G. Toby, met over a period of three months.

Eventually, an agreement dated May 30, 2000 was signed by the Bonny kingdom and NLNG, under the auspices of the Rivers State government.[39] This agreement focused on issues of such key concerns as the employment of 30 university graduates, and then some unskilled and semi-skilled staff, provision of boats for water transportation, CR and interaction units, Finima resettlement, and the danger of local people's demand for forest products in Grand Bonny Island. Other issues included implementation of the NLNG Base project's EIA mitigation measures relating to the Bonny GTS communities, health monitoring including the provision of health services arising from health hazards associated with NLNG's operations, and the influx of strangers into Bonny. There are also such other issues as the development of rural roads, patronage of local contractors, payment of adequate compensation to communities situated along the NLNG water wells area, provision of adequate social amenities for the NLNG-employed labour force at the NLNG workers camp, and remedial measures regarding the NLNG exclusion zone reserved for purposes of LNG shipments on the Bonny Sea.

Other provisions of the agreement include solid waste removal, preparation of a contingency plan in the event of gas disaster, vibration of light and noise in the course of NLNG's operations, and declaration of a nature conservation area. Some provisions of the agreement are political issues which include relocation of the NLNG headquarters from Lagos to Bonny, representation of Bonny kingdom on the LNG Board of Directors, and management positions

---

38 *See* the following Tide newspaper reports; (a), September 20–21, 1999, entitled 'Uncertainty Trails NLNG Commissioning', and 'Odili Unhappy with NLNG', pp. 1–3; (b), September 22–23, 1999, entitled 'Protest Rocks Bonny . . . As Youths Barricade NLNG Site . . . Gov Odili Intervenes, Re-assures', pp. 1–2; and (c), September 24–25, 1999, entitled 'Bonny Chiefs Deny Claim', and 'Bonny Suspends Protest', pp. 1–3. *Also see* the area of the NLNG homepage, captioned 'News & Media', with the subtitle 'Press Releases – 1999', for the publications entitled 'Incident at the NLNG Plant Site (i) [Statement I]' dated 20/09/1999, and 'NLNG Plant Shut-Down Incident at Bonny (ii) [Statement II)', dated 23/09/1999, *op cit. See* D. N. Zillman *et al* (eds), *Human Rights in Natural Resources Development: Public Participation in Sustainable Development of Mining and Energy Resources*, New York, Oxford University Press, 2002, pp. 582–583.

39 *See* the Bonny versus the NLNG agreement consummated consequent upon the Bonny kingdom versus the NLNG crisis, under the auspices of the Rivers state government reconciliation panel, dated May 30, 2000, (hereinafter called the 'Bonny versus the NLNG agreement consummated consequent upon the Bonny kingdom versus the NLNG crisis of September, 1999 [under the auspices of the Rivers state government reconciliation panel]').

for citizens of Bonny and other parts of Rivers state. The major obligation of the citizens of Bonny kingdom in this agreement is for them to grant NLNG 'a conducive environment [*ie*, social licence] to carry out its operations'.[40] The agreement also has provisions for channels of CR and interaction, and for dispute resolution in the event of future misunderstandings or crisis between the kingdom and NLNG.[41]

Mention may at this juncture be made about NLNG's 'Bonny Emergency Response Plan (BERP)', dated October 15, 2006. It was after the Bonny versus NLNG crisis that NLNG prepared this plan in part compliance with the risk control mitigation measures expressed in the ES of its plant complex and the Bonny versus NLNG agreement consummated consequent upon the crisis (under the auspices of the Rivers state government).[42] A glance at the BERP

40 *See* 'Bonny versus the NLNG agreement consummated consequent upon the Bonny kingdom versus the NLNG crisis of September, 1999 (under the auspices of the Rivers state government reconciliation panel)', *op cit*, p. 8, para 24.

41 Ibid, p. 8, para 25, entitled 'Disputes and Arbitration'. This paragraph provides that: *If at any time, any dispute or difference arises between the community and NLNG, either party shall as soon as reasonably practicable give notice to the other in writing of the existence of such a dispute or difference, specifying its nature and the point at issue and if within thirty (30) days such issue is not resolved, the dispute or difference shall be referred to the Presidential Committee on Oil & Gas Company/Community Relations for resolution which said decision shall be final and binding on both parties.* There are two areas where this paragraph is weak. One, this dispute resolution process can only prevail better without ousting the jurisdiction of the courts of law as expressed under section 6 of the 1999 Constitution of the FRN. Two, citizens and citizen groups of the kingdom such as Finima community and other vulnerable, as well as neglected minority groups, are entitled to directly participate in the IA and other processes of environmental decision-making affecting them. Ironically, the right of such directly affected citizens and groups to participate is ousted in paragraph 6, p. 3 of this agreement, entitled 'Community Relations & Interactions,' especially where they are not the GTS communities of NLNG, as provided in paragraph 9, p. 4 of the agreement. *See* A. G. McFarlane, '*When Inclusion Leads to Exclusion: The Uncharted Terrain of Community Participation in Economic Development*', 66 Brook. L. Rev. 861, 2000/2001, pp. 861–932. *Also see* the report of the WBG on the Extractive Industrial Review (EIR), which requires free, prior and informed consultation with the people and communities affected by extractive industrial projects, so as to enlist their broad support for these projects. *See* this report entitled 'Striking a Better Balance – The World Bank Group and Extractive Industries: The Final Report of the Extractive Industries Review, World Bank Group Management Response', found (in the area of the WBG homepage captioned 'Oil, Gas, Mining and Chemicals', with the subtitle 'Extractive Industries Review', at http://siteresources.worldbank.org/INTOGMC/ Resources/finaleirmanagementresponse.pdf visited on 04/04/05. *Also see* R. Goodland, *Sustainable Development Sourcebook for the World Bank Group's Extractive Industries Review: Examining the Social and Environmental Impacts of Oil, Gas and Mining*, Washington DC, WBG, 2006, especially pp. 10–24 and 167–173. *See* the International Association for Oil & Gas Producers (OGP) Report No. 2.85/322 of October 2002, entitled 'Key Questions in Managing Social Issues in Oil & Gas Projects', found at http://www.ipeca.org/downloads/social/ impact_assessment.pdf visited on 31/12/06, pp. 5, 20–23, and 55. *See 'Doing Better Business through Effective Public Consultation and Disclosure: A Good Practice Manual*, Washington DC, IFC Environment Division, 2000, found at http://ifcln1.ifc.org/ifcext/enviro.nsf/AttachementsByTitle/ppubconsult/$FILE/ PublicConsultation.pdf visited on 29/10/04. *See* the *IFC* 'Guidance for Preparation of Public Consultation and Disclosure Plan' dated December 1998, found at http://www.ifc.org/ifext/enviro.nsf/AttachementsByTitle/gf_pcdp/$FILE/GuiF_PCDGuidance.pdf visited on 31/12/06.

42 *See* the 'Nigeria LNG Project ES of the LNG Plant Complex, prepared by SGS Environmental Ltd.', *op cit*, p. 123. *Also see* the 'Bonny versus the NLNG agreement consummated consequent upon the Bonny kingdom versus the NLNG crisis of September, 1999 (under the auspices of the Rivers state government reconciliation panel)', *op cit*, para.7, p. 20.

reveals the need for continuous enlightenment and communication between NLNG and its host, Bonny kingdom, as well as with its GTS communities in a lesser capacity. A need thus arises for NLNG to create special communication units in its primary host Finima and Bonny Island communities, including at least two other units in its GTS communities in the western and eastern zones of Bonny kingdom. Besides, the scope of the Plan requires to be expanded to include the other two major MNOCs in Bonny (ie, Shell Nigeria and MPN), for it to be more comprehensive and effective. Also, examples of such plans elsewhere may be considered by NLNG,[43] as it is its responsibility to properly educate and prepare its host communities on the dangers of LNG plants.[44]

9.5 COMMUNITY INVOLVEMENT IN THE EIA PROCESS OF THE NLNG TRAINS

CI during the EIA process of the NLNG Base project was weak. As such, there was no interactive involvement of the affected, concerned and interested public in Bonny kingdom. The main instances of CI during the conception phase of the project included meetings held between the Finima Relocation Committee (FRC) and the NNPC, and the involvement of the Finima and other host communities during compensation payment for land acquisition for the project. Relatively low levels of consultation also took place with the apex traditional council of Bonny kingdom (ie, the Bonny Chiefs' Council [BCC]), especially as the kingdom had no king at the time. CI with the council however improved with the enthronement of a new monarch of the kingdom, Edward A. W. D. Pepple, in 1996.[45]

Consequently, an MoU between Bonny community and the JIC led by NLNG was signed on November 5, 1998, regarding certain CD projects. After the signing of this MoU (discussed in Chapter 8), execution was slow, and the people of Bonny felt more frustrated by adverse effects of the NLNG Base project such as environmental, health, socio-economic and other related effects, aggravated by the influx of some 6,400 strangers in search of construction jobs during the peak of the project. For instance, this situation resulted in the spread of communicable diseases and other health and socio-economic and traditional problems, such as the overstretching of available public utilities. The adverse effects of the NLNG Base project, complemented by those of Shell Nigeria at the BGOT and MPN at the BRT, created serious tension in Bonny. The EIA of the Base project indicates that the influx of strangers would impact on the culture, language and entire traditional livelihood of Bonny

43 *See* the 'B. C. Oil and Gas Commission Response Plan Requirements' dated December 13, 2004, and the Emergency Planning & Community Right-to-Know Act, 1986, of the USA.

44 *See* A. Gilpin, *Dictionary of Environmental Law*, Cheltenham, Edward Elgar, 2000, p. 91.

45 *See* I. K. Jumbo, 'Chronicle of a Grand Coronation', being an article published in the Tide newspaper, dated December 29, 1996, p. 2.

people.[46] The ES of the project indicates the commitment of NLNG to embark upon CI.[47] However, apart from the EIA process of the Shell Nigeria BTIP project, which gave detailed instances of community consultations (CCs), the ES of the NLNG Base project gave only a profile of the NLNG's CI programme. The summary of this profile, not backed by any concrete evidence of implementation, provides that:

> *Nigeria LNG Ltd. through their Public Affairs Department have a full programme of public consultation concerning the project. This process has already commenced and the Company are prepared to develop their consultation activities further in relation to the LNG Project and their future developments.*[48]

More detailed information of the ES on the NLNG CI process entitled 'Programme for future consultation/information' provides as follows:

> *Both during construction and over the life of the project, Nigeria LNG is firmly committed to expand the information and consultation process which has been launched. In follow-up consultation meetings, the interested groups will be briefed on company's intentions and actions in support of the population needs before implementation.*
>
> *To give effect to the programme, the company established a Community Relations Committee, which will serve as an interface between Finima, Bonny, the communities along the gas transmission System and the Nigeria LNG by:*
>
> *furthering and maintaining the lines of communications with the communities; monitoring developments within the communities, aggregating their demands, discussing them along corporate realities and making recommendations to Management;*
>
> *communicating company decisions on demands and other issues to the communities through their opinion leaders; implementing company decisions in ways that meet company policy and the expectations to the communities.*
>
> *The initiative will be taken by the NLNG but others can approach the company to put subjects on the agenda.*[49]

---

46 Limited public utilities/amenities in Bonny constituted a key reason for the provision of the MoU water, electricity and road projects by the JIC. Beside these amenities provided by NLNG, its main EPC contractor – TSKJ Nigeria Ltd., and TSKJ's numerous minor MNOCs such as CBI Nigeria Ltd., Julius Berger Nigeria (JBN) Plc, and Willbros Nig. Ltd. were independently providing public amenities in varying degrees at Finima and Bonny Island community, in the ongoing construction process of the NLNG project.

47 *See* the 'Nigeria LNG Project ES of the LNG Plant Complex, prepared by SGS Environmental Ltd.,' *op cit*, Executive Summary, pp. 104–124 on the mitigation measures of the NLNG project.

48 *See* the 'Nigeria LNG Project ES of the LNG Plant Complex, prepared by SGS Environmental Ltd.', *op cit*, Executive Summary.

49 Ibid, pp. 131–132.

The NLNG further indicates how its Public Affairs Department will improve communications:

> *In addition, the Public Affairs Department will implement a number of communication initiatives which include the following:*
>
> *enlightenment on expected influx of large numbers of people from different cultures [ie, about 6,400 workers – during the peak of employment of the construction process – along with other citizens and members of the public in search of employment, were expected to be in Bonny Island community and Finima community during the ongoing construction period of the NLNG in the communities] and how the communities can best respond to this;*
>
> - *the organisation of conferences and exhibitions to disseminate information and promote awareness;*
> - *the publication of brochures about Nigeria NLG's activities;*
> - *the establishment of a complaints system whereby members of the public or communities can make representations to the Company.*
>
> *Nigeria LNG is fully prepared to develop their consultation activities further in relation to the LNG Project and other future developments.*[50]

The foregoing CI commitments expressed by the NLNG were indeed far from being implemented before and immediately after the completion of the Base project. This generated the Bonny kingdom versus the NLNG crisis discussed above.[51]

As already indicated, after this crisis, NLNG began to make efforts to improve its CR in Bonny kingdom, in conformity with the provisions of paragraph 6 of the reconciliation agreement of the kingdom with NLNG. The NLNG CR strategy, designed after the crisis, slightly extends to the NLNG GTS communities of the kingdom, in fulfilment of paragraph 9 of the agreement drawn up by the Rivers state government.[52] Thus, regarding PI, the NLNG held the two forms of CCs discussed in Chapter 7.[53] Besides, regarding EIA mitigation measures, NLNG has designed two forms of stakeholders' involvement forums. First is the community forum involving the representatives of the BECC, BKDC, Finima Development Committee (FDC), and other stakeholders which NLNG decides to involve from such other stakeholder groups as the

---

50 Ibid, pp. 132–133, and the Executive Summary.

51 This crisis would also have been occasioned against Shell Nigeria and Mobil Producing Nigeria Unlimited (MPN), as exemplified later by the Finima community versus the MPU crisis which took place in June, 2001. *See* the report of the Human Rights Watch (HRW), entitled 'Nigeria: Niger Delta: No Democratic Dividend', Vol. 14, No. 7 (A) dated October 2002, found (in the publications area of the HRW homepage) at http://www.hrw.org/legacy/reports/2002/nigeria3/nigerdelta.pdf visited on 31/12/06, pp. 10–14.

52 *See* the 'Bonny versus the NLNG agreement consummated consequent upon the Bonny kingdom versus the NLNG crisis of September, 1999 (under the auspices of the Rivers state government reconciliation panel)', *op cit*, pp. 3–4. Paragraph 6 of this agreement is entitled 'Community/Relations & Inter-actions', while paragraph 9 is entitled 'GTS Communities'.

53 These are the NLNG production phase start-up workshop and the NLNG SCD workshop.

Bonny local government, Rivers state and the federal environmental regulatory authorities, including the representatives of environmental NGOs, and the leading women and youth groups of Grand Bonny.[54] Second is the critical stakeholders' consultation committee.[55] However, these forms of PI are mainly convened at the discretion of NLNG. Besides, although NLNG states that the purpose of engaging its critical stakeholders is participation, and that the key to its consultation approach at the local level is inclusivity 'to ensure that the viewpoints of as many different interest groups are gathered as practicable';[56] NLNG does not truly fulfil these commitments.

Although the CI process of NLNG before the Bonny kingdom versus the NLNG crisis was weak and non-compliant with its commitments expressed in its Base project EIA report, after this crisis NLNG began to improve its CCs in and overall CR with the kingdom and its other host communities outside the kingdom. However, considering that NLNG's ongoing CCs in the kingdom do not fulfil its acclaimed social responsibility commitments as a world-class NLNG company abiding by or upholding recognised international standards and practices associated with its operations, its forms and measures of CC are not too distinct from those of Shell Nigeria and MPN in the kingdom.[57]

9.6 SPECIFIC EXAMPLES OF NLNG'S SOCIAL INVESTMENTS (IE, SOCIAL AND ENVIRONMENTAL PERFORMANCES) IN BONNY KINGDOM

Apart from the MoU CD projects sponsored by the JIC led by NLNG, there are other social investments being embarked upon by NLNG in Bonny kingdom, especially in the interests of its primary host, Finima and Bonny Island communities, including its GTS communities of the kingdom.[58] It is important to give

54 The youths are traditionally represented by the Bonny Youths Federation (BYF), while the women are represented by their major umbrella organisations such as the Bonny Women Patriotic Movement (BWPM) and the Bonny LGA chapter of the National Council for Women Societies (NCWS).

55 NLNG defines its critical stakeholders as 'mainly the people living/working in the neighbourhood of the . . . NLNG] project, but also neighbouring industries, gas suppliers and shareholders. . . ' *See* the NLNG Train 7+ Project, 'Stakeholder Identification and Management Plan', *op cit*, p. 19.

56 Ibid, pp. 18–19. Notably, NLNG's categorisation of 'high awareness stakeholders' indicates NGOs, labour unions, neighbouring industries and licensing authorities. This categorisation excludes experts in relevant disciplines as stipulated in section 7 of the EIA Act, Laws of the Federation of Nigeria (LFN) 2004, entitled 'Opportunity for Comments by Certain Groups'. It thus undermines the input of these experts belonging to affected, concerned or interested community groups in Bonny kingdom, in the course of NLNG's operations in the kingdom.

57 While NLNG is so far leading in terms of social responsibility initiatives in Bonny kingdom, MPN is lagging behind it and Shell Nigeria. The MPN BRT site at Finima, Bonny Island, is almost inaccessible to Bonny people, as the site operates as a near-closed system. This requires MPN to improve upon its CI strategy and overall social and environmental performances in the kingdom.

58 *See* the area of the NLNG homepage captioned 'News & Media', with the subtitle 'Press Releases – 2001', regarding the press release entitled 'NLNG Kicks Off N500 Million Micro-Credit Scheme for Host Communities', dated September 18, 2001, found at http://www.nlng.com/NLNGnew/news/Press+Releases/2001/Micro-Credit+Scheme.htm visited on 24/09/08. *Also see* 'NLNG 2007: Facts and Figures on NLNG', p. 44.

a brief account of some of these investments being embarked upon by NLNG in the spirit of good neighbourliness in the kingdom.[59]

9.6(I) RESETTLEMENT OF FINIMA COMMUNITY FOR THE NLNG PLANT COMPLEX

Finima community (now called old Finima community) was involuntarily resettled by the NNPC, to create space for the NLNG plant complex mainly situated at old Finima community, along Grand Bonny Island.[60] The Finima people were resettled at an adjoining area of their ancestral homeland now called new Finima. To resettle the people, the NNPC held consultations with them, particularly with their paramount chief and elders, between January and February, 1978. Following these consultations, the NNPC's General Manager (Commercial), S. M. Akpe, wrote a letter of offer, reference no. GID/001/13.1/21, dated March 3, 1978, through the paramount chief of the community, Chief Idamiebi Brown, reaffirming the consultations held with the people, in the following words:

> *I am writing in connection with our discussions both in your office on 20th January, 1978, and at the meeting with the Finima community on 5th February, 1978. The position as discussed is that the area around Finima is physically the best for siting the proposed NLNG plant. It has also been stressed to us that the site can only be used for this purpose if Finima can be relocated. . . .*[61]

The NNPC, on behalf of NLNG, undertook certain responsibilities to resettle Finima community as follows:

---

59 NLNG's social investments for its GTS communities are embarked upon in these communities in a skeletal scale. These communities range from the Obiafu-Ubeta area (ie, from the Ogba-Egbema LGA where Obiafu is situated to the Ahoada-West LGA where Ubeta is situated) up to Rumuji in the Emouha LGA, and then to Bonny kingdom, Bonny LGA, through the GTS communities thereof to the NLNG plant complex at Finima, Bonny Island. Also, NLNG awards its Nigeria prize for literature and the Nigeria prize for science, as part of its generic CSR initiative in Nigeria. NLNG commenced the yearly award of these prizes worth US$30,000, in 2004. In the spirit of its Nigerianisation policy exemplified by these awards, the NLNG vessels are named after its primary host communities, host state, and some important cities and other states of Nigeria. *See* 'NLNG 2007: Facts and Figures on NLNG', p. 26. C/f NLNG's Nigerianisation social responsibility process with, for instance, that of Newmont Ghana (one of the world's largest gold mining companies) as expressed in the 'Ahafo Social Responsibility Agreement' by which Newmont Ghana committed in 2005 to allocate $1 per ounce of gold sold and one per cent of mine net profit to fund SCD projects in Ghana. *See* this Agreement found (in the 'Africa' area of the Newmont homepage captioned 'Our Global Presence' with the sub-title 'Business News') at http://www.newmont.com/africa/ahafo-ghana/news-events visited on 05/06/09.

60 *See* the area of the website of the 'hydrocarbons industry', entitled 'Bonny Island LNG Plant, Nigeria', found at http://www.hydrocarbons-technology.com/projects/bonny/ visited on 29/07/08.

61 *See* the letter of Offer/Understanding of the 'Siting of the LNG Plant at Finima', from the NNPC to paramount chief of Finima community, Chief Idamiebi Brown, dated March 3, 1978, p. 1.

(i). The parcels of land to be acquired from the Finima people for the project will be compensated for at reasonable commercial rates.

(ii). The provision of a helicopter for a day to enable representatives of Finima community locate a site of their choice in the areas belonging to them near Bonny.

(iii) The bull-dozing and general layout of the new site for construction purposes.

(iv) Historical graves and important shrines of the Finima people will be moved to the new site at the company's cost.

(v) Design and construction of bungalows/houses for displaced families/residents of Finima.

(vi). The provision of boreholes for domestic water supply.

(vii) The availability of electric power supply when the Bonny LNG Limited power plant is operating.

(viii). Employment opportunities for skilled and unskilled residents of Finima will be available.

(ix). Primary school places will be made available to Finima residents in the staff school to be established in the area by the Bonny LNG Limited when its operations get underway.

(x). Access to medical facilities in the hospital to be established by the Bonny LNG Limited for its operations would be given to the residents of Finima.[62]

This letter of the NNPC to the paramount chief of Finima community, further provided that:

> *Details of the assurances given in paragraph 2 above would be embodied in the Lease agreement to be entered into between the Bonny LNG Limited and the appropriate authorities in Finima for the parcels of Land to be acquired by the company. We also expect the Rivers State Government to give its full support for the proposals put to the Finima people by us.*[63]

In 1980, the NNPC set up the Finima Relocation Committee (FRC), to deal specifically with the physical issues of resettlement from old to new Finima community, which started in 1985.[64] The promises made to the people were far from being accomplished by the NNPC when they were forcefully resettled. Consequently, the paramount chief and elders of the community made a protest announcement for and on behalf of the community, in June 1990, decrying the people's plight, while recounting how they made a similar sacrifice in 1958,

62 Ibid, pp. 1–2.

63 Ibid. This letter reflected on the possibility of 'parameter surveys of the parcels of land required by the Bonny LNG and the assessment exercise of buildings and structures in Finima to start before the end of the third week of March, 1978'.

64 *See* the 'Nigeria LNG Project ES of the LNG Plant Complex, prepared by SGS Environmental Ltd.', *op cit*, Executive Summary, and p. 9.

when the land for the siting of the Shell BCOT was also compulsorily acquired. The protest announcement signed by the paramount chief of Finima, entitled 'To Mr. President and the Entire Nigerian Public', states:

> *Once again, the peace loving people of Finima, who inhabit their God given environment in the southern tip of Bonny river, have been robbed of their land by the Nigerian National Petroleum Corporation (NNPC).*
>
> *In 1958, the citizens of Finima, were called upon by the Federal Government, to surrender a good portion of their land, in the name of progress and co-operation, to accommodate what is now known as the Shell Export Terminal Tank farm at Bonny. The agreement struck on the occasion between Shell BP, their legal luminaries, and the then unsuspecting Chief and Elders of the community, were heavily weighed against the Finima community. Like the peace loving people we are, and continue to be, we bore and have continued to bear the heavy load of the outcome of this travesty of justice and fair-play, with forbearance, fortitude and grace, all in the name of one Nigeria, and being our neighbours keepers. Come 1978, exactly twenty years after, the Federal Government in the guise of the multi-million Oil conglomerate call[ed] the NNPC, came frantically knocking yet again on our door. This time around, soliciting for not only our entire ancestral home, to make room for the LNG plant, that will join hands with the petrochemical plant at Eleme, near Port Harcourt, to bail our country from crippling indebtedness. This move was initially resisted by the entire community but, forbearance and common sense won the day through dialogue initiated by the Traditional paramount ruler, Chief I. A. Idamiebi Brown, and the community elders, all in the name of making sacrifices in the interest of the entire country.*
>
> *Let it be categorically stated here and now, with all emphasis at our command, that the people of Finima did not ask to be moved. The experts at the LNG project chose our shores and deep waters as offering a most befitting economic environment, to harbour the LNG project. The 'ALMIGHTY NNPC' led by its then Managing Director, Chief F. Marinho and Mr. S. M. Akpe, the then General Manager Commercial, came knocking at our door and agreed on the Relocation terms with our chief and elders in a letter. .. of 3rd March, 1978,. .. It is pertinent to point out that while in the earlier cited correspondence, signed by Mr. S. M. Akpe, the then General Manager Commercial, it was emphatically stated in paragraph (3) to 'Design and construct bungalows/houses for displaced families/residents of Finima' only existing structures have been relocated so far, albeit poorly, leaving more than half the entire citizenry homeless.*[65]

65 *See* the protest announcement of Finima community signed on behalf of the people of the community by the paramount chief of Finima community, Chief Idamiebi Brown, entitled 'To Mr. President and the Entire Nigerian Public', published in the Vanguard newspapers of June 10, 1990, p. 4, (hereinafter called the protest announcement of Finima community entitled 'To Mr. President and the Entire Nigerian Public'), dated June 10, 1990.

This protest announcement describes how the people of the community were not against being resettled in the overall interest of Nigeria, while lamenting how they were being forced to do so, under undue influence, threat and intimidation, without the NNPC fulfilling its agreement negotiated with the community. Hence, the protest announcement continued thus:

> *It has taken 12 years of frustration and community stagnation for the NNPC and the Finima Relocation Committee, to come up with some uncompleted bungalow structures, with amenities that cannot in any way conform with civilized standards. The NNPC sub-committee on the movement headed by Chief Ernest Dublin-Green of Bonny and backed by the NNPC task force are now blatantly stampeding the community into moving into new Finima by dangling cartons of naira and threats of army invasion. New Finima located about ten kilometres from the nearest Bonny town, Bonny, is a place built on reclaimed mangrove swamps laced with sand dunes, with no roads, no water fit for human consumption, and with no commercial, medical or transport facilities. . . . in this 20th century, with threats and blatant bribes.*
>
> *. . . We have no wish to go back on our words, but all we are saying is that we will move only after roads, drinkable water, light and habitable dwellings have been put in place in [the] new town Finima, ...*[66]

Besides, before the Finima people were forced to vacate old Finima community, their paramount chief, Chief Idamiebi Brown, complained that the expanse of land being dredged and sand-filled for new Finima community was too small for them. In a letter to the chair and members of the FRC, dated February 20, 1985, Chief Idamiebi Brown also complained about the blockade of the Finima creek and the stagnation of the people's economic activities. While considering the small size of the landmass being dredged for new Finima community, Chief Idamiebi Brown compared it with the massive land areas being prepared to accommodate the NLNG construction workers and the land being designed as residential estate for the NLNG's main staff. Thus, while urging the NNPC to deal fairly with the people, the paramount chief's letter states that:

> *I therefore respectfully call upon you to please remove the blockade [of the Finima creek] which you have caused, and so save us from further suffering due to no fault of ours. If you cannot for now improve our lot, please do not make living more difficult for us.*
>
> *May I also draw your attention to my earlier request for adequate sand-filling at the New Finima. If you are providing about 534.54 acres of land for the housing estate of Bonny LNG workers of about 500 to 700 families, I do not see how the whole of Finima community with about*

66 Ibid.

two thousand or more families would be cramped into just 200 acres with no provision for expansion and no area for farming, and yet be expected to live a happy and contented life after being uprooted from their ancestral home. From all indications, the sand-filling so far done is not even adequate for the areas of which they are dispersed.

There is apparent stagnation of economic activities among Finima people as a result of the uncertainties surrounding the resettlement issues – to be or not to be. One would have thought that by now sand-filling would have been completed, so that surveyors could move in and do proper mapping out.

We have always welcomed the Bonny LNG Project. All we ask for is a fair deal in resettling the people. We are fellow Nigerians. So please treat us as brothers.[67]

The protest announcement of the paramount chief and elders of Finima concludes:

Finima is our only ancestral home, and we therefore respectfully call on MR. PRESIDENT and the entire citizenry of Nigeria, to prevail on the NNPC; its agents and the Rivers state Government, to restrain themselves in their bid to bulldoze the defenceless Finima people and trample on our inalienable rights. It is morally indefensible to condemn apartheid in South Africa and all it stands for on the one hand, while at home perpetrating ugly aspect of apartheid by forcefully evacuating and dumping the defenceless people of Finima in a harsh environment devoid of basic amenities.

What a reward for consenting to be partners in progress with the Federal Government.

. . . Here we rest our case.[68]

The foregoing confirms that the NNPC's responsibilities to the Finima people were far from being completely fulfilled, as certain basic social amenities were yet to be provided when they were involuntarily resettled[69] as from the second

67 *See* the letter of Chief Idamiebi Brown to the chair and members of the FRC, entitled 'Dredging of Creek and Dredge-Filling of Land', dated February 20, 1985.

68 *See* the protest announcement of Finima community entitled 'To Mr. President and the Entire Nigerian Public', dated June 10, 1990, *op cit.*

69 *See* the publication of Australian NGOs under the Australian Asia-Pacific Mining Network, entitled 'Principles for the Conduct of Company Operations within the Minerals Industry', in October 1998, found at http://www.natural-resources.org/minerals/csr/docs/csr/principles_for_mining_companies_by_aust_ngos.doc visited on 31/12/06, p. 5. On this note, under its Performance Standard 5, captioned 'Land Acquisition and Involuntary Resettlement', the IFC outlines the following as the objectives of involuntary resettlement. 1) To avoid or at least minimise involuntary resettlement wherever feasible by exploring other alternative project designs. 2) To mitigate adverse social and economic impacts from land acquisition or restrictions on affected persons' use of land by: (i) providing compensation for loss of assets at replacement cost; and (ii) ensuring that

half of 1990 to 1991, by the special task force of the FRC comprised of some NNPC personnel and Finima citizens.[70]

Given that these unfulfilled responsibilities were part of the grievances of Bonny people during the Bonny kingdom versus the NLNG crisis of September, 1999, paragraph 7 of the Bonny kingdom and NLNG agreement, consummated under the auspices of the Rivers state government, provides for the observance of such unfulfilled responsibilities inherited by NLNG. As NLNG is a worldclass multinational enterprise, it may be proper to briefly discuss how involuntary resettlement relates to these unfulfilled responsibilities and other internationally accepted or recognised commitments of NLNG to Finima community.

9.6(i)(a) Mining and Mineral Resources Development Project-induced Involuntary Resettlement and the Social Responsibility of NLNG to Finima Community

One of the major effects of the global mining and minerals development industry is the displacement (ie, development-induced displacement and resettlement [DIDR])[71] of resources-rich but poor-rural communities of developing countries.[72]

9.6(i)(b) Resettlement in EIA Process

The word 'resettlement' with respect to development projects is only indicted once in the EIA Act, Laws of the Federation of Nigeria (LFN), 2004. That is, under item 1(b) of the schedule of 'Mandatory Study Activities'. This schedule provides for 'Agricultural programmes necessitating the resettlement of 100 families or more'. Also, the '*Environmental Impact Assessment Sectoral Guidelines for Oil and Gas Industry Projects*', prepared by FEPA, provides for 'impacts due to project location/siting' involving the displacement of people, as one of the common environmental impacts associated with onshore petroleum

---

resettlement activities are implemented with appropriate disclosure of information, consultation, and the informed participation of those affected. 3) To improve or at least restore the livelihoods and standards of living of displaced persons. And 4) to improve living conditions among displaced persons through provision of adequate housing with security of tenure at resettlement sites. *See* the 'International Finance Corporation's Performance Standards on Social & Environmental Sustainability', dated April 30, 2006, found at http://www.ifc.org/ifcext/enviro.nsf/AttachmentsByTitle/pol_PerformanceStandards2006_full/$FILE+Performance+Standards visited on 31/12/06, p. 18.

70 *See* the protest announcement of Finima community entitled 'To Mr. President and the Entire Nigerian Public', dated June 10, 1990, *op cit*.

71 *See* J. Stanley, 'Development-Induced Displacement and Resettlement', found at http://www.forcedmigration.org/guides/fmo022.pdf visited on 31/12/06.

72 Refer to the area of the website of the International Institute for Environment and Development (IIED) on the MMSD project captioned 'Working Papers'. *See* the area of this website on the report of the MMSD Southern Africa, regional research paper compiled by D. Sonnenberg (Lims) and F. Munster, for the African Institute of Corporate Citizenship, entitled 'Involuntary Resettlement', dated August 2001, found at http://www.iied.org/mmsd/mmsd_pdfs/161_sonerberg.pdf visited on 31/12/06, p. 5.

development projects.[73] Besides, the United Nations Environment Programme (UNEP) *Environmental Impact Assessment Training Resource Manual*[74] provides that the evolving EIA process and practice seeks to enlarge its scope in such areas as resettlement. This manual categorises resettlement under 'equity and quality of life issues', which include 'resettlement, poverty alleviation and sustainable livelihoods'.[75] Also, while considering development project-induced displacement of people and other adverse effects on such vulnerable groups as ethnic minorities, the UNEP *Environmental Impact Assessment Training Resource Manual* provides that:

> *Often, in EIA, most attention is focused on such high profile issues, notably for projects which displace people and affect vulnerable minorities (as emphasised in the policy of the World Bank). These are unquestionably important internationally, not infrequently raising issues of human rights and social justice. . . . In particular, involuntary resettlement has extreme social impacts which in many cases warrant separate and specific study.*[76]

While outlining the reasons for public hearings as part of an Environmental Impact Statement (EIS) review procedure of the EIA process in Ghana, E. Appah-Sampong indicates situations where 'there will be relocation or dislocation of communities'.[77] In the Environmental Assessment (EA) or EIA process of mining and mineral resources development projects, lenders and sectoral industry-based groups require development-induced displacement such as resettlement to be treated as a special issue.[78] Internationally-accepted practice,

---

73 *See* the '*Environmental Impact Assessment Sectoral Guidelines for Oil and Gas Industry Projects*', Abuja, Federal Environmental Protection Agency (FEPA), 1995, pp. 6–7, especially p. 6. Other listed common potential environmental impacts of onshore petroleum development projects are damage to cultural and historical resources; interference with other utilities and with traffic; resettlement of population displaced; land-use conflict, interference with drainage patterns; and encroachment into other valuable lands. There are also such other impacts as encroachment into precious ecological zones (corals, reproduction) and interference with navigation; erosion hazards due to inadequate provision for resurfacing of exposed areas; and noise/vibration nuisance, especially at pump stations.

74 *See* M. McCabe and B. Sadler (eds), *Environmental Impact Assessment Training Resource Manual*, Geneva, The Economic and Trade Branch, Division of Technology, Industry and Economics (DTIE), UNEP, 2002.

75 Ibid, p. 6.

76 Ibid, pp. 466, 468, and 486, especially p. 466.

77 *See* M. McCabe and B. Sadler (eds), *Studies of EIA Practice in Developing Countries: A Supplement to the UNEP Training Resource Manual*, Geneva, DTIE, UNEP, 2002, p. 87.

78 Such projects-induced displacements as resettlement may be considered under environmental audits of SIAs in the EA process of development projects. *See* the OGP Report No. 2.85/322 of October 2002, entitled 'Key Questions in Managing Social Issues in Oil & Gas Projects', *op cit*, pp. 28–29. *See* the 'International Finance Corporation's Performance Standards on Social & Environmental Sustainability', dated April 30, 2006, *op cit*. *See* the Ilisu Dam and HEPP Environmental Management Plan (EMP), dated May 31, 2006, found at http://www.eigncon-sult.com/ilisu/themes/blue_style/images/force-download.php?file=./umwelt/pdf/EMP060604.pdf visited on 31/12/06, p. 2. Page 28 of the above-stated OGP report provides that major issues

established by leading international and intergovernmental bodies, requires that EA for involuntary resettlement provides for a full Resettlement Action Plan (RAP, which is sometimes referred to as Resettlement Management Plan [RMP]).[79]

Given that NLNG is committed to comply with such international standards as those of the WBG relating to its operations,[80] this book considers the performance standards of the International Finance Corporation (IFC) as a basis towards making some suggestions and recommendations on the resettlement of the Finima people in the course of the NLNG project.

9.6(i)(c) Multinational Financial Institutions and Development Project-induced Resettlements Emphasising the IFC Performance Standards

The IFC, founded in 1956, is a member and private sector arm of the WBG.[81] The IFC finances and provides advice on private sector ventures and projects

---

associated with resettlement may include: **More in-depth understanding of cultural and ethnic systems and values in order to correctly define appropriate family/social units and norms of households eligible for resettlement. *Evaluation of potential effects on communities by loss/gain of households. * Identification and evaluation of the thresholds at which economic effects make a household eligible for resettlement. *Fair and transparent compensation for land and resources. *Potential to offer attractive alternatives to resettlement. *Need for longer term monitoring of resettled families to ensure that they are economically the same or better off than prior to resettlement. * Consideration of cumulative impacts of projects if project-development is phased.*

79 *See* the submission by Corner House Research *et al*, entitled 'Review of EIAR for the Ilisu Dam and HEPP', found http://www.foe.co.uk/resource/reports/iIlsu_era_resettle.pdf visited on 31/12/06, especially p. 5.

80 Thus, the 'Stakeholder Identification and Management Plan' of the NLNGSevenPlus project provides that *International standards and benchmark practices, which apply to shareholder consultation and resettlement, include guidelines prepared by the International Finance Corporation (IFC) and the World Bank. The IFC's Good Practice manual [14] focuses on the benefits that early and effective consultation can offer a project. The World Bank Group's Environmental Assessment Policy [15] requires that project-affected groups and local non-governmental organisations (NGOs) be consulted during the ESHA* [Environmental, Social and Health Assessment] *process about the project's potential environmental and social impacts. The purpose of this consultation is to take local views into account in preparing environmental and social management plans as well as in project design. This is particularly important for complex projects, where the Policy [15] requires public consultation at least twice. Initial consultation should be undertaken following the environmental screening and prior to the terms of reference being prepared for the ESHA, followed by further consultation once the draft ESHA report has been issued. Other World Bank policies, broadly related to the Environmental Assessment Policy [15], such as Operational Policy 4.12 on Involuntary Non-Governmental Organisations in Bank-Supported Activities [18], also include provisions for public consultation. In summary; the policies include requirements for early consultation with affected people and NGOs, early disclosure of information, and provision of information in a way that allows informed consultation with stakeholders and project-affected people. With regard to resettlement planning, the World Bank policies require that all potentially displaced persons should be informed as early as possible about the resettlement aspects of the project and their views should be taken into account. See* the NLNG Train 7+ Project, 'Stakeholder Identification and Management Plan', *op cit*, p. 6.

81 The World Bank is a vital source of financial and technical assistance to developing countries of the world. It is not a Bank in the common sense. It is made up of two unique development institutions owned by its 185 member countries around the world. These two institutions are the International Bank for Reconstruction and Development (IBRD) and the International Development Association (IDA), each of which play different but supportive roles in the Bank Groups' mission of poverty reduction and the improvement of people's living standards around

in developing countries.[82] It promotes environmentally and socially sound and sustainable private sector developmental investments to help reduce poverty and to improve the quality of the lives of people in these countries.[83]

The WBG and other financiers of international development projects such as export credit agencies[84] have different but related standards regarding the financing of development projects. Such standards include EIA standards, which among other things, emphasise how to manage social issues associated with major natural resources development projects in ways that contribute to sound and equitable SD.[85] Hence, the IFC, the Organisation for Economic

---

the world. *See* the area of the website of The World Bank, on the IBRD, and another area of this website captioned 'What is IDA?', respectively found http://web.worldbank.org/WBSITE/EXTERNAL/EXTABOUTUS/EXTIBRD/0,,menuPK:3046081~pagePK:64168427~piPK:64168435~theSitePK:3046012,00.html and at http://web.worldbank.org/WBSITE/EXTERNAL/EXTABOUTUS/IDA/0,,contentMDK:21206704~pagePK:51236175~piPK:437394~theSitePK:73154,00.html visited on 31/12/06. The World Bank and the International Monetary Fund (IMF) are primary Bretton Woods institutions established during WW II in July 1944, to help rebuild the shattered post-war economy and to promote international economic cooperation. *See* the publication by the Bretton Woods Project, entitled 'Backgrounder: The World Bank, IMF and other Bretton Woods Institutions', found at http://thunderbay.indymedia.org/news/2002/07/1003.php visited on 31/12/06.

82 The WBG's President also serves as the IFC President. *See* the IFC homepage found at http://www.ifc.org/ including the area of this homepage captioned 'About IFC', with the subtitle 'President', found at http://www.ifc.org/about including the area of this website captioned 'Office of the President', with the subtitle 'Biography', http://web.worldbank.org/WBSITE/EXTERNAL/EXTABOUTUS/ORGANIZATION/EXTOFFICEPRESIDENT/0,,contentMDK:20519590~menuPK:51175739~pagePK:51174171~piPK:64258873~theSitePK:1014541,00.html visited on 31/12/06.

83 *See* the area of the IFC homepage entitled 'About the IFC', found at http://www.ifc.org/about and the sub-title of this area captioned 'What We Do', found at http://www.ifc.org/ifcext/about.nsf/Content/WhatWeDo visited on 31/12/06.

84 For instance, in terms of the cost and financing of the NLNG*Plus* (ie, the NLNG trains 4 and 5 projects) valued at the estimated cost of US$2.1 billion (excluding ship acquisition costs), the facilities of five international and six Nigerian banks were involved. The international facilities of the project comprise four international commercial bank loans supported by Export Credit Agency (ECA) guarantees or insurance totalling US$620 million involving an eight-year maturity period of the ECA facilities. These were accompanied by an uncovered international bank loan of US$180 million. These international and Nigerian local components of the cost and financing profile of the NLNG*Plus* project, emphasises the relevance of international financial and other operational conditions and standards to the operations of NLNG. *See* the area of the NLNG homepage captioned 'Operations & Strategies', with the sub-title 'Expansion Project: Trains 4 and 5 (NLNG*Plus*)', found at http://www.nlng.com/NLNGnew/operations/Expansion+Project.htm visited on 31/12/06.

85 *See* the World Bank Operational Policy/Bank Procedure 4.01 on Environmental Assessment (EA), dated January 1999, (updated in March 2007), found at http://wbln0018.worldbank.org/Institutional/Manuals/OpManual.nsf/toc2/9367A2A9D9DAEED38525672C007D0972?OpenDocument and at http://web.worldbank.org/WBSITE/EXTERNAL/PROJECTS/EXTPOLICIES/EXTSAFEPOL/0,,contentMDK:20543912~menuPK:1286357~pagePK:64168445~piPK:64168309~theSitePK:584435,00.html visited on 26/04/07. EA is one of the 10 environmental, social, and legal safeguard policies of the World Bank. EA is used in the World Bank to identify, avoid, and mitigate the potential negative environmental impacts associated with Bank lending operations. In the operational setting of the World Bank, EA is earmarked to improve decision-making, and to ensure that the options or alternatives considered in the course of development projects are sound and sustainable. Hence, it is mandatory for proper consultations to be held with the people

Co-operation and Development (OECD),[86] and sectoral industry groups such as the International Association for Oil and Gas Producers (OGP)[87] have certain guidelines, policies and standards on private sector development proposals in developing countries which govern the operations of multinational companies (MNCs) including multinational oil companies (MNOCs). The IFC developed eight performance standards on social and environmental sustainability,[88] to manage the social and environmental risks and impacts of private sector development projects which it is financing in its member countries. Other financial institutions may elect to apply these standards in the

---

affected by the development proposals based on the policy considerations and standards of the Bank. Regarding its safeguard policies, the World Bank states that its . . . *environmental and social safeguard policies are a cornerstone of its support to sustainable poverty reduction. The objective of these policies is to prevent and mitigate undue harm to people and their environment in the development process. These policies provide guidelines for bank and borrower staffs in the identification, preparation, and implementation of programs and projects. The effectiveness and development impact of projects and programs supported by the Bank has substantially increased as a result of attention to these policies. Safeguard policies have often provided a platform for the participation of stakeholders in project design, and have been an important instrument for building ownership among local populations. See* the area of the website of The World Bank captioned 'Safeguard Policies', found at http://web.worldbank.org/WBSITE/EXTERNAL/PROJECTS/EXTPOLICIES/EXTSAFEPOL/0,,menuPK:584441~pagePK:64168427~piPK:64168435~theSitePK:584435,00.html visited on 26/04/07.

86 The OECD, whose convention was originally signed on December 14, 1960, by 20 countries, is made up of 30 member countries, sharing commitments on democratic government and the market economy. It helps to tackle the economic, social and governance challenges of a globalised economy. It cooperates with the Commission for the European Union (EU), while in its global reach it has active relationships with about 70 countries and economies, NGOs and civil society. Hence, it has working relations with non-member countries in Africa, Asia, Europe, Latin-America, and the Middle-East, and conducts policy dialogue and capacity-building activities with non-member economies to share best policy practices and to bear on its policy debates. *See* the area of the OECD homepage captioned 'About OECD', found at http://www.oecd.org/about/0,2337,en_2649_201185_1_1_1_1_1,00.html as another area of this homepage captioned 'The OECD Centre for Co-operation with Non-Members', with the sub-title 'OECD Global Relations', found at http://www.oecd.org/pages/0,2966,en_36335986_36336523_1_1_1_1_1,00.html both visited on 31/12/06.

87 The OGP, formed in 1974 with headquarters in London, encompasses most of the world's leading publicly-traded, private, and state-owned oil and gas companies, oil and gas associations and major upstream service companies. Before it adopted the OGP as its name in 1999, it was originally called the E&P Forum. Its members produce more than half the world's oil and about one third of its gas. It promotes the safe, responsible and profitable performance of the global upstream industry. *See* the website of the OGP, found at http://www.ogp.org.uk/ and the area of this website captioned 'About OGP', found at http://www.ogp.org.uk/AboutOGP/index.html both visited on 31/12/06. *Also see* the OGP report No. 1.24/299 of November 1999 (Report No. 362 of January 2005), entitled 'Catalogue of International Standards used in the Petroleum and Natural Gas Industries,' found at http://www.ogp.org.uk/pubs/362.pdf visited on 31/12/06.

88 These Standards are 1) Social and Environmental Assessment and Management Systems; 2) Labour and Working Conditions; 3) Pollution Prevent and Abatement; 4) Community Health, Safety and Security; 5) Land Acquisition and Involuntary resettlement; 6) Biodiversity Conservation and Sustainable Natural resource Management; 7) Indigenous Peoples; and 8) Cultural Heritage. Performance Standard 7 also provides for marginalised ethnic minorities and vulnerable aboriginal minority groups, while Performance Standard 8 is applicable where the cultural heritage of displaced or resettled people and groups exist as well as the cultural heritage of people being endangered in the course of extractive industrial operations in general. Frequently therefore, the implementation of the IFC Performance Standard 5 may involve some or all the rest of the Performance Standards and Environmental Sustainability measures.

course of financing similar development projects. These standards establish certain criteria that the IFC clients are to accomplish throughout the life-cycle of an investment sponsored by it or other financial institutions associated with it. Clients of the IFC are to apply these standards and the applicable national laws and the obligations of host countries under international law, to improve on their performances while implementing development projects in emerging or developing countries.[89]

The 'IFC Performance Standards on Social & Environmental Sustainability', Performance Standard 5, deals with 'Land Acquisition and Involuntary Resettlement'.[90] Under this standard, the IFC defines involuntary resettlement in the following words:

> *Involuntary resettlement refers both to physical displacement (relocation or loss of shelter) and to economic displacement (loss of assets or access to assets that leads to the loss of income sources or means of livelihood) as a result of project-oriented land acquisition. Resettlement is considered involuntary when affected individuals or communities do not have the right to refuse land acquisition that results in displacement. . . .*[91]

If improperly managed, involuntary resettlement may occasion long-term hardship, impoverishment,[92] environmental damage and social stress where people are resettled. The IFC recommends that involuntary resettlement should be avoided or at least minimised; and that where it is unavoidable, environmental sustainability measures should be designed in good time, and appropriately implemented to mitigate adverse impacts on people and to improve their livelihoods and the welfare of communities. The IFC's advice to its clients includes the avoidance of the use of government authorities to forcibly displace or relocate people rather than embarking upon negotiated

---

89 *See* the 'International Finance Corporation's Performance Standards on Social & Environmental Sustainability', dated April 30, 2006, *op cit*, pp. i, 1 and 22–23. *Also see Investing in People: Sustaining Communities through Improved Business Practice: A Community Development Resource Guide for Companies*, Washington DC, IFC, 2000.

90 *Also see* the World Bank Policy on Involuntary Resettlement, Policy Directive OD 4.30, dated November 2002, found at http://www.ifc.org/ifcext/btc.nsf/AttachmentsByFile/Tur++AnX+3.3/$FILE/RAP++Annex+3.3++WB+Policy+Involuntary+Reset and the Bank's Operational Policy 4.12 on Involuntary Resettlement, dated December 2001, found at http://web.worldbank.org/WBSITE/EXTERNAL/PROJECTS/EXTPOLICIES/EXTOPMANUAL/0,,contentMDK:20064610~pagePK:64141683~piPK:64141620~theSitePK:502184,00.html both visited on 31/12/06. *See* Article 10 of the UN Declaration on the Rights of Indigenous Peoples on forced relocation which may basically apply to local community people as Finima. This Declaration provides that 'indigenous peoples shall not be forcibly removed from their lands or territories. No relocation shall take place without the free, prior and informed consent of the indigenous peoples concerned and after agreement on just and fair compensation and, where possible, with the option of return'.

91 *See* the 'International Finance Corporation's Performance Standards on Social & Environmental Sustainability', dated April 30, 2006, *op cit*, p. 18.

92 Ibid. *Also see* T. Downing, 'Avoiding New Poverty: Mining-Induced Displacement and Resettlement', found at http://www.iied.org/mmsd/mmsd_pdfs/058_downing.pdf visited on 31/12/06.

settlements.[93] The IFC urges that its Performance Standard 5 be applied during a social and environmental assessment process, while the actions necessary to meet the requirements of this standard should be expressed in a resettlement action plan (RAP) or a resettlement framework.[94] The IFC requires that a RAP be designed to identify the risks and other adverse impacts of resettlement processes, and that these should be integrated into the follow-up and monitoring processes as well as the environmental management plans (EMPs) and audit processes of development projects. It is the requirement of the IFC that a RAP be managed by a Social and Environmental Management System (SEMS) which involves social and environmental audits covering the life-cycle of development projects. The IFC require compliance with integrated life-cycle EAs within the framework of RAPs;[95] especially regarding resettlements taking place in environmentally and ecologically sensitive areas and where

---

93 *See* the 'International Finance Corporation's Performance Standards on Social & Environmental Sustainability', dated April 30, 2006, *op cit*, p. 18.

94 Ibid. *Also see Handbook for Preparing a Resettlement Action Plan*, Washington DC, IFC, 2002, found at http://.ifc.org/ifcext/enviro.nsf/AttachmentsByTitle/p-resettlement/$FILE/ResetlementHandbook.PDF visited on 31/12/06.

95 *See* some defects of the EIA report of the controversial Ilisu dam and hydro electric power project (HEPP – on the upper Tygris river, in the mainly Kurdish South-East of Turkey, 45 km from the Syrian border) as identified by Corner House research *et al*, among several other reviews of the EIA report of the project, are as follows. That, '. . . *a Resettlement Action Plan has yet to be made public, contrary to internationally accepted practice; . . . Key studies necessary to draw up a resettlement plan to internationally accepted standards have still to be undertaken or completed; . . . No provision has been made for independent monitoring, . . .*' The internationally-accepted practices breached include those of the World Bank, OECD, and the World Commission on Dams. The practices of the World Bank include the World Bank Operational Policy 4.01 on Environmental Assessment, the World Bank Operational Policy as well as the World Bank Operational Directive on Involuntary Resettlement. *See* the full report as well as its summary entitled 'Review of EIAR for the Ilisu Dam and HEPP', *op cit. See* one of the annexures to this Review report by Corner House Research *et al*, entitled 'Alternatives to Ilisu: Review of the EIAR for the Ilisu Dam and HEPP', found at http://www.iIisu.org.uk/alternatives_ response.pdf visited on 31/12/06. The BBC news states that this project of the Turkish Ministry of Energy has the following details. Height; 135 m, measuring 1,820m along the crest; predicted average annual energy generation 3.833 billion kWh; capacity to hold 11 billion cubic metres of water; reservoir to cover 313 sq km; and projected completion date 2013. This project, earmarked to be the second largest in Turkey, will devastate the environment and cultural heritage, cause flooding, lead to the displacement and resettlement of about 55,000 to 78,000 people, and some 1999 settlements, for which the government is to resettle the Hasankeyf community and thereby destroy the community's centuries-long cultural and archaeological heritage. The consultants who drew the resettlement plans had access only to limited information. *See* the BBC news report by L. Smith-Spark, entitled 'Turkey Dam Project Back to Haunt Kurds', found at http://news.bbc.co.uk/2/hi/europe/5243588.stm visited on 31/12/06. *Also see* Erhan Unlu, 'Tigris River Ichtyological Studies in Turkey: A Review with Regard to the Ilisu Hydroelectric Project', centred on the EIA Report of the project, dated May 2006, found at http://www.dwesigncon-sult.com/iIisu/themes/blue_style/images/force-download.php?file=./umwett/pdf/ProfUnlu_IchtyologicalStudies visited on 31/12/06. *Also see* B. Morvaridi, 'Social Review of the Ilisu Dam Resettlement Action Plan', found at http://www.ecgd.gov.uk/lrgtxt/ilisusocialreviewreport240602.doc visited on 31/12/06, and B. Morvaridi, 'Resettlement, Rights to Development and the Ilisu Dam, Turkey', Development and Change, vol. 35, No. 4, September 2004, pp. 719–741. *See* J. Stanley, 'Development-Induced Displacement and Resettlement', *op cit.*

there are disadvantaged groups such as minorities or other forms of marginalised or vulnerable groups or populations.[96]

The IFC Performance Standard 5 requires resettlement plans to address physical and economic displacements. Physical displacement involves the degree of compensation for land and such assets as dwellings and improvements made on or upon land and other fixed assets. Mitigation associated with development project-related displacements usually includes remedial measures regarding the loss of income and livelihoods of displaced or resettled persons and their communities. Thus, under economic displacement, issues such as the cost to business owners for re-establishing their businesses, credit facilities for the establishment and vitalisation of businesses, provision of alternative areas for dominant economic activities such as fishing and agricultural resources and areas, and the provision of employment opportunities and training and capacity-building

---

96 *See* the 'International Finance Corporation's Performance Standards on Social & Environmental Sustainability', dated April 30, 2006, *op cit*, p. 3. Considering that the Niger Delta region is ecologically sensitive and inhabited by vulnerable and marginalised groups, the entire eight 'IFC Performance Standards on Social & Environmental Sustainability', deserves to apply in the region in a comprehensive and integrated manner in the course of petroleum extractive operations in the region. Regarding the operations of NLNG in Bonny kingdom, apart from the Buoye-Omuso Brown major house and the citizens of Finima community, there are other marginalised groups identified in Chapter 8. These include the Bristol-Alagbarigha royal house which is complaining that it has been rendered vulnerable as an aboriginal minority entity, in the course of the operations and ongoing CCs of NLNG in Grand Bonny. Other marginalised groups include the ordinary citizens and citizen groups of Grand Bonny. UNEP has, for instance, outlined good practices on how to address equity issues in terms of addressing the impacts of development projects on ethnic minorities and other neglected and vulnerable groups under social impact assessment (SIA). *See* M. McCabe and B. Sadler (eds), *Environmental Impact Assessment Training Resource Manual, op cit*, pp. 466 and 486. The OGP Report No. 2.85/322 of October 2002, entitled 'Key Questions in Managing Social Issues in Oil & Gas Projects', *op cit*, p. 22, also makes provisions regarding vulnerable/indigenous populations to the effect that *more intensive consultation requirements are generally required with those groups considered to be vulnerable or indigenous. This is in part due to the fact that these populations are generally considered marginalised by larger population as a whole and/or have special consultation needs. Also see* the IFC's publication entitled 'World Bank Calls for the Improvement of the Impact of Extractive Industries on Women', found at http://web.worldbank.org/WBSITE/EXTERNAL/TOPICS/EXTOGMC/0,,contentMDK:21249024~menuPK:336936~pagePK:148956~piPK:216618~theSitePK:336930,00.html visited on 12/04/07. *See* the IFCs sustainability approach (eg, its Equator Principles: evolved as the benchmark for the financial industries regarding the management of social and environmental issues in project financing), found at http://www.ifc.org/ifcext/sustainability.nsf/Content/WhoBenefits_FI its revised 'environmental and social standards', found at http://www.ifc.org/ifcext/enviro.nsf/Content/EnvSocStandards and its policy on Social and Environmental Sustainability, found at http://www.ifc.org/ifcext/enviro.nsf/AttachmentsByTitle/pol_SocEnvSustainability2006/$FILE/SusainabilityPolicy.pdf all visited on 12/04/07. *See* the protest letter of the Bristol-Alagbarigha royal house to NLNG with Reference No. BARH/NLNG/2008-01, dated January 24th, 2008, entitled *inter alia* 'Re: The Socio-Economic Dislocation, Discrimination, Oppression, and Near Extinction of the Bristol-Alagbarigha Royal House (Founder of Your Grand Bonny Island Primary Host Community) in the Course of Your Operations in the Community'. *Also see* the publication of the World Rain Forest Movement entitled 'Nigeria: Gas Corporation NLNG Destroys Mangrove Forest in the Niger Delta', found at http://www.wrm.orguy/bulletin/68/Nigeria.html visited on 25/10/2005. *See* the MMSD Australia report, entitled 'Developing New Approaches for Stakeholder Engagement in the Minerals Sector', found at http://www.natural-resources.org/minerals/CD/docs/mmsd/australia/finalreport/stakeholderengagement.pdf visited on 17/11/04.

measures, are required to be provided.[97] The IFC Performance Standard 5 requires that displacement or resettlement processes in the course of siting or expanding development projects may, where permitted or possible, be carried out in collaboration with responsible government agencies or authorities. This performance standard also requires the setting up of a grievance mechanism designed to resolve disputes in an impartial manner, to which the people or communities being resettled may have recourse, independently of existing administrative or judicial dispute resolution measures. It requires informed participation of the affected persons and communities, so as to enable them to play an active role in the planning, implementation and evaluation process of resettlement. In the words of the IFC:

> *Following disclosure of all relevant information, the client will consult with and facilitate, the informed participation of affected persons and communities, including host communities, in decision-making processes related to resettlement. Consultation will continue during the implementation, monitoring, and evaluation of compensation payment and resettlement to achieve outcomes that are consistent with the objectives of this performance Standard.*[98]

Thus, the goal of the IFC is to help reduce poverty and to improve the quality of the lives of people and communities resettled in the course of siting or expansion of development projects in an environmentally sound and socially equitable manner.

9.6(i)(d) Concluding Remarks on Finima Resettlement

The controversial Finima community resettlement falls short of the NLNG's EIA commitments regarding stakeholder involvement and resettlement.[99] So far, the Community's resettlement process is at variance with the IFC Performance Standard 5 and other related standards on social and environmental sustainability which ought to have been integrated into the social and environmental RAP of the community. The IFC Performance Standards on Social and Environmental Sustainability and other relevant international good and widely accepted practices were breached or undermined by the NNPC in the course of resettling the people of Finima. For instance, such practices as the World Bank Operational Policy 4.12, including its Operational Directive 4.30, its Operational Procedure 4.12 on Involuntary

97 *See* the 'International Finance Corporation's Performance Standards on Social & Environmental Sustainability', dated April 30, 2006, *op cit*, pp. 21–22.
98 Ibid, p. 20.
99 *See* NLNG Train 7+ Project, 'Stakeholder Identification and Management Plan', *op cit*, especially pp. 2, and 4–6.

Resettlement,[100] and its Operational Directive on Environmental Assessment, were breached or undermined by the NNPC. Considering that the improper resettlement of the people of Finima from their old to new community remains a problem, NLNG inherited this problem when it came into operation. The fact that no RAP was made public by the NNPC or any other relevant government institution or agency, as required by widely acknowledged and accepted international standards and practices,[101] is a pointer that there was no RAP during the resettlement of the people of Finima.[102] The most concrete and relevant document in the custody of the people of Finima community, upon which the were resettled, is thus the above mentioned letter directed to the paramount chief of the community, Chief Idamiebi Brown, by S. M. Akpe, the NNPC's General Manager Commercial, with reference no. GID/001/13.1/21, dated March 3, 1978. This letter referred to the consultations held by the NNPC with the community and the responsibilities to be accomplished by the

---

100 *See* this Operational Policy dated December, 2001, and the Operational Directive dated November 2002, *op cit*, and the Bank's Operational Procedure on Resettlement 4.12 of January 2001, found at http://wbln0018.worldbank.org/Institutional/Manuals/OpManual.nsf/toc2/19036F316CAFA52685256B190080B90A?OpenDocument visited on 31/12/06. *See* the area of The World Bank website captioned 'Involuntary Resettlement', found at http:// web.worldbank.org/WBSITE/EXTERNAL/PROJECTS/EXTPOLICIES/EXTSAFEPOL/0,,contentMDK:20543978~menuPK:1286647~pagePK:64168445~piPK:64168309~theSitePK:584435,00.html visited on 31/12/06.

101 *See* the submission by Corner House Research *et al*, entitled 'Review of EIAR for the Ilisu Dam and HEPP', *op cit*, p. 3.

102 By and large, after committing themselves to uphold accepted international standards in their operational areas in developing countries, MNOCs do not often abide by these standards in practice. Briefly put, remedies open to the most helpless communities such as Finima lie in the persuasive effect of the court of public opinion on the MNOCs. Helpless communities may also persuade consumers in the developed countries to exert influence, via public opinion, on MNOCs and thereby make the companies comply with internationally-accepted standards and practice in favour of the communities. *See* the role of public opinion, as expressed during the World Summit 2002 online debate on the subject-matter of 'How can multinational companies be influenced to adopt corporate citizenship and accountability for sustainable development? Who are the key actors and what are the main barriers? What strategies could the Earth Summit 2002 develop to address this issue? ', found at http://www.earthsummit2002.org/es/life/Summary%20week%204.rtf visited on 31/12/06. Local communities may also secure a measure of relief by triggering the implementation of accepted international standards by enlisting the support of reputable financiers and financial institutions supporting development operations of the MNOCs in their communities. Regarding the financiers of the NLNG project, see the area of the NLNG homepage captioned 'The Company' (which indicates its shareholders), found at http://www.nlng.com/NR/exeres/F48DE9A7-F3F3-4A8E-929A-0C34F1CFF92B%2Cframeless.htm visited on 31/12/06. *Also see* the area of the NLNG homepage captioned 'Operations & Strategies', with the sub-title 'Finance', which shows some international financial facilities and international financial institutions involved in the financing of the NLNG project, *op cit*. The operations of these financial institutions in the advanced countries are governed by certain widely accepted guidelines and standards regarding development projects financing which NLNG should comply with in the course of its operations in its host communities. *See* D. Leipziger, *Corporate Responsibility Code Book*, Sheffield, Greenleaf, 2005. *See* J. Andriof and M. McIntosh (eds), *Perspectives on Corporate Citizenship*, Sheffield, Greenleaf, 2001. *Also see* W. Visser *et al* (eds), *Corporate Citizenship in Africa: Lessons from the Past; Paths to the Future*, Sheffield, Greenleaf, 2006. Besides, regarding how to remedy the continuing social cost of resettlement using the 'impoverishment risks and reconstruction (IRR) model/strategy, see G. Heggelund, 'Resettlement Programme and Environmental Capacity in the three Gorges Dam Project', Development Change, vol. 37, No. 1, 2006, pp. 179–199.

NNPC in favour of the community. However, these responsibilities do not satisfy such internationally-recognised standards as those of the IFC. Indeed, based on the requirements of the UNEP and those of such international sectoral industry-based groups as the OGP and development projects' financier-institutions such as export credit agencies and the WBG, the resettlement of the people of Finima requires a separate and specific study, namely an extreme social impact assessment (SIA) study, of the EIA process of the NLNG Base project.[103]

As a way forward, the NNPC is required to furnish NLNG with an inventory of the Finima resettlement process which the NNPC undertook before the start of NLNG's operations, if such an inventory was taken. Upon receiving this inventory, NLNG is required to comply with the prevailing international standards and practices to redress or remedy the process.[104] NLNG is required to prepare a social and environmental audit in order to produce a post-resettlement social and environmental management plan and SEMS capable of laying a better foundation for SD in new Finima community, in the course of its operations. To prepare this audit, NLNG is required to hold direct consultations with the Finima people, to interactively involve them along with other critical and high awareness stakeholders, such as government regulatory agencies, environmental NGOs and affected, concerned and interested relevant professionals, in the decision-making process.[105] The Finima community post-resettlement social and environmental management plan and SEMS, having an inbuilt alternative dispute resolution (ADR) mechanism, namely

---

103 *See* M. McCabe and B. Sadler (eds), *Environmental Impact Assessment Training Resource Manual, op cit*, pp. 466, 468, and 486, especially p. 466. The law suit, *Oronto Douglas vs. The Shell Petroleum Development Company of Nigeria Limited & Ors.* (1999) 2 NWLR, pp. 466–475), discussed in Chapter 5 and the Bonny kingdom versus the NLNG crisis of September, 1999, discussed in this chapter, demonstrates that the environmental and social performances of the NLNG in the kingdom during its Base project fell short of its world-class performance standards and commitments.

104 *See* 'When Displacement Ends: A Framework for Durable Solutions', being a publication of the Brookings Institution – University of Bern, Project on Internal Displacement, dated June 2007, found at http://www3.brookings.edu/fp/projects/idp/2007_DurableSolutionsFramework.pdf visited on July 16, 2007.

105 Excluding the chiefs and people of Finima community led by the paramount chief of the Buoye-Omuso Brown major house under paragraph 6 and in particular relation to paragraph 7 (ie, pages 3–4) of the 'Bonny versus NLNG agreement consummated consequent upon the Bonny kingdom versus the NLNG crisis of September, 1999 (under the auspices of the Rivers state government reconciliation panel)', *op cit*, constitute an omission that is contrary to existing local and international standards and practices on involuntary resettlement. *See* item no. 3 of the communiqué of the Bonny Island Foundation (BIF), entitled 'Communiqué Issued at the End of the Convention of Bonny Organisations held on Friday, December 23, 2005, at the Ibanise hall, Ogugumanga, Bonny Island', found at http://www.grandbonny.org/page1.htm visited on 31/12/06. This item provides that 'The Bonny Chiefs' Council should endeavour to resolve all disputes within Finima Community'. *Also see* the requirements for consultation and disclosure regarding resettlement as well as the setting up of grievance mechanisms, under the IFC Performance Standards 5 and 1, entitled 'Land Acquisition and Involuntary Resettlement' and 'Social and Environmental Assessment and Management Systems'. *See* the 'International Finance Corporation's Performance Standards on Social & Environmental Sustainability', dated April 30, 2006, *op cit*, pp. 5 and 20.

fully institutionalised environmental mediation expressed in the Preface and Chapter 1 and 10, requires to be implemented throughout the life-cycle of the NLNG project up to the project's decommissioning phase. As LNG projects world-wide are time bombs, this plan, along with its management system, is required to address the issue of gas explosion and other related dangers of the NLNG plant[106] in an environmentally sound and socially equitable manner. The plan needs to help reduce poverty and to improve the quality of the lives of people so as to enhance environmentally sound and socially equitable growth and development[107] in new Finima community. Generally, the operations of such MNOCs as Shell Nigeria, NLNG and MPN should help contribute to SD in Finima and Bonny Island communities.

9.7 THE NLNG FINIMA NATURE PARK (FNP)

As part of the NLNG Base project EIA mitigation, certain other resolutions and remedial measures were expressed in the Bonny kingdom versus the NLNG crisis agreement made under the auspices of the Rivers state government reconciliation panel. As part of the environmental protection and conservation responsibility of NLNG, it was resolved that a nature reservation area be declared in Bonny kingdom,[108] as expressed in paragraph 11 of this agreement captioned 'Declaration of Nature Reservation Area'. This paragraph states that:

---

106 Regarding the LNG explosion blast in Algeria, in January 2004, and other dangers of LNG plants to their host communities, *see* the publication of Tim Riley Law firm entitled 'LNG Danger to Our Communities: LNG History, Introduction & LNG Accidents', found at http://timrileylaw.com/LNG.htm visited on 31/12/06. *Also see* R. G. Bednarik, 'Facts About LNG Plants', found at http://mc2.vicnet.net.au/home/dampier/web/LNG.html visited on 31/12/06. *See* the publication by T. Riley entitled 'LNG Terminals – Danger to Our Communities', found at http://www.timrileylaw.com/LNG_PROLIFERATION.htm visited on 13/03/09. *See* N. Ismail and T. R. Stuart, 'The Train 7 Fire at PETRONAS LNG Complex, Bintulu, Malaysia', published in the Malaysian LNG Journal, dated July/August 2005, pp. 12–14, found at http://www.fwc.com/publications/tech_papers/files/Petronas%20LNG.pdf visited on 13/03/09.

107 For instance, regarding the contributions of the LNG plant and other industrial projects to the growth and development of Bintulu and the entire Sarawak State of Malaysia, *see* the area of the homepage of the Bintulu Development Authority (BDA) captioned 'Projects', found at http://www.bda.gov.my/investment/Projects.htm visited on 13/03/09.

108 *See* the 'Bonny versus the NLNG agreement consummated consequent upon the Bonny kingdom versus the NLNG crisis of September, 1999 (under the auspices of the Rivers state government reconciliation panel)', *op cit*, p. 5, para 11. *Also see* the 'Nigeria LNG Project ES of the LNG Plant Complex, prepared by SGS Environmental Ltd.', *op cit*, Executive Summary and especially pp. 109 and 116–117. According to the Nigerian Conservation Foundation (NCF), *a number of petroleum related companies have been involved in land consecrations during the course of their normal operations in Bonny Island. Nigeria Liquefied Natural Gas (NLNG) is no exception. The project's Environmental Impact Assessment (EIA) recommended forest conservation as one of the mitigation measures to cushion the adverse impacts of their development efforts. In an effort to show its commitment to environmental conservation of its area of operation while at the same time, implement part of the project's EIA report, the NLNG invited the Nigerian Conservation Foundation (NCF) to undertake a reconnaissance survey of Bonny Island and make necessary recommendation for conservation of forest reserves within the area of operation with particular emphasis on the conservation of Hippos which are seriously threatened by habitat destruction. See* the area of the website of the NCF, captioned 'Projects', found at http://www.ncfnigeria.org/projects.php#p3 visited on 31/12/06.

> *NLNG shall ensure the completion of preparation by its commissioned agent, the Niger Delta Wetland Centre [NDWC] of the proposal for the preservation of some part of the community as a Nature Preservation Area which proposal shall be made available to the community through the BECC one week after receipt of the said document for the Niger Delta Wetland Centre for the community input and participation before final decision is taken.*[109]

The NDWC had earlier, in 1998, been invited by NLNG to carry out a feasibility study of a designated location for a nature protection programme in order to address the nature conservation concern expressed by the Bonny people in the EIA process of the NLNG Base project. The background of the 'draft five-year management plan' of the FNP, Bonny Island, prepared by the NDWC, states:

> *Thirty-five years ago, the first oil industry activities started on Bonny Island with Shell establishing a tank farm for crude oil storage and export. The early operations of the oil industry activities on the Island were not labour-intensive and did not bring a great increase in population or economic activity. In 1996 following several years of preparation and contract negotiation involving multinational consortia and various sectors of the Federal Government of Nigeria (notably NNPC), construction of the Nigeria Liquefied Natural Gas (NLNG) plant started. With this huge state-of-the-art industrial development, there was a large population increase and concomitant pressures on all aspects of community life on Bonny Island. The entire village of Finima was uprooted from its ancestral lands and resettled nearby to provide the construction site for the plant at the mouth of the Bonny River estuary. A large expanse of land was cleared and transformed into a dedicated industrial area; since production began, construction of new trains has continued to meet increased production targets. At the same time, Shell continues to operate its tank farm and Chevron and Mobil also established operations in the area; it is expected that related down-stream industrial activity will follow.*
>
> *A comprehensive Environmental Impact Assessment (EIA) was carried out for NLNG's construction and operations. One of the recommendations of the EIA was that NLNG should assist in protecting some parts of the forest and wetland areas as a means of mitigating the damage done to previously forested areas. NLNG then decided to establish a protected area as part of its environmental programme to ensure that*

109 Ibid.

some areas of the Island are conserved as near as possible to their natural condition.[110]

NLNG describes the purpose of the FNP, including its size and present management, as well as its profile for public consultation and forest enlightenment campaign being undertaken with the BECC, as examples of its good neighbourliness in Bonny Island, in the following words:

> *The Park, named Finima Nature Park, is for conservation, recreational activities and research in the fauna, flora and cultural heritage of Bonny Island. It is approximately 700 hectares. At present, the nature reserve is managed by an NGO, the Niger Delta Wetlands Centre (NDWC), which undertook the feasibility study of the park area. In future, it will be managed by a Board of Trustees drawn from the host community.*
>
> *This is to ensure that the community has a sense of belonging and to make them appreciate that it is in their long and short term interest.*
>
> *The reserve area covers the rain forest and mangrove swamps, as well as an ecologically important area of sandy soil with fresh water ponds and tall timber between the swamps and the beach. This diversity is a good representation of the Niger Delta ecology, which will afford a unique opportunity for research and educational activities. Already, the reserve is harbouring some wild life species of high conservation value.*
>
> *There are also a variety of mammals, different bird species (mostly waterfowl) and reptiles, including crocodiles.*
>
> *In pursuing its environmental policies, the company considers public consultation and enlightenment fundamental to fostering good relationships with its neighbours. It has initiated a forest enlightenment campaign in accordance with EIA mitigation measures.*
>
> *The company is partnering with the Bonny Environment Consultants' Committee (BECC) on the campaign. Several billboards urging the preservation of the forests have been put at strategic locations on the Island.*
>
> *Use of wildlife resources [are] prohibited and wildlife concerned in fenced premises was relocated to the forest before construction work commenced.*[111]

The FNP is thus regarded as NLNG's contribution to the national and global conservation objective, towards complying with the provisions of UN Agenda 21, the Rio Declaration on Environment and Development, the Statement on Forest Principles, and the UN Convention on Biological Diversity, all of which resulted from the UN Conference on Environment and Development (UNCED), held at Rio de Janeiro, Brazil, in 1992. FNP is also regarded as an effort towards

---

110 *See* the 'Finima Nature Park, Bonny Island: Five Year Management Plan Prepared for NLNG (Nigeria Liquefied Natural Gas Limited), by Niger Delta Wetlands Centre, Port Harcourt, Nigeria', dated September 2001, hereinafter called the 'Finima Nature Park (FNP), Bonny Island: Five Year Management Plan Prepared by NDWC for NLNG', p. 2.
111 *See* 'NLNG 2007: Facts and Figures on NLNG', pp. 41–42.

addressing such international initiatives as the Ramsar Convention on Wetlands, 1971,[112] and the International Union for the Conservation of Nature and Natural Resources (ie, the World Conservation Union, IUCN).[113] While commending FNP as a good nature conservation initiative,[114] the management and operational processes of the Park should reflect benchmark global standards on nature reservation.[115] Also, NLNG, as the financier of the reservation initiative, and the apex rulership of Bonny kingdom, should ensure, without compromising professionalism and other relevant standards, that the board of trustees and other key management and operation personnel of the Park represent an equitable reflection of the chieftaincy houses of the kingdom. Following such examples as the effort of Natural England,[116] the MNOCs along with the federal, states and local governments in the Delta region are required to work in partnership to establish a nature reservation trust to enhance environmental conservation, rehabilitation and renewal in the region, due to accumulating adverse impacts of petroleum development operations.[117] Such a nature reservation trust, which may have strategic divisional units in the region, is capable of preserving the nature, culture, history and other aspects of natural heritage in

---

112 This Convention is an inter-governmental treaty signed in Iran in 1971. The mission of the Convention is the conservation and wise use of all wetlands through local, regional and national actions and international cooperation, as a contribution towards SD throughout the world. *See* the website of the Convention captioned 'The Ramsar Convention on Wetlands', found at http://www.ramsar.org/ visited on 12/04/06.

113 *See* the International Union for the Conservation of Nature and Natural Resources (IUCN –World Conservation Union), as well as its regional office for Africa, are established to conserve nature and its wetlands and forests resources as well as ecology and ecosystem protection and preservation measures, etc. *See* the area of the website of the IUCN, captioned 'IUCN Overview', found at http://www.iucn.org/en/about/ visited on 28/12/06. Regarding other related nature conservation efforts, *see*, the website of the global conservation organisation known as the World Wildlife Fund (WWF) of Canada, found at http://www.wwf.ca/ visited on 31/12/06.

114 Also, the initiative of NLNG to propagate and preserve the cultural heritage of Bonny kingdom by embarking on the revival of the Ibani (Bonny) language among the people of Bonny, deserves to be commended and encouraged by the people. *See* the 'NLNG 2007: Facts and Figures on NLNG', p. 42.

115 *See* the nature conservation effort of the global conservation organisation known as the World Wildlife Fund (WWF), Canada, see the website of the WWF, found at http://www.wwf.ca/ visited on 31/12/06.

116 *See* the Natural England homepage found at http://www.naturalengland.org.uk/ visited on 31/12/06. *Also see* the English Nature Research Reports, Report No. 160, produced by David Tyldesley and Associates, entitled 'Good Nature Conservation Practice in the Mineral Industry: Working Today for Nature Tomorrow', dated December 1, 1995, found at http://naturalengland.twoten.com/naturalenglandshop/docs/R160%20part%201.pdf visited on 31/12/06.

117 The objectives of Natural England are to conserve and enhance the natural environment in England –including the landscape biodiversity, geology and soils, natural resources, cultural heritage and other features of the built and natural environment, for the intrinsic values of these and the well-being and enjoyment of people and the economic prosperity which arises from them. Natural England works for people, places and nature to conserve and enhance biodiversity, landscapes and wildlife in rural, urban, coastal and marine areas. *See* the area of Natural England's homepage captioned 'conservation' found at http://www.naturalengland.org.uk/conservation/ default.htm visited on 31/12/06. *Also see* the homepage of the Minerals and Nature Conservation Forum, United Kingdom, found at http://www.mineralsandnature.org.uk/index.php visited on 31/12/06. This forum is a working group in the United Kingdom comprising representatives from the English Nature and the Minerals industry, through the Quarry Products Association and the Silica and Moulding Sands Association.

the region. By and large, the FG is required to encourage a systematic process of nature conservation by developing relevant policy, legislative and regulatory frameworks throughout the federation.[118]

9.8 NLNG'S SOCIAL INVESTMENTS REGARDING HUMAN, BUSINESS AND INFRASTRUCTURAL DEVELOPMENT AND SOCIAL SERVICES

The implementation of the Bonny versus NLNG crisis agreement (consummated under the auspices of the Rivers state government reconciliation panel – after the NLNG Base project), involves social investments to be implemented by NLNG in the interest of its Finima and Bonny Island primary host communities.

NLNG categorised its social investments under business and human development and the provision of infrastructure. NLNG's infrastructure/human development programme involves such activities as the encouragement of indigenous contractors, employment of skilled and unskilled labour, economic empowerment through micro-credit and skills acquisition, and the award of scholarships and educational support.[119] Other components of NLNG's infrastructural programme are the upgrading of existing infrastructure, road construction, provision of public water, and electricity power generation, distribution and maintenance.[120]

NLNG categorised the social investments which it executed in its primary host Finima and Bonny Island communities under its various trains, particularly ranging from its train 3 (*ie*, the NLNG Expansion project) to its train 6 (ie, the NLNG*Six*) project.[121] Following the MoU projects associated with the era of the NLNG Base project, the main social investments or impact-benefit projects stated under the NLNG train 3 include the establishment of the BVC, construction of Coal Beach Roundabout, and the rehabilitation of certain roads. These are the road to Finima, Court Road, Lecox/Isowari Road, new layout road, King Jaja Road, Park Road, Government School/Hospital Road by-pass, and the King Perekule Road.[122] Under the NLNG trains 4 and 5 (ie, the NLNG*Plus*), are outlined the construction of the Bonny Sandy Road, Bonny Land Reclamation, Finima Soccer Field Upgrade, and Finima Land Reclamation, including general road repairs in Finima, as aspects of its continuing social investments effort in Bonny and Finima communities. Accordingly, the impact-benefit projects provided under the NLNG's train 6 project are the

---

118 *See* the Nature Conservation (Scotland) Act, 2004.
119 *See* 'NLNG 2007: Facts and Figures on NLNG', p. 44.
120 Ibid.
121 NLNG's social investments in Grand Bonny and Finima communities include the MoU projects jointly sponsored by the NLNG and the two other major MNOCs (ie, Shell Nigeria and MPN) operating in these communities. *See* the 'NLNG 2007: Facts and Figures on NLNG', p. 46. *Also see* the area of the NLNG homepage entitled 'Community Relations', with the subtitle 'Community Projects', *op cit.*
122 *See* the 'NLNG 2007: Facts and Figures on NLNG', p. 52.

extension of the Jerusalem Road, Bonny, and the Bonny Land Reclamation project.[123] Regarding social services, the NLNG perfoms such services as the use of its boats to convey memebers of the public, especially citizens of Bonny kingdom, in the course of its operational activities between Bonny Island and Port Harcourt. Beside the foregoing, there are sundry social investments which are being accomplished by the NLNG in its host communities.

9.9 SUNDRY SOCIAL INVESTMENTS REGARDING HEALTH, EDUCATION AND ECONOMIC EMPOWERMENT

Under sundry social investments are the healthcare and educational programmes and services as well as socio-economic empowerment schemes being embarked upon by NLNG in its host Bonny kingdom and its pipeline communities outside the kingdom.

9.9(I) HEALTH CARE SERVICES

As already indicated above, the impact-benefit CD initiatives outlined by NLNG under health are the HIV/AIDS programme, the Roll Back Malaria Campaign, immunisation, and the provision of medical equipment.

Under the NLNG HIV/AIDS programme, the NLNG acknowledges that its ongoing construction phase resulted in the influx of migrant commercial sex workers from within and outside Nigeria, and among them are some without families. The presence of these migrant commercial sex workers generated several socio-cultural and other problems, such as HIV-AIDS infection in Bonny. For instance, a survey of the Rivers state Ministry of Health recorded an alarming increase of HIV-AIDS-infected expectant mothers, the ratio of which moved from 1.2 per cent in 1996 when the NLNG construction phase started, to 8.3 per cent in 2002. Thus, NLNG introduced several programmes to check the spread of the HIV-AIDS virus in Bonny Island. These programmes are the baseline study of knowledge, attitude and practice; training of health peer educators who serve promulgators of social knowledge; and the campaign targeted at different citizens' and resident groups in Bonny. Among these are the Youth against Aids Club (YAAC) groups formed in secondary schools, and the direct support given to people with the HIV-AIDS virus. Also, NLNG sponsored registration, under Part C of the Companies and Allied Matters Act (CAMA), 1990, of a Community-based Organisation (CBO) known as the 'Ibanise [Bonny Kingdom] HIV-AIDS Initiative' to focus on the prevention and treatment of HIV-AIDS in Bonny kingdom.[124] The JIC led by NLNG undertook to fund the first year of operation of this initiative whose objectives are to:

123 Ibid, p. 53.
124 Ibid, p. 47.

> *Reduce the transmission of HIV/AIDS among sectors of the population in Bonny kingdom; ensure close linkage and partnership with [the] national HIV-AIDS policy through collaboration with the National Action Committee on AIDS (NACA), State Action Committee on AIDS (SACA), and [the] Local Government Action Committee on AIDS (LACA); and develop a model of community-based public-private partnership on HIV-AIDS that can be adapted to other settings.*[125]

This Initiative has a Board of Trustees, a Technical Advisory Board and a Community Interface Committee, to help to realise its objectives.[126]

NLNG embarked upon its Roll Back Malaria Campaign to support the FG and the Rivers state Government in this regard. It launched its campaign in the Bonny and Emohua LGAs, during which it educated over 3,000 participants from its host communities on the need for improved sanitation and other preventive measures aimed at reducing the rate of malaria attacks in the communities. NLNG distributed mosquito and insecticide-treated bed nets and anti-malarial drugs to the participants.[127]

NLNG has also been supportive of the national immunisation programme in Rivers state through the provision of personnel and drugs for the immunisation of over 39,000 children against preventable childhood diseases.[128]

Regarding medical equipment, NLNG provided mattresses and bed linen to improve healthcare delivery services in the Bonny General Hospital[129] It also donated an Electrocardiogram (ECG) machine to the hospital for diagnosing and treating heart-related diseases.[130]

9.9(II) EDUCATIONAL PROGRAMMES AND SERVICES

Scholarships are awarded annually by NLNG to students of its host communities, as well as to other Nigerian students, in post-primary and tertiary institutions. Over 2,400 students from NLNG's host communities have benefited

---

125 *See* NLNG outlined the goals, status, structure and activities of the Ibanise HIV-AIDS partnership. The responsibility of the partnership included to design programmes earmarked to focus 'on such issues as information about the epidemic, combating false information and ignorance, overcoming denial, stigma and silence about the epidemic, providing access to voluntary counselling and testing for HIV, providing access to free anti-retroviral therapy to those who are HIV-positive'.

126 *See* the certificate of incorporation of this initiative signed by the Registrar General of the CAC, A. Almustapha, with reference no. CAC/IT/NO23234, is dated March 9, 2007. Along with Dr. Donald de Korte, chair of its Board of Trustees, the Initiative has the following other trustees, viz: Dr. Furo Ibiama, Dr. Brian Buckley, Professor Babantunde Osotimehin, Dr. Chimezie Murphy Okeh, Dr. (Mrs.) Ibimina Victor Akan, Dr. Dimulak Mwanmut, Chief (Dr.) Marcus Green, Dr. T. A. T. Allison, and Mrs. Nne Furo Kurubo.

127 *See* 'NLNG 2007: Facts and Figures on NLNG', p. 47. *Also see* the publication entitled 'Pro Natura in Bonny: Malaria Awareness Training /Social Baseline Assessment project', found in the area Pro Natura International (Nigeria) homepage at http://www.pronatura-nigeria.org/bonny.html visited on 29/11/08.

128 *See* 'NLNG 2007: Facts and Figures on NLNG', p. 47.

129 Ibid, p. 48.

130 *See* 'Facts and Figures on NLNG 2008', p. 78.

from this scholarship scheme. In 1977, NLNG launched the Bonny Educational Endowment Fund (BEEF), by which the salaries of teachers in the kingdom are slightly increased, to cushion the effects of inflation being experienced as a result of its operations in Bonny kingdom.[131] BEEF was expanded to support schools and their pupils through the supply and provision of such needs as books, school desks, science equipment and the building and rehabilitation of school blocks. Also, under education, the NLNG's Bonny Vocational Centre (BVC) is designed to promote vocational/entrepreneurial skills acquisition, development of technical competences and self-reliance in the young people of Bonny and their counterparts from other areas of Rivers state.[132]

9.9(III) ECONOMIC EMPOWERMENT

NLNG has Economic Empowerment impact-benefit CD initiatives designed in the interest of the citizens of its host communities. As stated above, these include the micro-credit scheme, Youth Empowerment Scheme (YES), the Nigeria LNG Agro Development Action (N-AGENDA), Business Development/ Advisory Support Services, Right of Way (ROW) Maintenance Contracts to landlord families, and the Nigerian NLNG Local Content Plan discussed in Chapter 6.

9.9(iii)(a) Micro-credit Scheme

This scheme and other NLNG social investment schemes for its host communities were announced by its Managing Director, during the NLNG commissioning ceremony on September 21, 2000. The speech, entitled 'Partnership for Success', provides that:

> *To mark Nigeria LNG's commissioning, he said, 'I am pleased to announce that we will expand our education programme by making a sum of fifty million naira (N50,000,000) available for improvements and upgrading of primary schools in the communities, distributing sixty thousand commemorative notebooks to all secondary schools in Bonny and along the GTS communities and doubling our university scholarship programme from 250 to 500. He also announced the provision of five hundred million naira (500,000,000) over a period of ten years to set up the Nigeria LNG Micro Credit Scheme to promote business development in Bonny and the GTS communities.*[133]

---

131 Teachers are thus encouraged by NLNG to concentrate on teaching rather than seeking oil and gas development construction employments in order to earn higher salaries.

132 Training at the NLNG Bonny Vocational Training Centre (BVC) started on March 10, 2005, with 20 students. The BVC's curriculum is designed to meet the aspirations of Bonny kingdom towards producing graduates with the award of International Vocational Level 3 Certificate of the London City and Guilds and/or the Nigerian Skills Technical Certificate. *See* the website of the City and Guilds Institute (which provides vocational training in the UK), found at http://www.city-and-guilds.co.uk/cps/rde/xchg/cgonline visited on 31/12/06. *Also see* 'NLNG 2007: Facts and Figures on NLNG', p. 49.

133 *See* the area of the NLNG homepage entitled 'News & Media: Past Events', with the sub-title 'Plant Commissioning Ceremony: President Obasanjo Commissions Plant', found at http://www.nlng.com/NLNGnew/news/pastevents/Plant+Commissioning+Ceremony.htm visited on 31/12/06.

Consequently, while describing the aims and objectives, advantages, management process, and concluded first phase of the micro-credit scheme, NLNG states that:

> *The micro-credit scheme is aimed at assisting those in the NLNG's host communities, who cannot raise funds to start business. It is meant to provide start-up credit facilities for this category whose propensity to save is low.*
>
> *This scheme has a distinct advantage of creating jobs in the informed sector with its multiple effects. It also promotes banking habits, since it focuses on mobilising savings and linking it to credit. The scheme also produces strong credible and accountable leaderships at the village level, as members are chosen on trust, based on known history and proven integrity.*
>
> *To manage this programme, the NLNG contracted the Community Development Foundation (CDF) and a bank to operate the scheme. CDF is a mentoring organisation with objective of formalizing the traditional village-level banking culture in a manner that is transparent, accountable and verifiable. The bank warehouses, disburses and manages the funds.*
>
> *In the just concluded first phase of the Micro Credit Scheme, over N110 million was disbursed to 248 groups, out of which N67 million representing 78% of due loans have been recovered. In the second phase, it is planned to scale up the level of financial and non financial support through partnership with and linkage of the participants to other micro finance service providers.*[134]

9.9(iii)(b) Youth Empowerment Scheme (YES)

This scheme was launched in October 2004 by NLNG to encourage unemployed youngsters between the ages of 18 and 25 years of its host communities to acquire self-employment skills through specific technical training and the promotion of small-scale businesses. Successful applicants are attached to accredited centres for training in such specified areas as basic computer training, application and maintenance; photography and video production; catering; hairdressing and cosmetics; fashion design and sewing; welding and fabrication; horticulture and landscaping; and woodwork and carpentry. Successful youngsters are given monthly allowances for transportation and other sundry needs during training. While describing the structure and starter packs given to graduates of the scheme, NLNG states:

> *The scheme is structured in three phases. The first phase is the acquisition of vocational training skills. In the second phase, the youths undergo leadership and citizenship training for attitude re-orientation and the inculcation of entrepreneurial skills. This takes place at the Leadership Training Centre [LTC] Aluu, Port Harcourt. The final stage is the graduation where*

134 *See* 'NLNG 2007: Facts and Figures on NLNG', pp. 49-50.

> *the youths are provided with Starter Packs. The Starter packs are tools in different trade areas and a small start-off capital to help the graduates start their businesses. For instance, those in computing go home with a complete computer system comprising a monitor, CPU, printer and UPS. Those in welding receive 200 amps voltage welding machines. About 78 of the 108 youths undergoing training under the scheme graduated in November 2005.*[135]

To complement YES, the NLNG has embarked upon skills acquisition and capacity-building follow-up schemes for indigenous businesses through training, seminars and micro-credit administration, to create employers and thereby enable them to transfer the skills which they have acquired through the scheme to others in the host communities.[136]

9.9(iii)(c) Agro Development Action (N-AGENDA)

The N-AGENDA is an empowerment tool designed to help rural dwellers by exposing them to best practices of agricultural production. This scheme is designed to promote market linkage, product diversification, encourage value adding services and initiate the required change and modernisation of traditional agriculture. About 100 participants were trained and supported in aqua culture through the African Regional Aqua Centre, (ARAC), Aluu, Rivers state, and crop farming through the International Institute of Tropical Agriculture (IITA) during the first phase of the scheme, while the second was designed to train another 1,000 agro-based business entrepreneurs in business development and management processes. The scheme was to enable NLNG to partner with excelling farmers yearly, so as to set up five model agro-based businesses as diffusion centres.[137]

9.9(iii)(d) Business Development/Advisory Services

This scheme was designed by NLNG to provide accessible, high quality and complementary business development and management support services to entrepreneurs in its host communities. It was designed to serve as a warehouse of information on business opportunities and emerging markets and to support entrepreneurs with new business ideas, including how to manage their products and embark on feasibility studies and business cash-flow analysis. NLNG's objective was to support forty entrepreneurs from two of its host kingdoms during the first phase of the scheme.[138]

135 Ibid, p. 50–51.
136 Ibid, p. 51.
137 Ibid, pp. 50–51.
138 Ibid, p. 51.

9.9(iii)(e) EPC and Right-of-Way Contracts based on the NLNG Local Content Plan

The NLNG Local Content Plan (LCP) is designed to fulfil the objectives of the Nigerian Content Policy (NCP) so as to generate the impact-benefits of its operations in favour of its host communities and their citizens, before considering other Nigerian indigenous businesses or entrepreneurs in the award of contracts. NLNG describes this impact-benefit CR strategy in the award of its Engineering, Procurement and Construction (EPC) contracts in the following words:

> *The rapid expansion of NLNG's business has brought about a change in its community relations strategy. NLNG has put in place a contract policy that ensures that contractors from the host communities take the first shot at contracts before the search widens to Rivers state, Nigeria and the world. This is adequately captured in the Nigerian Content Plan.*
>
> *Each of the EPC contracts for the new trains has a Community Relations component – a direct benefit from the train. The attendant community projects, . . . are carried out alongside the construction of the train.*[139]

Thus, technical evaluations of NLNG's CD interventions have their respective CR plans directed by designated CR officers. NLNG's principle of impact-benefit operates in the interest of its pipeline (GTS) right-of-way (ROW) landlord-families within Bonny kingdom and elsewhere by awarding them ROW maintenance contracts. As NLNG puts it:

> *NLNG has adopted an approach in its pipeline communities which recognises the African attachment to land and the obvious fact that no legislation, no matter how well intended, captures all the expectations of the people.*
>
> *To meet the communities' expectations, NLNG, after paying compensation for Right of Way, trees and crops, went the extra mile to ensure that feelings of dispossession and deprivation are assuaged.*
>
> *Holders of GTS Right of Way (ROW) Maintenance Contracts, which rotate among the land owning families, employ members to execute the jobs which cover: Pipeline Right of Way surveillance and inspection, Asset maintenance: painting of signposts and markers, grass cutting, etc.*[140]

9.10 REMARKS ON NLNG'S SOCIAL INVESTMENTS/IMPACT-BENEFITS

NLNG's social investment initiatives in the interest of its host communities and their citizens are either designed as EIA mitigation measures or the generic

---

139 Ibid, p. 52.

140 Ibid, pp. 46–47. The NLNG ROW contractors, while considering their contracts as good CR gestures, would like NLNG to increase the value of their contracts so as to realise its economic empowerment objectives in their interests.

impact-benefits accruing from its construction and operational processes. Indeed, as the Brent Spar incident which took place in 1995, in the North Sea, Europe, and the Ogoni crisis of the same year which led to the judicial execution of Ken Saro-Wiwa and his eight Ogoni kinsmen in Nigeria, constituted a wake-up call for Shell Nigeria, so is the Bonny kingdom versus the NLNG crisis of September 1999 a wake-up call for NLNG. As demonstrated in Chapter 7, these wake-up calls triggered Shell Nigeria and NLNG to become more alive to the concerns and agitation of their host communities by prompting them to embark on improved social responsibility measures in the communities.

So far, considering the social investments implemented by NLNG, Shell Nigeria and MPN in the kingdom, MPN may be described as a far less socially responsible corporate citizen of Bonny kingdom, while NLNG is relatively more socially responsible than Shell Nigeria. The relatively improved social and environmental performances of NLNG in Bonny is thus gradually influencing other MNOCs such as Shell Nigeria and MPN as well as other minor MNOCs operating in Bonny kingdom to improve their social responsibility performances in the kingdom. Hence, the lesser socially responsible operational strategy of MPN resulted in the attack launched on its operational site (the BRT) at Finima, Bonny Island, by Finima youths in June 2001.[141]

Regardless of the fact that NLNG is striving to increasingly improve its social and environmental performances in Bonny kingdom and its other host communities, an assessment of its social investment reports exemplified by the case of Bonny kingdom, somewhat portray these reports as self-congratulatory tools. For instance, NLNG states that by virtue of its host communities' benefits from social investments, it 'believes it has made the concept of good neighborliness come alive in its host communities in a manner that reflects its principle of stakeholding, partnership and sustainability'.[142] While the concept of good neighbourliness has thus come alive, NLNG's partnership and sustainability initiatives in its host communities require more pragmatic efforts on its part. A broader assessment of the NLNG reporting pattern tends to prove that other MNOCs operating in Nigeria have learnt from Shell Nigeria how to spend fortunes on the publication and advertisement of exaggerated social responsibility achievements in their host communities. The Executive Director of Friends of the Earth (FoE), Tony Juniper, while acknowledging how MNOCs are striving to improve on their social and environmental performances in their host communities, comments on this exaggerated reporting pattern. Juniper states that what matters to communities playing host to

---

141 Although this attack took place due to the demand made by the youths of Finima community for compensation for the operational site acquired by MPN in their community, the general issue which gave rise to the attack was the refusal or reluctance of MPN to respond favourably to the plight and concerns of the entire people of Bonny kingdom concerning its near closed-door operational strategy in the kingdom.

142 *See* 'Facts and Figures on NLNG 2008', p. 82.

extractive industrial operations is not what companies say in their glossy brochures, but the real change in the attitude and approaches of the companies that citizens of the communities can see and feel. In Juniper's words:

> *Friends of the Earth welcome genuine attempts by companies to improve their social and environmental performance.*
>
> *We congratulated Shell eight years ago for committing itself to sustainable development, and five years ago for finally pulling out of the Global Climate Coalition lobby group. Three years ago, we even stood up at the Shell Annual General Meeting [AGM] and recognised that the company had done some good thinking on sustainable development.*
>
> *But, the shocking reality is that for many communities living near to Shell refineries and depots little has changed over the past eight years. People in Durban in South Africa and Manila in Philippines and Louisiana in the US are still breathing polluted air, feeling the pain of skin diseases and worrying about accidents. In Nigeria and Argentina, communities are still waiting for real changes that they can see and feel. And in Texas and in China, people are fed up because they think that, despite nominal community work, Shell lacks commitment to the people whose health and/or livelihoods are threatened by refineries and pipelines.*
>
> *The communities affected by Shell's operations demand that the company addresses the problems directly. Where requested, Shell must send its most skilled and experienced international officials to meet with representatives from the communities of people who live nearest to Shell's facilities.*
>
> *What matters to these communities is not what the company says in glossy brochures. When people have asthma because they live next to a refinery or their rivers are polluted, promises don't mean much. Similarly, it is difficult to see how Shell's welcome recognition of the global threat posed by climate change squares with its policy to continue expanding oil and gas exploration and production.*
>
> *Friends of the Earth supports these communities' demands and also calls for a change in UK company law so that the right to trade is integrated with appropriate duties and responsibilities to ensure that communities can hold corporations fully accountable for their impacts on people and the planet.*
>
> *Then, we will see a real change in how Shell – and the rest of UK plc[s] – [do] business.*[143]

---

143 *See* the FoE report entitled 'Failing the Challenge: The Other Shell Report 2002', found at http://www.foei.org/publications/pdfs/shellfailingthechallenge.pdf visited on 23/12/04. *See* J. A. Zerk, *Multinationals and Corporate Social Responsibility: Limitations and Opportunities in International Law*, Cambridge, Cambridge University Press, 2006, p. 297. By and large, NLNG needs to improve on its operational performances by constantly addressing the criticisms against MNCs by civil society activists and activist groups and other forms of public opinions anchored on the adverse effects of extractive industrial operations in local communities of developing countries. *See* the publication of the World Rainforest Movement entitled 'Nigeria: Gas Corporation

Considering the self-praising (*ie*, the 'Agama Lizard' type)[144] orientation of Shell Nigeria and other MNOCs operating in Nigeria, the need arises for the NLNG to improve on its pattern of reporting its social investments by following the ethics of corporate sustainability reporting.[145] To do so properly in the context of the UN's ongoing effort towards achieving SD, NLNG needs to take such steps as becoming a member and participant of the UN Global Compact, as Shell Nigeria has already done (as indicated in Chapters 7 and 8, albeit with gradual improvements regarding its social and environmental performances).[146] Accordingly, as Shell Nigeria has already done, NLNG needs to be interested in the activities of such international organisations as the International Association for Impact Assessment (IAIA), to improve upon its IA and SD initiatives and practices. NLNG's membership of and interest in the IAIA is crucial, considering (as indicated in Chapter 3) that the IAIA is a leading global authority on IA for informed decision-making regarding policies, programmes, plans and projects.[147] The NLNG's interest in the IAIA and such other leading institutions as the New Partnership for Africa's Development (NEPAD) and UNEP discussed in Chapter 5 is important, considering that the 'oil and gas sector is a global leader in the application of impact assessment'.[148] Accordingly, to improve its strategies on PP and in effect CI, NLNG needs to develop interest in the International Association for Public Participation (IAP2), discussed in Chapter 3.[149]

NLNG Destroys Mangrove Forest in the Niger Delta', found at http://www.wrm.org.uy/buletin/68/nigeria.html visited on 25/10/05. *Also see* the publication by D. Wittenberg, entitled 'In Bonny It Never Becomes Night Anymore', found at http://www.eca-watch.org/documents/BonnyIsland130704.html visited on 29/11/04.

144 *See* the article of J. Osai entitled 'Shell as Agama Lizard' found at http://www.waado.org/Environment/OilCompanies/Shell-Communities/ShellsFalsePR.html visited on 22/03/04.

145 Regarding corporate sustainability reporting, *see* the Global Reporting Initiative (GRI) homepage, found at http://www.globalreporting.org/AboutGRI/ visited on 31/12/06.

146 *See* D. A. Rondinelli and M. A. Berry, 'Environmental Citizenship in Multinational Corporations: Social Responsibility and Sustainable Development', *European Management Journal*, Vol. 18, No. 1, 2000, pp. 70–84.

147 *See* the area of the IAIA homepage captioned 'About the IAIA' (which specifies the Association's vision, mission and values), found at http://www.iaia.org/modx/index.php?id=318 visited on 31/12/06.

148 *See* the 'Final Programme' of the 24th Annual Conference of the IAIA (held from April 24-30, at Vancouver, Canada), tagged 'Whose Business is it? Impact Assessment for Industrial Development', Fargo, International IAIA, p. 3. The NLNG's interest in the activities of the IAIA, is capable of enabling it to improve and consolidate upon its Local Content Plan anchored on the principle of impact-benefit towards greater public good in its host communities. *See* 'NLNG 2007: Facts and Figures on NLNG', p. 52. *Also see* the report and various papers delivered in the course of a series of five workshops held at the Oxford Policy Institute (OPI), London, captioned 'Adding Public Value: The Limits of Corporate Responsibility', from March to June, 2006, found at http://www.opi.org.uk/seminars.shtml visited on 31/12/2006. *See* the report of these workshops (prepared by P. Crowson), entitled 'Adding Public Value: The Limits of Corporate Responsibility' dated April 2007.

149 *Also see* the Calabash project (of the Southern African Development Community [SADC]) on PP in EA discussed in Chapter 3.

Considering the enormous adverse effects of petroleum development operations in the oil-rich Delta region, the IA process of petroleum development projects is required to conserve and protect the ecosystem of the region. IA is required to rehabilitate the traditional fishing, fish-farming and agricultural occupations of the people of the region and other oil-producing areas, while designing new sources of livelihood for the people.[150] Thus, to abide by widely, internationally-recognised and accepted industry standards and practices, NLNG and other MNOCs operating in the oil-producing areas of Nigeria need to comply with the findings of various sectoral efforts and other related initiatives[151] designed to improve the operations of the global oil and gas and mining industrial sector. Such a measure of compliance is capable of enhancing the efforts of the MNOCs to contribute to SCD, by appropriately integrating social concerns regarding their operations into their decision-making processes.[152]

9.11 CONCLUSION

This chapter appraises the social investments of NLNG in its primary host Bonny kingdom, especially in the Finima and Grand Bonny Island communities of the kingdom. It attempts to demonstrate how these investments are associated with the IA process of the various NLNG construction trains and entire operations of NLNG in its host communities. The chapter highlights the economic empowerment strategy of NLNG, among its other impact-mitigation and impact-benefit measures in the communities. This strategy emphasises the impact-benefit orientation of the NLNG Local Content Plan and the Shell Nigeria Local Content Policy from which this Plan was designed.

Regarding discussion on the agreement made between Bonny kingdom and NLNG, following the kingdom versus the NLNG crisis of September 20–22, 1999, it is obvious that while participating to protect the environment and their future, and to benefit from the operations of MNOCs, citizens of the

150 Regarding the vitalisation of such sea foods as shrimps, *see* the 'Subsector Assessment of the Nigerian Shrimp and Prawn Industry', prepared by Chemonics International Incorporated, for the United States Agency for International Development (USAID/Nigeria, dated November 2002, found at http://www.usaid.gov/ng/downloads/markets/shrimpandprawnssubsectorassessment.pdf visited on 24/04/06. Accordingly, regarding aquaculture and other SD strategies associated with fisheries, *see* the South Australia's Fisheries Research Advisory Board (FRAB) homepage, found at http://www.fishresearch.sa.gov.au/home visited on 26/09/08.

151 These include the efforts and/or initiatives of the MMSD project and the WBG Extractive Industries Review (EIR) process discussed in Chapter 3. *Also see* Principle 27 of the Johannesburg Declaration on SD. With regard to SCD in the Niger Delta, see the publication entitled 'The Institute of Sustainable Development', in the area of the Pro-Natura International (Nigeria) homepage, found at http://www.pronatura-nigeria.org/isd.htm visited on 29/11/08.

152 *See* K. McPhail and A. Davy, *Integrating Social Concerns into Private Sector Decision making: A Review of Corporate Practices in the Mining, Oil, and Gas Sectors*, Washington DC., The World Bank, 1998. *Also see* R. Goodland, *Sustainable Development Sourcebook for the World Bank Group's Extractive Industries Review: Examining the Social and Environmental Impacts of Oil, Gas and Mining, op cit.*

oil-producing communities have, in turn, a responsibility towards these companies. This responsibility lies mainly in the provision of an enabling environment, by ensuring industrial peace and harmony which represent the grant of social licence to enhance the operations of the MNOCs in the communities. Other responsibilities which citizens of the oil-producing communities include administering their communities in conformity with the principles and practices of SD, so as to enhance the achievement of SCD. One of these principles is that of public or citizens' participation. Participation involves transparency and accountability in decision-making. As indicated in Chapter 4, transparency and accountability are, for instance, required in the management of compensation, CD trust funds and other benefits accruing to the communities in the course of MNOCs' operations, so as to achieve greater or overall public good in the communities.

As identified in this chapter, where the social responsibility measures of NLNG are weakest in Bonny are in its effort towards addressing the legacy issues of its defective Finima community relocation exercise, considering the complaints of the people of the community being spearheaded by the community's founding family – the Buoye-Omuso Brown major house. Other weak social responsibility measures include NLNG's reluctance to address genuine complaints being made by some ordinary citizens and other directly affected, concerned or interested citizens' and vulnerable minority groups such as the Bristol-Alagbarigha royal house, regarding their exclusion and marginalisation in the course of NLNG's ongoing CCs in Grand Bonny Island community founded by the house.

The inability or unwillingness of the MNOCs to address genuine concerns of individuals and groups, who have become vulnerable and marginalised as a result of their operations, demonstrate non-compliance with their social responsibility commitments and widely recognised and accepted environmental and social performance standards governing extractive industrial operations worldwide. Conversely, among several other IA commendable efforts of NLNG is its nature conservation initiative establishing the Finima Nature Park (FNP). Given the suggestions already made in this chapter, NLNG and other MNOCs operating in Bonny kingdom and other areas of the Delta region need to enhance and preserve biodiversity in the region. This is essential to safeguard the endangered fisheries and other aquatic and terrestrial lives in the Delta region by evolving such SD-oriented measures as aquaculture, so as to enhance sustainable livelihoods and ecosystem preservation in the region.

The IA process and social investments of NLNG and Shell Nigeria discussed in Chapter 8 and this chapter demonstrate that PI (which includes CI) is a significant pillar of EA and IA in general. Accordingly, these two chapters confirm the conclusion reached in Chapter 5, that EA or IA is a significant pillar of SD. The IA process is a means towards enhancing or achieving SD of petroleum resources as well as SCD in Nigeria, including the promotion of PI, especially CI, in decision-making processes. IA thus needs to be encouraged and enhanced by improved CSR, so as to promote CI and strategic stakeholder partnerships with the JV partners of the petroleum resources development business in Nigeria, towards SD of these resources as well as SCD in the Delta region and other oil-producing areas of the country. On this basis, IA requires to be sustained and strengthened by strategic, stable and transparent government regulatory measures, in compliance with the provisions of the NEPAD 'Action Plan for the Environment Initiative' discussed in Chapter 5, and Article 29 of the Johannesburg Declaration on SD, 2002, in order to enhance Nigeria's realisation of the UN Millennium Declaration and the Millennium Development Goals (MDGs) discussed in Chapters 1 and 2. Besides, as LNG development yields high revenues, the multi-billion USD NLNG project has earned over N187 billion for Nigeria in eight years. Also, as LNG development operations are prone to disaster, LNG plants worldwide are time bombs. NLNG, therefore, needs to take its emergency response plan seriously in the interests of its primary host Finima and Bonny Island communities, including its GTS communities within and outside Bonny kingdom.

In a way, Chapters 4, 8 and this chapter demonstrate that the CIs designed by the MNOCs in the course of their development projects in Bonny kingdom make it essential for CBOs to be alive to the plight of local communities endowed with major natural resources in developing countries. As vehicles of grass-root social engineering, the existence of such CBOs may distinguish communities equipped with the potential to internalise laudable initiatives of the MNOCs, governments and other development partners, from other communities that are not so equipped, in the efforts to achieve SCD in the oil-producing areas of Nigeria.

PART F

Conclusions

CHAPTER 10

Key Issues, Findings and Recommendations

10.1 KEY ISSUES

One key issue of this book is how community participation, considered as 'community involvement' (CI), is discussed as an aspect of public involvement (PI, *ie*, citizens' or public participation (PP) in environmental decision-making, so as to examine the role of corporate responsibility and impact assessment (IA) regarding petroleum development in Nigeria, in order to enhance sustainable community development (SCD) in the oil-rich ethnic minority Delta region.

Citizens of the Delta region, the main producers of petroleum resources in Nigeria, have for over five decades of the resources development operations in their communities been concerned about the adverse effects on the environment in the region, their welfare and the well-being of their future generations. One of their major concerns is the right to properly (*ie*, interactively) participate in Nigeria's affairs, especially those that concern them directly, in a fair, just and equitable manner. They are aggrieved that the existing measures of CI in petroleum development are incapable of generating SCD in the region.

Based on continuing effort by the United Nations (UN) on the environment and development designed to achieve SD, which effort led to the Stockholm, Rio de Janeiro and Johannesburg (SRJ) Conferences, PP in environmental decision-making is increasingly becoming a fundamental aspect of policy, law and state practice in global nations. Due to the ongoing worldwide 'participation explosion' (*ie*, the globally recognised need for PP, especially the need for PP in energy and major natural resources [oil and gas, and mineral resources] development projects), participation is increasingly becoming an accepted cost of doing business, towards environmentally-sound and socially-equitable SD in resources-rich developing countries.

As a result of the adverse effects of petroleum development in the hitherto calm and peaceful communities of the Delta region, citizens of the region started in the 1990s to agitate against these effects on the environment, themselves and their future generations. Protracted community agitation, protests, conflicts, resistance movements, and so on, otherwise referred to as 'crises' in the Delta region, reveal that the neglect, marginalisation and oppressive measures being occasioned on the people of the region in the Federal Republic of Nigeria (FRN) are associated with the fact that they are minorities who are not empowered to influence or direct decision-making processes in the federation. Consequently, bills of right, charters, accords, resolutions and other related demands, declarations and pronouncements are being made by various ethnic groups and communities of the Delta region. These pronouncements, which began with the Ogoni Bill of Rights of 1990, include the Kaiama Declaration of 1998, the Resolution of the First Urhobo Economic Summit, the Warri Accord, the Aklaka Declaration of the Egi People, Oron Bill of Rights, the Demand of the First Niger Delta Indigenous Women's Conference for Women of Bayelsa state, the Declaration of the Ikwerre Rescue Charter, and the Declaration of the Niger Delta Bill of Rights. These pronouncements do not only express the environmental, socioeconomic and political concerns of the people of the Delta region regarding adverse effects of petroleum development; they also represent the views and aspirations of the people on how the FRN ought to be properly governed, especially regarding petroleum development in the region. Thus, whilst focusing on the true Delta region, this book identifies it as the South-South ethnic minority region of the FRN and thereby distinguished it from the artificial Delta region created by the Niger-Delta Development Commission (NDDC) Act, 2004 (formerly Cap. 6 Laws of the Federation of Nigeria [LFN] 2000).

The history of resistance movements in the Delta region dates back to the period of British imperial incursion in pre-colonial Nigeria. The British colonial era marked the beginning of the marginalisation and neglect of the people of the region in decision-making processes, contrary to those prevailing in the people's traditional social systems identified in Chapter 4. The degree of neglect and marginalisation suffered by the people gave rise to resistance movements against the British colonial government and thus the reaction of the government against such monarchs of the Niger Delta as Dappa Pepple of Bonny in 1854, Jaja of Opobo in 1887, Nana Olomu of Itsekiri in 1894, Koko of Nembe (Brass) in 1895, and Overanwen of Benin in 1897. Other resistance movements of the Delta minorities at that time included such mass protests as the women's riot at Igwenga (popularly called the Aba women's riot) of 1929, and the Akassa Raid of 1895 spearheaded by King Koko. During the Nigerian regional era, from 1939 to 1967, when the will of the three major ethnic groups reigned supreme, resistance movements of the Delta ethnic minorities against the right to be heard in the Eastern region led to the formation of the Cross-River-Ogoja (COR) state movement led by the Hon. Justice Udo Udoma, and the movement for the creation of Rivers state led by the Rivers Chiefs and Peoples' Conference (RCPC). There were also the eastern regional ethnic minority political party known as the Niger Delta Congress (NDC) established by Chief H. J. R. Dappa-Biriye, and the Isaac Adaka Boro's 12-Day Niger Delta revolution of 1966. Thereafter, in the 1990s, dominant resistance movements against the adverse effects of petroleum development in the Delta region included the Movement for the Survival of the Ogoni People (MOSOP). Ongoing umbrella resistance tagged the 'resource-control movement' – a name coined from the deliberations and networks of Southern Nigeria Governors – has become the order of the day in the region. This umbrella movement, for improved PP or CI in the decision-making process of petroleum development in the Delta region is being championed by militant youth groups such as the Movement for the Emancipation of the Niger Delta (MEND) and the Niger Delta Volunteer Force (NDVF). Although the resource-control groups do not have a common set of pronouncements, key among their demands is the enthronement of true fiscal federalism, enhanced by stable, transparent and accountable democratic governance, based on equity, social justice and fair play, between and among the diverse ethnic groups and citizens. The resource- control movement is, in effect, based on the fact that various constitutional and political development dialogues (from the 1953/54 Nigeria Independence Constitutional Conferences [NICCs] to date) have not sufficiently addressed the plight and predicaments of the Delta ethnic minorities; thus revealing the failure of such duly constituted dialogues in the country. Hence, as expressed in Chapter 2, there are calls by several citizens and citizen groups for a Sovereign National Conference (SNC), in order to decide Nigeria's future.

As Africa's largest oil-producing and the world's eighth largest oil-exporting country, Nigeria's economic back-bone is petroleum resources development, which accounts for 95 per cent of its export earnings and 80 per cent of its revenue. Considering the contributions of these resources to the Nigerian and global economy and as a source of huge profits to the multinational oil companies (MNOCs) operating in the country, the significance and consequences of the crises in the oil-rich Delta region cannot be over-emphasised. These crises constitute a great source of concern in Nigeria and the international community. It is obvious that Nigeria's future is inextricably linked to what her governing authorities do or do not do to resolve these crises. Thus, despite the military intervention posture of the Federal Government (FG) in the crisis-riven region, incumbent President Umaru Musa Yar'Adua created the Ministry of Niger Delta in September 2008. This Ministry is to coordinate government environmental, infrastructural development and youth policy initiatives, to enhance the development of the Delta region. It is the second ministry to concentrate on a particular area of the federation, following the Ministry of the Federal Capital Territory (FCT) created to address the developmental needs of the federal capital. Before the creation of the Ministry of the Niger Delta, the predecessor of Yar'Adua, President Olusegun Obasanjo, pronounced in April 2006 that successive FGs of Nigeria had failed the Delta region. As expressed in Chapter 2, President Obasanjo lamented the age-long neglect of the region, while admitting that the efforts of the FG towards solving the region's development problems and challenges are yet to make any appreciable impact on the lives of citizens of the region. President Obasanjo, who considered the crises in the region as a national challenge, established the Council for the Socio-economic Development of the Coastal States of the Niger Delta (SEDCOSND). The opinion of the author is that President Obasanjo had to set up this council, having realised that the NDDC, established in the interest of the entire oil-producing states (some of which do not belong to the true Delta region), is a misrepresentation. The setting up of the SEDCOSND justifies the focus of this book on the ethnic minority composition of the Delta region. As expressed in Chapter 2 and especially under the sub-heading of Chapter 1 entitled 'The Niger Delta Region', this book indicates that two out of the nine NDDC states (*ie*, Abia and Imo states) do not truly belong to the Delta region. There is thus a need for Nigeria to distinguish its other oil-producing areas from its true and main oil-producing Delta region, to properly address the problems and challenges confronting the region, its citizens and communities.

It is considered in this book that the FG's establishment of one intervention institution after another (*ie*, from the setting-up of the Niger Delta Development Board, NDDB, in 1961, the Oil Mineral Producing Areas Development Commission, OMPADEC, in 1992, the NDDC in 2000, and the SEDCOSND in 2006) has not solved the problems of the Delta region. These intervention institutions have not fully fulfilled the recommendations expressed in the Sir Henry Willink Commission report of 1958. As demonstrated in Chapter 3, the Willink Commission was set up by British colonial government at the end of the 1957 NICCs held at Lancaster House, London, to enquire into the fears of the ethnic minorities of Nigeria and the means to allay these fears towards the grant of political independence in the country. The Commission found that the Delta region was 'poor, backward and neglected'. This state of the Delta region has become more deplorable in the course of more than five decades of petroleum development, as the region is poorer, more neglected, underdeveloped, and crises-riven. The seriousness of the ongoing crises reveals that its state and the plight of its people are now worse than those that obtained during the period of the Willink Commission, due to the same historical problem; that is, the marginalisation of the interests of the region and its people by the major tribes whose elites control political power and authority, and in effect decision-making processes in the federation. The new Ministry of Niger Delta therefore has a Herculean task if it is to make a difference from previous FG's intervention measures and not merely to thrive as a bureaucratic structure.

Due to the concerns of many in Nigeria, the efforts of the FG along with those of the state and local governments exercising jurisdiction over the Delta region are being assessed by civil society, especially non-governmental organisations (NGOs). As expressed in Chapter 8, 92 per cent of Nigerians who expressed their opinion in a poll conducted by NOI Polls (a Nigerian-based not-for-profit organisation partnering with Gallup Poll of the USA) stated that various levels of government exercising jurisdiction over the Delta region are not doing enough for the region and its citizens. As expressed in Chapter 1 and reinforced in Chapter 2, the problems of the region are mainly lack of political will and sustained commitment of successive FGs. These are, for instance, evidenced by the divide and rule strategies and marginalisation of the region and other minority areas by the ethnic majority political rulers presiding over the affairs of the federation at the federal level of governance. Thus, considering how the Niger Delta crises are associated with governance, natural resources development and conflicts in Nigeria and other major natural resources-rich developing countries characterised by the resource curse,

Chapter 2 echoes the view of Karen Ballentine that 'for developing countries, natural resources are [often] the 'only game in town'.' In resources-rich developing countries suffering from the resource curse, intrigues regarding the control of revenues accruing from the development of major natural resources are indeed the main games generating crisis and conflicts in town.

Community crises in the Delta region are further complicated by the inability or unwillingness of state and local governments in the region to properly address the region's deplorable state and the plight of its poor citizens. Besides the role of state and local governments and that of MNOCs operating in the region, some citizens and citizen groups have a certain measure of blame to bear. While agitating that the FG should enforce the principles of social justice, equity and fair play in favour of the region and its citizens, such citizens and citizen groups are unwilling to enforce these principles, which constitute the basis of the resource-control movement in their respective interpersonal and inter-group relations in the region. The author's critical assessment on how several of these groups are addressing the principles of the resource-control movement reveals that these principles are being greatly undermined in various interpersonal, as well as intra- and inter-communal relations in the region. Such groups are engaged in resource-control in an incomplete manner or from a limited perspective (*ie*, based on the relationship of Niger Deltans with the FG, the major tribes and the MNOCs operating in the region). These groups disregard the way in which the principles of the resource-control movement relate to them, especially in social capital relations among them. Social capital relations undermining public good in the region, frustrate environmentally-sound and socially-equitable CI in petroleum development in the Delta region.

To overcome the negative effects of social capital relations and other challenges hindering the success of CI, the win-win environmental consensus and conflict resolution strategy may be applied by development proponents while interactively involving citizens of each directly-affected community in environmental decision-making processes, so as to translate the community's collective vision into these processes of petroleum development proposals. This strategy promotes consensus-building based on common grounds, which satisfies the powerful and vociferous citizens and citizen groups as well as supports and encourages the weak, voiceless or less powerful ones – who would otherwise have been neglected or excluded from participation. Government regulatory agencies and project proponents thus have a role to be diligent so as to ensure fair play between and among directly-affected citizens and citizen groups, in the course of CIs. In turn, powerful and vociferous community groups have a responsibility to restrain themselves from frustrating the process of due diligence designed by government regulatory agencies and project proponents to ensure the success of CIs regarding petroleum development projects in the Delta region.

This book does not contend that relationships among people should not be mutually advantageous; rather, it demonstrates how certain relationships (*ie*, social capital relationships) constitute internal contradictions in the Delta region, as these relationships undermine collective interpersonal and intra- and inter-group relations in the region. In other words, the book discusses where social capital relationships have reared their heads and generated internal contradictions in the Niger Delta. Social capital relations determine how some governments (including traditional governments), social institutions and community-based organisations (CBOs) either function or are organised and administered in the region against overall public good in the Niger Delta. Such contradictions determine how relationships among citizens and groups thrive, especially the relationships among some influential citizens and citizen groups, relative to the advantages they are deriving from impact-benefit and other social investment initiatives of the MNOCs operating in the region. These internal contradictions aggravate poverty and misery inflicted on the ordinary citizens of the region. As demonstrated in Chapter 4, in the Eastern Delta kingdom of Bonny, internal contradictions have the effect of worsening the crises in the Delta region. Besides, the state of affairs in Bonny kingdom reveals that even though the kingdom has been participating in IA and other environmental decision-making processes since the 1990s, the involvement of the citizens in these processes is being undermined under the house system of governance because of the system's diluted and misdirected nature from the seventeenth century, after the era of King Halliday (Awusa). Hence, Chapter 8 reveals that the house system no longer represents the true will and/or vision of Bonny citizens, considering the views of the citizens on how their inputs were ignored in decision-making processes, when they commented in the EIA process of the upgrade of Shell Bonny Terminal Integrated Project (BTIP). There is thus a need to improve the ongoing pattern of decision-making so that the voice of traditional rulers of Bonny kingdom would truly represent the voice of the people of the kingdom. The apex traditional rulers of Bonny kingdom need to command such natural law attributes as virtue and commitment to the service of their people, as demonstrated by the founding fathers and premier kings who established the kingdom's house system. Based on contemporary challenges, more rational, trustworthy and public-spirited decisions are required of the apex traditional rulers of the kingdom. Thus, if properly managed by the JV partners with the aid of a visionary traditional leadership, public interest-spirited state and local governments and vibrant CBOs partnering towards collective public good, the BTIP, Nigeria LNG and Mobil Producing Nigeria Unlimited (MPN) Bonny River Terminal (BRT) projects ought to sustainably boost socio-economic development, rather than poverty, misery and crisis in the kingdom. Besides, these multi-billion USD projects and other FG's JV petroleum development operations have greatly polarised the traditional Bonny society. Consequently, the FG has commissioned the military to protect these development operations.

Other instances of internal contradictions in the Delta region include those cited in Chapter 1, from the report of the Human Rights Watch entitled 'Nigeria Chop Fine: The Human Rights Impact of Local Government Corruption and Mismanagement in Rivers state, Nigeria', dated January 2007. This report charts the failures of local government administrations in Rivers state, whose government is wealthier than most Nigerian states. According to this report, the contradiction of the wealth of Rivers state, which is the heart of the Nigerian oil industry, is the material deprivation being experienced by the majority of its citizens. The report is complemented in Chapter 1 by the account of the deplorable nature of the plight of the entire less privileged, marginalised and impoverished citizens of Nigeria. Given that internal contractions are worsening the Niger Delta crises in ways which the outside world may not easily appreciate, the need arises for social capital relations to support the welfare of the citizens and productive activities towards environmentally-sound and socially-equitable SCD in the region. Such social capital relations are equally needed in other areas or regions of Nigeria.

Regarding international concerns about the Niger Delta crises, Chapter 2 points out how the USA, whose National Intelligence Council (NIC) in 2004 predicted the collapse of Nigeria, entered into a joint security compact to address the associated issues of security, peace and prosperity; while in 2008 the British government agreed to provide training and logistical support to the Nigerian military to combat anti-oil production militancy in the Delta region. The NIC November 2008 report indicates the need for foreign military intervention to end the Niger Delta crises so as to stabilise petroleum exports in Nigeria. The role of the advanced countries in the growth and development of Africa and African nations is also considered in Chapter 7, where proponents of corporate social responsibility (CSR) identified the significant role of business to Africa's development over centuries. CSR proponents contend that the future of Africa and African countries may be enhanced with the assistance of the advanced countries and Africans in diaspora.

The diverse nature of the key issues associated with the community crises in the Delta region is thus overarching, complex and complicated. These crises have generated several negative consequences, including the insecurity of lives, livelihoods and property in the region, as well as insecurity of supply of Nigeria's petroleum resources to its consumer-countries, as indicated in the Preface and Chapter 1. In the process, the lives of citizens of the region and those of foreign multinationals, and the joint venture (JV) investments of the FG with the MNOCs, are endangered. Considering these and other negative effects and challenges of petroleum development on the people of the region and their future generations, including the environment in the region, some citizens and citizen groups started making efforts to improve the situation. Among such efforts is the initiative to educate the outside world about the state of affairs in the region. On this note, Chapter 2 examines the presentation made by the Rivers Chiefs and Peoples Conference (RCPC) at the UN Earth Summit on Environment and Development (UNCED) which took place in Rio de Janeiro, in 1992. The high point of this presentation, centred on the historic and continuing multifaceted problems and challenges confronting the region, was a declaration by the RCPC that the environment in the region is endangered, and that the region is perhaps the most endangered delta region in the world, due especially to the adverse effects of petroleum development.

The crises in the Delta region require being fully and practically resolved in a way that will achieve environmentally-sound and socially-equitable SCD in the region. To do so by virtue of the internationalisation of petroleum resources-development operations, the need arises for the FG to implement internationally recognised norms, standards and practices designed to enhance the resources development to SD in the region. In this regard, improved CI is required to be practised in conformity with the globally identified need and the widely accepted principles of PP in environmental decision-making, espoused in Principle 10 of the Rio Declaration on Environment and Development, 1992, and elaborated in the Aarhus Convention of 1998 on participation. Considering therefore Nigeria's responsibilities in the context of the ongoing worldwide participation explosion, her National Assembly is required to enshrine provisions in her emerging petroleum law (the Petroleum Industry Bill, PIB) to improve environmental democracy in a way to enhance sustainable petroleum development and SCD. The improvement of CI towards SD of petroleum resources and SCD in Nigeria's oil-producing areas is an idea whose time has come. Consequently, the author advocates the emergence of a truly democratic and socially just and equitable FRN in which, regardless of elected, selected and/or appointed representatives, ordinary citizens are guaranteed the right to participate in decision-making processes to enthrone transparency, accountability and responsibility in governance, towards achieving SD in their communities, local government areas, states and the entire federation. Regarding compensation and other payments or revenues being derived by individuals, families and community groups from the MNOCs and other extractive industries, there is urgent need for Nigeria to initiate pro-active and practicable measures, in order to ensure that such revenues are made with the knowledge of all interest groups in the affected resources-producing areas. The reasons for such payments or revenues should accordingly be published within a stipulated time, in the interest of the general public. Governments are also required to be prudent and transparent in the management of the revenues accruing to them from extractive industrial operations, so as to be properly accountable to the governed. The Nigeria Extractive Industries Transparency Initiative (NEITI) Act, 2007, should therefore be amended to incorporate these and other necessary measures, in order to make governments (including traditional governments) and other representatives and agents of resources-producing communities, to be duly and fully accountable to the citizens, especially those excluded from participating in decision-making processes. The enforcement of these and other needful transparency measures require the efforts of civil society activists and groups and judicial activism in the country.

10.2 IMPROVED COMMUNITY INVOLVEMENT ENHANCED BY GREATER CITIZENS' EMPOWERMENT IN DECISION-MAKING AND THE STAKEHOLDER PERSPECTIVE

The questions designed to address the crises in the Delta region are aimed at identifying the existing forms or measures of CI in petroleum development in the communities of the region. The author examines whether or not these forms or measures of CI are capable of fulfilling the globally-recognised need and widely accepted principles of PP in environmental decision-making, so as to suggest necessary improvements. Focused on the stakeholder theory in business relations, the author identifies three major stakeholders of the petroleum development business in Nigeria. As indicated in Chapter 1, these stakeholders are the oil-producing communities and the JV partners of the business (*ie*, the MNOCs and the Nigerian National Petroleum Corporation (NNPC), representing the FG for and on behalf of the FRN).

Studies are continually revealing that the results of development proposals are better when the affected, concerned and interested members of the public are empowered to participate in the decision-making process of such proposals. There is thus no alternative to interactive CI in petroleum development in Nigeria, the lack of which is the root cause of marginalisation and poverty in the Delta region and hence the crises in the region. Similarly, there is no alternative path to Nigeria's prosperity than greater citizens' empowerment in the country's decision-making processes. As the oil-producing communities are stakeholders (of the petroleum development business in Nigeria), whose interactive involvement cannot be ignored or undermined in the decision-making process of the business, so are the entire citizens of Nigeria stakeholders whose interactive involvement in the governance of the country cannot be ignored or undermined.

10.3 IDENTIFIED FORMS AND/OR MEASURES OF COMMUNITY INVOLVEMENT IN PETROLEUM DEVELOPMENT IN THE DELTA REGION AND OTHER RELATED ISSUES

The author identifies two main forms or measures of CI in petroleum resources development in the Delta region. Including other instances of CI, these are designed to enable citizens of the resources-producing communities to make input into the ancillary decision-making processes of the resources development projects sited in the communities. The main measures of CI are those statutorily designed by the FG, and the CSR or industry-driven measures designed by the MNOCs operating in the region. For example, the EIA process identified in Chapter 5 and the public objection hearing system identified in Chapter 6 are statutory forms of CI designed by the FG. Another form or measure of CI designed by the FG is the Nigerian (Local) Content Policy (NCP), which involves the generality of Nigerians. The NCP evolved from the FG's economic self-reliance policy based on equity participation of Nigerians and Nigerian businesses in all spheres of Nigeria's economy, especially in the petroleum and other sectors of the economy dominated by foreigners, was designed to enhance the industrial development and advancement of the country as a sovereign entity. Other forms and measures of CI identified are those increasingly being designed by the MNOCs to fulfil their social responsibility (CSR) initiatives following those of their parent companies and groups, such as their sectoral groups. Most of these initiatives are designed outside and introduced into Nigeria by individual companies (such as Shell Nigeria) or by individual corporate groups (such as the Shell companies in Nigeria, of which NLNG is a part). CSR measures, increasingly designed by the MNOCs to address the crises in the Delta region, include memoranda of understanding (MoUs) entered into with host communities. Other CSR measures mentioned in passing in Chapter 6 include the involvement of professional CBOs in the EIA process of development projects in the communities, and the employment of the services of land-owning families and communities to provide surveillance services to protect the MNOCs' oil and gas installations. These three measures are discussed in Chapter 9. Other measures discussed in Chapter 6 include the National Content Plans of the MNOCs, as exemplified by the NLNG Local Content Plan designed from the Shell (*ie*, Shell Nigeria) Nigerian Content Policy (NCP). The Shell Project-Advisory Committee (PAC) system is discussed in Chapter 6 as a voluntary CI measure. Other voluntary CSR measures identified in Chapter 7 include the engagement of local NGOs and other community-based organisations such as community development committees (CDCs) to execute the Community Developments (CDs) and other community relations (CR) initiatives of the MNOCs in the oil-producing communities. The main CSR CI measures discussed in Chapter 7 are the Shell Nigeria stakeholders' workshops, the NLNG stakeholders' workshops, and the Niger Delta Environmental Survey (NDES) initiated by Shell Nigeria and almost entirely funded by the MNOCs under the umbrella of the Oil Producers' Trade Section (OPTS) of the Lagos Chamber of Commerce and Industry. Also, the FG is involved in the NDES. This makes the NDES a hybrid form of CI in petroleum development.

The identified CSR forms of CI may directly or indirectly fulfil the government's policy initiatives, such as its poverty alleviation, economic empowerment and SD initiatives. For instance, the NCP is designed by MNOCs such as Shell Nigeria and NLNG in a way to implement the objective of the Environmental Impact Assessment (EIA) process by providing impact-benefits for the communities directly affected by petroleum development projects. By so doing, the Shell Local (ie, Nigerian) Content Policy and the NLNG Local Content Plan are able to promote the poverty alleviation and economic empowerment programmes of the FG in the Delta region and other oil-producing areas of the country. In spite of the shortcomings of the project level EIA process being practised, this process stands remarkable as the most vibrant form of CI in petroleum resources development in Nigeria. Therefore, as expressed in Chapter 5, there is need to further develop the EIA, EA, or IA process of the resources development projects at strategic levels of the resources development proposals (*ie*, at the levels of policies, plans and projects), to enhance SD of the resources and sound and equitable SCD in the oil-producing areas.

Broadly speaking, as compared to project level EIA process, strategic environmental assessment (SEA) has a better prospect of enhancing SD of Nigeria's major natural resources and overall SD in the country. Given that IA is a source of CD and socio-economic empowerment of citizens of the oil-producing communities, Chapters 8 and 9 demonstrate how CI in the IA process of oil and gas development projects in the Delta region enable communities to bargain for or to derive social investments from the MNOCs. The author demonstrates that these investments are being provided by the MNOCs mainly because of the lack of GSR measures in the form of provision of basic infrastructures and other public utilities in the communities. These investments help to foster CD and to socio-economically empower citizens of the communities, so as to alleviate poverty in, and government's neglect of, the Delta region. By placing more emphasis on the provision of social investments, the MNOCs appear to be ignoring or compromising the degree of environmental protection required of them. The MNOCs therefore need to improve upon their environmental performance measures towards SD of petroleum resources, as well as their social performances beyond public relations, so as to contribute more meaningfully to environmentally-sound and socially-equitable SCD in the oil-producing areas. The FG's contribution to social investments through its JV partners does not relieve the government of its direct and traditional responsibility of providing public utilities in oil-producing areas and other areas of the federation. Besides, as expressed in Chapters 1 and 7, corporate accountability (*ie*, corporate environmental and social performance) should take place in a transparent and stable regulatory framework. It is the responsibility of government to develop this framework in accordance with the provisions of Article 29 of the Declaration of the World Summit for Sustainable Development (WSSD), *ie*, the Johannesburg Declaration on SD, 2002. By emphasising CSR and IA, and thus the inevitable role of government, the author demonstrates how the IA process may improve environmental decision-making. This shows that the MNOCs need to improve upon their social and environmental performances, and that GSR is needed to ensure proper regulation of the MNOCs, and to boost well-designed CSR measures in the course of petroleum development. The cries of neglect from the ordinary citizens of Bonny in the course of community consultations (CCs) designed into the IA process of the Shell Nigeria BTIP expressed in Chapter 8, demonstrate the weakness of prevailing CCs in IA petroleum development projects in the Delta region. These cries deserve to be addressed by an improved Social Impact Assessment (SIA) regime, namely strategic social impact assessment (SSIA), designed to achieve environmentally-sound and socially-equitable SCD, given that an underlining factor of the crises in the Delta region is lack of or inadequate SIA in the course of petroleum development in the region. This calls for the practice of strategic SIA through the introduction of SEA in the federation.

Efforts aimed at sustainable petroleum development in the Delta region need to take on board relevant lessons from other wetlands or deltaic regions. These include those of the Mekong Delta in Vietnam, and the Mississippi river, Florida Everglades and the Tennessee Valley Authority in the USA. Applicable lessons from these may help to improve the state of affairs in the Niger Delta and the performance of the newly-established Ministry of the Niger Delta and the NDDC established after the failure of the Niger Delta Development Board (NDDB) and the Oil Minerals Producing Areas Development Commission

(OMPADEC). The conservation, rehabilitation and renewal measures required in the Delta region and other coastal areas of Nigeria also suggest the relevance of the World Conservation Union and the Ramsar Convention on wetlands referred to in Chapter 2, and the need to establish nature reservation trusts based on the example of Natural England discussed in Chapter 9. Besides, PI in petroleum and other major natural resources development in Nigeria needs to be improved by the development of citizens' or PI toolkits or models. Other models that should be introduced into the Nigerian municipal system include impact-benefit agreements (IBAs) or other forms of Good Neighbour Agreements (GNAs) such as the Whitehorse Mining Initiative (WMI) of the Federal Republic of Canada, and the Ahafo Social Responsibility Agreement by which the Newmont gold mining corporation committed, in 2005, to allocate $1 per ounce of gold sold and one per cent of mine net profit to fund SCD projects in Ghana. These forms of GNAs are being increasingly negotiated, entered into and consolidated upon, to protect cultural heritage and to strengthen the bargaining position of indigenous peoples, local communities, and other neglected peoples being adversely affected by extractive industrial operations. Agreements like these are needed in jurisdictions or developing countries like Nigeria where municipal systems have not been able to address the plight of neglected resources-producing communities and integral interest groups within such communities. It would be better to cement Good Neighbour Agreements (GNAs) in Nigeria between the MNOCs and the oil-producing communities rather than the MoUs that are presently causing confusion and misunderstanding among these parties. GNAs are capable of creating a sense of belonging, greater fulfilment and sustainable partnerships enhanced by mutual trust, cooperation and commitment among stakeholders of major natural resources-development projects. GNAs may be drawn up and made subject to the JV agreements of the various MNOCs with the NNPC. As with the WMI, GNAs may be designed to involve wider stakeholder groups, such as communities, labour, and environmental organisations, as well as the industry and government. SD-oriented GNAs are capable of promoting environmental democracy and the socio-economic empowerment of citizens in the development of petroleum and other major natural resources serving as the economic backbone of resource-rich developing countries. Referring to page 14 of Nigeria's *EIA Procedural Guidelines, 1995*, GNAs constitute a category of contractual control for mitigating the adverse effects of petroleum development projects on citizens of oil-producing areas. To enhance the smooth introduction of GNAs, existing MoUs between the MNOCs and the oil-producing communities may be temporarily adopted as binding agreements, and eventually replaced by SCD-oriented GNAs.

It cannot be overemphasised how important it is to introduce GNAs in Nigeria to help generate an end to the crises in the Delta region, especially as the FG has initiated the move to grant Ondo and Ogun states, including Delta state, the opportunity to invest equitably in the Olokola (Ok) LNG project. As stated in Chapter 1, this FG's initiative primarily masterminded in favour of the Yoruba tribal majority of Ondo state and Ogun state makes it more incumbent on the government, led by the elites of the three major ethnic groups, to be fair and just to the Delta ethnic minorities who started agitating to have equity participation in petroleum development operations which have been going on in their communities since 1956. It is against this background of the injustices of major tribes against minority tribes, that the book figuratively presents the plight of the ethnic minorities of the oil-rich Delta region as that of the proverbial mother whose abundant breast milk has for over five decades been used to feed other children of the family, while her own children are largely deprived of its nourishment. The FG should therefore grant equity participation investment opportunities in petroleum development operations and introduce other fair, equitable and socially-justifiable benefits to the citizens of the Delta region and those of other oil-producing areas, considering that petroleum is a finite resource which will eventually run out. This is all the more so, as petroleum and other major natural resources development constitute the foundation for further developments (*ie*, the advancement of resources-rich developing countries and their peoples). The benefits from petroleum resources development also need to be extended to local governments of the resources-producing areas, as for instance specified in the Papua New Guinea (PNG) Petroleum Policy Handbook, 2003, and Sections 49(d), 170(3) and Part IV (Sections 164–179) and Sections 50 and 52 of the PNG Oil and Gas Act, 1998 (as amended in 2002), mentioned in Chapter 7.

Chapter 1 cites Principle 1 of the Rio Declaration on Environment and Development, 1992, which provides *inter alia* that 'man is at the centre of the concerns for sustainable development'. Hence, Nigeria's petroleum SD strategy should be directed towards the welfare of all of its citizens, especially the poor masses of the country, and humanity at large. As a source of energy supply to consumer-countries, Nigeria's petroleum requires to be developed in a way that will ensure security of supply, in order to demonstrate Nigeria's contribution to energy resources sustainability, as demonstrated in Chapter 1.

10.4 OTHER KEY FINDINGS AND RECOMMENDATIONS

Given that the main hypothesis of the book is that CI in petroleum resources development in the Delta region is mainly consultative rather than truly participatory, there is an attempt here to identify the forms or measures of CI in resources development in Chapters 5 to 7, elaborated on in Chapters 8 and 9 in the context of CSR initiatives. The findings are that in spite of the existing forms or measures of CI, the crises in the Delta region increasingly persist because decision-makers merely listen to the concerns of communities during community involvements without properly acting on these concerns in the course of the implementation of petroleum development projects in the region. It is in this same manner that governments in the country treat the inputs of the ordinary citizens, affecting their wellbeing, in decision-making processes, contrary to the social contract theory. Consequently, the existing forms or measures of CI do not fulfil the globally identified need and widely accepted principles of PP in environmental decision-making discussed in Chapter 3. Improved CI through improved CSR is therefore needed as well as GSR embedded in good governance (GG) in the course of the resources development in the Delta region and other oil-producing areas of Nigeria. The fulfilment of the identified need and accepted principles will enable the MNOCs to obtain the free, prior and informed consent of the communities which are directly affected by their operations, to enhance their smooth operations in the communities.

The author recommends that MNOCs should implement their widely published and publicised environmental and social responsibilities as discussed in Chapters 1 and 7, in the interest of their host communities. In this regard, Article 27 of the Johannesburg Declaration on SD, 2002, cited in Chapters 1, 2, 7 and 9, enjoins companies, including MNCs, 'to contribute to the evolution of equitable and sustainable communities and societies'. Regarding EA, it is recommended that the quality of the EIA process of petroleum development projects in Nigeria should be enhanced by improvement in CSR. This will properly demonstrate that PI (of which CI is a part) is a significant pillar of the assessment process aimed at enhancing the quality of the process towards SD, as identified in Chapter 5 and demonstrated in Chapters 8 and 9. Chapters 5, 8, and 9 also demonstrate that it is not typically an effective way of practising IA for MNOCs to obtain statutory permits from government regulatory agencies in order to implement their development proposals without equally obtaining social licence from the oil producing communities, in the course of their operations in the communities. Such a way of practising IA (*ie*, embarking on IA of petroleum development projects as well as any other extractive industrial operation) hinders SD. Accordingly, there should be life-cycle impact assessments of development projects – enhanced by such sustainability-assessment measures as proper follow-ups built into the Environmental Management Systems of development proponents, so as to strengthen and ensure greater effectiveness of the EA process towards SD. Sustainability assessments, from the design and conception stage to the decommissioning stage of development proposals, are required in the FRN, to properly implement the federation's SD principles. These are the Precautionary Principle, Pollution Prevention Pays Principle (3P +), Polluter Pays Principle (PPP), User Pays Principle (UPP), Principle of Inter-generational Equity, Principle of Intra-generational Equity, and the Principle of Participation. These principles, expressed in *Nigeria's Policy on the Environment*, demonstrate Nigeria's appreciation of the interdependent linkages among development processes, environmental factors, and human and natural resources. Formal introduction of SEA is also needed in Nigeria, in compliance with the New Partnership for Africa's Development (NEPAD) Action Plan on the Environmental Initiative discussed in Chapter 5. These and other internationally-identified environmental protection, preservation and SD measures require proper implementation in the course of all major natural resources development projects in the country.

Improvement in CSR in the Delta region and other oil-producing areas of Nigeria must be enhanced by GSR. Chapter 7 therefore concludes that the social investment being accomplished by the MNOCs in the communities of the oil-rich Delta region needs to be properly engineered, encouraged and sustained by GSR, towards SD of petroleum resources and environmentally-sound and socially-equitable SCD. The author demonstrated in Chapter 7 that there are limitations as regards CSR measures. No matter how well designed or intended, and no matter how well implemented, CSR is not an alternative to GSR embedded in GG, or that CSR is certainly not an alternative to good and responsible government. Development is primarily a domestic responsibility, so it is the role of government to generate citizen-oriented development policies, plans and programmes/projects. Generally, there is a need for governments in Nigeria to place priority on people-centred SD which is knowledge-based (*ie*, state-of-the art knowledge driven), so as to properly build bridges between theory and practice in ways that are capable of avoiding negative trends in the country. As expressed in Chapters 1 and 7, 'good governance and sustainable development are indivisible', as indicated by the former UN Secretary General, Kofi Annan, during his inaugural address at the UN 'International Conference on Governance for Sustainable Growth and Equity', held in New York, July 28–30, 1997. GG was identified at the WSSD, held at Johannesburg, South Africa, from August 26 to September 4, 2002, as a critical factor for ensuring successful SD. By virtue of the duty of companies (*ie*, the private sector) expressed in Article 27 of the Johannesburg Declaration on SD, 2002, cited above, business can enhance GSR embedded in GG, by embarking on good practice in the interest of society, especially the public directly affected by business operations, so as to achieve business sustainability. Thus, as expressed in Chapter 7, traditionally 'soft' issues such as human rights, the environment and other imperative social and ethical dimensions of business have now become 'hard' for business to ignore, manage or get them wrong, in the ongoing efforts designed to enhance and ensure mankind's and society's greater wellbeing.

Improved CSR measures backed by GSR and other GG measures require the support and encouragement of the oil-producing communities, as indicated in Chapters 1 and 9. The need for the communities to do so to provide an enabling environment for the operations of the MNOCs is identified in Chapter 9, under clause 24 of the Bonny kingdom versus NLNG agreement made under the auspices of the Rivers state government reconciliation panel, on May 30, 2000, following the kingdom versus NLNG crisis of September 1999. The author considers the support and encouragement of the oil-producing communities (to enhance the operations of the MNOCs in the course of petroleum development in the communities) to mean community social responsibility (SRC). CSR and SRC, generated by GG, will in turn generate cooperation, mutual trust and commitment between the MNOCs and the communities as well as consensus-building and strategic development partnerships between the three major stakeholders of the petroleum development business in Nigeria. Chapter 1 thus indicates the need for tri-sector development partnerships among the major stakeholders, to improve their so-far frosty relationships. The chapter indicates the need for tri-sector development partnerships in the course of major natural resources development in developing countries, in conformity with the provisions of Article 26 of the Johannesburg Declaration on SD, 2002, which echoes the significance of broad-based and long-term partnerships for SD. These partnerships constitute one significant finding of this book: that there is need for a conflict resolution strategy designed to achieve win-win situations among the three major stakeholders of the petroleum development business in Nigeria. Win-win situations such as reaching environmental consensus are bridge-building measures. They are ingredients of collaborative or multi-stakeholder partnerships (MSPs) required to govern the relations between the three major stakeholders. Chapter 1 demonstrates that so far the FG and communities are both unyielding, while the MNOCs are reluctant to do all that is required of them by governments and the communities (*ie*, to implement more social investment than they are willing to embark upon), in the course of their operations in the Delta region. Win-win environmental consensus and conflict resolution alliances, which require the commitment of each of the three major stakeholders in the performance of their respective roles and responsibilities, are amicable ways of resolving the crises in the Delta region, considering the relatively-uncompromising stance of each of these stakeholders. The stakeholder theory seeks to impose a measure of social responsibility on the international community, especially countries of the globe relying on Nigeria's petroleum resources to serve their needs, to persuade governments and MNOCs in Nigeria to properly fulfil their obligations and responsibilities to the oil-rich Delta region and other oil-producing areas of Nigeria. The fulfilment of these would accelerate the achievement of industrial peace and harmony in the oil-producing areas, especially as peace and prosperity in these oil-rich areas are intertwined with the prosperity of Nigeria and security of supply of Nigeria's petroleum resources to the consumer-countries. Considering the leadership question of the Delta region expressed in Chapter 1, to promote the interests of the people of the region require capable, credible and efficient, elected and appointed representatives in the realm of national politics and decision-making processes.

Placing the book in a more meaningful and proper national context, the enlarged/ancillary hypothesis expressed in Chapter 1 provides that the overwhelming majority of Nigerian citizens, especially the poor masses and the intelligentsia, are (along with the ethnic minorities, especially those of the Delta region) being excluded from participating in decision-making processes in the country. This hypothesis is verified, especially as participation means empowering citizens politically and otherwise. Lack of participation or improper participation means non-empowerment of citizens and is thus the basis for marginalisation, neglect, poverty, and misery being inflicted upon or suffered by the overwhelming majority of Nigerians. Hence, the book considers that the plight and predicaments of the minorities of the oil-rich Delta region regarding environmental democracy in relation to petroleum development can only be more meaningfully or effectively addressed in the context of overall citizens' participation in Nigeria. This also implies that the paradox of poverty in the midst of plenty in the Delta region needs to be more properly addressed by governments at all levels in the overall context of poverty in the midst of the plentiful wealth accruing to Nigeria from petroleum development.

Chapter 1 also indicates that the principle of permanent sovereignty has inherent rights and responsibilities, although these rights are enjoyed by the government of Nigeria and those of other major natural resources-rich developing countries without the political will or commitment of these governments to fulfil the corollary duties and responsibilities of this principle in favour of their citizens. These duties and responsibilities include the promotion of economic development, ensuring the protection of the environment, and enhancing SD, in the interest of the citizens. Thus, Article 21 of the African Charter of Human and Peoples Rights, Cap. 10, LFN, 1990 (ie, Article 17 of the UN Universal Declaration of Human Rights, 1948), provides that sovereignty over natural resources in the FRN be exercised in the interest of the people of the federation. Accordingly, Section 14(2) (b) of the 1999 Constitution of the FRN, cited in Chapters 1 and 9, states that 'the security and welfare of the people shall be the primary purpose of government'.

Chapter 1 indicates that Africa is a centre of crises and contradictions, and major natural resources development by extractive industries occupies a key place at the centre of these crises, as exemplified by sovereign and other ancillary governance control of petroleum resources development and the revenues from it in the FRN. The solution to these twin problems of crises and contradictions from the perspective of this book is improved CI in petroleum development vis-à-vis improved PI derived through greater citizens' empowerment in decision-making processes in the federation. Improved PI is capable of empowering the minorities of the oil-producing Delta region and the producers of other major natural resources in the FRN, environmentally, economically and socio-politically, as well as enhancing transparency and accountability in the overall governance of the federation. As expressed in Chapter 1, improved citizens' or public involvement is capable of resolving the leadership question of the FRN, considering that the key problem with PP in decision-making and the overall 'trouble with Nigeria' 'is simply and squarely the failure of leadership', using the words of Nigeria's erudite writer, Chinua Achebe. Leadership failure triumphs at all levels of governance from the federal to regional, state, local and community levels. Indeed, since the attainment of Nigeria's political independence, one of its greatest problems is the absence of public-spirited leaders capable of governing the country in the interest of all; consequently, the ethnic minorities and the poor citizens of the country are worse-off. Nigerian leaders are thus confronted with the challenge of truly representing the interests of Nigerian citizens, rather than their self-serving interests. Self-serving leaders in Nigeria should be united in promoting the common good of Nigerians and Nigeria, rather than their common greed; as the only item on the agenda of leadership is service to the people. Nigerian leaders are thus required to improve governance, in compliance with the provisions of Article 30 of the Johannesburg Declaration on SD, and the commitment of poor countries expressed in the UN Millennium Declaration based on the UN General Assembly Resolution 55/2 of September 8, 2000, in the interest of humanity in the country.

The three major stakeholders of the petroleum development business in Nigeria need to take advantage of the win-win environmental consensus and conflict resolution strategy recommended above as a way forward to resolve the crises in the Delta region, as this will persuade militant protagonists of the resource-control movement to reappraise their strategies. On this note, there is need for Nigeria to fully institutionalise environmental mediation as a form of Alternative Dispute Resolution (ADR), in order to enhance the resolution of environmental disputes and conflicts between and among the major stakeholders of the petroleum development business in the country. Environmental mediation as extensively practised in the United States of America (USA), Canada, and Australia, has become necessary in the FRN. Time is also at hand for the major stakeholders led by governments to embark upon fruitful negotiations toward mutual cooperation and collaboration, to bring to an end or at least minimise the protracted crises in the Delta region. This is indeed the time for the FG and the state and local governments presiding over the affairs of the communities in the region to develop these communities and to rehabilitate the citizens, including the freedom fighters, of the region, in pragmatic terms of multi-stakeholder partnership (MSP). In the process, as identified in the context of Bonny kingdom in Chapter 4 and generally regarding the entire Delta region, citizens of the region must address the challenges of the resource-control movement by practising the principles of the movement in the region. That means practising, as a form of SRCs, the principles of social justice, equity and fair play in their interpersonal and intra- and inter-group relations, to enhance the efforts of the government and the MNOCs towards overall public good in the region.

In Chapter 7 and in such other isolated cases in Chapter 8, the author discusses how activist civil society groups such as NGOs sensitised the world about the crises in the Delta region, especially during the judicial execution of the environmental and civil rights activist, Ken Saro-Wiwa, and his eight Ogoni kinsmen, in 1995. NGOs, therefore, need to continue to sensitise the world, and thereby persuade the MNOCs operating in Nigeria, as well as the federal government and the state and local governments in the Delta region, to generate environmentally-sound and socially-equitable SCD in the course of petroleum development in the region. SCD may be feasible in the oil-producing areas if the JV partners of the petroleum development business in Nigeria, and the state and local governments of these areas, fine-tune their SD strategies by sponsoring capacity-building and providing venture capital as CD trusts to encourage these areas to produce some of their basic needs and services so that they can achieve a measure of economic self-reliance. On this note, as public-spirited civil society groups, CBOs and leaders in the petroleum resources-producing areas are required to be alive to the plight of their people, by implementing laudable initiatives of the MNOCs, the government and other development partners at grass roots, so as to enhance the realisation of SCD in oil-producing communities.

By and large, the book confirms the proposal made in Chapter 1, on the strength of the enlarged/ancillary hypothesis, that there is a need for improved CSR in the Delta region and other oil-producing areas; and that there is a greater need for GSR embedded in GG so as to prevent the FRN from further decline or stagnation, in the interests of its entire component ethnic groups. Section 14(2)(c) of the 1999 Constitution of the FRN should be amended to empower citizens to make greater inputs in decision-making as regards all aspects of nation-building, to improve upon their wellbeing. Such empowerment will generate greater accountability, transparency and responsibility in governance, while promoting the loyalty and sense of belonging of the citizens. Along with the provisions of Section 14(1) of the Constitution, the proposed amendment has the potential to boost such subsidiary laws as the EIA legislation, which has provisions on PP, and thereby bridge the gap between PP laws and the policy and regulatory frameworks associated with them. The proposed Freedom of Information (FoI – *vis-à-vis* citizens' right-to-know) Act may be significant in this regard, by empowering all Nigerian citizens to have unfettered access to information. This would enhance unencumbered PI in decision-making and unfettered access to justice in the federation. Also, following the prevailing state of affairs in the Republic of South Africa, for instance, it is on the basis of GSR, anchored on GG that the amendment of the 1999 Constitution of the FRN is recommended in Chapter 1, in order to make economic and socio-cultural (ESC) rights enforceable on government in the interests of the citizens. Interactive CI enhanced by integrative social and environmental justice, towards environmentally-sound and socially-equitable SCD in oil-producing areas, cannot be achieved in the absence of GSR generated by a socially just, accountable, and transparent system of governance in the federation. SCD is so far yet to be achieved in the Delta region, as is the case in other parts of Nigeria. SCD in the oil-rich Delta region and SD in the entire FRN could not have been achieved in the absence of basic public utilities and other means of livelihood, processes and steps which are required to achieve the Millennium Development Goals (MDGs) in the interest of humanity, especially poor citizens of the federation. If SD is achieved in Nigeria it will be self-evident on the wellbeing of the citizens, particularly the poor citizens of the country. Accordingly, if SCD is eventually achieved in the Delta region, it will not require the exaggerated publicity being made by governments and MNOCs, as it will be obvious from the wellbeing of the citizens of the region in their various villages, towns and cities. Sustainability indicators, which include transparent and stable government regulation of petroleum and other major natural resources development, need, therefore, to be designed and implemented to properly streamline Nigeria's effort towards SD. Considering that the world is in an era of peak oil and climate change, and that SD is an illusion or incompatible with petroleum and other extractive industrial development operations in developing countries suffering from the resource curse, there is limited time within which to accomplish so much to achieve environmentally-sound and socially-equitable SCD in the oil-producing areas. Since

2015 is fast approaching, there is equally limited time to achieve the MDGs in Nigeria.

The author's perspective demonstrates that the more citizens of the oil-producing communities can benefit from petroleum development through interactive public involvement (PI) and other SD strategies, the more they would, as genuinely-recognised stakeholders and partners in progress, take part in ensuring the success of the development operations in their communities. The same applies to all Nigerian citizens, especially the poor masses, in terms of benefiting from the enormous revenues being derived from petroleum and other major natural resources development in the country. SCD in the Niger Delta and other parts of Nigeria therefore presupposes greater or improved citizens' involvement in all aspects of Nigeria's nation-building, in compliance with the dictates of the ongoing world-wide participation explosion associated with transparency and accountability in governance. This would involve empowering all Nigerian citizens, including the country's intelligentsia, such as experts in various fields of endeavour, and thereby make their voices to be truly heard and duly integrated into decision-making processes affecting their lives and well-being. To achieve this state of affairs require a visionary FG to exhibit the desired political will backed by commitment and a pro-active approach, and thereby motivate the state and local governments in the federation, to resolve the Nigerian leadership question in the interest of all. In the process, the FG and the relevant state and local governments will take more appropriate steps to resolve the crises in the Delta region. Governance, both civil and traditional, would thus be required to operate at a strategic level where the consequences of proposed policies, plans and programmes/projects would be considered and evaluated at the earliest possible stage of decision-making. With such improvements, PP/PI will surely become a proper way of governance and an accepted way of life, and thus steer Nigeria into true nationhood and prosperity, and to achieve SD vis-à-vis the MDGs by 2015.

10.5 AGENDA FOR FUTURE STUDIES

Following the key issues, findings and recommendations expressed above, there is a need for specific studies associated with some aspects of this book. As indicated in the introductory part, such studies may include the designing of CI models such as toolkits and guidelines based on identified good practices in community participation, CD and SCD, in the course of major natural resources development. Such models need, however, to be adapted to suit the circumstances of marginalised and neglected communities endowed with major natural resources in developing countries suffering from the resource curse. Thus, as recommended in Chapter 1, there is a need to develop PI guidelines and other such models regarding the development of petroleum and other major natural resources such as solid minerals, in order to promote industrial peace and harmony through partnership of the major stakeholders of these resources development businesses in Nigeria. Future study is needed on the development of policy and the enactment legislation on CSR, so as to enhance the development of Nigerian company law and practice. Such a study might address how the increasing emphasis on CSR in relation to MNOCs is a challenge to the Nigerian and other national oil companies (NOCs), in the ongoing efforts to achieve SD in the country. There should be future study on the Delta region's resource-control movement in relation to enthroning the principles of equity, social justice and fair play in the region. This study could among other things consider the unsustainable nature of militancy (*ie*, violence) in the region and address it through reorientation, capacity-building and other laudable initiatives designed to engage militant youngsters and to employ them gainfully and sustainably in their own best and the overall interests of society. Future studies should also be carried out on other ways of evolving sustainable communities, cities and towns, based on the peculiar circumstances of and situations in Nigeria. Finally, there should be more studies, backed by citizens' activisms based on due process, on how to achieve GG, including true federalism, in Nigeria.

Bibliography

Abubakar J. J., *Guns and Wars: Proliferation of Small and Light Weapons in Internal Conflicts in Nigeria*, London, Adonis & Abbey, 2008

Achebe C., *The Trouble with Nigeria*, Enugu, Fourth Dimension, 1983

Afigbo A. E., *The Warrant Chiefs: Indirect Rule in Southern Nigeria 1891–1929*, London, Longman, 1972

Agyeman J., Bullard R. D. and Evans B. (eds), *Just Sustainabilities: Development in An Unequal World*, London, Earthscan, 2003

Ahmed K. and Sanchez-Triana E. (eds), *Strategic Environmental Assessment for Policies: An Instrument for Good Governance*, Washington DC, The World Bank, 2008

Aina E. O. A. and Adedipe N. O. (eds), *The Petroleum Industry and the Environmental Impact in Nigeria*, Abuja, Federal Environmental Protection Agency (FEPA), 1996

Ajomo M. A. and Adewale O. (eds), *Environmental Law and Sustainable Development in Nigeria*, Lagos, Nigerian Institute of Advanced Legal Studies and the British Council, 1994

Akande J. O., *Introduction to the Constitution of the Federal Republic of Nigeria 1990*, Ebute-Metta, Lagos, MIJ, 2000

Akinrele A., *Nigeria Oil and Gas Law*, Dundee, Oil, Gas & Energy Law Intelligence (OGEL), 2005

Alagoa E. J., *A History of the Niger Delta: An Historical Interpretation of Ijo Tradition*, Port Harcourt, Onyoma Research, 2005

Alagoa E. J., *The Small Brave City-State*, Ibadan, Ibadan University Press, 1964

Alagoa E. J. (ed.), *The Land and People of Bayelsa State: Central Niger Delta*, Port Harcourt, Onyoma Research, 1999

Alagoa E. J. and Derefaka A. A. (eds), *The Land and People of Rivers State: Eastern Niger Delta*, Port Harcourt, Onyoma Research, 2002

Alagoa E. J. and Fombo A., *A Chronicle of Grand Bonny*, Port Harcourt, Onyoma Research, 2001

Ali S. H., *Mining, the Environment, and Indigenous Development Conflicts*, Tucson, The University of Arizona Press, 2003

Amachree I. T., *Effective Community Relations: Focus on Project Advisory Committee (PAC) of the Cawthorne Channel Drilling Campaign and other Issues Affecting the Oil and Gas Industry plus A Practical Guide to Claims for Oil Spillages, Acquisitions, Blockades, Agency, etc*, Umuebule, I. T. Amachree, 2004

Anand R., International Environmental Justice: A North-South Dimension, Aldershot, Ashgate, 2004

Anderson D., *Good Companies Don't Have Missions*, London, The Social Affairs Unit, 2000

Anderson D., *What Has 'Ethical Investment' To Do With Ethics?*, London, The Social Affairs Unit, 1998

Andre P., Delisle C. E.. and Reveret J., *Environmental Assessment for Sustainable Development: Processes, Actions and Practice*, Quebec, Press Internationales Polytechnique, 2004

Andriof J. and Mcintosh M.. (eds), *Perspectives on Corporate Citizenship*, Sheffield, Greenleaf, 2001

Andiof J. S. Waddock B. Husted and S. S. Raman (eds), *Unfolding Stakeholder Thinking: Theory, Responsibility and Engagement*, Sheffield, Greenleaf, 2002

Andiof J. S. Waddock B. Husted and S. S. Raman (eds), *Unfolding Stakeholder Thinking 2: Relationships, Communication, Reporting and Performance*, Sheffield, Greenleaf, 2003

Anghie A., *Imperialism, Sovereignty and the Making of International Law*, Cambridge, Cambridge University Press, 2005

Ascher W., *Why Governments Waste Natural Resources: Policy Failures In Developing Countries*, Baltimore, John Hopkins University Press, 1999

Asher W. and Healy R., *Natural Resources Policymaking in Developing Countries: Environment, Economic Growth, and Income Distribution*, Durham, Duke University Press, 1990

Asher W. and Mirovitskaya N. (eds), *Guide to Sustainable Development and Environmental Policy*, Durham, Duke University Press, 2001

Atkinson G., Dietz S. and Neumayer E. (eds), *Handbook of Sustainable Development, Cheltenham*, Edward Elgar, 2007

Atkinson G., Dubourg R., Hamilton K., Munasinghe M., Pearce D. and Young C., Measuring *Sustainable Development: Macroeconomics and the Environment*, Cheltenham, Edward Elgar, 1999

Atsegbua L. A., *Nigerian Petroleum Law – The Acquisition of Oil Rights in Nigeria*, Benin City, Renstine, 1993

Atsegbua L. A., *Oil and Gas Law in Nigeria: Theory and Practice*, Benin City, New Era, 2004

Ayaji S. (ed.), *Attah On Resource Control*, Lagos, Bangee Ventures, 2004

Ayida, A. A., *Rise and Fall of Nigeria*, Oxford, Mathouse, 1999

Ayre G. and Callway R. (eds), *Governance for Sustainable development: A Foundation for the Future*, London, Earthscan, 2005

Azaike S., *Inequities in Nigerian Politics*, Yanagoa, Treasure Communications Resource, 2003

Baderin M. A. and Mccorquodale R. (eds), *Economic, Social and Cultural Rights in Action*, Oxford, Oxford University Press, 2007

Bakan J., *The Corporation: The Pathological Pursuit of Profit and Power*, London, Constable & Robinson, 2004

Baker S., *Sustainable Development: Routledge Introductions to Environment Series*, London, Routledge, 2006

Bang J. M., *Ecovillages: A Practical Guide to Sustainable Communities*, Edinburgh, Floris, 2005

Bang J. M., *Growing Eco-communities: Practical Ways to Create Sustainability*, Edinburgh, Floris, 2007

Bannon I. and Collier P. (eds), *Natural Resources and Violent Conflict: Options and Actions*, Washington DC, The World Bank, 2003

Barber B. R., *Strong Democracy: Participatory Politics for a New Age*, Berkeley, University of California Press, 1984

Barbier E. B., *The Economics of Environment and Development: Selected Essays*, Cheltenham, Edward Elgar, 1998

Bartelmus P., *Environment, Growth and Development: The Concepts and Strategies of Sustainability*, London, Routledge, 1994

Bartkus V. O. and Davis J. H. (eds), *Social Capital: Reaching Out, Reaching In*, Cheltenham, Edward Elgar, 2009

Bartoli H., *Rethinking Development: Putting an End to Poverty*, Paris, United Nations Educational, Scientific and Cultural Organisation (UNESCO), 2000

Barton H. (ed.), *Sustainable Communities: The Potential for Eco-Neighbourhoods*, London, Earthscan, 2005

Barton B., Barrera-Harnandez L., Lucas A. R. and Ronne A. (eds), *Regulating Energy and Natural Resources*, Oxford, Oxford University Press, 2006

Bascur. O. A., *Latin American Perspectives: Exploration, Mining, and Processing*, Littleton, Society for Mining, Metallurgy and Exploration, 1998

Bass S., Reid H., Satterthwaite D. and Steele P. (eds), *Reducing Poverty and Sustaining the Environment: The Politics of Local Engagement*, London, Earthscan, 2005

Bastida E, Walde T. and Warden-Fernandez J. (eds), *International Comparative Mineral Law and Policy: Trends and Prospects*, The Hague, Kluwer Law International, 2005

Bee O. J., *Petroleum Resources of Indonesia*, Oxford, Oxford University Press, 1982

Beierle T. C. and Cayford J., *Democracy in Practice: Public Participation in Environmental Decisions*, Washington DC, Resources for the Future, 2002

Bekhechi M. A. and Mercier J., *The Legal and Regulatory Framework for Environmental Impact Assessments: A Study of Selected Countries in Sub-Saharan Africa*, Washington DC, The World Bank, 2002

Bell S. and Morse S., *Sustainability Indicators: Measuring the Immeasurable?*, London, Earthscan, 2008

Bilchitz D., *Poverty and Fundamental Rights: The Justification and Enforcement of Socio-Economic Rights*, Oxford, Oxford University Press, 2007

Birne W. P. and Boyle A., *Basic Documents on International Law and the Environment*, New York, Oxford University Press, 1995

Birnie P. W. and Boyle A. E., *International Law and the Environment*, Oxford, Oxford University Press, 2002

Blackburn W. R., *The Sustainability Handbook: The Complete Guide to Achieving Social, Economic and Environmental Responsibility*, London, Earthscan, 2008

Blair J. P., *Local Economic Development: Analysis and Practice*, Thousand Oaks, Sage, 1995

Blanpain R. (ed.), *Multinational Enterprises and the Social Challenges of the XX1st Century: The ILO Declaration on Fundamental Principles at Work, Public and Private Corporate Codes of Conduct*, The Hague, The Netherlands, 2000

Blewit J., *Understanding Sustainable Development*, London, Earthscan, 2008

Blowfield M. and Murray A., *Corporate Responsibility: A Critical Introduction*, Oxford, Oxford University Press, 2008

Bohi D. R. and Toman M. A., *The Economics of Energy Security*, Boston, Kluwer Academic, 1996

Bowen H. R., *Social Responsibilities of Businessmen*, New York, Harper and Brothers, 1953

Brass P. R., *Ethnicity and Nationalism: Theory and Comparison*, New Delhi, Sage, 1991

Brass, P. R. (ed.), *Ethnic Groups and the State*, London, Croom Helm, 1985

Breton A., Brosio G., Dalmazzone S. and Garrone G. (eds), *Environmental Governance and Decentralisation*, Cheltenham, Edward Elgar, 2007

Breton A. and Scott A., *The Design of Federations*, Montreal, The Institute for Research on Public Policy, 1980

Brolmann C., Lefeber R. and Dordrecht M. Z. (eds), *Peoples and Minorities in International Law*, Dordrecht, Martinus Nijhoff, 1999

Brownsword R. (ed.), *Global Governance and the Quest for Justice: Human Rights*, Oregon, Hart, 2004

Bruch C. (ed.), *The New 'Public': The Globalization of Public Participation*, Washington DC, Environmental Law Institute, 2002

Buchanan P. G., Grainge M. A. and Thornton R. C. N. (eds), *Papua New Guinea's Petroleum Industry in the 21st Century: Proceedings of the 4th PNG Petroleum Convention, 2000*, Port Moresby, PNG Chamber of Mines and Petroleum, 2000

Bullard R. D. (ed.), *The Quest for Environmental Justice: Human Rights and the Politics of Pollution*, San Francisco, Sierra Club, 2005

Bunter M. A. G., *Host Communities, Native Title and Petroleum Licensing*, Dundee, Centre for Energy, Petroleum and Mineral Law and Policy (CEPMLP), 2003

Burgess M., *Comparative Federalism: Theory and Practice*, Oxon, Routledge, 2006

Burgess M. (ed.), *Canadian Federalism: The Past, Present and Future*, Leicester, Leicester University Press, 1990

Burgess M. and Gagnon A. (ed.), *Comparative Federalism and Federation: Competing Traditions and Future Directions*, Hertfordshire, Harvester Wheatsheaf, 1993

Burns A., *History of Nigeria*, London, George Allen & Unwin, 1969

Campbell B. (ed.), *Regulating Mining in Africa: For Whose Benefit?*, Nordiska Afrikainstitutet (The Nordic Africa Institute), Uppsala 2004

Cannon T., *Corporate Responsibility: A Textbook on Business Ethics, Governance, Environment: Roles and Responsibilities*, London, Pitman, 1994

Caratti P., Dalkmann H., Jiliberto R. (eds), *Analysing Strategic Environmental Assessment: towards Better Decision-making*, Cheltenham, Edward Elgar, 2004

Carew-Reid J., Prescott-Allen R., Bass S.M.J. and Dalal-Clayton D.B., *Strategies for National Sustainable Development: A Handbook for their Planning and Implementation*, London, Earthscan, 1994

Carter N., *The Politics of the Environment: Ideas, Activism, Policy*, Cambridge, Cambridge University Press, 2004

Castiglione D., Deth J. W. and Wolleb G. (eds), *The Handbook of Social Capital*, Oxford, Oxford University Press, 2008

Chambers R., *Participatory Workshops: A Sourcebook of 21 Sets of Ideas & Activities*, London, Earthscan, 2007

Christian D. L., *Creating a Life Together: Practical Tools to Grow Ecovillages and Intentional Communities*, Gabriola Island, New Society, 2008

Clark A. L. and Johnson C. J., *Mineral Resource Assessment for National Planning and Policy Formulation*, Tokyo, Resource System Institute East-West Centre, 1988

Coenen F. H. J. M. Huitema D and O'Toole, Jr. L. J. O (eds), *Participation and the Quality of Environmental Decision Making*, Dordrecht, Kluwer Academic, 1998

Cooke B. and Kothari U. (eds), *Participation: The New Tyranny?*, London, Zed, 2004

Collier P., *The Bottom Billion: Why the Poorest Countries Are Failing and What Can Be Done About It*, Oxford, Oxford University Press, 2007

Connor D. M., *Constructive Citizens Participation: A Resource Book*, Catalina Terrace, Victoria, 1999

Connor J. A. and Kadel-Taras S., *Community Visions, Community Solutions: Grantmaking for Comprehensive Impact*, Saint Paul, Amherst H. Wilder Foundation, 2003

Cooke B. and Kothari U. (eds), *Participation: The New Tyranny?*, London, Zed, 2002

Corbett J. and Corbett M., *Designing Sustainable Communities: Learning from Village Homes*, Washington DC, Island, 2000

Cotula L. and Mathieu P. (eds), *Legal Empowerment in Practice: Using Legal Tools to Secure Land Rights in Africa*, London, Food and Agricultural Organisation of the United Nations (UNFAO) and International Institute for Environment and Development (IIED), 2008

Craig S., *Making Partnership Work: A Handbook on Involvement in Local Development Partnerships*, Dublin 2, Combat Poverty Agency, 1995

Crane A., McWilliams A., Matten D., Moon J. and Siegel D. S. (eds), *The Oxford Handbook of Corporate Social Responsibility*, Oxford, Oxford University Press, 2008

Creighton J. L., *The Public Participation Handbook: Making Better Decisions through Citizen Involvement*, San Francisco, Jossey-Bass, 2005

Crow H., *Memoirs of the Late Captain Hugh Crow, of Liverpool; Comprising A Narrative of His Life, Together with Descriptive Sketches of the Western Coast of Africa; Particularly Bonny; The Manners and Customs of the Inhabitants, the Productions of the Soil, and the Trade of the Country, to Which are Added, Anecdotes and Observations, Illustrative of the Negro Character*, London, Frank Cass, 1970

Crow H., *The Memoirs of Captain Hugh Crow: The Life and Times of a Slave Trade Captain*, Oxford, Bodleian Library, 2007

Crowther M., *The Story of Nigeria*, London, Faber and Faber, 1978

Crump A. *Dictionary of Environment and Development: People, Places, Ideas and Organisations*, London, Earthscan, 1991

Dalal-Clayton B. and Sadler B., *Strategic Environmental Assessment: A Sourcebook and Reference Guide to International Experience*, London, Earthscan, 2005

Dalal-Clayton B. and Bass S., *Sustainable Development Strategies: A Resource Book*, London, Earthscan, 2007

Dale A. and Onyx J. (ed.), *A Dynamic Balance: Social Capital and Sustainable Community Development*, Vancouver, University of British Columbia (UBC) Press, 2005

Dasgupta B., *Structural Adjustment, Global Trade and the New Political Economy of Development*, New Delhi, Vistaar, 1998

Daud H., *Protecting the Marine Environment from Land-based Sources of Pollution: Towards Effective International Cooperation*, Aldershot, Ashgate, 2006

Davis J. M., Ossowski R and Fedelino A (eds), *Fiscal Policy Formulation and Implementation in Oil-Producing Countries*, Washington DC, International Monetary Fund, 2003

Dawson J., *Schumacher Briefings 12: Ecovillages: New Frontiers for Sustainability*, Foxhole, Green, 2006

De Sadeleer N. *Environmental Principles: From Political Slogans to Legal Rules*, Oxford, Oxford University Press, 2002

Deirag I. (ed.), *Corporate Responsibility, Accountability and Governance: Global Prospects*, Sheffield, Greenleaf, 2005

Derefaka A. A. and Okorobia M. A. (eds), *History Concourse 2007: The Future of Niger Delta: The Search for A Relevant Narrative*, Port Harcourt, Onyoma Research, 2008

Dike K. O., *Trade and Politics in the Niger Delta 1830–1885: An Introduction to the Economic and Political History of Nigeria*, Westport, Greenwood Press, 1956

Donnelly J. *Universal Human Rights: In Theory & Practice*, Ithaca and London, Cornell University Press, 2003

Douglas O. and Okonta I., *Where Vultures Feast: Shell, Human Rights, and Oil in the Niger Delta*, New York, Sierra Club, 2001

Down C. G. and Stocks J. *Environmental Impact of Mining*, London, Applied Science, 1978

Dresner S., *The Principles of Sustainability*, London, Earthscan, 2008

Dwivedi O. P. and Vajpeyi D. K. (eds), *Environmental Policies in the Third World: A Comparative Analysis*, London, Mansell, 1995

Ebeku K. S. A., *Oil and the Niger Delta People in International Law – Resource Rights, Environmental and Equity Issues*, Koln, Rudiger Koppe Verlag, 2006

Eggert R. G. (ed.), *Mining and the Environment: International Perspectives on Public Policy*, Washington DC, Resources for the Future, 1994

Eide A., Bergesen H. O. and Goyer P. R. (eds), *Human Rights and the Oil Industry*, Oxford, Intersentia, 2000

Eide A., Krause C. and Rosas A., *Economic, Social and Cultural Rights: A Textbook*, The Hague, Kluwer Law International, 2001

Ejituwu N. C., *A History of Obolo in the Niger Delta*, Oron, Mason, 1991

Elaigwu J. I., *The Politics of Federalism in Nigeria*, London, Adonis & Abbey, 2007

Elliott J. A., *An Introduction to Sustainable Development: The Developing World*, London and New York, Routledge, 1994

Emberland M., *The Human Rights of Companies: Exploring the Structure of ECHR Protection*, Oxford, Oxford University Press, 2006

Eneyo S., *The Andoni Monarchy: An Introduction to the Kingship Institution of the Andoni People*, Port Harcourt, Riverside Communications, 1991

Erekosima T. V., Kio-Lawson W. H. and MacJaja O. (eds), *Hundred Years of Buguma History in Kalabari Culture: Buguma 1884–1894*, Lagos, Sibon, 1991

Eromosele V. E., *Nigerian Petroleum Business: A Handbook*, Surulere-Lagos, Advent Communications, 1977

Etekpe Ayotamuno Y. M., Nwala U. E., Kariboro J. and Jumbo M. C., *Harold Dappa-Biriye: His Contributions to Politics in Nigeria*, Port Harcourt, Onyoma Research, 2003

Etikerentse G., *Nigerian Petroleum Law*, London, Macmillan, 1985

Etikerentse G., *Nigerian Petroleum Law (*2nd edn.), Dredew, 2005

Farmer A., *Handbook of Environmental Protection and Enforcement: Principles and Practice*, London, Earthscan, 2008

Fekumo J. F., *Principles of Nigerian Customary Law*, Port Harcourt, F & F, 2002

Fiberesima J. A., *Okrika on Biography*, Port Harcourt, Newsfair, 2007

Finapiri G., *Forgotten Heroes of Grand Bonny*, Lagos, CSS, 2001

Finnis J., *Natural Law and Natural Rights*, Oxford, Clarendon, 1980

Finnis J. (ed.), *Natural Law: Volume I*, Aldershot, Dartmouth, 1991

Finnis J. (ed.), *Natural Law: Volume II*, Aldershot, Dartmouth, 1991

Fischer B. T., *Theory and Practice of Strategic Environmental Assessment: Towards A More Systematic Approach*, London, Earthscan, 2007

Fisher D., *Paradise Differed: Environmental Policymaking in Central and Eastern Europe*, London, Royal Institute of International Affairs, Energy and Environmental Programme, 1992

Fitzmaurice M. and Szuniewicz M. (eds), *Exploitation of Natural Resources in the 21st Century*, The Hague, Kluwer Law International, 2003

Flint J. E., *Sir George Goldie and the Making of Nigeria*, London, Oxford University Press, 1960

Forsyth M. (ed.), *Federalism and Nationalism*, Leicester, Leicester University Press, 1989

Francis D., Grayson J. and Henderson P. (eds), *Rich Seam: Community Development in Coalfield Communities*, London, Community Development Foundation, 2002

Fredrich C. J., *Trends of Federalism in Theory and Practice*, London, The Pall Mall Press, 1968

Freeman R. E., *Strategic Management: A Stakeholder Approach*, London, Pitman, 1984

Freeman M., *Truth Commissions and Procedural Fairness*, Cambridge, Cambridge University Press, 2006

French D., *International Law and Policy of Sustainable Development*, Manchester, Manchester University Press, 2005

Friedman A. L. and Miles S., *Stakeholders: Theory and Practice*, Oxford, Oxford University Press, 2006

Frynas J. G., *Oil in Nigeria: Conflict and Litigation between Oil Companies and Village Communities*, Piscataway, Transaction, 1993

Frynas J. G., *Beyond Corporate Social Responsibility: Oil Multinationals and Social Challenges*, Cambridge, Cambridge University Press, 2009

Frynas J. G. and Pegg S. (eds), *Transnational Corporations and Human Rights*, Basingstoke, Palgrave Macmillan, 2003

Gamman J. K., *Overcoming Obstacles in Environmental Policymaking: Creating Partnership through Mediation*, Albany, State University of New York Press, 1994

Gao Z., *Environmental Regulation of Oil and Gas*, London, Kluwer Law International, 1998

George C. and Kirkpatrick C., *Impact Assessment and Sustainable Development: European Practice and Experience*, Cheltenham, Edward Elgar, 2007

Ghai D. (ed.), *Development & Environment: Sustaining People and Nature*, Oxford and Cambridge, Blackwell, 1994

Gibson R. B., Hassan, S., Holtz, S., Tansey, J. and Whitelaw, G., *Sustainability Assessment: Criteria, Processes and Applications*, London, Earthscan, 2005

Gidado M., *Petroleum Development Contracts with Multinational Oil Firms: The Nigerian Experience*, Maiduguri, Ed-Linform Services, 1999

Gillespire A., *International Environmental Law Policy and Ethics*, Oxford, Oxford University Press, 2000

Gilpin A., *Dictionary of Environmental Law*, Cheltenham, Edward Elgar, 2000

Gilpin A., *Environmental Impact Assessment (EIA): Cutting Edge for the Twenty-First Century*, Cambridge, Cambridge Cambridge University Press, 1995

Girardet H., *CitiesPeoplePlanet*, Chichester, Wiley-Academy, 2004

Girardet H., *Schumacher Briefings 2: Creating Sustainable Cities*, Foxhole, Green, 2008

Glasson J., Therivel R. and A. Chadwick, *Introduction to Environmental Impact Assessment*, Abingdon, Routledge, 2005

Glazewski J., *Environmental Law in South Africa*, Durban, Butterworths, 2005

Golfzen, K. G. (ed.), *The Niger River Basin: A Vision for Sustainable Development*, Washington DC, The World Bank, 2005

Goodland R., *Sustainable Development Sourcebook for the World Bank Group's Extractive Industries Review: Examining the Social and Environmental Impacts of Oil, Gas and Mining*, Washington DC, The World Bank Group, 2006

Goodrich L. M. and Fox W. T. R. (eds), *Legal Effects of United Nations Resolutions*, New York, Columbia University Press, 1969

Gray D. E., *Doing Research in the Real World*, London, Sage, 2004

Guo Z. (ed.), *Environmental Regulation of Oil and Gas*, London, Kluwer Law International, 1998

Halfon R., *Corporate Irresponsibility: Is Business Appeasing Anti-Business Activists?*, London, The Social Affairs Unit, 1998

Hamilton K. and Atkinson G., *Wealth, Welfare and Sustainability*, Cheltenham, Edward Elgar, 2006

Hamilton M. S. *Mining Environmental Policy: Comparing Indonesia and the USA*, Hampshire, Ashgate, 2005

Hannesson R. R., *Investing for Sustainability: The Management of Mineral Wealth*, Boston, Kluwer Academic, 2001

Hassan D., *Protecting the Marine Environment from Land-Based Sources of Pollution: Towards Effective International Cooperation*, Hampshire, Ashgate, 2006

Haufler V., *Public Role for the Private Sector: Industry Self Regulation in a Global Economy*, Washington DC, Carnegie Endowment for International Peace, 2001

Hayward T., *Constitutional Environmental Rights*, New York, Oxford University Press, 2005

Henson R., *The Rough Guide to Climate Change: The Symptoms, The Science, The Solution*, London, Rough Guides, 2008

Heineccius J. G., *Natural Law and Enlightenment Classics: A Methodological System of Universal Law, with Supplements and a Discourse by George Turnbull*, Indianapolis, Liberty Fund, 2008

Hemmati M., *Multi-Stakeholder Processes for Governance and Sustainable Development: Beyond Deadlock and Conflict*, London, Earthscan, 2002

Hewawasam I., *Managing the Marine and Coastal Environment of Sub-Saharan Africa: Strategic Directions for Sustainable Development*, Washington DC, The World Bank, 2002

Hickey S. and Mohan G. (eds), *Participation: From Tyranny to Transformation – Exploring New Approaches to Participation in Development*, London, Zed, 2008

Higgins R., *Problems and Process: International Law and How We Use It*, Oxford, Clarendon, 1994

Holder J., *Environmental Assessment: The Regulation of Decision Making*, Oxford, Oxford University Press, 2004

Hopkins M., *Corporate Responsibility & International Development: Is Business the Solution?*, London, Earthscan, 2009

Hood C. and Heald D. (eds), *Transparency: The Key to Better Governance*, Oxford, Oxford University Press, 2007

Horsfall A. K., *The OMPADEC Dream*, West Sussex, Imprint, 1999

Hossain K. and Chowdhury S. R. (eds), *Permanent Sovereignty Over Natural Resources in* International Law, London, Frances Pinter, 1984

Howes M., *Politics and the Environment: Risk and the Role of Government and Industry*, London, Earthscan, 2005

Hughes D. J., Jewell T., Lowther J., Parpworth N. and de Prez P., *Environmental Law*, London, Butterworths, 2002

Ikein A. A., *The Impact of Oil on a Developing Country: The Case of Nigeria*, New York, Praeger, 1990

Ikein A. A., Alamieyeseigha D. S. P., and Azaiki S. (eds), *Oil, Democracy, and the Promise of True Federalism in Nigeria*, Lanham, University Press of America, 2008

Ikein A. A. and Briggs-Anigboh C., *Oil and Fiscal Federalism in Nigeria: The Political Economy of Resource Allocation in a Developing Country*, Vermont, Ashgate, 1998

Isichei E., *A History of Nigeria*, London, Longman, 1983

Johnston, J. F., *No Man Can Serve Two Masters: Shareholders versus Stakeholders in the Governance of Companies*, London, The Social Affairs Unit, 1998

Jones G. I., *The Trading States of the Oil River: A Study of Political Development in Eastern Nigeria*, New Brunswick, Transaction, 2000

Jones S. and Carswell G. (eds), *The Earthscan Environment, Development & Rural Livelihood*, London, Earthscan 2004

Jorre J., *The Nigerian Civil War*, London, Hodder and Stoughton, 1972

Joseph S., *Corporations and Translational Human Rights Litigation* Oxford, Hart, 2004

Kallhauge A. C., Sjostedt G. and Corell E., *Global Challenges: Furthering the Multilateral Process for Sustainable Development*, Sheffield, Greenleaf, 2005

Kaner S., Lind L., Toldi C., Fisk S., and Berger D., *Facilitators Guide to Participatory Decision-Making*, San Francisco, Jossey-Bass, 2007

Kant S. and Berry R. A. (eds), *Economics, Sustainability, and Natural Resources: Economics of Sustainable Forest Management*, Dordrecht, Springer, 2005

Khan S. A., *Nigeria: The Political Economy of Oil*, Oxford, Oxford University Press, 1994

Kirkpatrick C. and Lee N. (eds), Sustainable Development in a Developing World: Integrating Socio-economic Appraisal and Environmental Assessment, Cheltenham, Edward Elgar, 1997

Korten, D. C., *When Corporations Rule the World*, California, Berett-Koehler, 2001

Kotler P. and Lee N., *Corporate Social Responsibility: Doing the Most Good for Your Company and Your Cause*, Hoboken, John Wiley & Sons, 2005

Kumar S., *Methods for Community Participation: A Complete Guide for Practitioners*, Rugby, Practical Action, 2008

Krile J. F., *The Community Leadership Handbook: Framing Ideas, Building Relationships, and Mobilizing Resource*, Saint Paul, Fieldstone Alliance, 2006

Kumar R., *Research Methodology: A Step-by-Step Guide for Beginners*, London, Sage, 2005

Lafferty W. M. and Eckerberg K. (eds), *From the Earth Summit to Local Agenda 21: Working Towards Sustainable Development*, London, Earthscan, 1998

Lang W., Neuhold H. and Zemanek K., (eds), *Environmental Protection and International Law*, Norwell, Kluwer Academic, 1991

Langton M., Mazel O., Palmer L., Shain K. and Tehan M. (eds), *Honour Among Nations?: Treaties and Agreements with Indigenous Peoples*, Carton, Melbourne University Press, 2004

Langton M., Tehan M., Palmer L. and Shain K. (eds), *Settling with Indigenous People: Modern Treaty and Agreement-making*, Annandale, The Federation Press, 2006

Lawrence D. P., *Environmental Impact Assessment: Practical Solutions to Recurrent Problems*, Hoboken, John Wiley & Sons, 2003

Layard A., Davoudi S. and Batty S. (eds), Planning for a Sustainable Future, London, Spon, 2001

Leipziger D., *Corporate Responsibility Code Book*, Sheffield, Greenleaf, 2003

Lessonoff M. (ed.), *Social Contract Theory*, Oxford, Basil Blackwell, 1990

Lewis D (ed.), *Global Governance and the Quest for Justice: International and Regional Organisations*, Oxford, Hart, 2006

Liebenthal A., *Promoting Environmental Sustainability in Development: An Evaluation of the World Bank's Performance*, Washington DC, The World Bank, 2002

Lineberry W. P. (ed.), *Assessing Participatory Development: Rhetoric Versus Reality*, Boulder, Westview/IFAD, 1989

Long C., Participation of the Poor in Development Initiatives: Taking their Rightful Place, London, Earthscan, 2001

Lovan R. W., Murray M. and Shaffer R. (eds), *Participatory Governance: Planning, Conflict Mediation and Public Decision-Making in Civil Society*, Aldershot, Ashgate, 2004

Lucas C. and Hoskins L., *The Wilder Nonprofit Field Guide to Conducting Community Forums: Engaging Citizens, Mobilising Communities*, St. Paul, Amherst H. Wilder Foundation, 2003

Lucas J. R., *Democracy and Participation*, Middlesex, Penguin, 1976

Luhmann N., *Writing Science: Social Systems*, Stanford, Stanford University Press, 1984

Lynn R., *The Secret of the Miracle Economy: Different National Attitudes to Competiveness and Money*, London, The Social Affairs Unit, 1991

MacDonnell J. L. and Bates S. F. (eds), *Natural Resources Policy and Law: Trends and Directions*, Washington DC, Island, 1993

Mackintosh J. P., *Nigerian Government and Politics*, London, George Allen and Unwin, 1966

Macleod S. (ed.), *Global Governance and the Quest for Justice: Volume 11: Corporate Governance*, Oxford, Hart, 2006

Malcolm R., *A Guidebook to Environmental Law*, London, Sweet & Marxwell, 1994

Markandya A. and Halsnaes K. (eds), *Climate Change & Sustainable Development: Prospects for Developing Countries*, London, Earthscan, 2002

Marks S. and Clapham A., *International Human Rights Lexicon*, Oxford, New York, Oxford University Press, 2005

Mattessich P., Monsey B. and Roy C., *Community Building: What Makes It Work: A Review of Factors Influencing Successful Community Building*, Saint Paul, Amherst H. Wilder Foundation, 1997

Mayer J., Chambers B. and Farooq A. (eds), *Development Policies in Natural Resource Economies*, Cheltenham, Edward Elgar, 1999

McAllister M. L. and Alexander C. J., *A Stake in the Future: Redefining the Canadian Mineral Industry*, Vancouver, University of British Columbia (UBC) Press, 1997

McBarnet D., Voiculescu A. and Campbell T. (eds), *The New Corporate Accountability: Corporate Social Responsibility and the Law*, Cambridge, Cambridge University Press, 2008

McCabe M. and Sadler B. (eds), *Environmental Impact Assessment Training Resource Manual*, Geneva, The Economic and Trade Branch, Division of Technology, Industry and Economics (DTIE), UNEP, 2002

McCabe M. and Sadler B. (eds), *Studies of EIA Practice in Developing Countries: A Supplement to the UNEP Training Resource Manual*, Geneva, DTIE, UNEP, 2002

McPhail K. and Davy A., *Integrating Social Concerns into Private Sector Decision-making: A Review of Corporate Practices in the Mining, Oil, and Gas Sectors*, Washington DC, The World Bank, 1998

Middleton N. and O'Keefe P., *Redefining Sustainable Development*, London, Pluto, 2001

Midgley K., *Companies and their Shareholders – The Uneasy Relationship*, London, The Institute of Chartered Secretaries and Administrators, 1975

Mirovitskaya N. Asher W. (eds), *Guide to Sustainable Development and Environmental Policy*, Durham, Duke University Press, 2001

Mol A. P. J., Lauber V. and Liefferink D., *The Voluntary Approach to Environmental Policy: Joint Environmental Approach to Environmental Policy-making in Europe*, Oxford, Oxford University Press, 2004

Montanheiro L., Haigh B., Morris D. and Linehan M. (eds), *Public and Private Sector partnerships: Furthering Development*, Sheffield, Sheffield Hallam University Press, 1999

Moore N., *How to Do Research: A Practical Guide to Designing and Managing Research Projects*, London, Facet, 2006

Morrison-Saunders A. and Arts J. (eds), *Assessing Impact: Handbook of EIA and SEA Follow-up*, London, Earthscan, 2006

Muchlinski P., Ortino F. and Schreuer C. (eds), *The Oxford Handbook of International Investment Law*, Oxford, Oxford University Press, 2008

Mullen J., *Rural Poverty, Empowerment and Sustainable Livelihoods*, Aldershot, Ashgate, 1999

Munn R. E. (ed.), *Environmental Impact Assessment: Principles and Procedures*, New York, Wiley, 1979

Murdie A., *Environmental Law and Citizen Action*, London, Earthscan, 1993

Na'Allah A. (ed.), *Ogoni's Agonies: Ken Saro-Wiwa and the Crisis in Nigeria*, Asmara, Africa World Press, 1998

Nelson N. and Wright S. (eds), *Power and Participatory Development: Theory and Practice*, London, Intermediate Technology Development Group (ITDG), 1995

Newman P., Beatley T. and Boyer H., *Resilient Cities: Responding to Peak Oil and Climate Change*, Washington DC, Island, 2009

Nicolaidis K. and Howse R. (ed.), *The Federal Vision: Legitimacy and Levels of Governance in the United States and the European Union*, Oxford, Oxford University Press, 2003

Nnoli O., *Ethnic Politics in Nigeria*, Enugu, Fourth Dimension, 1978

Nwabueze B. O., *Constitutional Law of Nigeria*, London, Butterworth, 1964

Nwokedi A. E., *Community Relations in Oil Producing Companies in Nigeria*, Abuja, Daylight Media Services, 1999

Ogan C., *Okrika: A Kingdom of the Niger Delta*, Port Harcourt, Onyoma Research, 2008

Ogbuigwe A., *Offended: Legal Issues in the Niger Delta Struggle*, Port Harcourt, Anpez Centre for Environment and Development, 1999

Okonta I., *When Citizens Revolt: Nigerian Elites, Big Oil and the Ogoni Struggle for Self-Determination, Trenton*, Africa World Press, 2008

Okorodudu-Fubara M. T., *Law of Environmental Protection*, Ibadan, Caltop, 1998

Olisa M. M., *Nigerian Petroleum Law and Practice*, Festac Town, Lagos, Jonia Ventures, 1997

Omeje K., *High Stakes and Stakeholders: Oil Conflict and Security in Nigeria*, Aldershot, Ashgate, 2006

Omeje K. (ed.), *Extractive Economies and Conflicts in the Global South: Multi-Regional Perspectives on Rentier Politics*, Aldershot, Ashgate, 2008

Omorogbe Y., *Oil and Gas Law in Nigeria*, Lagos, Malthouse Press, 2001

Omorogbe Y., *The Oil and Gas Industry: Exploration & Production Contracts*, Ikeja-Lagos, Malthouse Press, 1997

Omoweh D. A., *Shell, the State and Underdevelopment of Nigeria's Niger Delta: A Study in Environmental Degradation*, Trenton, Africa World Press, 2005

Onuoha A., *From Conflict to Collaboration: Building Peace in Nigeria's Oil-Producing Communities*, London, Adonis & Abbey, 2005

Onuoha A., *When Communities Confront Corporations: Comparing Shell's Presence in Ireland and Nigeria*, London, Adonis & Abbey, 2008

Orebech P., Bosselman F., Bjarup J., Callies D., Chanock M. and Petersen H., *The Role of Customary Law in Sustainable Development*, Cambridge, Cambridge University Press, 2005

Osborn D. and Bigg T., *Earth Summit 11: Outcomes and Analysis*, London, Earthscan, 1998

Osha S., *Ken Saro-Wiwa's Shadow: Politics, Nationalism and the Ogoni Protest Movement*, London, Adonis & Abbey, 2007

Oshita O. O., *Conflict Management in Nigeria: Issues and Challenges*, London, Adonis & Abbey, 2007

Otite O. and Albert I. O. (eds), *Community Conflicts in Nigeria: Management, Resolution & Transformation*, Ibadan, Spectrum, 1999

Otto J. and Cordes J., *The Regulation of Mineral Enterprises: A Global Perspective on Economics, Law and Policy*, Westminster, Rocky Mountain Mineral Law Foundation (RMMLF), 2002

Otto J. M. and Cordes J. (eds), *Sustainable Development and the Future of Mineral Investment*, Paris, United Nations Environment Programme Division of Technology, Industry and Economics, 2000

Oxford M., *Developing Naturally: A Handbook for Incorporating the Natural Environment into Planning and Development*, Somerset, The Association of Local Government Ecologists (ALGE), 2000

Oyovbaire S. E., *Federalism in Nigeria*, London, Macmillan, 1985

Parra F., *Oil Politics: A Modern History of Petroleum*, London, I. B. Tauris, 2004

Pateman C., *Participation and Democratic Theory*, Cambridge, Cambridge University Press, 1995

Penner J. E., *Mozley & Whiteley's Law Dictionary*, London, Butterworths, 2001

Petschow, J. Rosenau and E. U von Weizsaker (eds), *Governance and Sustainability: New Challenges for States, Companies and Civil Society*, Sheffield, Greenleaf, 2005

Phuong C., *The International Protection of Internally Displaced Persons*, New York, Cambridge University Press, 2004

Pitchford M. and Henderson P., *Making Spaces for Community Development*, Bristol, The Policy, 2008

Porter A. L. and J. J. Fittipaldi (eds), *Environmental Methods Review: Retooling Impact Assessment for the New Century*, Fargo, The Press Club, 1998

Pound R., *An Introduction to the Philosophy of Law: Based on the Storrs Lectures Delivered at Yale University*, New Haven, Yale University Press, 1965

Ravindranath N. H. and Sathaye J. A., *Climate Change and Developing Countries (Advances in Global Change Research)*, Kluwer Academic, 2002

Register R., *Ecocities: Rebuilding Cities in Balance with Nature*, Gabriola Island, New Society, 2006

Rex J. and Mason D. (eds), Theories of Race and Ethnic Relations, Cambridge, Cambridge University Press, 1988

Richardson A., *Participation: Concepts in Social Policy 1*, London, Routledge & Kegan Paul, 1983

Rieu-Clarke A., *International Law and Sustainable Development: Lessons from the Law of International Watercourses*, London, IWA, 2005

Reitbergen-McCracken J. and Narayan D., *Participation and Social Assessment: Tools and Techniques*, Washington DC, The World Bank, 1998

Robinson N. A. (ed.), *Agenda 21: Earth's Action Plan*, New York, Oceana, 1993

Rochmat R., *Contractual Arrangements in Oil and Gas Mining Enterprises in Indonesia*, Rockville, Sijthoff & Noordhoff International, 1981

Rodney W., *How Europe Underdeveloped Africa*, London, Howard University Press, 1972

Rogers P. P., Jalal K. F. and Boyd J., *An Introduction to Sustainable Development*, London, Earthscan, 2008

Rogovsky N., *Corporate Community Involvement Programmes: Partnerships for Jobs and Development*, Geneva, International Institute for Labour Studies, 2000

Rowell A., Marriott J. and Stockman L, *The Next Gulf: London, Washington and Oil Conflict in Nigeria*, London, Constable & Robinson, 2005

Rugg G. and Petre M., *A Gentle Guide to Research Methods*, Berkshire, Open University Press, 2007

Samuel L., *Fundamental Social Rights: Case Law of the European Social Charter*, Strasbourg Cedex, Council of Europe, 2002

Sand P. H. (ed.), *The Effectiveness of International Environmental Agreements: A Survey of Existing Legal Instruments*, Cambridge, Grotius, 1992

Saro-Wiwa K., *On the Darkling Plain: An Account of the Nigerian Civil War*, London, Saros International, 1989

Schaltegger S. and Wagner M. (eds), *Managing the Business Case for Sustainability: The Integration of Social, Environmental and Economic Performance*, Sheffield, Greenleaf, 2006

Schrijver N., *Sovereignty over Natural Resources*, Melbourne, Cambridge University Press, 1997

Schrijver N. and Weiss F. (eds), *International Law and Sustainable Development Principles and Practice*, Leiden, Martinus Nijhoff, 2004

Schwarz F. A. O., *Nigeria: The Tribes, the Nations, or the Race – The Politics of Independence*, Massachusetts, Massachusetts Institute of Technology (MIT) Press, 1965

Seidman A., Seidman R. B., Walde T. W. (eds), *Making Development Work: Legislative Reform for Institutional Transformation and Good Governance*, The Hague, Kluwer Law international, 1999

Sharma S. and Starik M. (eds), *Stakeholders, the Environment and Society: New Perspectives in Research on Corporate Sustainability*, Cheltenham, Edward Elgar, 2004

Smith E. E., Dzienkowski J. S. anderson O. L., Conine G. B., Lowe J. S. and Kramer B. M., *International Petroleum Transactions*, RMMLF, Denver, 2000

Sidaway R. S., *Resolving Environmental Disputes: From Conflict to Consensus*, London, Earthscan, 2005

Simmons M. and Obe A. (eds), *The Guardian Nigerian Handbook 1982–83*, London, William Collins Sons, 1982

Smith G. (ed.), *Federalism: The Multiethnic Challenge*, New York, Longman, 1995

Spash L. C., *Greenhouse Value and Ethics Economics*, London, Routledge, 2002

Stallworthy M., *Sustainability, Land Use and Environment: A Legal Analysis*, London, Cavendish, 2002

Stec S. (ed.) *Handbook on Access to Justice Under the Aarhus Convention*, Szentendre, the Regional Environmental Centre for Central and Eastern Europe, 2003

Sternberg E., *Stakeholding: Betraying the Corporation's Objectives*, London, The Social Affairs Unit, 1998

Suberu R. T., *Ethnic Minority Conflicts and Governance in Nigeria*, Ibadan, Spectrum, 2003

Suberu R. T., *Federalism and Ethnic Conflict in Nigeria*, Washington DC, United States Institute of Peace, 2001

Sullivan R. (ed.), *Business and Human Rights: Dilemmas and Solutions*, Sheffield, Greenleaf, 2003

Synder F. and Slinn P. (eds), *International Law of Development: Comparative Perspectives*, Oxon, Professional, 1987

Tar Hon. S., *Constitutional Law and Jurisprudence in Nigeria*, Port Harcourt, Pearl, 2004

Tarr P., *Environmental Impact Assessment in Southern Africa*, Windhoek, Southern African Institute for Environmental Assessment (SAIEA), 2003

Therivel R., *Strategic Environmental Assessment in Action*, Sterling, Earthscan, 2004

Therivel R. and Partidario M. R., *The Practice of Strategic Environmental Assessment*, London, Earthscan, 1996

Tully S. (ed.), *International Documents on Corporate Responsibility*, Cheltenham, Edward Elgar, 2005

Tully S. (ed.), *Research Handbook on Corporate Legal Responsibility*, Cheltenham, Edward Elgar, 2005

Udoma U., *History and the Constitution of Nigeria*, Lagos, Malthouse Press, 1994

United Nations Economic and Social Commission for Asia and the Pacific (UNESCAP), *Public Involvement Guideline for Natural Resource Development Projects*, New York, UN, 1997

Vattel de E., *Natural Law and Enlightenment Classics: The Law of Nations*, Indianapolis, Liberty Fund, 2008

Victor G. D., Raustiala K. R. and Skolnikoff E. B., (eds), *Implementation and Effectiveness of International Environmental Commitments: Theory and Practice*, Laxenburg, International Institute for Applied Systems Analysis, 1998

Visser W., Business Frontiers: *Social Responsibility, Sustainable Development and Economic Justice*, Hyderabad, ICFAI University Press, 2006

Visser W., Matten D., Pohl M., and Tolhurst N., *The A to Z of Corporate Social Responsibility*, Chichester, John Wiley & Sons, 2008

Visser W., McIntosh M. and Middleton C. (eds), *Corporate Citizenship in Africa: Lessons from the Past, Paths to the Future*, Sheffield, Greenleaf, 2006

Vogel D., *The Market for Virtue: The Potential Limits of Corporate Social Responsibility*, Washington DC, Brookings Institution, 2005

Warburton D. (ed.), *Community & Sustainable Development: Participation in the Future*, London, Earthscan, 1998

Warden-Fernandez J., *Indigenous Rights Vs Development of Natural Resources: Which Will Be the Best Solution to Resolve Conflicts*, Dundee, CEPMLP, 2000

Warhurst A. and Noronha L (eds), *Environmental Policy in Mining: Corporate Strategy and Planning for Closure*, Florida, Lewis (imprint of CRC Press), 2000

Warner M. and Sullivan R. (eds), *Putting Partnerships to Work: Strategic Alliances for Development between Government, the Private-Sector and Civil Society*, Sheffield, Greenleaf, 2004

Watchendorfer-Schmidt U. (ed.), *Federalism and Political Performance*, London, Routledge, 2000

Welford R., *Hijacking Environmentalism: Corporate Responses to Sustainable Development*, London, Earthscan, 1997

Weller M. (ed.), *The Rights of Minorities: A Commentary on the European Framework Convention for the Protection of National Minorities*, Oxford, Oxford University Press, 2005

Wessling H. L., *Imperialism and Colonialism: Essays on the History of European Expansion*, Westport, Greenwood, 1997

Westra L., *Environmental Justice and the Rights of Unborn Future Generations: Law, Environmental Harm and the Right to Health*, London, Earthscan, 2006

Whitaker B., *Participation and Poverty*, London, Fabian Society, 1968

Wilson F. A. (ed), *Towards Sustainable Project Development*, Cheltenham, Edward Elgar, 1997

Wood C., *Environmental Impact Assessment: A Comparative Review*, Harlow, Pearson Education, 2003

Worika I. L., *Environmental Law & Policy of Petroleum Development: Strategies & Mechanisms for Sustainable Management in Africa*, Port Harcourt, Anpez for Environment and Development, 2002

Wunder S., *Oil Wealth and the Fate of the Forest: A Comparative Study of Eight Tropical Countries, London*, Routledge Explorations in Environmental Economics, 2003

Young O. R., *International Cooperation: Building Regimes for Natural Resources and the Environment*, Ithaca, New York, Cornell University Press, 1989

Young O. R. and Osherenko G. (eds), *Polar Politics: Creating International Environmental Regimes*, Ithaca, New York, Cornell University Press, 1993

Zerk J. A, *Multinationals and Corporate Social Responsibility: Limitations and Opportunities in International Law*, Cambridge, Cambridge University Press, 2006

Zillman D. N., Lucas, A. R. and Pring, G. (R.), (eds), *Human Rights in Natural Resources Development: Public Participation in Sustainable Development of Mining and Energy Resources*, New York, Oxford University Press, 2002

Zuckerman A. S. and Cranston R. (eds), *Reform of Civil Procedure: Essays on 'Access to Justice'*, New York, Oxford University Press, 1995

Index

Note: Entries which are references to footnotes are in *italic type* in this index.